PATHS OF FAITH

PATHS OF FAITH

Second Edition

JOHN A. HUTCHISON
Claremont Graduate School

McGraw-Hill Book Company

New York   St. Louis   San Francisco   Düsseldorf   Johannesburg
Kuala Lumpur   London   Mexico   Montreal   New Delhi   Panama
Paris   São Paulo   Singapore   Sydney   Tokyo   Toronto

PATHS OF FAITH

Library of Congress Cataloging in Publication Data
Hutchison, John Alexander, date
    Paths of faith.

    Includes bibliographies.
    1. Religion—History.   2. Religions.   I. Title.
BI.80.2.II78   1975   200'.9   74–2432
ISBN 0–07–031531–0

    2 3 4 5 6 7 8 9 K P K P 7 9 8 7 6 5

This book was set in Fairfield by Holmes Typography, Inc. The editors were James F. Mirrielees and Alison Meersschaert; the designer was Holmes Typography, Inc.; the production supervisor was Judi Frey. The photo editor was Susan Johns. Kingsport Press, Inc. was printer and binder.

ACKNOWLEDGMENTS

George Allen & Unwin, Ltd.: M. Pickthall (tr.), *The Meaning of the Glorious Koran.*
The Bobbs-Merrill Company, Inc.: Wing-Tsit Chan (tr.), *The Way of Lao Tzu.*
The Bodley Head, Ltd.: Rex Warner (tr.), *Furipides, Hippolytus.*
Columbia University Press: Wm. T. de Bary (ed.), *Sources of Indian Tradition, Sources of Chinese Tradition, Sources of Japanese Tradition.*
Humanities Press: S. Radhakrishnan (tr.), *The Principal Upanishads.*
The Macmillan Company: Y. L. Fung, *A Short History of Chinese Philosophy.*
John Murray, Ltd.: Duchesne-Guillaume, *The Hymns of Zarathustra.*
National Council of Churches of Christ: *Revised Standard Version of the Holy Bible.*
Oxford University Press: Henry Bettenson, *Documents of the Christian Church;* H. A. R. Gibb, *Mohammedanism.*
Princeton University Press: Khushwant Singh, *History of the Sikhs;* II. Zimmer, *Philosophies of India;* W. T. Chan, *A Source Book of Chinese Philosophy.*
Random House, Inc.: Lin Yutang, *The Wisdom of China and India, The Wisdom of Confucius.*
F. Ross, *Shinto: The Way of Japan.*
Charles Scribner's Sons: G. F. Moore, *History of Religions.*
Walter Stace: *The Teachings of the Mystics.*
Vedanta Society of Southern California: Prabhavananda-Isherwood, *The Song of God.*

CONTENTS

LETTER TO THE READER

As the work of writing this book draws to a close, I add a word here at the beginning which I hope may facilitate communication between author and reader. What have I sought to accomplish in this book? This question has been before my mind throughout the process of study and writing which has its fruition in the volume now before you.

My primary aim has been to provide a book that will be a reliable and adequate guide for the general reader and beginning student of the world's religions. My own interest and study grew out of teaching in this field in several colleges and universities. I hope my book may serve as a textbook for such courses. In addition to the classroom student, however, I have also had in mind the general reader who would like a survey of the wide field within the covers of a single volume.

Fundamentally the history of religions is a variety of the species history. I have sought to write accurate and adequate history. However it is necessary immediately to add that there is no such thing as uninterpreted history. The ideal of naked fact altogether divested of interpretive context is a will-o'-the-wisp. While I have sought to hold the interpretive aspect of this study to a minimum, I have not hesitated to interpret wherever necessary. Fact and interpretation are inseparable aspects of all historical study, but they are distinguishable elements within the total inquiry. I have sought to keep this distinction clearly before myself and my reader, and I hope he will be able to read my exposition with a view toward forming his own interpretation.

Courses in the history of religions are so well established in American universities and colleges that they need no special advocacy here. Yet the textbooks for such courses suffer from a number of defects. Perhaps the commonest fault is the gap which has opened up in recent years between existing textbooks and scholarship in the field. My effort has been to put the beginning student in touch with forms of research and study now going on.

Another defect of many textbooks is their adherence to an obsolete viewpoint often labeled "comparative religion" or more properly "comparative study of religion," according to which the author lays all the relevant data before the reader and then seeks by comparative study to find the "best" or "purest" religion, or even at times to discover the common essence among the world's many existing religions. Space does not permit here even a listing of the many false and misleading assumptions inherent in this approach. It must suffice to say that it is the effort to correct some of these defects which has led to the viewpoint of the present study, which is set forth in some detail in Chapter 1.

Still another defect in textbooks on religions of the world, though by no means limited to this subject matter, is special pleading for a particular viewpoint. I can only say that in the pages that follow, I have earnestly pursued fair-minded and critical exposition of all the faiths studied. What is even more important, my own deepest commitment here is not to my own conclusions, but rather to the whole ongoing process of study. This implies an open invitation to every reader to join the cooperative process of inquiry, making whatever contributions he can, and criticizing and correcting the mistakes of other contributors.

My book is based upon the assumption that the religions of mankind represent a form of human experience sufficiently important and pervasive to warrant their study as a part of any education which claims the name "liberal." Along with politics, art, economics, and science, religion is a basic and recurring aspect of man's culture. In every human culture of which reliable knowledge exists, there is evidence of religious behavior of some sort. Hence it follows that its study makes a claim on humane or liberal education.

Incidentally, this approach to religion as a pervasive aspect of human experience seems to me a good starting point for study in an age when religious opinion is divided among the believers, the nonbelievers, and also the many equally honest and thoughtful people who cannot place themselves in either of the first two camps. Whatever else and whatever more religion may, or may not, be, it is a pervasive and recurring form of human experience. Let critical inquiry begin at this point.

It is a fact of some importance that ours is an age of unprecedented religious illiteracy. This is particularly true of the American academic community. While religion, along with sex and politics, continues as a perennial subject for discussion, it is also true that in such discussion a shocking lack of ordinary factual knowledge is often shown. Men who would feel disgraced to be ignorant of science, art, or politics show no compunction about harboring the grossest and crudest misconceptions in the field of religion. This book is written as a modest contribution toward combating this contemporary religious illiteracy. Let the rebel continue to rebel, but let him at least know what he is rebelling against. Let the believer continue to believe, but let him at least give critical attention to what he believes. Both groups owe it to themselves to be acquainted with the range and variety of mankind's religious attitudes, practices, and beliefs.

Obviously these are ambitious goals which I have set for myself. Taken as a whole they constitute a large order for any book to fill; and the reader will have to make his own judgment as to whether I have even come close. Yet I must add that to have attempted less would have been to concede failure before the task began.

Adequately understood, the title of my book expresses the main emphases of my approach to the subject matter. The word *path* or any of its numerous translations is a recurring metaphor in the literature of the world's religions. China has its *tao,* and the Japanese have the analogous term *michi.* Buddhists speak of their faith as the path of the Buddha, and Muslims characterize Islam as the straight path. In both Old Testament and New Testament, this same metaphor is used extensively. Thus men have envisaged their religions as paths through the mortal woods.

As it is used in my title, I have understood path to mean a cluster of life values which provides man with a convincing and illuminating answer to the fundamental human question: Why am I alive? These values are expressed symbolically in each of the world's faiths. Each distinct cluster of such values and symbols constitutes a path to be walked. Men set their feet on it and make their way to a destination. In effect, their path defines their journey of life. Such I believe to be the historic function of the world's faiths. The religions of mankind are so many paths of life.

What is the meaning of the word *faith* as used in the title? Thirty years ago, Paul Tillich coined the phrase "ultimate concern" as a definition of faith. Understood as Tillich expounded and qualified it, the definition is, I believe, still valid, useful, and sufficiently general for our purposes. By the word *concern* Tillich sought to designate the active or volitional area of human experience. Interests, loyalties, allegiances, values have all been proposed as synonyms. However characterized, this region of human experience provides the human raw material from which all man's religions are made.

My own preference is for the term *value* because it establishes connection, validly as it seems to me, with the current interest in values among social scientists and also with the philosophic discipline known as value theory, or axiology. Faith or religious experience is, accordingly, experience of ultimate valuation.

Faith defined or interpreted as ultimate concern or valuation still remains ambiguous. It will clarify our usage of the word to point out three facets of meaning. (1) Faith in its most general and basic sense is experience of ultimate concern or valuation as just defined. As such it is a general religious phenomenon, embracing all the world's religions. Indeed it may be argued that this experience is universal. Not only all religions but all men experience faith in this sense of the word. They do so, it may be added, whether they are conscious of the experience or not. (2) Men seek to express faith in the first sense through the symbols of some historic community—Christian, Buddhist, Marxist, or other. Hence in the second sense we speak of Buddhist faith, Christian faith, or Marxist faith. In this second sense, faith is a label designating a distinctive way of expressing faith in the first and most general sense. (3) The word faith is used in still a third sense as a set of statements or propositions which endeavor to set forth the content of the first two meanings of the term. The third meaning might be characterized as propositional faith, or belief. Its function is to analyze or explore the meaning of the experience. However, this analysis often takes place amid divided and conflicting views, with attack of one position and defense of another. As a consequence, some communities of faith demand of their adherents an unquestioning acceptance of a particular set of such propositions, thus fastening upon faith the meaning of unreasoning belief, beyond or against reason or evidence.

The word "paths" points to the irreducible plurality of faiths in the world. Some of these faiths show large and impressive similarities with one another. Yet invariably there are differences as well. In the apparently irreducible plurality of faiths, each faith is addressed "to whom it may concern." This means that the student of religion must normally expect to find adherents of the various religions in a state of ultimate concern, directed to different, often mutually incompatible objects. Yet whatever the particular understanding of the religious object, the concern is ultimate. That is to say, men really believe their faiths, rather than living in the state of mingled accommodation, questioning, and sentimentality which often characterizes the modern liberal attitude toward the historic faiths.

Considering the title *Paths of Faith* perhaps the reader has already asked himself the question: Why faith rather than religion? This issue will be before us recurrently throughout our study. Here it must suffice to observe that virtually every one of the faiths discussed denies for one reason or another that it is a religion. In contemporary Western study, both theologians and historians of religion join in questioning or rejecting the term *religion* as radically distorting the forms of experience that it seeks to communicate. Yet problematic as it is, I do not think we can entirely dispense with it. Therefore I have sought in Chapter 1 to give it careful and guarded definition.

Still a further caution is necessary concerning the term *religion*. If it is to be used at all, it must be used descriptively and not with either affirmative or negative valuation. Many readers will approach this book either "for religion" or "against religion." Both parties must be prepared for discussion which seeks to explore what the phenomenon is, apart from these affections and disaffections. In the popular culture of America today, it is fashionable to be for religion, whatever that may mean. In the academic subculture of contemporary America, it is almost as fashionable to be against religion, whatever that may mean. For the present task of critical understanding, few popular affections and disaffections have muddied the waters of discussion more than these. Such attitudes place urgent items on the agenda of study.

The faiths described in my book may be characterized as adventures of the human spirit and also as explorations of man's humanity. Like all processes of exploration, they involve risk and experiment. Sometimes experiments end in negative results, explorations come to a dead end, and adventures end in disaster. The reader must be prepared to see such results in mankind's religious history. Yet the history of man's faiths show great fulfillments as well. There have been and still are great paths through the mortal woods, leading to unique fulfillments or, as the religions often say, to salvation. Whatever the reader's view of man's humanization and dehumanization, which is to say of those lifelong and age-long processes which sustain his essential humanness and those opposite processes which threaten it, he will find much to learn concerning both from the paths of faith described in this book.

I wish also to make personal acknowledgment to many people who have rendered valuable help in the writing of this book: to David Polk, who composed the glossary, read proof, and made innumerable suggestions for the improvement of the text; to my wife, who labored long over this text and endured the author's long preoccupation with this book; to many secretaries who deciphered my handwriting and produced a readable manuscript; and to students past and present whose questions and discussion have stimulated and clarified my study of the world's faiths.

John A. Hutchison

POSTSCRIPT FOR THE SECOND EDITION

As copy for the second edition goes to the publisher, I wish to thank the many readers who have made suggestions and corrections to improve my book. Substantive changes have been made in Chapters 3, 5, 6, 8, and 9 to enhance accuracy and coverage. An important feature of this revision is the brief section, *Concluding Comment,* which has been added at the end of each chapter, summarizing content and relating it to major themes of the book. In addition, revisions have been made throughout the text designed to clarify language, improve precision of thought, and correct facts as well as typographical errors. It is my hope and expectation that these changes will increase the effectiveness of this text in introducing the reader to the fundamental features of man's religions.

1

ON BEING STUDENTS
OF RELIGION

TOWARD A WORKING DEFINITION OF RELIGION

What is religion? How shall we study it? What does it mean to be a student of religion, and more particularly of the world's religions? Throughout the following pages we shall be immersed in these questions and the many answers that we and other men give to them, so it is well at the outset to place them clearly and squarely before our minds. These questions are large and difficult and in some ways asked better at the end than at the beginning of our study of the world's religions. For the whole enterprise of this book constitutes an actual and functioning attempt to answer precisely these questions. Yet any study of the world's religions will proceed more reasonably and adequately if we approach it with some idea, however inadequate, of what we are doing. Hence we shall devote this first chapter to questions and issues of this sort. What does it mean to be a student of man's religions in the second half of the twentieth century?

Formal definitions of religion are as numerous, as various, and often as conflicting as are students of religion. Often too, such definitions illustrate the Oriental parable of the blind men describing the elephant, each man taking hold

1

of a part of the beast and defining the whole in terms of this part. Like the elephant, religion is a large and complex phenomenon. In this connection, some historians of religion question or reject the word *religion* as a distortion of the form of experience which it seeks to communicate. Several of the world's major languages lack any word which can adequately be translated as "religion." The common noun *religion* imputes a unity or homogeneity of experience that does not exist. In a notable recent discussion, *The Meaning and End of Religion,* Wilfred Cantwell Smith recommends the abolition of the term *religion* and a substitution of the faith of individual men, which is then expressed in those concrete traditions or communities of faith, which others call the religions of mankind.

Acknowledging the force of these and other difficulties of the word *religion,* it still appears impossible to dispense with it completely. At least, it is necessary as a provisional term to get the process of study under way. Then at appropriate stages, qualifications will be introduced to guard against some of its misleading implications. Such at least will be the procedure of the present volume.

It is convenient at this point to begin with religious experience, in Paul Tillich's memorable but highly controversial phrase, as "ultimate concern."[1] Tillich chose *concern* as a neutral and descriptive word to designate the affective or motivational aspect of human experience. Concerns are what move men to action. R. B. Perry has used the more colorless term *interest* for this same aspect of experience.[2] Other writers employ various other terms, such as *values, allegiances,* or *loyalties.* There are important distinctions among these words; yet whatever term and interpretation are chosen, the crucial assertion is that this area of human experience provides men with the human raw material out of which religions are constituted. Religious experience, and religions, are made out of human interest or value. Let this assertion be held in mind as the student makes his way through the world's faiths, testing it on the factual data there to be encountered.

What is the meaning of the adjective *ultimate* in the phrase *ultimate concern?* Tillich has suggested *unconditional, absolute,* and *unqualified,* as synonyms.[3] It is well to note that these are adjectives modifying *concern.* In other words, the primary meaning of the term *ultimate* or *absolute* is a quality of human experience rather than an object or a substantive reality. The latter meaning, if it is to be affirmed at all, must be approached through the former.

The structure of interests, concerns, or values which constitutes a human self shows many levels or strata. The idea of ultimate concern implies that if we dig deep enough we will come upon an underlying value or interest which constitutes the final ground of validation or justification for a man's whole life, giving meaning and orientation to all his other interests, providing him with a functioning answer to the question, Why am I living? Of experiences of this kind, religions are made. Such at least is our thesis or hypothesis.

CHARACTERISTICS OF ULTIMATE CONCERN

TOP PRIORITY

Ultimate concerns or values possess several identifying characteristics. The first is that an ultimate concern has top priority in the system of concerns which constitutes a personality. From this it follows that an ultimate concern has the function of giving meaning, purpose, and direction to a man's life. An ultimate concern is one to which in a crisis a person willingly sacrifices every other value, including life itself. It is a concern for which a man is willing to die. Historically it may be observed that all such values tend to take on religious significance, whether officially labeled religious or not. For example, one thinks of family loyalty or of patriotism as values which tend to take on such religious quality.

Again, an ultimate value is not derived from or dependent upon other values. Rather is it the case that from it all a man's other values are derived. Hence etymologically it is more accurate to speak of *primary* rather than *ultimate* values. To employ a mathematical metaphor, a primary value, or ultimate concern, provides the coordinate system or frame of reference for other values.

Questions of many sorts are raised by this approach to religion as ultimate valuation. Are there in fact such values? Is it not rather the case that men devote themselves at one moment to one concern, and at the next moment to another? Accordingly, is not the relation between the values of a person or a culture simply one of mutual accommodation rather than hierarchical organization under a single supreme value? Is not man's value problem simply the juggler's problem of keeping several balls in the air without dropping any of them?

The real answers to these critical questions must, of course, be factual answers, that is to say, to whatever the actual, detailed observation of human personality, valuation, and religion leads us. At this point in our study, let us take ultimate concern as an initial hypothesis to be tested on the facts. Meanwhile it may be observed that the state of commitment to many values or value systems is strikingly similar to the religious phenomenon of polytheism. One writer has even proposed the hypothesis of "momentary gods." [4] Yet against a purely polytheistic faith or value system it may fairly be urged that human personality needs some functioning unity or integration if it is to continue at all. Such a unity, like the hub of a wheel which holds the spokes together, is provided by what we have here termed an ultimate concern or value.

Ultimate or religious concerns are thus unifying concerns for both persons and cultures. Perhaps too it may be observed that the fact which is decisive against a pure "polytheism of values" is the kind of human situation which demands unconditional decision and allegiance. Such "all or nothing" decisions, where one's whole life and life's meaning are at stake, presuppose unity. Such for example, is the decision for or against a totalitarian political system, or for or against human freedom. In such situations one chooses or decides, as the Bible suggests, with all one's heart, soul, mind, and strength.[5]

Another suggestion for understanding this area of human experience is to imagine a straight line along which one can locate various kinds of concerns. If he places at one end of the line those concerns which have an absolutely serious quality, at the other end he must place those which have only a passing, or in the literal and etymological sense, a superficial quality. As one moves along this line from the superficial to the serious concerns, he will observe the increasing emergence of religious quality. Also if the latter end of the line represents what has been called ultimate concern, then one may perhaps call those interests near this end "penultimate," or possessing an "almost religious" quality.[6]

PERVASIVENESS

A second trait of ultimate values, as the term is used here, is that such interests or values are spread over the totality of experience. Some interests or values are limited to a part of experience, while others claim dominance over all of human existence. The most obvious illustration is the contrast between political allegiance as construed by free and by totalitarian societies. In the former case, political concern is one partial human interest among others. Exactly the opposite is the case in totalitarianism, as indicated by the word itself. The Communist Party member, for example, agrees to guide *all* his activities by the directives of the Party. It is precisely the unlimited, unrestricted, or total quality suggested by *all* which gives to communism and to other forms of totalitarianism their often observed but little-understood religious character. Religious concerns are by nature total, all-embracing concerns.

HOLINESS

A third observable feature of ultimate concerns is their emotive or affective accompaniment, namely, the holy. Like *religion,* the terms *holy* and *sacred* are commonly used with many and variable meanings. Here it is convenient to begin with Rudolph Otto's approach to the holy as a unique emotion.[7] Like any unique entity, it is therefore strictly speaking indefinable. Nevertheless it is possible to point to a unique object and say that it is like this or that other object of experience. In this way, Otto says that the experience of the holy is like the experience of fear, wonder, awe, or mystery. As the study of this book unfolds, the reader will be able to see for himself how infinitely various are the forms of the holy. In this variety, perhaps the highest expression of the holy is the quality of reverence. Chapter 2 will return to the holy in some of its concrete manifestations.

Probably the most significant way of pointing to the holy is to indicate its relation to ultimate concern. The holy is the emotive accompaniment of ultimate concern and commitment. Wherever men commit themselves unconditionally, there this emotion emerges in their lives. Conversely, wherever we come upon this emotion, we have reason to believe that ultimate concern is occurring. Some writers distinguish between the sacred and the holy, asserting that the holy is an emotive response and the sacred a volitional or valuational response.[8] In this usage of terms, sacred values may be characterized as ultimate values plus their unique emotive quality of holiness.

This relation between ultimate concern and holiness is extremely useful to students of religion. It may be likened to the relation between atmospheric temperature and the height of the mercury column in the thermometer. Thus, the presence or absence of the holy in human experience is an accurate indicator of ultimate or religious concern. If this emotion is absent, the student may assume that living religious experience is absent. Wherever it does occur, even in response to such officially nonreligious symbols as a nation's flag, there ultimate or religious concern may be presumed to be present.

Called by many names, the holy designates not only the source but also the common feature of mankind's diverse faiths. This latter fact provides a decisive clue for definition. Among well-nigh innumerable definitions of religion perhaps the least inadequate and least misleading is in terms of human experiences which exhibit the quality of the holy. *A religion may thus be defined as an existent system of holy forms.* These forms are patterns or structures of human attitudes, beliefs, or practices; they are organized or structured ways of thinking, feeling, or doing. Sometimes they are individual forms of experience, sometimes they are social; most often they are a mixture of both. In the wide world, and in the long course of history, these systems or structures of holy forms have exhibited enormous variety. Yet their common and defining feature is their embodiment of the holy. Systems which exhibit this quality are religions, while systems which lack this feature are thereby rendered nonreligious in character.

SYMBOLIC EXPRESSION

A fourth feature of religious experience has to do with its expression and communication. Here a distinction must be made between the participant and the observer, or between the religious adherent and the student of religion. While it is legitimate for the student or observer to speak of religious experience, or ultimate concern, this is seldom the language of the participant or adherent. Men rarely say, "Let us have a religious experience," or "Let us be ultimately concerned." Rather, religious experience takes place in a context of powerful symbolic objects and words. These objects elicit the participant's religious responses. How natural, then, for him to assume that the holy or sacred actually dwells in these symbolic objects. For it is these objects which mediate his experience of the holy. Conversely, it is the function of eliciting ultimate concern which constitutes these objects as symbols.

In the history of man's religions, how infinitely various are these religious objects or forms! No object or event is so bizarre or so commonplace but that somewhere (and somewhen) men have treated it as a holy symbol. Rocks, trees, mountains, rivers, caves, and territories—these are only a few of the holy symbols of the world's religions. Similarly, commonplace actions like eating, drinking, or dancing (or doing nothing), not to speak of particular persons, groups, seasons, and times of life all have served as symbolic vehicles of holiness or ultimate valuation for some individual or community. What is meant by the term *symbol* is a large and difficult question. It is sufficient here to observe that symbols are poetic or imaginative words or other kinds of objects which have the power to evoke and sustain deeply moving forms of experience.

CELEBRATION AND CULTURE

A fifth and final trait of religious experience is its double aspect as celebrated and as lived. On the one hand ultimate concern may be *said* or celebrated in ritual and myth; but on the other hand it may also be *lived out*. The latter aspect sets important problems for the whole structure of both personality and culture. In respect to personality, ultimate concern means those convictions which give unity and meaning to a man's life. Such presumably is the basic function of religion in individual life. In respect to culture, ultimate concern signifies the convictions which create and sustain the life of a culture, and which also make it a shared life or community. So it is that culture is "lived faith" or "lived religion." [9] Ultimate concern is in this respect another name for those convictions which create and sustain the common life of a people. Hence, as Tillich has said, no great work of culture can hide its religious foundation.[10] That is to say, it is an expression of ultimate concern, or valuation.

MAN—THE RELIGIOUS ANIMAL

Religious experience of some sort seems common and peculiar to the human species. Attempts to show religion as an aspect of some animal species have collapsed, and now it is generally conceded that only man is religious. Within the human species all the cultures or societies of which we possess reliable knowledge show some form of religious behavior. Often, to be sure, these forms differ vastly from the forms of our own society. Also, there are in some societies, such as our own, individuals who in varying degrees reject these forms. Yet for the overwhelming majority of men in history, religious experience of some sort is a fundamental and common fact of life. Man is *Homo religiosus,* the religious animal.

Granting this conclusion, it is a promising clue to seek the source of religious experience in those features of the human situation which are unique in man. This suggestion goes counter to the thought of much modern social science, which has placed emphasis on the massive continuities of man with other forms of life, and indeed with nonorganic nature. Is not man only a single twig on the great tree of life? Is not the human body made of the same matter and subject to the same laws as nonorganic nature? Surely, one must understand and accept the full force of these assertions before he may legitimately proceed to consider any unique or distinctive features of the human species.

Yet that there are unique features of Homo sapiens is undeniable. For example, simple tools are present in some animal species, but tools are elaborated with an utterly new complexity in human technology. Hence man is *Homo faber*. Again, animals signal to each other in many ways, yet only in the human species is there evidence that signals are formally organized in syntax and grammar. Thus animal signals become human language. As Ernst Cassirer has persuasively argued, man is *Animal symbolicum*.[11] Still again, learning and training are important features of the life of many animal species, yet between animal training and human education there opens up a difference of kind as well as of degree. The former develops new means to the ends of life, while the latter is concerned with ends or goals of life as well as means. To cite just one more distinctive trait among the innumerable possibilities, man alone among living species appears to be aware of his own death and to face it as a conscious problem. From this awareness spring such diverse forms of human behavior as funerary customs and the erection of monuments to oneself or others. Thus too, almost unknown to other species, suicide is a human problem of considerable magnitude.

All of these and doubtless many more differences between man and his nearest animal relatives may be seen to be rooted in a single fact, namely, a new quality of human consciousness. In man alone among the animal species, awareness is turned not only outward upon the objective environment but inward upon the self. Indeed, it is precisely at the moment when awareness is turned inward that the self is born. In the words of G. H. Mead, the human self may be defined as that form of reality which can be an object to itself.[12] Most of the distinctive features of the human situation spring from man's capacity for self-awareness.

Out of this unique fact of human self-awareness emerges the perennial question Why? which is the source of religion. From Why? emerge Whence? Whither? Who am I? and the central religious question: Why am I alive? In the pages which follow, religion will be interpreted as the functioning answer to these questions. It must immediately be added that the answer is invariably given in symbolic form.

The definition or characterization of religion just given is substantially similar to that of the previous section. For in fact, the answer which men give to the religious question, Why am I alive? will be a set of values taken as providing a "reason for living." Such values thereby assume a functioning ultimacy in the life of the person who holds them.

A similar conclusion is derivable by means of the concept of *life orientation*.[13] What is the meaning of this phrase? Life has for most animal species a determinate meaning, usually definable in terms of the satisfaction of a finite number of definite biological drives, for activity, food, sex, and the like. Grant the satisfaction of these needs, and the animal appears to have a good life. With man the situation is radically different. To be sure, man as a biological organism still possesses these drives, yet in human life they are set in a wider context, so that while there is no good life for man without at least minimal satisfaction of biological needs, a whole new field with new kinds of "needs" and "desires" opens before man. Furthermore many of these new needs and drives are indeterminate and ultimately insatiable in character. What tyrant ever achieves enough power? What miser ever accumulates enough gold? What scientist ever achieves enough knowledge? What saint ever achieves enough virtue?

At the emergent human level, life becomes open and free, and the guidance of biological necessities and needs, while necessary, is no longer sufficient. So it is that a conscious relation to the wider human world, including the world of ideal possibilities, becomes a fundamental need for man. It is precisely the function of the ultimate values of religious experience to meet this need. Religious experience may thus be characterized as experience of total life orientation.

This function of total life orientation has been expressed as the activity of plotting and then walking a "path of life." Charles Morris's book entitled *Paths of Life* is devoted to the interpretation of the world's religions as alternative ways of life, or different systems of life orientation or life valuation.[14] In actual life each of these paths is invariably expressed in symbols which are distinctively its own. Conversely, it is the function of life orientation which imparts religious significance to a symbol or system of symbols.

This definition, or redefinition, of religion as a functioning answer to man's question, Why am I alive? will seem to many readers a radical relocation of religious issues from God to man. This is a problem which will be developed throughout the study which follows. Important aspects of this idea will be discussed in the final two chapters. Meanwhile, it is pertinent to observe that the fundamental question of how man will achieve and sustain his human character or essence—as well as the negative question of man's potential dehumanization—is deeply involved in his religious questions. To put this approach to religion in a single phrase, religions may be approached as so many attempts to achieve and maintain humanization. Such at least is the hypothesis here proposed. From this it follows that within each of mankind's civilized religious traditions is to be found a humane or humanistic tradition. It is therefore correct to speak not of humanism, but of humanisms. There are as many humanisms as there are major civilized religious traditions. These traditions may well differ widely from each other in the answers which they propose to the question, What must man do and be in order to be genuinely human? But they will agree on the centrality of the question.

THE STUDY OF RELIGION

Attention must now be turned from the question What is religion? to the question How do we study it? What is the proper attitude of the student of religion toward his subject? How does this attitude differ from that of the religious participant or adherent? With what tools does the enterprise of study proceed?

There are many ways to study religion, each of which has its own merits and limits, and all of which may contribute to the goal of understanding. Yet underlying all the methods are certain general issues and problems, one of which is the tension between commitment and objectivity and the closely related tension between the attitude of the religious adherent or participant and that of the student of religion. As previously noted, the former attitude is one of ultimate concern. Is there not a head-on conflict between this attitude of passionate attachment on the one hand and, on the other hand, the detached and fair-minded objectivity which is required of the student of religion? That there is a genuine tension here is undoubtedly true, but it is by no means unique to the religious region of experience. Rather it holds true for all areas of experience where significant forms of human value are involved. It is true, for example, of politics and of art. Can a man be a student of politics and at the same time a member of an active political party? Or in the case of art, is it possible to behold or enjoy art, to take in the meaning of a work of art, and also to engage in critical analysis and dissection of it?

This book is written in the conviction that in all such cases, the tensions between objectivity and commitment, between the attitudes of participant and observer, while they are real facts of life, can be creative and not destructive for both parties. In the case of religion, a faith can be the better for the searching, critical scrutiny of reason; and on the other hand, without religious participation the study of religion would soon wither and die. Unless there be religious practice, the student of religion will soon find himself unemployed!

Even more immediately the viewpoints of participant and observer are both integrally involved as aspects of all good study. Here as in other fields of liberal learning, the student must identify with his subject matter, at least to the degree necessary to establish its existence and significance. But then he must step outside and look in critical detachment at this same subject matter. From this point onward, the work of understanding alternates, as in a kind of leapfrog game, between the attitudes of attachment and detachment.

These comments will impinge differently upon different people. For the religious adherent who seeks to be a student of his own faith, it will doubtless be difficult to step outside and look with critical detachment at values to which he is unconditionally committed. Yet the adherent may be reminded that unthinking faith is a curious offering to make to the Creator of the human intellect. Speaking more affirmatively, the many fair-minded and reasonable men who adhere to some one of the world's great faiths testify to the possibility of a faith which is critically, reasonably held.

For the person who claims no religious adherence or who seeks to study a religion different from his own, the problem will be the very different one of seeking by imaginative sympathy to identify with his subject. He must strive to reproduce in some measure by imagination or empathy the viewpoint which the adherent possesses by his real participation. Doubtless this is very difficult, and no one achieves it perfectly. Yet some such act is necessary if significant study is to get under way at all.

Once it is under way, what are the characteristics of good study? Here follow in summary form three maxims for the study of religion in all its manifold varieties. The first is that *students of religion ought to seek the facts as objectively, as fully, and as freely as is humanly possible.* Stated negatively, the student of any subject ought not to hide, suppress, or distort facts. Rather he will seek them as freely and fully as he is able, and he will invite other inquirers to do likewise. This maxim is particularly necessary in the study of religion in order to dispel deeply rooted prejudices. The charge is often made that the putative or supposed study of religion is simply a massive structure of rationalization raised after the fact. Against all such charges and insinuations, the best possible defense is the actual day-to-day practice by the student of openness to fact, of freedom in the presence of facts.

In this connection it may be asked: What is a fact? To answer very briefly, a fact is whatever the human mind *finds* and does not *make, discovers* and does not *invent,* in its encounter with the world. Facts are *data,* literally and etymologically, "things given." Facts are thus pieces of reality. Beyond this general remark, what the facts are is a matter to be settled within each discipline.

It is a commonplace of discussion that there are no naked facts, denuded of all interpretation. To change the metaphor, facts do not grow like berries on a bush, waiting to be picked. Rather they are more like nuggets buried deep in the ground waiting to be dug out, polished, and exhibited to the world. It must also be observed whenever we exhibit them we do so in an interpretive context. Hence, the second maxim is *seek those explanations or interpretations which best illuminate the factual data, and form judgments on the basis of factual evidence.* The student should seek explanations which really explain; among the various alternative explanations in any given situation he should choose that which explains most adequately. It will sometimes be difficult to apply this rule to specific situations; but at least it provides a common goal of explanation or understanding.

A third general maxim for students of religion is *distinguish between fact and value, or between factual judgments and value judgments.* Factual judgments assert that something *is* or is *so,* while value judgments assert that in some way something is good or valuable, or that in some way it *ought* to be, or to exist. In actual human experience, fact and value are seldom or never separated. Values are built into factual situations; factual situations impinge upon human beings in ways which are good or evil, valuable or the opposite. Yet for purposes of study, it is sometimes important to distinguish fact from value, or more strictly, factual judgments from value judgments.

A fundamental distinction among the methods of studying religion is based upon this distinction between fact and value. Some methods seek to approach religion factually as an existing human phenomenon, abstracting it from all questions of validity or invalidity, good or evil, while other methods are deliberately normative or value-oriented in their approach to the subject.

APPROACHES TO THE STUDY OF RELIGION

What now are some of the specific approaches to the study of religion?

THEOLOGY

Theology is probably the oldest form of such study. Both the word and the idea are Greek in origin, going back to Aristotle, Plato, or perhaps even Socrates, for whom theology was the "ology" dealing with *theos. Ology* derives from the Greek word *logos* whose meanings range from "speech" to "study" or "inquiry" to "rational structure" which may be apprehended by human speech or mind. Thus the proper aim of any inquiry or study is to set forth the logos of the subject matter. *Theos* in Greek means "god," or "deity" or "things pertaining to deity." Theology was thus for the Greeks rational inquiry into things pertaining to the gods.

In this wide and generic sense, theological study has probably accompanied religious experience from its earliest human occurrences to the present moment. This is so for the good reason that the same human self which commits itself in ultimate concern is also a mind seeking critical understanding of its own commitments and those of other men as well. In this sense every man is perforce his own theologian. So conceived, theological study combines factual and value judgments in comprehensive synthesis.

During the Christian ages of the West, theology acquired a more limited meaning, coming to mean in effect the effort of the Christian faith at self-understanding. As a corollary, it has often been asserted that participation in theological study is limited to adherents of Christian faith, for surely only a Christian can truly understand the faith. However, in more modern times the attempt of theology to understand "from within" has given theology an exceedingly bad name. Hostile critics ask if it is not thus simply a vast enterprise of justifying a previously held position. Is not the theologian committed in advance to rationalizing some of the most provincial and prejudiced viewpoints of the medieval past? How then can he claim the intellectual freedom so essential to fair-minded, objective study? No candid observer would deny that theology has often deserved this bad reputation. On the other hand, these vices are by no means limited to theology, and at its best theological study is as rigorous, as critical, as free and fair-minded as any other intellectual discipline.

PHILOSOPHY

Philosophy is in some of its manifold aspects concerned with the study of religion. In ancient Greece, which is the historical source of Western philosophy, critical reflection upon religious mythology was a primary source of philosophical study. Similar relations will be observed in the history of both India and China. Since Hegel (1770–1831), "philosophy of religion" has been the customary label for a philosophic approach to religious issues and problems. Contemporary philosophy, particularly in the West, has not infrequently been scornful or hostile toward religion. Nevertheless, the philosophic exposition and appraisal of religious issues continues to be a major context and method for the study of religion. Sometimes in the contemporary situation the label "philosophical theology" is applied to this form of study. Whatever the label, this kind of thought impinges upon the subject of this book in two ways. In several of the religious traditions to be studied, the emergence of philosophical thinking will be observed as an important part of the tradition. In addition to this, the student will wish to make his own philosophical judgments concerning the subject matter. Philosophical thinking is thus part of the subject matter to be studied, and also an aspect of our study of it.

Many questions come to mind concerning the nature of philosophy and its relation to religion. Where does philosophy stand relative to the distinction between factual study and value-oriented, or normative, study? What indeed is the relation of philosophy to religion? On these and similar questions there exist vast disagreements among contemporary philosophers and theologians. Here it must suffice to observe that we shall follow the traditional view of philosophy as a form of study which seeks to embrace fact and value in a synoptic unity of all reality. Philosophic thinking about religion, or anything else, has an indefeasibly normative character.

What then, it may be asked, is the relation of philosophy to religion? This question will be with us for the duration of our study. At this point it must suffice to note both a similarity and a difference between these two activities. The similarity is that in contrast to other limited (and properly *delimited*) concerns such as art, science, and politics, both religion and philosophy make total claims upon men's lives, or in some way involve the widest possible totality of experience. The difference between religion and philosophy lies in their characteristic attitudes. As we have seen, that of religion is an attitude of faith or ultimate concern, while that of philosophy may be described as one of critical inquiry. The philosophic attitude is one of question asking while that of religion is one of question answering. It is not surprising to note that historically the recurring questions of philosophy are the abiding assurances of religion.

HISTORY

From ancient times history has constituted an important method and medium for the study of religion. Once more, both the word and the discipline are Greek in origin. Greek and Roman historians often dealt with religious beliefs and practices as aspects of their historical studies. In the ancient Greco-Roman world the Stoics were preeminent for their interest in the diverse religious phenomena of their world.

When, in early modern times, following the Middle Ages of Europe, historical study began again, it placed great emphasis on a critical evaluation of the sources from which the historian derives his data. Modern historical study and writing have shown a very great many emphases and varieties. Among these has been a noteworthy concern with the history of religions. Applied to Western religions, this study has emphasized free and critical study of Biblical and Christian sources. However, history of religions has also sought to embrace all of mankind's religions in its scope. It has been particularly concerned with the critical reconstruction (as well as the communication to Occidental readers) of essential aspects of the various Oriental faiths. It also has produced a persistent interest in the comparative study of the world's religions. With many changes of emphasis, these historical forms of study continue to the present moment. It is an important part of the task of this book to put the student in touch with the main conclusions of these historical forms of study.

How does historical study stand with respect to the distinction between fact and value? Clearly many kinds of valuation impinge upon the mind of the historian, influencing his study in innumerable ways, from the selection of data to be studied to his concluding appraisals. Yet despite all these influences, history is in its central aims a form of factual study, which seeks the factual reconstruction of this or that part of the human past. The final test of historical study is adequacy as to facts. Such tests and aims stand in contrast to the systematic evaluations of the philosopher and theologian. Similarly factual in method and aim are the sciences of man to be described in the next paragraph.

BEHAVIORAL SCIENCES

In modern times scientific methods of study have been extended to include man and society, producing bodies of knowledge variously labeled social sciences, sciences of man, or more recently, behavioral sciences. These are large, various, and important enterprises, yet they are pertinent here only as they bear upon the study of religion.

At least three of the behavioral sciences have done notable work in the study of religion, namely, psychology, sociology, and anthropology. All three of these disciplines laid their scientific foundations in the nineteenth century. The first psychology laboratory was established in Leipzig under Wilhelm Wundt in 1879; and Wundt's student, Tichner, established the first American department of psychology at Cornell University. Among the American pioneers of psychology was William James (1842–1910), whose wide interests ranged over both psychology and philosophy. James was one of the first, and surely one of the greatest, psychologists of religion. His book *The Varieties of Religious Experience,* which was the Gifford lectures of 1901–1902, has remained a classic in this field. James worked from the manuscript collections of E. D. Starbuck, which embraced all sorts of religious experiences, and deliberately emphasized bizarre and pathological forms. James sought in his psychology of religion to develop inductively from factual data the categories and generalizations essential for scientific understanding of religion. He was joined in this enterprise by such diverse workers as J. H. Leuba and J. B. Pratt. Despite some continuing interest along these lines, it must be added that in recent decades psychological interest in religion has shifted to other approaches and tasks.

Much recent experimental psychology, especially of the behaviorist school, has been either scornful or indifferent toward religion. Meanwhile other schools, as for example, that including Gordon Allport and centering around the psychology of personality, as well as those influenced by psychoanalysis, have continued a lively though critical interest in religious phenomena. This interest has operated both at a theoretical and a practical, or clinical, level, and has often provided fresh critical perspectives on religion and religious experience.

Sociology derived not only its name and many of its basic categories but also a critical concern with religion from Auguste Comte (1798–1857) and his "positive" philosophy. It has been concerned with religious belief and behavior as aspects of the society and social groups which it aims to study. Pioneering work in this area was done by Max Weber (1864–1920), whose book, *The Protestant Ethic,* discovered a close relation between the ethics of Calvinistic Protestantism and the rise of capitalism. Weber turned the same categories of social analysis on the religions of ancient India and China and on ancient Judaism. His influence continues in such contemporary sociologists as Talcott Parsons.

Anthropology is, as the etymology of the word implies, the science of man. Cultural anthropology has tended to be the comparative study of man in different cultures. Dating from Darwin's *Descent of Man* (1871) and E. B. Tylor's *Primitive Culture* (1875), it has maintained a special interest in primitive or preliterate cultures. The geneticism and evolutionism which characterized nineteenth-century anthropology have been largely replaced in the twentieth century by an interest in varieties of human culture and cultural patterns and in the human function performed by a society's many structures and processes. The next chapter will discuss some of the current findings of the anthropology of religion.

PHENOMENOLOGY

At the present time in Europe and America a notable synthesis of the various sciences of religion appears to be taking place under the title, "phenomenology of religion." This approach derives from the philosophic movement known as phenomenology which was originated and led by Edmund Husserl (1859–1938). Husserl's phenomenology was constituted by what the author believed to be a new method for philosophic study, among whose more important aspects were (1) the proposal to "bracket" or set aside all questions of evaluation, interpretation, and speculation, thus (2) to concentrate attention on the data of consciousness as they are presented to man's mind. Such data or "things given" are the phenomena which phenomenology is concerned to study. This study proceeds by rigorous, exhaustive description of these data as they present themselves to human consciousness.

Phenomenology provides a new approach in its descriptive study of the human phenomenon of religion. It proposes to study religion as a basic and pervasive aspect of human experience, systematically excluding all issues of philosophic or theological interpretation or validation.

If one thinks of religious experience metaphorically as a telephone conversation, phenomenology of religion proposes to set aside all questions which are concerned with the party at the other end of the wire. Does God exist or not? Is deity personal or impersonal? What, if anything, does he say to man? Such questions are simply beyond the scope of phenomenological study of religion, though this study must note as an aspect of the experience the transcendent claims made by religious experience. Yet the phenomenological student must deliberately avoid all judgments as to the validity of these claims, limiting his attention to religion as an observable aspect of human personality, society, and history.

Meanwhile, concentrating attention on the study of religious experience, phenomenology brings to its task the combined skills and achievements, the methods and results of all the social sciences. Their common purpose, simply and plainly stated, is to understand religion as an aspect of human experience. If the reader notes that the discussion of religion and religious experience in the first part of this chapter is influenced by phenomenology of religion, his observation will be entirely correct. Indeed, this influence will be apparent throughout this study of the world's faiths. In other words, religion will be treated as a pervasive aspect of human history and experience. Whatever else or more religion is, it is this. Descriptive, factual study of religion begins with this assumption. An understanding of whatever else it may—or may not—be will be erected on this foundation. To the descriptive, factual study of religion and religious experience this book is devoted.

TYPES OF RELIGION

As noted in the first section of this chapter, religious experience demands and receives symbolic expression for itself. In any specific situation these symbols are not symbols in general, but certain altogether concrete, particular symbols, around which gathers a community of people who express their ultimate concern through them. By some such process as this, the adjective *religious* is transformed into the noun or substantive *religion*. In other words *a religion* comes into being and maintains itself as a community centering in some concrete symbol or symbol system for the expression of ultimate concern.

Among the many implications to be drawn from this fact is one which has to do quite practically with the selection of religions to be studied in books like this one. Obviously all such selections and distinctions contain a conventional element. Yet properly the student will divide the field in terms of existing religious communities, as defined above. A glance at the table of contents will show a list of the existing religious communities of the contemporary world. These communities vary enormously in size, from a few thousand to many millions of adherents. They also vary in their relations to each other. The relations of Protestant and Roman Catholic Christianity to each other and to Judaism differ vastly from the relations between the religious communities of India, China, and Japan. The common feature in all this variety, once more, is that the religions selected for study in this volume (except for the explicit exception of Chapter 2) constitute actual living religious communities.

Many religions have been born and lived, and some have died during the long course of human history. They may be classified in many ways, each of which doubtless serves some particular use or purpose. In this section, there will be proposed a threefold classification based upon the location of the religious object, or object of ultimate concern. This object (or these objects) may be located (1) within the common world of nature and society, (2) beyond or above this world, or (3) both beyond and within the common world. There are accordingly three types of religion.[15]

The first type usually has a plurality of religious objects or gods; in other words, it is polytheistic. Its many deities are located within the common world of nature and society, and are more or less personified statements of man's relation to this world or to specific aspects of it. This type of religion has often been accurately characterized as "nature-culture religion." It has also been termed "cosmic religion." [16] The limiting case for this type of religion is that which takes the universe or world itself as divine. Something like this apparently was the view of the philosopher Aristotle. Chapter 17 will present the faith of Spinoza, who achieved his own highly distinctive formulation of this view.

Prehistoric and primitive religions are clearly of this first type, as will be seen in the next chapter. So are ancient Mesopotamian and Greek religions. China's classical faith is of this type. Among the world's living religions, Shinto in Japan, to be discussed in Chapter 9, most clearly exemplifies the nature-culture religion. It may also be asserted that whatever their formal professions, the actual functioning faith of most men in human history is of this type. It is so even when they formally profess different types of faith, such as those of the second and third types.

The second type of religion locates the religious object beyond the common secular world of nature and society. Here, in contrast to the first type, the religious object is usually conceived as singular rather than plural. It is *one* rather than *many*. Sometimes it is understood as deity, but sometimes not. In either case this type of religion represents the achievement by the human mind of a kind of Archimedean standpoint outside the world. As Archimedes asserted, if he could find a place to stand outside the world, he could move the world. Sometimes this type of religion is labeled "transcendent monism." The clearest historical illustrations are Buddhism, Jainism, and philosophic Hinduism. Popular Hinduism doubtless continues as a religion of the first rather than the second type. Various kinds of mysticism of both East and West also exemplify the second type.

The third type of religion finds the religious object both beyond and within the common world. With the second type, it shares an Archimedean standpoint beyond the common world; yet with the first type it asserts the reality and goodness of the world of nature and culture. The fundamental concern of this type of religion with one God makes appropriate the label "monotheism." The monotheistic religions of human history are Judaism, Christianity, Islam, and Zoroastrianism.

As subsequent chapters of this book will show, many further important distinguishing features cluster around the defining characteristics of the three types. Yet historical study also reveals many mixed types. Human history, it seems, tends to blur the sharp outlines of typological distinctions. At least one living religion, Sikhism, began as a deliberate attempt to mix a religion of the second type, Hinduism, with one of the third type, Islam. Much interest in Sikhism derives from this fact.

The differences implied by the threefold classification of religions by no means preclude the possibility of similarities of many sorts extending across the boundaries of the types. If a musical metaphor be permitted, it may be said that there are three main keys in which religions are composed, but that in these keys a great many themes and images recur. Some of these recurring features of the world's faiths will be discussed in the next section of this chapter.

The geographical source regions and distribution of the three types of religion is a subject of interest. Religions of the first type are scattered widely over the face of the earth, embracing all prehistoric and primitive religions, as well as the religions of archaic civilizations from Greece and Mesopotamia to China. South Asia, or the subcontinent of India, seems to be the leading source region of religions of the second type, though such exceptions or possible exceptions as ancient Taoism in China or Neoplatonism in Rome come readily to mind. The map in the front cover of this book shows the main distribution of religions of this type. The source region of monotheistic religions is the ancient Near East, extending from Iran westward, which may be seen on the map inside the back cover. However, the present distribution of these religions of the third type tends to be global—the historical relation of Christianity to the West notwithstanding. There are communities of Jews, Christians, and Muslims on every continent of the earth.

RECURRING QUESTIONS AND THEMES

The world's faiths show not only differences but many similarities. In some cases these similarities derive from common human situations. For example, for all men birth and death are crucially important events; hence birth and death are given religious interpretation in most or all religions.[17] So too are coming of age and marriage. Other significant occasions of human life are frequently invested with religious significance. In many societies the chief or head man and the laws of the group are holy. Frequently those aspects of nature upon which the group is dependent for life and livelihood are regarded as sacred. Illness and health, war and peace, disaster and prosperity—these are only a few of the recurring human situations invested with religious significance.

In general it may be said that these recurring human situations set problems or put questions to which the world's faiths offer solutions or provide answers.

Hence the dialectic of question and answer, of problem and solution, will be useful throughout the pages which follow. Frequently the student of religion will wish to dig out the question which is latent in the human situation and then show how this or that religion provides an answer to this question. It will be helpful at the beginning of this study to make a list of some of the questions or problems which will recur throughout. The list which follows here makes no claim to be complete or indeed to be a definitive list of recurring issues but rather seeks to be suggestive; the reader is encouraged to compile his own list as study proceeds.

It may also be pointed out that this or any other similar list of questions remains within the limits of descriptive or factual study. To be sure, each of the world's faiths makes its own normative answer to these questions. And in other contexts each man will wish to make his own answer in faith or ultimate valuation to these questions. Yet as students of religion our work is done when we have noted both the recurring human questions and the answers given by the world's faiths.

These issues are stated here to provide the student with a sample set of pegs, as it were, on which to hang the fabric of his study of religion. By no means do all the following themes recur in all the world's faiths. Nor will we feel obligated to point to every last occurrence of each theme or question. It must suffice to state these issues or themes here, and then to point occasionally to significant illustrations as they occur.

IS THIS A RELIGION?

Is this a religion, and if so, of what sort? This question may well sound artificial and pedantic to the beginning student. Such readers will be interested to know that in point of fact this question arises in the primary literature of virtually every religion to be studied. Indeed, virtually every one of the world's faiths denies, for one reason or another, that it is a religion. Something is obviously problematic about so questionable a word. One of the objectives of this study will be to work at this question, seeking an answer which accords with the facts of the world's faiths. Meanwhile, we begin with the provisional definition of a religion as a system of holy forms. Insofar as any system of phenomena has these properties, it will fall within our field of inquiry. Yet these assertions must also be regarded as hypotheses whose adequacy will be tested as inquiry proceeds.

WHAT IS THE RELIGIOUS OBJECT?

What is the nature of the religious object? This fundamental question, already broached in the previous section's typology, will be asked of each of the faiths to be studied. Is there, for example, a conception of deity? To the great surprise of many Western students of religion, some religions appear to have no deity at all, and in others deity is incidental and not central to the faith. If God or gods occur in the religion being studied, how are they conceived, and how do they function? More generally, under what circumstances do religions produce a deity and under what circumstances do they not?

HOW SHALL WE BE SAVED?

Religious experience may be formulated in terms of man's problem and its so-lution. If the terms *sin* and *salvation* may be stripped of all specifically Judeo-Christian interpretation and taken as general words for what is wrong with man and how man may be set right, then all the religions may be characterized in terms of sin and salvation. For all religions assert that there is a fundamental human problem which needs to be solved. There is a sin from which man needs to be saved. To use a still different metaphor (which was in fact used by Buddha) the religions of the world assert that man is sick, and each presents its own distinctive diagnosis and therapy. Religions may be approached as ways of salvation (a word which literally means "healing" or "wholeness"), though *from* what and *to* what man is saved are matters of specific interpretation in each of the faiths to be studied.

WHAT IS MAN?

Closely related to this question is another: What is man? In some cases this question is implied or suggested by the previous one. Yet in many of the world's religions the questions Who am I? and What is man? become a conscious focus for thought. In some sense, men have always asked these questions, demanded answers, and indeed have lived out their answers, as was noted in the second section of this chapter. Yet they are asked with a peculiar poignancy and urgency amid the storms of the twentieth-century world. It will not be false to the contemporary situation to imagine man in the center of a circle, asking pre-cisely these questions, with the different faiths of the world located around the circumference of the circle, each giving its answer. Among these answers man must choose, and in these terms he must live out his life. From a particular faith's answer to this question arise many other characteristic features of the faith, ranging from its puberty rites to its funerary customs to its ethical com-mandments. All such features bear a significant and understandable relation to the view of man.

RELIGIOUS FORMS

Another kind of question is posed by the observable recurrence of certain forms or structures among the different religions. Among the most frequently recurring structures are (a) myth, (b) ritual, (c) morality, and (d) religious community. Most if not all of man's religions tell sacred stories, engage in symbolic actions deemed to have religious meaning, live by certain commandments both affirmative and negative which derive from faith, and carry on these and other religious activities together in distinctive communities. The life values which constitute the human content of religion and which are sung or said in myth are enacted or celebrated in ritual. In morality these same life values become the standard goals of action; and in religious communities they become the integrating center which draws men together into the community.

The student's interest in these recurring forms is to see in what distinctive ways they emerge in the various faiths studied. What kind of songs are sung or tales are told? What kind of ritual occurs? What kind of ethics emerges and what place does ethics play in the whole religion?

The issues of religious community are even more complicated. While in one of its aspects religion is, as Whitehead reminds us, "What a man does with his solitariness," [18] religion is never completely solitary. Rather there is invariably some community of religious practice or faith. What is the nature of this community? What are its common practices, what is their significance? What is the relation of this community to the wider society of which it is a part? For some religions the religious community is simply the whole society performing or celebrating its faith. Such was the case in ancient Mesopotamia or Greece; with qualifications, such is the case with Shinto. In other cases, the religious community separates itself in ascetic withdrawal from the world. Such are the monastic communities in various faiths. Still other religious communities engage in missionary activity to the wider world, as do Christianity, Buddhism, and Islam. In every case the social structures, processes, and relations of a religion are an extremely important aspect of its whole nature, and are accordingly well worth study.

PHILOSOPHY

Another kind of theme which, while by no means universal is nonetheless widely recurrent, has to do with the emergence of theological or philosophical thinking in the world's faiths. Instances of this phenomenon will be visible in religious traditions as different as those of India, China, Greece, and medieval Christianity. The source of these forms of religious thinking lies in the fact that man, who as a self commits himself in ultimate concern or valuation, is also a mind concerned to understand this experience. In tracing the implications and bearings of the religious experience, men have been led to concepts of an altogether inclusive totality, and this is a type of thinking that constitutes the distinctive feature of philosophy. It is precisely the ultimacy or absolute quality of ultimate concern which leads the human mind to these widest generalities of which it is capable. Within this inclusive context, religious faith and experience are then critically appraised and either validated or invalidated. Such at least has been the course of events as philosophical thinking has emerged in several different cultural traditions. Accordingly, as he makes his way from faith to faith the student will be concerned to ask: Does philosophy occur here, and if so what are its distinctive features?

ARTISTIC EXPRESSION

Similar in many respects to the relation of religion to philosophy is that of religion to the arts. In many of the world's cultures faith has found significant expression in such arts as painting, sculpture, architecture, music, and literature; conversely, these arts have often been accorded a religious significance. Indeed the world's great art has more often than not been religious art. When the reader recalls the assertion that the religious experience demands and receives symbolic expression, this historic fact of the relation of religion to art is not at all surprising. It is, moreover, an extremely significant relation for both art and religion. Frequently through great and distinctive works of art in the various faiths we may (if we have ears to hear or eyes to see) perceive what these faiths have to say to us and to mankind. Illustrations will be given throughout our study of great works of the world's art which possess religious significance.

MYSTICISM

Another significant recurring theme is mysticism. Among the world's religions and also among students of religions this subject is a hardy perennial. Yet few terms in this whole vast field are subject to more variant and conflicting usage than "mystic" and "mysticism." At this point in our inquiry, it is sufficient to indicate a few general categories in terms of which this phenomenon may be identified and its analysis begun. The adjective *mystical* may be applied broadly but justifiably to any form of religious experience in which immediacy of apprehension (or cognition) is strongly emphasized. By *immediacy* is meant directness, or intuitive quality, in knowing.

Incidentally this definition collides head-on with the popular misconception to the effect that mystical means necessarily nonrational or irrational, that in effect, reason and mysticism are mutually exclusive. From the definition here given it may be correctly inferred that intuitive forms or qualities of knowing vary independently with rationality. Some mystical states are clearly irrational, and stoutly resist attempts at rational checking or testing. But others appear to be quite the opposite. Beyond the wide use of *mystical* as synonymous with *immediate* (not mediated), the noun *mysticism* is applied to two contrasting types of experience. One of these is sometimes called mysticism of communion, and the other is termed mysticism of ontological union, or absorption. Mystics speak characteristically of *union* with the religious object. Yet they appear to have in mind either one of two different meanings of this word. First is the intimate communion of friends who are "at one" with each other. Second is absorption in an Object so that all separate identity or selfhood disappears. In the latter, the self is frequently compared to a drop of water which returns to the great ocean of Being, or Reality. This distinction between absorption and communion will prove to be extremely important in several of mankind's religions.

The mysticism of communion has frequently served as a revitalizing force in a religious tradition. Examples of this will be forthcoming in several of the following chapters. The mysticism of absorption has also frequently had the further implication of suggesting a distinctive philosophic outlook. The late Aldous Huxley wrote of this outlook as the "perennial philosophy" recurring in many different times and places.[19] The distinctive features of this outlook will be sketched out later as discussion proceeds. At this point it is sufficient to note the recurrence of mystics and mysticism in all or most of mankind's faiths.

CONCLUDING COMMENT

This chapter on methods and approaches—in short on the tools of study—has been so long that the reader may well be impatient to move on to the use of these tools in the study of religions. This is an impatience that the author shares. For surely the justification of any tool is in the work that it enables us to do.

We have been concerned in this chapter with three main issues that will recur throughout our study. First, we have sought in however preliminary a manner to locate and identify our subject, and we have endeavored to relate it to man or humanity.

On this first issue, we have defined religious experience in terms of ultimate concern or ultimate valuation, then drawn out a few implications of this definition. Among these implications, none is more important than the assertion that the human content of mankind's religions is a cluster of values whose human function is to give meaning to life, and whose form is powerful expressive images or symbols. In the case of each of the religions which follow in this book we shall call attention to both of these elements, namely their value content and their symbolic expression.

Second, we have asserted that the religions of mankind—each in its own specific and concrete way—have functioned to answer the fundamental human question, why am I alive? What is the meaning of life? In this specific sense, all of mankind's religions have a humanistic function. However, a further distinction will be useful. Some religions like China's Confucianism (Chapter 8) place man in the center of the universe, saying in effect that "man is the measure of all things." Others assert a Reality above or beyond man, to which human life must conform. For these latter religions human life must be transcended, which means, both etymologically and literally, "to go beyond." Perhaps the clearest, starkest illustration of this type of religion is Indian Jainism (Chapter 4). Yet among the religions of transcendence, as we may call them, a further distinction will be useful. Of these religions some find human life fulfilled or realized in the encounter with higher reality, and so constitute a kind of humanism, while in others, notably Jainism, human values are simply transcended, and thus in effect wiped out.

Third and finally, we have asserted a threefold classification of the world's religions as (a) cosmic, (b) acosmic, and (c) historical. In the chapters which follow we shall seek to place each of mankind's religions in this classification.

NOTES

1. Paul Tillich, *The Protestant Era,* The University of Chicago Press, Chicago, 1948, pp. xv, 58, 87, 273.

2. Ralph B. Perry, *General Theory of Values,* Longmans, Green & Co., Inc., New York, 1926, pp. 115f.

3. Tillich, *op. cit.* See also numerous references to this topic in Paul Tillich, *Systematic Theology,* vols. I, II, III, The University of Chicago Press, Chicago, 1951–1963.

4. E. Cassirer, *Language and Myth,* Dover Publications, Inc., New York, 1946, pp. 22f.

5. Mark 12:30.

6. *Penultimate* is a term I first came across in an unpublished paper by Professor Thomas O'Dea of Columbia University.

7. R. Otto, *The Idea of the Holy,* Oxford University Press, London, 1923.

8. John Oman, "The Sphere of Religion," in Joseph Needham (ed.), *Science, Religion and Reality,* The Macmillan Company, New York, 1925.

9. T. S. Eliot, *Notes on the Definition of Culture,* Harcourt, Brace & World, Inc., New York, 1949, p. 30.

10. Tillich, *The Protestant Era,* p. 58.

11. E. Cassirer, *An Essay on Man,* Yale University Press, New Haven, Conn., 1944, p. 26.

12. G. H. Mead, *Mind, Self, and Society,* The University of Chicago Press, Chicago, 1934, p. 140.

13. J. Hutchison, *Language and Faith,* The Westminster Press, Philadelphia, 1963, pp. 101f.

14. Charles Morris, *Paths of Life,* George Braziller, Inc., New York, 1956.

15. Hutchison, *op. cit.,* pp. 248f.

16. M. Eliade, *Cosmos and History,*

Harper Torchbooks, Harper & Row, Publishers, Incorporated, New York, 1959.

17. Arnold van Gennep, *The Rites of Passage,* The University of Chicago Press, Chicago, 1960.

18. A. N. Whitehead, *Religion in the Making,* Living Age Books, Meridian Books, Inc., New York, 1960, p. 16.

19. Aldous Huxley, *The Perennial Philosophy,* Harper & Row, Publishers, Incorporated, New York, 1945.

SUGGESTIONS FOR FURTHER STUDY

Bergson, H.: *The Two Sources of Morality and Religion,* Anchor Books, 1954.

Burtt, E. A.: *Man Seeks the Divine,* Harper & Row, 1964.

Cassirer, E.: *An Essay on Man,* Yale, 1944.

————: *Language and Myth,* Dover, 1946.

Dawson, H. C.: *Religion and Culture,* Meridian Books, 1947.

Eliade, M.: *Patterns in Comparative Religion,* Sheed, 1958.

————: *Cosmos and History,* Harper & Row, 1959.

Frankfurt, H., and others: *Before Philosophy,* Penguin, 1951.

Hocking, W. E.: *Living Religions and A World Faith,* Harper & Row, 1940.

Huxley, A.: *The Perennial Philosophy,* Harper & Row, 1945.

James, E. O.: *History of Religions,* Harper & Row, 1957.

James, W.: *The Varieties of Religious Experience,* any edition.

King, W. L.: *Introduction to Religion,* Harper & Row, 1954.

Langer, S.: *Philosophy in a New Key,* Harvard, 1951.

Lessa, W., and E. Vogt: *Reader in Comparative Religion,* Harper & Row, 1958.

Moore, G. F.: *Birth and Growth of Religion,* Scribner, 1927.

Morris, C.: *Paths of Life,* George Braziller, 1956.

Needham, J. (ed.): *Science, Religion and Reality,* Macmillan, 1925.

Niebuhr, H. R.: *Christ and Culture,* Harper & Row, 1956.

Noss, J. B.: *Man's Religions,* Macmillan, 1963.

Otto, R.: *The Idea of the Holy,* Oxford, 1923.

Parrinder, G.: *Worship in the World's Religions,* Faber, 1961.

Smith, W. C.: *The Meaning and End of Religion,* Macmillan, 1963.

Spiegelberg, F.: *Living Religions of the World,* Prentice-Hall, 1957.

Stace, W. T.: *Mysticism and Philosophy,* Macmillan, 1961.

Tillich, P.: *The Protestant Era,* University of Chicago Press, 1948.

————: *The Courage To Be,* Yale, 1952.

————: *Theology of Culture,* Oxford, 1964.

Van der Leeuw, G.: *Religion in Essence and Manifestation,* Harper & Row, 1963.

Wach, J.: *Sociology of Religion,* University of Chicago Press, 1944.

Whitehead, A. N.: *Religion in the Making,* Meridian Books, 1960.

————: *Adventures of Ideas,* Cambridge, 1942.

Zaehner, W. C.: *Mysticism, Sacred and Profane,* Oxford, 1957.

2

SOME PAST RELIGIONS

Contemporary issues are often illuminated by a backward glance at history. Hence it is useful in a study devoted to the world's living religions to look briefly at some religions of the past. This chapter will glance quickly at prehistoric and primitive religion, and two samples of religions of ancient civilizations. This material will not only help to achieve historical perspective for the whole study, but will also provide a factual test for the previous chapter's assertion that man is *Homo religiosus*. It will also serve at the beginning of our study to underscore the fact that in the long course of human history religions are born, and some religions at least have died.

PREHISTORIC RELIGION

The scientific study of man's prehistory is only a century old; yet already it has gone through several stages of development with no end yet in sight. It began in the nineteenth century's interest in evolutionary development, aroused by the monumental achievement of Darwin. Following his success, a host of investigators sought to apply genetic and evolutionary models of explanation to every aspect of human experience, including religion.

One result of this interest was a greatly intensified study of human pre-history. Paleontologists, archaeologists, and anthropologists scrutinized extant human remains and turned up new evidence from many different parts of the world, rigorously analyzing and appraising even as the digging continued. They also eked out these somewhat meager bodies of factual evidence by carefully controlled inferences drawn from several related sciences. The result today is a fuller and probably more accurate picture of man's prehistoric past than ever before available.

The chronology which emerges from this reconstruction of the human past begins with the Paleolithic or Old Stone Age, which coincides approximately with the Pleistocene geologic era and extends approximately from a million years ago to 10,000 B.C. According to recent systems of classification,[1] this was followed by the Mesolithic or Middle Stone Age, ca. 10,000 B.C. to ca. 2500 B.C., which in turn was followed by the Neolithic or New Stone Age, whose more highly developed cultures showed such traits as crude agriculture and do-mestication of animals. Neolithic cultures were succeeded in several regions of the world by mankind's first civilized societies.

What does this reconstruction of the prehistoric past tell us about those re-mote and vast stretches of time? First, it makes clear that along with fire, simple tools, language, and culture, prehistoric man had religion. The earliest surviving human remains, dating from middle Paleolithic times, provide unequivocal evi-dence of behavior that may be termed religious or magico-religious.[2] These shreds of factual evidence from many parts of the world indicate at least three religious concerns, namely, (1) death, (2) birth and sex, and (3) man's re-lation to nature. Possibly there were others as well, evidence for which has long since perished.

Among the oldest human remains yet turned up are those of the so-called Peking man and Java man, both from a period estimated to be 400,000 to 500,000 years ago. The latter discoveries began in 1892 and extended through the 1930s and produced a number of skulls and other human bones. Meanwhile a cave near the village of Choukoutien some forty miles from Peking, China, in the late 1920s yielded skulls and other skeletal remains of some three dozen human beings from approximately the same prehistoric period.

The Choukoutien scene provided clear evidence of fire and simple tools. Furthermore the bodies had apparently been decapitated and the heads pre-served for ritual purposes. The skulls from both China and Java show injury, indicating that they had apparently been hacked open for a sacramental meal. Other bones had also been split open, presumably to get at the marrow. Ap-parently these Paleolithic men were cannibals, and the oldest known form of religious behavior is what one investigator has termed the cult of skulls.[3]

Other somewhat later Paleolithic remains from many parts of the world provide several additional and independent lines of evidence for prehistoric man's concern with death. Near the Bavarian village of Noerdlingen was found embedded in red ocher a cluster of some twenty-seven skulls, all facing westward.[4] Many other discoveries show this same red color which, as the color of blood, is inferred to be prehistoric man's magic instrumentality to preserve or reestablish life. At Le Moustier in France the skeleton of a Neanderthal youth was discovered under fragments of animal bones, lying face down with fore-

Willendorf Venus

Courtesy of the American Museum
of Natural History, New York

arm under the head and surrounded by stone tools and weapons.[5] These are only samples of the extensive evidence from widely separated regions of the world. From this evidence the student of religion may conclude that Paleolithic man was aware of death, and responded to its mystery and its threat in the only ways he could conceive.

Birth and the related phenomena of sex constituted another realm of mystery for prehistoric man, as may be seen from the so-called Venus figures, small female statues from all parts of the world whose exaggerated and sometimes voluptuous lines suggest fertility, sex, and pregnancy. It has been argued that these figures functioned as magical charms to guarantee successful pregnancy or safe birth. Scholarly controversy continues as to their precise significance, though there seems general agreement that they symbolize some sort of magico-religious concern with the origin of life in an age long before the emergence of the Earth-Mother as a goddess.

This interest found other expressions in Paleolithic times, as for example, in the fertility dance depicted in the rock shelter near Lerida, Spain.[6] In this fresco a group of nine women, narrow-waisted and wearing skirts, are shown dancing around a smaller naked male figure. Similar fertility dances and other rituals recur in folk religions throughout the world. A modern echo from this prehistoric tradition may be heard in such continuing ceremonies as dancing around the Maypole.

Of comparable significance to birth, sex, and death was Paleolithic man's relation to environing nature. Most immediately this involved the food supply, without which our prehistoric ancestor would speedily have starved. As has been said, nature was his "living larder." [7] In the absence of agriculture and domestication of animals, Paleolithic man was a predator upon nature. But he was also dependent upon nature in other ways as well. He was ever at the mercy of larger, stronger animal species. From summer's heat to winter's cold, and from flood to drought, prehistoric man's dependence upon nature was inexorably driven home to him.

Many of these concerns became the subject of magico-religious ritual, memorialized in Paleolithic cave art. In various regions, notably southern France and Spain, painting and sculpture from later Paleolithic times has been discovered deep within nearly inaccessible, dark caves. It was originally put there as an aspect of magico-religious ritual whose themes ranged from fertility and sex to hunting. One such painting depicts a dying bison with missiles being hurled at him. Another particularly notable painting from the same region has been called "The Sorcerer." It shows a figure with human face and feet but with stag's antlers, ears of a wolf, claws of a lion, and tail of a horse. Whether this figure was a human shaman who guaranteed good hunting, or whether some less obvious unity of human and animal life was intended is not clear. In either case, man's relation to environing animal species was in some way being celebrated here.

There is much factual evidence that by Neolithic times man's imagination was grasping at larger features of the nature which environed him. Sun, moon, and stars were engraved on tools and weapons. The arrangement of ritual stones, as in Stonehenge, argues a ritual relation to nature's wider aspects. The sky, or heaven, became an expression of the ultimate power and mystery upon which man was dependent. In many instances the gods were thought to live "up there." The metaphor of height for deity was destined to retain its symbolic power for a long time—perhaps until those very recent times when man turned his telescope on the heavens and then began to fly through the sky. How far back into the prehistoric past the symbolic meaning of height may be pushed is still an open question, for direct evidence is meager. Yet if the theories of

Wilhelm Schmidt and Andrew Lang are correct, a high sky god is among man's earliest prehistoric tenets.[8]

Prehistoric man's religion was made of such homely stuff as birth, copulation, death, and food supply, or, more precisely, of a magico-religious concern with these needs and values. There was a genuine realism in all this, for man's

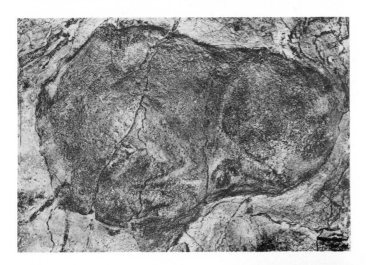

Bison cave paintings from Altamira, Spain: Actual photograph and artist's sketch

Courtesy of the American Museum of Natural History, New York

whole stake in existence consisted in these concerns. They constituted the meaning of his life, his ultimate concern. Prehistoric man's faith thus expressed his will to live in the midst of a capricious and often hostile environment.[9]

In the course of time, and particularly in the Neolithic age, cultural and social concerns developed greatly in range and complexity. Animals were do-

The Sorcerer: Cave painting from Les Trois Freres, France

Wall painting in prehistoric rock shelter

mesticated, and agriculture made an effective beginning. Man ceased to be simply a predator on nature and began to be a cultivator. He became a maker and a remaker—and also a defacer of nature. Human societies and cultures grew in size and diversification. With all of this it is not surprising that religion took on new dimensions, for again, it is the function of religion to express the total meaning of man's life. Nature in its various aspects continued to be regarded as sacred.[10] New gods and goddesses, new rituals and priestly functions, new myths all made their appearance.

Yet prehistoric man's religion remained what Chapter 1 termed the first, or nature-culture, type. It continued to be cosmic religion. The Greek term *cosmos,* usually translated as "world," designated the world of society surrounded and supported by nature under the unifying cover of heaven. Religions of the first type, from prehistoric times onward, have sought to orient man to this world, providing meaning for human life within this encompassing context.[11] Within the context of the cosmos, the adventure of humanity began.

SEARCH FOR THE ORIGIN OF RELIGION

As previously noted, nineteenth-century anthropology included a strong interest in the origin and development of religion, approaching this subject with full confidence that scientific answers would be forthcoming to questions of how religion began and how it developed from its origin to its present forms. With the epoch-making impact of Darwin's theory of evolution in biology, it was inevitable that men should extend this idea of evolutionary development to other fields of study. The pattern for this type of genetic and evolutionary explanation consisted of finding a theoretical origin and then showing the evolutionary growth and development of subsequent forms from this source. In some fields of study, this method was highly successful; in others it succeeded only in causing misunderstanding and distortion of the subject matter.

In the anthropology of religion, many investigators sought theories of how it all began and then how it evolved from primitive beginnings to nineteenth-century Europe. Some anthropologists confidently predicted that the new scientific forms of study would soon displace older prescientific philosophy and theology. Often, too, these investigators equated evolution with progress, either consciously or unconsciously. Here we shall list several such genetic theories.

Of the many specific hypotheses for the origin of religion, none was more influential than E. B. Tylor's *animism,* first propounded in his pioneering volume, *Primitive Culture,* published in 1871.[12] Tylor found the beginning of religion in primitive man's view of a soul, or ghostly double (the word *anima* being Latin for "soul," "mind," or, significantly, for "breath"). Seeing his dead friend in dreams or observing the difference between living and dead bodies, primitive man concluded that life consisted in the soul which left the body at death and which resided in breath or blood. According to Tylor's hypothesis, once the idea of a soul existed, primitive man proceeded indiscriminately to populate the world of nature with souls; and from animism evolved other, later forms of religion such as polytheism and monotheism.

Despite their initial plausibility, his views drew immediate critical fire. For one thing, the hypothesis of animism made primitive man more of a detached scientist or philosopher than there is any reason to suppose him to have been. More seriously, there soon appeared wide regions of religious belief and behavior not describable in terms of souls. In this context emerged the important alternative hypothesis of *animatism* or *manism*. The initial suggestion was made by Bishop R. H. Codrington, a missionary to Melanesia who observed that extensive areas of Melanesian religion which seemed unexplained by Tylor's animism were explicable in terms of a mysterious, impersonal power called *mana* which resided within holy or religious objects.

Once stated, the theory that religion originated in mana was taken up and developed extensively by many investigators. F. Max Mueller read Bishop Codrington's suggestion with approval, applying it to his own studies on Indian religion.[13] Codrington explained mana as a kind of mysterious power which flowed through all sorts of unusual or extraordinary objects, people, or events, setting them apart from ordinary or everyday things and happenings.[14] Codrington was particularly concerned to point out that mana varied independently of moral good and evil. It might be good or evil or morally neutral, its defining feature being simply mysterious power.

Other investigators were not slow to point out parallel ideas in the religious traditions of many other folk societies. The Sioux Indians called it *wakanda,* the Iroquois *orenda,* and the Algonquins *manitou;* but whatever the label, it turned out to be a similar idea and experience. In a notable development of mana as the source of religion, R. R. Marett placed it, in the terms of his book title, on "the threshold of religion." [15]

Still another kind of hypothesis was proposed by James G. Frazer in his multivolumed *The Golden Bough.* Following an unhistorical suggestion from Hegel's writings, Frazer postulated an age of magic antedating the age of religion.[16] Frazer distinguished magic from religion in their respective attitudes toward the world of mystery and spirit with which both purport to deal. The characteristic attitude of magic is one of control or manipulation for specific human purposes. Incidentally, this view established a line of continuity between magic and science, for the scientist as well as the magician seeks to control his subject matter. In these terms the modern natural scientist might be characterized as a magician who has made good. According to Frazer's views, religion differs from both magic and science, since its characteristic attitude is not one of control but of appeasement. Religion seeks to adjust man to the religious object and not vice versa. In short, magic says, "my will be done," while religion says, "thy will be done." With these differences in mind, Frazer was able to locate the beginning of religion in the failure of magic. The effort of magic to control the powers of the spiritual world failed and out of this failure emerged the radically different attitude of appeasement which characterizes religion.

Other students of primitive religion proposed still different hypotheses. The redoubtable philosopher of evolution, Herbert Spencer, found the origin of religion in the worship of ancestors, arguing that the gods were rulers and benefactors of mankind who after death were elevated to divine rank.[17] But other students of primitive religion tended to move away from genetic and evolutionary theories to other types of inquiry and explanation. For example, E. Durkheim's *Elementary Forms of the Religious Life* sought the source of religion in the relation of the individual to society, and more widely to humanity.[18]

For this purpose Durkheim drew upon *totemism,* which is a widely recurring phenomenon of the primitive world in which a group or tribe of people envisages itself as descended from an animal or other natural object, and celebrates this relation in a sacramental meal in which the animal, normally taboo, is ritually eaten. Other forms of ritual as well as social organization and ethics were derived from the totemic relation. Durkheim drew heavily upon Spencer's and Gillen's studies of totemic forms among the Aruntas of Australia. He also drew heavily upon the sociological philosophy of Auguste Comte.

Still other investigators of mankind's religions, from Feuerbach to Freud, found its source in man's deep and ineradicable tendency to wishful thinking.[19] Thus Feuerbach characterized the gods as "wish-entities," and Freud spoke of religion as originating in an infantile neurotic father fixation.

However, more important than any particular theory or change in theories has been the shift of twentieth-century anthropology away from genetic and evolutionary methods and models. During the past half century in anthropology, evolutionism has to a great extent given way to such other types of thought as the cultural relativism of Benedict and Herskovitz and the functionalism of Malinowski, Kluckhohn, and others.[20] The cultural relativists resisted the attempt of evolutionists to place all cultures and cultural forms somewhere in an all-embracing scheme of evolution, asserting on the contrary the relative validity of all the various cultural forms which mankind shows. The functionalists seek to explain cultural forms not in terms of origin but in terms of the human needs, functions, or purposes which they satisfy.

As a result of these massive shifts in outlook, the nineteenth century's hypotheses concerning the origin of religion no longer claim either interest or

validity. Most contemporary anthropologists would say simply and plainly that
they do not know how religion began. Yet though the evolutionary hypotheses
are no longer meaningful as theories of how it all began, they are not therefore
valueless. Rather they retain great value as descriptions of pervasive aspects or
recurring themes in mankind's religions. As such, they have continuing significance. Often, too, they shed useful light on civilized as well as precivilized
religions.

A further important consequence of the contemporary shift in viewpoint has
been a widespread questioning or outright denial of the evolutionists' assertion
of analogies between prehistoric and contemporary primitive man. Present-day
primitive societies are the end result of complex and often unique histories;
therefore it is often misleading to assume before factual study that they are
analogous to this or that stage of prehistoric society. Such evolutionary assumptions, whether conscious or unconscious, frequently also carry negative value
judgments in their use of the term *primitive* to mean "at a lower stage of evolutionary development."

Recent and current studies place their emphasis upon full investigation of
specific factual aspects of primitive societies and religions. In this connection,
several recent investigators, notably V. Gordon Childe and Robert Redfield,
have pointed to an important observable similarity between prehistoric and
contemporary primitive societies, namely, that they are both folk societies, and
their religions are religions of folk societies.[21] By "folk society" is meant the
small human group whose members still maintain face-to-face relations, where
wealth is severely limited and social functions and distinctions are little developed. Primitive societies, let it be noted, include those of the present as well
as the past. The folk societies of the prehistoric and primitive world stand
in contrast to the larger and more differentiated societies of civilized human
history.

SEVEN RECURRING THEMES IN FOLK RELIGION

Meanwhile it will be useful here to list several significant recurring themes of
folk religion. No claim is suggested that these are universal features of folk
religion or that the following list constitutes the whole of any folk religion. Indeed other similar recurring themes will come to the reader's mind. Of the
seven recurring features which follow here, the first four are in effect reformu-
lations of earlier evolutionist studies of origin. The attempt to trace significant
recurring themes through different religions has been carried out with great
success by such phenomenologists of religion as G. van der Leeuw and M.
Eliade.[22]

THE HOLY

Probably the most pervasive pattern observable in folk religion is the holy or sacred. Chapter 1 found reason to define religion in these terms. In the present chapter's discussion of genetic theories, reference was made to Melanesian mana and to analogous concepts in other traditions. Mana and its parallels elsewhere in the world may be characterized as concretions of holiness, or holy power. As such, while clearly not the beginning of religion, the holy or sacred is probably religion's most widely recurring feature. So van der Leeuw defines religion as "man's encounter with Power." [23] By this he means mysterious or extraordinary power. In folk religions, power comes in many guises and dwells in an infinite variety of objects, persons, or events which thereby acquire power and also acquire symbolic significance. Roger Caillois's study, *Man and the Sacred,* traces some of these varieties.[24] Among his illustrations is the sacredness of sex among the Thonga, a Bantu tribe for whom sexual behavior imparts sacredness to all the innumerable objects, events, and persons which it touches.[25] This sacredness is ritualized in many sorts of bizarre ceremonies. Caillois also points out the sacredness of war for primitive man—and not quite incidentally for man in the modern world.[26] In suicidally negative ways war becomes both a divinity and a sacrament. Among the most frequently recurring forms of the sacred are those relating to birth and death. As Caillois says, "the sacred is what gives life and takes it away." [27] It is beginning and end.

Of the many facets of the holy power, none is more important than *taboo,* by which objects charged with holiness are set apart from ordinary usage, forbidden to common approaches. In many folk societies the person of the chief as well as the symbols of social authority are taboo. Often the taboo is extended to the chief's personal property, his living utensils, and even at times to his living quarters or to the ground on which he walks. Human embodiments of taboo range from criminals to culture heroes, and it occurs from the rites of birth to funeral ceremonies. Taboo seems to vary independently with moral good or evil, or with promise or threat. The powerful or the extraordinary is the vehicle of taboo. Because taboo is a powerful inhibition or proscription of human action, it has sometimes been regarded as the origin of morality.

ANIMISM

Animism, while by no means coextensive with religion and clearly not its origin, nevertheless does recur significantly throughout history. The idea of soul, spirit, or person will be significant throughout this study, as it is throughout mankind's religions. The phenomenon of animism might thus be characterized as the premature identification of things with souls, or the attribution of selfhood to objects of nature. Tylor's observation that nature is "possessed, pervaded and crowded with spiritual beings" is verified in many folk religions.[28] Yet Tylor's interpretation of the situation as a mistaken hypothesis concerning the causation of events may well be questioned. It can be argued that pre-civilized man like his civilized brother had direct experience of person-person relations as well as person-thing relations and that his mistake was to misapply the idea of self or of person-person relations to aspects of experience which civilized man has learned to be impersonal or person-thing relations. Hence animism may be characterized as misplaced personalism rather than as mistaken, prescientific explanation of events.

MAGIC

Magic and religion recur together regularly in mankind's history. If Frazer's view of the origin of religion in the failure of magic must be rejected as a genetic or evolutionary hypothesis, it nonetheless forcibly calls attention to this recurring relation; it also suggests an alternative hypothesis for magic as what we may term misused religion.

In contrast to secular or nonreligious experience, both magic and religion involve the holy; but as Frazer's theory points out, where religion seeks to adjust man to the holy or religious object, magic does precisely the opposite, seeking to control the object for definite human purposes. It is this purpose to control which led Frazer to see in magic the forerunner not of religion but of science. According to this view, magic is in effect science which fails to achieve its object due to its failure correctly to perceive causal relations.

It must be added that whereas science is secular or nonreligious in spirit, magic covers itself with the same spirit of holiness which characterizes religion. To Frazer's distinction, Malinowski has added a further difference between magic and religion, namely, that while religious purposes are public and social, those of magic tend to be private and individual as well as specific.[29] Nevertheless, it is true to say that magic as misused religion recurs with great frequency throughout all the world's religions.

When this happens, the holy objects of religion become *fetishes,* holy objects, charms, and the like designed to achieve one specific result or to avert another. The priest or prophet of religion tends to become the *shaman,* or *sorcerer,* who by spell, incantation, and magical ritual seeks to cure illness or to cause it, to secure good fortune, or avert evil, in any of the innumerable ways known to magicians. Magic is the dark shadow cast not only by folk religion but by civilized religion as well. In recent times the rise of modern natural science has forced upon men's minds a clearer distinction than ever before in human history between religion and magic. Yet despite the rise of science, magico-religious attitudes and behavior still persist in popular religion as they have throughout the ages.

TOTEMISM

Totemism has already been identified as a recurring cluster of social practices centering in belief in a tribal animal or plant or other object from which all members of the group are descended and around which group life centers. Frequently the totem object is eaten in a sacramental meal which celebrates the bond of brotherhood. Usually a strict taboo is placed upon the ordinary or secular eating of the totem animal. Stories of the totem animal constitute the tribal myth, from which are also derived many of the basic forms of social organization. Likewise from these mythical sources are derived the prescriptions and proscriptions which form the society's moral code.

While totemism and folk religion are by no means coextensive, totemic forms constitute an important recurring pattern, as may be seen in such works as Robertson Smith's *The Religion of the Semites*[30] and Durkheim's *Elementary Forms of the Religious Life*. These totemic forms serve to underscore the religious character of the bond between the individual and his society. Such forms find exemplification in contemporary society in such phenomena as patriotism or civic loyalty.

MYTH

Similarly social in character are three further significantly recurring features of folk religion: myth, rite, and morality. Through all three of these runs a continuity of fundamental values which forms the human raw material and content of religions. The values which are sung out in myth and danced out in ritual become in morality the norms for interpersonal or social action. These elements will be discussed in order.

Myth or mythology may be defined as sacred story or narrative whose social function is the authoritative expression of values. To say this is to distinguish between myth and folklore or diverting fiction.[31] It is also to oppose alternative interpretations of myth, such as the popular view of myth as primitive man's prescientific attempts at explanation. That such elements may at times be present in myth is undoubtedly true, but the central and defining function of myth is that of a vehicle for those central values which give meaning and direction to human life. Malinowski points out this function of myth as religious and moral instruction for each rising generation among the Melanesians whom he knew so well.[32] This appears to be the function of myth not only in folk societies but in civilized traditions as well.

RITUAL

Ritual consists of symbolic actions fitted to some occasion of individual or social life. Often in folk societies the distinction between individual and society is not clearly drawn, or it is drawn in different terms from those of modern Western society. For the individual, rites of passage consecrate the milestones of a man's journey from birth onward through puberty and marriage to death, asserting the meaningful character of life to the individual and to his society.[33] But the society also has its ritual occasions. Times of triumph or disaster, of victory or defeat in war, as well as the celebration of the cycle of the year or of the four seasons are examples of public occasions for ritual celebration.

Ritual, for both individual and society, develops its own functions or uses. One such use is purification. Purification rituals, both individual and social, recur widely throughout the world and employ many symbolic forms, from washing to flagellation to verbal confession, which have apparently an equal number of meanings. The common feature in all this variety is the need which men feel for purification.

Similarly various in its recurrent forms is sacrificial ritual. Foods or other useful objects are burnt on an altar, water or wine is poured out in a libation, useful objects of various sorts are given to the gods in whatever ways are customary. Sometimes sacrifice is construed as a bargain with the gods; at other times it is understood as a communal meal to which the gods are invited, and at other times still other interpretations are indicated. In these various ways men are impelled to enact the symbolic meanings of ritual. In their various rites and ceremonies men act out the meaning of life.

MORALITY

Morality consists of norms which govern interpersonal relations. So various are these norms and their relations to religion that some students of folk religion have denied any significant relation of religion to morality.[34] There is no intention here to understate the variety of moral norms among different folk societies, ranging as they do from vegetarianism to cannibalism, from celibacy to polygamy and polyandry, and from pacifism to holy war. Yet in all this, what does seem to be generally true is that the basic norms for social action carry religious sanction. The idea of a secular morality appears not to have occurred to the men of folk society.

The values which form the content of this morality are characteristically those of the particular society. Hence the purpose of folk morality is to fit the individual into his society. It is a morality of "my station and its duties." In terms of H. Bergson's *The Two Sources of Morality and Religion,* it is the morality of a closed society rather than an open society.[35] In Eliade's alternative formulation, the morality as well as the religion of folk society is one of "cosmos" rather than "history." In terms of Chapter 1 of the present study, it is an orientation of the first, or nature-culture, type.

MESOPOTAMIAN RELIGION

Several recent investigators of human origins have focused attention upon the
"urban revolution," by which is meant the first emergence independently, but
concurrently, in several regions of the world of civilized city-state societies
which contrast sharply with the folk societies that preceded them. Compared
with the small face-to-face societies of the prehistoric and primitive world, these
ancient civilizations show several important distinguishing traits.[36] (1) The size
of the settlement is greatly increased. (2) There is an increase in amount and
importance of tribute or taxation. (3) As a direct result of the increase in wealth
there are large public works. (4) Writing emerges as an essential social function. (5) Related to writing are the beginnings of mathematics and science.
(6) There is greatly increased differentiation of economic activities and structures. (7) Metalworking becomes an important activity for both war and peace.
(8) A privileged ruling class makes its appearance. (9) The state emerges as a
distinct social structure and function. Other features of the urban revolution
will come readily to mind, but these are sufficient to make clear its nature and
its epoch-making importance in human history. Specific examples of these features will doubtless come to the reader's mind from ancient civilizations, ranging geographically from China to Egypt and to Yucatan.

Our concern is with the impact of the urban revolution upon religion. In
this chapter two illustrations, ancient Mesopotamia and Greece, will be briefly
examined. Subsequent chapters will call attention to analogous religious developments in ancient China, India, Iran, and Israel. The present selection of
Mesopotamia and Greece is based upon two considerations—the existence and
availability of archaeological knowledge and the relevance of this knowledge to
the inquiry of this volume as a whole. Also, Mesopotamian and Greek religions
afford significant similarity and contrast to each other.

Mesopotamia has been both cradle and tomb of many civilizations during its
more than six millennia of history. The Fertile Crescent is a crescent-shaped
band of habitable land bordering the Arabian desert. From Mesopotamia it
extends northwestward to Syria then bends southward along the Syrian coast
to the border of Egypt. The Fertile Crescent has been the scene of struggles for
possession and habitation from before the dawn of history. It has also been important as a source region of religions. At least four world religions may be
traced to sources in or near this region, namely, Judaism, Christianity, Zoroastrianism, and Islam.

The first civilized inhabitants of Mesopotamia were Sumerians, a people
associated with Sumer, which was one of the many city-states that sprang into

being around 4500 B.C. in the fertile land between the rivers (*Mesopotamia* means in Greek "between the rivers"). Sumerian, apparently unrelated to other languages, used an alphabet of wedge-shaped or cuneiform characters. In addition to Sumer there were other city-states, such as Kish, Lagash, and Erech, as well as Ur, from which, many centuries later (ca. 2000 B.C.), Abraham is said to have made his westward migration to Canaan.[37]

Beginning around the middle of the fifth millennium B.C. these Sumerian city-states maintained civilized cultures for approximately 1500 years. This was followed by decline culminating in successful invasion and conquest about 2200 B.C. by a Semitic people whose Mesopotamian base was Akkad. The newcomers spoke a Semitic tongue known as Akkadian. Under King Sargon I of Akkad they conquered and held extensive sections of Mesopotamia. However, in another few centuries the cycle of rise and fall of empires carried the new conquerors to downfall. Then another turn of the same wheel brought still another Semitic dynasty to power.

The most important king of this new dynasty was Hammurabi (1728–1686 B.C.), famous for his law code. As Moses received the Ten Commandments from the Lord, so Hammurabi received his code from Shamash, Babylonian sun god. These two ancient law codes are similar in their avowal of the *lex talionis,* or law of equal vengeance, prescribing an eye for an eye and a tooth for a tooth. Soon after Hammurabi's time, Babylon fell to another invading group, the Kassites, whose brief triumph gave way in turn to the Assyrians, then the Chaldeans, and after them the Persians.

Throughout these vast and violent changes, Mesopotamian religion maintained remarkable stability. Its populous pantheon of gods and goddesses dating from early Sumerian times gained some new names and new functions, and the basic myths were altered from time to time to fit new situations and new needs, yet the overarching fact was continuity.

Most of the many deities of ancient Mesopotamia were expressions of some natural or social force or object, or a combination. The social forces were those of the urban or city-state civilization, which was the new emergent order of the Mesopotamian world. The gods were transcendental rulers modeled after their earthly counterparts, and the council of the gods was also drawn from earthly models. It is not too much to say that Mesopotamian religion was a kind of transcendental reflection of the new order of social life.

The gods also continued to be the rulers of the nature which was the persistent and encompassing environment of society. For example, Anu was the god of heaven and also chief deity of Erech. In some early pantheons he was also the ruler of the gods. Enlil, god of the air, ruled at Nippur. Sin was a moon goddess who ruled at Ur. Shamash was the sun god of Lachish. Ea, or Enki, was a water god whose home was Eridu. Nintud, later to become Ishtar, was the mother goddess of Kish. These and other deities were said to gather in a celestial council, like the councils of leading men of a city. These deities also were regarded as the superior citizens of a kind of cosmic state whose other members included men on earth and even objects of nature as well.[38] In this cosmic state the principle of continuity, described in the last chapter, prevailed among all elements of the whole. From the highest deity down through human-kind to the humblest object of nature, all were members together of a single homogeneous and ordered society.

In many documents the Mesopotamian pantheon featured divine couples, each god being paired with a goddess. Thus familial (and also extrafamilial) relations were assumed as matters of fact for the gods. Often in Mesopotamia and elsewhere in the ancient world, these assumptions produced erotic forms of ritual. The ritual marriage of god and goddess was widely believed to induce the fertility of the earth which brought forth each year's crop. In emulation of god and goddess, erotic rituals with priests or priestesses of the gods were customary religious practices. Temple prostitution was frequent in ancient Mesopotamia.

Probably the most prominent and important later arrival in the Mesopotamian pantheon was Marduk of Babylon. His rise coincided with that of the city of Babylon under the second Semitic dynasty in the late centuries of the third millennium. That Marduk was a war god constituted a religious recognition of the historic fact that war was becoming an increasing preoccupation of the Babylonian servants of the gods. Marduk was also a god of the light of the heaven and of the city of Babylon. The ancient Sumerian creation story was probably altered by Marduk's priests to give their god a central place in its dramatic liturgy. Again we note the impact of the urban revolution on Babylonia's religious thought and practice.

Beside Marduk was Ishtar, the great mother goddess. She was wife and mother of Tammuz, god of the spring, and she presided over fertility in nature and man. The planet Venus was sacred to her, and her annual descent to the underworld and return to earth marked the seasonal cycle of the year. Ishtar was one of the great deities of the ancient Near East. We shall meet her repeatedly elsewhere under other names.

The lively imagination of Mesopotamia produced a luxuriant variety of myths and other literature, among which were two of the great documents of the world's religious literature, the creation story (often called by its first two words, *Enuma Elish*, meaning "when on high") and the Gilgamesh epic. The Babylonian creation story is significant both in itself and for its similarities and contrasts with the Biblical creation story and with stories of origin in other religions. The present text is a seventh-century B.C. version from the library of the Assyrian king Ashurbanipal, but the original may be traced back to the early part of the second millennium B.C.[39]

The Babylonian story begins with the original divine pair, the god Apsu and the goddess Tiamat, the former a deity of fresh water and the latter of the salt sea. From these two are derived the host of gods and goddesses who inhabit the regions on high. The dramatic conflict which forms the plot of the *Enuma Elish* begins when Apsu is disturbed by the noise of his children. He and his mate resolve to destroy their offspring. However, the god Ea acts first, killing his father, Apsu. Gathering allies, Tiamat resolves upon revenge. The opposing gods, gathering for council of war, find a leader in Marduk, who accepts the role of mortal combat with Tiamat, but only on condition that he be accorded chief place among the gods.

The combat between Marduk and Tiamat forms the highly dramatic climax of the story. Tiamat draws into her service many of the monsters of the deep. She covers herself magically with a protective red paste which recalls the red color of prehistoric art and religion. But Marduk is equal to the situation. When Tiamat opens her mouth, he drives in his sword so that she cannot close it. Then he slits Tiamat apart, placing the one half over man as the heavens above and the other half under foot as the earth. The outlines of cosmogonic myth are clearly present in this episode, interpreting heaven and earth in terms of Tiamat's body.

Having begun the task of fixing the definite outlines and forms of the cosmos, Marduk continues the work of creation by making man. He does so, speaking words similar to those in Genesis:

> *Marduk opened his mouth and unto Ea he spoke*
> *That which he conceived in his heart he made known unto him:*
> *"My blood will I take and bone will I fashion*
> *I shall create man who shall inherit the earth."* [40]

From man Marduk proceeds to complete the work of creating the world culminating in the city of Babylon. The creation story comes to dramatic completion with the recitation of the fifty names of Marduk. This and other features of the story make clear its ritual use as a part of the Babylonian New Year's Day celebration. The recitation of the myth was conceived as an essential feature in sustaining the orderly cosmos of which Babylon and its way of life constituted the center.

The Gilgamesh epic differs from the *Enuma Elish* in that its characters are more human than divine. Gilgamesh, the hero, is like many of the Greek heroes part god and part man. He is ruler of the city-state of Uruk. The plot of the epic consists of his futile, tragic pursuit of a medicine of immortality. Here is history's first story of man against death. Seeking an answer to the problem of mortality, Gilgamesh sets out toward a western land guarded by a divine monster named Hubaba. His friend and travel companion, Enkidu, offends Ishtar and is condemned to die. In his wanderings Gilgamesh comes to an ancient ancestor, Utnapishtim, who tells him a flood story which is at several significant points identical with the Biblical story. Both stories tell of a uni-

Mesopotamian seal showing sacred tree flanked by priests
Courtesy of the Pierpont Morgan Library, New York

versal deluge from which a few people and animals escape by means of an ark. The main difference between the Hebrew and Babylonian stories is the monotheism of the former and the polytheism of the latter. Utnapishtim also gives Gilgamesh an herb of immortality, which Gilgamesh carelessly leaves on the shore of the pool while he bathes, only to have it swallowed by a serpent. The conclusion apparently is that man has no alternative but to endure his mortality, to continue to live in the face of the death which is human fate.

Magic, which was by no means absent from the two great epics, was also a pervasive element in Babylonian popular religion. The people were provided with spells or incantations for every occasion of life, there were priests to administer the spells, and there were innumerable gods, godlings, and demons who effectively carried them out.

The orders and corporations of priests constituted an important class of Babylonian society. Many of the temples in which these priests worshiped, lived,
and worked have been uncovered by modern archaeology. The temple compound, consisting of numerous buildings for worship, for schools, libraries, and
numerous other activities of the priests, centered in a *ziggurat,* which was a
pyramid-shaped structure with a shrine at the top. Similar to religious edifices
from the pyramids of Egypt to the stupas of India or pagodas of the Buddhist
world, the ziggurat appears to have symbolized the earth mountain. The Akkadian word *ziggurat* meant "mountain-top" or "pinnacle." At the summit was an
axis mundi or axis of the world. The ziggurat was probably a remote ancestor
of the steepled church.

In their temple compounds, the Babylonian priests not only prayed, recited
their endless spells, and made oracular forecasts of the future, but pursued lore
and scholarship which led them to the beginnings of astronomy. Their knowledge was passed on to their students in the first known schools of history.[41]
These priests also carried on extensive business and commercial activities.

Like many other chapters of the human past, ancient Mesopotamia was destined to be gone beyond and left in oblivion to await the spades of modern
archaeology. The ancient Mesopotamians lacked the adventurous minds of
Greece or the adventurous faith of Israel. Yet within this Mesopotamian cosmos
—and others like it in many other regions of the world—the journey of civilized
humanity began. From these ancient sources, mankind took its beginning.

GREEK RELIGION

In contrast to Mesopotamia, elements of ancient Greece still live. Twentieth-
century Western languages, arts, philosophy, science, and politics all still bear
living and powerful Greek influence. In religion, while no one worships Zeus,
Apollo, or Dionysus, they too live on in many aspects of contemporary religious
and cultural life.

Modern historical and archaeological study is radically revising our understanding of the origins and early days of Greece and Greek religion. Before the
city-states of the Hellenic age, indeed before the earlier Homeric age, lies a
long period of migrations and movements of peoples which historians are only
beginning to understand. Perhaps as early as the twentieth century B.C. invaders
swept into Greece from the north, subjugating the so-called Helladic peoples.
The term *Aryan* or *Indo-European* is a label which identifies the speech of
these invaders as one of a family of languages extending from Sanskrit in India
to Greek, Latin, and modern European languages. The first civilization of
which there is detailed and reliable knowledge is that of the Minoans of Crete
(ca. 2200–1100 B.C.) and the related Bronze-age Aegeans of the mainland and

the Greek archipelago. Around 1400 B.C. disaster overtook Cnossus on Crete. Perhaps it was an earthquake, perhaps a new wave of invaders, but Crete never regained its previous glory. However, Minoan influence spread to the mainland in the form of Mycenaean civilization. The Homeric age may be understood as a later stage of this culture. Again, however, invasion from the north, this time from the Dorians, was the spur to change. It overthrew Mycenaean culture, but at the same time dispersed Mycenaean influence to the western shores of Asia Minor. From the new combination of elements emerged the city-state civilization of Greece's golden age.

Greek history from this period onward is better known to us. Among the Greek city-states Athens led the heroic resistance to Persia, and thereby gained both glory and the leadership of the Greek world. The great age of Athens lasted approximately from the time of the Persian wars (490–480 B.C.) until the Peloponnesian War (430–404 B.C.). The fratricidal strife of the latter war sealed the doom not only of the great age of Athens but of the Greek city-states. The next century saw the rise of Philip of Macedon and his son, Alexander, whose far-flung conquests marked the historic transformation from Hellenic to Hellenistic Greece. The Hellenic age was the great creative period of Greek thought and life; and the Hellenistic age was the later period (usually dated from the death of Alexander, 321 B.C.) in which Greek language, literature, and thought were spread over the whole Mediterranean world. Greek culture combined with Roman power to produce a more or less unified civilization which endured for eight centuries, until Rome fell; and then in turn out of the Dark Ages a new civilization called the West or Christendom came into being.

Gilbert Murray has called attention to the historical changes and developments of Greek religion in his book *Five Stages of Greek Religion*.[42] While much of Murray's analysis has been changed and corrected by more recent scholarship, his five stages remain useful as an outline for historical development. We shall use them for this purpose.

PRE-HOMERIC RELIGION

The first stage was the early pre-Homeric period during which successive waves of invaders swept into Greece from the north, mixing their own religious beliefs and practices with those of previous inhabitants. It was a time of local gods, who were often envisaged not as definite persons but as vague powers, and before whom (or which) men bowed in primitive and fearful awe, appeasing by sacrifice and celebrating in a wide variety of folk festivals. These holy powers provide significant illustration of the definition of religion given in Chapter 1 and elaborated in the section on folk religion of this chapter. Many of these gods or powers were chthonic, or derived from the earth and dwelling in the earth rather than in the sky. Murray reconstructs this very ancient period of Greek religion by inference from later Athenian folk festivals such as the Diasia, which was devoted to Zeus Meilichus, or Zeus of Placation; the Thesmophoria, devoted to Demeter and Persephone; and the Anthesteria, devoted to placating the spirits of the dead. He concludes:

> In each of these great festivals we find that the Olympian gods vanish away and we are left with three things only: first with an atmosphere of religious dread; second with a whole sequence of magical ceremonies which in at least two or three cases produce a kind of strange personal emanation of themselves, the appeasements producing Meilochos, the charm-bearing Thesmophoros; and thirdly with a divine or sacred animal. In the Diasia we find the old superhuman snake who reappears so ubiquitously throughout Greece, the regular symbol of the underworld powers, especially the hero or the dead ancestor. Why the snake was so chosen we can only surmise. He obviously lived underground: his home was among the Chthonia the Earth-People.[43]

Some of the gods of the later Homeric times go back to this early period, but their characters and functions differed from those of subsequent ages. Zeus was Father Sky, but he also assumed many local roles and functions in different regions. At Dodonna he gave oracles through a sacred oak tree. In other places he was a fertility deity, a quality preserved in his later philanderings. He was the guardian of several city-states. He was also the god of clouds, rainmaking and the thunderbolt.

At this period Zeus was not yet married to Hera, who in some regions appears to have been a cow goddess. In the Peloponnesus she was a maiden who made love with the hero Hercules. Some myths connected her with Jason and his quest for the golden fleece. Hera's subsequent marriage to Zeus has been interpreted by Jane Harrison as a mythical expression of the subjugation of indigenous peoples by northern invaders.[44] Thereafter Hera became the jealous wife and Zeus the henpecked and philandering husband. Somewhat ironically, the Greeks came to regard the marriage of Zeus and Hera as the archetypal holy union. Hera became the patron of married women, affording divine protection of marriage and the family.

Apollo also had a pre-Homeric history. In early times he was a god of shepherds and farmers, playing his lyre for rural and pastoral followers. He was also an archer whose arrows brought deadly illness. He was probably not Greek in origin, for as late as the *Iliad* he sided not with the Greeks but with the Trojans. Apollo killed a python on the slopes of Mount Parnassus, and became the patron deity of Delphi, most famous of Greek oracles. Thereafter he became the god of revelation whose priestesses foretold the future and spoke his words in trance to human seekers. Much later he became also a sun god.

There were many other deities as well. Artemis was a virginal goddess of wild nature and a protector of animals as well as lover of children. Poseidon was probably a horse deity before he became ruler of the sea, Athena was a warrior maiden and owl goddess who came to be patron and protector of Athens. Demeter was Mother Earth, and so presided over agricultural fertility, husbandry, and the seasonal cycle. She was also the mother of the maiden Persephone. There was Dionysus, god of wine and ecstatic rites. There were innumerable local heroes who after death hovered in protection over their local regions. In these and innumerable other divine figures, what the Greeks added

Three deities from Mycenae

Courtesy of the National Archeological Museum, Athens, Greece

to the recurring theme of nature-culture gods was their own sharp and sensitive perception. As a result, their gods came in time to be extremely interesting and vivid people.

From this earliest period Greek religion involved rites or ceremonies which formed integral parts of the common life of family, clan, and state. Families had their own gods and ritual forms, as did clans and states, in which participation was as much a civic duty as a religious practice. The cult of the dead united the living with the departed members of the group. Offerings of food and wine were presented at graves. Animal sacrifice, with an accompanying sacrificial meal, was the most frequent ceremony. Divination also played a part in Greek religion from earliest days. In addition to innumerable local oracles throughout Greece, there was the great oracle at Delphi, which gave a semblance of unity to Greek religion and to the Greek people. In order to participate in religious ceremonies, it was necessary to be ritually pure, so purification rites abounded. Some of these very ancient rituals continued to exist throughout Greek history at the foundation of Greece's many-layered religious structure. Greek people continued in these various ways to act out the values that gave meaning to individual and common life.

FROM HOMER TO GREEK TRAGEDY

In Gilbert Murray's second stage of Greek religion the gods came to live their immortal lives on Mount Olympus in the divine household presided over by Zeus. While they differed from mankind in not having to die, like men they were subject to the impersonal law of fate, or *moira*. Such at least was the view of Homer, who more than any other man was responsible for the organization of the Olympian pantheon in the form which is familiar and traditional in Greece and the West.

The Homeric pantheon was a characteristically Greek achievement in order and humanism. Few religious traditions of mankind have achieved a genuine and widely accepted order for their pantheons. The Babylonians had only minimal success; and the experience of other peoples will be noted as our study proceeds. As noted above, Homer's Olympian deities often represented new characters and functions attached to early pre-Homeric deities. What emerged in the Olympian pantheon were gods and goddesses who were interesting and vividly etched personalities even in their amours, their squabbles, and other outlandish activities—as interesting and human as the people who created and listened to the Homeric epics.

Yet this achievement was purchased at a price. The Olympian deities still maintained relations to various aspects of nature, as Zeus to his thunderbolt, Apollo to the sun, and Artemis to wild nature. But now a gulf was fixed between nature and the gods. The old, primitive awe and mystery were gone, or greatly reduced. Likewise, Homer's reinterpretation of traditional mythical themes often replaced the earlier emotions with a characteristically Greek sense of esthetic measure and beauty. It is also probable, as Murray argues, that the Olympian pantheon was the expression of a new conquering people who cast out old rites and myths as they completed their work of conquest. In any case, it is a historic fact that the Olympian pantheon gave to Greece, divided into many city-states and regions, the unity of a common tradition and a common civic faith. Society equally with nature found expression in Greek religion.

The sturdy Boetian farmer-poet, Hesiod (ca. 750 B.C.), as well as Homer, left his imprint on Greek religion. Arranging the innumerable multitude of deities in a family tree, beginning with the origin of the world, Hesiod showed how they formed parts of the orderly cosmos which arose out of the original chaos.[45] From chaos came gods and goddesses as well as elements of the cosmic order, and frequently the two are identical. Hesiod's *Theogony* has been significantly contrasted with the Babylonian *Enuma Elish*.[46] Where the latter expressed a static world, Hesiod's depiction of the world is full of dynamic tensions, pushing onward to new developments. Where the *Enuma Elish* is a story of order emerging from chaos, the *Theogony* also depicts conflicts among divine authorities. Also, Hesiod's myth is well on the way to becoming philosophy.

As many writers have pointed out, the Olympian gods ignored a crucial human need. This missing element, a strong sense of individual participation and destiny, was provided by the mystery religions. The word *mystery* is from a Greek verb meaning literally "to put one's hand over the mouth," i.e., to be silent. The Greek mystery cults in all their variety seem to have involved certain common elements: (1) preparatory purification such as ritual bathing, (2) instruction in knowledge given behind closed doors and held as the secret possession of members, (3) a secret and solemn beholding of sacred symbolic objects which are closely related to this knowledge, (4) narrating or dramatic enactment of a sacred story, and (5) a crowning or wreathing of initiates as full members of the brotherhood, with the promise of a blessed immortality hereafter.

There were three main traditions of mystery religions in ancient Greece —Eleusinian, Dionysian, and Orphic—all dating from the sixth century B.C. or before, and lasting for most or all of Greece's long history. The first took its name from the seaside town of Eleusis where its ritual was enacted and to which its sacred processions made their way. The Eleusinian mysteries combined the myth and ritual of Demeter and Persephone with that of Dionysus, and they assured adherents of a "better lot," that is, immortality hereafter. The Dionysian mysteries involved their members in more violent rites. Intoxication with wine was regarded as possession by Dionysus. Was he not god of wine? Often, too, an animal, kid or bull, was torn apart while still alive, and its blood was drunk, and its flesh eaten by maddened worshippers in a rite called *omophagia*. For these reasons the Dionysiac rites maintained throughout Greek history their reputation for wildness and fury, and Dionysus remained a god apart, largely unrelated to the Olympian pantheon.

Orpheus, the traditional founder of the Orphic rites, was himself said to have been the victim of the Dionysiac rite. The Orphic mysteries, as they spread over the Greek world, took the opposite path of asceticism. By following Orphic rules of purity, wearing white garments, abstaining from meat-eating, from sexual indulgence, and other pollutions, a man might avoid hell and secure a blessed portion in the hereafter. Orphic influences were strong upon such other groups in Greece as the Pythagorean brotherhood of mathematicians and philosophers and Plato and his followers. In their forms of thought and worship, the mysteries exerted great influence upon Western religion and philosophy. For ancient Greek people they expressed dimensions of life lacking in Olympian religion.

Another distinctively Greek development which took place during Murray's second stage of Greek religion was the emergence of tragic drama. Modern, secular theatergoers often forget the religious origin of drama, even when they view modern presentations of Greek tragedy. In ancient Greece tragic drama grew out of religious ritual and maintained a relation to Greek religion. Indeed it must be viewed as a distinctively Greek religious development—in its time, a new and boldly original development of Greek religion.

The idea of tragedy was a probing of the issues of man's fate under the gods; and the tragic dramatists all asserted, with their individual emphases and accents, that when man overreaches himself in pride (*hybris*), he is overtaken by doom (*nemesis*) acting in accordance with the law of fate (*moira*). The Greek tragic hero is a great man whose inexorable doom is brought about by a fatal flaw in his nature. While human fate is inevitably tragic, the man who meets and undergoes this fate achieves his own dignity. The Greek tragedians were humanists in the highest sense.

Extant works of Greek tragedy are from three writers, Aeschylus (d. 455 B.C.), Sophocles (d. 406 B.C.), and Euripides (d. 406 B.C.), each of whom developed and modified the central theme of tragedy in his own way. For example, at the end of Aeschylus's three plays comprising the *Oresteia*, Orestes is acquitted by the Athenian court (of which Athena is judge) of the murder of his mother. At the end of Sophocles's cycle of three plays on the life of Oedipus and his family, King Oedipus accepts his tragic fate with more inner peace than at any previous time of his restless life.

Not only man's fate but man's relation to deity and to divine justice are explored by the tragedians. The chorus in Aeschylus's *Oresteia* declares:

> *Sing sorrow sorrow; but good win out in the end.*[47]

Yet the same dramatist in *Prometheus Bound* represents Zeus as the cruel tyrant who keeps Prometheus chained to a rock in never-ending agony, and Prometheus's attitude toward his tormentor is one of mortal defiance toward an immortal power which is cruel and antihuman in quality. Of all the tragedians, it was Euripides who raised the problem of evil in sharpest form. Euripides's character, Hippolytus, cries out in words like those of the Biblical Job:

> *Ah pain pain pain*
> *O unrighteous curse*
> *Thou Zeus dost thou see me? Yes it is I.*

The proud and pure, the server of god
The white and shining in sanctity
To a visible death, to an open sod
I walk my ways
And all the labor of saintly days
Lost, lost without meaning.[48]

In the view of many students of Greek tragedy, Euripides's seeking, probing mind pushes him beyond the other tragic dramatists in the direction of some new form of faith, intimated but never fully articulated.

PHILOSOPHY

Murray classifies as the third stage of Greek religion "the great schools of the fourth century," that is, the philosophic schools such as the Platonists, the Aristotelians, the Cynics, Stoics, and Epicureans.[49] Behind these schools lay several centuries of philosophic history of which they were the culmination. Like tragic drama, Greek philosophy must be viewed as a distinctive emergent from Greek religion. Alone among the peoples of the ancient Near East, the Greeks made the journey from myth to philosophy and set philosophy on its own distinctive path.[50]

Hesiod's *Theogony* has been noted as myth on the verge of transformation into philosophy. Greek philosophy began with Thales (ca. 500 B.C.) and his view that the underlying substance of all things was water. Thales apparently made the decisive step from saying that Poseidon was god to asserting that water was the underlying metaphysical substance. In contrast to Thales's identification of water as the substance underlying all things, Anaximander argued that this substance was "the boundless"; and Anaximenes maintained that it was air.[51] Still other proposals were made and developed, but underlying all the specific assertions and systems was philosophy's concern with the nature of being-as-such. It was the ancient Greek way of thinking and expressing the unique sort of all-inclusive totality, which Chapter 1 identified as the distinctive feature of philosophical thinking. To this concern the name *metaphysics* or *ontology* has traditionally been given in Western philosophy.

Early in Greek philosophy there emerged a critical concern with Greek religion and an attempt at philosophic reconstruction of religion. Xenophanes wrote a philosophic poem critically attacking anthropomorphic views of the gods.[52] Other philosophers such as Pythagoras and his followers sought philosophic constructions, or reconstructions, of religion.

A new, more extensive and intensive criticism of tradition, not only in religion, but in ethics and politics as well, emerged with the Sophists of the fifth century. The Sophists, literally the "wise ones," were also the first professional teachers of Greek history. They were interested not so much in metaphysical views of the universe as in systematic criticism of popularly held views. As a consequence, the Sophists were viewed with suspicion by traditionally minded Greek people. The views of different Sophist philosophers varied widely, though they tended to skepticism toward traditional metaphysics and religion. Some of them attacked traditional Greek religion as both unreasonable and immoral.

Sophist criticism set the context for Socrates (d. 399 B.C.), who was both Sophist and supreme anti-Sophist. Socrates must be viewed as an important figure in Greek religion as well as in philosophy. He used arguments and ideas similar to those of the Sophists, and like the Sophists was devoted to unremitting criticism of traditional religion. Moreover, he sought to push the process of criticism to its conclusion, which he viewed as the emergence of necessary general definitions in logic and general norms of action in ethics. This task of making a new beginning Socrates apparently viewed as his calling, or vocation, and he attributed its source to the promptings of his god (or *daimon*). Socrates viewed his philosophic task of criticism as a mission to be "a gadfly to Athens." [53]

Plato (d. 347 B.C.) continued Socrates's and the Sophists' criticism of traditional Greek religion, charging it again with irrationality and immorality. Yet in the *Republic* and the dialogs of Plato the reader finds not only criticism, but also the clear outlines of a reconstructed religion. Plato offers a view of reality in which the unchanging realm of Platonic ideas lies beyond the realm of changing appearances. In this unchanging realm are the archetypal ideas which are exemplified in the forms of the objects of experience. Over all the ideas, like the sun above the world, shines the Idea of the Good. The realm of ideas constituted for Plato a timeless dwelling place for the souls of good men and for gods. It was a kind of city of God, of which it is said:

> In heaven . . . there is laid up a pattern of it, methinks, which he who desires may behold, and beholding may set his own house in order. But whether such an one exists or ever will exist in fact is no matter; for he will live after the manner of that city, having nothing to do with any other.[54]

Plato did not call the Idea of the Good divine or God, but in later ages, the theologians of three of the world's religions (Christianity, Judaism, and Islam) used Plato's philosophy as a theological vehicle for expression of their monotheistic faiths. In one of his later works, the *Timaeus*, Plato sketched his view of a divine artisan or Demiurge.[55]

Plato's philosophy also set forth a view of man's nature as intellectual or spiritual, and hence not limited to the body. Among the numerous other religious suggestions in Plato's philosophy is his view of Socrates as the idealized figure in whom philosophy was incarnated. In the *Symposium,* Socrates appears as the hero of a new kind of philosophic-religious orientation.[56] Plato's account of the trial and death of Socrates sufficed to place the figure of Socrates at the source of the Western tradition of philosophy and indeed of all humane knowledge.

Plato's student Aristotle (d. 322 B.C.) gave a different direction to philosophy. He was the son of a physician and himself a scientist of wide and varied interests, which found expression in his philosophic writings. As a consequence, his writings do not show religious themes or qualities comparable to those of Plato. Yet Aristotle's writings as well as Plato's were destined many centuries later to be used by Muslim, Jewish, and Christian theologians for their own purposes.

In addition to Platonists and Aristotelians, the schools of philosophy of which Murray writes as the third stage of Greek religion included Cynics, Stoics, Epicureans, and others too numerous and too unimportant for mention. These schools were a significant feature of the Hellenistic, or Greco-Roman, world and had considerable influence on that world. Each school had its own body of philosophic teachings received from its founder and carried on in the tradition and community of the school. Each had its list of worthies who had advanced the teachings. These teachings ran the full range of philosophical reflection from metaphysics through epistemology and logic to ethics. The Platonists held to the doctrine of ideas and the spiritual nature of reality. They also produced a wide range of epistemological and ethical doctrines. The Epicureans held to their idea of atoms and the void and to a hedonistic ethic. All of this, they said, resulted in a quieting of needless fears and in a peaceful mind. The Cynics held a view of nature which led them to scorn society and its conventions. While the Stoics maintained an interest in the full range of ideas from metaphysics through logic to ethics, they placed primary emphasis upon their distinctive ethical teachings. Stoic ethics made a clear and sharp cut between reason on the one hand and emotion on the other, maintaining that man should guide his life by reason and not by passion. The good is the rational, argued the Stoics, and they did not doubt that human reason sufficed for the purpose of rational guidance. They also made a fundamental distinction between goals which are under human control and those which are not. In the latter realm, man is called simply to endure what cannot be altered while he cultivates the inward and self-sufficient life of reason.

These philosophic schools had many of the traits of religious communities. They maintained attitudes of respect amounting to reverence for their founders —even the Epicureans termed their founder, Epicurus, a savior. In effect they were communities of disciples. All of them maintained an attitude of religious veneration for the figure of Socrates. They also maintained a common life not unlike that in monastic brotherhoods of many of the world's religions. In short, they functioned religiously for many people throughout the Greco-Roman world; so doing, they formed the environment and the main competition in that world for both Judaism and Christianity.

"FAILURE OF NERVE"

Murray characterized the fourth stage of Greek religion, in a celebrated and controversial phrase, as a "failure of nerve," seeking to embrace within this characterization a wide variety of religious phenomena ranging from a notable revival of mystery cults to a great influx of Oriental cults such as Manichaeism and Mithraism, a greatly enhanced popularity of astrology, and a widely shared mood of fatalism.[57] Whereas the great schools of the third stage preserved a faith in man and reason, the newer faiths surrendered this tenet for a belief in some transhuman deity who was alleged to reveal himself supernaturally to man. Murray included the rise of Christianity among the symptoms of failure of nerve, for Christianity found the meaning of life in the service of God rather than in the fulfillment of human life. In this judgment, Murray's preference for Stoicism over Christianity becomes apparent, for Stoicism is a faith centering in the fulfillment of man rather than primarily in the service of God. From this viewpoint, Christians' service of the one transcendent God has seemed to many men a form of escapism and a failure of nerve.

NEOPLATONIC MYSTICISM

The final stage of Greek religion, according to Murray, occurred in late antiquity and centered around such figures as the philosopher Plotinus (d. A.D. 270) whose *Enneads* sought a systematic statement of Plato's philosophy, culminating in a description of a mystical experience of the One.[58] The teachings of Plotinus constituted still another philosophical-religious school which attracted wide allegiance throughout the Greco-Roman world. Neoplatonism, as Plotinus' system of thought came to be called, was also destined for a long and notable career in the Western world as a vehicle of mystical religion. Plotinus taught the supreme reality of the One, with various grades of being emanating in concentric circles from this center and returning to it. The congeniality of this system to what Chapter 1 termed the mysticism of absorption, or ontological union, has been apparent to many great mystics of the Western world.

Among the ancient adherents of this Platonic or Neoplatonic view of reality was the fourth-century Roman Emperor Julian the Apostate (A.D. 332–362), who sought to oppose the growing power and influence of Christianity. Julian sought, in vain as it turned out, to return his people to the old gods and to the old way of life which they bequeathed to their followers. From this time onward, Greek influences were exerted through the Christian movement which Julian sought to combat. For as we shall see in Chapter 13, the Christian movement constituted a synthesis of Greek and Hebraic sources.

The late Dean Inge once characterized the Christian church as the last great achievement of Hellenistic culture. It was also the first great work of Western culture, but that is a matter which must await discussion in later chapters. Meanwhile it may be observed here that Greek influence has been strong in Western religion as in all other aspects of Western culture.

CONCLUDING COMMENT

This chapter has provided valuable documentation and confirmation for all three of the main theses set forth in the first chapter. First, on the issue of the nature of religion as ultimate concern or valuation, in prehistoric and primitive religions as well as those of ancient civilizations we have observed significant and often highly distinctive configurations of value taken as ultimate or final by different human groups. Birth, sex and family, and death are three such recurring clusters of concern. So too is the common life of one's society as embodied in its laws or in its head-man. Man's relation to his natural environment with its animal species, its seasons of the year, its sky above and earth beneath are also recurring concerns. In every case that which is taken as ultimate is thereby holy or sacred.

The symbolic forms of these ultimate and holy values vary widely. Apollo, for example was Greek, and Marduk was Mesopotamian. These gods and all their divine relatives in other societies bear the distinctive marks of the particular people who served them. So too do the various and innumerable myths and rites, as well as the sculptured likenesses and architectual forms related to their worship. And these forms are only a suggestion of many more to come in religions and cultures around the world. Once again, in these symbolic forms, men's ultimate values have found powerful and lively expression.

As to the second main theme, namely the existential question, why am I alive? in many of the religions of this chapter it tends to be changed to the plural form, why are we alive? The emphasis is on the human group rather than the individual. In human history men have been members of society before they have been individuals. Yet individual selfhood, with the corollary of self-awareness, does emerge, certainly not all at once but by gradual and often fragmentary steps. In this chapter we have noted this emergence in ancient Greece with its achievement of rational selfhood. In future chapters we shall see a similar emergence in distinctive ways in such various places as ancient India, China, and Israel. Yet however it emerges and whatever symbolic form it assumes, why live? does constitute the inevitable religious question. To it the many religions of man may be regarded as functioning answers.

As to the third question, concerning the three types of religion, virtually all the religions studied in this chapter were of the cosmic or nature-culture sort, celebrating this or that value of the cosmos, and asserting the meaning of life in these terms. The sole significant exception occurred in ancient Greece where in Plotinus and his Neoplatonism an acosmic outlook became visible, and also influential for the future.

NOTES

1. Edwin Oliver James, *Prehistoric Religion,* Thames and Hudson, London, 1957, p. 291.

2. Edwin Oliver James, *History of Religions,* Harper & Row, Publishers, Incorporated, New York, 1957, p. 4.

3. *Ibid.,* p. 17.

4. *Ibid.,* p. 20.

5. *Ibid.,* p. 21.

6. *Ibid.,* p. 149.

7. Bronislaw Malinowski, "Magic, Science and Religion," in Joseph Needham (ed.), *Science, Religion and Reality,* The Macmillan Company, New York, 1925, p. 44.

8. W. Schmidt, *The Origin and Growth of Religion,* Methuen & Co., Ltd., London, 1931; A. Lang, *The Making of Religion,* Longmans, Green & Co., Ltd., London, 1898.

9. Malinowski, *op. cit.*

10. Robert Redfield, *The Primitive World and Its Transformations,* Cornell University Press, Ithaca, N.Y., 1953, p. 61.

11. Mircea Eliade, *Cosmos and History,* Harper & Row, Publishers, Incorporated, New York, 1959.

12. Edward B. Tylor, *Primitive Culture: Researches into the Development of Mythology, Philosophy, Religion, Language, Art and Custom,* Henry Holt and Company, Inc., New York, 1889.

13. Bishop R. H. Codrington's letter concerning mana in William A. Lessa and Evon Z. Vogt (eds.), *Reader in Comparative Religion,* Harper & Row, Publishers, Incorporated, New York, 1958, p. 207.

14. *Ibid.,* pp. 207f.

15. Robert R. Marett, *The Threshold of Religion,* Methuen & Co., Ltd., London, 1929.

16. J. G. Frazer, *The Golden Bough,* The Macmillan Company, New York, 1958.

17. Herbert Spencer, *Principles of Sociology,* D. Appleton & Company, Inc., New York, 1899, vol. I, pp. 422, 437.

18. Emile Durkheim, *Elementary Forms of the Religious Life,* The Free Press of Glencoe, New York, 1965.

19. Ludwig Feuerbach, *The Essence of Christianity,* Harper & Row, Publishers, Incorporated, New York, 1957.

20. See *inter alia* Ruth Benedict, *Patterns of Culture,* Mentor Books, New American Library of World Literature, Inc., New York, 1946; Clyde Kluckhohn, *Mirror for Man,* McGraw-Hill Book Company, New York, 1949.

21. V. Gordon Childe, *Man Makes Himself,* New American Library of World Literature, Inc., New York, 1951.

22. G. van der Leeuw, *Religion in Essence and Manifestation,* George Allen & Unwin, Ltd., London, 1938; Mircea Eliade, *Patterns in Comparative Religion,* Sheed & Ward, Inc., New York, 1958.

23. Van der Leeuw, *op. cit.,* p. 28.

24. Roger Caillois, *Man and the Sacred,* The Free Press of Glencoe, New York, 1960.

25. *Ibid.,* pp. 139–151.

26. *Ibid.,* p. 173.

27. *Ibid.,* p. 138.

28. Tylor, *op. cit.,* vol. II, p. 185.

29. Malinowski, *op. cit.*

30. W. Robertson Smith, *The Religion of the Semites,* Black, Edinburgh, 1889.

31. Bronislaw Malinowski, *The Foundations of Faith and Morals,* Oxford University Press, London, 1936, pp. 9f.

32. *Ibid.*, pp. 25f.

33. Arnold van Gennep, *Rites of Passage,* The University of Chicago Press, Chicago, 1960.

34. Ruth Benedict in Franz Boas, ed., *Anthropology and Modern Life,* W. W. Norton & Company, Inc., New York, 1928.

35. Henri Bergson, *The Two Sources of Morality and Religion,* Henry Holt and Company, Inc., New York, 1935.

36. Redfield, *op. cit.*

37. Genesis 12:1.

38. Henri Frankfort and others, *Before Philosophy,* Penguin Books, Inc., Baltimore, 1949.

39. Isaac Mendelsohn, *Religions of the Ancient Near East,* The Liberal Arts Press, Inc., New York, 1955, p. 17.

40. As quoted in John B. Noss, *Man's Religions,* The Macmillan Company, New York, 1949, p. 56.

41. Samuel N. Kramer, *History Begins at Sumer,* Doubleday & Company, Inc., Garden City, N.Y., 1959.

42. Gilbert Murray, *Five Stages of Greek Religion,* Columbia University Press, New York, 1925.

43. *Ibid.*, pp. 33–34.

44. Jane Harrison, *Mythology,* Marshall Jones, Boston, 1924, p. 94.

45. Hesiod, *Theogony,* trans. Norman O. Brown, The Liberal Arts Press, Inc., New York, 1953.

46. *Ibid.*, pp. 37f.

47. Aeschylus, *The Oresteia,* The University of Chicago Press, Chicago, 1953.

48. Euripides, *Hippolytus,* The Bodley Head, Ltd., London, 1949.

49. Murray, *op. cit.*, p. 103.

50. Frankfort, *op. cit.*, pp. 248f.

51. Milton Charles Nahm, *Selections from Early Greek Philosophy,* Appleton-Century-Crofts, Inc., New York, 1947, pp. 65–66.

52. *Ibid.*, p. 109.

53. Plato, "Apology," in B. Jowett, *The Dialogues of Plato,* Random House, Inc., New York, 1937, vol. I, p. 329.

54. *Ibid.*, vol. II, p. 377.

55. *Ibid.*, vol. II, pp. 524f.

56. *Ibid.*, vol. III, pp. 293–358.

57. Murray, *op. cit.*, p. 153.

58. Murray, *op. cit.*, p. 17.

SUGGESTIONS FOR FURTHER STUDY

Albright, W. F.: *From the Stone Age to Christianity,* Johns Hopkins, 1957.

Angus, S.: *Religious Quests of the Greco-Roman World,* Scribner, 1953.

Benedict, R.: *Patterns of Culture,* Mentor Books, 1946.

Breasted, H.: *The Dawn of Conscience,* Scribner, 1933.

———: *Development of Religion and Thought in Ancient Egypt,* Harper & Row, 1959.

Caillois, R.: *Man and the Sacred,* Free Press, 1960.

Childe, V. G.: *Man Makes Himself,* New American Library, 1951.

Durkheim, E.: *Elementary Forms of the Religious Life,* Free Press of Glencoe, 1965.

Eliade, M.: *Patterns in Comparative Religion,* Sheed, 1958.

———: *Cosmos and History,* Harper & Row, 1959.

Evans-Pritchard, E. E.: *Nuer Religion,* Oxford, 1956.

Ferm, V. T. A. (ed.): *Forgotten Religions,* Philosophical Library, 1950.

Feuerbach, L.: *The Essence of Christianity,* Harper & Row, 1957.

Finegan, J.: *Light From the Ancient Past,* Princeton, 1947.

Frankfort, H., and others: *Before Philosophy,* Penguin, 1949.

Frazer, J. G.: *The Golden Bough,* Macmillan, 1958.

Freud, S.: *The Future of an Illusion,* Anchor Books, 1957.

Goode, W.: *Religion among the Primitives,* Free Press, 1957.

Grant, F. (ed.): *Hellenistic Religion,* Liberal Arts, 1954.

Harrison, Jane: *Prolegomena to the Study of Greek Religion,* Cambridge, 1903.

James, E. O.: *Prehistoric Religion,* Harper & Row, 1957.

Lessa, W., and Vogt, E.: *Reader in Comparative Religion,* Harper & Row, 1958.

Malinowski, B.: *Magic, Science and Religion,* Doubleday, 1955.

———: *The Foundations of Faith and Morals,* Oxford, 1936.

Marett, R. R.: *The Threshold of Religion,* Macmillan, 1914.

Mendelsohn, I. (ed.): *Religions of the Ancient Near East,* Liberal Arts, 1955.

Murray, Gilbert: *Five Stages of Greek Religion,* Columbia, 1925.

Nilssen, Martin: *Greek Popular Religion,* Columbia, 1940.

Raden, Paul: *Primitive Religion,* Viking, 1937.

Redfield, Robert: *The Primitive World,* Cornell, 1953.

Rose, H. J.: *Religions in Ancient Greece and Rome,* Harper & Row, 1959.

Schmidt, W.: *The Origin and Growth of Religion,* Dial Press, 1931.

Tylor, E.: *Primitive Culture,* Holt, 1889.

3

THE BEGINNINGS OF
INDIAN RELIGION

As we embark for our passage to India, most of the familiar landmarks and labels of Western religion must be left behind. Not even the familiar terms *Hinduism* and *Hindu religion* remain. The English term *Hinduism* was first used in 1829.[1] The related word *Hindu* is of somewhat more ancient and more common usage in India, though in origin it appears to be a Persian rendering of the name given to the Sindh, or Indus, river and region. There is no adequate Sanskrit word for *religion*. For etymological reasons—and other reasons as well—many scholars deny that what popular usage designates as Hinduism is a religion at all, arguing that it is, rather, a total way of life. We will not be able completely to avoid some of these vexing and problematic words but must use them, at least provisionally, for the purpose of getting the process of study under way. These linguistic observations may serve to put us on guard against the characteristic Western vice of reading Western meanings into Indian words, ideas, and practices. Stated more affirmatively, our aim is to listen while the Indian tradition speaks for itself through the documents and artifacts, the men, ideas, and events treated in the next five chapters.

One particular difference of terminology must be specifically noted. Some writers use *Hinduism* for the total complex of Indian religion, while others restrict it to the major tradition of Indian religion. This volume follows the latter course. *Hinduism* as here used is a label for the religious phenomena to be discussed in Chapter 6. Yet here as elsewhere labels, once understood, are less important than what they indicate or describe.

Somewhat ironically, we shall approach the Indian religious tradition historically. This approach is ironical for the reason that ancient India was little concerned with history.[2] Our contemporary account, fragmentary as it is, of "the wonder that was India"[3] has been reconstructed only very recently, and with tools of historical study constructed largely by modern Western scholars. Yet to the twentieth-century Western student, hence to most readers of this book, the historical approach will be most illuminating.

The history of Indian religion may fruitfully be compared to a landscape seen by a geologist. As he makes his way over a countryside, noting the strata of rocks, the hills, the valleys, and innumerable other features of the landscape, using them all as data from which to reconstruct the geological history of the region, so the student of religion must approach India. The next five chapters will be concerned in one way or another with the complex landscape of Indian religious history. As the geologist speaks of successive layers or strata of rock, laid down during long geological ages, so we shall speak of successive strata of religion laid down during Indian history. At least six such layers or strata can be identified and distinguished.

(1) The oldest is the religion of the Indus Valley peoples of the third and early second millennium B.C. (2) The second is that of the Aryan invaders who poured into India through the northwest passes about the middle of the second millennium, subjugating previous inhabitants, quarreling among themselves, singing their songs and performing their sacrifices, leaving the Vedas as their one monument. (3) The third stratum is the philosophic religion of the Upanishads dating from the end of the second millennium to the middle of the first. (4) The fourth consists of the religious thought, documents, and movements stemming from men like Buddha and Mahavira, who lived in what has been called the Axis age, or Axis time, i.e., the seventh and sixth centuries B.C. Later ages were to call this period in India the age of the great heresies. (5) The fifth layer consists of Indian responses to these heresies, notably in the *Bhagavad Gita* and the *Code of Manu.* (6) The sixth and most recent stratum consists of the practices and attitudes originated in the centuries which the West calls A.D. which are sometimes labeled "Hinduism," or "popular Hinduism." This designation is somewhat misleading, since this religious complex contains elements, like Vedic *mantras,* or prayers, that go back to the ancient Vedic past. Yet the analogy of a geological landscape can help us here, for sometimes the most ancient rocks lie on the surface of the ground as outcroppings alongside

newer features from many different ages. So it is with the Indian religious landscape.

In this chapter we will deal with the three most ancient strata of Indian religion, while Chapters 4 and 5 will deal respectively with Mahavira and Buddha, Chapter 6 with Hinduism, and Chapter 7 with the newest Indian religion, Sikhism.

INDUS VALLEY CIVILIZATION

Remnants of the most ancient stratum of Indian culture and religion are visible to the twentieth century as a series of mounds in northwest India, notably at Harappa in Punjab and Mohenjo-daro in Sind. There is sufficient similarity in the remains to posit a uniform civilization over the whole region, extending for almost a thousand miles along the Indus River basin. Archaeological excavation of these sites has begun only in the present century, and much digging and interpretation remain to be done before anything like an adequate account of these ancient people is possible. For example, their language remains undeciphered to date.

Present evidence points to an archaic urban or city-state culture not unlike that of Mesopotamia and of the other great river valleys of the ancient world. Despite these similarities, there is little reason to conclude that the Indus Valley civilization was greatly influenced from Mesopotamia. This civilization seems to have flourished from approximately 2500 to 1500 B.C. Apparently an intense social conservatism dominated these people, for in their millennium or so of existence their pattern of life appears to have changed only very slightly. Remains of houses indicate a structure of social classes ranging from working people to an opulent merchant class whose plumbing excelled anything else prior to Rome. Their public buildings included a fortified citadel and a large public bath. The cities were laid out on a grid pattern. Technology was of a relatively advanced sort, producing a highly efficient saw. Crops included wheat, barley, peas, and cotton. There is also evidence of several of the main species of domestic animals.[4]

Among the archaeological findings are female figurines, presumably fertility images of the kind which are widely distributed over the world of antiquity. There are also sculptured figures of the Mother Goddess who apparently was a favorite deity, and whose icons adorned the homes of the people. She was doubtless the lineal descendant of the Venus figures of the last chapter; and she has reappeared many times and under many names in subsequent Indian history.

These and other figures testify to a well-developed interest in sculpture and other arts as well. The representation of animals was remarkably lifelike. As in other cultures and in subsequent Indian religion, these people apparently regarded some animals as holy. Particularly noteworthy are icons of the bull, often depicted with a single horn. The cow, so generally revered in later Indian religion, is nowhere depicted in Harappa and Mohenjo-daro.

Particularly noteworthy in this culture is the so-called horned god. He is depicted on seals, usually in the seated posture of devotion well known to later

Indus Valley seal of the horned god
Courtesy of the National Museum, New Delhi

Indian holy men. His body is nude except for necklaces, and on some of the seals he is surrounded by four wild animals. His face has a fierce aspect, which has led to the suggestion that he is meant to be superhuman. Protuberances on the sides of his head have led to the suggestion of some modern students that these were second and third faces. One authority has boldly termed the horned god "Proto-Shiva," and the name has gained wide acceptance. In any event, this figure has much in common with the later Indian god, Shiva.[5]

Phallic worship may be inferred to have been an important element of Indus Valley religion; at least there were many cone-shaped objects similar to the *lingam* of later Indian religion. It is also a fair inference that these objects were related to the cult of Proto-Shiva, as the lingam later became the symbol of

Shiva. The horned god is depicted with an erect phallus. It has also been suggested, with perhaps less factual basis, that certain large ring-shaped stones were female sex symbols related to the Mother Goddess, as was the *yoni* of later Indian religion.

In Harappa, a cemetery with fifty-seven graves was discovered in 1947. The dead were buried in extended posture with pottery and personal ornaments—

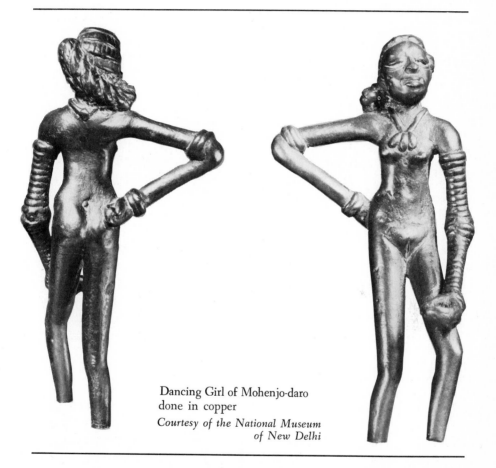

Dancing Girl of Mohenjo-daro
done in copper
*Courtesy of the National Museum
of New Delhi*

a notable difference from the general practice of cremation in later Indian history. Many other supposed features of Indus Valley religion, ranging from sacred trees to sacred ablution rituals, suggested by the large public baths at Mohenjo-daro, have been advanced by different investigators. Yet in the absence of deciphered written record, the whole scene remains somewhat vague and speculative.

The Indus Valley civilization apparently came to a violent end at approximately the middle of the second millennium B.C. Harappa and Mohenjo-daro were defended throughout their history by citadels, but toward the end of their existence there is evidence of greatly increased fortifications and other military activity. There is also other concurrent evidence of violent destruction of many villages in the region. One recent archaeological expedition reports finding a group of huddled skeletons, strongly suggesting the final sack of the city. While the evidence is by no means conclusive, it is persistently suggested that the destroyers of the Indus Valley civilization were the Aryan invaders, to whom we must turn attention in the next section.

As we do so, let us note the hypothesis proposed first by Heinrich Zimmer of a continuous tradition of distinctive ideas and attitudes stemming from pre-Aryan India and maintaining its identity against the more powerful, dominant Aryan tradition throughout the long course of Indian history.[6] Zimmer and others explain many characteristic features of Indian religion and culture in terms of the interaction of these two traditions. In Zimmer's formulation of the hypothesis, the Vedic thought and faith brought to India by the Aryan invaders is dominantly monist and idealist in outlook, meaning that reality is conceived in unitive terms and that the human self or mind is regarded as a part of this great unity. By contrast, the thought and faith of the pre-Aryan peoples show an outlook which is dualist or even pluralist, meaning that reality has an irreducible diversity. Also in contrast to Aryan idealism, the pre-Aryan outlook is realist, that is, man's self and mind are considered to be in some way independent of the reality they envisage. Other scholars continue to question and argue different aspects of the Zimmer hypothesis. The pages which follow will raise some of these critical questions. Nevertheless the hypothesis is valuable as a way of focusing attention upon significant aspects of Indian religious history. Whatever his conclusions, the serious student of Indian religion will learn much in the course of coming to terms with Zimmer's hypothesis.

THE VEDIC ARYANS AND THEIR RELIGION

Around 1500 B.C. a group of barbarians broke through the mountain passes from central Asia and fought their way into northwest India. In later centuries they moved eastward as far as the plain of the Ganges. The invaders called themselves Aryans, a word meaning "lord" or "noble." Linguistic evidence links them with other groups who swept off the central Eurasian plain at about this time and established themselves in such different lands as Iran, Greece, Rome, and Germany. The Sanskrit language of the Aryan Indians is closely related to Iranian, Greek, Latin, and German, and is generally recognized as the oldest of the Indo-European, or Aryan, language group.

The literature of the Aryans, which constitutes the sole body of evidence from which to construct our picture of their life and faith, consists of the four Vedas and certain closely related documents called *Brahmanas, Aranyakas,* and

Upanishads. Of the Vedas, the most important is the *Rig Veda,* which consists of 1028 hymns or poems composed by a great many seers, or *rishis,* all anonymous, during the period of approximately 1500 to 1000 B.C., for use in the religious ritual of the Aryans. Originally composed for oral recital, these hymns were not written down until many centuries later. Scholarly discussion of the date of the Vedas still goes on. One extreme Indian estimate pushes the date back to 6000 B.C. and asserts that they were the work of a people then inhabiting an arctic region, who only later undertook the long migration to India. Western scholars tend to hold to a period in the second half of the second millennium B.C. as the most likely period of origin. For example, W. Norman Brown feels that the *Rig Veda* was complete by the year 1000 B.C.[7]

Of the other three Vedas, the *Sama Veda* is an arrangement for ritual purposes of certain verses of the *Rig Veda.* The *Yajur Veda,* later than the *Rig Veda,* contains sacrificial formulas in prose and verse to be chanted by the priest. The *Atharva Veda* consists of magical spells and incantations in verse, covering a wide variety of situations which range from conceiving a child to preventing conception, from winning in gambling to confounding one's enemies, and to averting many assorted kinds of ill-fortune.

In the Indian tradition, the massive Brahmanas (or "Priestlies") are regarded as appendices to the Vedas. The Aranyakas (or "Forest Books") are in turn appendices to the Brahmanas, and the Upanishads bear a similar relation to the Aranyakas. All of these writings were included by those who later established Hindu orthodoxy within the category of Veda, or Vedic literature. The poems are Veda Samhita, and the other elements, respectively, Veda Brahmana, Veda Aranyaka, and Veda Upanishad. As Vedic, these documents constitute the most sacred writing in Indian religion. They are *shruti,* meaning "heard," since the inspired seer was supposed to hear the sacred words which he recited or composed. Writings which are shruti are to be distinguished from writings which are *smriti,* literally "remembered," a category which embraces traditional Indian religious classics such as the *Bhagavad Gita.*

Between the lines of the Vedas lies the story of the Aryan invasion of India, as well as the exploits and common life of these invaders. Their enemies, called the Dasas, are described as dark-skinned and ill-favored, yet rich in cattle and dwelling in fortified places that have been conquered by the Aryans. The Vedas tell the story of this conquest as well as that of internecine warfare among the Aryan tribes.

The Aryans lived by a mixed pastoral and agricultural economy. The Vedas contain many references to cattle, thus providing a beginning for the devotion accorded in subsequent ages in India to the cow. There are also references to other domestic animals such as sheep, goats, and horses, and also to stock breeding. Horses were apparently used in warfare, as also were chariots.

Aryan society did not involve, at least for some centuries, either writing or cities. Political organization centered in a chief, called a *rajah,* who was head of the larger family. Marriage was apparently monogamous and permanent. Priestly tasks were not involved in the chief's functions. The rajah's political power was limited by a council of leading men, of the sort common in ancient societies.

Like most traditional cultures, Aryan society had four main classes: warriors or nobles, priests, workmen and a middle class, and serfs. This division is particularly important in India, for it developed subsequently into the caste system. In this traditional Indian system the priestly, or Brahman, caste subsequently achieved and maintained a position of primacy, subordinating the noble class as well as the others.

The Aryans were a simple, warlike people, singing, gambling, brawling, and generally loving life. Their religious ceremonies and their gods were of a piece with their life. The sacrificial ritual which was the central feature of their religion was performed in the open air and was conceived as a means of securing the favor of their gods, who were thought to descend and join the human participants in the ceremonies, sitting on straw mats set out for them in the sacrificial enclosure. Though the gods were invisible, men knew them through their effects. They knew the demons in a similar way, and took precautions to avert the effects of their pranks and misdeeds. Both deities and demons were expressions of natural and social forces. There was, in short, little or nothing in this Vedic religion which might not be reproduced in religions of the first, or nature-culture, type around the world.

The Vedic gods have often been compared with the Olympian Greek pantheon, several deities being similar in both name and function. For example, the Vedic sky god, Varuna, resembled the Greek Uranus, and the Vedic Dyaus Pitar is like the Greek Father Zeus. Yet there were differences as well. The Vedic Indians never successfully ordered their pantheon as did the Olympian Greeks; and despite their similarity, these Vedic gods were never as clear, as sharply defined, or as interesting persons as their Greek relatives, leading one authority, Maurice Bloomfield, to the characterization of the Vedic pantheon as "arrested anthropomorphism."[8] Furthermore, as Zimmer has pointed out, ancient India, unlike Greece, never underwent a period of religious skepticism. Rather, the gods were "melted down" by philosophical speculation to a single metaphysical substance. The many Vedic gods and goddesses became in the course of time manifestations of a single supreme deity or principle—a distinctive Indian development of the greatest significance for her whole religious tradition.

Among the Vedic deities was Dyaus Pitar, or Father Heaven, to whom there are numerous references, but not a single hymn, in the *Rig Veda.* Apparently he was already in eclipse even in early Vedic times. As Father Heaven, he was often linked with the goddess Prithivi, or Mother Earth, thus illustrating a recurring pattern of devotion to two fundamental aspects of man's natural environment. Vedic deities were often classified into three groups, of the sky, air, and earth.[9]

Clearly the most important and characteristic deity of the Aryans was the hard-fighting, hard-drinking god Indra, to whom some 250 hymns of the *Rig Veda* were dedicated. He was probably the son of Father Sky and Mother Earth and was both war god and storm god. In more recent times, Indra has receded to the position of a minor rain deity. In ancient times, however, he led the Aryan warriors in battle, celebrating their victory over their enemies by drinking great draughts of potent *soma*. His wife, Indrani, was less well known, but many of his attendants, lesser spirits of the storm called Maruts, shouted and sang martial songs as they accompanied their leader into battle. A luxuriant mythology celebrated Indra, rider of the storm and Aryan champion.

Probably the most important single myth of the *Rig Veda* centers in Indra's slaying of the demon Vritra, thus releasing the cosmic waters and setting the stage for the emergence of the cosmic order. This battle was the climax of the agelong struggle between two kinds of forces. Vritra was the champion of the demons of restraint, bondage, and nonbeing, while Indra was the leader of the forces of light, life, and being. Immediately after he was born, Indra's aid was sought for this crucial battle. He accepted on the condition that he should be king of the gods. Then he took three great draughts of soma, which gave him overpowering strength and vast size. By means of these newly acquired powers, he split apart heaven and earth, so that he might occupy the intervening space. For the battle with Vritra, he was armed by Tvashtar, blacksmith of the gods, with the weapon of lightning.

After a fierce struggle Indra conquered and slew Vritra, bursting his belly and thus releasing the seven cosmic waters or rivers. These waters were pregnant with the sun, whose light and heat were essential to sustain life. Soon the earth too was spread out and stabilized, and the sky attached at the four corners of earth. Over this whole order Indra reigned as supreme ruler. In the course of events, man was fashioned as a servant of the gods. Though Vritra, chief of demons, has been slain, the demons still exist in the dark underworld, from which they sally forth to tempt and mislead man. So the age-old battle between Good and Evil, between Being and non-Being (*Sat* and *Asat*) continues.[10] (As an example of dualism which plays a basic role in Vedic thought, this myth poses important negative evidence for the Zimmer hypothesis.) This Indra myth bears important similarity to ancient Mesopotamia's mythical narrative of Marduk, as described in Chapter 2.

Comparable in importance to Indra, but very different in nature, was the sky god, Varuna. The heavens and sun constituted his primary domain, but as a sun god he came in time to preside over the days and seasons, and so, with the help of Rita, to preside over the order and law of the universe. Rita was conceived either as cosmic law or as a more or less definite personification of it. It was only a step from cosmic order to moral order, or righteousness. Varuna took that step. In many hymns he appeared as the revealer of sin, the judge of truth to whom were addressed man's prayers for forgiveness. Varuna sent his agents to all parts of the world, receiving reports of the deeds of men. Not even the secrets of the individual heart were hidden from Varuna; wherever two people planned together, there Varuna stood, judging their plans. Like Yahweh in the Bible he punished sin and rewarded righteousness. Before him man bowed in penitence and humility. An attendant of Varuna watched as men were brought at their life's end either to the "house of clay" or to the "place of blessing."

Another sun god, Surya, appears to have been primarily the shining sun. He prolonged life and drove away both disease and evil dreams. He was the priestly figure who declared man righteous in the presence of the gods. One of India's most famous and splendid ancient temples is that of Surya at Konarak. There were still other deities of the sun and solar functions. Savitar has been since Vedic times the stimulator, to whom is still addressed the Gayatri, perhaps the best-known and most important prayer in Hindu devotional practice (*Rig Veda* III.62:10): "We meditate upon that adorable effulgence of the resplendent vivifier, Savitar, may he stimulate our intellects." The Asuras were the "bright ones" whose chariot bore the sun. Ushas, the dawn, was a beautiful lady, sometimes said to be Surya's wife.

Agni the fire god (note the similarity to the Latin, *ignis*) was the fire of sun and thunderstorm as well as of hearth and altar. As god of sacrificial fire it was Agni who carried to the gods the sacrifices consumed by the fire. Some said there were many Agnis. It is hard at times to see when there is personification and when Agni is simply sacred or deified fire. The connection of fire with altar and sacrifice gave Agni a relation to priestly ritual, so that as priests increased in importance, so did Agni.

Two deities important in later Indian religion, Vishnu and Shiva, occupied only a minor place in the Vedic pantheon. To Vishnu only five Vedic hymns were addressed. He did not come into his own until later times. Like Vishnu, Shiva was a minor Vedic deity, and his early name was Rudra. At least the equation of Rudra and Shiva is widely accepted among students of the Vedas. His later name, Shiva, means "the shining one," or "auspicious one." In the Vedic period Rudra was primarily a storm god. He also shot arrows of plague and disaster, but he could bring healing as well. He dwelt in remote mountains and visited men according to his wishes.

Among the many other Vedic deities were Tvashtar, the heavenly blacksmith, like Hephaestus in Greece, Vayu, the wind, Yama, lord of the dead, and Soma, lord of the potent drink which found its way into Vedic ceremonies, producing visions and feelings of exaltation. Sometimes Soma is personified; sometimes it appears to be simply the holy or deified object itself. During Vedic times, these and almost innumerably many other gods and half-gods dwelt in the sky, in the air, or on the earth around man, influencing him for weal or woe.

The most important ritual of Vedic religion was sacrifice. Doubtless many attitudes and ideas played a part in the sacrificial cultus. Awe and wonder were important, but so was the desire to gain the favor of gods. As we have seen, the gods were thought to descend and fraternize with the men who sacrificed to them. There were no temples in Vedic times, the ritual taking place in the open air. Offerings were of milk or ghee (clarified butter), or grain, and of animals. There is no reason to believe that at first the priests were more important than in any other ancient society. Yet as masters of the sacred formula which rendered the sacrifice effective, the priests possessed an incalculably valuable monopoly which in the course of time established for the Brahman caste the dominant position in Indian society. Many of the priestly elements in Indian religion were already visible in Vedic times. Already there was an elaborate division of labor among four types of priests: the *adhvaryu,* or altar-builder, the *hotar,* who invoked the gods, the *agnidh,* who kindled the fire, and the Brahman, who presided and offered the central *brahma,* or prayer.

Already in the Vedas we meet the sacred syllable *Om,* or *Aum.* As with many another sacred word, the origins of *Aum* are buried in antiquity. However, in the course of time its three letters came to symbolize the three major Vedas, and also the three major deities, Vishnu, Shiva, and Brahma. More philosophically, it was understood to body forth into sound the fundamental reality of the universe. Obviously such a potent sound could exert mystical power upon the minds of those who meditated upon it.[11]

The later part of the Vedic period brought notable changes. Place-names in the later hymns of the Vedas change, and one infers that the Aryans were moving eastward toward the Ganges. Also the power of the kings or chiefs grew at the expense of the earlier tribal assemblies, and around the kings gathered courts and courtiers. Priestly power also grew apace, and with it the elaborate ritual of sacrifice took on endless elaboration. A new sacrifice, the *ashva medha,* or horse sacrifice, appears in later Vedic ritual. In this ceremony a consecrated horse was set free to roam at will for a year, followed by a chosen band of warriors. Tribes on whose land the horse wandered were forced to do homage or fight. At the year's end, the horse, if not captured, was brought back home and sacrificed. Despite its great expense, it was the ambition of every aspiring monarch to perform this ritual. The final climactic ceremony involved the slaughter of over one hundred horses. The whole practice was said to guarantee full salvation to those who completed it. A. L. Basham comments that it bedeviled Indian politics for a millennium. There were other royal consecrations, and *vajapeya,* which was a sort of rejuvenation ceremony designed to restore the vital energies of a middle-aged monarch.[12]

Several new developments in later Vedic thought are intimated in the Vedic texts. There were tendencies toward ritualism, toward monotheism, toward skepticism, and toward philosophic monism. As already noted and as will be seen in the image of cosmic sacrifice, some Vedic seers pushed in the direction of increasing ritual domination. Other seers, however, took up the idea of deity, and pushed in the direction of a single supreme God. There were even some skeptics among these ancient poets who questioned the whole system. Most important of these movements at least in the light of subsequent development, was the trend toward philosophic monism.

The ritual tendency is intimated by the name Brahmanaspati (or Brhaspati), which occurs with increasing frequency in later portions of the *Rig Veda.* The Sanskrit root, *brh,* denotes the holy prayer or devotional utterance which was a central feature of Vedic sacrifice, and the whole name, Brahmanaspati, has been rendered as "lord of the ritual." Here was a kind of deification of the sacrifice, probably set up by priests as a supreme principle in deliberate rivalry to Indra. Such was the increasing power of the priests!

Tendencies of a more theistic sort were expressed in Prajapati (literally "lord of creatures") and Vishvakarman (literally "maker or doer of all"), though the nature and implications of these tendencies may only be guessed. At least it can be inferred that the Indian mind was casting about in search of new forms. Skeptical tendencies are apparent in many of the hymns which raise questions or cast doubt on the power of virtue of Indra and other deities. There is even a hymn addressed to Ka (literally the interrogative pronoun *Who?*) in which the author presses home his questionings regarding the traditional deities. There are even some straightforward personifications, such as Kala (Time) and Skambha (Frame), suggested for membership in the Vedic pantheon.

The two most important hymns of the later Vedic writings are X.90 and X.129 of the *Rig Veda,* the so-called Hymn to Purusha and Hymn to Creation respectively. *Purusha* is the Sanskrit term for "person" (though one translator has rendered it as "male," which is one of its meanings); and the hymn turns upon the idea of microcosm and macrocosm. Purusha is represented as the cosmic person, and then to compound the metaphor the cosmic person is treated as both priest and sacrifice in the cosmic, or universal, sacrifice. Yet the interest of this hymn is not simply hieratic but cosmogonic as well, for from Purusha are derived the seasons of the year, the four Vedas, and the three-storied Indian universe. If this imagery is too compact and complex for the imagination of Western readers, its influence on Indian imagination—and Indian practice— can hardly be overestimated, for this notable hymn contains the first reference in Indian history to the four castes, Brahman, Kshatriya, Vaishya, and Shudra, deriving respectively from the head, shoulders, abdomen, and feet of the cosmic person.

Equally important as a harbinger of things to come was *Rig Veda* X.129:

CREATION

*Then was not non-existent nor existent: there was no
   realm of air, no sky beyond it.
What covered in, and where? and what gave shelter?
   Was water there, unfathomed depth of water?*

*Death was not then, nor was there aught immortal: no
   sign was there, the day's and night's divider.
That one thing, breathless, breathed by its own nature:
   apart from it was nothing whatsoever.*

*Darkness there was: at first concealed in darkness,
   this All was indiscriminated chaos.
All that existed then was void and formless: by the
   great power of warmth was born that unit.*

*Thereafter rose desire in the beginning, Desire, the
   primal seed and germ of spirit.
Sages who searched with their heart's thought discovered the existent's kinship in the non-existent.*

*Transversely was their severing line extended: what was
   above it then, and what below it?
There were begetters, there were mighty forces, free
   action here and energy up yonder.*

*Who verily knows and who can here declare it, whence
   it was born and whence comes this creation?
The gods are later than this world's production. Who
   knows, then, whence it first came into being?*

*He, the first origin of this creation, whether he
   formed it all or did not form it,
Whose eye controls this world in the highest heaven, he
   verily knows it, or perhaps he knows not.*[13]

"That One," or "that one thing" (in the Sanskrit language *tadekam*, the neuter third-person singular demonstrative pronoun joined to the neuter form of "one"), is here boldly taken to designate the original reality from which all other entities derive their existence. This is even true of the gods, concerning whom we are assured that they are "later than this world's production." In the imagery of this remarkable philosophic poem, out of darkness and water, which constituted the original chaos, first emerged "that one thing," and from this primal reality all the various phenomena of the universe have derived successively, by means of desire. Of equal importance are the dualistic references to nonexistence and existence (*asat* and *sat*), and to death and immortality. Here is the dualism of the India myth; and monism is represented as being prior and dominant to it. Of equal significance in this ancient Indian account of the origins of things is the spirit of skeptical inquiry in which the anonymous poet wrote. The last lines are the record of his bold skeptical questioning.

Another feature of the later Vedic age was the body of literature called Brahmanas. It is impossible to assign a definite date for these documents, estimates ranging from 1000 to 300 B.C. It is even harder for the modern Western reader to make sense of these vast rambling documents, apparently so totally lacking in order or coherence. They were probably guidebooks or textbooks for Brahman priests. There are occasional hints of philosophic meaning, jumbled together with esoteric meanings, word magic, and what often seems sheer verbiage. A. B. Keith remarks that "they are works in which the imagination of successive generations of priests has been allowed to run riot."[14] A twentieth-century Hindu scholar speaks of the "extreme conservatism and the stagnant ritualism of these documents."[15]

Yet some patterns of meaning and order are detectable. For one thing, the rise to prominence of the Brahman priesthood and their innumerable sacrifices as well as their priestly caste status all appear here. The image of cosmic sacrifice of *Rig Veda* X.90 was apparently an intimation of things to come, for it was elaborated in great and intricate detail in the Brahmanas. In successive metaphors the *Shatapatha Brahmana* treats the universe as a vast fire altar, and as a sacred, sacrificial horse. One particularly poignant and characteristic statement of this Brahmana asserts that the sun would not rise if the Brahman priest did not correctly perform the daily sacrifice! To this, we must hastily add that this imputed relation between ritual and reality is by no means unique to India. In Chapter 2, we saw that the Babylonian New Year's festival was regarded as necessary to sustain the structure of the cosmos. However, only in India has priestly power gained dominance so completely and for so long a time. Although a long succession of rebels, from Buddha to Gandhi, have arisen to speak against caste, none of them has succeeded in breaking the hold of this massively sacred custom on the mind and practice of India. What the reader sees in the Brahmanas is the sacred power of priests asserting its domination over the whole of life.

Other tendencies are also visible. Vishnu, whom we have seen in earlier Vedic times as a minor deity, now rises to prominence as god of the sacrifices.

Shiva's identification with the Vedic Rudra here becomes a fact. Also in the Brahmanas one catches occasional glimpses of notable philosophic ideas such as that of the self-existent Brahman of which all other gods and all realities are transitory manifestations. These ideas demanded further expression and development. In the course of time they formed the content of a new stratum of Indian religion, namely, the Upanishads.

PHILOSOPHIC VISION OF THE UPANISHADS

Priestly ritual was not the only nascent tendency of the later Vedic period. In addition to the Brahmanas, there were other documents, the Aranyakas and the Upanishads. The Aranyakas ("Forest Books") are the record of men who drew away from civilized society and toward the forests, there to meditate, to practice asceticism, and to seek salvation. Their thought found expression in the Upanishads. The word *upanishad* means to "sit apart," i.e., at the feet of a teacher, and the image is that of teacher and students sitting apart in the forests, discussing the great themes of human existence. *Upanishad* also clearly implies the esoteric nature of the teaching, limited to a closed circle of teachers and students, not for general public consumption. As these ancient Indian teachers and students discussed, meditated, and practiced asceticism, a new perspective, that of philosophic vision, opened before them. Hence the Upanishads constituted a new stratum of religion in ancient India.

The figure of the ascetic who seeks salvation by the practice of austerities is present in the earliest Vedic documents. These records tell of several kinds of holy men, including "the silent ones" who left civilized life for the forests, as well as others who traveled from village to village, teaching and demonstrating their ways. In all cases, the ascetic was believed to possess a special kind of power, often plainly magical, and his influence was based on this widespread belief.[16] Yet in the Upanishads his austerities and meditation were transformed into something new.

As already observed, the coming of philosophy in ancient India, unlike ancient Greece, brought no head-on collision of priest and philosopher. The viewpoint of the Upanishads did involve a devaluation of priestly ritual; and at least one Upanishad characterizes sacrifices as uncertain or leaky vessels to salvation.[17] Presumably, philosophic speculation or contemplation was better. Unlike the Sophists of ancient Greece, these ancient Indian philosophers did not attack the popular religion. Rather they did something far more characteristic of Indian thought: they treated both Vedic deities and Brahmanic ritual as symbolic manifestations of a supreme philosophic principle.

Some 108 Upanishads are said to exist, but of this number only a dozen or so are truly important. Among them are the *Brihad Aranyaka,* the *Chandogya,* the *Katha,* the *Isha,* the *Kena,* the *Mandukya,* the *Mundaka,* the *Shvetasvatara,* the *Taittiriya,* and the *Aitareya.*[18] The earlier Upanishads such as the *Brihad Aranyaka* and the *Chandogya* are in prose, while later ones are in verse. They vary in length from the very short *Kena* and *Mandukya* to the long and rambling *Brihad Aranyaka.* Most of them contain dialog of some sort. Many persons, including even some women and members of different castes participate in the dialog. While a few of the characters are historical persons, as for instance the philosophically minded King Janaka of Videha, traditional father-in-law of Rama of the *Ramayana,* most are either fictional or are unknown to us.

RECURRING THEMES

Clearly no unified system of philosophic doctrine emerges from these ancient dialogs; indeed the ideas which are proposed often clash with each other. Western readers have compared them to Plato's dialogs. In both there is questioning and argument which constitute a kind of drama of ideas, sometimes resulting in solution or agreement, but sometimes not. The reader encounters in both Plato and the Upanishads several recurring themes of great importance. These themes of the Upanishads became in many cases the systems of later Indian philosophy. Here we shall sketch and illustrate eight such recurring themes, though others will occur even to the casual reader of the Upanishads.

ABSOLUTE REALITY

The first and perhaps dominant theme of the Upanishads is the Absolute Reality which we have already met in "that one thing" of Hymn X.129 of the *Rig Veda.* This idea is by no means a unique achievement of these ancient Indian explorers of the mind's life. Rather, the conception of a self-subsistent reality beyond the common objects of everyday life, yet pervading them and giving them whatever reality they possess, recurs in many times and places and under many names. We shall meet it in many of the world's faiths as our study proceeds. Indian thought called it *Brahman,* which is derived from the magic word of the sacrifices, but which came to mean for the philosophers of the Upanishads "the Supreme Reality." Brahman as Supreme Reality is to be distinguished from the Brahman priesthood, and from the four-faced deity Brahma. If the word *God* be shorn of its personal, Judeo-Christian meanings and assigned an impersonal or transpersonal sense, their *Brahman* may be freely translated as "God."

The limited, finite character of all the objects of everyday life, not to speak of one's own self, point toward a Supreme, or Absolute, Reality, which does not change or pass away but simply and supremely *is.* It is that which supremely or absolutely *exists,* in its own power, not dependent on other existing things.

Indeed, the *via negativa* so popular in the philosophic thought of India consists of stripping away all qualifying predicates from this verb *to be*, or *to exist*, until one comes at last to the idea of being-as-such, or Supreme Being. As the *Brihad Aranyaka Upanishad* puts the matter, the Supreme Reality is *"neti, neti,"* "not this, not this." It lies at the end of the road of philosophic abstraction when we have stripped away from the verb *to be* every last predicate adjective and predicate nominative and are left simply with Being. Here again is *tadekam*, "that one thing" of *Rig Veda* X.129.

There are other paths which lead to the same goal, among them the path of religious devotion. So, for example, the devotee in the *Brihad Aranyaka Upanishad* is admonished to utter the prayer, "From the unreal lead me to the real, from darkness lead me to light, from death lead me to immortality."[19] Here one sees the same struggle of the forces of unreality, darkness, and death against reality, light, and immortality which characterized *Rig Veda* X.129; but here as there, the single divine principle of Reality, Light, and Immortality wins out.

Here is the way the *Mundaka Upanishad* puts this same fundamental matter:

> *Two kinds of knowledge are to be known, as indeed, the knowers of Brahman declare—the higher as well as the lower.*
>
> *Of these, the lower is the Rig Veda, the Yajur Veda, the Sama Veda, the Atharva Veda . . .*
>
> *And the higher is that by which the Undecaying is apprehended.*
>
> *That which is ungraspable, without family, without caste, without sight or hearing, without hands or feet, eternal, all-pervading, omnipresent, exceedingly subtle, that is the Undecaying which the wise perceive as the source of beings.*
>
> *As a spider sends forth and draws in (its thread), as herbs grow on the earth, as the hair (grows) on the head and the body of a living person, so from the Imperishable arises here the universe.*[20]

To cite just one more expression of this theme from the innumerable possibilities, the *Chandogya Upanishad* says this:

> *In the beginning, my dear, this was Being alone, one only without a second. Some people say "in the beginning this was non-being alone, one only; without a second. From that non-being, being was produced."*
>
> *But how, indeed, my dear, could it be thus? said he, how could being be produced from non-being? On the contrary, my dear, in the beginning this was being alone, one only, without a second.*
>
> *It thought, May I be many, may I grow forth. . . .*[21]

While many, if not most, references to this Supreme Reality suggest an impersonal Being, others, like the following from the *Brihad Aranyaka,* clearly reflect a personal, or theistic, concept:

> *Verily, he is the great unborn Self who is this (person) consisting of knowl-edge among the senses. In the space within the heart lies the controller of all, the lord of all, the ruler of all. . . .*[22]

In the later poetic Upanishads this characterization of the World Spirit or Ultimate Reality in personal rather than impersonal terms is even more frequent and emphatic, thus providing a source for a distinctive Indian path to salva-tion, that of *bhakti,* or religious devotion, which came in the course of time to differ fundamentally from the way of philosophic knowledge.

SELFHOOD

The Supreme Reality which lies beyond all the specific objects of the uni-verse as a World Spirit may also be sought in the depths of the human self. Here it is not Brahman but *Atman,* which is the Sanskrit word for self, or soul. Yet the term appears to mean to the philosophic seers of the Upanishads not any particular self or any particular aspect of the experience of selfhood but rather the experience of selfhood in its widest, deepest, and most general sig-nificance. Again, one may approach the true nature of the Atman best by stripping away one by one all the predicates which make any self particular —make it this self rather than that self. At the bottom of this deep well of the self lies the universal Self, or Atman. To the exploration of the Atman are devoted many passages of the Upanishads.

Like Brahman, the Atman is to be approached by a process of negation (neti, neti). Atman is not easily known, for the good reason that it lies beyond every normal waking act or attitude. The serious seeker of the Self must by means of ascetic discipline detach himself from the pursuits of the world and from an interest in his own existence. Gradually as he treads this path of de-tachment and introspection the Atman opens before him.

In the metaphor of the *Katha Upanishad,* the Self is compared to chariot and charioteer:

> *Know the Self as the lord of the chariot and the body as, verily, the chariot, know the intellect as the charioteer and the mind as, verily, the reins. The senses, they say, are the horses; the objects of sense the paths (they range over); (the self) associated with the body, the senses and the mind—wise men declare—is the enjoyer. . . .*
>
> *He who has no understanding, whose mind is always unrestrained, his senses are out of control, as wicked horses are for a charioteer.*
>
> *He, however, who has no understanding, who has no control over his mind (and is) ever impure, reaches not that goal but comes back into mundane life.*

He, however, who has understanding, who has control over his mind and (is) ever pure, reaches the goal from which he is not born again. . . .

Beyond the senses are the objects of the sense, and beyond the objects is the mind; beyond the mind is the understanding and beyond the understanding is the great self.[23]

IDENTITY OF SELF AND REALITY

The climactic and characteristic declaration of the Upanishads is the identity of Atman and Brahman, or in the words of the *Chandogya Upanishad,* "tat tvam asi," "that art thou."[24] In other words, there is a complete identity between the absolute or universal reality underlying the objective world and that which every man may find at the foundation of his subjecthood. These are two paths to the same Supreme Reality. Of this Reality each human soul is a broken fragment. Hence man's highest destiny is to realize this fact and so to realize the great identity or unity which is fulfillment, salvation, and blessedness. The *Chandogya Upanishad* puts it this way in dialog between father and son:

These rivers, my dear, flow the eastern toward the east, the western toward the west. They go just from sea to sea. They become the sea itself. Just as these rivers while there do not know "I am this one," "I am that one." In the same manner, my dear, all these creatures even though they have come forth from Being do not know that "we have come forth from Being." Whatever they are in this world, tiger or lion or wolf or boar or worm or fly or gnat or mosquito that they become.

That which is the subtle essence, this whole world has for its self. That is the true.

That is the self. That art thou, Shvetaketu. . . .[25]

This same dialog pursues the theme by means of two other metaphors, that of the seed of the nyagrodha tree, and that of salt dissolved in water. In both cases the illustrations arrive at the conclusion, "that art thou," meaning that the human self is one with universal reality. As the salt pervades the water in which it is dissolved, or as the whole tree is implicitly given in its smallest seed, even so the Self and Reality, or the Atman and Brahman, are ultimately equivalent to each other.

No more important or characteristic words than these are spoken throughout the Upanishads. These ideas echo and reecho through many of the most important systems of Indian philosophy. The path to salvation by emancipation from all finite things ends in absorption in the Absolute Reality. This way was discovered and explored by the philosophic seers of the Upanishads; and it was destined to be trodden by Indian seekers and pilgrims from that day to this. Thinkers and seers of many schools and sects devoted themselves to making explicit some of the implications of the Upanishadic vision. Some of these further implications or corollaries were developed by the Upanishads themselves.

STAGES OF CONSCIOUSNESS

Among these is the idea of stages of consciousness. First is ordinary waking consciousness, which is the lowest rung on the ladder to salvation. Next above it is dreaming consciousness, and above that dreamless sleep. Above dreamless sleep, however, lies a fourth and nameless form of consciousness recognizable only to those who have experienced it, to whom it is understood as that absorption of the individual in Absolute Reality which constitutes salvation. From the Upanishads onward, Indian religious and philosophic thought has never ceased to explore the nature of consciousness with a view to understanding and achieving this fourth state. So it is that these early insights of the Upanishads led onward in the course of time to such detailed systems as Yoga.

The *Mandukya Upanishad,* whose twelve brief verses are descriptions of the four stages, characterizes the fourth state thus: "The fourth is that which has no elements, which cannot be spoken of, into which the world is resolved, benign, non-dual. Thus the syllable *aum* is the very self. He who knows it thus enters the self with his self."[26]

For the Upanishads the experience of absorption in Brahman-Atman constituted salvation, or *moksha.* Most of India's philosophers and seers have had their own version of salvation as emancipation. As we shall see in coming chapters, the founders of Jainism and Buddhism had their own distinctive interpretations. In this ancient argument of the schools the authors of the Upanishads spoke of it as the great identity, "tat tvam asi," and as the top of the ladder of ascent through the four stages of consciousness.

SAVING KNOWLEDGE

This same salvation is also characterized as the highest and truest form of knowledge; conversely, perdition is characterized as a state of ignorance, or the absence of this supreme knowledge. To be sure, this is not ordinary secular knowledge, nor is it simply intellectual knowing of this or that metaphysical proposition. Rather it may be characterized as a living awareness on the part of the whole mind, or self, of the great identity of Atman and Brahman. In this supreme awareness, mind is not so much conscious of this identity as actually absorbed in it. In this unique form of awareness everything is unified and transcended.

This unique knowledge has its own distinctive moral prerequisites. If a man still clings to finite life, or to any of the concerns pertaining to mortal existence, he will be unable to rise to the higher state. The discipline of asceticism is necessary to break the fetters which bind the self to the lower world. Then by the discipline of meditation the mind may be directed to its true object, the Supreme Reality. Awareness of this true object also contains the implication that all else is illusory and delusory appearance. All sense experience and all objects of finite reality are only relatively true, for they are the products of the illusion-maker. The veil of illusion must be torn away if the Real is to be found. Such, said the seers of the Upanishads, is the saving knowledge which is man's proper aim or goal!

DESTINY BEYOND DEATH

Closely related to this supreme experience was the question of what lay beyond death. Many of the Upanishads allude to this perennial question but the *Katha* is devoted specifically to it. The boy Nachiketas was about to be sacrificed by his father and asked Yama, the lord of the underworld, to grant him three boons. The first was that his father should be pacified and the second, that the fire sacrifice be named for him; but the third was that he be told what lies beyond death. Yama was reluctant, but Nachiketas was presistent. So Yama was led to set forth the view of man's destiny beyond death as absorption in the Absolute Reality. This blessed destiny was asserted to go beyond both extinction and continued finite existence in some supramundane realm. From this viewpoint, finite existence was regarded as a form of bondage which man must transcend if he is truly to be saved. Only if a man has risen beyond all finite desires for survival or extinction is he truly saved. The *Katha Upanishad* puts the matter thus:

> *The knowing self is never born; nor does he die at any time. He sprang from nothing and nothing sprang from him. He is unborn, eternal, abiding and primeval. He is not slain when the body is slain.*
> *If the slayer thinks that he slays or if the slain think [sic] that he is slain, both of them do not understand. He neither slays nor is he slain.*
> *Smaller than the small, greater than the great, the self is set in the heart of every creature. The unstriving man beholds Him, freed from sorrow. Through the tranquility of the mind and the senses [he sees] the greatness of the self.*[27]

COSMOGONY

We have already noted some of the cosmological and cosmogonic suggestions of the Vedas and Brahmanas, that is, suggestions concerning how the world began and what it is made of. *Rig Veda* X.129 derived the world from chaos and desire. Ever and again the Upanishads suggest that all things derive from

Brahman. A wide variety of other suggestions are strewn throughout the Upanishads. Among teachings which subsequent generations called orthodox, creation was ascribed to Purusha, the cosmic person who felt loneliness and need for companionship and so took a wife. This primordial couple procreated the whole phenomenal universe. Somewhat similar to this imagery is the idea of creation from a primordial cosmic egg. The *Brihad Aranyaka* says it was a golden egg!

Other less orthodox minds put forward other less traditional cosmogonic suggestions. Some said the world began as water; others that the universe had begun as fire, wind, or ether; still others put forward fate, or time, or chance as the ruling principle of all things, while some skeptically questioned the possibility of any knowledge of these matters. Materialists also appeared on the scene, tracing all things to a source in matter. We shall have occasion in the next three chapters to sketch in more detail some of the systems of thought which had their origin in this seminal period of Indian religions and philosophic history.

KARMA-SAMSARA

One theme is delineated in the Upanishads which overlaps both cosmology and ethics and has very great importance for the future of Indian thought and life; it is *karma-samsara*. *Karma* is the law of the deed; it occurs in many religious traditions as the perception that moral deeds carry their consequences, "as you sow, so will you reap." Ancient Indian thought asserted this insight to be an inexorable law and joined it to belief in transmigration (*samsara*). The result was the traditional Indian view that evil deeds have consequences through many incarnations. One Upanishad puts the matter in the following words:

> *If you thus indicate the greatness of this self then there is that other, different one also called self, who, affected by the bright or dark fruits of action, enters a good or evil womb, so that his course is downward or upward and he wanders about, affected by the pairs [of opposites like pleasure and pain].*[28]

The *Chandogya Upanishad* asserts karma-samsara in specific detail:

> *Those whose conduct here has been good will quickly attain a good birth [literally "womb"], the birth of a Brahman, the birth of a Ksatriya or the birth of a Vaisya. But those whose conduct here has been evil, will quickly attain an evil birth, the birth of a dog, the birth of a hog or the birth of a candala [outcast].*[29]

Compared with this grim prospect it was small wonder that emancipation from all finite existence seemed a joyful prospect!

MORALITY AND ETHICS

While the main concern of the Upanishads was with salvation, or blessed-ness, nevertheless morality was dealt with as an important aspect of the journey to salvation. Thus for example, indulgence of material or sensual desire is evil, as is attachment to the things of the world. Conversely, sacrifice, study, and charity are great goods; so too are discipline, austerity, and celibacy. These qualities are good because they lead the soul upward on the path to salvation. The *Maitri Upanishad* has this to say concerning the body and its needs:

> In this foul-smelling, unsubstantial body, a conglomerate of bone, skin, muscle, marrow, flesh, semen, blood, mucus, tears, rheum, feces, urine, wind, bile, and phlegm, what is the good of the enjoyment of desires? In this body which is afflicted with desire, anger, covetousness, delusion, fear, despondency, envy, separation from what is desired, union with the undesired, hunger, thirst, old age, death, disease, sorrow, and the like, what is the good of the enjoyment of desires? . . . But, indeed, what of these? . . . Among other things, there is the drying up of great oceans, the falling away of mountain peaks, the deviation of the fixed pole-star, the cutting of the wind-ropes [that hold the stars in their places], the submergence of the earth, the departure of the gods from their sta-tion. In such a world as this, what is the good of enjoyment of desires? For he who had fed on them is seen to return [to this world] repeatedly. Be pleased, therefore, to deliver me. In this world [cycle of existence] I am like a frog in a waterless well. Revered Sir, you are our way [of deliverance], you are our way.[30]

In a notable passage, the *Brihad Aranyaka Upanishad* moves through a long list of goods such as husband, wife, sons, wealth, love of the gods, and the like, asserting that they are not dear for their own sake but for love of Self (or Atman). The conclusion is an ethic which harmonizes many human goods under an ideal detachment, concluding in these words:

> Verily, not for the sake of all is all dear but all is dear for the sake of the Self. Verily, O Maitreyi, it is the Self that should be seen, heard of, reflected on and meditated upon. Verily, by the seeing of, by the hearing of, by the think-ing of, by the understanding of the Self, all this is known.[31]

The ethical spirit of the Upanishads is admirably summed up in a notable passage of the *Brihad Aranyaka*, which incidentally is echoed in T. S. Eliot's poem, "What The Thunder Said," from "The Wasteland."

> The threefold offspring of Prajapati, gods, men and demons, lived with their father Prajapati as students of sacred knowledge. Having completed their studentship the gods said, "Please tell [instruct] us, sir." To them then, he

uttered the syllable da [*and asked*] "*Have you understood?*" *They* [*said*] "*We have understood, you said to us* 'damyata,' '*control yourselves.*'" *He said,* "*Yes, you have understood.*"

Then the men said to him, "*Please tell* [*instruct*] *us, sir.*" *To them he uttered the same syllable* da [*and asked*] "*Have you understood?*" *They said,* "*We have understood. You said to us* '*give.*'" *He said,* "*Yes, you have understood.*"

Then the demons said to him, "*Please tell* [*instruct*] *us, sir.*" *To them he uttered the same syllable* da *and asked,* "*Have you understood?*" *They said,* "*We have understood, you said to us,* 'dayadhvam,' '*be compassionate.*'" *He said,* "*Yes, you have understood.*" *This very thing the heavenly voice of thunder repeats* da, da, da, *that is, control yourselves, give, be compassionate. One should practice this same triad, self-control, giving and compassion.*[32]

CONCLUDING COMMENT

Glancing backward over this chapter and over the centuries of Indian religious history it has described, what conclusions may we draw? First of all the values of Vedic religion seem to be those of cosmic religion as characterized in Chapters 1 and 2. The gods of the *Rig Veda,* like those of Homeric Greece and of many other ancient societies, are more or less personified powers of nature and society. As we have seen, Indra in particular embodied the main values of the Aryan invaders of India. Insofar as we can reconstruct them, the religious values of the earlier Indus Valley civilization seem to have been similar in this respect.

The most important single development in ancient Indian religion was the achievement of a point in human thought above the common world of nature and culture. Let us call it an Archimedean point, recalling the words of the ancient Greek scientist that if he could find a point outside the world he could lift the world. *Tadekam,* or "that one thing" is the designation for this point in *Rig Veda* X, 129. In the Upanishads it is called both Brahman and Atman, and we have seen the classic assertion *tat tvam asi,* "that art thou." All of these designations point toward the concept of *moksha* or salvation by emancipation from all mortal or finite bonds. This idea is intimated by several of the seers of the Upanishads, and in coming chapters we see it again in such figures as Mahavira and Buddha. It will also be developed in the central tradition of Hindu philosophy and devotion, namely Vedantism. Moksha implies a negative valuation of the common world of nature and culture. One practical corollary of this negative valuation has been India's preoccupation with ascetic practices of many sorts.

This development in Indian religion is variously evaluated by different modern scholars. Many have characterized it bluntly as world-denial or world-negation. However, Heinrich Zimmer declares ecstatically that ancient India achieved a viewpoint above the common life of human culture, in terms of which all things human might be calmly adjudicated, and which only now, several millenia later, the West is approaching. Perhaps one issue in these conflicting evaluations is that the sources, the Upanishads, do not speak with a single voice. In any case it is sufficient at this point to raise the issue and urge the student to work on it for himself as our study proceeds.

As to our second main issue, we see the existential question, why live? raised in unequivocal and also distinctively Indian fashion by the seers of the Upanishads, and we will see it again in such figures as Mahavira and Buddha. These individual men in ancient India pushed away the tight embrace of their society and in their own way asserted individual life and destiny with all its questions and issues. This is a theme that will be with us in one form or another throughout this book.

Finally we see in ancient India's concept of moksha or emancipation a move from the first to the second or acosmic type of religion. Indeed ancient India is one of the world's chief source regions of this type of religion.

NOTES

1. W. C. Smith, *The Meaning and End of Religion*, The Macmillan Company, New York, 1963, p. 62. See also *Hinduism* in *Oxford English Dictionary*, vol. 5, p. 293.
2. William H. Moreland and Atui C. Chatterjee, *A Short History of India*, Longmans, Green & Co., Inc., New York, 1957, pp. 34–35.
3. A. L. Basham, *The Wonder That Was India*, Grove Press, Inc., New York, 1959.
4. *Ibid.*, pp. 14–28.
5. J. Marshall and others, *Mohenjo Daro and the Indus Civilization*, 3 vols., London, 1931. Quoted from Basham, *op. cit.*, p. 23.
6. Heinrich Zimmer, *Philosophies of India*, Meridian Books, Inc., New York, 1957, pp. 59–60.
7. W. Norman Brown, *Man in the Universe: Some Continuities in Indian Thought*, Oxford and IBH Publishing Company, Calcutta, 1966, p. 7.
8. M. Bloomfield, *The Religion of the Veda*, G. P. Putnam's Sons, New York, 1908, p. 83ff.
9. Arthur B. Keith, *The Religion and Philosophy of the Vedas and the Upanishads*, Harvard University Press, Cambridge, Mass., 1925, vol. I, chap. 8.
10. Brown, *op cit.*, pp. 21–23.
11. Zimmer, *op. cit.*, pp. 372–378.
12. Basham, *op. cit.*, p. 42.
13. Quoted from Lin Yutang, *The Wisdom of China and India*, Modern Library, Inc., New York, 1942, p. 15.
14. Keith, *op. cit.*, vol. II, p. 440.
15. Kenneth W. Morgan (ed.), *The Religion of the Hindus*, The Ronald Press Company, New York, 1953, p. 30.
16. Basham, *op. cit.*, p. 244.
17. Mundaka Upanishad I.2.7, in S. Radhakrishnan, *The Principal Upanishads*, Harper & Row, Publishers, Incorporated, New York, 1953, p. 676.
18. Robert E. Hume, *The Thirteen Principal Upanishads*, Oxford University Press, Fair Lawn, N.J., 1958.
19. Brihad Aranyaka Upanishad, I.3.28., Radhakrishnan, *op. cit.*, p. 162.
20. Mundaka Upanishad I.1.4–7, in Radhakrishnan, *op. cit.*, pp. 672–673.
21. Chandogya Upanishad, VI.2.1–3, in Radhakrishnan, *op. cit.*, p. 447.
22. Brihad Aranyaka Upanishad, IV.4.–22, in Radhakrishnan, *op. cit.*, p. 279.
23. Katha Upanishad, I.3.3–10, in Radhakrishnan, *op. cit.*, pp. 623–625.
24. Chandogya Upanishad, VI.8.4, 6, 7, in Radhakrishnan, *op. cit.*, pp. 457–459.
25. Chandogya Upanishad, VI.10.1–3, in Radhakrishnan, *op. cit.*, pp. 460–461.
26. Mandukya Upanishad 12, in Radhakrishnan, *op. cit.*, p. 701.

27. Katha Upanishad, I.2.18–20, in Radhakrishnan, *op. cit.*, pp. 616–617.

28. Maitri Upanishad, III.2, in Radhakrishnan, *op. cit.*, p. 805.

29. Chandogya Upanishad, V.10.7, in Radhakrishnan, *op. cit.*, p. 433.

30. Maitri Upanishad, I.3.4, in Radhakrishnan, *op. cit.*, pp. 796–797.

31. Brihad Aranyaka II.4.5, in Radhakrishnan, *op. cit.*, p. 197.

32. Brihad Aranyaka V.2.1, in Radhakrishnan, *op. cit.*, pp. 289–290.

SUGGESTIONS FOR FURTHER STUDY

Basham, A. L.: *The Wonder That Was India*, Grove Press, 1959.

Brown, W. N.: *Man in the Universe*, University of California Press, 1966.

Danielyou, A.: *Indian Polytheism*, Bollingen, 1963.

Dasgupta, S.: *Indian Idealism*, Cambridge, 1933.

de Bary, W. T. (ed.): *Sources of Indian Tradition*, Columbia, 1958.

Deussen, P.: *The Philosophy of the Upanishads*, T. & T. Clark, 1906.

Eliot, Sir Charles: *Hinduism and Buddhism*, Routledge, 1954.

Griffith, R. T. H.: *The Hymns of the Rig Veda*, Lazarus, 1897.

Hume, R.: *The Thirteen Principal Upanishads*, Oxford, 1923.

Keith, A. B.: *The Religion and Philosophy of the Vedas and the Upanishads*, Harvard, 1925.

Marshall, J., ed.: *Mohenjo Daro and the Indus Civilization*, Oxford, 1931.

Morgan, K. (ed.): *The Religion of the Hindus*, Ronald, 1953.

Piggott, S.: *Prehistoric India*, Penguin, 1950.

Prabhavananda, S., and F. Manchester: *The Upanishads*, Mentor Books, 1957.

Radhakrishnan, S.: *History of Indian Philosophy*, G. Allen, 1929–1931.

—— (ed.): *History of Philosophy, Eastern and Western*, G. Allen, 1952.

——: *The Principal Upanishads*, Harper & Row, 1953.

—— and C. Moore: *Sourcebook of Indian Philosophy*, Princeton, 1957.

Renou, L.: *Religions of Ancient India*, Oxford, 1953.

Smart, N.: *Doctrine and Argument in Indian Philosophy*, G. Allen, 1964.

Zaehner, R. C.: *Hinduism*, Oxford, 1963.

—— (ed.): *Hindu Scriptures*, Everyman, 1966.

Zimmer, H.: *Philosophies of India*, Meridian Books, 1957.

4

MAHAVIRA AND JAINISM

THE AXIS AGE IN ANCIENT INDIA

This chapter begins with the period of human history around the world which Karl Jaspers has called the Axis age or Axis time, that is, approximately the seventh and sixth centuries B.C., when in several different regions of the world there were significant new beginnings, new stirrings of life.[1] The Axis age was marked by the emergence of several historic individuals and new movements stemming from them in regions as far separated as Greece and Israel from India and China. The first philosophers of Greece, the prophets of Israel, and such Chinese figures as Lao-tzu and Confucius were men of the Axis age. So too were Buddha, Mahavira, and other Indians. It was an age whose importance to the history of religions can hardly be overstated.

The twentieth-century student can only guess as to the causal factors of this ancient age of genius. The urban revolution, sketched in Chapter 2, had produced a kind of traditional civilization which had held sway for over two millennia. During this time the individual had been held within the close embrace of traditional society. Now individual men began to chafe at these bonds and in various ways asserted their individuality. It was a time of ferment and change around the world. What technical and social factors spurred the change can only be surmised. Perhaps new forms of commerce contributed, for the businessman has often been a revolutionary figure in history—sometimes in spite of himself. Whatever the causes, out of the Axis age emerged new men, new ideas, and new directions for humanity.

In India the period has been called the "age of the great heresies." [2] This is a somewhat anachronistic designation, since Buddhism and Jainism, which came into being at this time, were not formally declared heresies until many centuries later. (They were declared heresies for two reasons: they did not acknowledge the sacred authority of the Vedas and they rejected that touchstone of Hindu orthodoxy, caste.) In India the Axis age was a time of world-weariness and restiveness, when not only Buddha and Mahavira, but a great many other men as well shook the dust of society from their feet and sought the solitude of the forest, there to practice asceticism, to meditate—and, significantly, to think new thoughts about the nature and destiny of man.

India's Axis time produced a wide range of teachers, each with his own group of followers and his own body of distinctive teaching about the proper conduct of life, the goal of life, and the kind of fulfillment or blessedness this goal would bring. Among these teachers Mahavira, the founder of Jainism, Buddha, and the anonymous seers of the Upanishads are outstanding and have left enduring marks on Indian thought and life. Others were more like Makkali Goshala. founder of the Ajivikas sect, who exerted significant influence for a millennium in India until it finally died out in the fourteenth century. While well known in India, the Ajivikas are little known in the West. [3]

The historical sources testify to many other notable figures, some known, but many unknown to us. For example, the Buddhist *Digha Nikaya* lists no less than six different teachers who offered themselves as instructors to Buddha during his seven-year search for salvation. [4] One was Purana Kassapa, an antinomian who taught that the moral or immoral quality of a man's life had no influence on his karma. The second was Goshala, founder of the Ajivikas sect already alluded to, whose tenets included a rigid fatalism and an equally rigid atheism. A third teacher was Ajita Kesakambala, a materialist who railed against India's already heavily sacral religious tradition. A fourth, Pakuda Kacchayana, was an atomist and apparently the forerunner of other philosophies of this sort in later Indian history. The fifth was none other than Natuputta Vardhamana, rigid and extreme ascetic, and founder of Jainism. The sixth was a man named Sanjaya Belatthiputta, whose teachings centered in philosophic skepticism.

Other historical sources mention still other teachers, such as Kapila, the founder of Sankhya philosophy, and Gautama, founder of the Nyaya philosophy. Undoubtedly there were still others whose names and ideas have perished but who participated in this ancient age of intellectual ferment and wide-ranging speculation.

Despite the great diversity of doctrines, some patterns of similarity do emerge. All these ancient teachers (except the materialists and skeptics) acknowledged as man's chief goal his emancipation from mortality, or from finitude. This goal, called *moksha* in the Sanskrit language of ancient India and variously interpreted by these teachers, pointed to a realm of blessedness or salvation beyond all the limitations of man's human, relative world. Many of these systems provided their own distinctive paths of meditation and of ascetic practice leading to this goal. Most of them also accepted the idea of karma, which was the law of the deed ("as you sow, so will you reap"), and applied it with ironclad rigor to all man's life; many of them like the philosophic seers of the Upanishads extended its application to many incarnations, past and future.

Among these ancient teachers, Nataputta Vardhamana, known also as Mahavira, stands out for the extreme rigor of his ascetic practice and the clear, bold outlines of his philosophy. Also, he was, along with Buddha, the first of a long line of Indian rebels against caste. Above all he was the founder of the religious community and tradition of Jainism.

A STUDY IN EXTREMES

Zimmer places Mahavira and Jainism as first among those traditions of philosophy, art, and religion which go back to the ancient pre-Aryan past of India, citing as evidence the realism and dualism of this philosophy in contrast to the monistic idealism of the Aryan tradition and pointing also to Jainism's own insistent tradition of a long line of twenty-four *tirthankaras,* or "ford-finders," of whom Mahavira was only the last.[5] By "ford-finder," Jains have meant a great man who has discovered a way across the stream of mortal misery to the farther shore of salvation. The images of the ford and the ford-finder are strong not only in Jainism but also in Buddhism and throughout other Indian faiths. Once the ford has been discovered, other, lesser mortals may make their passage through it to the farther shore. Jainism has always insisted that each man must do this for himself, in his own power, without the help of any god or savior. Hence Jainism honors Mahavira and the long line of some twenty-three tirthankaras before him but resolutely refuses to deify them. Particularly notable for Jainism is the probably historical figure of Parshva, who is honored as the twenty-third ford-finder, and who lived ca. 872–772 B.C.[6]

Jain thought and practice present themselves to students of mankind's religions as a study in extremes. Jainism is extreme even within its Indian environment in its atheism, its asceticism, and its devotion to *ahimsa,* the ethic of noninjury. Western students of the world's religions are sometimes puzzled by the attitudes of indifference and negation toward God which are to be found among the Oriental faiths. Jainism goes beyond indifference and agnosticism and asserts a dogmatic atheism. It was not alone in this respect, for Goshala of the Ajivikas apparently asserted a similar negation. Modern students can only speculate what led these Indian teachers to such dogmatic rejection of the traditional gods of their people. Two possibilities appear in the sources. First, they regarded the gods as unnecessary, for man could achieve salvation through his own power and without neurotic dependence on powers beyond himself. Second, the gods seemed even at this early stage of history an irrational principle of explanation. Consider the naturalism of the following bold declaration from the *Gaina Sutra*:

> A monk or nun should not say: The god of the sky! the god of the thunderstorm! the god of the lightning! the god who begins to rain! the god who ceases to rain! may rain fall or may it not fall! may the crops grow or may they not grow! may the night wane or may it not wane! may the sun rise or may it not rise! may the king conquer or may he not conquer!
>
> But knowing the nature of things he should say: The air . . . a cloud has gathered or come down; the cloud has rained.[7]

Ascetic practice (*tapas*) is of widespread occurrence in mankind's faiths and nowhere more frequent or intensive than in India. Yet here again, Jain theory and practice stand out as extreme. Two general patterns of motivation lead to asceticism. On the one hand it is a kind of spiritual athleticism; the Greek word *askesis* originally denoted the training which athletes underwent in preparation for the games. On the other hand, some forms of asceticism posit a dualism of matter and spirit and then seek to rescue the human spirit from its prison house of flesh. In fact, both of these interpretations converge in Jain thought, and as a consequence Jain practice is more extreme than any other on earth. The greatest Jain heroes or saints are recorded with approbation as having ended their lives by fasting to death. The Jain monk traditionally has worn a piece of cheesecloth over his mouth to prevent swallowing and thereby destroying insects, and has carried a small broom to sweep living things from his path.

In these practices there is a convergence of asceticism and noninjury to living beings. The latter may be said to be based upon the idea of the unity of all life and the feeling of reverence for life. Again, most of mankind's faiths have taught these precepts in some qualified form, but only Jainism has carried this tenet to the extreme of absolute noninjury to *all* living beings. Indeed some Jain source documents find souls imprisoned in such inorganic things as fire and stones. The Jain doctrine of ahimsa has influenced Hindu tradition, and was acknowledged by Gandhi as an influence on his own ethical thinking. Yet Jainism's own extremes of practice are vividly summarized in a paragraph by Heinrich Zimmer:

> *Non-violence (ahimsa) is thus carried to an extreme. The Jaina sect survives as a sort of extremely fundamentalist vestige in a civilization that has gone through many changes since the remote age when this universal piety and universal science of the world of nature and of escape from it came into existence. Even Jaina lay folk must be watchful lest they cause unnecessary inconvenience to their fellow beings. They must, for example, not drink water after dark; for some small insect may be swallowed. They must not eat meat of any kind, or kill bugs that fly about and annoy; credit may be gained, indeed, by allowing the bugs to settle and have their fill. All of which has led to the following bizarre popular custom, which may be observed even today in the metropolitan streets of Bombay. Two men come along carrying between them a light cot or bed alive with bedbugs. They stop before the door of a Jaina household, and cry: "Who will feed the bugs? Who will feed the bugs?" If some devout lady tosses a coin from a window, one of the criers places himself carefully in the bed and offers himself as a living grazing ground to his fellow beings. Whereby the lady of the house gains the credit, and the hero of the cot the coin.*[8]

Historically Jainism is notable among India's religions for the vigor and vitality of its community and consequently for the tenacity with which it has resisted the absorptive powers of Hinduism and maintained its own existence. It remains today a small but vital community of some 1,680,000 people, almost all of them in India.[9] However, like some other minority groups it has made contributions to Indian culture out of all proportion to its numerical strength. Indian ethics, philosophy, literature, architecture, and sculpture all show significant Jain influence. The observer of Indian religions gets the impression that the Jain community is still very much alive. One reason among others for that vitality is that this community owes its origin to a personal founder, or as the Jains would correct us, to twenty-four founders. Here apparently history is the lengthened shadow of several great men. Among them was Mahavira, the last ford-finder, the founder of the Jain community and tradition, and discoverer of the Jain path.

LIFE OF THE FOUNDER

Jain tradition places Mahavira at the end of a succession of twenty-four saviors, or ford-finders, extending back to the very ancient pre-Aryan past of India. While evidence for the full historicity of this view is less than compelling, it

fits with what is known of Indian history, and it does point instructively to the
diversity of Indian religious thought and faith.

Whatever his antecedents, Mahavira appears as a contemporary of Buddha
and a participant in India's Axis age. Jain tradition assigns to his life the dates
540–468 B.C.[10] Mahavira and Buddha shared a common heritage, and a common geographical origin in northeast India, as well as many striking similarities of both biography and thought.

Temple icon of the Jain
ford-finder
*Courtesy of the Government
of India Tourist Office*

It is often impossible to discern the outlines of real human life amid the
formal and stylized recollections which constitute the life story of the founder
according to the *Gaina Sutra* and other Jain source documents.[11] A summary
of this traditional material runs somewhat as follows. Nataputta was born to
noble parents in northeastern India in the region of Magadha, or modern Bihar.
As a noble, he was reared in courtly luxury and destined apparently to succeed
to his father's throne, but his heart was with a band of ascetics of the order of
Parshva who inhabited a park outside his town. As a filial and obedient son,
he could not join them—yet. At length, and by divine prearrangement, his

parents died. One source says they met death by the approved Jain method of self-starvation.

Nataputta was now free to join the monks and to set out on the ascetic path to salvation. Ironically, a retinue of servants carried him to the park on an expensive litter. There he abandoned his ornaments and finery, threw off his clothes, plucked out his hair in five handfuls, and took the vow to live a life of complete detachment from all worldly things, saying: "I shall for twelve years neglect my body and abandon care of it. I shall with equanimity bear, undergo and suffer all calamities arising from divine powers, men or animals." [12]

The Venerable One, as his followers call him, observed two basic rules on this rigorous quest for salvation by emancipation: (1) asceticism, conceived as a way of liberating the soul from the contamination of matter, and (2) noninjury to all living things. His asceticism was of the strictest sort. Refusing shelter he became literally the "houseless one," exposing his body to wind and rain, to summer's heat and winter's cold. Even the temporary refuge of sleep was scornfully minimized, for after brief moments of sleep he would wake himself again to endure (one is tempted to say, masochistically to *enjoy*) the misery of consciousness. His body went altogether uncleansed and unclothed. He maintained the strictest detachment from human society, refusing even to answer when other people addressed him. Villagers set their dogs on him, threw dust on him, even lit a fire under him and drove nails through his ears, but through all these innumerable miseries he remained steadfastly imperturbable.

Just as scrupulously he avoided injury to any and all living things. As will soon be seen, ahimsa is an essential feature of Jain philosophy; it is based presumably on the founder's precept and practice. He distinguished between living beings (*jivas*) and nonliving beings (*ajivas*) in order to avoid all possible harm to living things. Here too his way was absolute, uncompromising. Carrying a small broom he swept insects from his path. He strained his drinking water with a piece of cloth to avoid swallowing living things. Thus did Vardhamana establish a kind of world's record for his practice of tapas and ahimsa.

At the end of this hard, twelve-year journey was the experience of emancipation. Giving precise details of time and place, the Jain source describes this climactic experience: ". . . in a squatting position with joined heels exposing himself to the heat of the sun with the knees high and the head low in deep meditation in the midst of abstract meditation he reached *nirvana,* the complete and full, the unobstructed, unimpeded, infinite and supreme, best knowledge and intuition called *kevala.*" [13] Thus he became Jina (Conqueror), Mahavira (Great Hero), and the twenty-fourth tirthankara, the titles by which he has been known among his followers ever since. Jain tradition has understood the nature of this crucial and definitive experience as a final breaking of the fetters which bound Vardhamana to the world of mortal misery. To employ Jainism's other root metaphor, in this experience he made his way across the ford to the farther shore of emancipation and salvation. In Jain metaphor and idea, the liberating experience, far from being one of absorption, was rather one of total isolation or separation.

His achievement of emancipation impelled Mahavira to set forth on a thirty-year period of teaching and preaching in which he proclaimed to others his way of salvation by ascetic detachment. He also gathered followers about himself and sent them forth in their turn to teach the way of salvation. Mahavira died at the age of seventy-two and is now, according to his followers, in a state of bliss called *Isatpragbhara,* a place at the top of the Jain universe and beyond the grim cycle of death and rebirth. In contrast to other Indian faiths, Jainism teaches the continuance of individual selves in this state.

MAHAVIRA'S FOLLOWERS

For a period of two centuries or so Mahavira's disciples remained a small community of monks and lay followers, less numerous and less important than other rival groups such as the Ajivikas and Buddhists. Jain tradition asserts that the great king Chandragupta, founder of the Maurya dynasty and grandfather of the Buddhist king Ashoka, became a Jain monk after abdicating his throne. Jain records show a marked increase in members during this period. It is also recorded that during the Maurya period a famine impelled an exodus of Jain monks southward to the Deccan with consequent increase in numbers and influence. Gradually they scattered, spreading over the whole Indian subcontinent.

In the first century of the Christian era occurred the great split between the two main sects of Jainism, the Shvetambaras (or Whiteclad) and the Digambaras (Skyclad). Monks of the former group condone the wearing of at least minimal clothes, while those of the latter insist, in fidelity to the founder, on total nudity. Jain nudity, be it added, has nothing whatever to do with sensuality. Rather it symbolizes a final break with clothes as a symbol of man's bondage to the world. The stylistic abstraction of the nude figures of Jain sculpture underscore this conclusion.

Much later, still a third sect, called the Sthanakvasis, came into existence in the eighteenth century, opposing in iconoclastic, protestant fashion all temples and all ritual and claiming to worship everywhere by inward meditation. Nowadays the Sthanakvadins have assembly halls lacking any images, where the faithful gather for devotional exercises or to hear expositions of Jain teaching. In other respects their precepts and practices resemble those of other Jains.

Having been transmitted orally for many centuries, Jain sacred literature was finally committed to writing in the fifth century. This aroused a dispute between the two main sects, the Shvetambaras accepting the traditional canon, and the Digambaras rejecting these documents and subsequently producing many new sacred writings of their own. The Jain canon as preserved by the Shvetambaras consists of forty-five texts in the Ardhamagadha dialect of Prakrit, some in prose and some in poetry. Some of it may come from Mahavira's time, though much of it is from a later time. In addition to the canonical writings there is a considerable body of literature which, while not sacred scripture, is cherished by Jains for its celebration of pious themes.

JAIN PHILOSOPHY

The system of thought which has formed the core of Jainism might be accurately characterized as a philosophy of salvation. It is a cluster of general ideas about man and the world which if believed and acted upon will guide a man's footsteps along the hard, steep path out of the world's misery to emancipation and salvation. Such at least is the claim of Jainism. How much of this thought goes back to the founder and how much consists of later accretion is impossible to say. Yet Mahavira emerges from the records of Jain history as a bold and original philosophic mind arguing his case amid the schools and arguments of his time.

Notice has already been taken of Zimmer's hypothesis that Jainism belongs in a tradition of ideas and attitudes going back to India's ancient, pre-Aryan past. A part of his evidence is the realist and pluralist outlook of Jain philosophy, in contrast to the monistic idealism of the Upanishads and the Vedantist tradition. This realism and pluralism, Zimmer argues, represents the philosophic outlook of the pre-Aryan, Dravidian peoples. In Chapters 5 and 6 we shall encounter several other systems which fit into this pattern and tradition, including Buddhism and the Nyaya, Vaishesika, Yoga, and Sankhya philosophic systems of Hinduism.

THE WAY TO SALVATION

If Jainism is a philosophy of salvation, *from* what and *to* what is man saved? The Jain view is that man is to be freed *from* bondage or attachment to this world of complete misery, and *to* the blessedness called *kevala* or *kaivalya*, meaning, as we have said, isolation or separation. This means a release from bonds, which is the Jain version of the common Indian idea of emancipation from mortal enslavement. It is completed in a transcendental realm of bliss called Isatpragbhara, at the top of the universe. It entails continued individual existence rather than absorption, though this tenet is not greatly emphasized in Jain teaching and is unknown to many Jains.

The world out of which man seeks salvation is a thoroughly miserable, wretched place, inhabited by an infinite number of souls, most of whom have no hope of rescue from the hell which is existence. Jainism has a fivefold classi-fication of living beings according to their number of senses. Thus men, gods, and demons have five senses; a second class contains creatures of four senses—touch, taste, smell, and sight. The three-sense creatures include such small or-ganisms as fleas, ants, and moths. Two-sense creatures include worms, leeches, and shellfish. The one-sense beings comprise a vast class including vegetable bodies ranging from trees to turnips, earth bodies which include stones, clay, and jewels, water bodies, fire bodies, and wind bodies. Indeed it is hard to think of any existing entity which is excluded from this comprehensive classification of putative living forms. Thus the Jain claim appears to be that the whole universe is alive. One writer speaks of this view as hylozoism.[14] Every object contains a soul which is imprisoned in wretchedness within its body, groaning in misery, vainly seeking escape. This cosmic misery is regarded as the inex-orable working of the iron law of karma.

> *Thus say all perfect souls and blessed ones, whether past, present, or to come—thus they speak, thus they declare, thus they proclaim: All things breathing, all things existing, all things living, all beings whatever, should not be slain or treated with violence, or insulted, or tortured, or driven away.*
>
> *This is the pure unchanging eternal law, which the wise ones who know the world have proclaimed, among the earnest and the not-earnest, among the loyal and the not-loyal, among those who have given up punishing others and those who have not done so, among those who are weak and those who are not, among those who delight in worldly ties and those who do not. This is the truth. So it is. Thus it is declared in this religion.*
>
> *When he adopts this Law a man should never conceal or reject it. When he understands the Law he should grow indifferent to what he sees, and not act for worldly motives. . . .*
>
> *What is here declared has been seen, heard, approved, and understood. Those who give way and indulge in pleasure will be born again and again. The heedless are outside [the hope of salvation]. But if you are mindful, day and night steadfastly striving, always with ready vision, in the end you will conquer.*[15]

Jainism says that the world has no beginning and no end, holding this tenet in common with Buddhism and other Oriental philosophies. The world exists eternally as a kind of permanent cosmic receptacle for the misery of its creatures. For man alone there is a possibility of salvation. The state of humanity is a kind of escape hatch from the world. One Jain religious poem bids its readers:

> *After tossing on the ocean of being, of which birth and death are waves,*
> *You have come to man's estate.*
> *Avoid the things of sense and pluck the fruit of human birth.*[16]

"The fruit of human birth" refers to the salvation that is possible to man alone.

Jainism is thus first of all an ascetic way of life; and as we have seen, the manner in which emancipation may be achieved is by the practice of tapas and ahimsa. A Jain Sutra expresses the ideal way of life in these words:

> If another insult him, a monk should not lose his temper,
> For that is mere childishness—a monk should never be angry.
> If he hears words harsh and cruel, vulgar and painful,
> He should silently disregard them, and not take them to heart.
> Even if beaten he should not be angry, or even think sinfully,
> But should know that patience is best, and follow the Law.
> If someone should strike a monk, restrained and subdued,
> He should think, "[It might be worse—] I haven't lost my life!" . . .
> If on his daily begging round he receives no alms he should not be grieved,
> But think, "I have nothing today, but I may get something tomorrow!" . . .
> When a restrained ascetic, though inured to hardship,
> Lies naked on the rough grass, his body will be irritated,
> And in full sunlight the pain will be immeasurable,
> But still, though hurt by the grass, he should not wear clothes.
> When his limbs are running with sweat, and grimed with dust and dirt
> In the heat of summer, the wise monk will not lament his lost comfort.
> He must bear it all to wear out his karma, and follow the noble, the supreme
>   Law.
> Until his body breaks up, he should bear the filth upon it.[17]

To ascetic practices the Jain monk seeks to add fortitude.

> Oh man, refrain from evil, for life must come to an end.
> Only men foolish and uncontrolled are plunged in the habit of pleasure.
> Live in striving and self-control, for hard to cross are paths full of insects.
> Follow the rule that the Heroes have surely proclaimed.
> Heroes detached and strenuous, subduing anger and fear,
> Will never kill living beings, but cease from sin and are happy.
> "Not I alone am the sufferer—all things in the universe suffer!"
> Thus should man think and be patient, not giving way to his passions.
> As old plaster flakes from a wall, a monk should make thin his body by fasting,
> And he should injure nothing. This is the Law taught by the Sage.[18]

The monk articulates his ascetic way of life in the traditional Five Great Vows. In the *Gaina Sutra* each vow has its own detailed fivefold application, spelling out its application to all possible circumstances. In summary fashion the vow is as follows:

> I renounce all killing of living beings whether subtle or gross, whether movable

or immovable. Nor shall I myself kill living beings (nor cause others to do it, nor consent to it). As long as I live, I confess and blame, repent and exempt myself of these sins in the thrice threefold way in mind, speech and body. . . .

I renounce all vices of lying speech (arising) from anger or greed, fear or mirth. I shall neither myself speak nor cause others to speak lies nor consent to the speaking of lies by others. . . .

I renounce all taking of anything not given either in a village or a town or a wood, either of little or much, of small or great, of living or lifeless things. . . .

I renounce all sexual pleasures, either with gods or men or animals. I shall not give way to sensuality. . . .

I renounce all attachments, whether little or much, small or great, living or lifeless; neither shall I myself form such attachments nor cause others to do so, nor consent to their doing so. . . .[19]

For lay adherents of Jainism there are twelve vows, notably less severe than those of the monk: (1) never knowingly to take the life of a sentient being, (2) never to lie, (3) never to steal, (4) never to be unchaste, (5) to check greed, (6) to avoid temptations, (7) to limit the number of things in daily use, (8) to guard against all avoidable evil, (9) to keep stated periods of meditation, (10) to observe periods of self-denial, (11) to spend occasional periods as a monk, and (12) to give alms.[20] For the devout Jain layman, ahimsa involves a strict vegetarian diet, extending even to a prohibition on eating eggs.

Whether practiced by monk or layman the Jain ethic has been accurately characterized as a kind of higher egoism. In the conduct of life and the pursuit of salvation, it is each man for himself. True, he observes the rule of ahimsa, but he does it, as Jains say, to reduce his own karma, to wipe the stain of karmic matter off his own soul, or to use Jainism's other root metaphor, to break the fetters which bind his soul to the material universe.

ATHEISM

In this way of life and salvation there is no help from any savior or God, for as previously noted, Jainism dogmatically rejects the existence of God. To be sure, there may be gods or superior beings in the universe, but they are fellow prisoners along with men and other living beings, and subject to the same iron law of karma. What Jain atheism denies is that God either made the world or rules it. Jain thought argues this conclusion with great conviction and by means of arguments which in the West have usually been associated with Humean skepticism. It is asked, If God created the world where was he before creation? It is asked whether any single being could have the skill to make the world, or whether or not God used raw materials to fabricate the world. If so, this is independent of God; if not, whence comes this stuff of which things are made? Moreover, if God created the world out of love for human things, why did he not make the creation wholly blissful? Indeed the fact of evil leads us to the conclusion that God commits great sin in killing the children he has made. The conclusion of these lines of thought is that the very idea of a Creator and Lord is self-contradictory, that the universe itself is uncreated and indestructible, enduring by the compulsion and necessity of its own nature.

> *Some foolish men declare that Creator made the world.*
> *The doctrine that the world was created is ill-advised, and should be rejected.*
>
> *If God created the world, where was he before creation?*
> *If you say he was transcendent then, and needed no support, where is he now?*
>
> *No single being had the skill to make this world—*
> *For how can an immaterial god create that which is material?*
>
> *How could God have made the world without any raw material?*
> *If you say he made this first, and then the world, you are faced with an endless regression.*
>
> *If you declare that this raw material arose naturally you fall into another fallacy,*
> *For the whole universe might thus have been its own creator, and have arisen equally naturally.*
>
> *If God created the world by an act of his own will, without any raw material,*
> *Then it is just his will and nothing else—and who will believe this silly stuff?*
> *If he is ever perfect and complete, how could the will to create have arisen in him?*
> *If, on the other hand, he is not perfect, he could no more create the universe than a potter could.*
>
> *If he is formless, actionless, and all-embracing, how could he have created the world?*
> *Such a soul, devoid of all modality, would have no desire to create anything.*
>
> *If he is perfect, he does not strive for the three aims of man,*
> *So what advantage would he gain by creating the universe?*
>
> *If you say that he created to no purpose, because it was his nature to do so, then God is pointless.*
> *If he created in some kind of sport, it was the sport of a foolish child, leading to trouble.*
>
> *If he created because of the karma of embodied beings [acquired in a previous creation]*

He is not the Almighty Lord, but subordinate to something else. . . .

If out of love for living things and need of them he made the world,
Why did he not make creation wholly blissful, free from misfortune?

If he were transcendent he would not create, for he would be free;
Nor if involved in transmigration, for then he would not be almighty.

Thus the doctrine that the world was created by God
Makes no sense at all.

And God commits great sin in slaying children whom he himself created.
If you say that he slays only to destroy evil beings, why did he create such
beings in the first place? [21]

The idea of an atheistic religion is so foreign to the Western mind that the question inevitably arises: Is this a religion, and if so in what sense? One answer is that in the terms of Chapter 1's hypothesis it is an existing system of holy forms. It is also a path to salvation. Indeed Jainism is a highly distinctive and an extremely difficult path of faith and life.

DUALISM OF MIND AND MATTER

Jain metaphysics is characterized by a fundamental dualism of mind and matter, or as Jains put it, of jivas and ajivas. This duality extends metaphysically to the entire universe, but it also goes through the heart of each human being, dividing him into a soul and a body which imprisons the soul. Life is enmeshed in nonlife. From the prison house, it is barely possible that one's soul, or life-monad, may be liberated by tapas and ahimsa.

PLURALISM AND KARMIC MATTER

Beyond its basic matter-spirit dualism, Jain metaphysics is realist and monadic, or atomistic, in character. That is to say, reality is asserted to be made up of many irreducible units independent of each other and of the human minds which know them. As one Jain document says, "There are many souls, just as there are many pots and other things." [22] In contrast to the monism of Aryan philosophy, Jain thought asserts many kinds of living and nonliving beings, of spirit and matter. Against the monism of Aryan thought Jainism maintained an irreducible pluralism, not only of souls, but also of elements in the universe beyond man. In addition to souls, the universe is composed of matter, space, *dharma, adharma* (good and evil), and time.[23]

We have already noted Jainism's acceptance of the common traditional Indian idea of karma-samsara. Jain metaphysics added a novel theory concerning the way in which this grim and endless process took place. It taught that in general karma was due to a mixing of jivas, or soul, with ajivas, or matter, and that karma might be stopped by cleansing the matter from one's soul. In the course of time Jainism elaborated a theory of special kinds of matter, called karmic matter, which clings to the soul like barnacles to a ship, causing karma and bondage. Over 148 kinds of karmic matter, each causing its own destructive kind of bondage, have been listed by Jain thinkers.[24]

They also elaborated an ingenious theory of the way in which karmic matter stains the soul, or life-monad, a variety of different colors. Thus different colors of karmic matter were thought to correspond with different types of persons. At the bottom of the scale is black, the color of merciless and cruel persons. Next above are dark blue characters who are roguish and venial. Gray typifies the reckless and thoughtless soul. Fiery red is the color of prudent, honest, and devout persons; while yellow is the color of compassionate character. White souls are disinterested and impartial and thus best of all karmic types. Yet the highest aim is to cleanse all the stain of karmic matter from the soul in order to facilitate release from bondage. Also, as we have seen, karma has its cosmic as well as its individual results; as souls go on transmigrating eternally, they generate the vast cosmic cycles of history.

CYCLIC VIEW OF HISTORY

No less fantastic than these psychological speculations is the Jain view of history, which is also characteristically pessimistic. It centers attention on the wheel of time (kalacakra) which is of enormous size and is unceasing in its cyclic motion. The wheel is said to have twelve spokes; while six of them are turned toward man's world, there is improvement, but while the other six are turned, there is degeneration and evil. A single twelfth-turn of the wheel is called a palyopama and is estimated by the Jains to take as many years as would be needed to fill a container 4 miles high and 4 miles in circumference with fine, tightly packed human hair, if a single hair is added every 100 years. Truly the Jains seem intent upon outdoing other competing faiths in their description of the human predicament!

Somewhat more comprehensible to human imagination are the effects of evolution and devolution on the human body and the duration of human life. In the supremely good periods of history, human bodies are 6 miles tall, and men live for three palyopamas. However, as the wheel of time turns to its negative phase, bodies reduce gradually to a mere 18 inches, and life-span shrinks to sixteen years.

The coming of Jain saviors, or ford-finders, is also related to this cyclic move-ment of history. The world was good enough to get along without saviors until the third period in the downward course when the first savior arose. During the third and fourth periods came the succession of twenty-four saviors, Mahavira arriving just before the close of the fourth period. The world is now regarded as too evil to permit the coming of another savior, and it will remain so for another 80,000 years. Only then will the upward course of history permit men to achieve salvation.[25]

DOCTRINE OF MANYSIDEDNESS

A further and final aspect of Jain philosophy which has often baffled Western students is its subtle logic and epistemology, featuring the doctrines of "View-points" (*nayavada*) and of "Perhaps," or "Conditional Predication" (*syadvada*), which taken together are the doctrine of "Manysidedness" (*anekantavada*).[26] Considered as a whole this aspect of Jain thought constitutes a recognition that the world is more complex than simple black-and-white distinctions allow. Also, human limitations resulting from karma condition and make relative man's knowledge of his world.

The doctrine of Perhaps entails a sevenfold view of predication, beginning with simple affirmation, simple negation, a qualified combination of the two, and a recognition that the truth or falsehood may be unknown to us, the last three of the seven forms being odd combinations of these first four forms.

The doctrine of Manysidedness is a recognition of the thoroughly conditioned and relative aspects of all human thought and speech. It may be illustrated by the Indian parable of the blind men describing the elephant. The attempts of the blind men at truth reflect their specific, limited situations, which in turn are the result of karma. While all their efforts contain some truth, yet none is the whole or final truth. In short it is argued that man here on earth knows in part and imperfectly. Only when he has achieved kaivalya does his knowledge attain perfection.

Here then, in summary, is the philosophy which is offered as a road map for the hard, ascetic Jain path to salvation, or emancipation. It is a path which leads through that vast and dismal swamp which is the world and in which innu-merable wretched and suffering creatures are mired forever. Yet to man is given the hope—slender though it be—of escape. It is an escape by each individual's power of knowledge and self-mastery. Man can plot this path only by correct knowledge, namely, that of Jain philosophy, by which he must then resolutely live. For the few who successfully traverse this difficult path, salvation lies at the end.

THE JAIN COMMUNITY

As the student turns from Jain philosophy and teaching to the community and tradition of people who profess to live by it, many questions and tensions arise. How can people derive guidance and orientation from such unworldly doctrines? What is the source of the persistent vitality of the Jain community? Part of the answer to the latter question lies in the fact that the Jains have always been a small minority group, which here as elsewhere in human history

Jain ford-finder, Parshva

Courtesy of E. Eilefson

has maintained its vigor by swimming against the stream. Another significant fact is the middle-class character of the Jain community.

Early in their history the Jains were barred by their view of ahimsa from the traditional pursuit of agriculture. Somewhat ironically perhaps, they turned to trade, commerce, and banking, where they have greatly prospered. The discipline of their faith prepared them for the discipline of the marketplace. While their white-clad monks and nuns have stood at the spiritual center of their community, the practical affairs of the community have been in the capable hands of laymen. The Jains are governed by popularly elected regional councils in which the laity predominates.

The Jain community devotes itself to manifold activities of education and philanthropy directed to its own members and also to the larger Indian society. Jain schools provide both secular and religious instruction for children of adherents. Monastic institutions are well supported. Jains also support such various enterprises as rest houses for pilgrims, orphanages for children, and even, in devotion to ahimsa, hospitals for sick and defective animals. All of these activities testify to the extent and quality of lay participation.

Jain worship centers in its temples and assembly halls. For the Sthanakvadins, assembly halls having no images are the meeting places where Jain teaching is expounded and devotions, both individual and corporate, are performed. For the Digambaras and Shvetambaras, their temples are in many ways similar to those of Hindus. The central object is an icon of a Jain savior, which is daily bathed, garlanded, and cared for like a Hindu god. However, the attending priest is careful to inform the visitor that this is no deity but a discoverer of the path. Like the Hindu temple, much (though not all) of the worship is by individuals. Jain temples are notable throughout India for their spotless cleanliness as well as for the rich ornamentation of their furnishings.

Jain devotion also includes periodic fasts and other ascetic practices and pilgrimages to famous places. Parasnath in the region of Calcutta is celebrated as the burial place of Parshva, the twenty-third ford-finder. At Shatrunjaya there is a veritable city of temples—863 of them—to Rishabha, the first in line of succession; and at Girnar there are temples to Nemi, the twenty-second. Pilgrims throng to many such places.

Jains have made distinctive contributions to Indian art. For example, at Ellora there are several Jain cave temples along with those of Buddhist and Hindu inspiration and origin. The observer soon develops an eye for the distinctive style of Jainism. Probably the most notable feature is the standing posture for the ascetic saint. Unlike his Buddhist and Hindu cousins, the Jain ascetic does not sit in the lotus posture, but stands erect in all his nudity, with hands at his sides and looking straight ahead. Apparently the Jain ascetic was not even permitted the comfort of a sitting posture, but rather must stand in complete immobility and passivity as he meditated. The abstraction of these Jain figures constitutes a powerful artistic expression of Jain detachment from the world. The most famous such Jain figure, the Gomatesvara at Sravana Belgola in south India, is more than 50 feet high. The sculptor has depicted vines growing around the legs—so long has the ascetic saint stood in contemplation. The Gomatesvara is a notable center for Jain pilgrimages and devotions.

Jains carry on an active campaign of writing and pamphleteering to explain their faith to the outsider. While they seek converts, their efforts to date have not been notably successful. Their apologetic literature recommends fasting in terms of its benefits to health. Not even the strict Jain vegetarian diet, which includes a prohibition on the eating of eggs, need involve a protein deficiency. Jain monks and nuns are extolled as athletes of the spiritual life. The Jain philosophy is advocated as an adequate way of understanding the existing

Relief from the top of a Jain stele

Courtesy of Metropolitan Museum of Art,
Gift of Mrs. John D. Rockefeller, Jr., 1942

world and as a guide to the breaking of fetters along the upward path to emancipation.

The Jain shopkeeper or professional man may not be a monk, and his wife may not be a nun, but they can participate in the activities of the community. They can keep their own laymen's vows, such as to observe periodic fasts, and they can go on pilgrimage. They can honor Mahavira and other ford-finders as the great conquerors; then setting their own feet on the Jain path they can hope that someday they too will be conquerors.

CONCLUDING COMMENT

Jainism has its own distinctive interpretation of the basic Indian conception of moksha, as discussed in Chapter 3. Around this center clusters a group of distinctive values, which taken together constitute the Jain way or path. Jain ascetic practices, even by Indian standards, have been judged extreme. As we shall see in the next chapter, this trait contrasts with Buddhism's middle way. Jain atheism has in effect asserted that man must walk the path to salvation by his own light and strength. Jain philosophy has functioned as a guide to this path. This philosophy has achieved distinctive formulations of such Indian themes as karma-samsara and the vast repeating cycles of historical time. Jain contributions to Indian sculpture, architecture and other arts have been outstanding. As a minority group in Indian history, the Jain community has clung tenaciously to its distinctive tenets—resisting the absorptive powers of Hinduism. Also, while it honors its monks and nuns, the Jain community is ruled by lay leaders. Such is the Jain path to salvation, or ultimate concern, Jain style.

As to our second main issue, namely the questions, why live? or what must I do and be to be genuinely human? we must respond first by rejecting the latter formulation of this question. For Jainism, humanity is at best an escape hatch from an essentially evil existence. Humanity is something to be utterly transcended. Or better, it is a disease for which Jainism claims to have both diagnosis and cure. Why live? In order to rise above human existence to blessedness yonder. The Jain answer is clear and forthright.

An equally clear answer is forthcoming to our third main issue. Jainism is indeed the clearest example of an acosmic faith that we shall meet in all our study of the world's religions.

NOTES

1. Karl Jaspers, *The Origin and Goal of History*, Routledge & Kegan Paul, Ltd., London, 1953, pp. 51f.

2. George F. Moore, *History of Religions*, Charles Scribner's Sons, New York, 1948, vol. I, chap. XII.

3. A. L. Basham, *The Wonder That Was India*, Grove Press, Inc., New York, 1959, pp. 294f.

4. *Digha Nikaya* 1.47f, as quoted in William T. de Bary (ed.), *Sources of Indian Tradition*, Columbia University Press, New York, 1958, pp. 41–43.

5. Heinrich Zimmer, *Philosophies of India*, Meridian Books, Inc., New York, 1957, pp. 181f.

6. *Ibid.*, p. 183.

7. *Gaina Sutras*, trans. H. Jacobi, Sacred Books of the East, vol. XXII, Oxford University Press, London, 1884, p. 152.

8. Zimmer, *op. cit.*, p. 279.

9. W. Norman Brown, *India, Pakistan, Ceylon*, rev. ed., University of Pennsylvania Press, Philadelphia, 1951, p. 93.

10. Basham, *op. cit.*, p. 288.

11. *Gaina Sutras, op. cit.*, vol. XXII.

12. *Ibid.*, p. 200.

13. *Ibid.*, p. 201.

14. de Bary, *op. cit.*, p. 49.

15. *Ibid.*, pp. 61–62.

16. *Ibid.*, p. 91.

17. *Ibid.*, pp. 64–65.

18. *Ibid.*, p. 64.

19. *Gaina Sutras, op. cit.*, vol. XXII, pp. 202–210.

20. John B. Noss, *Man's Religions,* The Macmillan Company, New York, 1963 (3rd ed.), p. 163.

21. de Bary, *op. cit.*, pp. 79–80.

22. *Ibid.*, p. 82.

23. *Ibid.*, p. 76.

24. Zimmer, *op. cit.*, pp. 248–252.

25. W. Norman Brown, *Man in the Universe,* Oxford and IBH Publishing Company, Calcutta, 1966, pp. 76f.

26. See *inter alia* de Bary, *op. cit.*, pp. 74–75; Sarvepalli Radhakrishnan and Charles A. Moore (eds.), *Source book in Indian Philosophy,* Princeton University Press, Princeton, N.J., 1957, p. 261.

SUGGESTIONS FOR FURTHER STUDY

Barodia, V. D.: *History and Literature of Jainism,* Bombay, 1907.

Basham, A. L.: *The Wonder That Was India,* Grove Press, 1959.

————: *History and Doctrine of the Ajivakas,* Luzacs, 1951.

Brown, W. N.: *Man in the Universe,* University of California Press, 1966.

Buhler, J. G.: *On the Indian Sect of the Jains,* Luzacs, 1903.

Dasgupta, S.: *History of Indian Philosophy,* Cambridge, 1922–1935.

de Bary, W. T. (ed.): *Sources of Indian Tradition,* Columbia, 1958.

The Gaina Sutras, trans. H. Jacobi, Sacred Books of the East Series, Oxford, 1884.

Hiriyanna, S.: *Essentials of Indian Philosophy,* G. Allen, 1949.

Jaini, J.: *Outlines of Jainism,* Cambridge, 1916.

Pratt, J. B.: *India and Its Faiths,* Houghton Mifflin, 1916.

Radhakrishnan, S.: *History of Indian Philosophy,* G. Allen, 1929–1931.

———— (ed.): *History of Philosophy, Eastern and Western,* G. Allen, 1952.

———— and C. Moore (eds.): *Source book in Indian Philosophy,* Princeton, 1957.

Renou, L.: *Religions of Ancient India,* Oxford, 1953.

Smart, N.: *Doctrine and Argument in Indian Philosophy,* G. Allen, 1964.

Stevenson, S.: *The Heart of Jainism,* Oxford, 1916.

Zimmer, H.: *Philosophies of India,* Meridian Books, 1957.

————: *The Art of Indian Asia,* Bollingen, 1955.

5

BUDDHA AND EARLY BUDDHISM

Buddha belongs along with Mahavira to the Axis age of Indian history. There are striking similarities in the biographies and teachings of these two men. Both were born and lived in the same northeastern region of India. Both were nobles born to rule; both renounced the throne for the austere life of the religious ascetic, seeking and then finding emancipation. Both were rebels against hardening caste lines and increasing Brahman domination of Indian religion and life, with the result that later ages of Hinduism judged both men heretics. Indeed so similar are these biographies that some observers have concluded that Buddha and Mahavira were the same man.

But there were all-important differences too. While both Mahavira and Buddha were boldly original philosophic minds, their philosophies differed fundamentally. While both founded ascetic, monastic movements, Jainism is as we saw in the last chapter a path of extreme asceticism, while Buddhism in deliberate contrast and opposition has described itself as a middle way to emancipation. For this as well as other reasons, these two religions have developed historically in profoundly different ways. The Jains have remained a small community of less than 2 million adherents, all within India, while Buddhism

claims between 300 million and 400 million followers. It has interacted significantly with most of the great civilizations of Asia, it has adherents in all parts
of the world, and constitutes one of mankind's universal religions.

For many Occidental students, the comparison of Buddhism and Christianity
has provided a natural focus for study. Both are personally founded religions,
and in both cases the founders have been regarded as saviors.[1] In both cases
there has been considerable pious concern with the founder's life. There are
stories of preexistence, of miraculous birth, and of divine guidance for both
Buddha and Christ. In both cases there are theological or philosophical theories
dealing with the founder's significance.

But there are irreducible differences as well. Christianity has consistently
maintained the uniqueness of the single figure of Christ and has delved deeply
and critically into specific factual details of his life. Buddhism, by contrast, has
multiplied Buddha figures almost without limit, and has been less interested in
specific historical events than in ideas. In the modern West, scholars both inside
and outside the Christian church have pursued both intensively and extensively
a quest for the historical Jesus. There has been no similar quest for the historical
Buddha. In the main, Buddhism has contented itself with traditional recollections of Buddha. From these traditional recollections, contained in the source
documents in Pali and Sanskrit languages, the student must seek to piece
together the life and teachings of the Buddha.

THE FOUNDER'S LIFE

As was the case with Mahavira, the primary source documents on Buddha provide us at best with a few highly stylized and traditional recollections of the
founder's life. The first reaction of the modern Western reader is that there is
little or nothing of genuine biography. Yet this same reader has perforce to
add that this apparently is what the Buddha has meant to the people who told
these stories in the first place and have passed them on ever since. They constitute a kind of traditional portrait painted by many artists over long periods
of time. Around this portrait, often without any reference to the man who sat
for it, Buddhist devotion has centered.

Yet as he wrestles with these problems, the modern, critically minded student
of Buddhism begins to see in these recollections of the Buddha the point of
impact of a uniquely forceful mind and personality. While it is admittedly
impossible to discern or reconstruct the outlines of a historical Buddha, it is
possible to see beneath the many layers of tradition the seismic impact of a
uniquely great man's mind and life. That Buddhism is a personally founded
religion is a fact of the greatest importance. A summary of the traditional
material relating to Buddha's life follows here.

Buddha was born to noble parents in the region of Magadha of northeast India, in the foothills of the Himalaya Mountains, in what is now the state of Bihar. The dates 560–480 B.C. for his life must be understood as approximate or probable only. Traditional Buddhist stories of many preexistent lives of the Buddha have been gathered into the Jataka tales, some 550 of which exist. Buddhist tradition also recounts stories of Buddha's miraculous birth.[2] In a dream his mother saw a heavenly white elephant with a lotus flower in his trunk, who approached and entered her side.[3] The next day the dream was interpreted by the astrologers, who said that she had conceived a son who would be either Universal Teacher or Universal Emperor. The baby was named Siddhartha (meaning "wish fulfilling"). Seven days after his birth, his mother died, leaving him in the care of her sister.

Brahman astrologers prophesied that the child would see what Buddhism has called the "four passing sights," which would wake him to the grim facts of human misery. Accordingly, his father took every possible precaution to shelter him from the world. He was reared in luxury and destined to succeed to his father's throne. He married his cousin, Yashodhara, whose hand he won in a contest of feats of strength. She bore him a son named Rahula (meaning "fetter"). Even then apparently, he desired detachment.

Yet Prince Siddhartha was not inwardly happy with his princely life. His restiveness came to climactic expression when he was twenty-nine. Despite paternal protectiveness, he saw the "four passing sights," namely, an old man, a sick man, a dead man, and a monk. The first three expressed to the future Buddha the misery of human existence, and the fourth symbolized emancipation from it. Siddhartha's mind was made up. Indifferent to his father's redoubled efforts to distract him by means of parties and dancing girls, he roused a faithful servant and rode off into the night. Putting the city far behind him, he dismounted, stripped off his fine clothes, cut off his hair, and assumed the meager garments of a wandering ascetic. Thus occurred what Buddhist tradition has called the Great Renunciation or the Great Retirement.[4] Thus also began Buddha's seven-year quest for salvation.

As noted in the last chapter, Buddhist scriptures tell of no less than six teachers who during this time sought to instruct Gautama in their ways. One of them represented Jain teaching and in some sources is identified as Mahavira himself. But his way did not bring salvation to the seeking Siddhartha. Other teachers instructed him in Brahman speculation and Yoga discipline, still others in different philosophic systems popular at the time. But, alas, none of those ways communicated salvation to the princely ascetic.

Influenced by fellow ascetics, he embarked upon the way of extreme asceticism. One day, worn out by hunger, he fainted. His fellow ascetics believed he was dead. Yet as he recovered consciousness he concluded that this way too was futile. He secured a little food by begging, and his body regained some of its strength. The other ascetics turned in disdain from this backslider. Yet Siddhartha was actually on the threshold of the great discovery which would make him the Enlightened One, or the Buddha.

There are several accounts and as many different interpretations of this decisive and climactic experience.[5] Siddhartha was now thirty-five years old and

The Great Departure and Buddha's Temptation
Courtesy of the Metropolitan Museum of Art,
Fletcher Fund, 1928

had followed successively many paths that failed to lead him to his goal. Could there be still another way? Seated one day under a pipal tree on the outskirts of Gaya in the realm of King Bimbisara of Magadha, he vowed to remain there until his quest was achieved, until he had solved the problem of mortal misery. For forty-nine days he sat beneath the tree, known ever since as the bo tree, or wisdom tree. According to Buddhist theology the guardian spirits and gods fled, while for many days Buddha struggled with Mara the tempter, whose strategies ranged from attack by whirlwind and tempest to the seductive appeals of his three beautiful daughters, Desire, Pleasure, and Passion.

At length the enemy retired vanquished, and Gautama, left alone, sank into deep meditation. Finally on the forty-ninth day he knew the truth. He had discovered the secret of misery and what must be done to overcome it. By this knowledge he became the Buddha, the Enlightened One, or in more precise etymology the Awakened One. This experience of supreme insight constituted his Great Awakening, or Great Enlightenment.

What was the content of this experience? Buddha's answer resembled a physician's terse diagnosis and prescription of therapy for a disease.[6] Buddhist tradition has communicated Buddha's truth in the form of the Four Noble Truths and the Noble Eightfold Path. The first two of the Four Truths may be termed diagnosis and the third and fourth, therapy. The first asserts that all existence is misery, or *dukkha,* and the second that misery is rooted in ignorant craving, or *trishna.* The third truth asserts that misery may be abolished by abolishing ignorant craving, and the fourth truth asserts that this can be done by the Noble Eightfold Path. Thus as one Buddhist writer puts it, Buddha "had found the sovereign remedy for all the major ills of mankind." [7]

The Noble Eightfold Path is understood as a Middle Way to Nirvana, being the mean between the two extremes of Jain asceticism on the one hand and worldliness on the other. This Eightfold Path consists of (1) right understanding, (2) right-mindedness, (3) right speech, (4) right action, (5) right livelihood, (6) right effort, (7) right meditation, and (8) right emancipation. The first two steps have to do with understanding and the attitude of the human mind toward the Buddhist Way; they are called the Higher Wisdom. The next three taken together constitute the Ethical Disciplines and have to do with the moral quality of Buddhist life. The final three steps are called the Mental Disciplines because, based upon the previous ones, they prepare, direct, and then move the seeking mind onward to the achievement of its goal, Nirvana.

The significance of this experience of awakening in the life of Buddha and all who reproduce it in their lives is once and for all to break the iron chain of karma-samsara, or the fated cycle of rebirths. Mahavira had spoken analogously of the stoppage of karma; Buddha and his followers spoke of breaking the chain of cause and effect which holds men in bondage to delusion. Buddhists believe that Buddha's great insight opened up a new chapter in the history of man's spiritual life. Once this path to salvation had been discovered and opened up by Buddha, other men might also walk it.

To Western ears Buddha's goal of Nirvana sounds extremely negative. Etymologically it means "blowing out" (of the flame of passion). Does it not then clearly imply extinction or the desire for a quiet death? Buddhists reply that this is by no means the case. Buddha himself expressly denied that Nirvana meant annihilation. What is extinguished is only the ignorant cravings which produce misery. What is left is bliss beyond the comprehension of all save those who know it by direct experience. Words serve here only to indicate the path which man must walk; and they are meaningful only to those who set their feet on the path to Nirvana.

Buddhist tradition tells of Buddha's subsequent meditation for another seven weeks during which he went through a period of doubt as to whether this new wisdom should be proclaimed to mankind. The question at issue was whether, having experienced Nirvana, he should immediately seek its full realization (a state which Buddhists call *Parinirvana* and believe he achieved at death) or whether out of compassion for suffering humanity he should tell others the good news of deliverance from misery. The latter course won out, and out of compassion for suffering humanity the Buddha embarked upon what turned out to be a forty-five-year mission.

He preached first to his five former fellow ascetics in the Deer Park near Banaras, thus setting in motion the Wheel of the *Dharma*. As he approached, the ascetics resolved to show scornful indifference to one who had defected from their austere way, but Buddha's attitude of victorious calm and peace won first their attention, then their respect, and finally their adherence. The conversion of these men marked the beginning of the *Sangha,* or Buddhist monastic order. Some days later fifty-three more converts were added, and Buddha sent them out in all directions to teach the new way to deliverance.

At Rajagaha King Bimbisara and many of his royal court became lay followers and supporters of the order. There too, Buddha received his two chief disciples, Shariputta and Moggallana, together with a large group of their friends Each new monk took the vow which has become traditional throughout the Buddhist world: "I take refuge in the Buddha, the Dharma and the Sangha." Members of the order were bound together by a common discipline, by their saffron robes, but most of all by their common allegiance to Buddha. The discipline is summarized in the traditional Ten Precepts:

1. I take the vow not to destroy life.
2. I take the vow not to steal.
3. I take the vow to abstain from impurity.
4. I take the vow not to lie.
5. I take the vow to abstain from intoxicating drinks, which hinder progress and virtue.
6. I take the vow not to eat at forbidden times.
7. I take the vow to abstain from dancing, singing, music, and stage plays.
8. I take the vow not to use garlands, scents, unguents, or ornaments.
9. I take the vow not to use a high or broad bed.
10. I take the vow not to receive gold or silver.[8]

Lay followers are committed to the first five of these Ten Precepts. Abstention from "impurity" means for monks strict celibacy, but for laymen it means abstention from extramarital sex relations.

Returning home, Buddha converted his royal father, his wife and son, and other members of the court, including his jealous cousin Devadatta. Despite formal conversion, Devadatta's heart remained full of jealousy and evil. In many

Deer Park Sermon
Courtesy of the Government of Andhra Home

stories of the Buddha, Devadatta appears as the villain. In one tale he set loose a mad elephant in Buddha's path, but the beast was so impressed by Buddha's gentleness that he bowed calmly at his feet.

The Sangha was, in the words of one Buddhist writer, a democracy, "the earliest monastic institution governed by perfect democratic principles which continues to the present day." [9] Its brotherhood ignored barriers of caste and class; Buddha's son Rahula was a member, but so was the former court barber Upali, and the former noble Ananda. Each new monk was placed under the tutelage of an older member of the order. There were fortnightly public confessions of shortcomings.

Buddha's practice was to gather his monks for intensive instruction during the four months of the rainy season. During the balance of the year, they traveled through the towns and countryside of north India, teaching Buddha's message of deliverance from misery.

The earliest Buddhist records are ambivalent concerning miracles of Buddha and his monks. There are many stories of wonders attributed to Buddha, yet he is also recorded as sternly forbidding his monks to perform miracles. There are innumerable stories of the Buddha's beneficent powers; for example, once he converted a notorious bandit, and another time he achieved an armistice between two armies drawn up for battle. There are also many stories of philosophic controversy between Buddha and other teachers and schools, notably the Jains.

The consistent image of the Buddha contained in these stories is that of an irenic and compassionate spirit, a sharp and highly original philosophic mind, and above all, a man dedicated in single-minded fidelity to his own emancipation and that of his fellowmen. So passed years of teaching, preaching, and organization. The brotherhood grew. It gained lay followers who provided material support for the monks. Buddha's influence spread throughout northern India. The earliest Buddhist sources also show a clear beginning for the idea of Buddha as a celestial or divine figure.

The Buddha's death, or Parinirvana, occurred at the age of eighty on a journey with a group of monks to the obscure village of Kusinara. Details of different accounts differ. According to one he took his midday meal at the home of Chunda, a goldsmith, and was afflicted with mortal illness. In his illness he lay down between two sal trees and died, surrounded by devoted followers. Buddhist tradition attributes to both Buddha and his followers prescience of his impending death. His last words were: "And now, O priests, I take my leave of you; all the constituents of being are transitory; work out your salvation with diligence." [10] His disciples cremated his body and scattered his ashes over the region.

BUDDHA'S TEACHING

It is impossible to distinguish precisely between the teachings of Buddha and later tradition which developed in the course of time. What is possible is to discern at the source of this tradition the impact of a powerful individual mind and life. The essence of Buddha's teaching has already been summarized as his insight into the nature of mortal misery and of its cure, which was also his message of deliverance to others. There seems no good reason to deny this core of teaching to the historical Buddha and every good reason to affirm it. While an earlier generation of Western students of Buddhism tended to regard the later Sanskrit documents as inherently less reliable sources of the Buddha's teaching than the earlier Pali documents, there is a tendency among contemporary scholars to believe that these later sources may contain accurate recollections of the Buddha—sometimes perhaps more adequate than earlier documents.

The key to Buddha's thought lies in his single-minded vision of misery and its cure. Misery (*dukkha*) is rooted in ignorant craving, or the delusory, itching

Standing Buddha
*Courtesy of the Archeological
Survey of India*

will to exist, to get, and to possess. Ignorance (*avidya*) of the true state of reality leads to craving, which in turn attributes reality to transitory and unreal things. If this root of ignorant craving is cut, the whole vast tree of misery will wither and die. What is left is not extinction—though it will seem so to those ignorant minds still held fast in their bondage to the world. Rather it is the bliss of Nirvana, which despite its negative etymology (noting the parallels between Latin and Sanskrit, Coomaraswamy has coined the term for Nirvana, "despirated," as the negative of "aspirated") is not in actuality negative, but super-affirmative. Such, at least, is the testimony of Buddha's followers.

Buddha wanted just enough philosophy to serve as a vehicle for this vision of emancipation—and not one sentence more. Whatever was useless for his purpose was effectively pruned away. When his disciples asked him whether the world is eternal or not, whether there is a substantial soul independent of the body or not, whether this soul exists after death, and whether there are gods or not—questions, be it noted, which other men have regarded as of religious significance—he replied that these were questions "which do not edify." [12] In the philosophical style of the twentieth century they are meaningless questions.[13] What was meaningful to the Buddha was misery and its cure, that and only that.

In the historical context of his time, this must be read as a rejection of traditional Brahman metaphysics with its fantastic speculations concerning gods, future lives, immortal souls, and substantial realities. Buddha's rejection of all this bears striking analogy to modern philosophic positivism and its rejection of metaphysics. To be sure, the twentieth-century Western reader seems to observe much residual metaphysics in Buddha's teaching, such as the teaching of karma-samsara. Yet to Buddha those doctrines were apparently not matters for speculation but were of direct experience. The fact that this assertion seems incredible to the modern reader simply serves to underscore the chasm which yawns between people of different times, places, and cultures.

Buddha likewise rejected Indian *bhakti,* or devotion to a god, as an unhealthy dependence on external realities. Rather, each person must climb the ladder of salvation for himself; he must use his own resources of perception and strength for the achievement of Nirvana. In fact, no other resources are available. As has been remarked, this is "the strictest sort of humanism in religion." [14] Here indeed was a bold and original philosophical mind.

As a part of the ancient Indian tradition, Buddha accepted the ideas of karma and samsara, but he gave to these traditional ideas his own original and distinctive interpretation. Most important, he parted company from the hardening lines of Indian orthodoxy in his teaching that a man of any caste can experience an awakening of heart so complete as to destroy karma and thus effectively, at one stroke, eliminate future rebirth. Negatively stated, it is those men who have not conquered ignorant craving who still live on in the ceaseless treadmill of rebirth, or samsara. Stated affirmatively, enlightenment and emancipation may come for a man of any caste who will meet its hard but simple conditions.

Buddha's philosophical outlook sought to provide a supporting context for this vision of deliverance from misery. The basic categories were *anatta* and *anicca,* or the ideas of (1) no substantial soul, and (2) no substantial realities in the world. The concept of anatta, no-ego, or no-soul, denies the existence of a substantial self or soul and asserts the apparent self or soul to be a temporary configuration of five components (called *skandha* in Sanskrit and *kandha* in Pali) which are (1) body, (2) feelings, (3) perceptions, (4) states of mind, and (5) awareness. These elements are asserted to enter into combination at the individual's birth and to separate at death. This analysis of the human self is the foundation of Buddhist psychology. Incidentally, it shows striking similarity to modern Western behaviorist views of the self.

Buddha denied substantial reality not only to the human self, but to the external world and all the things or objects in it. The idea of anicca asserts the transitory, impermanent nature of all things in the universe. There are no substances, no abiding entities; as with Heraclitus in ancient Greece, all is flux. Buddha would agree with the Christian hymn-writer: "Change and decay in all around I see." As has been said, the Buddhist universe knows no being, but only becoming.

The implications of these Buddhist themes are drawn out in what has traditionally been called the chain of dependent origination. The links of this chain are claimed to show how the original state of ignorance produces in succession all the appearances of the delusory world. Perhaps it might be characterized as an attempt to show metaphysically how one damned thing leads to another! Out of (1) ignorance arises (2) imagination, which in turn produces (3) self-consciousness. From self-consciousness come in turn (4) name and (5) form (i.e., corporeal existence or the appearance of it). Thence in succession arise (6) the six senses (Buddhism includes thought as one of the senses), (7) contact, (8) feeling or emotion, (9) craving, (10) attachment, (11) becoming or appearance, and finally (12) rebirth. The conquest of ignorance leads to the breaking of this chain and thence to the final dissolution of delusory self and world. In the end only Nirvana remains.[15]

Buddha bequeathed to his followers a lofty and distinctive system of moral ideals, whose central and characteristic feature is a tension between detachment and compassion. This tension was rooted apparently in the experience of the founder, who having achieved Nirvana was confronted by the alternatives of immediate and final entrance into Nirvana or of delaying this consummation in order compassionately to communicate this message of deliverance to suffering humanity. He was, in short, confronted by the choice between detachment and compassion; and his solution was to seek a balance in tension between these goals.

Both for Buddha and his followers, the tension between detachment and compassion must be judged creative rather than destructive. The two ideas support each other. For it is by the breaking of the fetters which fasten man to misery that one can achieve compassion. Negatively, it is the bondage to craving which leads to cruel action and prevents compassion. Knowledge (*vidya*) is the insight which overcomes attachment and self-centeredness, making possible both individual fulfillment and compassion for fellow human beings. It is the balance between these two elements which distinguishes Buddhist morality from that of Jainism, imparting to Buddhism the notes of moderation and even quiet joy lacking in Jainism.

Both detachment and compassion have specific applications in Buddhist ethics. How many of these teachings may be traced back to the historical Buddha it is impossible to say. As expressions of detachment, Buddhism lists the Three Intoxications, the Five Hindrances, and the Ten Fetters. The Three Intoxications, or Defilements, are in one formulation, evil attitudes, evil thoughts, and evil actions.[16] The Five Hindrances are (1) sensual desires, (2) hatred, (3) sloth, (4) restlessness and worry, and (5) doubts.[17] One version of the Ten Fetters is as follows: (1) delusion of self, (2) doubt, (3) dependence on works, (4) sensuality, bodily passions, (5) hatred, ill-feeling, (6) love of life on earth, (7) desire for life in heaven, (8) pride, (9) self-righteousness, (10) ignorance.[18]

Detachment points to the transmoral goal of Nirvana. In Nirvana there is no individual existence, and hence there are no moral relations. So it is that the ideal of detachment generates in Buddhist social attitudes a tendency toward passivity and withdrawal. In this spirit the Buddha encouraged his followers to "wander alone like a rhinoceros." [19] This attitude is also illustrated by the well-known Buddhist parable of Kisi Gotami, a poor mother whose only child, a baby son, died. Refusing to give up, she went from place to place and from teacher to teacher seeking medicine to bring the dead son back to life. She came at length to the Buddha who told her to go around the city until she found some grains of mustard seed from a house in which no one had ever died. She sought in vain from house to house until in a moment of insight the Buddha's lesson became clear to her.

> *Thought she: In the entire city this alone must be the way! This the Buddha, full of compassion for the welfare of mankind, must have seen! Overcome with emotion, she went outside of the city, carried her son to the burning-ground, and holding him in her arms, said: "Dear little son, I thought that you alone had been overtaken by this thing which men call death. But you are not the only one death has overtaken. This is a law common to all mankind."* [20]

Yet Buddhism from the first included the cultivation of love for fellowmen as well as detachment, though in early Buddhism the former was clearly subordinated to the latter. Its compassion was founded upon the archetypal example of Buddha's own sympathy for suffering humanity. The root ideas are those of compassion, literally "feeling with others" (*karuna*), and of friendliness or loving-kindness (Pali *metta* and Sanskrit *maitri* mean "friend"). By these moral ideals the whole human family is bound together in its interdependence of misery, and also need and aspiration for well-being or health. So it is that Buddhism follows its founder in being "a religion of infinite compassion." [21] Says the *Metta Sutta*:

> As a mother, even at the risk of her own life, protects and loves her child, her only child, so let a man cultivate love without measure toward all beings. Let him cultivate love without measure toward the whole world, above, below, and around, unstinted, unmixed with any feeling of differing or opposing interests. Let a man remain steadfastly in this state of mind all the while he is awake, whether he be standing, walking, sitting, or lying down. This state of mind is the best in the world.[22]

This ideal is given more specific social application in the following passage from the *Sutta Nipata*:

> Husbands should respect their wives, and comply as far as possible with their requests. They should not commit adultery. They should give their wives full charge of the home, and supply them with fine clothes and jewellery [sic] as far as their means permit. Wives should be thorough in their duties, gentle and kind to the whole household, chaste, and careful in housekeeping, and should carry out their work with skill and enthusiasm.
>
> A man should be generous to his friends, speak kindly of them, act in their interest in every way possible, treat them as his equals, and keep his word to them. They in turn should watch over his interests and property, take care of him when he is "off his guard" (i.e. intoxicated, infatuated, or otherwise liable to commit rash and careless actions), stand by him and help him in time of trouble, and respect other members of his family.
>
> Employers should treat their servants and workpeople decently. They should not be given tasks beyond their strength. They should receive adequate food and wages, be cared for in time of sickness and infirmity, and be given regular holidays and bonuses in times of prosperity. They should rise early and go to bed late in the service of their master, be content with their wages, work thoroughly, and maintain their master's reputation.[23]

The spirit of Buddha's ethics is well summarized in some well-known lines from the *Dhammapada*:

> All that we are is the result of what we have thought: it is founded on our thoughts, it is made up of our thoughts. If a man speaks or acts with a pure thought, happiness follows him, like a shadow that never leaves him.
>
> "He abused me, he beat me, he defeated me, he robbed me"—in those who harbor such thoughts hatred will never cease.

"He abused me, he beat me, he defeated me, he robbed me"—in those who do not harbor such thoughts hatred will cease.

For hatred does not cease by hatred at any time; hatred ceases by love—this is an old rule.

The world does not know that we must all come to an end here; but those who know it, their quarrels cease at once.[24]

THE FIRST TWO CENTURIES IN INDIAN BUDDHISM

Buddhist tradition asserts that there was a great assembly of 500 Buddhist monks at Rajagaha in 480 B.C., the first of a long succession of such councils, comparable to the ecumenical councils of Christianity. Tradition claims that these monks recited the Pali canon of scripture, called the *Tipitaka* (Sanskrit, *Tripitaka,* meaning "Three Baskets"), thus fixing or codifying this document. The same Buddhist tradition goes on to say that the Tipitaka was transmitted by oral tradition until the fourth council, when it was put into writing. The Tipitaka, or Tripitaka, consists of three main parts, the *Vinaya Pitaka* (Obedience, or Discipline, Basket) consisting of rules for the Sangha, the *Sutta Pitaka* (Teaching Basket) consisting of expositions of the Buddhist way of life, and the *Abhidhamma Pitaka* (Metaphysical Basket) consisting of philosophical treatises. According to one Buddhist source this last part of the Pali scriptures was not formally adopted until the third council.

The second great council was held a century later, in 380 B.C., at Vesali. It witnessed the first signs of a split destined to widen in the course of time between what were to become Theravada and Mahayana forms of Buddhism. This council was also marked by disputes over monastic discipline, some monks asking for relaxation of rules forbidding gold and silver, liquor, beds, and meals after midday. They also asked for private rather than public confession of shortcomings.

A third council was convened ca. 240 B.C. at Paliputra under the sponsorship of King Ashoka. Led by this great king, it was a milestone in the history of Buddhism, transforming it from an Indian movement to a universal religion.

Ashoka, the third king of the Maurya dynasty, was the grandson of the founder, Chandragupta Maurya, who had carved out a kingdom in northwest India as Alexander the Great's armies withdrew. Ashoka began as King of Magadha but achieved by conquest an empire which embraced most, if not all, of the vast Indian subcontinent. He came closer to the political unification of India than any other ruler until the arrival of the British in the seventeenth and eighteenth centuries, A.D.

Ashoka's conquests included what he subsequently came to regard as a particularly bloody victory over the Kingdom of Kalinga on the Bay of Bengal. Apparently the carnage pricked his conscience. In penitence he renounced his warlike ways and reformed the extravagant practices of his luxurious court. The royal hunt was abolished, and the allowance of meat for the court reduced to two peacocks and an antelope daily. These actions as well as Ashoka's establishment of hospitals for men and animals expressed his avowal of the traditional Indian idea of noninjury, or ahimsa. Significantly it did not entail complete pacifism.

East gate of Sanchi stupas
Courtesy of the Archeological Survey of India

Ashoka's activities are recorded on the rock edicts and pillar inscriptions by which he communicated his deeds and reforms to the people of his far-flung realm.[25] These records constitute (except for Harappa and Mohenjo-daro) the oldest extant historical monuments of Indian civilization. They also reveal Ashoka's intensely interesting personality. He was apparently much concerned with religion in general and with all the varieties of religion within his realm. His rock edicts proclaim religious freedom and toleration for all the numerous sects of his realm in a manner which is altogether unique in ancient history.

While a Buddhist adherent and patron, Ashoka's religion was a layman's faith, emphasizing moral practice and social service. His records mention planting fruit trees along the roads of his realm, digging wells, and setting up rest houses. To insure the morals of his subjects he established a new class of officials, the "Officers of Righteousness" whose duties included inspection and supervision of the morals of his subjects. For Ashoka religion seems to have meant moral conduct in this life and heaven in the next. Significantly, his records speak of *svarna,* the Sanskrit word for "heaven," rather than of Nirvana.

Ashoka's relation to Buddhism was momentously important. Some authorities believe that he actually entered the Buddhist order, though this is far from certain. What is more probable is that he conceived and called the Council of Paliputra. He did not hesitate to prescribe reading for the Buddhist order; he also ordered unworthy monks to be unfrocked. He erected shrines at Buddha's birthplace and place of enlightenment, and encouraged pilgrimages to these and other sacred places.

From Ashoka's time onward, Indian Buddhism assumed more of the distinctive features of a religious movement than previously, including temples, rituals, and many other institutional appurtenances of a religion. These in turn led to some of the great and characteristic forms of Indian Buddhist art such as the *stupa* and the *chaitya.* The latter is a kind of chapel or temple built to celebrate some holy place and often housing a relic of the Buddha. Not infrequently, as in the case of Karla, such chaityas were carved out of live rock. In many cases a chaitya was accompanied by a *vihara,* or monks' living quarters. The stupa is basically an earth mound built over a relic of the Buddha, to be visited and circumambulated by the faithful. Among the greatest works of Indian art are the stupas at Sanchi.

Ashoka seems to have conceived of Buddhism as a universal faith rather than as simply an Indian movement. He sent missionaries to many distant places. Most notably, he sent his son (some accounts say his brother) Mahinda to Ceylon. Whatever Mahinda's relation to Ashoka, Ceylonese Buddhism, with its manifold implications for the culture of that land, dates from this time.

Ashoka's period was crucial for the division between Theravada (or Hinayana) and Mahayana as the two major historical forms of Buddhism. The former is the Buddhism of Ceylon and southeast Asia, and the latter is the Buddhism of Tibet, China, Korea, and Japan. The terms *Mahayana* and *Hinayana* were coined by Indian Mahayana adherents; and they mean respectively the Great Vehicle and the Small Vehicle, or as Heinrich Zimmer has suggestively rendered them, the "Great Ferryboat" and the "Small Ferryboat," whose functions are to carry people across the stream of mortal misery to the bliss of the farther shore.[26] Adherents of the faith called Hinayana regard this term as reflecting a somewhat negative valuation and prefer the name *Theravada,* meaning the "Way of the Elders." By using the latter term they assert their claim to being in a direct line of transmission in a kind of apostolic succession from the Buddha. They further deny this succession to many of the beliefs and practices of Mahayana, asserting them to be later accretions.

Lion capital by King Ashoka
*Courtesy of the Archeological
Survey of India*

The breach between Theravada and Mahayana did not come simply or quickly. One of the first splits, occurring in the second century A.N. (After Nirvana) or the third century B.C., was that between the *Mahasanghikas* (Great Assembly-ites) and the *Sthaviras* (Elders, in Pali *Thera*); it seems to have centered in the agelong issue of the layman's relation to the Sangha, or community of monks. The former group pressed for a greater role for laymen and the latter maintained the supremacy of the monks. The *Sthaviravadins* continued the process of frag-mentation in the centuries immediately following. Among other groups to branch away were the *Pudgalavadins* (Personalists), who asserted the reality of the per-son apart from the five skandhas of other Buddhist thought, the *Sarvastavadins* (All-is-ists), who asserted the reality of time against other Buddhists, and the

Vibhajyavadins (Distinctionists). A century later still another group called *Sautrantikas* denied scriptural authority to the Abhidharma Pitaka, and asserted it for the *Sutras*, from which their name was derived. Still another group splitting away from the *Vibhajyavadins* and finding its way to Ceylon ca. 240 B.C. first applied the name *Theravada* to itself. The name was extended in the following centuries to cover all of southeast Asian Buddhism. Meanwhile developments destined to produce Mahayana continued in India. In the next section we shall characterize Theravada, and in the following section do the same for Mahayana.

THE WAY OF THE ELDERS

Theravada claims to stand in direct succession from Buddha and his disciples. This succession is embodied in the great councils, the first three of which have been described. A fourth, the Council of Matale was held in Ceylon in 25 B.C. There the Tipitaka, previously transmitted orally, was committed to writing. There was another council in northwest India under King Kanishka in the first century, but its authority is not recognized by Theravada Buddhists. The fifth great Theravada council was held in 1891 in Mandalay, Burma, and the sixth in 1956. Both of the latter grew out of modern reassertions of Buddhist vitality.

The Pali canon fixed at Matale consists, as we have seen, of the Three Baskets, or Tipitaka, each of which has several main subdivisions as follows:

1. The Basket of Discipline (*Vinaya Pitaka*): This contains five main subdivisions, all devoted to monastic discipline.
2. The Basket of Discourses (*Sutta Pitaka*): This contains narrative and didactic material, notable among which are *Jataka* and *Dhammapada*.
3. The Basket of Ultimate Things (*Abhidhamma Pitaka*): This contains seven books of Theravada philosophy.[27]

It is significant to note that the Pali scriptures were preserved in Ceylon while they were lost in India. As a consequence the great fifth-century Indian Buddhist scholar, Buddhaghosa, came to Ceylon in order to retranslate them from Sinhalese to Pali, and take them back to India.

Ceylonese Buddhism dates from the third century B.C. when King Ashoka's son or brother Mahinda, together with six companions, came to Ceylon as missionaries. Mahinda proclaimed the *dhamma* (the Pali term for the Sanskrit *dharma*) with such eloquence that King Tissa and his court embraced the new faith. Monasteries were founded, and stupas and temples were erected. Nuns were brought from India to found an order for women. Tradition says that they brought a sprig of the original bo tree from Bodhgaya, which still lives and grows at the monastery at Anuradhapuna. Buddha's collarbone and other relics are said to have been brought to Ceylon at this time. Later, in A.D. 310

the tooth relic was brought from India and given a place of honor in the Temple of the Tooth in Kandy.

Buddhist fortunes in Ceylon have ebbed and flowed with the changing centuries. Social disorders, invasions, and religious decline brought Buddhism to the point of extinction around A.D. 1000. However, a devout king imported a new order of monks from Burma. Later, during the Dutch domination of Ceylon in the eighteenth century, still another new order was introduced from Thailand. British rule in the eighteenth and nineteenth centuries brought increased Christian missionary activities, but this stimulated new life and thought in Ceylonese Buddhism which continues to the present day. Theravada Buddhism continues as the national faith of Ceylon.

From Ceylon Buddhism found its way to the lands of southeast Asia. Tradition tells many tales, but reliable history concerning the origins of Burmese Buddhism is meager or lacking. Buddhist legend tells the story of two merchants named Tapassu and Bhallika who gave the Buddha his first meal after his enlightenment and who, having been converted by the Buddha, went on to Burma to lay the foundations of Buddhism in that country. Another legend says that the Buddha gave them a few hairs from his head which are now properly enshrined in the celebrated Shwedagon Pagoda of Rangoon. Still another story asserts that two missionaries of King Ashoka first brought Buddhism to Burma. It is said, presumably with better basis, that the fifth-century missionary scholar, Buddhaghosa, visited Burma and planted the seeds of Burmese Buddhism.

What can be historically established is that under the eleventh-century King Anawrahta, who first unified Burma, Buddhism enjoyed a golden age. Ever since this time Buddhism has been the established religion of Burma. It has had its ups and downs, but has never been seriously challenged as Burma's major faith.

Similar tales are told concerning Thailand where, since the fourteenth century, Buddhism has been the established religion. This has meant governmental support, but often also a large measure of governmental control for the 165,000 monks in 20,000 Thai monasteries.

From Ceylon, Burma, and Thailand, Buddhism made its way to Cambodia, Laos, and Vietnam. Since these lands show extensive Indian influence, their Buddhism has also shown an important mixture of Hinduism. The world-famous Angkor Wat was a twelfth-century achievement of Cambodian Buddhism. From these southeast Asian lands Buddhism penetrated Malaya, Sumatra, Java, Borneo, and Bali. The great stupa at Borobudur in Java is a monument to this movement. However, from the fifteenth century to the present Islam has displaced Buddhism as the living religion of Indonesia.

In Theravada lands the center of Buddhism remains the brotherhood of Buddhist monks. In these lands Buddhism is essentially a monastic brotherhood

surrounded and supported by lay followers, and radiating its influence into the
surrounding society. The characteristic institutional structure for Theravada is
the monastic complex called in Thai language the *wat* (and in Burmese,
phongyi chaung).[28] Within the complex the chief building is the *bot*, which
is a hall for worship or meditation, as well as teaching and preaching. Here
the most prominent feature is the image of the Buddha seated high above the
altar and surrounded by images of Buddha's disciples. On the altar are candle-
sticks, incense burners and other equipment for ritual. Also there is likely to
be a bouquet of flowers brought as homage to the Buddha. In some prominent
place in the meditation hall is a raised seat for the teachers or preachers who
dispense instruction and inspiration to members of the order and at times to
the public. Other parts of the monastic complex include living quarters for the
members, as well as a number of stupas, *dagobas,* or pagodas, whose graceful
towers tapering upward give the whole structure its characteristic appearance.

Authorities disagree as to the origin of the pagoda, but the most probable
guess is that it began as the stupa or relic mound, such as that at Sanchi, India,
and that the multiform roof began as a series of parasols placed over a relic.
Whatever their beginning, pagodas are characteristic features of the southeast
Asian landscape—and also as we shall see of China and Japan.

While the pagoda retains its function as a relic shrine, it has also gathered
to itself other functions. It is the center of ritual and public festivals of many
sorts. The Perahera festival at Kandy in Ceylon features music, dancing, and
processions in which relics are taken from the pagoda and returned to it. Ceylon
also has a New Year's festival (similar to the Hindu Holi) in which cars or
floats bearing images of the Buddha are paraded about the streets. The Buddha
is also honored by exhibitions of national dance. As in India people splash
each other with colored water.

The most important popular festival of Theravada Buddhism is Wesak, usually observed in the full moon of May, and celebrating the birth, enlightenment,
and Parinirvana of the Buddha. Houses and streets are decorated, and gifts are
given to monks and to the poor.

Theravada Buddhism has struck deep roots in these cultures, influencing art,
ethics, politics—indeed, all aspects of the common life. In Thailand and Burma
it has been customary for young men to spend at least a few weeks in study
and meditation in a monastery before assuming the duties of citizenship. Others
may go to the monastery for periods of meditation or instruction. Buddhist
religious practices of many sorts, ranging from retreats and pilgrimages to marriages and funeral ceremonies and to public holidays or festival days are established features of the society.

What is Theravada's view of the Buddha, whose images line the meditation
halls of monasteries and dot the landscape of southeast Asia? Buddha is honored
and reverenced by his Theravada followers as the great discoverer of the path

to salvation. Yet having discovered it and walked it, Buddha is now in Nirvana, beyond the reach of human adoration or petition. Hence, while Theravada religious followers honor and reverence him and even meditate before his image, they do not, properly speaking, worship him or pray to him. The flowers on his altar, as well as the many Buddha images are ways of paying homage to the discoverer of the path which leads from mortal misery to the blessedness of *Nibbana* (the Pali version of *Nirvana*).[29]

Theravada has lagged far behind Mahayana in its speculation about Buddha and other Buddha figures. Yet the beginnings of such speculation are present in Pali sources. They affirm the Buddha's preexistence and his descent to earth from the Tushita heaven in order to bring enlightenment to mankind. They also affirm the existence of other Buddha figures, notably Bodhisattvas, or Buddhas-in-the-making. Gautama himself was a Bodhisattva in a long series of transmigrations before achieving his final birth and enlightenment. While Gautama Buddha clearly continues to occupy the central place, Theravada Buddhism finds place in its devotion for Metteya (Sanskrit, *Maitreya*), now a Bodhisattva and, more specifically, the Buddha of the next age. In Pali sources there are a few allusions to other Bodhisattvas, ranging from six to twenty-four in number. They are said to be candidates for Buddhahood, or enlightenment, who delay their entrance into Nibbana in order to help suffering fellow creatures. As will presently be clear, the Bodhisattva figure assumed other meanings in Mahayana Buddhism.

Theravada philosophy—if this term be permitted—has consisted largely of reflection upon the main themes of Buddha's thought, such as the nature of misery and of deliverance to Nibbana, the transitory, unsubstantial character of self and world, and the nature and transmission of *kamma* (Sanskrit, *karma*). Beyond these limits it has, in obedience to Buddha, refused to venture.

Theravada thought has made much of the silence of the Buddha in response to questions whose answers would have taken him into speculative answers which do not edify. Buddha's silence may be taken as his rejection of the Indian speculative philosophy of his time. Such thought contributed nothing to man's way out of misery to deliverance.[30] Buddha would presumably agree with the modern philosophic formulation: "What we cannot speak about we must pass over in silence." [31]

Yet despite themselves Theravada Buddhists did in their way speak concerning these matters; they elaborated Buddha's doctrines of anatta and anicca, as a kind of philosophic explication and guide for the Buddha's way to salvation. One celebrated Theravada source compares the soul to a chariot which is composed of wheels, frame, reins, spokes, etc.; when the chariot is dismantled—one is tempted to say dissolved—into these component parts, nothing of the chariot remains. So, analogously, the human self is analysed into the five kandhas, or components; [32] they come together in a temporary configuration to

constitute the self which appears, but they separate at death and nothing remains. Hence, death signifies the end of a temporary phenomenon.

This view of selfhood raised significant questions for personal identity. Is
the grown man really the same person as the infant of many years ago? Buddhist
thought replied with the metaphor of a light which burns continuously through
the night.[33] Further, the continuity of the body provides a pragmatic unity of
self.

This uncompromising denial of a substantial self seemed to leave the issue of
rebirth dangling. How can there be rebirth if nothing transmigrates? Again
Buddhist thought used the metaphor of a light—this time the light passed from
one lamp to another. The lamps might crumble and disappear, but the light
continues. Even so does kamma pass from one transitory configuration of selfhood to another.[34] Despite the absence of substantial existence, Theravada
thought managed to say a great deal concerning kamma. As there are different
kinds of seeds so there are many kinds of kamma, some good, some bad, each
producing its own kind of character and behavior. Other refinements and elabo-
rations of the idea arose in the course of time.[35]

More affirmatively, Theravada Buddhist thinkers formulated the Noble Eightfold Path as stages of development for the soul passing through the realms of
morality, concentration, and wisdom.[36] In this process, Theravada has changed
the traditional order of the Eightfold Path, to begin with right speech, right
action, and right livelihood. From these a person goes on to wisdom preparatory
to meditation and thence to his goal in emancipation. Theravadins also emphasize
that this is a journey of the soul undertaken and carried out in man's own
strength. No gods are available for help or guidance on man's journey.

Theravada ethics continued the tension between the goals of individual
emancipation and compassionate love for mankind. The latter is by no means
lacking. There is an attitude of quiet friendliness, if not of outgoing generosity,
in Theravada virtue.

> *This a man should do who knows what is good for him,*
> *Who understands the meaning of the Place of Peace—*
> *He should be able, upright, truly straight,*
> *Kindly of speech, mild, and without conceit.*
>
> *He should be well content, soon satisfied,*
> *Having few wants and simple tastes,*
> *With composed senses, discreet,*
> *Not arrogant or grasping. . . .*
>
> *In his deeds there should be no meanness*
> *For which the wise might blame him.*

May all be happy and safe!
May all beings gain inner joy—[37]

As previously noted, this Buddhist love can sometimes become the virtue that returns good for evil. Yet in Theravada, Buddhist compassion continues to be fundamentally the impartial goodwill of the man who has delivered his own soul from craving and wishes to show others how they may do the same.

While its goal has remained a clearly transsocial and transmoral salvation, Theravada ethics has generated significant moral teachings and social values. It continued the hostility to caste. So for example the *Sutta Nipata* says:

No brahman is such by birth.
No outcaste is such by birth.
An outcaste is such by his deeds.
A brahman is such by his deeds.[38]

It has continued to hold up the fivefold rule for laymen: (1) Do not take life; (2) Do not take what is not yours; (3) Do not act basely in sexual matters; (4) Do not tell falsehoods; (5) Do not drink spirits.[39] For the Buddhist layman this rule as traditionally interpreted has meant that he cannot be a butcher, though he can eat meat provided by non-Buddhist butchers. While not strictly pacifist in its teaching, Buddhism has been among the most peaceful and peace-loving of the world's religions. It has been remarkably successful in promoting abstinence from alcohol.

Despite its somewhat nonpolitical nature, Buddhism has discouraged the pretensions of kings to divine or semidivine status. Like other Indian faiths and philosophies of its time, Buddhism sees the historical origin and development of man's world within a vast and pulsating universe in which periods of growth and decay, of improvement and degeneration seem to follow each other in an endless succession of ages. As for the recent past and present, the times are becoming worse, as is evidenced in the increase of immorality and in people's shorter life-spans. They will continue to worsen until a climax of evil is reached. Then the wheel will turn again.

Yet Theravada teaches that man's destiny and blessedness lie beyond all the ups and downs of the world of ceaseless becoming. In this world, which is without beginning or end, men live and labor as prisoners until they reach the state of Nibbana, where sorrow and illusion exist no longer. To lay bare the great illusion is the work of man. To contemplate life without being enmeshed in worldly things and then to go forth into higher spiritual life is the Path of the Buddha and his Theravada followers. To be united with what is real and permanent—that is, to attain Nibbana—is the goal of that Path.

THE GREAT VEHICLE

While Theravada was developing and spreading over southeast Asia, Mahayana, the Great Vehicle, was assuming its distinctive forms and moving toward
domination in India. Once more, one must not assume that this was a simple
or rapid process. Adherents of many forms of Buddhism lived and worked together in India and doubtless argued with each other for a period of several
centuries. A Chinese visitor to India in the early fifth century found Theravada
still very much alive.[40] Nevertheless in Indian Buddhism, Mahayana won out
in the end. Zimmer's translation of *yana* as "ferryboat" and his relating this
metaphor to that of the river crossing already encountered in Jain thought, will
help the Western student understand this whole aspect of ancient Indian
thought as well as the more specific issue of Mahayana, or the Big Ferryboat,
and its superiority over the Little Ferryboat:

> *The gist of Buddhism can be grasped more readily and adequately by
> fathoming the main metaphors through which it appeals to our intuition than
> by a systematic study of the complicated superstructure, and the fine details
> of the developed teaching. For example, one need only think for a moment
> about the actual, everyday experience of the process of crossing a river in a
> ferryboat, to come to the simple idea that inspires and underlies all of the
> various rationalized systematizations of the doctrine. To enter the Buddhist
> vehicle—the boat of the discipline—means to begin to cross the river of life,
> from the shore of the common-sense experience of non-enlightenment, the
> shore of spiritual ignorance (avidyā), desire (kāma), and death (māra), to
> the yonder bank of transcendental wisdom (vidyā), which is liberation (moksa)
> from this general bondage. Let us consider, briefly, the actual stages involved
> in any crossing of a river by ferry, and see if we can experience the passage
> as a kind of initiation-by-analogy into the purport of the stages of the Buddhist
> pilgrim's progress to his goal.*
>
> *Standing on the nearer bank, this side the stream, waiting for the boat to
> put in, one is a part of its life, sharing in its dangers and opportunities and in
> whatever may come to pass on it. One feels the warmth or coolness of its
> breezes, hears the rustle of its trees, experiences the character of its people,
> and knows that the earth is underfoot. Meanwhile the other bank, the far
> bank, is beyond reach—a mere optical image across the broad, flowing waters
> that divide us from its unknown world of forms. We have really no idea what
> it will be like to stand in that distant land. How this same scenery of the river
> and its two shorelines will appear from the other side we cannot imagine. How
> much of these houses will be visible among the trees? What prospects up and
> down the river will unfold? Everything over here, so tangible and real to us
> at present—these real, solid objects, these tangible forms—will be no more
> than remote, visual patches, inconsequential optical effects, without power to
> touch us, either to help or to harm. This solid earth itself will be a visual,
> horizontal line beheld from afar, one detail of an extensive scenic view, beyond
> our experience, and of no more force for us than a mirage.*

> *The ferryboat arrives; and as it comes to the landing we regard it with a feeling of interest. It brings with it something of the air of that yonder land which will soon be our destination. Yet when we are entering it we still feel like members of the world from which we are departing, and there is still that feeling of unreality about our destination. When we lift our eyes from the boat and boatman, the far bank is still only a remote image, no more substantial than it was before.*[41]

If now it be asked why this ferryboat is more adequate for its purpose than the other, the answer is that it can carry more people, it is a larger vehicle, embracing more of man's life in the world. It was even enough of an omnibus to embrace the charms, the prayers, the ceremonies, and the mythologies which formed so large a part of popular religion in Mahayana. Hinayana—such is the charge of Mahayana—is a vehicle on which only a few selected and very dedicated individuals make their passage to the further shore. Mahayana is a vehicle for all men. Many Mahayana sources also opine that it is a more effective vehicle of salvation. Hinayana, the lesser vehicle, does not really secure the full salvation of its people, say these sources.

The historical development of Mahayana in India took place under the beneficent influence of a group of monarchs whom Zimmer has called "the great Buddhist kings." [42] We have already noted the career of King Ashoka and his decisive impact upon Buddhism. Shortly after his death, the Maurya dynasty and empire disintegrated and disappeared. But other, lesser kings arose to take his place as royal patrons of Buddhism, principally in northwest India. From the few shreds of archaeological evidence they are labeled Greco-Bactrian, since their remains, from coins to sculptured likenesses of Buddha, show possible Greek influence, and since they lived and reigned in the region of Bactria. One of these Greco-Bactrian kings, perhaps the greatest, King Milinda (125–95 B.C., whose Greek name was Menander), is known to us through a notable document, *The Conversations of King Milinda,* which reports the king's serious questions concerning Buddhist thought, addressed to his guide and tutor, the monk Nagasena. Many aspects of these conversations are more sympathetic to Theravada ideas than to Mahayana; clearly there was no unanimity among these royal patrons of Buddhism. Another such Buddhist king was Kanishka (78–123 A.D.) of Kushana. From these and presumably similar royal adherents and patrons of the faith, one sees in development a relation of faith to culture somewhat different from that of Theravada. There is in the case of Mahayana a notably greater affirmation of the varied life of human culture. Increasingly this affirmation was extended to all aspects of the culture.

Other differences also emerged, including a different attitude toward Buddha. As early as Ashoka we note in some Buddhist documents an attitude of personal devotion toward the Lord Buddha which is similar to bhakti in Hinduism.

From this root grew several new and significant developments. One was the development of great new Buddhist arts. Early Buddhism had been reluctant to make sculptured or painted likenesses of the Buddha. At Sanchi, whose devotion was Theravada, there was a careful avoidance of any likeness of the Buddha. This reticence was overcome by Mahayana. In northwest India from the first century of the Christian era onward, a great new tradition of sculpture celebrated the main events of Buddha's life, and the different aspects of his many-sided message. The sculptors who created this art owed a debt to Greek sculpture, but they developed their own new and highly distinctive style. Similarly in the early centuries of this era fresco paintings such as those which adorn the walls of the monastic caves at Ajanta celebrated the new Mahayana devotion to the Buddha.

The central and determining feature of Mahayana was its new Sutra literature which came into being from ca. 100 B.C. to ca. A.D. 400. While its adherents claimed it to be the revealed word of the Buddha, to the historical student of Buddhism it shows many significant new religious and philosophical features.

One such feature of Mahayana is what may be called the path of the bodhisattva. Both the term and the idea antedated Mahayana. As we have seen, the word "bodhisattva" means "being or body of light," and we have already noted in Theravada the presence of such figures as Maitreya, the Buddha of the next age. In both Theravada and Mahayana the proliferation of Buddha-figures who come from heaven to earth seems to be rooted in the conviction of Buddha's transmundane nature and significance, or in other words that he is greater than mere man—in western terms, divine.

In Mahayana the bodhisattva path was based upon the assumption that every man is a potential Buddha. The path to Buddhahood might be extremely hard and eons long, but laymen and monks alike may set their feet upon it. The motives were aspiration for enlightenment and compassion of mankind. The characteristic bodhisattva vow promised not to enter full Buddhahood until all others are saved.

The six perfections to which the bodhisattva is committed are: (1) giving, (2) morality, (3) patience, (4) vigor or zeal, (5) meditation, and (6) wisdom. The last, called in Sanskrit, *prajna paramita* ("the wisdom of the further shore") is a necessary ingredient of all the others, defining the spirit in which they are to be sought, namely without ulterior motivation and without attachment to the unreal world. Mahayana Sutras assert that *prajna* or wisdom is a subtle and difficult perfection to achieve. Wisdom is also personified as a goddess who is asserted to be the mother of all the Buddhas.

To the perfections Mahayana added the theory of *bhumis* or stages on the way to becoming a Buddha. In different formulations the number and order of stages varied, but they all began with the bodhisattva's first thought of enlightenment, and culminated in the final achievement of Buddhahood. The intervening time might be eons or *kalpas* long; it involved such requirements as declaring one's vows in the presence of a Buddha, thus necessitating waiting until a Buddha arrives in the world. Yet perhaps the most significant feature of the bodhisattva ideal is its implication of universal compassion and salvation. Compassionately the bodhisattva seeks the salvation of all, and in the end all will be saved. Truly Buddhism is a religion of infinite compassion and universal salvation!

For mortals just setting their feet on the bodhisattva path there is encouragement in the contemplation (and the grace!) of heavenly bodhisattvas or mahasattvas ("great beings"). These savior gods and goddesses are both more numerous and more significant in Mahayana than in Theravada. Some sound Christlike in their expression of suffering love, as the following passage illustrates:

> *I take upon myself . . . the deeds of all beings, even of those in the hells, in other worlds, in the realms of punishment. . . . I take their suffering upon me, . . . I bear it, I do not draw back from it, I do not tremble at it, . . . I have no fear of it, . . . I do not lose heart. . . . I must bear the burden of all beings, for I have vowed to save all things living, to bring them safe through the forest of birth, age, disease, death and rebirth. I think not of my own salvation, but strive to bestow on all beings the royalty of supreme wisdom. So I take upon myself all the sorrows of all beings. I resolve to bear every torment in every purgatory of the universe. For it is better that I alone suffer than the multitude of living beings. I give myself in exchange. I redeem the universe from the forest of purgatory, from the womb of flesh, from the realm of death. I agree to suffer as a ransom for all beings, for the sake of all beings. Truly I will not abandon them. For I have resolved to gain wisdom for the sake of all that lives, to save the world.*[43]

Of the virtually innumerable celestial bodhisattvas there is space for only the briefest mention of the most important and widely known. *Maitreya*, the Buddha of the next age, has been mentioned in the section on Theravada. He was historically the earliest bodhisattva to gain a following, and his human followers include both Mahayanists and Theravadins. He appears frequently in the Buddhist sculpture of Gandhara and of central Asia. Maitreya became Mi-lo-fu in China.

Of equal influence and popularity is *Manjusri*. His name means "sweet glory," and he is also known as *Manjughosa* ("sweet voice"). He is the patron of wisdom whose sharp sword cuts through ignorance and illusion and whose book depicts the bodhisattvas' perfection. Followers say that very long ago and very far away he began his bodhisattva path as a devout king. Now even though he has completed the path he stays in the samsara-world until all are saved. Manjusri became Wen-yu in China.

Avalokiteshvara or *Lord Avalokita* (this word means "descender to the world") was early an attendant of other Buddha figures and only later achieved independent status. He is said to grant boons to those in distress or trouble, and to save his followers from lust, hostility and folly. He was symbolized in art as a be-jeweled layman with a high crown, and was later represented with eleven heads and many arms. In China he changed sex, becoming the goddess Kuan yin, deity of mercy. In Japan Kuan yin is Kwannon.

Bodhisattva Maitreya

Courtesy of the Archeo-logical Survey of India

Samantabhadra ("universal sage") has been associated with the teaching and practice of the *Lotus Sutra*. He watches over its devotees, protecting those who keep its teaching and admonishing those who forget. He became Pu-hien in China. *Kshitigarbha*, who is Ti Tsang in China and Jizo in Japan, delivers people from the sufferings of the samsara-world. *Vajrapani* ("thunder-hand") is the stern foe of sin and evil; he bears the weapon of the thunder-bolt in his hand.

In addition to the heavenly bodhisattvas there are other heavenly Buddha figures with important roles in Mahayana. Of these among the most important is *Amitabha* ("unlimited light") who is known as Amita or Amida in China and Japan. He is the blessed Lord of Sukhavati, or the Pure Land or Heaven of devo-tional Buddhism, whose adherents confidently proclaim that if a person will meditate on Amida with a faith-filled mind Amida will meet him when he dies and guide him to Sukhavati.

Vairocana ("shining out") was, as his name indicates related to the sun as well as to Shakyamuni Buddha. He achieved a separate identity in later Mahayana and played an important role in tantric Buddhism. Still later in Japan he came to be identified with the Shinto sun goddess Amaterasu.

The proliferation of Buddha figures in Mahayana inevitably suggests a contrast to Christianity, which (though it has multiplied angels and saints) has steadfastly maintained the uniqueness of Christ. Yet as we observed above, if the solutions were different the root issue was similar. In the case of both Christianity and Buddhism the root of these developments was a conviction of what we have termed the celestial or transmundane significance of the founder. Believers were convinced that Jesus and Gautama respectively were more than mere men! It was this connection which generated in early Christianity such doctrines as the incarnation and trinity. Holding a similar conviction in the very different intellectual and spiritual climate of ancient India, Buddhists arrived at the very different outcomes sketched in the preceding paragraphs.

Still a further comparison may be indicated. In the Apostles' Creed and again in the Nicene Creed Christians affirmed Christ to be both truly divine and truly human. Somewhat analogously Buddhists asserted of Buddha a *Dharmakaya* ("Dharma body" or "Body of Reality") and a *Nirmanakaya* "(Body of Appearance"). In other words Buddha "appeared" here on earth. That was all that was needed. This idea contrasts with the Christian claim that Christ was "truly man," or fully incarnated as a man. From a Christian viewpoint Buddhism is accordingly a gnostic or docetic religion, while Buddhists might reply that Christianity is still bogged down in the unreal world of matter. To the twentieth-century student of man's religions these claims constitute very different visions of human existence!

Later Mahayana philosophers added to the *Dharmakaya* and *Nirmanakaya*, still a third "body," namely *Sambhogakaya* ("Body of Bliss"), thus constituting a kind of Buddhist trinity. However the similarity with the Christian trinity is numerical only; in content these ideas are utterly dissimilar, as we have seen above.

Mahayana Buddhism brought into being not only new forms and objects of devotion but new philosophies as well. These Buddhist philosophers believed that they were really fulfilling Buddha's philosophic intention, and did not hesitate to attribute their words to him. But to the modern student their ideas seem new, going far beyond Buddha's teachings.

Among these new philosophies none was more important than the *Madhyamika* ("Central Way") of Nagarjuna (ca. A.D. 150–250), so-called because it maintained Buddha's middle way between being and nonbeing. Nagarjuna was apparently court philosopher to an Indian king, and he sought to argue the Mahayana case against both Hinayanists and non-Buddhists. His method of argument was to show that all opposing views—and indeed the whole samsara-world—are riddled with self-contradiction, and therefore lack substantive reality or being.

All is Shunya, argued Nagarjuna, and his philosophy is sometimes called *Shunyavada* (the "Way of Emptiness"). *Shunya* is the Sanskrit word for zero in the number series, and is variously translated as "empty" or "void." Philosophically it means that all things lack *svabhava* or self-existence; they have only a relative being. Indeed one translator has rendered Shunya as "universal relativity."

It is important to note Nagarjuna's religious motivation. Buddha had argued that both the self and the external world are delusory appearances. The teaching of Shunya carries this program to its logical conclusion. Nagarjuna did not shrink from declaring that both Buddha and Nirvana are Shunya, and thus not objects to which one may be attached or on which one may be "hung-up." Shunya frees man from the samsara world for the world of liberation and enlightenment. Indeed, declared Nagarjuna, these are not two different realms but the same world seen under different aspects!

Nagarjuna has been called the Immanuel Kant of Indian philosophy. Kant criticized all preceding European philosophies; Nagarjuna did likewise in India. Also as Kant's criticism led onward to idealist philosophies of the nineteenth century, so Nagarjuna's thought led onward to Buddhist idealism. Most important of these idealist philosophies of Indian Buddhism was the *Yogacara* ("Practice of Yoga") or *Vijnanavada* (the "Way of Consciousness") of the fourth or fifth centuries A.D. The basic or foundational idea of this philosophy was that of *alaya vijnana* ("receptacle consciousness") from which in successive derivations all things are produced or derived. This absolute consciousness was a positive rendering of Nagarjuna's Shunya or Void. It was also termed *Tathata* ("Suchness"), and in relation to Buddha as Dharmakaya. From this source were drawn out successively in order all the various forms and things of the world of appearance. The eight stages of derivation are: (1) receptacle or absolute consciousness, (2) mind-consciousness, (3) consciousness of touch, (4) consciousness of sight, (5) consciousness of hearing, (6) consciousness of smell, (7) consciousness of taste, and (8) sense-center consciousness. Like philosophic idealisms of other times and places, all things are of the nature of mind; from this original cosmic Mind they derive and to it they return. This idealist Buddhist philosophy was destined to profoundly influence the thought of China and Japan.

THE THUNDERBOLT VEHICLE

It is important to realize that during the centuries of Buddhism's power in India there was never a clear or sharp separation between Buddhism and Hinduism. These two faiths—as they have seemed to later generations—overlapped and mingled together in many ways. Fa Hsien, Chinese traveler and student of Buddhism, early in the fifth century observed that Buddhist monks joined in many Hindu processions and rituals.

During these centuries of Indian Buddhist influence there grew up in both Buddhist and Hindu communities a new way called *tantrism,* or *Vajrayana* (meaning the "thunderbolt vehicle"). The first name is from the word *tantra,* meaning book, or manual; and *thunderbolt vehicle* is an allusion to the violence of passion often aroused and involved in this way. The origins and chronology of tantrism are obscure. By the fifth century the new way was much in evidence, and two centuries later another Chinese visitor to India, Hsüan Tsang, comments on its continued incidence.

Tantrism, whether of the Buddhist or Hindu variety, consisted of a curious combination of mystical and magical practices designed to achieve salvation. Magic had never been absent from the quest for salvation in India; and in tantrism it attached itself to the formulas or manuals (*tantras*), to diagrams or pictures (*yantras* or *mandalas*), and to sacred words (*mantras*). Together these forces were thought to guarantee salvation or emancipation of the sort traditionally sought in India. Among the potent mantras *"Om mani padme hum"* was a formula believed to possess peculiar mystical potency. *Om* or *Aum* is the mystical syllable we have observed from the time of the Upanishads onward. The other words are variously translated "the jewel is in the lotus," or "the jewel of the lotus." Whether or not the allusion is sexual is the subject of much scholarly argument.[50] Allied with the sacred words and diagrams were mystical and magical postures and practices related to Yoga.

Many of these practices had both a sexual and an antinomian significance. The former was based upon an idea, of ancient origin in India, that each god possessed a source of power termed *Shakti.* This power was regarded as feminine in character and was often regarded as the deity's wife or consort. In tantric Buddhism this led to the emergence of *taras,* or savioresses, as consorts for many of the Buddha figures. In both Hindu and Buddhist tantric groups this concern with male and female principles in myth and rite was expressed sometimes in sublimated, and sometimes in unsublimated, forms, known in Indian terms as Right-hand and Left-hand Shaktism respectively.[51]

These religiously derived erotic practices may be characterized as ways of catharsis by indulgence. The religious devotee went through the experience of passion, sexual or of another sort, with his eyes fixed on what we have called the farther shore of emancipation. To pursue this metaphor, he deliberately immersed himself in passion, seeking eventually to swim to the farther shore. As one tantric source says:

> The mystics, pure of mind,
> Dally with lovely girls,

Infatuated with the poisonous flame of passion,
That they may be set free from desire.

. . . .

The mystic duly dwells
On the manifold merits of his divinity,
He delights in thoughts of passion,
And by the enjoyment of passion is set free.[52]

Such indulgence which aimed at salvation, in order to be effective, had to take place under the direction of a trained guru and as a part of secret, esoteric rituals. These rites involved not only sex, but the five prohibited things or "M's", *madya* (wine), *mamsa* (meat), *matsya* (fish), *mudra* (parched grain), and *maithuna* (sexual intercourse), all partaken as a kind of sacrament of forbidden things.[53] Often the sexual rites were asserted to reproduce in human life the experience of the god and goddess in their union. Such union placed the religious devotee beyond all the dualities of human experience, giving him a direct experience of the union promised by mysticism. Often these rituals took place at night as a kind of Black Mass, Indian fashion.

The antinomian character of these secret tantric beliefs and practices illustrates a pattern which recurs not only in Indian religions but throughout the world. However we may seek to render it comprehensible, it is apparently the expression of some human need. A concern with these and similar questions on the part of a wide variety of students has sustained Western interest in Indian tantrism, whether of the Hindu or Buddhist variety.

Tantrism was only one of several signs of decline in Indian Buddhism. Hsüan Tsang, Chinese visitor to seventh-century India, commented on Buddhism's waning vitality. Hindu devotees, particularly in southern India, mounted an increasing opposition to the way of the Buddha; Shankara's writings from the early ninth century are studded with passages strongly hostile to Buddhism. Yet the grand strategy of Hinduism was not to oppose but to absorb—or to re-absorb. And in the end it proved effective. Buddha became for many devout Indians an avatar of Vishnu.

Despite these shreds of evidence, the well-nigh total decline of Indian Buddhism remains an enigma. Apparently it lost the original vitality which carried it to every part of India and then sent its missionaries forth to every corner of Asia. Another factor was a vigorous new assertion of Hindu devotion. As a result of these—and doubtless other factors of which the modern student is ignorant—Buddhism virtually perished in the land of its birth.

The final blow to Indian Buddhism was struck in successive waves by invading Muslims beginning with the eleventh century. The servants of Allah smashed the monasteries and slaughtered the "shaven-headed brahmans," as they called

Buddhist monks. While Buddhism had a firm base in lands beyond the mountains and beyond the sea, it was virtually extinguished in the land of its birth.

Only within the past century have Indians sought to reclaim their Buddhist heritage. King Ashoka's pillar now appears on the Indian flag, and contemporary Indian writers speak proudly of "Hindu-Buddhist civilization." But this is another and a more recent story, to which we will return in different context.

TIBETAN BUDDHISM

Buddhism found its way to Tibet in the reign of King Songtsan-Gampo who came to the throne in A.D. 642. As a social reformer he sought for his people the benefits of both Indian and Chinese civilizations. His two wives, Indian and Chinese respectively, were both Buddhist. So he sent to both India and China for Buddhist books, teachers, and ideas. He sought to introduce Buddhism to his people along with other benefits of civilization.[54]

The indigenous religion of Tibet, called Bonism (or Pönism in some formulations), was a kind of polydemonism devoted to placating the spirits of that bleak and austere land. It featured animal sacrifice and sometimes human sacrifice, and other ritual offerings to the spirits. Magic words and magic dances were all part of a pattern of averting the damage that evil or capricious spirits could bring to humankind. The advance of Buddhism in Tibet was interrupted in the eighth century by an epidemic which supporters of Bonism persuaded the people was due to the wrath of the old gods. Temples were destroyed and Buddhist leaders were forced to flee the country.[55]

Buddhism returned in force with the arrival, in the same century, of the great Indian Buddhist tantric scholar, Padma Sambhava. The tantric forms which he introduced replaced a great many of the Bonist rites and skillfully incorporated the others. As a result of the latter process, Tibetan Buddhism, particularly in its popular form, has been preoccupied with the efficacy of diagrams and formulas such as "Om mani padme hum." Instead of the demons, there were now Buddha figures, often of austere appearance and hard to know or placate. Tibetans have sought these ends by a variety of rites and practices, including innumerable sacred formulas, prayers, and prayer wheels. The last may not be a Tibetan invention, but has become a characteristic feature of Tibetan religion. It is essentially a cylinder revolving on its axis and containing a sacred formula or prayer which is presented to the Buddhas on each revolution. Some Tibetans have even had their prayer wheels turned by water power. In such ways the old magic returned in the new faith.

The Tibetan Buddhist monks are called *lamas* (meaning "one who is superior"). From the time of Padma Sambhava the monastic orders have been the central feature of Tibetan religion and society. It was traditionally regarded as a great honor for a son to become a lama. It has been estimated that prior to the Chinese Communist invasions of Tibet in 1950 and 1959, 20 percent of the male population were monks.

The monastic orders dwelt in vast, thick-walled monasteries designed for protection from Tibet's bleak climate. However, they soon became veritable fortresses held by powerful hereditary abbots whose temporal power was greater than that of the kings. Within these walls tantric beliefs and practices often made monastic celibacy the exception rather than the rule.

As is the case with monastic orders and movements in all faiths and all parts of the world, worldliness and reform have alternated in Tibetan Buddhism. Among the great names in Tibetan history are those of men who arose to call the monks back from fighting, politicking, and wenching to their vocation of meditation and compassion. One such was the great Indian monk, Atisha, who arrived from Nalanda in 1042 and instituted fundamental and thorough reform. Atisha taught Tantrayana as the third vehicle, the sequel and culmination of both Hinayana and Mahayana.[56] Yet his interpretation of Tantrayana was a purified version, purged of its overt eroticism and reinfused with spiritual meaning. Atisha's work of reform and revitalization was carried further by the Tibetan monk Marpa (1020–1097) and his student and successor, Milarepa (1040–1123). Both are still reverenced as religious and also as cultural leaders. Milarepa's religious poetry is still read and cherished. It has been translated into English.[57]

An event which Tibetan Buddhists recall with pride was the appointment by the Chinese Emperor Kublai Khan of the Grand Abbot of Tibetan Buddhism as Kuo-Shih, "instructor of the nation," i.e., to all of China. Kublai Khan was an interested inquirer into many faiths, but he apparently concluded that lamaism was best adapted to the needs of his people. This abbot, Phakpa by name, was also given by Kublai Khan supreme authority over all of Tibet, making him the first lama who was sovereign ruler of the country.[58]

Still another significant wave of monastic reform swept over Tibetan Buddhism in the fourteenth century under the great monk and reformer, Tsong-kha-pa. From this reform Tibetan Buddhism emerged in substantially the form it held until its recent destruction by the Chinese Communists. There are three main orders of monks. The largest is the Gelukpa school often called by Westerners the Yellow Hat sect, founded by Atisha, reformed by Tsong-kha-pa, and ruled by the Dalai Lama. Next in size is the Old Translation school, which goes back to Padma Sambhava, and is sometimes erroneously identified by Western scholars as the Red Hat school. The third in size is the Kagyupa school founded by Marpa, and accurately designated as the Red Hat school. The Grand Lama of the Yellow Hat monastery at Lhasa acquired the name *Dalai Lama* in the sixteenth century. In response to a request from a Mongol chieftain, the Lama journeyed to Mongolia to revise and revive Buddhism. The grateful chieftain gave him the title *Dalai,* meaning "the sea," that is, measureless and profound.

The Dalai Lama was until his flight to India in 1959 the temporal as well as the spiritual leader of his people. He was conceived to be an incarnation of Avalokita, while the Panchen Lama, abbot of the Tashilumpo monastery, who stood second in the hierarchy, was regarded as an incarnation of Amitabha. It is worth noting that the latter abbot and order have throughout modern Tibetan history been sympathetic to China, while the Dalai Lama has, by contrast, looked to India. For some years after the Chinese conquest the Panchen Lama was maintained by the conquerors as a puppet ruler and leader of Tibet, but recent reports indicate that he too has been liquidated.

Tsong's fourteenth-century reform of Tibetan monasticism led to the strict imposition of celibacy, thus ending hereditary monastic rule and creating the problem of succession. It was solved by the Tibetans with the world-famous theory of the reincarnation of the head lamas in their successors. The present Dalai Lama is the fourteenth in succession. A Tibetan account of his selection tells of signs and miracles perceived by a Tibetan governmental official called the State Oracle indicating the location of the Dalai Lama's new birthplace.[59] Other visions and oracles were perceived, and in response a searching mission disguised as ordinary pilgrims set out for the distant Amdo Province of China. Finding the supernaturally indicated house, they came to the boy, who was said to greet the travelers with recognition. He also identified belongings of the previous, recently deceased Lama. Securing permission from the lad's parents, the embassy took him back to Lhasa and with pomp and ceremony installed him as Dalai Lama.

Tibetan Buddhist devotion has been directed to many figures in addition to Avalokita and Amitabha. The former has in Tibet, in accordance with tantric tradition, a wife named Tara, who is a goddess of great power and equal goodness. For those who need and want theology, there are elaborate bodies of speculation which seek to systematize or rationalize these religious practices. Over wide areas of both practice and belief, Tibetan Buddhism does not greatly differ from Mahayana Buddhism elsewhere.

Tibetan Buddhism as well as traditional Tibetan life came to a sudden and violent end with the invasions by the Communist Chinese in 1950 and 1959. For many centuries Tibet had been claimed by both India and China. Since the fall of the Manchu dynasty in China, Tibet had asserted her autonomy, and both India and China had recognized it. However, in 1950 the Chinese invaded the little land and placed a puppet government in power, thus forcibly securing Chinese hegemony. The Tibetans remained restive and rose in hopeless rebellion in 1959 under the leadership of the Dalai Lama. Chinese arms promptly and ruthlessly destroyed the opposition. The Dalai Lama and some of his followers made good their escape to India, where they remain today as refugees. A United Nations investigation condemned the Chinese action as genocide, but was unable to do anything about it. The future of Tibetan Buddhism as of the Tibetan nation today remains clouded.

At this point we must temporarily terminate our story of the way of the Buddha, promising to resume it later in other contexts. So far we have seen its rise and fall in ancient India, and its establishment both in southeast Asia and in Tibet. Yet, long as this chapter has been, it is only a beginning. The story of Buddhism will be resumed in Chapter 8 on Chinese religion and Chapter 9 on Japanese religion.

Meanwhile enough has been said for the student to begin to construct his picture of the Buddhist way or path. It is a way in which not God but man and his salvation (or health) are central. For this reason Buddhist devotion is meditation rather than worship or prayer defined as communion with deity. The differences between Buddhist values and Judeo-Christian values may be seen by comparing Buddhist Nirvana with the Judeo-Christian heaven, for teachings about the hereafter frequently illuminate the ways in which men think about the "herein." The Buddhist faith (or more accurately, vision) has shown a persistent power to interact with different human societies, producing notable traditions of art, ethics, philosophy, religion, and other cultural forms.

CONCLUDING COMMENT

Like Mahavira and the anonymous seers of the Upanishads, Buddha was a man of ancient India's Axis age. He appears as the boldest mind and spirit of the time, and his influence is still strong upon the system of devotion and thought which he originated.

Is there an identifiable cluster of values or concerns which is taken as ultimate by the Buddha and his early and Indian followers? The center of this cluster is Nirvana, which was Buddha's way of saying moksha or salvation by emancipation from mortal existence. Around this center are grouped Buddha's other teachings. In contrast to Jain extremism, he sought a middle way to salvation; he consciously avoided extremes of practice and teaching. His philosophy, challenging other contemporary ways and problems, may be described as a series of pointers toward salvation or emancipation. He had his own distinctive interpretation of karma-samsara, and of the vast, beginningless and endless cycles of historic time. His ethic was poised in creative tension between the values of detachment and compassion for fellow creatures. Such was Buddha's path or pattern of ultimate values.

As we have seen, Buddha embodied and exemplified his teachings, and hence was early regarded by his followers as a more than human figure. Of the two main forms of Buddhism, Mahayana pushed this tendency vastly further than did Theravada; these two contrasting Buddhist ways or paths were constituted largely in terms of this distinction regarding the Buddha and other Buddha figures.

As to our second main question, why live? or what must I do and be to be human? we see a clear difference between Buddhism and the last chapter's Jainism. There is indeed such a thing as Buddhist humanism. Its basic values are compassion and intuitive wisdom, which in varying combinations constitute human fulfillment or realization, even though the full perfection of these values lies, as Buddhists would say, on the further shore. By his partial realization of these values, Buddhist man fulfills his humanity.

On the third question, namely which of our three main types Buddhism is, we must give a qualified answer. Clearly Buddha's teachings are of the second or acosmic type. Yet his followers in varying degrees made concessions to the cosmos. Of the two main groups, Theravada seems to have maintained its acosmic character with more consistency than Mahayana. The latter may perhaps be characterized as a central core of acosmic teaching surrounded and qualified by cosmic attitudes and ideas—and in the case of devotional or Pure Land Buddhism even by theistic or type-three elements as well.

NOTES

1. Burnett H. Streeter, *The Buddha and the Christ,* Macmillan & Co., Ltd., London, 1932; Masutani, *Buddhism and Christianity: A Comparative Study,* Young East Association, Tokyo, 1954.

2. Henry C. Warren, *Buddhism in Translations,* Harvard University Press, Cambridge, Mass., 1922, pp. 38f.

3. A. L. Basham, *The Wonder That Was India,* Grove Press, Inc., New York, 1954, p. 257.

4. Warren, *op. cit.,* pp. 66–67.

5. For different interpretations of the experience of enlightenment see Warren, *op. cit.,* pp. 67f.; Basham, *op. cit.,* p. 258; Kenneth Morgan (ed.), *The Path of the Buddha,* The Ronald Press Company, New York, 1956, p. 8.

6. Morgan, *op. cit.,* p. 8.

7. *Ibid.,* pp. 3f.

8. T. W. Rhys Davids, *Buddhism,* Society for Promoting Christian Knowledge, London, 1903, p. 160.

9. Morgan, *op. cit.,* p. 35.

10. Warren, *op. cit.,* p. 109.

11. Heinrich Zimmer, *Philosophies of India,* Meridian Books, Inc., New York, 1957, p. 473.

12. Warren, *op. cit.,* p. 101.

13. Ninian Smart, *Doctrine and Argument in Indian Philosophy,* George Allen & Unwin, Ltd., London, 1964, chap. II, pp. 34f.

14. John B. Noss, *Man's Religions,* rev. ed., The Macmillan Company, New York, 1956, p. 167.

15. Morgan, *op. cit.,* pp. 25–26.

16. *Ibid.,* p. 107.

17. *Ibid.,* pp. 109–110.

18. Davids, *op cit.,* pp. 109–110.

19. V. Fausböll, *Sutta Nipata,* Sacred Books of the East Series, Oxford University Press, London, 1881, pp. 6f.

20. Clarence H. Hamilton (ed.), *Buddhism: A Religion of Infinite Compassion,* The Liberal Arts Press, Inc., New York, 1952, p. 99.

21. *Ibid.,* title.

22. *Metta Sutta,* quoted from Morgan, *op. cit.,* p. 94. This passage is also in *The Sacred Books of the East,* Charles Scribner's Sons, New York, 1897–1903, vol. X, part 2, p. 25.

23. Basham, *op. cit.,* p. 286.

24. Hamilton, *op. cit.,* p. 65.

25. *Ibid.,* pp. 100–103.

26. Zimmer, *op. cit.*, p. 474.

27. Morgan, *op. cit.*, pp. 68–70.

28. James Bissett Pratt, *The Pilgrimage of Buddhism*, The Macmillan Company, New York, 1928, p. 129.

29. Morgan, *op. cit.*, p. 75.

30. T. R. V. Murti, *The Central Philosophy of Buddhism*, George Allen & Unwin Ltd., London, 1955, p. 35.

31. Ludwig Wittgenstein, *Tractatus Logico-Philosophicus*, The Humanities Press, Inc., New York, 1961, p. 151.

32. William T. de Bary (ed.), *Sources of Indian Tradition*, Columbia University Press, New York, 1958, pp. 106–108.

33. *Ibid.*, pp. 108–109.

34. *Ibid.*, p. 109.

35. Morgan, *op. cit.*, p. 86.

36. *Ibid.*, pp. 104–107.

37. de Bary, *op. cit.*, p. 120.

38. *Ibid.*, p. 143.

39. *Ibid.*, p. 138.

40. *Ibid.*, p. 191.

41. Zimmer, *op. cit.*, pp. 474–476.

42. *Ibid.*, p. 488.

43. Basham, *op. cit.*, p. 275.

44. For discussion of analogous issues in the history of Christian thought, see H. Bettenson, *Documents of the Christian Church*, Oxford University Press, Fair Lawn, N.J., 1947.

45. See *inter alia* Alice Getty, *The Gods of Northern Buddhism: Their History, Iconography and Progressive Evolution Through the Northern Buddhist Countries*, Oxford University Press, London, 1928.

46. Sarvepalli Radhakrishnan and Charles A. Moore (eds.), *Sourcebook in Indian Philosophy*, Princeton University Press, Princeton, N.J., 1957, p. 340.

47. Zimmer, *op. cit.*, p. 521.

48. Murti, *op. cit.*, pp. 123–124.

49. Radhakrishnan and Moore, *op. cit.*, pp. 333–337.

50. Basham, *op. cit.*, p. 280.

51. de Bary, *op. cit.*, p. 193.

52. *Ibid.*, pp. 198–199.

53. Zimmer, *op. cit.*, p. 572.

54. Morgan, *op. cit.*, p. 238.

55. *Ibid.*, p. 239.

56. *Ibid.*, p. 243.

57. Garman C. C. Chang, *Hundred Thousand Songs of Milarepa*, Universal Books, Hyde Park, N.Y., 1962.

58. Morgan, *op. cit.*, p. 248.

59. *Ibid.*, p. 257.

SUGGESTIONS FOR FURTHER STUDY

Arnold, Sir Edwin: *The Light of Asia*, any edition.

Bharat, A.: *The Tantric Tradition*, Rider, 1965.

Buddhist Scriptures, trans. E. Conze, Penguin, 1951.

Burtt, E. A. (ed.): *The Teachings of the Compassionate Buddha*, Mentor Books, 1955.

Conze, E.: *Buddhism, Its Essence and Development*, Philosophical Library, 1954.

Coomaraswami, A.: *Buddha and the Gospel of Buddhism*, Putnam, 1913.

Davids, T. W. Rhys: *Buddhism*, Society for Promoting Christian Knowledge, 1903.

de Bary, W. T. (ed.): *Sources of Indian Tradition*, Columbia, 1958.

Hamilton, C. (ed.): *Buddhism: A Religion of Infinite Compassion*, Liberal Arts, 1952.

King, W.: *Buddhism and Christianity*, Westminster Press, 1962.

———: *A Thousand Lives Away*, Oxford, 1964.

Lin Yutang: *Wisdom of India and China*, Modern Library, 1945.

Morgan, K. (ed.): *The Path of the Buddha*, Ronald, 1956.

Murti, T. R. V.: *The Central Philosophy of Buddhism*, G. Allen, 1955.

Pratt, J. B.: *The Pilgrimage of Buddhism*, Macmillan, 1928.

Radhakrishnan, S.: *History of Indian Philosophy*, G. Allen, 1929–1931.

——— (ed.): *History of Philosophy, Eastern and Western*, G. Allen, 1952.

——— and C. Moore (eds.): *Sourcebook in Indian Philosophy*, Princeton, 1957.

Saunders, K. J.: *Gotama Buddha,* Association Press, 1920.

Smart, N.: *Doctrine and Argument in Indian Philosophy,* G. Allen, 1964.

Soothill, W. E.: *The Lotus of the Wonderful Law,* Oxford, 1930.

Streeter, B. H.: *The Buddha and the Christ,* Macmillan, 1932.

Waddell, L. A.: *The Buddhism of Tibet,* Heffer, 1958.

Warren, H. C.: *Buddhism in Translation,* Harvard, 1922.

6

HINDUISM

WHAT IS HINDUISM?

The problem of terminology with which we have wrestled in preceding chapters becomes acute in the present chapter, for several reasons. *Hinduism* is, as previously noted, a modern Western term, dating from the early nineteenth century. While the word *Hindu* is of older and wider occurrence in India, its origin is Persian. (*India* is derived from the same source.) What this means is that few of the people included within the popular designations of Hindu or Hinduism have themselves used these labels. Some recent Indian writing has proposed the alternative term, *Sanatama Dharma,* meaning "eternal teaching or religion"; but this presents even more formidable problems.[1]

Another issue is raised by the extension of the terms *Hindu* and *Hinduism.* Just how much of the vast accumulation of religious phenomena in Indian history is to be embraced by these terms, and on what basis are the inclusions and exclusions to be made? Mention has already been made of the fact that Jainism and Buddhism are usually regarded as heretical and therefore excluded. Yet there are no formal authorities recognized by all or most adherents of the Hindu faith; Hinduism has no pope and no bishops to rule on such matters.

The sole effective authority seems to be the longtime operation of public opinion. The student has no alternative but to regard as within the bounds of this faith what its adherents have so regarded.

Another kind of issue is raised by the contention that Hinduism is, for one reason or another, not a religion. The claim is sometimes made that it lacks one or more of the necessary features of a religion; or it is alleged that this is not simply a religion but a total way of life. Neither of these strictures need delay us long. Chapter 1 guarded against the first by the definition of religion as a system of holy forms. Clearly Hinduism is such a system, though profoundly different from other such systems, particularly those of the West, and demanding to be understood in its own terms. Indeed, the term *dharma* as a synonym for Hindu religion will not be seriously misleading. The contention that the Sanskrit language has no term for "holy" appears not to be factual, there being at least several words which render this meaning.

Chapter 1 should also have prepared us for the contention that Hinduism is a total way of life or that its effects are spread widely throughout traditional Indian culture. As the student of man's religions sees the varieties of relation between faith and culture in the long course of history, he will not be greatly surprised at the fact that this central Indian religious tradition bears a unique and significant relation to virtually the whole of Indian society.

Chapter 3 likened Indian religious history to a geological landscape. The present chapter brings us to its most recent strata. Geological analogy can help us here with its concept of outcroppings. Just as very ancient layers of rock lie exposed on the surface of the earth as outcroppings alongside more recent strata, so in India's religious landscape, one may hear a Brahman priest chanting a Vedic mantra and see nearby a shrine or temple of more recent origin or see a procession devoted to some twentieth-century phenomenon. The leaders of Hinduism claim to be the inheritors of the whole Vedic tradition, as described in Chapter 3; and the only question which the student of religion would wish to raise is whether they are the sole legatees of this tradition. It is even possible to observe in contemporary Hinduism the influence of pre-Aryan Dravidian elements in such phenomena as the continuing vitality of the god Shiva. Not even Buddha and Mahavira can be excluded from these influences, for the historical development of Hinduism must be understood as among other things a reaction to these faiths. In order to absorb (or reabsorb) Buddhism, Hinduism incorporated into itself Buddhist elements. The Lord Buddha elicited a response of personal devotion from his followers—as many another religious founder before and since. One notable Hindu response was a new accent and emphasis on bhakti, or devotional religion. Hence it has been said of one group of devotees that they literally sang Buddhism out of south India.

During the crucial millennium of its historical development (roughly from

500 B.C. to A.D. 500) a great many different historical causes and conditions influenced emerging Hinduism. Caste lines hardened and castes proliferated, with the result that caste came to express in massively conservative fashion the interdependence of life within Indian society. *Bhakti marga,* or personal devotion, developed as a way of faith of enormously wider social appeal than the more aristocratic and austere ways of ritual works (*karma marga*) and knowledge (*jnana marga*). In these and countless other ways Hinduism came more and more to be an inclusive expression of the Indian community and tradition.

The main forms of belief, practice, and not least of all, feeling, which have constituted Hinduism were in existence before the end of the first millennium in the Christian era. Nevertheless Hinduism continued to serve as the Indian faith during two important succeeding periods—and to be significantly influenced by this historic function. First was the approximately 750 years of Muslim domination (999–1757) and second the 250 years of European domination (1757–1947).

Mahmud of Ghaznin broke into India in A.D. 999, beginning over two decades of raids and depredations and three-quarters of a millennium of Muslim rule, during which the relation between Islam and Hinduism was a centrally important issue, both religiously and politically. At first Islam was a hostile faith of alien conquerors who in the service of Allah smashed Hindu temples and massacred Hindu people. In later periods Islam put down its own roots in Indian soil; but the problem of its relation to Hinduism has never achieved a solution satisfactory to either religion. Muslims sought to convert Hindus, Hinduism sought to absorb Islam. Neither succeeded. One Indian reformer, Nanak, troubled at the ill will between Islam and Hinduism, sought to transcend these differences; ironically he succeeded in founding still another religion, Sikhism, which fought both Islam and Hinduism. (Sikhism is the subject of Chapter 7.) Meanwhile during the Muslim centuries, Hinduism was greatly strengthened in its historic role as India's faith.

The eighteenth and nineteenth centuries brought the European West in force to India and thus confronted Hinduism with a new challenge. Would India desert her ancestral faith for Western Christianity or for a modern, secular, nonreligious path of life? Indian answers to these questions have, as usual, varied over a wide spectrum, yet the dominant answer to date has linked Hinduism closely with emerging Indian nationalism. Yet to this it must be added that the voices of nationalism in Hindu faith have never completely drowned out those which seek to speak a Hindu message to all humankind.

Throughout its long history Hinduism has had few if any institutional forms which extended to all its vast and various community of adherents, who now number between 300 million and 400 million people.[2] Its unity is the unity and historical continuity of Indian culture. In its infinite variety of rites, attitudes, beliefs, and practices only two appear to be common to all Hindus: (1) acknowledgment of the validity of the Vedas and (2) the practice of caste. Even for these two recurring features, important qualifications will prove necessary.

SOURCES OF HINDUISM

To what documents and other sources shall the student look for the history of Hinduism? First he will recognize that Hinduism was the inheritor of much that had gone before, specifically of the Vedas and the whole Vedic tradition—though, one hastens to add, molded and interpreted in terms of later tradition. After the close of the Vedic period other documents emerged to give expression and distinctive shape to developing Hinduism. They were, and still are, for Hindus smriti and not shruti (literally "remembered" and not "heard"), that is, religious classics and not canonical scripture. Nonetheless their authority is very great, and in some cases they are more frequently read than the canonical Vedas. Among these classical documents, none has been more influential in the development and maintenance of religious practice than the Code of Manu (ca. 200 B.C.). The later Yajnavalkya Code (ca. A.D. 200) has wielded similar influence. They illustrate the type of literature known to Indians as *dharma shastra,* or manuals for moral guidance.

India's two great epics, the *Mahabharata* and the *Ramayana,* have been fruitful sources of religious images and ideas as well as tales of divine and human heroes and heroines in their never-ending adventures and misadventures. The *Mahabharata,* traditionally attributed to the sage Vyasa, is the story in Sanskrit poetry of the great Bharata War. (The Bharatas were one of the principal tribes of the ancient Aryan invasion.) Consisting of over 100,000 stanzas, the *Mahabharata* is the world's longest poem. Stripped of its many interpolations, it tells the ancient and heroic tale of internecine struggle and war in the Bharata tribe. The throne of the *Kurus,* or *Kauravas* (a leading group among the Bharatas), fell to Dhrtarashtra, who was blind and was therefore barred from the throne. Hence it went to his younger brother, Pandu, who as the result of a curse renounced the throne for an ascetic's life. By default the crown reverted to Dhrtarashtra. When Pandu died, the heirs-apparent were his five sons, Yudhishthira, Bhima, Arjuna, Nakula, and Sahadeva. However, the sons of the reigning Dhrtarashtra conspired against the true heirs.

The five sons of Pandu wandered forth for a time as soldiers of fortune. During their wandering, Arjuna won as wife Draupadi, who in order to avoid strife became the common wife of all five brothers. During the course of their wandering they also met their divine friend and helper, Krishna. Finally Dhrtarashtra recalled Pandu's sons and prepared to renounce his throne. His own sons, however, continued to connive to deny the succession to the sons of Pandu. Duryodhana enticed Yudhishthira into a gambling match in which with the help of a magician he won not only the kingdom, but also the brothers and their joint wife. A compromise settlement of this gambling debt was achieved

Arjuna's penance from *Mahabharata,* at Mahabalipuram
*Courtesy of the Government
of India Tourist Office*

according to which the five Pandavas went into exile for thirteen years after which they would return and receive the kingdom.

As this time approached, they sent word to Duryodhana demanding their kingdom. Receiving no answer, they began to prepare for the inevitable and climactic battle. All the kings and warriors of India and of kingdoms as far away as Greece and China lined up on one side or the other. The two armies met on the plain of Kurukshetra, traditionally located on the broad plain north of Delhi. There for eighteen days the great battle raged, until at the end no one on either side was left alive except the five Pandava brothers and their divine helper, Krishna. Yudhishthira finally received his kingdom, and with his brothers and their wife lived peacefully and gloriously. At the close of the poem, Yudhishthira renounced his throne in favor of Arjuna's grandson, and the five brothers and wife set out for the Himalayas where they climbed up to the City of the Gods.

The *Ramayana,* shorter than the *Mahabharata,* is attributed to the sage Valmiki. It tells the story of the trials and tribulations of the righteous Prince Rama and his equally virtuous wife Sita. Rama was cheated of his succession to the throne and retired to the forest with his wife, who was then abducted and carried off to Ceylon by the demon king, Ravana. She was rescued by her husband, who was assisted by the monkey god Hanuman and his army of valiant monkeys. Finally Rama was restored to his throne, where with Sita he reigned happily. There is a final book of the *Ramayana* in which Rama, while knowing fully his wife's innocence while she had been a prisoner in Ceylon, nonetheless yields to popular rumor and opinion and divorces her. Thus the *Ramayana* is given a somewhat tragic ending. Modern scholars are divided in their view of this ending, some holding that it formed no part of the original poem but was added later. However this may be, Rama and Sita have lived on in Indian imagination as the ideal king and queen, and husband and wife.

Not only have the epics served as sources for countless religious images and themes; they have, particularly in their more popular versions, served as vehicles of popular devotion and feeling for countless generations of Indians. They illustrate the fact that Indian literature lacks a precise line separating the sacred and the secular realms of life and thought.

Probably the most influential single document in Indian religious history is the *Bhagavad Gita.* Most scholars believe that it was originally one of many interpolations in the *Mahabharata,* but for many centuries it has been an independent document, and has been the classical source of bhakti, though it is by no means the first or only source. Dating from around the third century, it begins as a conversation between the Pandu warrior Arjuna and his charioteer, who turns out to be the god Krishna, and who also turns out to dominate the conversation with his expositions of traditional Hindu faith culminating in the bhakti marga, or way of devotion. The *Gita* gives clear evidence of multiple authorship in its inclusion of several distinguishable viewpoints. Many scholars find in it an attempt to combine monistic Aryan thought with the dualistic viewpoint of Sankhya philosophy. The *Gita's* repeated listing of virtues which are distinctively Buddhist suggests that the author was deliberately incorporating Buddhist elements in this statement of Hindu faith. Other commentators point to its attempt to affirm and combine the viewpoint of action with that of devotion. It may be characterized as the document into which flowed the whole previous tradition and out of which emerged virtually the whole subsequent Hindu tradition. The influence of the *Gita* is in important measure due to this synoptic viewpoint. To the analysis of the *Gita* we shall return later in this chapter.

Still another kind of document functioned as a Hindu source, namely, the *Puranas* (or Ancient Tales). Eighteen Puranas exist, of which the best known are the *Bhagavata,* the *Vayu, Vishnu,* and *Agni.* They do not antedate the Gupta period of Indian history (A.D. 300–500) and their content is a miscellany of tales, teaching, and other matters. While clearly not as great as many of the earlier works of Indian religion, their importance as sources of popular piety is very great.

To this list of source documents, it is important to add the qualification that significant aspects of Hinduism will elude us if we limit our study solely to literary sources, for Hinduism is above all a tradition of innumerable people, past and present, whose behavior has no significant relation to written sources. Their actual practices in the great cities and countless villages of India are the all-important source for the study of Hinduism. This is the importance of what is termed "popular Hinduism."

FOUR ENDS OF MAN

As has been repeatedly observed, the chief end of human life in Hinduism is moksha, conceived as emancipation from all those fetters, hindrances, and delusions which taken together constitute human experience and personality. Yet with Hinduism's inclination toward inclusiveness, it is not surprising that in the course of history other goals were added to form the traditional tetrad. It is Hinduism's claim to offer something to everyone and to every condition and stage of human life. The four ends of man help to make good this claim; together they provide scope and expression for all the varied capacities of man's life. The traditional four ends of man (*purushartha*) are duty, or righteousness (*dharma*), material success (*artha*), love, or pleasure (*kama*), and emancipation (*moksha*).

DHARMA

The first aim, dharma (from *dha,* meaning "to sustain"), is the moral law and order which sustain the world, society, and the individual. Construed as a human virtue, dharma is best translated as righteousness or duty. It is moral virtue, held and pursued in the religious context of Hinduism.

Dharma is a pervasive goal of Hinduism, and to its pursuit all men are exhorted. Hindu literature and philosophy are devoted to the study of the science of dharma. For example, the hero of the *Ramayana* is said to be a veritable incarnation of dharma;[3] and the hero of the *Mahabharata* proclaims dharma as its content and message: "With uplifted arms I cry, none heeds; from dharma, material gain and pleasure flow; then why is not dharma pursued? Neither for the sake of pleasure, nor out of fear or avarice, no, not even for the sake of one's life should one give up dharma; dharma stands alone for all time; pleasure and pain are transitory."[4]

The content of dharma varies with an individual's position in society and station in life. As traditionally interpreted, dharma appears to lack the assumption of human equality so basic to Western morality and ethics. While it assumes the unity of life and the universality of duty, it is duty construed within the context of inequality of different persons and classes (castes) and different stages of life. For the young man, dharma implies the duties of the student, for a mature man, those of the householder, and for an older man, possibly those of *sadhu* and *sannyasin*. It always includes observance of caste and of the religious ritual appropriate to one's position in life. The continuing and constant element in dharma may perhaps be described as harmonious but unequal order, first of the individual person, then of society, and finally of the universe, as these fields of experience are envisioned by Hinduism. Here truly is a morality of "my station and its duties."

ARTHA

Artha means material profit, but in many instances this idea is extended to include the necessary means or instrumentalities supporting any human activity. Notably it includes the instrumentality of politics and statecraft. Traditional Indian literature is studded with references to artha, but Kautilya's *Artha Shastra* (usually translated as "Treatise on Material Gain"), since it first came to light in 1905, has been taken as the classic statement of artha.[5] While it contains discussion of economic goods, it also includes many sections devoted to political problems.[6] The latter deal with the acquiring and maintaining of political power, in ways that read like Machiavelli's *The Prince*. Kautilya, the putative author of this document, is said to have been foreign minister of Chandragupta Maurya, grandfather of King Ashoka and founder of the Maurya dynasty.

The *Artha Shastra* lists three ends of human life, dharma, kama, and artha, but argues that the last is most important for the reason that on this foundation alone the other two can be realized.[7] The *Artha Shastra* and the subjects it treats are particularly important as a corrective for popular Western views of the Hindu mind as devoted solely to unworldly or superworldly goods. Here are a writer and a tradition within emerging Hinduism who bid us pursue worldly goods with open-eyed realism. In Zimmer's formulation, here is a "philosophy of time" rather than of eternity. The third end, kama, is also of time rather than of eternity.

KAMA

Kama is a protean thing, ranging from sexuality to the enjoyment of art.[8] *Kama* is the name of the Indian god of love. Like the Greek word *eros* it functions as both a proper and a common noun; and also like its Greek analogue, it embraces wide ranges of meaning. The *Kama Sutra* of Vatsyayana is a gentlemen's guide to sexual behavior and related topics.[9] This meaning of *kama* points to a significant strand of Indian tradition which may be characterized as a candid affirmation of sex as a human good. This attitude is also illustrated by erotic sculpture and painting such as those which adorn the temples at Konarak and Khajuraho.[10] Yet the main Indian tradition in sex morality, as illustrated by the Code of Manu and other dharma shastras, can only be characterized as conservative, indeed, austere to the point of asceticism. The reconciliation of these conflicting attitudes is no easier than of the many other dualities and diversities of Indian thought and life.

Kama includes not only overt sexuality but also what may perhaps be termed sublimated sexuality in art and culture. In this guise the pursuit of pleasure as the goal of life includes all the refinements of aesthetic experience and speculation as these occur in the various arts.[11] Again, it is not easy to reconcile this affirmation of pleasure with an overall view of life in which pleasure is regarded as a hindrance to emancipation or a fetter binding man to this passing world of flesh and matter. The Indians have not been unaware of these inner tensions among the four goals, and they have made many suggestions for harmonizing them. One suggestion takes the line that each end has its own proper time and place.[12] Another suggestion has been that both artha and kama exist in relation to dharma; if dharma be pursued, artha and kama will be added. Sometimes men have been enjoined to pursue artha and kama in ways conformable to dharma.[13]

MOKSHA

In any case the final and supreme goal remains moksha, or emancipation. The supremacy of moksha has been asserted by Hinduism in a variety of ways. The main image for this superworldly goal is that of absorption in Brahman, in which all finite and mortal conditions of life are overcome and transcended. Indian thought from the Axis age onward (including both Buddhist and Jain philosophies) has interpreted human freedom as emancipation and asserted it as man's supreme goal. (The sole exception, the Carvakas, or materialists, will be discussed later in this chapter.) The preoccupation of all these systems of thought and faith with the problem of time and the freeing of man from the "noose of time" may be cited as a specific illustration. Philosophic interpreta-

Wheel of the sun chariot
at Konarak

   *Courtesy of the Archeo-
   logical Survey of India*

tions may vary, but they are variations on the theme of human emancipation. While emancipation is regarded as a form of contemplative knowledge in which man sees, or sees through, the delusory character of mortal life, this knowledge has usually been achieved or at least accompanied by ascetic practices.

In addition to the achievement of moksha by saint or sannyasin, and to its envisagement by philosophers and seers, traditional Indian society has also placed its highest social valuation upon those individuals who are said to have achieved this supreme goal of emancipation. The common man, toiling amid the hindrances and illusions of this world, may not enjoy or immediately anticipate this fulfillment for himself, but he can acclaim those pioneers of the spirit who have done so. Sympathetically he can share in their achievement.

THREE PATHS TO SALVATION

The same Hindu tendency to inclusiveness which brought into being the four ends of man, has also created the three *yogas* (ways) or *margas* (roads). These roads of life may be characterized as configurations of thought, practice, and feeling designed to achieve emancipation for those who walk them. Which road a man chooses is a matter of temperament, tradition, individual aptitude, or social status. It is also important to note that the three paths are by no means mutually exclusive; the religious life of many devout Hindus is a combination of all three. The three paths are (1) personal devotion (bhakti), (2) works (karma) and (3) knowledge (jnana).

BHAKTI MARGA

The way of personal devotion is actually older and of wider occurrence than its classic statement in the *Bhagavad Gita*. The idea of a personal relation to a divine lord is at least intimated in several of the Upanishads and is clearly delineated in the *Shvetasvatara Upanishad*. It is as widely diffused as the idea and emotion of love in religious experience. Bhakti has a base, moreover, not only in Vedic tradition and in human nature, but also in Indian society. The practice of bhakti is more widely possible than the other two ways. The way of ritual works requires leisure time available only to an aristocrat, and the way of knowledge calls for both a guru, or teacher, and the intellectual capacity to respond to his teachings. However, the worker or tradesman going about his daily tasks is able to cherish and cultivate a love for his chosen lord.

From the *Gita* has stemmed a long tradition of devotional feeling, writing, and activity which continues to the present day. Yet the *Gita* itself is still widely read; it remains the prime source of bhakti.

The *Bhagavad Gita* is a Sanskrit poem of eighteen chapters or sections. As we have seen, it begins as a conversation between a Pandu warrior, Arjuna, and the Lord Krishna, who is an *avatara,* or incarnation, of Vishnu. Yet from the time of the *Gita* to the present, Krishna has been a deity in his own right. The portrait of Krishna in the *Gita* is accordingly an intrinsically important theme in Indian religion. The conversation moves from Arjuna's pacifism to the three paths of salvation, each of which is described and affirmed as in some sense valid. Yet bhakti is asserted as supreme.

In the *Gita*'s synoptic affirmation of all the options in every choice, many scholars have seen evidence for multiple authorship. Not only are all three margas affirmed, but there is acceptance and a fusion of two main philosophical viewpoints, of Sankhya-Yoga on the one hand and of Vedanta on the other. (These philosophic viewpoints will be sketched in the next section of this chapter.) Again, as we have seen, the *Gita* seeks to incorporate Buddhist values in its Hindu synthesis. Likewise all the gods are affirmed, though under the supreme lordship of Krishna. In this disposition to embrace every alternative, the *Gita* appears typically Indian.

The conversation between Arjuna and his charioteer which opens the poem takes place on the field where Kurus and Pandavas are drawn up for impending battle. Arjuna expresses dismay at the prospect of war's carnage and destruction as well as its evil social consequences (including the mixing of castes). He ends on the pacifist note that he prefers being killed to killing. Krishna's answer is that the real self, or atman, is essentially immortal, and that therefore both killing and being killed are illusory experiences. Both the words and the sentiments recall the *Katha Upanishad*.

> *Some say this Atman*
> *Is slain, and others*
> *Call It the slayer:*
> *They know nothing.*
> *How can It slay*
> *Or who shall slay It?*
>
> *Know this Atman*
> *Unborn, undying,*
> *Never ceasing,*
> *Never beginning,*
> *Deathless, birthless,*
> *Unchanging for ever.*
> *How can It die*
> *The death of the body?*
>
> *Knowing It birthless,*
> *Knowing It deathless,*
> *Knowing It endless,*
> *For ever unchanging,*
> *Dream not you do*
> *The deed of the killer,*
> *Dream not the power*
> *Is yours to command it.*[14]

In response, Krishna bids Arjuna to fight as a member of the noble or Kshatriya caste, whose divinely appointed duty is to fight. As the conversation continues, Krishna sketches two paths to salvation. One is the path of yogic meditation in which the human soul turns away from action to contemplation leading to absorption in Brahman, the Absolute Spirit, and the other path is that of action, but without concern for the fruits of action. As the argument continues, Krishna ranges widely over the main themes of Indian religion and philosophy. As the discussion turns from man to God or Brahman in Chapter VI the author makes a crucial distinction between lower Brahman and higher Brahman, identifying the former with Prakriti or Nature and the latter with Krishna, conceived even more clearly as a personal Lord or Savior. As the latter theme is developed, the monism of the Upanishads and Vedanta is depicted as a stage on the way to the personal relation to Lord Krishna, thus deliberately reversing the order of Vedantist monism. What is often called Indian theism begins clearly to emerge as an alternative religious option.

This view rises to dominance in Chapters XI and XII, which constitute the climax of the Gita. In XI Arjuna asks Krishna for a direct version of himself. Krishna responds by endowing Arjuna with a supernatural eye. Then follows the dazzling theophany of Krishna's universal forms. Arjuna exclaims:

> *Ah my God I see all gods within your body;*
> *Each in his degree the multitude of creatures,*
> *See Lord Brahma throned upon the lotus;*
> *See all sages and the holy serpent.*
>
> *Universal form, I see you without limit,*
> *Infinite of arms, eyes, mouths and bellies*
> *See and find no end, midst or beginning.*

The self disclosure or revelation of Lord or God to his human devotee is a theistic form or relation, similar to many such experiences depicted in the Judeo-Christian Bible or in the Qur'an. Similar too is the response of faith and love on the part of the human recipient. There is in all this one marked difference. The monotheistic religions depict God solely in ethically good forms. In sharpest contrast, Krishna's universal forms combine good and evil in bizarre and frightening combination, as Chapter XI of the *Gita* clearly shows.

As a personal Lord, Krishna claims Arjuna's loving devotion. While all three of the margas or puttis to salvation are affirmed as valid in the *Gita*, it is the way of devotion or bhakti which the *Gita* proclaims as supreme. Arjuna puts the central and crucial question:

Some worship you with steadfast love. Others worship God the unmanifest and changeless. Which kind of devotee has the greater understanding of yoga?[15]

Lord Krishna answers:

> *Those whose minds are fixed on me in steadfast love, worshipping me with
> absolute faith. I consider them to have the greater understanding of yoga.*
>
> *As for those others, the devotees of God the unmanifest, undefinable and
> changeless, they worship that which is omnipresent, constant, eternal, beyond
> thought's compass, never to be moved. They hold all the senses in check.
> They are tranquil-minded, and devoted to the welfare of humanity. They see
> the Atman in every creature. They also will certainly come to me.*
>
> *But the devotees of the unmanifest have a harder task, because the unmani-
> fest is very difficult for embodied souls to realize.*

> *Quickly I come*
> *To those who offer me*
> *Every action,*
> *Worship me only,*
> *Their dearest delight,*
> *With devotion undaunted.*

> *Because they love me*
> *These are my bondsmen*
> *And I shall save them*
> *From mortal sorrow*
> *And all the waves*
> *Of Life's deathly ocean.*

> *Be absorbed in me,*
> *Lodge your mind in me:*
> *Thus you shall dwell in me,*
> *Do not doubt it,*
> *Here and hereafter.*[16]

From bhakti is derived a high code of ethics which draws into its pattern many
threads from traditional Indian thought, ranging from the unity of all life to
the spiritual conquest of desire or pleasure, or the ideal of imperturbability.
All these are held together by the unifying insight of bhakti. Krishna declares
to Arjuna:

> *A man should not hate any living creature. Let him be friendly and compas-
> sionate to all. He must free himself from the delusion of 'I' and 'mine.' He
> must accept pleasure and pain with equal tranquillity. He must be forgiving,
> ever-contented, self-controlled, united constantly with me in his meditation.
> His resolve must be unshakable. He must be dedicated to me in intellect and
> in mind. Such a devotee is dear to me.*
>
> *He neither molests his fellow man, nor allows himself to become disturbed
> by the world. He is no longer swayed by joy and envy, anxiety and fear.
> Therefore he is dear to me.*

He is pure, and independent of the body's desire. He is able to deal with the unexpected: prepared for anything, unperturbed by anything. He is neither vain nor anxious about the results of his actions. Such a devotee is dear to me.

He does not desire or rejoice in what is pleasant. He does not dread what is unpleasant, or grieve over it. He remains unmoved by good and evil fortune. Such a devotee is dear to me.[17]

Not only has the *Gita* been India's most widely read and cherished religious classic, but from it has stemmed a continuing tradition of devotional poets, singers, and mystics who have kept the bhakti marga alive to the present day. To this company belong the *alvars* (poet-devotees of Vishnu) and the *nayanars* (poet-devotees of Shiva) as well as India's greatest modern poet, Rabindranath Tagore.[18]

KARMA MARGA

The way of works, or karma marga, is ancient, aristocratic, conservative, and for its adherents all-encompassing. Karma means both ritual and moral deeds, for Hinduism draws no sharp distinction between the two. One shades imperceptibly into the other. However, the primary emphasis is on ritual deeds. The most ancient sources of this way are the Vedas and the Brahmanas, but it is elaborated in precise detail in the dharma shastras, notably the Code of Manu. The way of works provides an appropriate ritual for every event of man's life, from cradle to the grave, and for every significant occasion of human society. To those who fulfill its requirements it promises salvation.

Here, as elsewhere in the infinite diversity of Hinduism, there are only a few recurring patterns. Among these are the five daily obligations, the offerings to the gods, to the seers, to the forefathers, to lower animals, and to humanity. The first is met by the performance of prescribed sacrifices. The offering to the seers consists of devotional reading and study of the Vedas. The offerings to animals and to humanity consist of giving food and alms.[19]

The offering to the forefathers consists of the Shraddha rites. These are sacrifices of water and food to one's father and other ancestors. For a year after the father's death these rites are required every month; thereafter, once a year. The offering of cooked rice balls covered with sesame and honey together with cereals and seasonal fruits is believed to restore the body of the deceased. It is deemed a great violation of filial piety not to perform Shraddha rites. A major motive for marrying and having children is to have one's Shraddha rites fully and correctly performed. Indian stories tell of confirmed celibates who married for this purpose.[20]

The life of an individual human being is invested with religious significance from the cradle to the grave by means of appropriate sacraments or symbolic ceremonies. One source lists forty such sacraments.[21] Of this number, particular importance is placed upon four or five which mark major milestones in the course of an individual life. The first is a birth ceremony performed by the newborn infant's father, in which Vedic prayers are repeated and the infant's tongue is rubbed with clarified butter and honey.[22] While there are ceremonies related to the naming of the child, to the first haircut, to the study of the Veda, the next major sacrament is that which celebrates a boy's coming of age in things religious. This age varies between eight and twenty-four years according to caste and other circumstances.[23] At this time members of the upper two castes receive their symbolic caste threads. The marriage ceremony is next in the course of an individual's life. The final sacrament is performed at death, and consists of the cremation of the body on a funeral pyre with appropriate mantras and expiation rites. Whenever possible, this sacrament takes place on the bank of a sacred river such as the Ganges.[24]

Beyond these common ritual activities, Hinduism entails wide varieties of religious practice, ranging from temple rituals to pilgrimages to sacred places and attitudes of reverential respect to the various kinds of holy men. A few of these practices will be described later in this chapter.

The Code of Manu and the various other source documents for the karma marga deal in detail with the obligation of moral as well as ritual actions. One primary duty is that of caste. The four main castes with their various duties and prohibitions are described in detail, and the massive authority of Indian religion is placed squarely behind the system.[25] Traditional Hindu defense of the caste system usually takes the form of asserting that caste is an expression of the interdependent character of human life and society, arguing that without caste Indian society might not have survived at all.[26]

The Code of Manu also deals with the status and duties of women. While a woman is by no means without rights, it is repeatedly asserted that she must remain throughout her life dependent upon men—first her father, then her husband. For a "woman is never fit for independence"; and "husband must be constantly worshipped as a god by a faithful wife." [27] These and innumerable other teachings are asserted as the content of dharma, or righteousness. The goal of a righteous life pursued with the guidance of the Code of Manu is the attainment of salvation. All three paths have this same destination.

JNANA MARGA

Jnana marga seeks salvation by philosophic knowledge. This is of course not knowledge in any ordinary secular sense. It is not knowledge which may be found between the covers of a book, but rather a contemplative intellectual vision of the sort first achieved by the seers of the Upanishads. Saving knowledge, or jnana, is the direct experience of this vision of the One Supreme Reality, together with the forms of study and the discipline of life which support and sustain it.

As saving knowledge consists of the vision of all-embracing unity, so the opposite of knowledge, avidya, consists of the delusion of separate, individual existence. The human individual may be compared to a single wave on the ocean, which during its momentary existence, may proudly assert its separateness from every other wave and from all else in the world. However, in the next moment the ocean reaches out and draws this wave back to itself. So indeed man's highest truth and greatest blessedness is to be emancipated from the delusion of separate, finite existence, and to be absorbed in Supreme Being.

To walk this path to salvation is the work of a lifetime, and requires not only hard study, but ascetic discipline of life. While the idea of the four stages of life, or *ashramas*, is by no means limited to jnana marga, they do find explicit exemplification here. (1) The first stage is that of the student of religion in which under the guidance of a guru the young man devotes himself to the study of the Vedas and Vedic tradition. (2) Upon completion of study, the young man takes a wife and enters upon the life of a householder. Here he must play out fully and faithfully the role of husband, father, and citizen. He must do so even though he realizes that this social way of life involves him in all sorts of stains, compromises, and injury to living beings. He will also perform faithfully all the appropriate rituals. Yet even in the midst of the world his heart is fixed on the distant goal of emancipation. (3) When his family has been reared and his skin is wrinkled and his hair white with age, the man is free to embark upon the third stage, a hermit's life. Then, detaching himself successively from all worldly objects, he seeks the fourth and final stage. His wife may accompany him up to this final stage, but presently seeing him liberated from all worldly bonds, she will depart, leaving him to meditate alone on the goal that lies before him. (4) The fourth stage is that of the sannyasin, who has achieved, in mind and heart at least, the final emancipation from mortality and union with, or absorption in, Ultimate Reality. While the final and complete absorption can only take place at death, the sannyasin is one who by following the jnana marga has achieved a direct experience of absorption in the trancelike state of *samadhi*. He is then *jivan mukti*; he has achieved emancipation while still living.

SIX VIEWPOINTS

Related to the jnana marga as specific applications and interpretations of its basic outlook are the six orthodox systems, or *darshanas*. Indian tradition has listed six philosophies as orthodox by their acknowledgment of the Vedas, and three as heretical, namely, Buddhism, Jainism, and Carvakas (India's indigenous tradition of materialism). Buddhist and Jain thought share some though not all of the assumptions of the orthodox systems.

The Carvakas tradition is significant for its virtually complete rejection of the orthodox traditions. Like philosophic materialism in the West from Lucretius onward, the major motivation of Carvakas seems to have been anticlerical and antireligious. In a tradition as sacral and often as extreme as that of India, such a critical tradition is at least understandable. Like many of its Western counterparts, this Indian tradition found in philosophic materialism a vehicle for its fundamental and often radical criticism of religion. The Carvakas philosophy is named for its supposed founder. But his dates and indeed his existence are matters of inconclusive argument. The *Carvaka Sutra* has been lost. The tenets of this philosophy have to be reconstructed from orthodox writings that describe it in order to refute it. Yet the existence of many orthodox refutations and polemics against Carvakas philosophy argue a continuing tradition. Men do not attack nonexistent philosophies.

Beyond its notes of ridicule and contempt for all persons and actions relating to things religious, the Carvakas philosophy mounted its attack, like many forms of Western materialism (and as the student will see in Chapter 8, like Chinese forms as well) by means of a combination of materialism, empiricism, skepticism, and an ethic of egoism and hedonism. In existing documents, there is little subtlety in blending these diverse and sometimes conflicting elements. At least a few twentieth-century Indian philosophers have sought to establish a continuity between this traditional philosophy and the dialectical materialism of Marxism.

Indians have termed the six orthodox systems *darshanas* (from the Sanskrit verb *drsh,* meaning "to see," hence, "viewpoints"). As one sees them in Indian history, they may also be characterized as different strands of tradition. In some areas they are mutually exclusive or incompatible, yet more often they overlap each other. All of them aim at the goal of emancipation, each offering its own interpretation of the knowledge necessary for this purpose. In this respect they might be called road maps for the journey to salvation. Not all of these viewpoints are equally alive today. Most recent and contemporary Indian philosophers tend to be followers of the sixth, or Vedanta, tradition and system, though in their varying formulations many have woven into their philosophies strands from one or more of the other traditions. Conversely, Vedantism may be said to have largely absorbed the other ways.

INDIAN LOGIC

The Nyaya philosophy is said to have begun with an ancient figure named Gautama, who was possibly a contemporary of the founder of Buddhism. He was nicknamed Aksapada (literally "footeyed," thus at least possibly one who spoke or lectured with his eyes fixed on his own feet). He was the traditional author of the *Nyaya Sutra*. However, the oldest authentic documents of this school are from the third century. Like other Indian philosophies, Nyaya seeks salvation by knowledge. However, Nyaya is distinctive in its concern with the problems of logic, semantics, and epistemology. *Nyaya* means "inference," and its adherents have been concerned to study and list the valid forms of inference, as well as the general conditions of knowing. Knowing, in turn, exists to facilitate emancipation. Nyaya recognizes four sources of true knowledge: (1) perception, (2) inference, (3) analogy, and (4) credible testimony. Inference is subdivided into inference from cause to effect, from effect to cause, and from perception to abstract principle. Three kinds of causes are recognized: (1) material, e.g., the wood of which this desk is made, (2) formal, e.g., the carpenter's blueprints, and (3) effective, or efficient, e.g., the carpenter's tools and activities.[28] Nyaya developed its own theory of the syllogism, as well as its interpretation of proof and doubt. It has a realist view of the relation of knowing to its objects, and hence illustrates the Zimmer hypothesis of a way which goes back in origin to India's ancient pre-Aryan past. It is also avowedly theistic in outlook. Both Nyaya and the closely related Vaishesika seek to establish the existence of deity by arguments from the design of the universe to a divine designer, and from the fact of motion to a prime mover. Yet all of its manifold distinctions and activities are aimed at the liberation of the soul.

ATOMISM

Vaisheshika philosophy is not only similar at many points to Nyaya, but has also been traditionally closely linked to it. Its originator was a third-century B.C. seer named Kanada. Like Nyaya, Vaisheshika has a realist view of knowledge; the object of knowing is regarded as independent of the mind of the knowing process. It is also pluralist in outlook; *Vaisheshika* means "particular," and refers to the belief that the world contains an irreducible plurality of real entities or atoms. Vaisheshika also contains what is probably history's oldest statement of an atomic system. Like Nyaya it aims at salvation as a result of true knowledge. The content of this saving knowledge consists of an awareness of the separateness of man's soul from all material existence. In this respect, Vaisheshika is often characterized as a matter-spirit dualism, like that of Jain philosophy, and also of Sankhya-Yoga.

DISTINCTIONISM

The Sankhya school is traditionally traced back to Kapila, a shadowy seventh-century B.C. figure, though its earliest reliable documents come from the third century of the Christian era. Like Vaisheshika, Sankhya seeks man's emancipation through knowledge of the separateness of the human soul from matter. The soul is inherently spiritual in nature, and salvation consists of an adequate realization of this fact. *Sankhya* means "distinction," that is, the capacity to distinguish spirit from matter. Originally Sankhya was nontheistic or atheistic. It had no God to effect or assist this realization; rather, each man must achieve it for himself. Bondage, on the other hand, was asserted to consist of a confusion, in fact as well as in ideas, of mind and matter. Actually, the soul as such can never be anything except free; but man's awareness of freedom is obscured and overlaid by matter, thus producing a state of ignorance which constitutes human bondage.

Surrounding this central core of teaching in Sankhya is a body of distinctive metaphysics and an equally distinctive and closely related psychology. This metaphysical system posits two basic elements of the universe, *Purusha* (or mind) and *Prakriti* (or matter). The interrelations of Purusha and Prakriti produce a kind of cosmic process which some Western students have likened to evolution. However, it is a cosmic process which repeats itself in undulating fashion, age after age, producing recurring cycles of evolution and devolution.

From this cosmic system and process are derived, by means of the various combinations of Purusha and Prakriti, the different types of individual human beings. Human souls differ in their combination of the three *gunas,* namely, intellect (*sattva*), active power or passion (*rajas*), and inertia (*tamas*). Taken together in distinctive combinations, the three gunas define a personality. Yet Sankhya regards them all as hindrances or impairments, that is, hindrances to emancipation. Hence it follows that personality, in the Western sense of that word, consists of a bundle of such hindrances or impairments, which bind man to the world. Accordingly it is the purpose of Sankhya to provide liberation from personality.[29]

In these three preceding darshanas, and in Yoga as well, the student observes the similarity of a realist and pluralist outlook. He will recall that this is also a feature of the heretical Jain philosophy. Again, in this connection attention is called to Zimmer's thesis that this outlook was originally part of the very ancient pre-Aryan past of India, in sharp contrast to the monistic idealism of the Aryan invaders which is to be seen in the sixth and last darshana, Vedantism.

YOGA

Yoga philosophy has traditionally been linked to Sankhya. In the view of some students, Sankhya provided the philosophy and Yoga the exercises and regimen for a single system or tradition. However, Yoga philosophy came in the course of time to have a Lord, an element which was originally lacking in Sankhya. The whole path of Yoga was then defined as a form of devotion or dedication to the Lord. Some scholars hold that originally Yoga was as nontheistic as Sankhya. Among the many traditions of Yoga, the Raja Yoga of Patanjali, second century of the present era, is perhaps the best known. Hatha Yoga is distinguished for its emphasis on physical exercises and control of the body.

Philosophically the two systems differ in terminology but agree in the basic feature of attributing human bondage to matter, and in seeking liberation by separating or distinguishing mind from matter. Yoga holds the human ego to be immersed in ignorance and affliction. From this bondage man can be emancipated by a realization of his spiritual nature. However, what is distinctive in Yoga is the way in which this realization is achieved, namely by an eightfold series of steps, demanding full participation of both body and mind. This eightfold way might be likened to an eight-rung ladder, at the top of which stands salvation. In order for the student of Yoga to make his way up these eight steps to salvation, he must have a guru who will impart to him through intimate personal relation the real meaning of the way of Yoga. While different traditions of Yoga differ at specific points and in their particular emphases, all would agree on these eight steps.

1. Restraint or self-control (*Yama*)
2. Observance of self-culture (*Niyama*)
3. Posture or control of the body (*Asana*)
4. Regulation of breath (*Pranayama*)
5. Restraint of the senses, or abstraction from sense objects (*Pratyahara*)
6. Concentration of attention (*Dharana*)
7. Meditation (*Dhyana*)
8. Emancipation (*Samadhi*) [30]

The similarity of Yoga to Buddhist meditation testifies to their common Indian origin. It is also strikingly similar to mystical disciplines in many of the world's traditions, which have also constructed their ladders to eternal blessedness. Often too they have been eight-rung ladders.

EXEGESIS (OR PURVA MIMAMSA)

Purva Mimamsa originated with Jaimini (fourth century B.C.) and is unique among the orthodox viewpoints for its deliberate rejection of speculative metaphysics and for its passionate belief in the absolute literal validity of the Vedas. *Mimamsa* means "interpretation," or as one writer has rendered it, "exegesis." [31] So completely true are the Vedas that there is no need for any deity to guarantee or establish their validity. Hence Purva Mimamsa is nontheistic or atheistic. In Western terms, this system might be characterized as atheistic fundamentalism.

The validity of the Vedas is explicated by a distinctive and subtle theory of verbal meaning. Words, this theory argues, are the outward expression of eternal, timelessly valid ideas. These Platonic ideas and their verbal expressions are altogether independent of the human processes of speaking and thinking by which they are apprehended and expressed. So, at least argues Purva Mimamsa.

In keeping with its characteristic literalism, Purva Mimamsa alone among the orthodox ways believes in a literal heaven inhabited by literal individual selves, thus rejecting the idea of unitive absorption so important to other orthodox systems. It believes this because the Vedas say so. In recent times Purva Mimamsa has made common cause with such organizations as Arya Samaj, which are devoted to the superiority of the Vedas and the India culture which has flowed from them, thus becoming in effect a religious expression of cultural nationalism.

VEDANTA

Vedanta means "end of the Veda" and refers to the source of this philosophy in such hymns of the *Rig Veda* as X.129, and the Upanishads. "End" here means fulfillment or realization. Vedanta derives also from the *Vedanta Sutras* of Bada-rayana (variously dated from the second century B.C. to the fourth century of the Christian era and also known as the *Brahma Sutras*), with their pithy, aphoristic comments and expositions of Upanishadic philosophy. Vedanta clearly is the most important, influential, and extensive of the six orthodox darshanas, both in the past and in the present.

In Western terms, Vedanta may be characterized as philosophic idealism both in its metaphysics and in its epistemology, that is, its approach to reality and to knowledge. Followers of Vedanta have differed in the degree of monism in their interpretations. Undoubtedly the most influential of interpreters was Shankara, author of the monistic, or *advaita*, Vedanta. There is no unanimity among experts concerning the dates of Shankara's life, yet the traditional dates (A.D. 788–832) seem as widely accepted as any alternative. He was a many-sided genius whose brief life left its imprint on many aspects of Indian culture. A devotee of Shiva and a poet as well as a philosopher, he was also a vigorous opponent of Indian Buddhism. His commentaries on the Upanishads and on the *Vedanta Sutras* emphasized the sole reality of Brahman, or Absolute Being. All else is *maya* (appearance). To be sure, many other things seem real enough from the viewpoint of everyday life. The trouble—or more specifically, the illusion—lies in this viewpoint. Looking from the aspect of eternity, or Brahman, we recognize the world for what it is, maya or delusory appearance. Shankara's philosophy is the most forthright expression in Indian philosophy of the transcendent One which (or whom) we meet in many guises among the world's religions. Stated in twentieth-century terms, this is a view of human experience which places supreme valuation on contemplation of the One, with corresponding devaluation of other forms of experience.

Shankara gave much attention to the relation of Brahman and maya. He likened the delusory appearance of the world to the apparent snake which turns out to be a rope, or to the magician's tricks. He also identified the world of appearance as the play or sport of the Absolute Reality.

Shankara conceded a qualified or partial reality to Brahman-with-personal-qualities (Saguna Brahman), to whom, as Lord, the religious devotee may relate himself in personal terms. Yet this aspect of Brahman is clearly subordinated to Nirguna Brahman, or Brahman-beyond-all-qualities, who (or which) must be apprehended by contemplative vision in a kind of transpersonal relation.

While Shankara's influence has constituted a major tradition in Indian philosophy, its monism has never gone unchallenged. Three centuries after him, the commentaries of Ramanuja (d. A.D. 1137) on the Upanishads and Sutras argued a higher degree of reality for individual objects and persons, both here and hereafter. Ramanuja's philosophy placed a higher valuation than Shankara's on the reality and significance of human personality, and also on man's personal relation to God. Later still Madhva (d. A.D. 1278) argued for an even plainer pluralism in philosophy. Many modern Indian philosophies such as those of Radhakrishnan and Aurobindo, while standing in the tradition of monistic idealism, make important qualifications in the direction of asserting affirmatively the reality of individual persons and objects and the common world of which they are parts.

POPULAR HINDUISM

All religions seem to show different faces to the intellectual and to the common man, so it is not surprising to find this true in Hinduism. Yet in Hinduism this distinction is more important than in many other religions, for a great measure of Hinduism's tenacious vitality lies in its hold upon the hearts of India's masses. Hence we must now ask what religion means to the average man in India as he goes about the business of life in the countryside, the villages, and the cities of the Indian subcontinent. In this connection, it is well to bear in mind the fact that India's population is still at least 75 percent rural.

As often is the case with large generalizations, some advance qualifications are in order. First, in a country as large as India regionalism is a fact of life, so we will not be surprised to find significant variants in Indian popular religion. Particularly important is the difference between north and south India. Second, life changes even in as massively traditional and conservative a society as India.

Some traditional patterns of caste are being eroded. These evidences of erosion are strikingly visible in the cities.

The religious practices of the common man and his innumerable brothers and sisters throughout India present a picture of infinite variety. There probably is an altar or shrine in the home (or in wealthy homes a room set apart as a chapel) where *puja,* or devotion, is performed by members of the family. In wealthier families there may be a Brahman priest who functions as a domestic chaplain. As the individual ventures forth into the community he may perform puja before roadside shrines to this or that god. He pauses to place a bouquet of flowers before a Shiva shrine with its lingam and yoni or to pour a libation of water or repeat a prayer before the symbol of some other god. He tosses a coin to a holy mendicant or perhaps joins a religious procession or enters the temple of some particular lord to do his devotions amid the buzzing confusion of other worshipers and then to go his way. The options that open before the individual are unlimited in number and variety.

He may join with others or go alone on pilgrimage to some famous temple or other holy place. An example of the latter is Hardwar in north India, where the holy Ganges River has its source. Pilgrims gather from all parts of India seeking purification from their sins by immersion in the icy waters. It may be the great cave of Shiva at Amarnath in Kashmir, where pilgrims gather by the thousand every August to worship at a frozen spring which forms a lingam of ice. Or it may be the sea at Cape Comorin, the southern tip of India, or the Magh Mela celebration at Allahabad in January, when hundreds of thousands of pilgrims crowd their way onto the beach and into the cold water where the Ganges and Jumna Rivers flow together.[32] All Hinduism's holy cities, Ayodhya, Dwarka, Mathura, Hardwar, Banaras, Kanchipuram and Ujjain are celebrated pilgrimage spots.

The Ganges is the most holy of India's many holy rivers, and its most holy place is at Banaras. So to Banaras people come from all parts of India to wash away their sins in the sacred waters of Mother Ganga. Not only does the pilgrim return home purified from past sins, but if he dies in this holy city his feet need only be immersed in the river's water for him to be assured of happiness hereafter. Thousands of pilgrims bottle some of the water to take home to friends or neighbors. For the faithful, Ganges water is a veritable medicine for all ills.

India has other sacred places to which the pilgrim may go to rekindle his faith or to acquire spiritual merit. There are innumerable hills and valleys, rocks, rivers, and caves sacred to some deity or sanctified by some reference in sacred scripture or legend. They dot the landscape from the Himalayas to Cape Comorin. Their faded and tattered yellow banners announce to the passerby that they are holy places where men pause to say a prayer, to do obeisance to higher—or in some cases lower—powers.

Times, days, and seasons are sacred in India. Probably no other religion or nation has so many holidays. Lord Krishna's birthday in September is celebrated in all parts of India. Likewise national in scope is Holi, which comes in late winter or early spring. It was originally devoted to Kama, the god of love, though now he has no apparent relation to it.[33] It is a kind of Hindu saturnalia, a time of universal merrymaking and license. Respectable citizens forget caste restrictions, scattering red powder over their neighbors, squirting them with red-colored water, and playing all kinds of practical jokes. The autumn festival to Durga is a notable holiday in Punjab. In some parts of Maharashtra the September festival to Ganesha or Ganpati takes on the proportions of contemporary Western Christmas with floats, parades, colored lights, and processions.

Indian piety has other kinds of attachments too, notably to sacred cows and to sacred men of various kinds. Reverence for cows, or cow protection as it is commonly called, is a widely occurring pattern. In many states of India it is forbidden on pain of capital punishment to kill cows. The sacredness of cows is historically rooted in their actual importance to the ancient Aryans and in the resulting references to cows in India's ancient and sacred writings. To most devout Hindus it appears sufficient to know that this is a part of their tradition.

This strict taboo has many consequences: it reinforces the traditional Indian vegetarian diet; it means that old and decrepit cattle cannot be dispatched; it means that the tanner's occupation is the lowest form of human life; it means continuing Hindu agitation against what is called "cow slaughter," that is, any killing of cows. Affection and respect for cows are shown by adorning them with flower garlands and anointing their hoofs with oil. It does not extend to such rational proposals as the development by scientific genetics of a better strain of cows. Cow dung and cow urine are sacred substances; a holy man may mat his hair with the former and anoint his body with the latter. In recent history Hindu reverence for cows has played a part in Hindu-Muslim tension. Hindu sensibilities are outraged by the fact that Muslims eat beef and also by the fact that most Indian butchers seem to be Muslims. No less a person than Gandhi has defended cow protection as a valuable and sacred symbol of the unity of life and of man's relation to the whole animal world.[34]

Men of many different sorts are sacred in Hinduism. First and most obvious in this category are members of the Brahman caste. In recent times there has been an erosion of the caste system, especially in the urban centers, but in the countless villages of India the Brahmans continue to claim and to receive from other men the traditional reverential respect. The four main castes are subdivided into hundreds and even thousands of subcastes which function in ways ranging from holy labor unions to exclusive clubs.

There are other kinds of holy men too. The sadhu and sannyasin are widely believed to be the repositories of spiritual and sometimes magic power, sometimes transcending the limitations of caste. The extremes of this pattern are well known even to people who know little or nothing else about India. Indian holy men recline on beds of spikes, skewer themselves with knives and swords, look into the sun until their eyes are blinded, sit in strange postures until their limbs are atrophied, and do countless other strange deeds to show their self-mastery. Yet such strange and masochistic extremes ought not to obscure the goal of Indian religion, to emancipate the spirit from the flesh, from time, and from mortal bondage of all sorts. It is this goal which gives religious significance to the activities of the sadhus. There are also countless holy men of humbler calling, whose holiness consists of the practice and the aphoristic teaching of traditional piety.

Indian popular religion shows a variety of gods equal to that of its religious practices. One Hindu scholar has written that in India the One Supreme Being is known in many ways and worshiped in many forms.[35] For India's masses these ways and forms are frankly polytheistic. Ancient efforts to order India's populous pantheon fixed the number of deities at thirty-three, eleven each in heaven, air, and earth. But later attempts increased the number to 33 crores, a crore being 10 million. So it is that deity may be conceived as one or as 330 million, according to one's viewpoint! Critically minded Hindus like to say that deity is one, but that the Supreme One is manifested in many forms.

A few deities stand out as particularly important. There is the mother goddess, known by many names and in many guises, some to be listed below. There is Ganesha the elephant, Nandi the bull, and Hanuman the monkey, and there is Kama, the god of love. As we have already observed, Krishna is a great god in his own right. So too are Rama and Sita. Yet preeminent among India's innumerable deities is the Hindu *Trimurti,* or Trinity, consisting of Brahma, Shiva, and Vishnu. This Trinity is often interpreted as Nature or the Universe in its three roles as creator, destroyer, and preserver.

Brahma, the creator, is not to be confused with Brahman, which is Absolute Reality. Brahma, while he has fewer than half a dozen temples and no contemporary cult of devotees, is important in both religion and art. Religiously, he stands in the background as the creator who set the world in motion. In art he is represented with four faces and often is depicted riding on a white swan or goose. His wife is named Sarasvati and is the patron of wisdom. In the guise of Prajapati, Brahma is said to have been born of the primal golden egg and in turn to have been the agent in creating the rest of the universe. The ordered structure of both nature and society derive from Brahma.

Shiva, the auspicious or shining one, is also known to his devotees as Mahadeva, the great god; and he surely is one of India's great gods. Descended from Rudra, the Dionysus of the Vedic pantheon, Shiva has retained many of Rudra's destroying and terrifying aspects. He is the expression of the vitality and dynamism of both nature and human nature, in both its destructive and creative aspects. Hence Shiva has both a terrifying and a gracious aspect. Innumerable groups of Shiva devotees have existed and do exist in all parts of India, including an enormous variety of people and religious attitudes, ranging in the past and present from asceticism to overt eroticism, from ascetics to bandits and prostitutes.

Around Shiva has grown up a luxuriant mythology. A well-known shrine, the eighth-century Elephanta cave temple on an island in Bombay harbor, displays the central lingam surrounded by nine massive pieces of sculpture depicting varying aspects of his many-sided life and activities. These are: (1) Shiva Nataraja, lord of the dance, (2) Shiva killing the demon of darkness, (3) the marriage of Shiva and Parvati, (4) Shiva as the source of the three rivers, Ganga, Jumna, and Sarasvati, (5) the Trimurti or three-form deity, Shiva, Brahma, and Vishnu, (6) Shiva as androgyne, that is, half male and half female, (7) Shiva and Parvati quarreling, (8) Mt. Kailasa shaken by the demon, Ravana, but stabilized by Shiva, and (9) Shivayoga, or lord of ascetics. The Shiva temple at Chidambaram in south India is sacred to the first of these roles, Shiva Nataraja. The figure of Shiva surrounded by a ring of fire, standing on the dwarf of world illusion and dancing the end of one world epoch and the beginning of the next is among the most familiar and popular figures in Indian art and religion.

Shiva has both wives and attendants, or *vehicles*. This last term is a technical word employed by Hinduism, meaning "carrier" or "that on or in which the deity rides." All major deities have such vehicles. In Shiva's case the principal vehicle is the bull, Nandi, who is frequently depicted in sculpture in front of Shiva temples. Shiva also has numerous consorts or wives. There is Kali, the black goddess, fierce and unapproachable, adorned with a necklace of skulls, and with four arms to flail her victims to pieces before she devours them. Yet Kali also has a kindly aspect; to her devotees she appears as the kindly mother. There is Parvati, gracious and kind; and Uma, the goddess of light. Among the incarnations of Parvati is Meenakshi, to whom the famous south Indian temple at Madurai is devoted. But there is also Durga, or Thaga, the fierce patroness of a cult of robbers and killers known as Thugs. For many centuries prior to their forcible suppression in the nineteenth century the Thugs served their goddess by making the waylaying and killing of travelers a fine art as well as a holy vocation.[36]

By means of these wives Shaivism has maintained a close relation to Shaktism, or the cult of the female. *Shakti* is a word of many meanings, ranging from the more or less personified idea of a god's power or energy to the mother goddess, and to a wife or consort of a god. In popular religion the word seems to embrace all or many of these varieties of meaning. In short, *Shakti* means "female power" and is exemplified by Durga, Kali, the goddesses Lakshmi (wife of Vishnu), Sarasvati (wife of Brahma), and many more as well. As Kali the mother goddess is a fierce fighter against demons, yet she is also depicted as a dispenser of grace. As Lakshmi she is the giver of good fortune; in this form she is depicted sitting on a lotus or being bathed by two attending elephants.

Nandi, the Sacred Bull
Courtesy of the Metropolitan Museum of Art,
Rogers Fund, 1946

As Sarasvati, the mother goddess is both the personification of the Sarasvati River and the patron of learning and wisdom.

Shaktism as the cult of female energy embraces a wide range of Hindu phenomena. Right-handed Shaktism might be termed the cult of sublimated eroticism whose characteristic emotions range from kindness and gentleness to aesthetic appreciation. To such attitudes and ways of life the mother goddess has inspired many Indians. Left-handed Shaktism, as it has traditionally been called, has been the cult of unsublimated eroticism, whose orgiastic forms of worship have been a matter of record in India for many centuries. These Hindu practices have sometimes made common cause with Buddhist forms of tantrism, as described in the last chapter. The central thought apparently was the same,

Trimurti, Elephanta cave temples, Bombay
Courtesy of the Government of India Tourist Office

namely, catharsis by holy indulgence. In this case the ritual had the additional dimension of serving the goddess who epitomized the female spirit.

Vishnu, who has rivaled Shiva in the number of devotees and the luxuriance of the mythology surrounding him, is also an expression of vital forces in nature and human nature. But it is vitality in kindlier ways and forms of expression than Shiva's. Vishnu is a god of love in several meanings of that many-faceted word. He is a lover of righteousness and a dispenser of divine grace to the aspiring human soul. But he also loves his wife Lakshmi as well as the innumerable maidens who gather admiringly around him. Vishnu's vehicle is the bird god Garuda. Vishnu has many great temples and groups of devotees in all parts of India.

Shiva, Lord of the Dance

Courtesy of the Metropolitan Museum of Art,
Purchase, 1946, Hicks Brisbane Dick Fund

A notable feature of the worship and mythology of Vishnu has to do with his many incarnations, or avatars. The word *avatara* means "descent," in this case that of the blessed Lord into the world of men and animals. Literally innumerable avatars are claimed and celebrated by Vishnu's followers. Yet myth and ritual have concentrated attention upon ten main ones, nine of which have occurred, with the tenth being expected in the near future. In some formulations each avatar defines a new age, the whole list thus constituting a Hindu view of history. The divinities and heroes composing the list were adopted by Vaishnavism at different times, though all were incorporated by the eleventh century. The total list and the mythology of each avatar vary in different formulations. In one formulation they are as follows:

Hindu princess worshipping a lingam
Courtesy of the Metropolitan Museum of Art,
Bequest of George D. Pratt, 1935

(1) The Fish (*Matsya*). The world being overwhelmed by a disastrous deluge, Vishnu took the form of a fish who saved Manu (the Hindu Noah), carrying him and his family to high ground in a ship fastened to his head. He also saved the Vedas from the flood. The Fish incarnation has never been widely popular.

(2) The Tortoise (*Kurma*). In the flood many treasures were lost, including the

ambrosia by which the gods renewed their youth. Vishnu transformed himself into a great tortoise and dived into the depths of the ocean. The gods placed Mount Mandara on his back and, turning a mythical serpent around the mountain, churned the ocean by pulling the serpent. From this churning emerged the ambrosia as well as many other treasures, including the goddess Lakshmi.

Hindu nymph from Bhubeneshwar
Courtesy of the Metropolitan Museum of Art, Purchase, 1965, Rogers Fund

(3)   The Boar (*Varaha*). The earth was cast into the ocean by an evil demon. Vishnu took the form of a boar who killed the demon and raised the earth to its former position by means of his tusk. The cult of the boar was popular in some parts of India during the Gupta period.

(4)   The Man-Lion (*Narasimha*). A demon having obtained a promise from

Brahma that he could not be killed by day or night, by man or beast, persecuted gods and men including his own pious son. Vishnu turned himself into a man-lion (thus neither man nor beast), burst from a pillar in the palace at sunset (when it was neither day nor night), and slew the villainous demon.

(5)   The Dwarf (*Vamana*). Still another demon, named Bali, gained power over the world of gods and men. Vishnu changed himself into a dwarf and asked the demon for as much of the world as he could cover in a stride. When the boon was granted he changed himself into a giant, taking two strides over heaven and earth and leaving only the underworld to the demon and his followers.

(6)   Rama with the Axe (*Parashurama*). Vishnu took the form of a Brahman named Rama (not to be confused with the hero of the *Ramayana*) whose father was robbed by an evil king. Killing the evil king, the enraged Brahman warrior turned upon the whole Kshatriya caste whom he wiped out twenty-one times in succession.

(7)   Rama, hero of the *Ramayana*. Vishnu transformed himself into the hero of this epic in order to save the world from the oppressions of the demon king Ravana. In this avatar Vishnu combined the virtues of faithful husband, brave leader, and beneficent king. This avatar and the next one are clearly the most important for Vaishnavate devotion.

(8)   Krishna, the god-hero of the *Mahabharata*. Throughout this epic Krishna appears as the friend and advisor of the Pandava warriors. Alongside the epic and supplementing it, a rich mythology grew up, celebrating Krishna, both as a warrior hero and a pastoral flutist calling women and girls to dance with him in the moonlight. In this manner, it was added in pious afterthought, the voice of god calls man to leave earthly things for the joys of divine love!

(9)   Buddha, founder of Buddhism. According to Hindu theology Krishna became Buddha in order to delude the wicked, leading them to deny the Vedas and ensure their damnation.

(10)   Kalkin, the avatar yet to come, will be a warrior mounted on a white horse with a flaming sword. He will judge the wicked, reward the virtuous, and restore the ideal age.[37]

This sketch of a few significant themes and patterns in popular religion has barely hinted at Hinduism's inexhaustible store of religious rites, myths, and movements. Yet enough has been said to classify popular Hinduism as predominantly a religion of the first, or nature-culture, type. Its gods and goddesses are expressions of one or another aspect of the world of nature and society. Its myths and rites celebrate diverse aspects and values of the same world.

Yet there is much evidence that the faith of many of India's sages, seers, and philosophers is that of the second type, transcendent monism, devoted to a blessedness which is yonder or elsewhere. It is also true that these same seers and sadhus are the culture heroes of the people of India. In other traditions more concerned with consistency, this relationship might cause embarrassment, tension, or conflict. Yet all that it appears to mean in India is that Hinduism enjoys the best of both worlds.

MODERN AND CONTEMPORARY ISSUES

The cluster of elements in Indian religion to which we have given the label "Hinduism" assumed its distinctive shape before the coming of Islam to India around the year 1000. For the approximately three-quarters of a millennium during which Islam was the faith of India's rulers, Hinduism maintained itself

Krishna overcoming the Snake Demon, Kaliya
Courtesy of the Metropolitan Museum of Art,
Rogers Fund, 1927

by the simple but effective strategy of resisting conversion and continuing to exist. There was some marginal interaction between Islam and Hinduism, particularly in the regions of India where adherents of the two faiths met and mingled. Yet the large historic fact is that Hinduism and Islam continued as living faiths of many millions of Indians, with the fateful result of conflict and, in the twentieth century, partition of the nation into India and Pakistan.

The coming of the West in modern times confronted Hinduism with many new challenges and issues. The Portuguese arrived first, landing on the Malabar coast in 1498. Their explorers were soon joined by Jesuit missionaries. The British and French were present in force by the seventeenth century. In mid-eighteenth century the English won out in the struggle for domination. In

1757 an army under Clive defeated the French at the Battle of Plassey, thus gaining control of the crucial region of Bengal. From this base the English moved out until they ruled all of India.

By the early decades of the nineteenth century Christian missionaries, both Protestant and Catholic, were in India in force. This century was to see several significant Indian responses to Christianity, ranging from liberal receptiveness to extreme nationalistic rejection. Hindu religion was a central component of all these responses. Taken together they constitute a great revival of Hinduism, the effects of which are still being felt.

The first response was illustrated by Ram Mohun Roy (1772–1833), founder of the Brahmo Samaj, reformer of Hinduism, and often called the father of modern India.[38] A Brahman educated in traditional Sanskrit learning and a devout Hindu, Roy entered the employ of the British and soon rose as high as an Indian could in the Bengal Civil Service. Of independent income by the age of forty-two, he went to live in Calcutta, and characteristically threw himself into a great number of humanitarian and religious causes. He founded and edited newspapers in English, Bengali, and Persian, he started schools, and led successful campaigns against such traditional evils as *sati,* or widow burning. He also argued the case of Hinduism against Christian missionaries so effectively that he converted to Unitarianism the Scottish missionary with whom he was translating the New Testament into Bengali.

In 1828 he founded the Brahmo Samaj (Society of God), for the reformed or purified worship of God and for the pursuit of humanitarian morality. Roy was convinced that the conception of deity as one and spiritual in nature was a common element of all high religions, including both Hinduism and Christianity. Hence no pictures, no images, and no animal sacrifices were used in religious sacrifices of the Brahmo Samaj. Its members met for congregational worship of the one God—a novel practice in Hinduism.

Roy remained a faithful Hindu, wearing his Brahman caste thread to his death. Yet he was a liberal who sought to learn from all religions, incorporating their elements of strength into his reformed version of Hinduism. He was particularly attracted to the humanitarian ethic which he saw in Christianity, but felt that this could be separated from Christian dogma and grafted onto Hinduism. From this viewpoint he mounted a vigorous counterattack against the Christian missionaries, maintaining Hinduism as in no way inferior to Christianity.

The Brahmo Samaj attracted to its membership some of the outstanding Indians of the time, among them Dwarkanath Tagore and his son Debendranath Tagore, and the fiery young Keshub Chunder Sen. The society fell into inactivity following Roy's death in 1833. It was revived by Tagore in 1843. But it was split in 1865 over differences between Debendranath Tagore and Keshub

Chunder Sen. Tagore was more devotional than activist in spirit and vastly
more conservative than Sen, who attacked the caste system root and branch.
Sen also disagreed with Tagore in his incorporation of extensive elements of
Christian faith. Sen and Tagore split the Brahmo Samaj into two competing
fragments. Sen's followers subsequently deserted him, forming still another
group, while he came to view his organization as what he termed a "new dis-
pensation," claiming to build upon a Christian foundation but going beyond
historic Christianity. These three groups continue a nominal existence in
present-day India.

A different and decisively negative response to the West as well as to Christianity may be seen in the life and ideas of Swami Dayananda Sarasvati (1824–
1883), founder in 1876 of the Arya Samaj.[39] Born a Brahman in the state of
Gujarat, he rebelled against family and religious tradition as a youth, running
away from home at the age of nineteen. He spent fifteen years as a wandering
ascetic, coming at length to view the four Vedas as absolute and final truth. He
spent the rest of his life proclaiming this message in all parts of India, arguing
the validity of the Vedas against all comers. His conviction that the Vedas were
for all Indians, and not just for Brahmans, brought upon him the wrath of
orthodox Hindus. As a result of his own strong and controversial views, numerous attempts were made on his life, one of which finally succeeded. In
1876 in Bombay he founded the Arya Samaj as an expression of his militant
faith in the Vedas. His ideas made contact with the Purva Mimamsa philosophy
of Jaimini. In the nineteenth and twentieth centuries it became a powerful vehicle of Hindu nationalism. Like Dayananda, his followers see the Vedas as
the source of all human truth. He asserted that firearms and electricity were
predicted in the Vedas and that whatever is valid in modern science and democracy is actually of Vedic origin. Such was—and is—Dayananda's sharp way
of expressing total rejection of Christianity and the West.

Still a different response found expression in Sri Ramakrishna (1836–1886)
and his follower Swami Vivekananda (1863–1902). Ramakrishna, though a
Brahman, was a child of the Indian countryside and its simple traditional piety.
But he was a mystic and a saint in whom India's ancient religious tradition
came to new and compelling life. Installed as a priest in a temple at Dakshines-
war near Calcutta, he became at once a devotee of Kali. He also became a
religious seeker who tried over a twelve-year period the novel experiment of
being a Christian, a Muslim, and a Hindu, in short, seeking to embody in his
own agonized life the forms of spirituality of all the world's religions. At length
he came home to his own reformed, revitalized interpretation of Hinduism.

He attracted as students and disciples many of the leading men, especially
young men, of India. His disciples transcribed his aphoristic teachings, published later as the *Gospel of Ramakrishna*.[40] It expresses the world as he saw it,

permeated by the presence of the Divine. Among his disciples was a young Indian lawyer who, when he first visited Ramakrishna, was about to sail to England for further legal study. He abruptly changed his plans and underwent a twelve-year discipleship, at the end of which he became Swami Vivekananda, apostle to the world of his master Ramakrishna's message. In 1893 Vivekananda attended the First World Parliament of Religions, held in conjunction with the Chicago World's Fair. His eloquence and his message made an immediate and forceful impression on his hearers. From Chicago he set out on four years of lecturing in America and England, as a kind of Hindu missionary to the West. Returning home, he founded the Ramakrishna Mission and with characteristic energy set about the task of reform and regeneration of India. He died at the age of thirty-nine, but his influence has continued and spread in India and throughout the world through the Ramakrishna Mission. Gandhi has acknowledged the influence on his own life of Vivekananda's zeal to serve India's downtrodden masses.[41]

As the nineteenth century wore on, the thinking and idealism of India's leaders became increasingly political in nature. The Indian National Congress was founded in 1885, and until India's independence in 1947 it served as a focus for Indian political leadership. The movement had begun with a moderate liberalism, in the spirit of Ram Mohun Roy. However, increasingly extreme views forced their way to the front. In the thinking of many of these men there was a close relation between Indian nationalism in politics and Hinduism in religion. For example, B. C. Chatterjee (b. 1838) edited anti-British magazines and wrote devotional poetry to the mother goddess, who now appeared in the guise of Mother India.[42] B. K. Tilak (1856–1920), imprisoned by the British for inciting India's masses to violence, wrote books entitled *The Mystic Import of the Bhagavad Gita* and *The Arctic Home of the Vedas*. He also reformed and reshaped Hindu festivals and other ritual to serve as a vehicle for his anti-British political views.

The career of Aurobindo Ghose (1872–1950) led from education to political agitation and prison, but soon thereafter to a career of religious meditation and philosophic writing. After an English education and posts in Indian higher education, he threw himself into Bengal politics, associating himself with the extreme nationalist group in the Indian National Congress of 1907. He was jailed by the British for suspected participation in a bombing plot. A mystical experience in jail led him after his release to withdraw from politics to an ashram at Pondicherry, to spend the rest of his life in religious exercises and philosophic writing through which he produced some striking new accents in Indian thought and faith.[43]

The twentieth century brought to the forefront of leadership in Indian political society and Hindu faith the great figures of Mohandas Gandhi (1869–

1948) and Rabrindranath Tagore (1861–1941). Gandhi stands as contemporary India's greatest political leader and the architect of the free Indian nation. He was reared in Gujarat as a member of the Vaishya, or merchant caste. Particularly important was the influence of his devout mother and Jain friends of the family. Gandhi studied law in England and then, after a brief return to India, spent twenty years in South Africa as the leader of the Indian minority. During that time his basic convictions and methods were being formed and tested, notably that of *satyagraha* (literally "truth-force") or, as he expressed it, "the force which is born of truth and love." [44] Returning to India in 1915 he soon became the unchallenged leader of the Indian National Congress. His leadership during three decades led to Indian independence.

Called a saint in politics, Gandhi replied that he was a politician trying to become a saint.[45] Religiously his great significance was his ability to reach back into Indian tradition for apparently dead ideas and to give them fresh and vital application in contemporary Indian life. Such were satyagraha and *swadeshi* (loyalty to one's own land or tradition), both major political weapons in Gandhi's arsenal. Gandhi's independent conscience led him to protest the inhuman custom of outcasting, as well as the bloody rioting between Muslims and Hindus which accompanied independence and partition between India and Pakistan. The latter position led to his death, for he was assassinated while at prayer by a fanatical Hindu nationalist, N. V. Godse, who felt he had made too many concessions to Muslims. Clearly the Hindu faith as well as the Indian nation owes an inestimable debt to the quickening influence of Gandhi's thought and life.

In many ways the great figure of Gandhi overshadowed that of the poet and mystic Rabindranath Tagore. Son and grandson of men prominent in the nineteenth century, Rabindranath Tagore grew up as a Bengali Brahman. He was given an excellent education by his father. As a youth he turned to the writing of mystical and devotional poetry in the classic, bhakti tradition. He translated his own poems from Bengali to English, publishing in 1912 the volume *Gitanjali* ("Song Offerings").[46] A year later he was awarded the Nobel Prize for literature, an event which made him a world figure as well as a hero to fellow Indians. In the years which followed, he lectured widely in America and Europe, dwelling on the twin evils of the West, as he saw them, nationalism and militarism. To these twin manifestations of Western materialism, he opposed India's spiritual heritage.

In India he came under increasing attack for his continuing criticism of Indian nationalism. In 1921 he and Gandhi disagreed on this issue. Tagore had previously hailed Gandhi as India's "frail man of spirit," an embodiment of Indian virtue against the vices of the West.[47] But as Gandhi moved toward such forms of Indian nationalism as swadeshi, Tagore raised his voice in criticism. He remained to his death a cosmopolitan and an internationalist. In this he believed that he had spoken not only for Asia against the nationalist West, but for India's religious heritage as well.

Gandhi's friend and protégé, Jawaharlal Nehru, never shared Gandhi's devout religious faith. His autobiography reveals an agnostic and a secular mind.[48] Nehru's leadership, among other important factors, led to an independent Indian government which is ostensibly completely secular in nature. Such a neutral political arena is in effect a new experience for Hinduism. Other aspects of contemporary Indian society, notably the introduction of science and technology with their inevitable concomitant of urbanization, continue to drive in the same direction, to a secular society. A coalition of secular forces and Gandhi's religiously based idealism led to the 1948 law of the Indian national government abolishing untouchability and forbidding its practice in any form. While social practice falls somewhat short of legal enactment, this is an important statement of social purpose and direction.

Hinduism in present-day India shows many facets and diverse tendencies. Political and military events, including partition and continuing friction with Pakistan, as well as the Chinese attack of 1963, have notably increased Indian nationalism and with it the nineteenth-century alliance between nationalism and various forms of Hindu religion. This alliance continues its existence in several organizations and minority political parties such as the Mahasabha, the Rashtriya Swayamsevak Sangh, the Jan Sangh, and the Ram Rajya Parishad. Gandhi's moral ideals live on in the saintly Vinoba Bhave (b. 1895) and his program of *bhudan,* the voluntary giving of land by wealthy landowners to landless peasants.[49] Conceived as a nonviolent, Gandhi-type alternative to Communism, it has had some slight influence in India's rural life. Still other Indians turn hopefully to a secularism which sees in religion only a combination of outmoded superstition with social reaction. Meanwhile India's masses continue in their traditional ways of piety and faith, oblivious to twentieth-century winds of doctrine. As the student observes their ways of worship he is impressed with the fact that however uncritical, extreme, and sometimes repugnant these ways may seem to him they do constitute a living, functioning part of individual and social life in present-day India.

CONCLUDING COMMENT

If to the western observer the three faiths originating in ancient India, namely Jainism, Buddhism and Hinduism, appear generally similar in outlook, this is not the case for adherents of these faiths who often point to sharp differences of emphasis and accent. Of the three, that which is known to us as Hinduism differs from the other two alike in its central position in India's historical tradition, and in the range and variety of ideas, attitudes and symbols incorporated within its inclusive and catholic unity.

This variety leads on directly to the question: Is there a single configuration of value, taken by Hindus as ultimate or final? Truly it is difficult to the point of implausibility to find this much unity in the infinite variety of Hindu thought and devotion! However, very tentatively two suggestions may be offered for the reader's consideration. The first is the Vedic maxim, Reality is one, but the sages speak of it in many ways. Taken in Indian context, this saying points first to the transcendent One, and then to all the phenomena of Hinduism as deployments of this underlying unity. Second, we may look at Hinduism's varied manifestations as so many expressions of what we have termed the central Indian tradition. In either of these ways—and are they not really one way?—there may be said to be a Hindu path to salvation or pattern of ultimate valuation.

Is there a Hindu humanism? Or on the other hand, is all conception of human fulfillment or perfection simply lost in the jungle variety of Hindu thought and practice? Certainly one such underlying value expressed by this tradition is precisely tolerance and the freedom of pluralism—especially when these values are asserted against western forms of unfreedom and intolerance. Beyond this there is again the vision of the One, which constitutes final fulfillment. Short of this final fulfillment, to glimpse the One from afar might perhaps be described as man's anticipated fulfillment.

Concerning our three main types of religion, it is not surprising to find all three in Hinduism, which is accordingly a mixed type. The religion of the Vedas is, as we have seen, cosmic, and India's popular or village religion remains so to this day. Vedantist philosophical thought constitutes a central core of acosmic ideas and attitudes. Bhakti, or devotional theism from the *Bhagavad Gita* to the poems of Tagore constitute an important tendency toward theistic or type-three religion.

NOTES

1. Swami B. K. Tirtha, *Sanatama Dharma,* Bhayatriya Vidhya Bhavan, Bombay, 1964.

2. "India: Religion and Philosophy," *Encyclopedia Americana,* 1963, vol. 15, p. 27.

3. William de Bary (ed.), *Sources of Indian Tradition,* Columbia University Press, New York, 1958, p. 212.

4. *Ibid.,* p. 212.

5. *Ibid.,* p. 237.

6. *Ibid.,* p. 237.

7. *Ibid.,* p. 236.

8. *Ibid.,* pp. 258–259.

9. *Ibid.,* pp. 259–261.

10. See *inter alia* Heinrich Zimmer, *The Art of Indian Asia,* Bollingen Series, Pantheon Books, a Division of Random House, Inc., New York, 1955, for illustrations of Khajuraho (vol. II, plates 309–318) and Konarak (vol. II, plates 348–375).

11. de Bary, *op. cit.,* pp. 261–275.

12. *Ibid.,* p. 266.

13. *Ibid.,* p. 212.

14. *The Song of God: Bhagavad-Gita,* trans. Swami Prabhavananda and Christopher Isherwood, Mentor Books, New American Library of World Literature, Inc., New York, 1954, p. 37.

15. *Ibid.,* p. 97.

16. *Ibid.,* pp. 97f.

17. *Ibid.,* p. 99.

18. Rabindranath Tagore, *Gitanjali,* Macmillan & Co., Ltd., London, 1916.

19. Kenneth W. Morgan (ed.), *The Religion of the Hindus,* The Ronald Press Company, New York, 1953, p. 139.

20. *Ibid.,* p. 139.

21. de Bary, *op. cit.,* p. 235.

22. Morgan, *op. cit.*, p. 181.

23. *Ibid.*, p. 182.

24. *Ibid.*, p. 183.

25. Sarvepalli Radhakrishnan and Charles A. Moore (eds.), *Sourcebook in Indian Philosophy,* Princeton University Press, Princeton, N.J., 1957, p. 172.

26. Morgan, *op. cit.*, pp. 147–148.

27. Radhakrishnan and Moore, *op. cit.,* p. 172.

28. See Heinrich Zimmer, *Philosophies of India,* Meridian Books, Inc., New York, 1957, pp. 610–612. See also, Radhakrishnan and Moore, *op. cit.*, pp. 356–385.

29. Zimmer, *op. cit.*, pp. 280–330.

30. *Ibid.*, pp. 433–436.

31. Ninian Smart, *Doctrine and Argument in Indian Philosophy,* George Allen & Unwin, Ltd., London, 1964, p. 236.

32. James B. Pratt, *India and Its Faiths,* Houghton Mifflin Company, Boston, 1915, pp. 37–42.

33. A. L. Basham, *The Wonder That Was India,* Grove Press, Inc., New York, 1959, p. 207.

34. W. Norman Brown, *Man in the Universe,* Oxford and IBH Publishing Co., Calcutta, 1966, p. 58.

35. Morgan, *op. cit.*, p. 51.

36. See John Masters, *The Deceivers,* Penguin Books, 1955, for a work of fiction depicting the practices of the Thugs.

37. Basham, *op. cit.*, pp. 302–307.

38. de Bary, *op. cit.*, p. 571.

39. *Ibid.*, p. 628.

40. *Ibid.*, pp. 638f.

41. *Ibid.*, pp. 646f.

42. *Ibid.*, pp. 707f.

43. *Ibid.*, pp. 725f.

44. *Ibid.*, p. 801.

45. *Ibid.*, p. 802. See also Mohandas K. Gandhi, *An Autobiography: The Story of My Experiments with Truth,* Beacon Press, Boston, 1957, p. 35.

46. Tagore, *op. cit.*

47. de Bary, *op. cit.*, p. 790.

48. *Ibid.*, p. 893. See also Jawaharlal Nehru, *An Autobiography,* The Bodley Head, Ltd., London, 1936.

49. de Bary, *op. cit.*, pp. 924f.

SUGGESTIONS FOR FURTHER STUDY

Basham, A. L.: *The Wonder That Was India,* Grove Press, 1959.

Bharat, A.: *The Tantric Tradition,* Rider, 1965.

Brown, W. N.: *Man in the Universe,* University of California Press, 1966.

Danielyou, A.: *Hindu Polytheism,* Bollingen, 1963.

Dasgupta, S.: *History of Indian Philosophy,* Cambridge, 1922–1935.

———: *Indian Idealism,* Cambridge, 1933.

de Bary, W. T. (ed.): *Sources of Indian Tradition,* Columbia, 1958.

Eliot, Sir Charles: *Hinduism and Buddhism,* Routledge, 1954.

Hindu Scriptures, trans. C. W. Zaehner, Everyman, 1966.

Hiriyanna, M.: *Essentials of Indian Philosophy,* G. Allen, 1949.

Morgan, K. (ed.): *The Religion of the Hindus,* Ronald Press, 1953.

Mueller, F. Max: *The Six Systems of Indian Philosophy,* Longmans, 1899.

Pratt, J. B.: *India and Its Faiths,* Houghton Mifflin, 1915.

Radhakrishnan, S.: *History of Indian Philosophy,* G. Allen, 1929–1931.

——— (ed.): *History of Philosophy, Eastern and Western,* G. Allen, 1952.

——— and C. Moore (ed.): *Sourcebook in Indian Philosophy,* Princeton, 1957.

Renou, L.: *Religions of Ancient India,* Oxford, 1953.

——— (ed.): *Hinduism,* Washington Square Press, 1963.

The Song of God: Bhagavad-Gita, trans. S. Prabhavananda and C. Isherwood, Mentor Books, 1954.

Zaehner, C. W.: *Hinduism,* Oxford, 1962.

Zimmer, H.: *Myth and Symbol in Indian Art and Civilization,* Pantheon, 1946.

———: *The Art of Indian Asia,* Bollingen, 1955.

———: *Philosophies of India,* Meridian Books, 1957.

7

SIKHISM

Sikhism is India's and the world's newest religion (excepting of course such newer movements as Bahai, Mormonism, or Christian Science which fall short of being "religions" in the full substantive and historical sense); Sikhism came into being during the sixteenth and seventeenth centuries. It is today the religion of some 6,200,000 people concentrated mainly in the Punjab in northwest India.[1] It continues to engender in its adherents a strong sense of community. A prominent Sikh writer characterizes it as the only wholly Indian religion and also the full maturity of Hindu and Muslim thought and faith.[2]

The term *Sikhism*, like so many isms in religion, must be regarded as an unfortunate but probably unavoidable label. *Sikh* is Punjabi for the Sanskrit *shisya*, meaning "student" or "disciple." *Sikhism* will be taken here as a shorthand label for the distinctive faith and tradition of the Sikh people.

This religious community presents the student with several highly significant and intriguing questions. (1) One such question has to do with the placing of this chapter within the present volume, which is to say, the classification of Sikhism among the religions of mankind. As indicated, Sikhism is an Indian religion, and for purposes of convenience is here classified as such. (2) Yet the historic Sikh attempt to combine elements of Hinduism and Islam constitutes

191

a kind of crucial experiment for Chapter 1's typology of religions. Do religions of different types really combine with each other; or like oil and water do they remain separate? (3) Even apart from this book's typology, Sikhism claims interest as an example of syncretism, or a mixing of religions which has succeeded. Many historical attempts at syncretism have failed to produce a faith which attracts or holds the allegiance of any considerable number of human beings. Judged by this standard, Sikhism has succeeded where other attempts have failed. Why? (4) Even apart from syncretism Sikhism claims interest as an example of the birth and growth of a religion "in the full light of history" (as Muslims like to say about their own faith). By several centuries, Sikhism is the most recent of mankind's living religions. Can it provide us with answers to the questions of the causal factors which make for the birth and growth of religions? (5) Still another significant feature of Sikhism is its transformation from a passive, quietist sect to a fighting theocracy. The history of religions has no more ironical or striking transformation than this.

THE FOUNDER'S LIFE

Nanak (1469–1539) was born in the village of Talwandi some forty miles from Lahore, and his life and influence are inextricably bound up with the Punjab. Nanak's life must be understood against the background of the history of this northwest Indian region. For several centuries this had been an area where Hindu and Muslim met and mingled—and also fought and killed each other. It is not by chance that Nanak raised his voice in protest against religious conflict.

Other currents of religious thought and feeling had their impact on Nanak. The bhakti tradition of Hinduism produced a succession of devotional poets and saints who went about the countryside singing their songs of faith. Muslim mystics, called sufis, sang similar songs and praised Allah in similar ways of devotion. To the common man—and Nanak was a common man—these devotional traditions must have seemed indistinguishable. Often their followers worshiped at the same shrines and marched and sang in the same processions.

Many of these saints of the Hindu and Muslim traditions raised their voices on common issues. They spoke against religious conflict and empty ceremonialism and for human brotherhood. The Hindu bhakti saints protested the evils of caste. Notable among these figures were the fifteenth-century Ramanand and his better-known disciple Kabir (1440–1518), who described himself as "a child of Rama and Allah," and devoted himself to the reconciliation of Hindu and Muslim.[3] Kabir was born a Muslim, but found no difficulty in worshiping with Hindus and others. He seems to have believed in one God, the supreme reality, beside whom all else was illusion. More important, he believed that man must find his way to God with the guidance of a guru as well as by meditation and singing hymns of praise and love. Over five hundred of Kabir's hymns have been incorporated into the Sikh Bible, the *Adi Granth;* and a small sect of Kabir's followers, the *Kabir panthis,* still exists. There is no evidence that Kabir and Nanak ever met, but Kabir's influence on his younger contemporary was strong. Both men owed much to a common tradition of devotional religion. This tradition of devotion influenced the development of Sikhism in many ways, not least of all in the Sikh emphasis on a personal teacher, or guru.

Nanak's parents were Hindus, and his father was a village accountant and farmer. His schoolmaster was a Muslim. Nanak was a dreamy and meditative child, and marriage at the age of twelve failed to turn his mind toward more worldly concerns. His wife came to live with him at the age of nineteen, and two sons were born to them. His father sought to settle Nanak into a stable occupation, but he failed as cowherd and as tradesman.

Leaving wife and children with his parents, he found his way to the district capital, Sultanpur, where he had better success as manager of a state store. He was joined there by a Muslim friend and musician, Mardana, and the two organized a group for the singing of hymns, which soon became a group of religious seekers.

The great crisis in Nanak's life occurred one day as he was bathing in the river before going to his daily work. The Sikh account of it is that God gave him a cup of nectar to drink and spoke to him in the following words:

> *Nanak, I am with thee. Through thee will my name be magnified. Whosoever follows thee, him will I save. Go into the world to pray and teach mankind how to pray. Be not sullied by the ways of the world. Let your life be one of praise of the Word, charity, ablution, service, and prayer. Nanak, I give thee my pledge. Let this be thy life's mission.*[4]

In response to the divine summons, Nanak uttered the words which introduce the Japji, the morning prayer which is repeated silently each morning by every devout Sikh to this day:

> *There is one God.*
> *He is the supreme truth.*
> *He, the creator,*
> *Is without fear and without hate.*
> *He, the omnipresent,*
> *Pervades the universe.*
> *He is not born,*
> *Nor does He die to be born again.*
> *By His grace shalt thou worship Him.*

Before Time itself
There was truth.
When time began to run its course
He was the truth.
Even now, He is the truth.
Evermore shall truth prevail.[5]

The divine voice spoke again, saying to Nanak, "Thou art the Guru, the Supreme Guru of God." At this time Nanak is said by his followers also to have received the robe of honor from the God who spoke to him. Meanwhile he was reported missing, and it was presumed that he had drowned in the river. On the fourth day he returned home and gave away all his possessions except a loincloth. From the gathering crowds he turned away in silence. Then he went with his friend Mardana and joined a group of mendicants. The next day he arose and spoke, saying only: "There is no Hindu and no Mussalman."

According to Khushwant Singh, this crucial experience took place in 1499 during Nanak's thirtieth year.[6] As a result of these experiences Nanak was ready to set out, accompanied by Mardana, to proclaim the truth he had received.

There is no reliable knowledge concerning the journeys of Nanak and his friend Mardana, though it is generally agreed that they traveled widely throughout India, making their way as far as Assam in the east, Ceylon in the south, and Tibet on the north. Wherever he went, Nanak preached and sang his message of God the True Name who sought the salvation of every man and the peaceful brotherhood of humankind. In order to dramatize the unity of Hindu and Muslim, Nanak devised and wore a ridiculously mixed costume, combining a Muslim mango-colored jacket with a white Hindu safa and dervish's hat, with Hindu caste marks on his brow. Mardana was the constant companion of Nanak's journeys, accompanying his songs on a small stringed instrument.

Wherever he went, Nanak labored to found communities of Sikhs, or disciples. He had his greatest success in his native Punjab, where first one then several such communities sprang up and flourished.

Later in life Nanak took Mardana and set out on the traditional Muslim pilgrimage to Mecca. They wore the garb of Muslim pilgrims and carried the customary carpet for prayer and cup for ablution. Sikh tradition tells a tale of what happened to Nanak on the way:

He was staying in a mosque and fell asleep with his feet toward the Ka'ba—
an act considered of grave disrespect to the house of God. When the mullah
came to say his prayers, he shook Nanak rudely and said: "O servant of God,

thou hast put thy feet toward Ka'ba the house of God; why has thou done such a thing?" Nanak replied: "Then turn my feet toward some direction where there is no God nor the Ka'ba." [7]

During the last fifteen years of his life Nanak settled down in the Punjab village of Kartarpur as guru of his community. He was teacher, preacher, and leader. He required a strict routine of his followers, each day beginning with a bath in cold water before daybreak, followed by worship. The day was then free for secular affairs until the evening prayers.

The death of his friend Mardana reminded him of his own advancing years. Knowing that his end was near, he chose as his successor a devoted follower named Lehna, to whom he gave the name Angad (meaning "of my own limb"). For the choice of succession, he passed over his own sons, who had not obeyed him. Nanak died in 1539, and his followers tell the following story about his demise:

Said the Mussalmans, "we will bury him"; the Hindus, "we will cremate him"; Nanak said: "You place flowers on either side, Hindus on my right, Muslims on my left. Those whose flowers remain fresh tomorrow will have their way." He asked them to pray. When the prayer was over, Baba pulled the sheet over him and went to eternal sleep. Next morning when they raised the sheet, they found nothing. The flowers of both communities were fresh. The Hindus took theirs; the Muslims took those that they had placed.[8]

In death as in life, Nanak proclaimed his gospel of man's oneness under the one God.

NANAK'S TEACHINGS

The source of Sikh teaching is the holy book called the Adi Granth, which is a remarkable collection of the writings of Nanak, of the Gurus who followed him, of Kabir, and of numerous other Sikh, Hindu, and Muslim religious teachers. The compilation of these writings was begun by the fifth Guru, Arjan, and the Adi Granth was given its position of unique holiness by the tenth Guru, Gobind Singh, who declared that after him there would be no more Gurus, but that the Granth would serve this function for the Sihk community. It has since been revered as a sacred or even divine book. It is not only the Sikh source book, but the center of its devotion and worship.

While the teachings of the Granth are by no means limited to those of Nanak, his writings do occupy a central place in it. His fundamental teaching was "God the True Name." Several motives may be detected in this formulation. The designation *True Name* was in part his effort to transcend such limiting and partisan names as Shiva, Rama, or Allah, though at times he did not hesitate to use these and other names. There were, furthermore, devotional traditions in both Islam and Hinduism which concentrated the devotee's attention on the names of God.

One student of Sikhism comments that Nanak's metaphors for deity are those natural to Hinduism, citing the line, "He Himself is the Relisher; He Himself is the relish." [9] Other traditional Hindu metaphors might be added, such as that of the formless one pervading all things. However, Nanak's poems also feature such clearly monotheistic metaphors as *sovereign, creator,* and *lord.* There are also a great many terms, such as *love,* sometimes clearly erotic love, which were common to both Sufi and Bhakti traditions.

To this, one must simply add that while the student of religion with an eye for the differences between faiths of the monistic and the monotheistic types can easily distinguish these different kinds of metaphors in the writings of Nanak and his followers, nevertheless, despite this volume's hypothesis of three types of religion, these metaphors appear to lie side by side with no suggestion of inner disharmony or conflict.

These differences are even clearer as we turn to the discussion of God's relation to the world, where Nanak spoke alternately of both maya and creation. For example, he wrote the following:

> *Maya, the mythical goddess,*
> *Sprang from the One, and her womb brought forth*
> *Three acceptable disciples of the One:*
> *Brahma, Vishnu and Shiva.*[10]

Nanak's view of maya seems to have been that of the deceptive force of illusion pervading all things other than the One. Yet alongside such references, and indeed much more frequently, the reader finds references to the world as the work and creation of the sovereign monotheistic Lord of all.

Again there are references to predestination, yet Khushwant Singh is probably correct in asserting that Nanak's view was that man's freedom under God conquers fate and predestination.[11] Here, in short, is the teaching of monotheistic freedom. Yet Nanak also clearly taught the Hindu doctrine of karma-samsara, asserting that evil conduct led to the bondage of continued rebirths, while obedience led to liberation.

One prominent teaching of Nanak derived from both Hindu and Muslim sources, that of the need for a guru who sustained a personal relation to his students or disciples. As we have seen, the word *sikh* means "disciple." The

Sikh gurus have also been charismatic leaders of their people in war and politics. Sikhism has imparted its own distinctive definition to the word *guru*. Nanak rejected many of the Hindu forms by which God is mediated to man, but he underscored men's need for a guru. The guidance of a guru is both necessary and sufficient to lead men to God:

> *O Man, repeat God's name and praises;*
> *But how shalt thou obtain this pleasure without the guru?*
>   *It is the guru who uniteth man with God.*[12]

This was a tenet which was destined to grow in importance with the historical development of Sikhism.

In his doctrine of man Nanak managed to combine a view of human dignity and fulfillment with a strong sense of human sin, folly, and evil. "Numberless are the ways of folly and vice," said Nanak.[13] His writings also trace evil to human pride, in ways sounding strangely similar to Christian descriptions of sin.

Nanak's ethical and social teachings enunciated several of his lifelong convictions. First and most notably, he never tired of criticizing empty ceremonialism in religion, as well as religious forms such as caste which he believed to conflict with human morality or righteousness. The story is told of Nanak that when on the banks of the Ganges he saw Hindus throwing water to the rising sun as an offering to their dead ancestors, he turned and began to throw water in the opposite direction. Asked what he was doing, he replied that he was watering his fields at home in the Punjab. For, he said, if these men could send water to heaven surely he could send it to his home village![14] Religion, he never ceased to say, consists not of things like this, but of deeds of kindness and goodness. At times Nanak used the traditional Indian word *ahimsa* for this moral quality.

One notable respect in which Nanak broke with Hindu moral values was his rejection of asceticism. He remained within the world and bade his followers to do likewise. Indeed, the ascetic way of his own son, Sri Chand, was doubtless a reason for the son's being passed over when a successor to Nanak was being chosen. Sri Chand's followers were destined to create differences of opinion in the Sikh fellowship. However, while Nanak commanded his followers to live within the world, he prescribed an austere and disciplined way of personal righteousness for them. While within the world, it was nevertheless at first a distinctly quietistic or passive way of life. However, this heritage which Nanak bequeathed to his followers was destined within two centuries to be transformed into an activist, fighting faith.

THE GREAT TRANSFORMATION OF SIKHISM

Nanak was succeeded in order by nine Gurus, making ten in all, as follows: [15]

 1. Nanak, 1469–1539
 2. Angad, 1504–1552
 3. Amar Das, 1479–1574
 4. Ram Das, 1534–1581
 5. Arjan, 1563–1606
 6. Har Govind, 1595–1644
 7. Har Rai, 1630–1661
 8. Har K'ishan, 1656–1664
 9. Tegh Bahadur, 1621–1675
10. Gobind Singh, 1666–1708

The great transformation of Sikhism came not suddenly, but gradually, step by step, in the Sikh community under these leaders.

The second Guru devised a new script and began the compilation of Sikh writings. He also emphasized physical fitness, making drill and competitive games a part of the community life. Amar Das, the third Guru, made the *langar*, or the communal meal, an integral part of Sikhism. In this, the human equality and casteless aspect of the community were emphasized. Visitors were required to accept the Guru's hospitality by eating with his disciples. Among Amar Das's visitors was the Moghul Emperor Akbar, who was himself much interested in religious reform. Amar Das also pursued such reforms as prohibition of *purdah* and *sati,* that is, of the veiling and seclusion of women, and the self-immolation of widows on their husband's funeral pyres. The fourth Guru, Ram Das, began the change of Sikh ethics from quietism to activism, teaching, "If anyone treat you ill, bear it. If you bear it three times, God Himself will fight for you the fourth time." [16] This same Guru, Ram Das, was notable for beginning both the famous Golden Temple at Amritsar and the city around the temple. He also sent missionaries to many parts of India. His son, the fifth Guru, Arjan, proved to be one of the greatest and most energetic of the ten leaders. He completed the temple and also the tank of Amritsar, making bathing a sacred ritual. He compiled the Adi Granth and installed it in the temple. He was himself a poet of high ability.

The death of Akbar and the accession of Jahangir to the Moghul throne brought bad times to Arjan and his Sikh community. Jahangir did not share Akbar's religious tolerance and sought an excuse to suppress the Sikhs. Arjan was implicated—just how deeply, and how serious the plot, historians disagree— in a plot to overthrow Jahangir and was summoned to Lahore, where he was imprisoned and tortured to death.[17] Arjan's dying injunction to his son, who became the sixth Guru, Har Govind, was to "sit fully armed on the throne and maintain an army to the best of his ability." [18] From this point may be dated the beginning of the gradual emergence of the fighting Sikh theocracy.

The young Har Govind, only eleven years of age at the time, took the seat of his father, girded with two swords, and began to gather soldiers, horses, and arms for the defense of his community. He carried on intermittent warfare against both Jahangir and his successor, Shah Jahan. No match for the Moghul armies in the open field, the Sikhs took to the hills and perfected the tactics of guerrilla warfare. Har Govind's leadership increased the solidarity as well as the military confidence and resolution of his people. Surrounded by increasingly hostile Muslims, the Sikhs increased in their own nationalism. Har Govind also increased the far-flung missionary activities of the Sikh community and provided efficient administration for its increasing numbers of adherents.

These trends continued during the terms of the seventh and eighth Gurus. The ninth Guru, Tegh Bahadur, like the fifth, was a martyr for his faith. He was a victim of the Muslim fanaticism of the Moghul Emperor Aurangzeb. The final step in the transformation of Sikhism to a fighting theocracy occurred under Bahadur's son, Guru Gobind, or as he came to be known, Gobind Singh, meaning "Gobind the Lion." A talented writer of verse, a courageous soldier and leader, and above all else a man who believed that he acted under divine authority, Gobind Singh provided leadership, military, religious, and social, for his people until his assassination by a Muslim fanatic in 1708.

Gobind took a decisive step for himself and for the Sikhs when in 1699 he instituted the Khalsa, or the Community of the Pure, by a new ritual called the Baptism of the Sword. The ceremony began after the morning worship when the Guru appeared before the congregation, drew his sword, and demanded five men for sacrifice. After some hesitation, one volunteer offered himself. He was taken into a tent, and a little later the Guru reappeared with his sword dripping blood and asked for another victim, and so on to the number of five. Only then did the Guru produce the five goats he had sacrificed, and gathered the five men about him for a new ritual of initiation, or baptismal ceremony.[19] Mixing sugar in plain water and stirring it with a dagger to the recitation of his own martial hymns, he made each of the five drink from the single bowl. Since they had come from different Hindu castes, this signified their initiation into the casteless community of the Khalsa. Their Hindu names were changed to the family name of Singh (from the Sanskrit *simha*, meaning "lion"), and they professed the martial creed of the Khalsa. Five symbols were prescribed: (1) unshorn hair and beard (*kes*), (2) comb (*kangha*) to keep the hair tidy, (3) knee-length breeches (*kach*, from which "khaki" is derived), (4) a steel bracelet (*kara*) on the right wrist, and (5) the saber (*kirpan*). Four rules were prescribed: (1) not to cut any hair of the body, (2) not to smoke or chew tobacco or drink alcohol, (3) not to eat meat of any animal slaughtered by the customary Muslim bleeding to death, (4) not to molest Muslim women or to have sexual relations with any women except a lawful wife. Having initiated the five Khalsa, Gobind asked them in turn to baptize him, to symbolize their equality with him in the new brotherhood.[20]

So began the new disciplined order of fighting Sikhs. Gobind threw membership in this austere new brotherhood open to all who wished to join and so gathered about himself a band of free and fearless fighting men. In the years that followed, there was ample opportunity to test their mettle in actual combat, for Gobind and his followers spent their lives in continual conflict with the Moghuls and other regional rulers. Thus the transformation from quietist sect to a fighting theocracy was completed.

The rest of Gobind's life was spent in mortal and tragic combat. In 1704, after three years of siege, his headquarters at Anandpur fell to the armies of Aurangzeb. His mother and his two youngest sons were among the victims. Gobind escaped to fight again at Chamkaur, where again his forces were surrounded and finally were destroyed. In this siege his two remaining sons as well as many devoted followers perished. When his fortunes were at low ebb, he was summoned to Delhi by Aurangzeb, but he replied by penning his famous *Zafar Namah,* or "victorious epistle" in which he hurled defiance at the emperor and assured him that one day the Khalsa would take vengeance upon him.

Gobind escaped through the siege lines and made his way to the Deccan, where later he joined with Aurangzeb's successor, Bahadur Shah, who had expressed interest in him and his cause. He spent the rest of his life with Bahadur Shah and was assassinated at Nanded by a Muslim fanatic. As the place of Gobind's death Nanded has become a Sikh pilgrimage spot.

The years which followed Gobind's death continued the violence of Sikh history. Not even the Golden Temple, which housed the Adi Granth, was exempt, for within the following century it was destroyed and rebuilt several times. Following Gobind's demise, the Sikhs rallied around a follower who sought to be Gobind's successor, Banda Singh Bahadur, but they fell away when he sought to assume the mantle of the Guru. He was executed in Delhi in 1716. During the greater part of the eighteenth century Sikh military power was divided among confederacies called *misls*.

Unity and domination came to the Sikh community again early in the nineteenth century under the leadership of one of the most colorful and romantic figures in Sikh history, Ranjit Singh. Ranjit was a brave soldier and a military leader of great ability. He was also a shrewd politician, who succeeded in carving out and maintaining a kingdom which included virtually the whole of the Punjab.

Ranjit's kingdom did not long outlive his death, which occurred in 1839. During his last years his most formidable opponents turned out to be no native rulers but the British, who were intent upon pushing their hegemony into northwest India. British diplomacy and arms checked Ranjit's expansion, and after his death British arms brought the Sikhs within British India. Two wars,

Portraits of Sikh warriors
Courtesy of the Museum of Fine Arts, Boston

in 1845–1846 and 1848–1849, brought Sikh recognition of British power. The Sikhs became valuable allies of the British, who put Sikh military propensities to work throughout their empire. In the Indian mutiny of 1837, the Sikhs remained loyal to the British, for in the Muslim and Hindu leaders of the mutiny they saw enemies rather than allies. Sikh soldiers and constabulary were

Assembly of Sikhs

Courtesy of the Museum of Fine Arts, Boston

important to British dominion in Asia through the nineteenth century and up to the First World War. However, British policies in the Punjab following that war turned support to alienation and hostility.

With the British to the Punjab came Christian missionaries. One notable Sikh response in the second half of the nineteenth century was the Singh Sabha (or Assembly), which carried on an active campaign of education and propaganda in defense of the Sikh faith. Khalsa College was organized in 1892, followed by the Khalsa Tract Society and a weekly newspaper called *Khalsa Samachar*. In the present century many of these activities have been taken over by other organizations.

The largest single issue in recent Sikh history has been the independence and partition of India. The 1947 line of division between India and Pakistan went through the middle of the Sikh homeland, and Sikhs found themselves in the middle of the disastrous and bloody riots which accompanied partition. For the Sikh community these events can only be described as an unmitigated disaster. Almost two and a half million Sikhs abandoned homes, lands, and temples, fleeing as refugees from Pakistan to India. In many cases they virtually exchanged places with landless Muslim peasants from Punjab.

With independence has come a secular Indian state in which traditional privileges enjoyed by some religious communities have been abolished. Sikhs have often found this to their disadvantage. One result has been a continuing agitation for a Punjab state in which there would be a Sikh majority. This was granted by the Indian government in 1966 with the division of Punjab into Punjab and Haryana. However, agitation has continued for more satisfactory conditions for this new Sikh state.

THE SIKH COMMUNITY TODAY

Whatever one's estimate of Sikh teaching, it is undeniable that the Sikhs have continued as a hardy and vital community. They have defended their faith and themselves heroically and often against great odds. Sikhs today are bound together by this tradition. Like the Jains and the Parsees, the Sikhs are today a vigorous and visible minority within the wider Indian society. In contrast to the Jains and Parsees, the Sikhs are not predominantly of the middle class. Rather they are farmers, mechanics, taxi drivers, and soldiers.

Most of their number continue in the traditional occupation of agriculture in their northwest Indian homeland, and they are some of India's best farmers. Within the past century, migration to the cities, often spurred by famine in the Punjab, has increased the numbers of Sikhs in the cities of India and indeed throughout Asia, where their beards, turbans, and names make them a highly visible social minority. Government service and politics have claimed some of them. Sikhs have also excelled in athletics. To themselves and to other Indians they are men of action.

The Sikh community is a culture centering in a faith whose home is the Sikh temple, or *gurdwara* (literally "gate of the guru"). The most famous is the Golden Temple of Amritsar, which houses the Adi Granth and continues as a popular pilgrimage place for Sikhs throughout India. Destroyed and rebuilt many times during the stormy history of the Sikhs, it maintains its original

The Golden Temple of Amritsar
Courtesy of the Government of India Tourist Office

design and function. It is of the Moghul style of architecture, and if it lacks the artistic distinction of the Taj Mahal, it continues to be a living house of faith for millions of men. Its worship service, as in all Sikh gurdwaras, is open to all who will observe the minimal conditions of covering their heads and baring and washing their feet.

Other celebrated gurdwaras are at Tarn Taran near Amritsar, at Nanak's birthplace, at Anandpur where Gobind Singh lived, and at Nanded in Maharashtra, where he died. Yet, probably more important are the local gurdwaras in the innumerable cities and towns of India. The central object of any gurdwara is the Granth, and it is sometimes charged that this holy book is treated like a Hindu deity, being aroused and reverenced in the morning and put to bed at night. Sikh defenders deny this charge, asserting that the Granth is the source and guide but not the object of faith. The Sikh worshiper upon entering the gurdwara goes up a gangway leading to the Granth and there leaves an offering and makes an obeisance. Then, without turning his back on the Granth he retraces his steps. Reading from the Granth is the central act of worship both in temple and in home. Often it is read through continuously for periods of from two to seven days. Other aspects of Sikh worship include daily prayers, public and private, and the singing of hymns.

Sikhs share many of the festivals of Hinduism, but have added some of their own, mainly related to celebrated figures and events in their history. In many of these ceremonies the Granth is taken out of the temple and is marched around the city in procession, often accompanied by musicians and singers. A notable feature of many Sikh holidays is the *guru ka langar,* or "kitchen of the guru," which is a mass meal at which all participants, sometimes numbering many thousands, eat together.

The life of the individual is guided by ceremonies at such milestones as birth, coming of age, marriage, and death. Most of these emphasize his membership in the Sikh community. The death ceremony is notable for its strict prohibition of unrestrained lamentation. Sikhs customarily practice cremation.

Pilgrimages are prominent among other religious observances of Sikhs. Yet probably for most members of this faith, the paramount religious facts are membership in the community and the duties of an active, social life. Sikhism is an ethical and social religion.

Like other religions of the modern world Sikhism has faced problems of attrition due to secularization. In recent times increasing numbers of its adherents have cut their hair, shaved their beards, and in varying degrees have broken with the traditional prohibition on the use of tobacco and alcohol. Even more fundamental has been an increasing neglect of prayer and worship. One study of a small Sikh village in the Punjab found only a small minority who prayed daily and even fewer who observed the formal morning and evening prayers.[21] In some quarters, education has eroded Sikh piety, with the result that pious Sikhs have taken a dim view of education.

Yet other historical forces, even more powerful than these, have supported Sikh faith. Events like partition and independence have thrown the Sikhs together in defense of themselves and their heritage. Even more important has been the emergence of several notable contemporary expositors and defenders of Sikh faith, such as Jodh Singh and Khushwant Singh. Hence the present question seems to be not whether Sikhism will survive, but the forms and shapes which its continued existence will take.

CONCLUDING COMMENT

In the light of the foregoing sketch of Sikh history and thought, some answers must now be essayed to the questions posed at the beginning of this chapter. Sikhism is a historically successful combination of elements drawn from Hinduism and Islam, which are, in our typology, religions of two different types. What does the fact of Sikhism lead us to conclude about our typology? Clearly the Sikh people have not felt any of the problems that might be predicted on the basis of this typology.

One conclusion which must be drawn is that the typology consists of ideal types rather than real types, that is to say, ideas drawn out of the fullness of experience and held in abstraction. Wherever such abstract ideas or ideals are referred back to actual human experience, their sharp edges are blurred and blunted. Actual religions tend to be mixed, involving elements from all three types. Yet the typology will be fruitful if it points to significant elements in experience that need to be analyzed and understood.

In these terms Sikhism presents a complex picture. Although its source documents contain elements drawn from both Muslim and Hindu traditions, there is little doubt that the Muslim source predominates. Speaking theologically, Sikhism is faith of the monotheistic type, as its active, this-worldly, social nature testifies. Its historic hostility to caste is a crucial clue.

Yet, on the other hand, historically the Sikhs have had good relations with Hindus and have generally been well treated by them, while they have been ill treated by Muslims. The result has been a vastly greater influence from Hinduism upon the Sikhs than from Islam. The common history of the Sikh community has given genuine unity to these diverse influences. Hence it is true that while Sikhism is theologically a monotheistic religion, its historical relation to Hinduism has seriously modified this nature.

As to the success of Sikh syncretism, the reasons are doubtless a combination of these same historical influences and the personal impact of its founder and Gurus. Clearly Nanak was what sociologists of religion have called a charismatic personality. So too was Gobind Singh, called by many Sikhs *the* Guru. These men spontaneously communicated to the people around them a sense of their own conviction; and upon this influence their authority was based. Religions begin and renew themselves by the power of such persons.

Even more important in Sikhism's vitality is the challenge of its destiny. Men are bound into living traditions and communities by a common history with its harsh necessities and its strenuous challenges. This truth about history or destiny, while illustrated by Sikhism, is by no means limited to this religion. It is perhaps fair to say of Sikhism that it has survived despite its syncretism, because it has been rooted in the history of a real community.

What has been said about Sikh tradition and community illuminates the more general question of the circumstances under which religions come into being. From the Sikh example as well as others, we may generalize to say that a religion comes into being as the way in which a community of men expresses the meaning of its life. It does so in symbolic terms, and the symbols express the values which give human life its meaning, providing what Chapter 1 called life orientation. For the individual, his community and tradition provide a context of meaning in terms of which he may grow and fulfill his life.

Sikhism's transformation from a passive sect to a fighting theocracy is harder to explain, constituting as it does a well-nigh complete reversal of basic values. A change so total testifies to the impact of historic circumstances upon men and religions. While men never live without values, apparently their values change ceaselessly in response to new historical circumstances and challenges.

The Sikh transformation also testifies to the vitality if not to the consistency of the men who effected it. Clearly it was a matter of fight or die, organize militarily or perish, and the Sikh leaders and their followers chose the former. Other men and other faiths we have studied might have made the opposite decision. Having made their decision and lived it out, the Sikhs continue to celebrate it in the myth and ritual of their faith. The Sikh values, which find embodiment in Sikh personality and community, constitute an expression of this historical tradition.

NOTES

1. W. Norman Brown, *India, Pakistan, Ceylon,* rev. ed., University of Pennsylvania Press, Philadelphia, 1960, p. 93.

2. Khushwant Singh, *The Sikhs Today,* Orient Longmans, Calcutta, 1964, p. xiii.

3. Khushwant Singh, *History of the Sikhs,* Princeton University Press, Princeton, N.J., 1963, vol. I, p. 24. See also William T. de Bary, ed., *Sources of Indian Tradition,* Columbia University Press, New York, 1958, p. 532.

4. K. Singh, *History of the Sikhs,* p. 31.

5. *Ibid.,* p. 32.

6. *Ibid.,* p. 36.

7. *Ibid.,* p. 36.

8. *Ibid.,* p. 37.

9. de Bary, *op. cit.,* p. 533.

10. *Selections from the Sacred Writings of the Sikhs,* trans. Trilochan Singh and others, George Allen & Unwin, Ltd., London, 1960, p. 46.

11. K. Singh, *History of the Sikhs,* p. 45.

12. de Bary, *op. cit.,* p. 537.

13. *Ibid.,* p. 537.

14. K. Singh, *The Sikhs Today,* p. 5.

15. *Selections from the Sacred Writings of the Sikhs,* p. 17.

16. M. A. MacAuliffe, *The Sikh Religion,* as quoted in J. B. Noss, *Man's Religions,* rev. ed., The Macmillan Company, New York, 1956, p. 283.

17. de Bary, *op. cit.,* p. 541.

18. K. Singh, *The Sikhs,* George Allen & Unwin, Ltd., London, 1953, pp. 27f.

19. *Ibid.,* p. 29.

20. *Ibid.,* p. 29.

21. John C. Archer, *The Sikhs in Relation to Hindus, Moslems, Christians and Ahmadiyyas,* Princeton University Press, Princeton, N.J., 1946, p. 291.

SUGGESTIONS FOR FURTHER STUDY

The Adi Granth, or Holy Scriptures of the Sikhs, trans. Ernst Trumpp, Trubner, 1877.

Archer, J. C.: *The Sikhs,* Princeton, 1946.

Brown, W. N.: *Man in the Universe,* University of California Press, 1966.

de Bary, W. T. (ed.): *Sources of Indian Tradition,* Columbia, 1958.

Field, Dorothy: *The Religion of the Sikhs,* J. Murray, 1911.

Gupta, H. R.: *History of the Sikhs,* Dawson, 1950.

Harbans Singh: *The Heritage of the Sikhs,* Bombay, 1964.

Khushwant Singh: *A History of the Sikhs,* Princeton, 1963.

Loehlin, C. H.: *The Sikhs and Their Book,* Lucknow, 1945.

————: *The Sikhs and Their Scriptures,* Lucknow, 1958.

MacAuliffe, M.: *The Sikh Religion,* Oxford, 1909.

Selections from the Sacred Writings of the Sikhs, trans. Trilochan Singh, and others, G. Allen, 1960.

8

CHINESE RELIGION

The transition from India to China presents one of the most massive contrasts in the history of religion. India's reaching for an Absolute Reality beyond the common world of nature and society with the accompanying alienation of man from this world stands in polar opposition to China's staunchly this-worldly attitude. The Chinese perception of particular realities contrasts with India's fondness for abstract speculation. In short, while the dominant attitude of the Indian tradition is acosmic, that of China is cosmic; in terms of our typology of religions India's is type two, while China's is type one.

In contrast to the heavily sacral quality of Indian culture, where holiness seems to suffuse and permeate everything, Chinese culture seems secular. There are holy or sacred objects in the Chinese tradition, but they have, as it were, a low-voltage holiness. In contrast to the widespread supernaturalism or transcendentalism of India, China presents a strong indigenous tradition of naturalism. *Naturalism* may be defined as the attitude which asserts that nature is all of reality and denies the existence of anything beyond. Along with this naturalism the Chinese tradition developed a vigorous criticism of popular religious forms (and religious abuses) for which there is all too little parallel in India.

In the Chinese tradition the great continuities are nature and society; taken

together they constitute the universe, or cosmos, which forms the enduring
context of man's life. For most men in the Chinese tradition it is unthinkable
even to conceive of man or anything else outside of this context. As one Chinese
scholar has remarked, from the Chinese viewpoint the Biblical creation story,
with its transcendent deity who brings the world into being from nothingness,
is meaningless, because in the Chinese view the universe has always existed.[1]

Shang ceremonial vessel
Courtesy of Freer Gallery of Art, Washington, D.C.

The world, or cosmos, just *is.* The basic symbols of this cosmic reality are
Heaven, Earth, the Central Kingdom, and Man. W. T. Chan has underscored
the last term, asserting "the one word which sums up the Chinese tradition is
humanism." [2] It is a humanism which affirms man in this cosmic context.

In studying China as in studying virtually every religious tradition discussed
in this volume, the question arises: But is this religion? Many scholars have denied that Confucianism is a religion, asserting that it is simply and plainly an
ethical philosophy. Y. L. Fung has written that whereas Western people are

religious in outlook, the Chinese are philosophical.³ At least a part of the controversy is a quibble over words. For if *religion* be defined in Western, or monotheistic terms, then clearly the word has little or no reference to China. In fact there is no word in the Chinese language which can properly be translated as "religion." However if *religion* be defined more generally, as proposed in Chapter 1, as a system of holy forms, then clearly the Chinese tradition does show observable phenomena which fit this definition. Heaven, Earth, the Central Kingdom, and Man, constitute such a system of holy forms—withal a distinctively Chinese system.

CHINESE BEGINNINGS

China stands as probably the oldest continuous civilized tradition in the world. In the sixth century B.C., when our study of its religion begins, it was already an old society in which men looked back to the "good old days" of an ancient past. The Chou dynasty had come to power in 1120 B.C., but back of the Chou lay the Shang, which had reigned from 1800 to 1120 B.C., and back of the Shang lay the prehistoric Hsia dynasty with its sage kings, Yao and Shun.

The Chou dynasty was destined to last until 221 B.C., when it was forcibly displaced by the Ch'in. (The word *Ch'in* is from the far western province of Ch'in, whose duke became the famous First Emperor, Shih Huang-ti, 221–210 B.C., founder of the Ch'in dynasty. From *Ch'in* is derived the Western word, *China*. The Chinese do not use this name, speaking rather of themselves as the people of the Central Kingdom, *Chung Kuo*.) Our story begins in the declining period of the Chou dynasty, often called the "warring states" period (ca. 600–250 B.C.), which was an age of feudal disintegration immediately preceding the rise of the Ch'in.

The Ch'in dynasty lasted only from 221 to 207 B.C., yet during this time it built the Great Wall, as well as canals and roads and much else. More than any single achievement, the Ch'in unified China for the first time. Yet this unity was bought at the price of cruel tyranny which brought about the downfall of the dynasty. An example of this tyranny was the famous, or infamous, Burning of the Books. Many traditionally minded scholars had resisted Ch'in efforts at unification. Their resistance was based upon their ancient classical texts. It was broken by a summary governmental order to turn over all books for destruction, on pain of death.

The great achievement of the Ch'in dynasty was the idea of a Chinese empire and of the bureaucracy necessary to carry the idea into effect. The Ch'in was succeeded by the classical dynasty of ancient China, the Han. With an interregnum from A.D. 9 to 23 dividing the Han into "earlier" and "later," this dynasty lasted from 202 B.C. to A.D. 220. It was ancient China's classical age, a time of greatest importance and achievement in all aspects of culture, including religion. During the Han dynasty Confucianism achieved the role of the established faith or philosophy, which endured until A.D. 1911.

THE CLASSIC TEXTS

As the student begins his study of Confucius, Lao-tzu, and the other Chou teachers and schools, he finds them presupposing a set of classical books or texts whose ideas and images served even in those ancient times as traditional premises of thought and the norms of action. The customary word *classic* (the Chinese term is *ching*) designates the reverential respect and authority ac-

corded these books from the ancient period onward. One list of classics included thirteen books; the better-known list of classics included five books.[4] The latter list is as follows:

(1)   The *Shih Ching,* or "Classic of Songs," was also known as the "Book of Poetry." It consisted of 305 songs or poems dating from the tenth to the seventh century. Many were simple love poems, others were ritual hymns, and still others had political or social significance. All testified to the importance of poetry to the Chinese even at this early time. The ability to recite and even to compose poetry remained the mark of an educated man in China. It has been claimed that Confucius edited the *Shih Ching,* though this is far from certain.

(2)   The *Shu Ching,* or "Classic of Documents," is known also as the "Book of History." It consisted of chronicles, speeches, and other similar matters from the early Chou period, though extensive sections have been shown to consist of later forgeries added to the text.

(3)   The *I Ching,* or "Classic of Changes," was a diviner's handbook of uncertain and mixed age which came into existence by gradual accretion and not all at once. Parts of it go back to the early Chou period. It was built around eight trigrams, or combinations of three horizontal lines, broken or unbroken, which served as a basis for foretelling the future. The *I Ching,* with its trigrams and hexagrams (composed

of two trigrams), served the purpose not only of divination but, later, of Chinese cosmology and cosmogony as well. Out of these materials developed a highly distinctive Chinese folk philosophy that envisaged the universe as a single, vast relational system.

(4)   The *Ch'un Ch'iu*, or "Spring and Autumn Annals," was a chronological record of important events in the state of Lu from 722 to 481 B.C. The chronology is factual, and it has often been asserted that Confucius either wrote or edited this document.

(5)   The *Li Chi*, or "Record of Rites," was a second-century B.C. compilation of earlier materials dealing with ceremonies. These rites constituted a key element in the Confucian view of social order.

A thousand years after the end of the Chou period, four shorter texts, The Four Books, were officially added to the Five Classics. These were (1) the

A Chinese landscape entitled "Streams and Mountains Without End"

Courtesy of the Cleveland Museum of Art,
Gift of Hanna Fund

"Analects," or "Sayings of Confucius," (2) the "Mencius Book," (3) the "Great Learning," and (4) the "Doctrine of the Mean." The last two were selected chapters from the *Li Chi.* The Four Books together with the Five Classics constituted the authoritative sources of the Chinese tradition. What is even more important, we have here in the process of writing, reading, and then honoring a body of writings, a clue to the nature of the Chinese tradition. The Chinese are a people who have looked for the answers to life's questions from ancient writings interpreted by scholars or sages.

RECURRING THEMES AND IMAGES

Pervading these classical writings and the culture which the writings informed and guided is a series of themes and images which, taken together, shed valuable light on the religious viewpoint and outlook of ancient China. The following summary makes no claim to completeness, but it will serve to bring the reader into touch with the Chinese attitude which speaks through them.

HEAVEN

The Chinese universe consisted, as noted, of Heaven and Earth, and in the middle of the flat disk of Earth, the Central Kingdom. Heaven was the vault of the sky, but it was also the source of human destiny and in an impersonal way also the object of natural piety. In the very early days of the Shang dynasty men spoke of *Shang-ti* (meaning "Lord on high"). But during the Chou dynasty *T'ien* became the customary term and idea. At least one translation of the "Sayings of Confucius" has translated *T'ien* into English as "Sky." [5] Yet perhaps the term *Heaven* as used in the somewhat impersonal phrases, "Heaven knows," or "Thank Heaven" is a more adequate rendering. One Chou dynasty school of philosophy argued that Heaven had a personal nature, but Confucius and the other schools held it to be impersonal in nature.

From very ancient times onward, the Emperor, acting as the representative of his people, performed prescribed sacrifices to Heaven, at the imperial Altar of Heaven outside the capital city on the days of the summer and winter solstice. At the spring and autumn equinox he performed similar sacrifices at the Altar of Earth. Analogous ceremonies to Earth were also performed in state capitals and local villages throughout China. In this manner was celebrated the dependence of Man on Heaven and Earth, and Man's place in this cosmic scheme of things.

TAO

Pervading the classical documents is the term *tao,* meaning "way" or "path." While Western students may despair of a truly adequate translation, nevertheless "cosmic way" comes close. Tao is the ongoing dynamic way of the universe, as well as its preordained rational structure. Hence to follow the tao is to follow the path of the cosmos, which leads to self-realization, and to diverge from the tao is to lose one's way. While one group of Chinese thinkers, the Taoists, developed their own highly distinctive views on the tao, they had no monopoly on either term or idea, both of which pervaded ancient Chinese thought.

YIN AND YANG

The components of the tao were the dual energy modes, *yin* and *yang,* which in different combinations came together to constitute all things in nature and society. Yang was the active, male principle, and yin the passive, female principle. Thus for example, the Heaven was yang, and the Earth yin. The sun was yang, and the moon was yin. Yang was bright and yin dark; hence the bright sunlit side of a hill was yang, while the dark, shadowed side was yin. Yin and yang were embodied in different combinations in the trigrams of the *I Ching,* the unbroken line being yang and the broken line yin. Combined with the traditional Chinese five agents, or elements, namely, metal, wood, water, fire, and earth, yin-yang speculation produced a kind of proto-scientific investigation of nature not unlike alchemy. Historical and human events were also analyzed by court astrologers in terms of yin and yang and the five agents, using the *I Ching* as their guide; and the future was forecast in these terms.

THE MANDATE OF HEAVEN

The mandate of Heaven (*T'ien Ming*) was ancient China's way of imparting divine sanction to the ruler. The idea recurs in the *Shu Ching,* and after Confucius it became a fundamental category of political thought and practice. The mandate of Heaven meant that the Emperor ruled with the sanction of Heaven, that he was veritably the Son of Heaven. It imposed special responsibilities and requirements on China's ruler, for it was asserted that if the Emperor did not properly perform the rituals, or if he were an evil man, the mandate would be withdrawn. It was a matter of controversy just how or when the mandate might be given or withdrawn. Mo tze, for example, taught the right of rebellion against a ruler who no longer sought his people's well-being. Realistic and cynical thinkers pointed out that any ruler who maintained himself in power seemed to have Heaven's mandate. Others argued that if China and her people suffered misfortune, it was a sign that the mandate had been withdrawn. However interpreted, the mandate was a powerful force for social unity under the Emperor.

FAMILY REVERENCE

The underlying social unit throughout Chinese history has been the family. Indeed, by extension, what was the Central Kingdom but a Great Family under the Son of Heaven? The solidarity of the family was guaranteed by reverential respect for one's father and for seniors in general. This reverence was not limited to living persons, but extended to the family ancestors, to whom prayers and sacrifices were regularly offered and who were visibly present in tablets over the family altar. Similarly, on important occasions of one's life a man consulted his ancestors (that is, visited their graves for reflection and meditation) on the decision to be made.

Perhaps the most important rituals of family reverence and solidarity were funerals, which traditionally in China were momentous—and also expensive—affairs. In very ancient times members of the nobility were buried with weapons, furnishings, and animal and human attendants. Such human sacrifices continued until late Chou times, when they were supplanted by pottery and subsequently paper substitutes. Even in relatively recent times the manufacture of paper money and paper images for funerals has been a major industry.

Family loyalty has been a massive stabilizing and conserving force throughout Chinese history. The "way of the fathers" has been a powerful sanction for ethics as well as a device for hallowing all tradition or custom. In all of this, the scholar, highly honored as he has been, has had the function of advising rulers and society on the ways of the past and the present.

ANIMISM

Much of the substance of the previous five themes has permeated Chinese society to its grass roots. Yet in China the popular level of religion has homelier ingredients as well. The worship of Heaven was present—in the background. The worship of Earth, often in the form of local fertility gods, was closer at hand. So too were the innumerable spirits, good, evil, and capricious, with which the world was populated. The popular religion of most societies is marked by animism; that of China was notably so. The spirits were classified as good spirits, or *shen,* and evil spirits, or *kwei.* Natural phenomena, from mountains and rivers to animals, both real and imaginary, were conceived as dwelling places of these spirits. Chinese people went to great lengths to keep the goodwill of the shen, and to avert evil at the hands of the kwei. Sacrifices, incantations, bonfires, torches, and firecrackers were only a few of the means of averting supernatural evil and securing good. This popular preoccupation with spirits had as one of its consequences a haughty condescension on the part of the intellectuals, who were led to look down upon popular religion with mingled detachment and scorn.

CHOU SCHOOLS OF PHILOSOPHY

According to the great Han historians, there was a notable flowering of philosophy during the declining period of the Chou dynasty extending, they asserted in typical hyperbole, to as many as "a hundred schools." The primary meaning of philosophy for these schools was ethics, though several of them included significant teachings in epistemology, logic, and philosophy of religion. The Chinese term used by modern philosophers, *che hsüeh,* literally "wisdom study," is modern and probably influenced by the West. Confucius used the term *che,* "wisdom". These ancient schools of philosophy were in effect bodies of teaching concerning the conduct of life. Disciples gathered in communities around leading teachers, and in traditions stemming from these teachers. Of the putative hundred schools or traditions, six turn out to be historically significant, and of the six, one, Confucianism, has had altogether central significance in Chinese history.

The pages which follow will consider the six Chou schools in turn, beginning with Confucianism.

CONFUCIUS, THE FIRST TEACHER

The main source for the life and teachings of Confucius is the Analects, or Sayings, which was written not by Master K'ung himself, but by immediate disciples. (The title *Analect* is a Latin rendering of the Chinese title *Lun Yü*. Like the name Confucius, the Latin title comes from the sixteenth- and seventeenth-century Jesuit missionaries to China.) The Analects are organized in twenty chapters, consisting in all of 479 aphoristic sentences.[5] There is also a biography of Confucius by the Han historian Ssuma Ch'ien (d. 80 B.C.). Fragments of teaching and recollections of the master's life are contained in the "Great Learning" and the "Doctrine of the Mean." There are also widespread traditions concerning Confucius scattered throughout ancient Chinese history and folklore; needless to say, all such materials must be critically sifted.

Confucius' traditional dates, 551–479 B.C., are doubtless not far wrong. He was born in the province of Lu at the base of the Shantung Peninsula. His ancestors are said to have been aristocratic refugees who had fled from Sung to Lu during a revolution, perhaps that which toppled the Shang dynasty and put the Chou in power. The twentieth-century scholar, Hu Shih, has advanced the thesis that Confucius was a *Ju*, or court intellectual of an ancient traditional type which had gone out of fashion and which, argues Hu Shih, Confucius succeeded in reviving in his own time.[6]

Confucius' father died shortly after his birth, leaving the family in straitened circumstances. Nonetheless his mother secured for her son a typical aristocratic liberal education. Apparently Confucius achieved all-round excellence as a student, his studies ranging from archery, chariot driving, and the like, through lute playing, to historical and literary scholarship, which together constituted the ideal of the educated gentleman. As a young man he held minor governmental posts. The death of his mother caused him great grief. Confucius mourned the prescribed twenty-seven months, but even after this time, when he took up the lute his grief prevented him from singing.

He opened a school which became the model of Chinese education. Its curriculum consisted of the traditional six disciplines: history, poetry, government, propriety, music, and divination. While the sons of many wealthy families were his students, Confucius was proud to say that no student was ever turned away for lack of money. The school was oriented toward government service as an application of ethics to society. Its graduates have been estimated at three thousand, of whom seventy-two became close personal disciples of Confucius.

Tradition (not verified by the Analects) asserts that he took public office at the age of fifty, rising through various posts to that of prime minister in the state of Lu, only to be framed by less righteous officials. Losing face, he resigned. However this may be, there is better historical evidence for a thirteen-year period of wandering beginning in his mid-fifties. Accompanied by three close disciples Confucius went from state to state, seeking a ruler wise enough to accept him as advisor. He could find none. During these years he was sustained by a very genuine sense of calling and mission. Beset by mobs and harried by police and other officials, he declared, "Heaven begat the power (*te*) that is in me. What have I to fear . . . ?" [7] The motivation and form of Confucius' mission were his obedience to the mandate of Heaven; its content was the application of morality to politics in order to restore the ancient and good order of the early Chou dynasty. This harmonious way of life seemed utterly lost in the disorder and violence of his lifetime. Confucius believed fervently that he was born to restore this original, virtuous, archaic order.

Apparently through a former student who was an official of Lu, and thus politically more successful than his teacher, Confucius was invited home to Lu in 484 B.C. He spent his last years in the scholarship he greatly loved, perhaps editing some of the classics, and died in 479 B.C. at the age of seventy-two. He died in apparent disillusionment, yet great success for his teachings lay in the history yet to come. Master K'ung was destined to live on in the impact of his teachings on China.

CONFUCIAN THEMES

The teachings of Confucius often seem flat and unexciting to the modern Western student, lacking the intellectual appeal of Socrates and the radical faith and love of Jesus. They seem blandly conservative, a complacent rationalization of the status quo. To the ancient Chinese student they held both relevance and power, expressing as they did the essential meaning of humanity set in the context of the Chinese cosmos. In the fabric of Confucius' teachings, eight recurring themes will be pointed out as main threads.

LI

First and perhaps most basic is *li,* hard to translate precisely, and variously rendered as "propriety," "courtesy," "rites and ceremonies," and "decorum." Actually it means, or can mean, all of these things. Perhaps "good form" is as accurate a translation as can be achieved. It begins with those good forms which constitute decorum or etiquette, and it continues without any discontinuity through morality to the nature of the universe. For in contrast to the West, classical Chinese thought saw no discontinuity between these two aspects of social relations. Nor indeed does the matter end there. The *Li Chi* quotes Confucius as asserting that li:

> . . . *is the principle by which the ancient kings embodied the laws of heaven, and regulated the expressions of human nature. Therefore he who has attained li lives and he who has lost it dies. . . . Li is based on heaven, patterned on earth, deals with the worship of the spirits and is extended to the rites and ceremonies of funerals, sacrifices to ancestors, archery, carriage driving, capping, marriage, and court audience or exchange of diplomatic visits. Therefore the sage shows the people this principle of a rationalized social order and through it everything becomes right in the family, the state and the world.*[8]

There is a good order or harmony of the universe in which man participates by his practice of li. Conversely, the pervasive and harmonious order of the universe finds illustration and application in human life in man's practice of good form.

HSIAO

It has already been noted that respect for one's father in particular and for elders in general constitutes a basic virtue of the Chinese tradition. Confucius gave eloquent expression and wholehearted assent to filial piety (*hsiao*) even to the extent of defending and concealing a father's crime from the government.

> *The Duke of She observed to Confucius: "Among us there was an upright man called Kung who was so upright that when his father appropriated a sheep, he bore witness against him." Confucius said the upright men among us are not like that. A father will screen his son and a son his father—yet uprightness is to be found in that.*[9]

At its best, filial piety consisted of an inward respect or reverence for one's parents. It was generalized to include elders of all sorts, and indeed all that was ancient or archaic.

> *Tzu Yu asked about filial piety. Confucius said: "Nowadays a filial son is just a man who keeps his parents in food. But even dogs or horses are given food. If there is no feeling of reverence, wherein lies the difference?"* [10]

A significant application of the virtue of filial piety to Chinese society lay in the traditional five great relations. In the *Li Chi*'s formulation, they are as follows:

1. Kindness in the father, filial piety in the son
2. Gentility in the elder brother, humility and respect in the younger

3. Righteous behavior in the husband, obedience in the wife
4. Humane consideration in elders, deference in juniors
5. Benevolence in rulers, loyalty in ministers and subjects [11]

It will be noted that none of these relations is symmetrical, or in other words, none is a relation between equals. Confucius' ethic is that of a well-ordered feudal hierarchy, where goodness consists in finding one's station and doing its duties.

JEN

The humane quality of Confucius' ethic is exemplified by the quality called *jen* in Chinese and variously translated as "humanity" or "human-heartedness." The Chinese character consists of the radicals for "man" and "two."

> *Fan Ch'ih asked about humanity. Confucius said: "Love men."* [12] . . . *Again, Confucius said: "Without humanity a man cannot long endure adversity, nor can he long enjoy prosperity; the wise find it beneficial."* [13]

Jen required properly conceived responses to all of the many human situations of social life. Someone inquired: "What do you think of requiting injury with kindness?" Confucius said: "How will you then requite kindness? Requite injury with justice, and kindness with kindness." [14]

In general, jen provided the moral foundation for Confucius' humanistic ideal, which included also excellence of many sorts.

SHU

Jen is fulfilled or realized in the closely related quality of *shu*, which is perhaps best translated as "reciprocity."

> *Tzu Kung asked: "Is there any one word that can serve as a principle for the conduct of life?" Confucius said: "Perhaps the word 'reciprocity': Do not do to others what you would not want others to do to you."* [15]

Western readers should not be confused by the negative formulation, which is largely the result of Chinese polite convention which seeks not to intrude upon the privacy of another person. The moral sentiment is remarkably similar to that of the Golden Rule of Christianity.

YI

Jen and shu are applied to specific social relations by means of *i* or *yi*, usually translated as "duty," "obligation," or "righteousness." It is by means of yi that the individual is related to other individuals in the precisely ordered society of ancient China. Yi is the form of social relations, while jen and shu are the human values communicated by this form. While other later thinkers such as Mencius developed this idea, the germ of it is present in Confucius' teachings.

CHIH

Still a further basic value of the good life, according to Confucius, is *chih,* or knowledge. While chih included book-learning and scholarship, it did not stop there, but extended both to artistic taste and to insight into the good life which constitutes wisdom. The wise man, for Confucius, was the man who could take the materials of human nature and shape them into humane patterns. "Confucius said by nature men are pretty much alike; it is learning and practice that set them apart." [16]

For a summary one cannot do better than to quote Confucius' first students and disciples: "There were four things that Confucius was determined to eradicate: a biased mind, arbitrary judgments, obstinacy and egotism." [17] Or again, "Confucius said: Having heard the Way (Tao) in the morning, one may die content in the evening." [18]

CHENG MING

Confucius found a social application of knowledge in the virtue which he called *cheng ming,* usually translated as "rectification of names." It means a kind of semantic honesty in social relations, and especially in political relations. Kings and their subjects should say what they mean and mean what they say. Indeed they should *do* and *be* what they say. The Sayings put the matter this way:

> *Duke Ching of Ch'i asked Confucius about government. Confucius replied:* "Let the prince be the prince, the minister be minister, the father, father, and the son, son."
>
> "Excellent," *replied the duke.* "Indeed if the prince is not prince the minister not minister the father not father and the son not son, then with all the grain in my possession shall I ever get to eat any?" [19]

He meant apparently that the country would be ruined.

CHÜN TZU

All of these values are summed up and embodied in the man whom Confucius called *chün tzu,* variously translated as "magnanimous man," "great man," or "man-at-his-best." It was this man who would put the Confucian teachings into practice and thereby achieve human fulfillment. In many respects this ideal man was similar to the magnanimous man of Aristotle's ethics in ancient Greece. Both ideal men were well-educated, wise, socially conscious aristocrats, whose greatest enjoyment lay in the goods of the mind, but who were willing to assume the tasks of political leadership in their community. Magnanimous man in ancient China and ancient Greece sought and found wise ethical solutions to political problems. He did so by avoiding extremes and cleaving consistently to the middle way, which is also the rational way.

RELIGIOUS ELEMENTS IN CONFUCIANISM

To what extent, if any, do these teachings constitute religion? Are there any religious elements in Confucius' teaching? Or shall we agree with many Chinese scholars who have argued that Confucius' teachings constitute an ethical philosophy but surely not a religion?

As previously noted, if we assume a monotheistic or Judeo-Christian definition of religion, Confucianism is obviously not a religion, but a moral philosophy. Yet in the broader sense of a distinctive system of holy forms which provide orientation for men's lives, Confucianism comes within the bounds of religion. In Western terms, Confucius might be described accurately as a humanistic agnostic. Not God or gods but man occupied the center of Confucius' attention. Concerning the shen and the kwei, he bade his followers to honor them but stay aloof.[20] Concerning prayer and afterlife Confucius was agnostic. Asked by his disciples about prayer, he replied cryptically: "My praying has been going on a long while." [21] Asked about life after death, he replied: "Before we are able to do our duty to the living, how can we do it by the spirits of the dead?" [22] Confucius' outlook was summed up precisely in his own aphorism: "To devote oneself earnestly to one's duty to humanity and while respecting the spirits to stay aloof from them may be called wisdom." [23]

Obviously these attitudes do not add up to burning religious zeal. However, at least three religious elements may be detected in Confucius' teachings. First was his love of ritual. His disciple Tzu Kung questioned the ritual sacrifice of sheep, to which Confucius replied, "You love the sheep and I love the ceremony." [24] Lin Yutang has remarked of this aspect of Confucius' teachings that if he had been a Christian, "he would surely have been a high churchman." [25]

A second religious element was Confucius' sense of historical meaning, which located the archetypal good age in the past and sought to return to this idealized past. With different symbols, this glorification of an ideal past has been a recurring attitude in many religions. In the thought of Confucius, the ideal age of the past was the early days of the Chou dynasty. As we have seen, Confucius sought to set the world right by returning to this archaic good time.

Yet the most unmistakably religious element in Confucius' thought was his sense of vocation and mission, his sense of being called and sent. This attitude is a primary symptom of living religious experience wherever it occurs. In Confucius' case, it was Heaven that called him and sent him forth—or so Confucius believed. Moreover this belief constituted the meaning of his life. Especially during his years of wandering and rejection, this mission sustained him. Hence despite his agnosticism and his scorn of popular religion or superstition, Confucius was in this sense a religious man.

LAO TZU AND CHUANG TZU

Like Confucianism, Taoism originated in the late Chou period. Throughout Chinese history it has been second in importance only to Confucianism, for which it has often served as a foil. Scholars have long argued whether the *Tao te ching* ("Classic of the Way and Its Power") could possibly have been written by Lao tzu, a somewhat shadowy figure who seems to have been an older contemporary of Confucius. While parts of the writing are clearly of later origin (showing the influence of schools and writers who are demonstrably of later times), the weight of scholarly opinion at the present time inclines to Lao tzu (the name means "the Old One") as a historical figure and the author substantially responsible for the *Tao te ching*.[26] However, many of the stories which cluster around Lao tzu are easily identifiable as pro-Taoist, anti-Confucian propaganda. Some sociologically minded writers have sought to identify the social class or group responsible for the *Tao te ching*. For example, Lin Mou-sheng says that the Taoists were "disillusioned intellectuals," in contrast to the successful gentlemen scholars of the Confucian school.[27] Y. L. Fung opines that the Taoists were "hermits." [28]

The *Tao te ching* is a brief, cryptic poem, usually divided into eighty-one stanzas (though there is a different textual tradition which divides it into sixty-five stanzas). It has been translated into English over forty times and, due both to the generally contextual nature of the Chinese language and to the language of the *Tao te ching* in particular, with widely varying results.

The key term of the *Tao te ching* is *Tao*, which the previous section of this chapter has identified as a widely recurring term in Chinese language and thought. "Way" or "Path" is perhaps the best English rendering of *Tao,* though one translator renders it as "System." [29] We have seen that Confucius used it to characterize the social system and way which he advocated and which he believed to be in accord with Heaven and Earth.

The Taoists gave their own highly distinctive mystical and metaphysical interpretation to the idea of Tao. Here we shall list five ideas which recur throughout this remarkable poem as aspects of the Tao.

(1)   The most fundamental theme is the nature of the Tao. What then is Tao? The opening lines of the *Tao teh ching* inform us:

> *The Tao that can be told of is not the eternal Tao;*
> *The name that can be named is not the eternal name.*[30]

The *Tao te ching* struggles through many stanzas with the problem of naming the unnameable. The Tao eludes literal designation or naming because it does not fall within the realm to which language primarily refers. However, once this fact is accepted, it is possible by means of metaphor and symbol to find some way to catch the Tao in the human net of words. Several suggestions are made.

(2)   One recurring suggestion is to call it the One since from the Tao comes One.[31] Another is to designate it by paradox and negation:

> *We look at it and do not see it;*
>   *Its name is The Invisible.*
> *We listen to it and do not hear it;*
>   *Its name is The Inaudible.*
> *We touch it and do not find it;*
>   *Its name is The Subtle (formless).*
> *These three cannot be further inquired into,*
> *And hence merge into one.*
> *Going up high it is not bright, and coming down low, it is not dark.*
> *Infinite and boundless, it cannot be given any name;*
> *It reverts to nothingness.*[32]

In addition to the One, these lines show the use of paradox in pointing to the Tao. It is a favorite device, running through the poem.

(3)   Other symbols for the Tao emerge from study of the *Tao te ching*, notably water, the female, the uncarved block, the valley, the void, and the infant. All significantly are, in terms of Chinese tradition, yin and not yang. This has led some commentators to see a controversy with the dominant Confucianist school whose terms and images are activist and yang. The *Tao te ching* says:

> *The best (man) is like water.*
> *Water is good; it benefits all things*
>   *and does not compete with them*
> *It dwells in (lowly) places that all disdain.*
> *This is why it is so near to Tao.*[33]

> *The spirit of the valley never dies.*
>   *It is called the subtle and profound female.*
> *The gate of the subtle and profound female*
>   *Is the root of Heaven and Earth.*[34]

Attain complete vacuity.
Maintain steadfast quietude.
All things come into being,
And I see thereby their return.[35]

He who knows the male (active force) and
*   keeps to the female (the passive force)*
Becomes the ravine of the world.
Being the ravine of the world,
He will never depart from eternal virtue,
But returns to the state of infancy.

.   .   .   .

He will be proficient in eternal virtue,
And returns to the state of simplicity (uncarved wood).[36]

(4)   Another closely related theme is the overtly anti-Confucian polemic of the *Tao te ching*. Many stanzas can only be read as deliberate argument against the activist humanitarian ethic of the Confucians. For example, the *Tao te ching* asserts:

Heaven and earth are not humane (jen)
They regard all things as straw dogs.
The sage is not humane.[37]

Even plainer are the following lines:

When the great Tao declined,
The doctrines of humanity (jen) and righteousness (i) arose.
When knowledge and wisdom appeared,
There emerged great hypocrisy.
When the six family relationships are not in harmony
There will be advocacy of filial piety and deep love to children.
When a country is in disorder,
There will be praise of loyal ministers.
Abandon sageliness and discard wisdom;
Then the people will benefit a hundred fold.
Abandon humanity and discard righteousness;
Then the people will return to filial piety and deep love.

.   .   .   .

Abandon skill and discard profit;
Then there will be no thieves or robbers.
However, these three things are ornament (wen)
*   and not adequate.*
Therefore let people hold on to these:
*   Manifest plainness,*
*   Embrace simplicity,*
*   Reduce selfishness,*
*   Have few desires.*[38]

(5)   In addition to the criticism of Confucianism with its deep involvement in

China's pyramidally organized society, the reader can also see in these stanzas the advocacy of a simple, natural way of life. Taoist morality is often termed one of inaction. The Chinese term *wu wei* means "inaction," or "action without action." Many of the texts, taken literally, mean just that. For example it is said that:

> *Therefore the sage manages affairs*
> *without action. . . .*[39]

Nevertheless, in context the meaning seems to be one of cooperating with the Tao. Just as a swimmer makes better progress by swimming with the waves than by fighting them, so man should swim with the wave of Tao. One should thus do what is natural, namely cooperate with the Tao. The implication is frequently that Confucianism is unnatural.

Taoist ethics emphasized the way of natural simplicity, and nature's harmony. Like most of the Chou schools it was antimilitarist and had a strong feeling of the evil of war, and also of the coercive processes of government. Taoism was committed to a laissez-faire view of government. "Ruling a big country is like cooking a small fish; that is to say, too much handling spoils it," asserted the *Tao te ching*.[40] The ideal social order for Lao tzu was a small rural community away from the urban life and high society so greatly valued by the Confucians.

> *Let there be a small country with few people.*
> *Let there be ten times and a hundred times as many utensils*
> *But let them not be used.*
> *Let the people value their lives highly and not migrate far.*
> *Even if there are ships and carriages, none will ride in them.*
> *Even if there are arrows and weapons, none will display them.*
>
> . . . .
>
> *Let them relish their food, beautify their clothing, be content with their homes,*
> *and delight in their customs.*[41]

The contrast with Confucian teaching could hardly be more complete!

The fourth-century wit and mystic, Chuang tzu (399–295 B.C.), stood in the tradition of Lao tzu, but in several important ways he pushed the Taoist logic onward to new conclusions. Chuang tzu's book combines mystical vision and mordant social criticism. It is the vision of One which leads to a profound— and comic—sense of the unreality of all else. Or beginning with everyday appearance, Chuang tzu reduced to ridiculous unreality everything which fell short of the One. To Western readers this blending of mystical vision and mordant satire—both metaphysical and social—is a most unusual combination. In China, Chuang tzu created a tradition which brought these two elements together, forming a compound of great power and historical significance.

Chuang tzu's book has many passages which express the vision of Tao. The following lines of paradox will suffice for illustration:

> *Great Tao has no appellation. Great speech does not say anything. Great humanity is not humane (through any special effort). Great modesty is not yielding. Great courage does not injure. Tao that is displayed is not Tao. . . .*[42]

Man's fulfillment lay in ordering his life according to this pattern.

> *He who knows the activities of Nature (T'ien, Heaven) and the activities of man is perfect. He who knows the activities of Nature lives according to Nature. . . .*[43]

True to the yin viewpoint of the Taoist tradition, Chuang found the source of things in the abyss of nonbeing.

> *In the great beginning, there was non-being. It had neither being nor name. The One originates from it; it has oneness but not yet physical form. When things obtain it and come into existence, that is called virtue (which gives them their individual character). That which is formless is divided [into yin and yang], and from the very beginning going on without interruption is called destiny (ming, fate).*[44]

It will be noted for Chuang tzu, as for his master Lao tzu, that in these discussions of the Tao or the One, the metaphor of height is conspicuous by its absence. Here is an immanent rather than a transcendent One, pervading all things. The Tao is here in our midst, not yonder, elsewhere, or above all things.

It is the vision of this One which generates in Chuang tzu's sharp mind an unremitting sense of the relativity of all things natural and human. If only the One truly *is*, all else is only apparent; its appearances turn out to be mutually contradictory and hence delusory. This led Chuang tzu to his theory of opposites which cancel each other out:

> *When there is life there is death, and when there is death there is life. When there is possibility, there is impossibility, and when there is impossibility, there is possibility. Because of the right, there is the wrong, and because of the wrong, there is the right. Therefore the sage does not proceed along these lines but illuminates the matter with Nature.*[45]

> *Pleasure and anger, sorrow and joy, anxiety and regret, fickleness and fear, impulsiveness and extravagance, indulgence and lewdness come to us like music*

from the hollows or like mushrooms from damp. Day and night they alternate within us but we don't know where they come from. . . . Without them there would not be I. And without me who will experience them? They are right near by. But we don't know who causes them. It seems there is a True Lord who does so, but there is no indication of his existence.[46]

Yet in this curious world of polar opposition and universal relativity each thing seems to find its relative place. So Chuang tzu asked:

If a man sleeps in a damp place, he will have a pain in his loins and he will dry up and die. Is that true of eels? If a man lives up in a tree, he will be frightened and tremble. Is that true of monkeys? Which of the three knows the right place to live? [47]

Sharp as were his jibes at mankind and society, it was to epistemology that he propounded the ultimately unanswerable question:

Once I, Chuang Chou, dreamed that I was a butterfly and was happy as a butterfly. I was conscious that I was quite pleased with myself, but I did not know that I was Chou. Suddenly I awoke and there I was, visibly Chou. I do not know whether it was Chou dreaming that he was a butterfly or the butterfly dreaming that it was Chou.[48]

For Confucius and his followers public service was a well-nigh sacred calling. When the messengers of the king came to ask Chuang tzu to become an official advisor, Chuang tzu was fishing. Without looking up, he asked about the fossil tortoise at the royal court. "Is this tortoise better off dead and with its bones venerated or would it be better off alive with its tail dragging in the mud?" The ministers affirmed the latter option, to which Chuang tzu replied, "Then go away and I will drag my tail in the mud!" [49]

To the Confucians and to the Chinese public generally, even more sacred than public service were funeral rites. Chuang tzu subjected them to biting ridicule. When his wife died, his friend Hui Shih came to offer condolence and to his horror found Chuang tzu squatting on the ground, singing, and beating on an earthen bowl. To the visitor's admonition Chuang tzu replied:

When she died, how could I help being affected? But as I think the matter over, I realize that originally she had no life; and not only no life, she had no form; not only no form, she had no material force (ch'i). In the limbo of existence and non-existence, there was transformation and the material force was evolved. The material force . . . was transformed to become life, and now birth has transformed to become death. This is like the rotation of the four seasons, spring, summer, fall, and winter. Now she lies asleep in the great house (the universe). For me to go about weeping and wailing would be to show my ignorance of destiny. Therefore I desist.[50]

From Lao tzu and Chuang tzu have stemmed a continuing tradition of mingled mysticism and wit.

Taoist divinity descends from Heaven
Courtesy of the Metropolitan Museum of Art,
Fletcher Fund, 1938

OTHER CHOU SCHOOLS

While the traditions of Confucius and Lao tzu have predominated in Chinese history, they have by no means been the whole story. The Han historians said there had been six Chou schools. In addition to (1) the Confucianists, or Ju, and (2) the Taoists, were (3) the Mohists, (4) the Naturalists, or Yin-Yang school, (5) the Logicians, or school of Names (in Chinese the *Ming chia*), and (6) the Legalists (in Chinese *Fa chia*).

THE MOHISTS

The first critic of Confucius was Mo tzu (470–391 B.C.), whose criticisms of Confucius stemmed from his own philosophical viewpoint. One of Mo tzu's most characteristic teachings was universal love. Each of us ought to love all men, said Mo tzu, and to love all men equally or, as he put it, indiscriminantly. This in turn was based on Mo tzu's belief in the innate goodness of man, a teaching he shared with all Chou philosophers except the Legalists.

Mo's equalitarian teaching clashed with the reigning Confucian view that each man's love for his fellowman must be precisely shaped by social relations. For example, I have an obligation to love my parents more than those of some stranger; and my duty to my ruler differs from my duty to a serf. Confucius' doctrine was that of discriminating love, in contrast to Mo tzu's teaching of equal and indis- criminating love for all men.

Mo declared boldly that for the individual and for society universal love would yield altogether desirable results. Part of this confidence came from his conviction that love naturally "worked" as a basis for human life. As many Western students of Mo tzu have said, he was a utilitarian. Yet Mo also believed that Heaven sanctioned love—and also placed a divine veto on other different and opposing ends or goals of life.

Mo tzu's views of Heaven were sharply critical of Confucius. Where Con- fucius looked upon Heaven in largely impersonal terms, Mo tzu (alone among the six philosophies) viewed Heaven as personal. Heaven, or God, wills right- eousness and also the well-being of the people. Men must obey Heaven as they obey the personal will of a human superior, declared Mo. They would also be well advised to heed the oracles by which Heaven's will is made known to us, he added.

In still another way Mo tzu set himself against Confucius. Where Confucius sought to turn men back to the ideal goodness of the early Chou dynasty, Mo tzu sought to return to the even earlier and simpler times of the Hsia. He outdid Confucius in his choice of the ideal age at the beginning of things.

In view of these features of his thought, it is not surprising that Mo tzu envisaged a simple way of life for his ideal society. Its citizens would be farmers living under a king who did Heaven's will, seeking above all his people's well-being. The good king would seek his people's welfare in literally every department of life, yet nowhere more than in his avoidance of the supreme evil and folly of war. Moreover, the elaborate and expensive rituals of later days would not be present in the ideal times; funerals were to be simple. Mo tzu had harsh words for expensive Confucian funerals.

THE NATURALISTS

The Yin-Yang school was in Chou times little more than a name, a book, and a list of terms. Tsou Yen (305–240 B.C.) was identified by Han historians as the founder. It was apparently a school devoted to metaphysics and cosmology which sought to explain things in nature and events in history by their combinations of Yin and Yang, and also by the five elements or agents: water, fire, wood, metal, and earth. Later, in Han times, this school came to prominence, but before then it is shrouded in obscurity.

THE SCHOOL OF NAMES

The school of Names, or *Ming chia,* was represented in Chou times by Hui Shih (380–345 B.C.) (the friend who visited Chuang tzu at his wife's death), and Kung-sun Lung (b. 380 B.C.). These men had no monopoly on the concern with names or words, for this interest was widespread in ancient China. Yet for the school of Names this was the dominant concern, although Hui and Kung-sun frequently disagreed with each other.

What comes down to us from these men are statements of some puzzles, problems, and paradoxes which have fascinated and bewildered men throughout subsequent Chinese history. Hui Shih for example propounded the following statement of limiting concepts:

> *The greatest has nothing beyond itself;*
>   *it is called the great unit.*
> *The smallest has nothing within itself;*
>   *it is called the small unit.*[51]

Was he thinking of the universal flux of all things in the following?

> *When the sun is at noon it is setting; when there is*
>   *life, there is death.*[52]

The cosmic orientation of his system of thought is apparent in the following:

> *Love all things extensively. Heaven*
>   *and earth form one body.*[53]

He also left a budget of debaters' paradoxes on which presumably his students sharpened their wits, such as the following:

> *The pointing of the finger does not reach [a thing];*
>   *the reaching never ends.*
>
> . . . .
>
> *A white dog is black.*
> *An orphan colt has never had a mother.*
> *Take a stick one foot long and cut in half every day*
>   *and you will never exhaust it even after ten thousand*
>   *generations.*[54]

Kung-sun Lung occupied himself with the closely related problem of predication. For example, a famous chapter in the Kung-sun Lung book dealt with the question of whether a white horse is a horse. His ideas were developed into a subtle theory of the relation of names (or marks) to the world of things. He seems to have distinguished between what modern Western philosophers call primary and secondary properties.[55]

While the school of Names ceased to exist after Chou times, its achievements were caught up and carried on by other schools and other philosophers.

THE LEGALISTS

Unique among the Chou schools was that known to Western students as the Legalists; in Chinese it was called *Fa Chia,* which Fung has translated as "men of methods," that is, realistic political methods. It was a school of Machiavellian realism, popular among ancient Chinese rulers and their advisors. Notable among its exponents were Lord Shang (d. 338 B.C.), Han Fei tzu (d. 233 B.C.), and Li tzu, who was the chief minister of the Ch'in Emperor, Shih Huang-ti. The Legalist school was the official school during the Ch'in dynasty, and seems indeed to have had significant influence upon the career of this dynasty. It fell from favor with the fall of the Ch'in. Han Fei tzu was influenced by his teacher Hsün tzu, who was known to history as a heterodox Confucian, but who shared important doctrines with the Legalists. Apparently Han Fei derived from this teacher the notion, rare in ancient Chinese thought, that human nature was not good but evil.

Basically the Legalist school believed in coercive power. Rejecting especially the moral standards of the Confucians and the religious sanctions of the Mohists, the Legalists taught that to be successful, a ruler must practice the art of power politics. His law must be clear, and backed by both generous rewards and severe penalties, well known to all. Individual violence, threats, warfare, and regimentation of people must be used by the ruler without hesitation when the need arises. The unforgivable crime of a king is weakness.

Man, according to the Legalist theory, is not good or righteous by nature, and hence he responds to the hope of reward or the fear of penalty. Man is, in short, by nature an egotist. The wise ruler knows this, and is able to take this refractory human material and mold it into something resembling a good life. But this good life is the ruler's achievement and not the gift of nature.

Legalism's social ethic envisaged a simple society consisting of farmers, soldiers, and rulers. In particular, the Legalists inveighed against merchants and scholars with their decadent and recalcitrant ways. In the words of Han Fei, they were the vermin of the state. Li tzu practiced this antipathy to scholars who opposed the harsh rule of the Ch'in First Emperor. In 215 B.C. he issued the order requiring scholars to turn in for destruction all books other than official Ch'in documents. It was a harsh episode in a tyrannical regime. Small wonder that later thinkers looked back upon the Legalists with disapproval amounting to horror.

CONFUCIAN TRADITION IN DEVELOPMENT

Fourteen centuries after they lived, Mencius and Hsün tzu were formally declared by Chu Hsi (A.D. 1130–1200) to be the "orthodox" champion and the "heterodox" champion respectively. In ancient times they were simply two writers who developed divergent interpretations of the growing Confucian tradition. Mencius, or Meng K'o (371–289 B.C.), was roused by the opposition to defend, explain, and amplify the teachings of Confucius. "The words Yang Chu and Mo tzu fill the land," he warned. Yang Chu was a fourth-century hedonist and cynic, and between this extreme and the simple-minded rustic virtue of Mo tzu, Mencius sought to recall his countrymen to the middle way of Confucius.

The life of Mencius bears striking resemblance to that of Confucius. Reared by a devoted and widowed mother, Mencius developed early in life a concern for ritual propriety. He is said even as a child to have played at funeral rituals. Like his master, he sought public office in order, as an advisor to rulers, to reform the government; but like Confucius he failed and wandered from state to state. Like Confucius he was a highly successful schoolmaster. He too retired to his home state, spending his last days in writing and scholarship. He died at the age of eighty-one.

His teachings may be regarded as underscoring and amplifying certain themes and issues of Confucius. He took the idea of the goodness of men and made it somewhat more explicit and emphatic than did Confucius. Man's inherently generous and social nature is illustrated by the fact that if a child falls into a well, all men instinctively rush to aid him. Similarly, Mencius asserted, men are properly remorseful when they have been selfish or cruel.

In interpreting this goodness, he sided in one very important respect with Confucius against Mo tzu. Where the latter asserted the duty of equal and universal love for all men, Mencius and Confucius argued that love must be discriminating. Its application must be related to the social rank and situation of its recipient. Love guided by reason and related to a well-ordered society is the fulfillment of man.

In society, the goodness of the people requires the knowledge of a wise ruler if it is to be realized. It is the duty of such a ruler to devote himself to the well-being of his subjects; if he rules to his own advantage he becomes thereby an evil ruler. This devotion to the well-being of his people is the distinguishing mark of a good and great ruler.

Mencius also spelled out with particular emphasis the evil of war. "War makers are robbers of the people," he said; good rulers are those who maintain the peace. Mencius viewed war as Heaven's punishment against the wrongs and evils of man. Yet he also taught the right of rebellion against an evil ruler who had apparently lost Heaven's mandate.

A final aspect of Mencius' teaching is often called his "mysticism." Like Confucius he taught the mandate of Heaven; but here again he pushed the teaching further, saying that in the will of Heaven there is an appointment for everyone and everything. This sense of calling was understood in terms of a man's inner disposition. The virtuous man knew his calling, or appointment, by means of inner awareness.

Hsün tzu (298–238 B.C.) disagreed with almost all the distinctive views of Mencius. He believed and taught that man is by nature evil. Therefore, to give expression to our nature is to set loose the forces of chaos and conflict. Rather, man's egotistical nature must be trained, guided, and controlled by a strong ruler. Out of such guidance comes whatever goodness men are capable of. As previously noted, Hsün tzu was the teacher of Han Fei, the Legalist.

Hsün tzu also pushed beyond Confucius in his teaching of the impersonality of Nature or Heaven. The processes of nature, from rainfall to the movement of the stars, take place in ways altogether indifferent to man and utterly heedless of his prayers, incantations, and sacrifices. Here was a naturalism which was radically critical of popular religion with its prayers, sacrifices, and good and evil spirits. Yet Hsün tzu would not abolish the rites and sacrifices, for they aroused human and useful feelings. They also had an aesthetic appeal. Hsün tzu seems never to have asked whether religious ritual could long persist on this basis.

Documents also made their contributions to the developing Confucian tradition, notably the "Great Learning" (*Ta Hsüeh*) and the "Doctrine of the Mean" (*Chung Yung*). The Great Sung scholar, Chu Hsi, selected these two texts along with Confucius' Analects and Mencius' book to constitute the so-called Four Books which for six centuries after Chu Hsi until the fall of the

Manchu dynasty in A.D. 1911, constituted the primer of Chinese education, studied and committed to memory before students began the Five Classics.

The "Great Learning" is a brief essay of somewhat uncertain authorship; its ideas if not its words go back to Confucius, and it stands clearly in the Confucian tradition. It is devoted to the Confucian ideal of self-cultivation or self-realization by means of study, or what the text itself calls the "investigation of things." As the "Great Learning" asserts:

> The extension of knowledge lay in the investigation of things. For only when things are investigated is knowledge extended; only when knowledge is extended are thoughts sincere; only when thoughts are sincere are minds rectified; only when minds are rectified are our persons cultivated; only when our persons are cultivated are our families regulated; only when families are regulated are states well governed; and only when states are well governed is there peace in the world.[56]

"The Mean" (*Chung Yung*) is a brief and anonymous essay in the Confucian tradition. Its key idea is that of "centrality" (*chung*), meaning moderation, balance, and suitableness in the conduct of life. A persistent emphasis of the *Chung Yung* is that in following this ideal, man places himself in accord with Heaven and Heaven's way.

The second important concept is that of "sincerity" or "truth" (*ch'eng*). This is essential to the full development of man's nature. Sincerity is self-completing and self-directing. "Sincerity is the beginning and end of things; without sincerity there is no existence." To cultivate sincerity is to walk in the way of Heaven and Earth which is "broad and deep, transcendental and intelligent, extensive and everlasting." [57]

THE HAN ESTABLISHMENT OF CONFUCIANISM

The Ch'in dynasty failed in its bold attempt to unify China. Cruel and high-handed methods carried out by Shih Huang-ti, and rationalized by the official Legalist philosophy, produced an inevitable reaction. After Shih Huang-ti's death in 210 B.C., his ministers strove in vain to continue the dynasty under his weak son. By 206 B.C. the Ch'in had disappeared. Out of rebellion and the struggle for power emerged Lin Chi, or Kao tzu, founder of the Han dynasty. Except for an interregnum under the usurper Wang Mang, A.D. 9–23, the Han dynasty lasted until A.D. 220. It was the great imperial, classical age of ancient China.

If we ask why and how the Han emperors succeeded where the Ch'in failed, at least a significant part of the answer lies in their willingness to consolidate power more slowly. In all of this, the Confucian philosophy played a significant role as the official philosophy. To be sure, the actual behavior of the Han emperors was sometimes guided by Legalist precepts, but it was rationalized in Confucian terms. The new Han synthesis of philosophies was not pure Confucianism, but a blend of elements of Legalist policies and Taoist metaphysics, as well as ingredients from the Five Agents school and the "Book of Changes."

The central theme of the emergent synthesis was the role of the Emperor in his relations on the one hand to the Central Kingdom and its people and on the other to Heaven and Earth. Official views gave to the Emperor a position of moral leadership and ritual representation of his people. Yet so far as the day-to-day business of government was concerned, this was assigned to bureaucrats, while the Emperor was pushed behind a screen of mystery. From this lofty position his office provided sanction for the activities of government.

Ritual sanction was given by the Emperor's leadership in ceremonial activities, including notably the sacrifices to Heaven and Earth. A crucial idea in this system was the mandate of Heaven, according to which Heaven's will was manifested in the acts and person of the sovereign. Theoretically at least this mandate might be lost by defects and misdeeds on the part of the sovereign. Successful and prosperous rule was widely interpreted as possession of the mandate. More cynical commentators pointed out that the mandate came to rest upon an emperor at the moment when the strength of his sword succeeded in placing him in governmental power.

At a more popular level of thought and feeling, power was rationalized in ancient China by omens, portents, and prodigies, reported and interpreted by court astrologers, philosophers, or oracles. Such omens might be either affirmative or negative, but they were widely believed to declare Heaven's will to the inhabitants of Earth.

Many minds and hands participated in the enterprise of creating and maintaining this official Han Confucian synthesis. The court historians Ssuma Tan and his son Ssuma Ch'ien contributed historical lore concerning the hundred schools of Chou times. Men pored over the "Book of Changes" with its trigrams and hexagrams, interpreting not only nature, but politics and history in its occult terms. They also added an appendix to the "Book of Changes," which was to prove very important to later ages.

Among the contributors none was more important than Tung Chung-shu, 179?–90? B.C., official court philosopher and counselor to emperors, author of a commentary on the "Spring and Autumn Annals," but most of all synthesizer of Han Confucianism. Tung's own thought seems to have contained important metaphysical ideas from the Five Agents school and also from Taoism. So he interpreted Han politics in terms of their supposed ingredients of wood, fire, earth, metal and water. Yet all this was held under the dominant Confucian ideas of Heaven, Earth, and Man.

On human nature and education, Tung had his own thoughts, which attempted to synthesize the views of Mencius with those of Hsun tzu. Noting that theorists disagreed on the question of the goodness of man, Tung developed the idea that good was a term which could not properly be applied to the raw material of human nature. Only by education and political guidance could goodness be achieved. For this reason Heaven ordains both education and politics for the high goal of human fulfillment. As Tung put it, "From Heaven the people receive their potentially good nature, and from the king the education which completes it. It is the duty and function of the king to submit to the will of Heaven, and thus to bring to completion the nature of the people." [58]

As advisor to the Emperor, Tung Chung-shu took important steps in the establishment of Confucianism. In 136 B.C. he submitted to Emperor Wu the memorial establishing Confucian teaching as the official system of the empire. It read in part: "Your unworthy servant considers that all that is not encompassed by the Six Disciplines and the arts of Confucius should be suppressed and not allowed to continue further, and evil and vain theories stamped out. Only then will unity be achieved, the laws made clear, and the people know what to follow." [59]

Tung followed this move twelve years later, in 124 B.C., with a proposal to found an official Confucian university at the capital. One of the purposes of this university was to supply a trained governmental bureaucracy. By the end of the first century B.C. there were 3,000 students in attendance, and in later Han times, the number rose to 30,000. In this way Tung built a bureaucracy well schooled in Confucian philosophy. Tung's work was later to grow into the famous examination system.

In later Han times Confucianism moved further toward its secure establishment by the adoption of official texts of the Confucian classics. Ever since the Ch'in book burning in 214 B.C. two sets of texts had existed: New Texts, written in the new script of Ch'in and Han times and doubtless incorporating the views of their newer redactors, and Old Texts, written in the archaic characters of Chou times and claiming to be the pure ancient texts. This situation produced a long-continued scholars' battle between proponents of the Old Texts and of the New Texts. It was a battle in which emperors intervened to support one set of views or to repress opposing views. Finally, in A.D. 79, in a document called "Discussions in the White Tiger Hall," an official and final recension was achieved. Yet silk scrolls were impermanent things in an impermanent world, and a century later, in 179, by imperial edict, the complete text of the Five Classics and the "Sayings of Confucius" were engraved in stone and set up in a place of honor at the imperial university.[60]

During the Han dynasty the official rites to Confucius began. In 195 B.C. Kao Tzu, founder of the Han dynasty, performed sacrifices at the tomb of

Confucius, though that doughty old warrior was doubtless motivated more by political expediency than by piety. Similar ceremonies at national and prefectural capitals began in A.D. 59 as part of the Han establishment of Confucianism. During the centuries which followed, the rites to Heaven and Earth and to Confucius provided a unifying cultus for the people of the Central Kingdom. The ceremonies to Confucius became progressively more elaborate. Instrumental music, ceremonial dances, libations of wine, and choral music were progressively added. Confucius himself was given progressively higher titles, first duke, then king. Scholars of the Sung dynasty, be it noted, withheld the title "emperor." Ming dynasty scholars reformed and simplified the rites, limiting Confucius to "Master K'ung the Perfectly Holy Teacher of Antiquity." This continued until 1906, when the Manchus in a last desperate effort to stabilize their tottering throne declared Confucius "co-equal with Heaven and Earth." All of this was destined to be swept away with the fall of the empire and the coming of the Republic of China in 1911.

While these developments were beginning in high official circles, popular piety also was according a higher and higher position to Confucius in its own way. From Han times onward he was accorded a supernatural birth, and miracle upon miracle was attributed to him. The wonder tales grew with the passage of time.[61] These movements in popular piety in China (as elsewhere in human history) often provoked reactions of skepticism and naturalism among intellectuals. We have already glimpsed the naturalistic views of Hsün tzu at the end of the Chou period. These views were taken up and given mordant expression in later Han times in the writings of Wang Ch'ung (A.D. 27–97). His *Lun heng,* or "Critical Essays" expressed a single continuous theme, "hatred of fictions and falsehoods." [62] Wang applied his theme to the religious issues of his time. He never tired of pouring scorn on anthropomorphic or personal views of Heaven. "Some foolish men say that Heaven produces silk and grain expressly for man's well-being," but, comments Wang scornfully, this is to "make Heaven a farmer or the mulberry girl of man." [63] The mature and reasonable man is led, rather, to the opposite viewpoint, to a thoroughly naturalistic, impersonal conception of Heaven.

Similarly Wang challenged the popular view that "when men die they become ghosts with consciousness and the power to harm others." [64] All the evidence leads to the opposite conclusion, that when the body dies and decays, consciousness ceases. The popular fear of ghosts is sheer, groundless superstition.

Wang also turned his sharp knife upon contemporary scholars who accepted doctrines on their teacher's say-so or because they were ancient. They ought instead to use their critical reason. In similar vein he looked with disdain upon the increasing honor paid to Confucius and his "Analects." Such honor leads to irrational obscurantism. Again, critical reason ought to be man's guide and authority.

NEO-TAOISM

With the fall of the Han dynasty in A.D. 220 began a period of more than three centuries of disorder and disintegration unprecedented in Chinese history and often referred to as the period of Three Kingdoms (220–280) and Six Dynasties (280–589). During these troubled centuries the Chinese tradition came closer to chaos and complete discontinuity than at any other time in its long history.

Our interest in these historical developments is in their impact upon religion. The rise to prominence of Taoism and the coming of Buddhism to China during this period are not matters of coincidence, but rather must be understood in large measure as responses to this time of troubles. Men sought refuge from the storms of their times either in Taoist gardens or in Buddhist monasteries.

Neo-Taoism is a Western scholars' designation for the revival of interest in the writings of Lao tzu and Chuang tzu during the third, fourth, and fifth centuries. The fall of the Han dynasty inevitably damaged the prestige of the Confucianism so closely connected with it. Yet it must also be pointed out that many of the men who wrote with fresh appreciation of Lao tzu and Chuang tzu during this period also continued to regard themselves as good Confucians. They found lines from Confucius' teachings to support their Taoist views; notable among such lines was Confucius' remark that "Yen Hui was nearly perfect but often empty." [65] Confucius did not disappear from the scene, but only receded into the background, while the "dark learning" (*hsüan hsüeh*) of Lao tzu and Chuang tzu came into new prominence. Three new accents or emphases were heard in Taoist thought. Y. L. Fung has spoken of rationalists and sentimentalists.[66] With these must be considered a third development, the emergence of a popular religious brand of Taoism.

RATIONALISM

One of the greatest philosophical works of the neo-Taoist period was the "Commentary on the Chuang tzu" attributed to Kuo Hsiang (d. A.D. 312). There seems to have been some confusion between Kuo and another figure named Hsiang Hsiu who lived a generation earlier and held similar views. Whatever the authorship, the result was a distinctive philosophical perspective which came to be known as the Kuo-Hsiang viewpoint, and which consisted of a systematization and development of suggestions made by Chuang tzu and Lao tzu.

The primary tenet of the Kuo-Hsiang viewpoint was that the Tao is "nothing" (*wu*). Lao tzu and Chuang tzu had said this centuries before, meaning probably that the Tao is not any particular thing. The Kuo-Hsiang pushed onward to the view that Nature (literally "Heaven," or *T'ien*) is simply "the general name for all things." [67] This meant that Nature, or Heaven, is not to be identified with any particular thing, either "here" or "up there." It is simply the scheme of things entire. Since it is literally not any thing, it is wu, or emptiness. Yet as the universe it simply and eternally *is*.

Negatively, Kuo-Hsiang argued that there is no Creator or Lord. Chuang tzu had questioned whether or not such a Lord existed; now Kuo-Hsiang answered with a definite negative. There is simply no adequate evidence for the existence of a Lord. [68]

The Kuo-Hsiang philosophy was one of flux and had a clear view of the process of change which embraced all things. This process was known as the self-transformation of things, which might be characterized as the way in which each thing comes to be and passes away in the never-ceasing process of becoming. Yet there is a relation between the universe and the flux of things. As Fung has put it, "everything that exists in the universe needs the universe as a whole as a necessary condition of its existence, yet its existence is not directly produced by any other particular thing." [69]

The Kuo-Hsiang viewpoint carried this idea of change into its view of human institutions and morals. Changing customs and morals may justifiably be regarded as man's response to ever-changing circumstances. In the face of the changing human world, Kuo-Hsiang recommended two attitudes, a Taoist simplicity of mind, and an alternation, as circumstances might demand, between activity and passivity (*yu-wei* and *wu-wei*).

The Kuo-Hsiang viewpoint drew out and made explicit still another suggestion of Lao tzu and Chuang tzu, namely, the absolute freedom of the individual. According to this view the individual has the sovereign possibility of withdrawing from social circumstances into his own individual and free life.

ROMANTICISM

Other followers of the dark learning were less philosophically inclined. Rather they were men of letters and aesthetes. Fung calls them romantics and sentimentalists devoted to *feng liu* (literally "wind and stream"), or nature. They drew upon the Taoist tradition of a "return to nature" as a way of escape from the evils, artificialities, and responsibilities of society. Writers of this school showed a refined and sophisticated hedonism as deliberate and explicit as any in human history. They wrote a famous forgery, the *Lieh tzu* book, attributing their ideas to the shadowy traditional fifth-century B.C. figure of Lieh tzu. The famous Yang Chu chapter of this book, translated into English under the title "Yang Chu's Garden of Pleasure," makes the refined and subtle pursuit of pleasure the chief end of man, or at least of wise men.

Similar in outlook was the group called the "Seven Sages of the Bamboo Grove," of the late third and early fourth centuries. In deliberate rejection of Confucian social responsibility they devoted themselves to *ch'ing t'an*, or pure conversation. Pleasure, conviviality, and wit sharpened to a razor's edge were the goals of these men. To their garden of pleasure, or bamboo grove, they withdrew from the turmoil of their times. One member of the group was said to have been followed by a servant with a jug of wine and a spade, the former to refresh him and the latter to bury him if he fell dead. Another story tells about Juan Chi and his nephew Juan Hsien, who with their families were great drinkers and who when they met did not bother to drink out of cups but sat on the floor and drank from a large jar. The story concludes on the following note of naturalism: "and then the Juans drank with the pigs." [70]

Another member of this group was fond of cranes. He was given two young cranes and in order to prevent their flying away clipped their wings. But the clipped cranes seemed despondent, and when their feathers had grown out, the master let them fly away.[71] Still another member of the group, Wang Hui-chih (d. 388) opened his window one night on a fresh snowfall whose gleaming whiteness made him think of a distant friend. Immediately he set out to visit the friend though the journey took the whole night. Reaching the friend's house he was about to knock on the door when, on a new impulse, he turned about and returned to his own home.[72]

POPULAR RELIGION

Still a third new development of the Taoist tradition was the emergence of a popular religious movement with its own myth and ritual and much given to magic, shamanry, and similar phenomena. This is only one of many instances in the history of religions in which magic follows mysticism. The reason apparently is that mystics speak in metaphors. They do so necessarily, for this is the only way in which to put into words of the ordinary world their supraworldly message. In the case of Lao tzu and Taoism, the claim to know the eternal Tao was central.

It was only a step from *knowing* the eternal to *becoming*, oneself, eternal or immortal. The Chinese have always had a hankering for elixirs and charms to produce earthly immortality, and Taoism greatly accentuated the trend. It was easy enough for earthly and literal-minded followers of Lao tzu and Chuang tzu to bend their words to this end. The result was that the Tao became a kind of recipe for endless life, which would be guarded and protected apparently forever against all hazards and evils.

These trends gathered momentum during Han times. The Emperor Wu Ti, despite his patronage of Confucianism, was much attracted to Taoism and was especially interested in the effort of alchemy to change cinnabar to gold. Chinese alchemy connected "edible gold," or cinnabar, with immortality, a connection that cost some men their lives, since cinnabar is poison. Wu Ti was informed by a court geomancer that if he would perform certain ceremonies to Heaven on a Taoist sacred mountain he would not die. The outcome of this experiment is unknown.

In the first century an enterprising religious leader named Chang Tao-ling founded a secret society devoted to the pursuit of immortality by means of alchemy combined with various techniques of meditation. Since all members of the society had to pay an admission fee of five bushels of rice, his sect came to be called the Five Bushels of Rice Way (*Wu Tou Mi Tao*). Under the successive leadership of his son and grandson this organization grew to considerable power. Members said that Chang had discovered the true elixir of immortality and had actually been assumed to heaven on the back of a tiger from the top of the sacred Dragon-Tiger Mountain (Lung-hu in Kiangsi Province). They added that Lao tzu had appeared to him and conferred on him the title "Celestial Teacher." Chang's successors became the line of Taoist "popes," actually chief necromancers living atop Dragon-Tiger Mountain, and in recent centuries doing little but blessing charms and talismans.

The fourth-century scholar Ko Hung wrote a book, *Pao P'o Tzu*, devoted to the exposition and defense of the Taoist search for immortality.[73] With ingenious arguments based on the putative immortality of animals such as the crane and turtle, Ko defended the possibility of man's living forever. He did scholarly research in the extensive lore on this subject in China, including even a volume which explored sexual techniques for achieving endless life.[74] Ko also carried on experiments with magic and alchemy, involving a pill for immortality. Small wonder that his followers told the story that when Ko was eighty-one a friend came to visit him and found only his empty clothes—apparently sufficient proof that he had joined the Taoist immortals!

Popular Taoism also developed an extensive myth and ritual, largely in reaction to the coming of Buddhism to China. Devotion to Buddha appealed to many Chinese people, but it led others to seek for a Chinese figure who might serve a similar function. This process had actually begun in A.D. 165 when the Han emperor made sacrifices to Lao tzu and built a temple to him. Later, in competition with Buddhism, Lao tzu was accorded virtually divine titles and heavenly associates. Taoist writings were compiled into a canon of holy scripture, and in short, Taoism was launched as a religion. In this process there are clear instances of fabrication of both myth and ritual. On at least three occasions Taoists also gained sufficient power in governmental circles to mount campaigns of harassment or persecution against Buddhism, first in 446, under Emperor T'ai Wu of the northern Wei dynasty, then in 574, under Emperor Wu of the northern Chou dynasty, and most extensive and important in 845, under the half-mad Emperor Wu Tsung of the T'ang dynasty.

Meanwhile, as a popular religion Taoism continued to flourish, thriving apparently on felt needs and wishes of the Chinese masses. Many of its gods and godlings have been for centuries a part of the Chinese tradition. There are the Eight Immortals, celebrated in legend, pictures, and images. According to Taoist myth these happy folk lived in the islands of the blessed, where they are pictured, some sipping wine heated by one of their number while another plays the flute. Often pictured alone is the maiden Ho Hsien Ku, who gained immortality through a diet of mother-of-pearl. There is Tsao Shin, the god of the hearth, who is the silent observer in chimney corners and kitchens throughout China. There is also Ch'eng Huang, city god, and innumerable others, gods, spirits, and guardians who claim a place in the Taoist pantheon.

In more recent centuries, popular Taoism has fallen on evil times, and appears to be headed for extinction. This is a topic to which we shall recur in the last section of this chapter. However, it is important in this connection to realize that many of the words, ideas, and images of Taoist philosophy and literature found lodgment and new life in Chinese Buddhism, especially Ch'an, or Zen.

CHINESE BUDDHISM

Chinese Buddhist tradition tells the story of the Han Emperor Ming Ti (A.D. 58–75), who saw a vision of a golden man who turned out to be Buddha. On the advice of his counselors, the Emperor sent to India for more details and received in return an embassy of Indian monks with Sutras and images. This story, however, has been traced to a forgery of ca. A.D. 200.[75] But there is authentic evidence of Buddhism in China even before this time. It traveled from India apparently by way of the trade routes of central Asia. In the second-century literature one begins to see the names of outstanding Buddhist missionaries and translators of Sanskrit texts into Chinese. Notable among such figures was a Parthian prince known to history by his Chinese name, An Shih-kao, who was active at the Chinese capital, Loyang, during the latter half of the second century. Two centuries later, Kumarajiva stands out as translator and missionary and one of the greatest transmitters of Buddhist faith to China. The son of an Indian father and a Kuchan princess, Kumarajiva studied Thera-

Sandstone figure of Eleven-headed Bodhisvatta. From the T'ang dynasty

Courtesy of the Cleveland Museum of Art,
Mr. and Mrs. Severance A. Millikin Collection

vada Buddhism in Kashmir, but was subsequently converted to Mahayana by a reading of Nagarjuna's philosophy. He was seized by an invading Chinese army and carried off to China as a prisoner of war. In the first years of the fifth century he was welcomed to the Chinese capital of Ch'ang'-an, and given the title of National Preceptor, i.e., teacher to the nation. From then until his death in 413, he was active in translation of Indian Mahayana Buddhist documents into Chinese.

Another development was the extensive travel to India by Chinese monks and students of Buddhism. Over the period from the third to the eighth century no less than 200 Chinese students made the perilous journey, many of them to the famous Buddhist university at Nalanda.[76] Two of these men are known by their travel records, namely, Fa Hsien who went to India in 399 by way of central Asia and returned by sea in 414, and Hsüan Tsang who made the round trip between 629 and 645, by way of central Asia. There were doubtless many others whose records are lost to us, but they returned to China laden with Buddhist texts, images, and ideas.

Buddhism found lodgment in China at this period of Chinese history for many reasons. The fall of the Han dynasty brought a great lowering of prestige to the Confucian teachings, which had been the established faith of the fallen dynasty. The three centuries which followed the fall of the Han were as chaotic and disordered as any period in Chinese history. In such periods men seek shelter from the storms of their times. As already noted, some sought escape in neo-Taoist gardens of pleasure. The rise of neo-Taoism, with its teaching of emancipation of the individual from his social context, was an additional factor favorable to the reception of Buddhism. Taoism provided similarity not only in ideas, but also in words for the difficult task of putting Buddhism's Indian message into the Chinese language.

It would be false to suppose that there was no resistance to the new faith. To many proud citizens of the Central Kingdom, Buddhism was nothing more than an outlandish doctrine of barbarian peoples to the west. They pointed for confirmation to the fact that neither Buddha nor his teaching was mentioned in the Chinese classics, and drew the conclusion that therefore Buddha and his teaching were unworthy of their notice.

One record of the arguments between apologists for Buddhism and Chinese opponents of the new faith is preserved in a document called the *Mou Tzu*.[77] It is a valuable record of Chinese charges against Buddhism, and of Buddhist answers to the charges. It noted the argument that Buddhist monasticism and

asceticism seemed to conflict with filial piety, for a monk had no family or family ties. His ascetic practices violated his body, which was the gift of his parents. Further his refusal to bow to the ruler seemed clearly subversive and un-Chinese. Such were the charges, and one by one the *Mou Tzu* sought rational answers to them.

Iron head of Buddha. From the Sung dynasty

Courtesy of the Metropolitan Museum of Art, Fletcher Fund, 1961

The Buddhist missionaries won their argument, at least in the opinion of great numbers of their countrymen who between the fourth and eighth centuries turned to Buddhism. So great were their numbers that in many books of history T'ang China was called Buddha land. To the Chinese mind, Buddhism brought a new dimension of transcendence. To the intellectuals it brought an Archimedean point or fulcrum above or beyond the traditional cosmos, or world of nature and society. To the populace it brought good news of a many-storied heaven which might be theirs—not to speak of an equally populated region of hell, as well as Buddhist saviors who would be man's friends and guides here and hereafter. To many Chinese people Buddhism also brought a more active compassion expressed in works of philanthropy. Conversely, Buddhism was transformed by its encounter with China.[78] The very process of translation, achieved, as we have noted, with the help of Taoist terms, aided in the trans-formation. To sum up this vast and complicated change, China brought Bud-dhism down to earth and gave it many new Chinese emphases and accents.

SECTS IN CHINESE BUDDHISM

One feature of Chinese Buddhism which is of considerable historical interest was it fragmentation into sects. Indian Buddhism, to be sure, had produced a variety of schools, each arguing the validity of its own teaching. Yet the sec-tarian divisions of Chinese Buddhism represented a new development. Each Chinese group centered in a particular Indian text which it held and taught as essential truth, and around which it gathered its adherents. These sectarian divisions in Chinese Buddhism are often compared to those of Protestant Chris-tianity. In some ways the analogy is accurate; however, in one respect it is misleading, namely, that Chinese Buddhist sects seldom or never made exclusive claims of the sort so frequent in Protestant Christianity. The Chinese Buddhist groups are also important as background of similar (but by no means identical) groups in Japan.

At least three Hinayana, or Theravada, sects sprang up in third- and fourth-century China as imports from India. But in the contest for the mind and heart of China, they proved no match for the Mahayana interpretation of Buddhism. In the case of both Theravada and Mahayana groups, the first ones were organ-ized around particular texts and bodies of teaching brought directly from India.

One such early Mahayana group was the *San Lun,* or Three Treatise sect, founded by Chi Tsang (A.D. 549–625). Of the three treatises, two were by Nagarjuna and one by his disciple Aryadeva. When this sect fell into extinc-tion, Nagarjuna's great influence was passed on through others. Another early sect was the *Wei Shih,* or Consciousness Only group, founded by the great traveler to India, Hsüan Tsang (596–664), who during his life was one of the leading Buddhists of China. This sect followed the doctrines of the Indian Yogacarya school of Asanga and Vasubandhu. Still a third early Mahayana sect was *Hua Yen,* or Flower Garland, so called from the name of its favorite Indian Sutra, the *Avatamsaka.* Its nominal founder was Tu-shun (557–640) but its great master was Fa-tsang (643–712). The influence of these men and groups penetrated Chinese Buddhism and has lasted on in other sects and traditions.

Three main families of sects have formed the main tradition of Chinese Buddhism, namely (1) *T'ien t'ai* (Heavenly Terrace, named for the mountain where its main monastery was located), (2) *Ching tu* (Pure Land, named for the Pure Land or Heaven promised to its followers) and (3) *Ch'an* (Meditation, or *Dhyana*, which is its central teaching).

T'IEN T'AI (HEAVENLY TERRACE)

T'ien t'ai Buddhism was founded by Chih-I, or Chih-k'ai (538–597), as he was sometimes called. He was a war orphan who turned to Buddhist religious practice. Possessed of a subtle and powerful philosophic mind, he was awakened by his teacher, Hui-ssu, to another and different dimension of Buddhism, namely, religious meditation. His synthesis of philosophy and meditation has characterized T'ien t'ai tradition in China and Japan ever since. Its followers have consistently maintained the double emphasis of "eyes of wisdom and legs of practice."[79]

Chih-k'ai's careful study of the *Saddharma Pundarika*, or "Lotus Sutra," convinced him that it contained the whole of essential Buddhist truth. His main writing was entitled *The Profound Meaning of the Scripture of the Lotus of the Wonderful Law;* his followers have continued to study, expand, and recite this document. Chih-k'ai also taught that Buddha, after he had achieved enlightenment, went successively through five periods of teaching beginning with the "Flower Garland Sutra," second the Hinayana canon, third the major Mahayana Sutras, fourth the Prajnaparamita Sutras, and finally the *Saddharma Pundarika*.[80] They constituted ascending steps on his road to truth or salvation.

Chih-k'ai's philosophy was a Chinese version of Nagarjuna's philosophy as transmitted by Kumarajiva. As such, his basic teaching might be characterized as mind defined as universal emptiness. By this was meant what Chapter 5 characterized in Nagarjuna as the teaching of universal relativity. From the absolute point of view, nothing truly is; all things are riddled with contingency, relativity, and internal contradiction. In other passages this was interpreted as a philosophy of universal flux, or as Chih-k'ai put it, as temporariness.

Yet the world of appearance or phenomena has at least a relative being. In an idealist cosmogony and cosmology, Chih-k'ai derived from Emptiness or Mind the ten dharma spheres of the world. In all, these ten spheres comprise the three-storied world of heaven, earth, and hell and their respective inhabitants. However, in other contexts, these levels of appearance or reality were interpreted by Chih-k'ai as a kind of ladder of ascent, beginning at the bottom with man's present forms of experience, the top being that absence of craving and of conditioned, finite reality, which is the supreme goal of man's seeking. They were similar to western ideas of degrees of being.

CHING-TU (PURE LAND)

A very different type of Buddhist thought and practice was represented by the Ching-tu, or Pure Land, group. Its traditional founder was Hui-yuan, who in the year 402 founded the White Lotus Society, composed of 123 monks and laymen united in a vow to be reborn in the pure land or western paradise of Amitabha, or Amida Buddha.[81] Yet the actual work of formulating the doctrine of Pure Land and spreading its message far and wide was done by T'an-luan (476–542). T'an-luan appears to have been seeking health by means of Taoist elixirs when an Indian monk impressed upon him the transitory character of all life and the truth of the Pure Land doctrine. T'an turned to the study of Vasubandhu's commentary on the *Sukhavativyaha Sutra* with its crucial lines:

> *Behold the phenomena of yon sphere,*
> *How they surpass the paths of the three worlds.*[82]

and its reference to the prospect of rebirth into that happy land. T'an-luan's *Commentary on Vasubandhu's Essay on Rebirth* shows all distinctive and characteristic traits of Pure Land thought and faith. Man is a sinner, guilty of the gravest violations and evils. Yet by personal relation to the Savior Amida, man may be rescued. For this he needs a trusting heart. Also he must call upon the name of Amida, repeating this name in fidelity of heart. All who call upon the name of Amida will be reborn in the Happy Land. In the Pure Land there will be a pleasant and good life for all. T'an-luan and other converts to Pure Land also pointed out the dire urgency of man's situation, and the need, up to one's dying breath, of confessing faith in Amida Buddha.

CH'AN (MEDITATION)

Perhaps most intensely Chinese of all was Ch'an, or Meditation, Buddhism, traditionally said to have been founded by the Indian monk Bodhidharma in the late fifth or early sixth century. One estimate puts him in China from 420 to 476, while another dates his coming to China in 520. He appears to have advocated meditation, in contrast to both knowledge and good deeds, as the way to enlightenment. Others, too, followed in his tradition with similar teachings, but Ch'an Buddhism owes its real impetus to the fifth and sixth Patriarchs. The fifth Patriarch, Hung-jen, was the leader of Ch'an Buddhism at the time of its split into northern and southern schools over the issue of sudden enlightenment. There is current scholarly debate over the interpretation of these crucial events.[83] According to one account Hung-jen was visited one day by an illiterate youth from the south who importuned the master to be allowed to stay and seek the Law of the Buddha. The youth's name was Hui-neng; and he stayed on to work in the monastery kitchen.

One day Hung-jen announced a contest of verses to decide his successor. A leading contender named Shen-hsiu wrote the following:

> Our body is the tree of Perfect Wisdom,
> And our mind is a bright mirror.
> At all times diligently wipe them,
> So that they will be free of dust.[84]

The fifth Patriarch expressed qualified approval of this contribution, but deferred judgment as to succession of leadership. Meanwhile Hui-neng wrote the following verse:

> The tree of Perfect Wisdom is originally no tree.
> Nor has the bright mirror any frame.
> Buddha-nature is forever clear and pure.
> Where is there any dust?

For good measure he also added the following verse:

> The mind is a tree of Perfect Wisdom.
> The body is the clear mirror.
> The clear mirror is originally clear and pure.
> Where has it been affected by any dust? [85]

His fellow monks were surprised by these verses of Hui-neng, who went back to pounding rice in the kitchen. The fifth Patriarch recognized in Hui-neng his successor, yet fearing for his safety he called him secretly at night, gave him the robe and law, making him the sixth Patriarch; but sent him away to the south. So began the split between southern and northern branches of Ch'an Buddhism, the former devoted to sudden enlightenment and the latter to gradual enlightenment.

Whatever the historicity of these stories, there was a historic split between northern and southern branches of Ch'an at this time and presumably over this issue. The northern branch went its own way, but the southern branch stemming from the impetus of Hui-neng developed its own distinctive interpretation of salvation by meditation. The living tradition was continued in the south.

Ch'an (as well as its Japanese progeny, Zen) has been summed up in four traditional maxims:

> A special transmission outside the scriptures;
> No dependence upon words and letters;

> *Direct pointing to the soul of man;*
> *Seeing into one's nature and attainment of Buddhahood.*[86]

The first maxim seems to argue for an oral tradition stemming from the Buddha, but apart from the written sources upon which other sects were based. The first two maxims taken together assert a tradition of the inwardness of spirit, independent of literal meanings or ideas. The third maxim might be paraphrased as an intuitive knowing of the self, beyond all intellectual knowledge. The fourth affirms the fruition of this knowledge as the attainment of Buddhahood or the achievement of the awakening or enlightenment which is open to all men and which constitutes man's highest fulfillment. Meditation Buddhism has consistently taught that Buddhahood or the Buddha nature is possible for all men.

The content of this experience may be described as the union of an individual human mind with Ultimate Reality in such a way that all craving is overcome, enabling one to see life steadily and see it whole. According to Ch'an and Zen, this experience is not the direct consequence of human seeking or contrivance; it is not under human control. On the other hand, there are no gods to offer supernatural assistance. Man must seek salvation in his own power. Yet having exerted himself to the fullest, he must at the last, relax and permit the experience of enlightenment to happen to him.

One distinctive aspect of Ch'an is the method by which enlightenment is pursued. It consists of disciplined obedience under a master who sets many tasks of labor, study, and devotion. The master may also resort to such extreme measures as shouting or beating. Most distinctive of all, he may set a *kung-an* (Japanese, *koan*) for his student. This is a particularly puzzling question on which the student must concentrate his attention, seeking an answer or solution. Many koans appear to be paradoxes, reflection upon which serve to jolt the student's mind free from its customary secular ruts, and thus prepare the way for enlightenment. Others are thinly veiled metaphors or allegories. In this latter category is the following dialog:

> *Question: "Whenever there is any question, one's mind is*
> *confused. What is the matter?"*
> *The Master said: "Kill, kill."* [87]

In this context the meaning of "kill" apparently is to overcome or destroy all particular entities along the path to awakening. It is apparently the Zen formulation of the *via negativa*.

The ontological or metaphysical identity between the worlds of salvation and delusion is the subject of the following koan.

> *A monk asked: "How is illusion true?"*
> *The master answered: "Illusion is originally true."*
> *The monk asked: "How is illusion manifested?"*
> *The master answered: "Illusion is manifestation and*
> *manifestation is illusion."* [88]

Other koans, like the following, seem simply to be enigmatic sayings:

> *A monk asked: "How can silence be expressed?"*
> *The master answered: "I will not express it here."*
> *The monk said: "Where will you express it?"*
> *The master said: "Last night at midnight I lost three*
> *pennies by my bed."* [89]

The koan became a widely used and characteristic teaching device in Ch'an Buddhism. It may be regarded as a distinctive formulation of the recurring religious theme of paradox, whose function is to shake a mind free of its habitual secular world and point it toward awakening. Often the koan was in effect an enacted paradox.

A fourth kind of Buddhism, *Chen yen,* or True Word, arrived late in China. In 712 three missionaries arrived in the capital city, Ch'ang-an, laden with charms, mandalas, and incantations guaranteed to induce the experience of enlightenment. Their background was the kind of tantric Buddhism and Hinduism which we have already seen in India. The new missionaries gained an initial following in the T'ang court, but as it turned out, esoteric Buddhism gained no continuing organized existence in China. Nevertheless many of its practices struck roots in the popular religion and continued in other forms. Also it soon made its way from China to Japan where as *Shingon* it has continued in vigorous life to the present.

By the ninth century Buddhism had made its decisive contribution to China. Some aspects of the new faith, like cremation and asceticism, China rejected; other aspects, such as a more active philanthropy and a new philosophic impetus, she accepted. Yet perhaps Buddhism's greatest contribution to the Chinese tradition was the stimulus it provided for the neo-Confucian revival which followed.

NEO-CONFUCIANISM

During the centuries of Buddhist ascendancy in China, Confucianism never disappeared, but only receded into the background. From this position in T'ang and Sung times, Confucianism mounted a counteroffensive against Buddhism and neo-Taoism to regain its former position of dominance. To this reassertion of China's classical tradition, the name neo-Confucianism has been given. The first stirrings of neo-Confucianism in the T'ang dynasty may be observed in that staunch old classicist, man of letters, and astringent critic of Buddhism, Han Yü (786–836). In his essay entitled, "What Is the True Way?" (*Yüan Tao*), Han vigorously attacked both Buddhism and Taoism as unfilial, unsocial, and escapist. Quoting China's ancient classics with approval, Han bade his fellow countrymen to return to the way of their fathers. He also denounced false and time-serving teachers as unworthy of the classical way of Confucius.

Han concentrated his attack on Buddhism, which was still spreading in the China of his time. His *Memorial on the Bone of Buddha* was a bitter protest to the Emperor against the honor which was being shown to a relic of Buddha. Most of all, the Emperor should not give aid and comfort by participating in these ceremonies! Rather let him give the order to seize this bone and have it cast into the fire. As for the Buddhists, they are a degenerate and immoral lot, with their ascetic practices and their superstitious ritual around this stinking bone.

In the T'ang, Han Yü was a lonely voice, but in the Sung dynasty, neo-Confucianism became a movement massively influential in both politics and philosophy. In many cases philosophers were advisors to emperors and other governmental officials. Was it not in the Confucian tradition that the philosopher should apply his wisdom to the solutions of social and political problems?

Sung neo-Confucianism began with Chou Tun-yi (1017–1073). Chou was much influenced by Taoism. It is said that his philosophic view of the Ultimate was given to him in a diagram by a Taoist priest. His ethic of tranquillity and "having no desires" show similar influence. Whatever his sources, Chou's writing expounded a cosmology in which all things proceed from the Great Ultimate (*T'ai Chi*). This term and idea may be traced in the Han dynasty "Great Appendix" to the "Book of Changes." [90]

Chou began with the exclamation, "The Non-Ultimate! And also the Great Ultimate." [91] By this he meant apparently the equivalence of non-Being, or Emptiness, and Absolute Being in a manner which both Taoist and Buddhist philosophy had made familiar. The Great Ultimate became for Chou and his neo-Confucian successors the generating source from which all else proceeded, as well as the goal to which it returned. Specifically, from the Great Ultimate are derived in succession *yin* and *yang* and the five agents—water, fire, wood, metal, and earth; and from the interaction of these forces arise all the myriad things of nature and society. By such a process the Great Ultimate gives birth to the world of everyday experience. The sage is the highest expression of humanity, and by the virtue of sincerity he establishes his oneness with Heaven and Earth.[92] By oneness is meant "having no desire," and having no desire, one is "empty." [93] In such assertions as the last the reader sees Chou's great debt to the Buddhism and Taoism which had come before him.

Shao Yung (1011–1077) continued many of Chou's interests, yet he emerges as a true Confucian, particularly in his view of the sage as the perfect man who with his mind grasps the underlying unity and structure of all being and thus is able to respond rationally to the universe around him in what Shao called the "observation of things." Of crucial importance was Shao's concept of number. Like that of Chou and others, it had esoteric and magical aspects. Yet what is philosophically important was Shao's view that numbers are embedded in the structure of the universe and thus determine reality.

Chang Tsai (1021–1077) produced a philosophy based not on number or principle (li) like that of Shao, but upon material force (ch'i). This term and the idea of material force had had a long history before Chang's time. The Han philosophers had described it as "limpid, colorless substance" which fills the universe and is the raw material of which determinate things are made. Now Chang picked up this idea and used it as the basis of a realistic metaphysics designed to oppose the views of Buddhism and Taoism. According to Chang, out of the never-ceasing flux of ch'i arise all the creatures and realities of the world, including man.

Chang's philosophy involved notable formulations of the moral and religious aspects of man's life. His "Western Inscription" (Hsi-ming), so called because it was inscribed on the west wall of his study, is an eloquent synopsis of the whole neo-Confucian view for which he spoke. It is well worth full quotation:

> Heaven is my father and earth is my mother, and even such a small creature as I finds an intimate place in their midst.
>
> Therefore that which extends throughout the universe I regard as my body and that which directs the universe I consider as my nature.
>
> All people are my brothers and sisters, and all things are my companions.
>
> The great ruler [the Emperor] is the eldest son of my parents [Heaven and earth], and the great ministers are his stewards. Respect the aged—this is the way to treat them as elders should be treated. Show affection toward the orphaned and the weak—this is the way to treat them as the young should be treated. The sage identifies his character with that of Heaven and earth, and the virtuous man is the best [among the children of Heaven and earth]. Even those who are tired, infirm, crippled, or sick, those who have no brothers or children, wives or husbands, are all my brothers who are in distress and have no one to turn to.
>
> When the time comes, to keep himself from harm—this is the care of a son. To rejoice in Heaven and have no anxiety—this is filial piety at its purest.
>
> He who disobeys [the principle of Heaven] violates virtue. He who destroys humanity (jen) is a robber. He who promotes evil lacks [moral] capacity. But he who puts his moral nature into practice and brings his physical existence to complete fulfillment can match [Heaven and earth].

He who knows the principles of transformation will skillfully carry forward the undertakings [of Heaven and earth], and he who penetrates spirit to the highest degree will skillfully carry out their will.

Do nothing shameful in the recesses of your own house and thus bring no dishonor to them. Preserve the mind and nourish the nature and thus [serve them] with untiring effort.

The great Yü hated pleasant wine but attended to the protection and support of his parents. Border Warden Ying cared for the young and thus extended his love to his own kind.

Emperor Shun's merit lay in delighting his parents with unceasing effort, and Shen-sheng's reverence was demonstrated when he awaited punishment without making an attempt to escape.

Tseng Ts'an received his body from his parents and reverently kept it intact throughout life, while Po-ch'i vigorously obeyed his father's command.

Wealth, honor, blessing, and benefit are meant for the enrichment of my life, while poverty, humble station, care, and sorrow will be my helpmates to fulfillment.

In life I follow and serve [Heaven and earth]. In death I will be at peace.[94]

The neo-Confucian movement made notable advances in the work of the two Ch'eng brothers, Ch'eng Yi (1033–1107) and Ch'eng Hao (1032–1085). The father of these two had been a friend of Chou Tun-yi, and they both studied with Chang Tsai. Both of the Ch'eng brothers were neo-Confucian philosophers, yet from their differing interpretations sprang the two significant and diverging directions of this tradition. From Ch'eng Hao came the school of Mind (*Hsin*) which led on to Wang Yang-ming (1472–1529), while from Ch'eng Yi came the school of Reason (li) culminating in Chu Hsi (1130–1200). The latter has been called by Y. L. Fung the school of "Platonic realism." [95] Perhaps it might more appropriately be called the school of Aristotelian realism.

Ch'eng Yi produced a philosophy based upon the idea of *li*, usually translated as "principle," but strikingly similar to "Platonic idea." All things under Heaven can be understood in terms of their li, or principles, said Ch'eng Yi. "Everything must have its li," [96] he quoted, from the *Book of Odes*. What Ch'eng Yi and others called "the investigation of things" consists in discovering, laying bare, and describing these principles which exist within the various structures and processes of the world. This process of inquiry was said not only to explain things, but also to fulfill the mind's life and thus produce self-realization. For Ch'eng Yi and others it came to have moral as well as intellectual significance.

As a further step, all li, said Ch'eng Yi, is ultimately one; in other words, there is one principle underlying and pervading the whole world. As he stated this matter, "You may extend it over the four seas, and it is everywhere true.

It is the unchangeable principle that can be 'laid before Heaven and earth' and is 'tested by the experience of the three kings.' " [97]

As a loyal Confucian, Ch'eng Yi held man's nature to be originally good. Yet this led to the problem of explaining why some men fulfill this potentiality and others do not. Ch'eng Yi explained this in terms of different qualities of their material force, saying that "men endowed with clear material force are wise while those endowed with turbid material force are stupid." [98]

According to Ch'eng Yi the moral fulfillment of human nature took place through the virtue which he called "seriousness," or "moral cultivation." Its goal is humanity, or humaneness.[99] Ch'eng went to great pains to distinguish Confucian seriousness from Buddhist tranquillity. While there may be superficial similarities, the former has a genuine content while the latter is admittedly empty in nature.

Ch'eng also engaged in sharp polemics on Buddhism and Taoism, which he charged with being against family and humanity. Hence they "can finally be reduced to a pattern of selfishness." [100] Taoism he found downright misleading in its slippery and paradoxical way of speaking. Hence "the Taoists carry with them an element of treachery." [101]

The philosophy that Ch'eng Yi began was brought to its definitive and culminating statement by the great Chu Hsi (1130–1200). Chu's philosophical system began in an assertion of the conjunction of li and ch'i as the form and matter of all things. In every existing thing may be detected li and ch'i. Li has a kind of logical priority; it is the timeless form of things. In the beginning was li, or as Chu Hsi put it, "before Heaven and earth existed, then was certainly only principle." [102] Furthermore, man's mind is a faculty for apprehending and containing li.

All nature was asserted by Chu to be a conjunction of li and ch'i or form and matter. Nature is principle only; but without the material force and solid substance of the universe, principle would have nothing in which to inhere. Like Ch'eng Yi before him, Chu distinguishes between clear and turbid material force; where there is clarity, li expresses itself freely, but where ch'i is turbid, there obstruction and confusion prevail.

Chu Hsi's fundamental concept was the Great Ultimate, or T'ai Chi, which he interpreted as "the principle of Heaven and earth and the myriad things." [103] The Chinese characters for T'ai Chi combine what was originally the sign for the ridgepole of a tent and the sign for pervasiveness. It will not be far off the mark to envisage the universe as a tent with T'ai Chi as its ridgepole. As Chu Hsi put it, "the Great Ultimate is similar to the top of the house or the zenith of the sky." [104] Chu asserted that while the Great Ultimate is one, its manifestations are infinitely many. For all things that exist in some sense express the Great Ultimate. For this relation Chu used the metaphor of the moon, which is one, but whose light is reflected on the myriad surfaces of the world. The Great Ultimate is at once the first and last reality and the highest good, in which all virtues are fulfilled.

Like other Chinese scholars before him, and like intellectuals in many of the world's traditions, Chu Hsi was scornful of anthropomorphic views of Heaven or deity. He shared the reticence and agnosticism of Confucius concerning the shen and kwei of popular religion as well as life after death. Like Confucius he proposed to continue the sacrificial rites for social and aesthetic reasons.

According to Chu the goal of man was the realization of humanity. He quoted with approval the maxim of Ch'eng Yi, "When man puts impartiality into practice that is humanity," and added that humanity is "the principle originally inherent in man's mind." [105] Out of impartiality and humanity are born altruism and love.

Chu Hsi was a statesman of note, but he preferred the life of the teacher and scholar. To his White Deer Grotto, students came from all parts of China, imbibing the philosophy which soon became in effect China's official view— challenged but never displaced for the next seven centuries. Chu was a great scholar, whose editions of the classical Confucian texts became the accepted ones. As we have seen, it was he who placed the Four Books alongside the Five Classics as required reading for all who would be scholars. It was also he who ruled Hsün tzu to be heterodox and Mencius to be orthodox.

Chu Hsi's philosophy was challenged during his lifetime by the school of Mind, deriving from Ch'eng Yi's older brother, Ch'eng Hao, and Lu Chiu-yüan (1139–1192), or as he was also known, Lu Hsiang-shan. Ch'eng Hao's philosophy expressed many of the same ideas and emphases as that of his younger brother. However, there was one notable difference, namely, a greater emphasis upon the identity of man's mind with the universe and upon the intuitive character of the thinking process by which this identity is achieved and sustained. Chang Tsai had said "that which extends throughout the universe I regard as my body and that which directs the universe I regard as my nature." Ch'eng Hao wrote analogously, "The humane man forms one body with all things comprehensively." [106] By the cultivation of sincerity and seriousness, a man finds his place in the scheme of things entire and is thus able to say, "All the operations of the universe are our operations."

What Ch'eng Hao began, Lu Chiu-yüan carried forward. He argued forcefully that humanity is by nature mind, and that mind consists in li. Hence as a man comes to see the identity of the li in his mind with the li of the universe, he comes to an intuitive sense of oneness with the universe. Lu's philosophy was clearly more subjective and more intuitive than that of Chu Hsi.

The school of Mind received its definitive statement some centuries later in the philosophy of Wang Yang-ming (1472–1529), or Wang Shou-jen as he is sometimes called. A general and statesman of great distinction and integrity as well as a philosopher, Wang sought in his philosophy to give expression to the principles by which he lived.

Like others before him in the school of Mind, Wang wrote eloquently on the unity of all things. "The great man regards Heaven and earth and the myriad things as one body. He regards the world as one family and the country as one person." [107] This sense of identity is to be realized in filial feeling, not only toward one's own father but toward the fathers of all men, in brotherhood with all men, and in attitude of sympathy toward every human being. Indeed, Wang extended this feeling of sympathy beyond the boundary of humanity to include every living being.

The intuitive sense of right and wrong he regarded as "innate knowledge" given to man by Heaven, and therefore "the original substance of my mind." [108] In this form of knowing, Wang asserted, is the unity of all things, for in all of this there is no separation of mind and li. Such dualities come about as a result of selfish desires which breed error. Hence, Wang concluded, "the innate knowledge of my mind is the same as the principle of Heaven." [109]

Perhaps Wang's most distinctive teaching was his doctrine of unity of knowledge and action. When men know truly, action follows naturally. Conversely "there have never been people who know but do not act." [110] Selfish desires intrude to distort and to separate knowing and doing. Truly to know entails doing, and vice versa. "Knowledge is the beginning of action and action is the completion of knowledge." [111]

RECENT AND CONTEMPORARY ISSUES

Modernity came late to China, being forced upon her at gunpoint by Western nations during the nineteenth century. Now, more than a century later, we can at least begin to assess its multiple impact upon the massively traditional culture of China. First it must be said that the coming of the modern age only aggravated the longtime problems of Taoism and Buddhism in China. Popular, or religious, Taoism has existed for several centuries in a dying condition. Hence the coming of modernity has only served to accelerate its death.

Taoist godlings have continued to elicit popular devotion, popular Taoist literature has continued to circulate, Taoist charms and fetishes have continued to be worn, and secret societies of dominantly (though by no means exclusively) Taoist inspiration have sprung up in recent centuries. Yet as W. T. Chan points out, since the thirteenth century there has been no reading or study of the Taoist classics, and there has been a steady deterioration of its schools. There has also been a lack of leadership.

There was a brief flare-up of Taoism in the Boxer Rebellion of 1900, for the Boxers, along with other secret societies, were a Taoist sect. The Dowager Empress was a leader in welding together Chinese nationalism and Taoist voodooism. The Boxers believed that their Taoist charms would protect them from the bullets of foreign devils. There are authentic records of Boxers, firm in this faith, who were shot down and arose and staggered on a few steps before falling again. Such apparently were the powers—and limits—of this faith.

Chan reports that in 1948–1949 the Taoist center at Dragon-Tiger Mountain and the White Cloud Temple were well kept.[112] Yet at the mountain, the "Heavenly Teacher" of Taoism, the sixty-third lineal descendant of Chang Ling, had disappeared and was completely forgotten. Under China's Marxist rulers there seems no prospect for Taoism except extinction.

Chinese Buddhism entered the modern world after several centuries of governmental discrimination and anti-Buddhist propaganda. In the present century it has suffered for several decades from what its leaders call "catastrophes"— special taxes, confiscation of property, destruction of temples, and forced secularization of monks and nuns.[113] It cannot be expected that any of these trends has been reversed by Chinese Communism.

Within the twentieth century there have been some notable efforts at reform and revitalization of Chinese Buddhism. The great Buddhist abbot, T'ai-hsü (1889–1947), was indefatigable in his effort to reform and rebuild Chinese Buddhism, seeking to redirect it toward this-worldly, humanistic, and scientific goals.[114] Buddhist laymen under the leadership of Ou-yang Ching-wu (1871–1943) worked toward similar goals. There was concurrently a notable increase in publication and circulation of Buddhist books and periodicals. These men and movements breathed new life into many traditional ideas and organizational structures. Yet their longtime influence in a China ravaged by war and then dominated by Communists is, to say the least, problematic. To date the Marxist rulers of China have given no indication of any attitude other than hostility toward Buddhism or any other traditional religious faith.

The situation, though somewhat more complicated, is not essentially different for China's other major faith, Confucianism. Confucian bureaucrats and philosophers were unable to make any effective response to the coming of Western nations, Western ideas, and Western guns.[115] They were also unable to extricate themselves—or Confucianism—from the downfall of the Manchu dynasty in 1911.

The Manchu, or Ch'ing, dynasty (1644–1911) was toppled by Sun Yat-sen's nationalist revolution of 1911–1912. Efforts which were made to have Confucianism established as a state religion in the new Chinese nation came to naught. The Constitution of 1913 asserted that "in the education of citizens the doctrines of Confucius shall be regarded as the basis of moral cultivation."

However, the 1923 Constitution said only that "a citizen of the Republic of China shall be free to honor Confucius and to prefer any religion." [116]

Meanwhile the ethics of Confucius, indeed, his whole philosophy, was subjected to an all-embracing critical attack. The New Culture Movement which began in 1916 under the leadership of Ch'en Tu-hsiu (1879–1942) and Hu Shih (1891–1963) vigorously attacked Confucian ethics, philosophy, and scholarship as hopelessly obsolete and an obstacle to China's progress. Both Ch'en and Hu were forthright partisans of modernity and hence opposed to Confucian traditionalism.[117]

Ch'en was the founder of the Chinese Communist Party, though he was later expelled and disowned by the Party. He was a lifelong iconoclast. Hu was American-educated, at Cornell and Columbia, and was an adherent of John Dewey's philosophy, which he pitted against Confucius. Through their periodical, *The New Youth,* these men and their colleagues poured a withering fire upon Confucian ethics, demanding personal freedom from bondage to the family system. Hu also initiated what he called a literary revolution against stilted and artificial ways of writing and scholarship. Hu also proposed a mode of thought called "doubting antiquity." [118] Soon the issues broadened into a debate on the issue of science versus traditional humanism.

Not all Chinese opinion was hostile to Confucius. When Sun Yat-sen died the leadership of the nationalist movement and Kuomintang Party passed to the more traditional Chiang Kai-shek (1887–   ). In addition to his expulsion of Russian advisors and opposition to Chinese Communists, Chiang undertook in 1934 a New Life Movement.[119] This was an effort to provide in more traditional terms a new basis for individual and social ethics. While this program was undoubtedly influenced by Chiang's newly found Christianity, the influence of Confucian ideas and ideals was also clearly present. The content of the new life was declared to be the four traditional Chinese virtues, *li* (decorum or good form), *i* (righteousness or duty), *lien* (integrity or honesty), and *ch'ih* (sense of shame for what is evil). The whole program was pervaded by the Confucian spirit of self-cultivation.

At the same time that Chiang was launching his popular movement, Professor Y. L. Fung (1895–   ) was constructing his own attempt at modern neo-Confucian philosophy. In the tradition and spirit of Ch'eng Yi and Chu Hsi, Fung sought to construct a new Confucian philosophic synthesis which would make China's tradition and its values available to the twentieth century. The attempt, admittedly ambitious, had some success. However, it came to a sudden and violent end in 1950 when Fung renounced Confucianism and his own lifework in order to embrace the Marxist philosophy.[120]

In 1949 the Communists came to power in China, Chiang Kai-shek and his government fleeing to Taiwan. As the Communists consolidated their position, they behaved in predictably antireligious ways toward China's traditional faiths.

The few bits of reliable information which filter through the bamboo curtain separating China from the West suggest that these antireligious attitudes persist, and that their impact increases.

As these words are written, Marxism seems secure in its hold upon China. The people of the Central Kingdom are being persuaded by the forcible persuasions of Mao Tse-tung and his followers to desert their old teacher Confucius for the new teachers, Marx and Mao. Therefore the foreseeable future is dark for all of China's traditional faiths. Yet students of history know that the intentions of even the most powerful rulers sometimes come to unexpected conclusions. Students of Chinese history also know that the Chinese anvil has outworn many hammers.

CONCLUDING COMMENT

As the student of religions looks back across the many centuries of China's history, what does he see? What does traditional China have to tell us about man and the forms of his ultimate concern? Our study suggests a fourfold answer. (1) The Chinese tradition constitutes a classical depiction of man in the cosmos. Regardless of his own faith or philosophy, no man can remain unmoved or unilluminated by China's statement of human excellence and fulfillment—in short by its humanism and humanistic tradition. At many points this humanism is like that of ancient Greece and Rome, and Confucius bears striking similarity to Aristotle. In both cases man is depicted as fulfilling or perfecting his life within the comprehensive context of the cosmos. China shows us the greatness and also the limitations of this way of construing the human situation. (2) The tradition of Taoist thought and expression is China's highly original statement of man's creative and transcendent freedom, the freedom to stand clear of the common life, to celebrate the unique individuality of one's own life, and in one's own way to celebrate one's unity with the universe. (3) Chinese Buddhism, while long eclipsed by Confucianism, nonetheless did bring the monk's gaze from heaven down to earth, directing Buddhist meditation upon the goods of this life and this world. This meditation provided an essential ingredient in neo-Confucianism. Without Chinese Buddhism, Chu Hsi could not have been. Chinese Buddhism was also an essential link in the transmission of Buddhism to Japan. (4) China also presents a distinctive view of the relation of faith to philosophy and of the uses of philosophy. Hsün tzu, Wang Ch'ung, and their followers join forces with Lucretius and Voltaire in the criticism of religious superstitions, weaknesses, and vices. Chu Hsi's capacious and comprehensive mind speaks across barriers of time and space, communicating to all men its synoptic and rational vision. Confucius still calls men to fulfill their humanity by lives of thought and service to humankind. To men with minds to learn, traditional China still has much to teach.

NOTES

1. Unpublished remark made in a Claremont Graduate School seminar by Chang Chuan-Yüan in 1964.

2. *A Source Book in Chinese Philosophy,* Wing-Tsit Chan, trans., Princeton University Press, Princeton, N.J., 1963, p. 3.

3. Yu-Lan Fung, *A Short History of Chinese Philosophy,* The Macmillan Company, New York, 1960, pp. 3–4.

4. Edwin O. Reischauer and John K. Fairbank, *History of East Asian Civilization,* Houghton Mifflin Company, Boston, 1960, p. 68.

5. James R. Ware, *The Sayings of Confucius,* Mentor Books, New American Library of World Literature, Inc., New York, 1955, III, 13.

6. Wing-Tsit Chan, *Religious Trends in Modern China,* Columbia University Press, New York, 1953, pp. 25–26.

7. Confucius, "Analects," VII, 22.

8. *Li Chi,* IX.

9. "Analects," XIII, 18.

10. *Ibid.,* II, 7.

11. *Li Chi,* XV.

12. "Analects," XII, 22.

13. *Ibid.,* IV, 2.

14. *Ibid.,* XIV, 36.

15. *Ibid.,* XV, 23.

16. *Ibid.,* XVII, 2.

17. *Ibid.,* IX, 4.

18. *Ibid.,* IV, 8.

19. *Ibid.,* XII, 11.

20. *Ibid.,* III, 13.

21. *Ibid.,* VII, 34.

22. *Ibid.,* XI, 11.

23. *Ibid.,* VI, 20.

24. *Ibid.,* III, 17.

25. Lin Yutang, *The Wisdom of Confucius,* Modern Library, Inc., New York, 1938, p. 14.

26. Philomene S. Harrison, "Lao Tzu and the Ch'un-Ch'in Period: An Inquiry into our Present Knowledge of the Tao Te' Ching," unpublished doctoral dissertation, Claremont, Calif., 1963.

27. Lin Mousheng, *Men and Ideas,* The John Day Company, Inc., New York, 1943, p. 9.

28. Fung, *op. cit.,* p. 9.

29. Ware, *op. cit.,* I, 2.

30. Chan, *A Source Book in Chinese Philosophy,* p. 139.

31. *Ibid.,* p. 160.

32. *Ibid.,* p. 146.

33. *Ibid.,* p. 143.

34. *Ibid.,* p. 142.

35. *Ibid.,* p. 147.

36. *Ibid.,* p. 154.

37. *Ibid.,* p. 141.

38. *Ibid.,* pp. 148–149.

39. *Ibid.,* p. 140.

40. *Ibid.,* p. 168.

41. *Ibid.,* p. 175.

42. *Ibid.,* pp. 186–187.

43. *Ibid.,* p. 191.

44. *Ibid.,* p. 202.

45. *Ibid.,* p. 183.

46. *Ibid.,* p. 181.

47. *Ibid.,* p. 187.

48. *Ibid.,* p. 190.

49. William T. de Bary and others (eds.), *Sources of Chinese Tradition,* Columbia University Press, New York, 1960, p. 79.

50. Chan, *A Source Book in Chinese Philosophy,* p. 209.

51. *Ibid.,* p. 233.

52. *Ibid.,* p. 233.

53. *Ibid.,* p. 234.

54. *Ibid.,* p. 235.

55. *Ibid.,* p. 242.

56. de Bary, *op. cit.,* p. 129.

57. *Ibid.,* p. 135.

58. *Ibid.,* p. 183.

59. *Ibid.,* p. 257.

60. *Ibid.,* p. 163.

61. *Ibid.,* pp. 246–247.

62. *Ibid.,* p. 251.

63. *Ibid.,* pp. 251–252.

64. *Ibid.,* p. 253.

65. "Analects," XI, 18.

66. Fung, *op. cit.,* chaps. 19, 20.

67. de Bary, *op. cit.,* p. 282.

68. Fung, *op. cit.,* p. 221.

69. *Ibid.,* p. 222.

70. *Ibid.,* p. 237.

71. *Ibid.,* pp. 236–237.

72. *Ibid.,* p. 235.

73. de Bary, *op. cit.*, pp. 298f.

74. *Ibid.*, p. 301.

75. Kenneth W. Morgan (ed.), *The Path of the Buddha*, The Ronald Press Company, New York, 1956, p. 184.

76. Reischauer and Fairbank, *op. cit.*, p. 146.

77. de Bary, *op. cit.*, p. 314.

78. H. Nakamura, *The Ways of Thinking of Eastern People*, compiled by Japanese National Commission for UNESCO, Tokyo, 1960.

79. Morgan, *op. cit.*, p. 202.

80. *Ibid.*, p. 200.

81. *Ibid.*, pp. 194–195.

82. de Bary, *op. cit.*, p. 376.

83. *Ibid.*, p. 390.

84. *Ibid.*, p. 391.

85. *Ibid.*, p. 391.

86. D. T. Suzuki, *Zen Buddhism,* ed. by William Barrett, Anchor Books, Doubleday & Company, Inc., Garden City, N.Y., 1956, p. 9.

87. de Bary, *op. cit.*, p. 408.

88. *Ibid.*, p. 405.

89. *Ibid.*, p. 406.

90. Fung, *op. cit.*, p. 283.

91. de Bary, *op. cit.*, p. 513.

92. *Ibid.*, pp. 514f.

93. *Ibid.*, p. 515.

94. de Bary, *op. cit.*, pp. 524–525.

95. Fung, *op. cit.*, chap. 25.

96. de Bary, *op. cit.*, p. 527.

97. *Ibid.*, p. 527.

98. *Ibid.*, p. 529.

99. *Ibid.*, p. 530.

100. *Ibid.*, p. 533.

101. *Ibid.*, p. 533.

102. *Ibid.*, p. 540.

103. *Ibid.*, p. 539.

104. *Ibid.*, p. 540.

105. *Ibid.*, p. 556.

106. *Ibid.*, p. 559.

107. *Ibid.*, p. 571.

108. *Ibid.*, p. 576.

109. *Ibid.*, p. 578.

110. *Ibid.*, p. 579.

111. *Ibid.*, p. 579.

112. Chan, *Religious Trends in Modern China*, p. 152.

113. de Bary, *op. cit.*, chaps. 24, 26.

114. Chan, *Religious Trends in Modern China*, pp. 118f.

115. *Ibid.*, p. 4.

116. *Ibid.*, p. 8.

117. de Bary, *op. cit.*, pp. 813f.

118. *Ibid.*, p. 844.

119. *Ibid.*, pp. 800f.

120. Chan, *A Source Book in Chinese Philosophy*, pp. 751f.

SUGGESTIONS FOR FURTHER STUDY

Bruce, J. P.: *Chu Hsi and His Masters*, Probsthain, 1923.

Chan, W. T.: *Religious Trends in Modern China*, Columbia, 1953.

Creel, H. G.: *Confucius: The Man and the Myth*, John Day, 1949.

de Bary, W. T. (ed.): *Sources of Chinese Tradition*, Columbia, 1960.

Dubs, H. H.: *Hsüntze, the Moulder of Ancient Confucianism*, Probsthain, 1927.

Fung, Y. L.: *A History of Chinese Philosophy*, Princeton, 1952.

————: *A Short History of Chinese Philosophy*, Macmillan, 1960.

Goodrich, H. C.: *A Short History of the Chinese People*, Harper & Row, 1943.

Hamilton, C. (ed.): *Buddhism: A Religion of Infinite Compassion*, Liberal Arts, 1952.

Lao-Tzu: *The Way of Life: Tao Te Ching*, trans. R. B. Blakney, Mentor Books, 1955.

Latourette, K. S.: *The Chinese: Their History and Their Culture*, Macmillan, 1934.

Legge, James: *The Texts of Taoism*, SBE, Oxford, 1891.

Lin Yutang: *The Wisdom of Confucius*, Modern Library, 1938.

————: *The Wisdom of India and China*, Modern Library, 1942.

Morgan, K. (ed.): *The Path of the Buddha*, Ronald, 1956.

Reichelt, K.: *Religion in Chinese Garment*, Lutterworth, 1951.

Soothill, W.: *The Lotus of the Wonderful Law*, Oxford, 1930.

A Source Book in Chinese Philosophy, trans. W. T. Chan, Princeton, 1963.

Waley, A.: *Three Ways of Thought in Ancient China*, Anchor Books, 1939.

Ware, J.: *The Sayings of Confucius*, Mentor Books, 1955.

Wilhelm, R.: *Confucius and Confucianism*, Harcourt, Brace, 1931.

Zuercher, E.: *The Buddhist Conquest of China*, Brill, 1959.

9

JAPANESE RELIGION

Compared with the long history of China, that of Japan is brief and recent; and it has been much influenced by China. Yet the Japanese have imparted their own distinctive shape to all the materials that have come to their shores from the Asian mainland and more recently from the West. Illustrations of this process of assimilation range from language and art to virtually every other significant element of Japanese culture; however, there is no more important example than Japanese Buddhism, which is surely as much Japanese as it is Buddhist.

Japanese and Chinese religions constitute a study in similarities and differences. In both Japan and China, as in other religious traditions of the first, or cosmic, type throughout the world, nature and society, taken together, are man's ultimate concern. For both China and Japan, furthermore, nature is primarily an aesthetic reality to be apprehended by the perceptive eye of the artist. The Japanese have given their own distinctive expression to this theme; as H. Nakamura has put it, the Japanese apprehend the "absolute in the phenomenal world." [1] That is to say, the absolute is not some remote entity beyond this world but is to be envisaged in and through the world of present appearance.

The Japanese tradition has worked with many materials imported from China, as for instance, the Confucian ethic, or emperor worship. However, the end result is something uniquely Japanese. Nakamura has spoken of the unique importance in Japan of the "concrete social nexus," the actual social context of the individual in family, community, and nation.[2] Correlated with this context has been the flexibility and pragmatism of the individual in fitting himself into the existing situation and living his life as a part of this concrete social whole. Nakamura speaks of this trait as the Japanese "acceptance of actuality."[3]

Modern Japan alone among Asian societies has succeeded in building and maintaining a highly efficient, advanced industrial society. One of the innumerable consequences of this achievement is a combination, which is unique on the face of the earth, of the old and the new in Japanese culture. It is a combination that the Japanese appear to accept with a maximum of harmony and a minimum of discord. Nowhere is this Japanese combination of the old and the new more important than in religion.

SHINTO MYTH AND RITUAL

The customary label for Japan's indigenous religious tradition is *Shinto*. This name is ironical, for it is Chinese (*shen* means "spirit" or "god"; *tao* means "way"; hence, "way of the gods"). The Japanese rendering of the same expression is *kami no michi*. In a recent book title, Professor Sokyo Ono has proposed "The Kami Way" as an adequate English rendering of *Shinto*.[4] The term *kami* needs explanation, for it is fundamental to Shinto, and it is an elusive term for Western students. It surely does not mean "God", and even "god" does not render it accurately. The Greek term *daimon* comes closer, but this word too has been largely lost to modern speech and thought. In terms of Chapter 1, *kami* may be rendered as "power" or "holy power." Sometimes this power is somewhat personal—at least personal enough to be invoked or prayed to—but in other situations kami is an object as impersonal as a river, a mountain, or a stone, or it is a pervasive ethos. Perhaps the truth of the matter is that the early Japanese found no necessity to become clear or definite on these issues and so left them vague—to the bewilderment of modern Western students of religion. Hence having sought to characterize kami, we shall leave it untranslated throughout this chapter.

There are many—innumerably many—kami, and the Japanese have never felt the necessity of ordering this thickly populated pantheon beyond the assertion of a functional primacy of *Amaterasu Omikami*. And this, as we shall see, derives largely from the rise to dominance in ancient Japan of the Yamato clan which worshipped Amaterasu. Speaking generally, the dwelling places of the kami are nature or society or some combination of both. Any mysterious, strange, or impressive aspect of the social or natural world is likely to reveal the presence of a kami. But the best summary of this matter is from a celebrated Shinto scholar, Motoori Norinaga (1730–1801):

> *I do not yet understand the meaning of the term* kami. *Speaking in general, however, it may be said that* kami *signifies, in the first place, the deities of heaven and earth that appear in the ancient records and also the spirits of the shrines where they are worshipped.*
>
> *It is hardly necessary to say that it includes human beings. It also includes such objects as birds, beasts, trees, plants, seas, mountains, and so forth. In ancient usage, anything whatsoever which was outside the ordinary, which possessed superior power, or which was awe-inspiring was called* kami. *Eminence here does not refer merely to the superiority of nobility, goodness, or meritorious deeds. Evil and mysterious things, if they are extraordinary and dreadful, are called* kami. *It is needless to say that among human beings who are called* kami *the successive generations of sacred emperors are all included. The fact that emperors are also called "distant kami" is because, from the standpoint of common people, they are far-separated, majestic, and worthy of reverence. In a lesser degree we find, in the present as well as in ancient times, human beings who are* kami. *Although they may not be accepted throughout the whole country, yet in each province, each village, and each family there are human beings who are* kami, *each one according to his own proper position. The* kami *of the divine age were for the most part human beings of that time and, because the people of that time were all* kami, *it is called the Age of the Gods* (kami).[5]

As in the case of all faiths, Shinto has its distinctive myth and ritual. Indeed Shinto *is* this myth and ritual. It is also the distinctive cluster of values which is the human substance of what is recited in the myth and enacted in the ritual. These values might be summarized in the phrase "the Japanese way of life." As this chapter proceeds we shall seek to unpack this phrase and inspect some of its contents. Meanwhile, it may be remarked that Shinto is the clearest example among mankind's living religions of a type-one, or nature-culture, religion.

Shinto also involves the student once more in the recurring question: What is religion? More specifically it raises questions about the extension of this concept, for it involves many activities which in other societies would not be conventionally classified as religious. For example, most Americans would not classify community observances such as Memorial Day parades and decoration of military graves, or July Fourth gatherings as religious. Neither would they feel that a visit to Washington's home at Mount Vernon or to the Lincoln Memorial were religious exercises. (In passing, it may be noted that recent writers as different in outlook as Will Herberg, Lloyd Warner, and Robert Bellah have spoken of America's new civic religion in which in popular myth and ritual the American way of life is celebrated.[6]) In such observances the parallel to Shinto becomes explicit. Yet whatever the case for America or other peoples or nations, the analogous activities in Japan take place within the religious auspices of Shinto.

SHINTO MYTH

If one turns to Shinto myth, he may observe significant analogy to American stories of origin and destiny from the landing of the Pilgrims to the legends of Washington, Lincoln, or even more recent heroes. In the case of Shinto, there are no canonical scriptures analogous to the Judeo-Christian Bible; however, there are sacred writings, notably the Kojiki, "Record of Ancient Tales," and the Nihongi or Nihon Shoki, or "Chronicle of Japan." Precise dates can be assigned to both, the former being produced in A.D. 712 and the latter in A.D. 720. Both show the influence of Chinese historical writing of the time. Together they contain the main mythological sources of Shinto. Here we shall summarize briefly six of these mythical episodes or themes which have historical and contemporary importance.

COSMOGONIC MYTH

The cosmogony of the Kojiki speaks of the primordial chaos as like an ocean of mud out of which three kami sprang. All three were born apparently without progenitors, and left no posterity. Other kami sprang into being and in the characteristic manner of kami, became invisible. Among these subsequent kami were *Iza nagi* (the Male Who Invites) and *Iza nami* (the Female Who Invites), the Japanese versions of the recurring Sky Father and Earth-Mother. They were ordered by their heavenly colleagues to give birth to the earth. Provided with a spear, they descended to the floating bridge of heaven where they thrust the spear into the brine. As they drew up the spear, the tip formed the island of Onogoro, where they erected a palace and a pillar. Exploring their bodies, they discovered their sexual differences and desired union. Going around the sacred pillar, they embraced, and from their union were born innumerable kami as well as the islands of Japan, mountains, rivers, sea, and finally the Fire Kami. In this last birth Iza-nami was so badly burnt that she died and withdrew to the nether world.

A well-known student of Japanese religion comments accurately on stories of beginnings that they are not in any precise sense a creation story similar to that in Genesis, where a sovereign Lord calls the world into being out of nothingness.[7] Creation stories of this sort seem limited to the third, or monotheistic, type of religion. By contrast, these Japanese stories like many other tales from type-one, or cosmic, religions simply and artlessly recount the beginnings of the things of nature and culture.

IZA NAGI IN THE UNDERWORLD

A sequel to the cosmogonic myth is the story of Iza nagi's descent to the underworld in search of his wife. Finding her place, he talked with her, asking her to return to the world. She asked him to wait, meanwhile pleading with him not to look upon her present decomposed state. Disobeying, Iza nagi lit the end-piece of his comb only to see his wife's hideous decaying body. In horror at what he saw, he fled, pursued by the ugly forces of the nether world.

What is the meaning of this story, so similar to Mesopotamian, Greek, and other stories of descent to the underworld? Is this a myth of the seasons? Is Holtom right in regarding it as a picture poem depicting a terrific thunder-

Haniwa, or ancient Japanese grave figure representing deceased family member

Courtesy of the American Region News Bureau, Japan Airlines

storm? [8] Or is Ross correct in suggesting a psychological interpretation of man's coming to definite consciousness? [9] As is so often true with mythical materials, it seems impossible to make a definite decision on the basis of the document itself. It is possible that several elements are involved.

AMATERASU AND SUSA-NO-O

When Iza nagi reached the upper world he paused by the sea in characteristically Japanese fashion to cleanse himself. Ablution and purification are recurring themes in Shinto. In the course of Iza nagi's ablutions, several kami were born. From the dirt washed from his left eye was born the most important kami of all, Amaterasu. From the dirt washed from his right eye was born the moon kami, Tsukiyomi, while from his nose was born the storm kami, Susa-no-o (or Susa-no-wu). The moon kami is not heard from again in the Kojiki, but the relations between Amaterasu and her brother Susa-no-o are developed in detail. As befits a storm deity, Susa-no-o was violent and capricious, doing great damage to mountains and rivers. Then according to the Nihongi he and Amaterasu each produced children, Susa-no-o by chewing up Amaterasu's string of curved jewels, and Amaterasu by chewing up Susa-no-o's sword.

Susa-no-o continued his pranks and depredations, breaking down the divisions of his sister's heavenly rice fields, filling the ditches, and polluting with dung the hall in which she held the feast of the first fruits. His misdeeds achieved a climax when he broke through the roof tiles of her weaving room, and threw in a flayed colt. A council of kami, called to deal with the refractory deity, expelled him from heaven to dwell in the region of the Izumo shrine in western Japan.

AMATERASU IN HIDING

Meanwhile the enraged Amaterasu had hidden herself in a rock cave. A myriad of kami sought to entice her out. Their efforts culminated in an obscene dance that evoked roars of laughter and excitement and caused the offended Amaterasu to peer out in curiosity. Thereupon a rope was stretched behind her, beyond which she could not again withdraw.

What is the meaning of these myths? The reader will not be wrong in seeing here the free play of primitive or archaic imagination on perennial themes of nature and society. From the beginning Amaterasu has been a sun goddess. As noted above, she was the deity of the Yamato clan; when this clan won military and political leadership in ancient Japan, their deity assumed primacy as well. Susa-no-o was related in early history to the Izumo shrine. These, and doubtless innumerable other suggestions, are implicit throughout these artless stories.

FOUNDING OF JAPANESE EMPIRE

A politically important myth was the story of Amaterasu's sending her grandson Ninigi to the earth to rule the islands of Japan. Her charge to him was contained in words which many a patriotic Japanese has learned by heart: "The Luxuriant Land of Reed Plains is a country which our descendants are to inherit. Go, therefore, Our Imperial Grandson, and rule over it! And may Our Imperial lineage continue unbroken and prosperous, coeternal with Heaven and Earth!" [10] Pious tradition reckons these events of the beginning of the Japanese empire to have taken place in 660 B.C., though critical historical study lends no support to this or any other date.

ISÉ SHRINE

Of comparable significance was the story of the enshrinement of Amaterasu at Ise, a shrine connected thenceforth with the imperial house. The shrine was built, and in it were placed the three symbols of Amaterasu and the Japanese imperial house, a mirror, jewels, and a sword. Through many centuries of Japanese history, men have made pilgrimages to Ise and there have personally verified this myth. Many more tales both local and national might be added, but these are sufficient to make clear the nature of Shinto myth as a celebration of Japanese history and values, in short, of the Japanese way of life.

Ise Shrine
Courtesy of the Japan National Tourist Organization

SHINTO RITUAL

Shinto ritual may be characterized as the enactment in symbolic actions of these same values. Shinto ritual like the myth is of diverse origins and combines a wide variety of interests. Elements of animism, fertility worship, worship of ancestors and heroes, and nature worship are only a few of its ingredients. The sun goddess herself combines in her own person many roles. She is the chief deity of Japan and of the imperial house as well as sun goddess.

Shinto rite and myth exhibit an impressive regional diversity. Local shrines and celebrations have always played an important part in Shinto. We have already alluded to two of the most important regional shrines, at Izumo on the west coast and Ise on the inland sea, which came also to nationwide significance.

While Shinto ritual has changed along with all things historical, there have been few if any radical mutations in its long history. Contemporary Shinto ritual thus provides a point of living relation between twentieth-century Japan and its ancient past.

Shrine buildings have been characteristically simple in structure, usually constructed of wood with whole tree trunks for beams. Traditionally they consisted of a single room, though they were sometimes partitioned. Often ceremonial objects, such as the mirror at Ise, are enshrined within, symbolizing the kami who lives there. But at times the building has served simply as a place where people might go singly or in groups to worship the kami. The most prominent and best-known feature has been the *torii* gateway which serves as a sign of the shrine. Near the entrance there is running water or a water basin where the mouth and hands of worshipers may be ceremonially cleansed.

Shinto worship has traditionally consisted of two elements, attendance and offering. The former term refers to all the forms of participation in the ritual, whether procession, dance, or other appropriate ceremony. Offerings in ancient times consisted of such things as first fruits, first catch of fish, or booty of war brought as food for the kami. In modern times the offerings have been food or money. Offerings also include prayers which are punctuated by a clapping of hands in order to attract the kami's attention. Many of the ritual prayers and liturgies preserved from early times show a simple and archaic beauty of language which is characteristic of Shinto.

The festivals of Shinto as well as the values they celebrate are innumerable and diverse, ranging from Kyoto's *Gion* festival, which recalls an eighth-century deliverance from pestilence, to the cycle of the agricultural year. Foods, most notably rice, figure prominently as themes. Among the festivals of national scope is the New Year's celebration during which millions of Japanese visit the Meiji shrine adjacent to the imperial palace grounds of Tokyo or other shrines throughout the land.[11]

Among other important observances are the *Nii-name-sai*, or Festival of New Food, celebrated November 23 and 24 as a thanksgiving for the harvest, and the

Three Shinto shrines in the mountains of South Nara

Courtesy of the Cleveland Museum of Art,
John L. Severance Fund

Dai-jo-sai, or Great Food Festival, which confirms a new Emperior's authority. In the latter, a series of year-long symbolic activities relating to the rice harvest culminate in a ceremonial meal eaten by the new Emperior.[12] Again the observer sees in all this a fusion of social and natural values.

Shinto goes back to the prehistoric past of Japan, and in many ways it is not essentially different from other folk religions. What is unusual in Shinto is its persistent vitality. Buddhism pushed it into the background but by no means displaced or destroyed it. Rather, in the background it continued to function as an ethos, or climate of opinion, and even more important, as a climate of feeling and sensibility for the whole Japanese cultural tradition. Also, at significant

Torii gateway at Shinto shrine, Miyajima
Courtesy of the Japan National Tourist Organization

period• of Japanese history it has thrust its way into the foreground of important structures and events.

BUDDHIST BEGINNINGS

Buddhism came to Japan along with written language and other arts of civilized life in approximately the fourth and fifth centuries. Two particular episodes in this process are recounted in the Nihongi. The first occurred in A.D. 552, when the King of Paekche in Korea sent to the Japanese court an envoy with an image of Buddha, along with some writings and a hearty recommendation to try the new faith. The Emperor was delighted, but his court was sharply divided. The new worship began, but a pestilence occurring shortly thereafter was interpreted as being due to the hostility of the national gods; as a consequence the image of Buddha was thrown into a moat and his new temple razed. It was not until 584 that a second start was made. New images and books were sent from Korea. Again forcible measures were taken to suppress Buddhism, but this time to no avail. Learned priests began to arrive from Korea as missionary teachers. Buddhism survived and grew.

Among the most avid students of the new faith was Prince Shotoku (573–621), regent during the reign of Empress Suiko (592–626). As a convert to Buddhism, Shotoku encouraged the building of temples, and lectured and wrote commentaries on Buddhist Sutras. His so-called Seventeen Article Constitution promulgated in 604 admonished the Japanese people to reverence the three treasures. For, it asserted, "the three treasures, viz. Buddha, the Law, and the Monastic orders, are the final refuge of the four generated beings, and are the supreme objects of faith in all countries." [13] The reader also observes that the influence of Confucian ethical and political ideals as well as Buddhism is apparent throughout Prince Shotoku's constitution.

Evidence of Chinese influence of many sorts, including not only Confucian ethics and Buddhist religion but also the Chinese calendar and the precisely graded Chinese hierarchical system of the royal court, may be observed in Japan from the time of Prince Shotoku onward. Successive embassies to the Asian mainland imported into Japan the T'ang culture of China.

These Chinese influences, and notably the impact of Chinese Buddhism, achieved a climax in the Nara period (710–783). The city of Nara, established as capital in 710, was modeled after the T'ang Chinese capital of Ch'ang-an. Travelers from China brought to Nara not only Buddhist Sutras that were currently the focus of Chinese study and meditation, but much else, ranging from the Buddhist custom of cremating the dead (first practiced in Japan on the Buddhist monk Sosho) to new ceremonies for ordaining monks and new methods of road and bridge building and irrigation.

Many notable features of Japanese Buddhism and other aspects of Japanese life and culture date from the Nara period. Among these are the public bath and the Bon festival. The latter celebrates offerings by Buddha's disciple Moggallana, who was effective in releasing his mother from suffering in hell. This ceremony has celebrated the release of persons from nether-worldly suffering. It is analogous to Christ's harrowing of hell. From the Nara period comes the great Buddha Vairocana statue, planned in 741 by Emperor Shomu and completed a decade later. This statue, housed in the Todaiji temple, was the central feature of Emperor Shomu's nationwide program of Buddhist temple building.

Japanese Buddhists of the Nara period probably understood little of the subtle philosophy contained in the Sutras which they brought from China. However, they were active in organizing sectarian groups around each new

Wooden figure of ancient Japanese Buddha. From the Koryuji Temple, Kyoto

Courtesy of the Japan National Tourist Organization

document. In this manner emerged the traditional six Nara sects. Two of these groups never had real or effectual existence in Japan, and none has significant existence today. However, the influence of some of these groups and of their documents has continued to the present in other Buddhist organizations. The six Nara sects were as follows: (1) *Sanron* or "Three Treatises" was introduced in 625 and was based on the Chinese *San lun* sect. (2) *Hosso* or "Consciousness Only" was brought to Japan about 660 and was based on the *Wei Shih* sect of China, whose founder, Hsüan Tsang, had brought its source documents and ideas from India to China in 645. (3) *Kegon* was based upon the *Hua Yen* or "Flower

Garland" sect of China and upon the *Avatamsaka Sutra* which was translated into Japanese in 722. The sect has headquarters at Todaiji in Nara, and exists as a custodian of antiquities. (4) *Ritsu* was based upon the *Vinaya Pitaka* and was concerned with problems of obedience such as the ordination, discipline, and morality of monks. (5) *Jojitsu* and (6) *Kusha* were based on specific Mahayana documents and had no separate historical existence in Japan.

The Nara period also saw the beginning of the continuing process of fusing Buddhist and Shinto forms of religious practice and thought into a single Japanese tradition. For example, the Empress Shotoku, daughter and successor of the Buddhist Emperor Shomu and herself a devout Buddhist, declared in a famous statement that she and her people should serve the Three Treasures with their highest devotion, should next reverence the gods of the shrines of heaven and earth, and should next cherish and love the princes, the ministers, the officials of the hundred departments, and all the people of the land.[14] Buddhism was thus given top priority but was incorporated into a structure which had a Shinto component.

The close relation of church and state in Nara Buddhism, amounting to a virtual Buddhist religious establishment, brought the same abuses which have accompanied established religions elsewhere. As a result the Emperor Kammu resolved in 783 to move his capital in order to escape the influence of the Buddhist groups. In 794 Heian-kyo, or Kyoto, became the capital. So began the Heian period of Japanese history.

MAIN FORMS OF JAPANESE BUDDHISM

During the Heian period (794–1192) and the Kamakura period (1192–1338), Buddhism in Japan became Japanese Buddhism. That is to say, the religious forms and ideas which had been imported from China during the preceding centuries took root and grew in Japanese soil. It is worth noting that no major new forms of Japanese Buddhism have come into being since Kamakura times. Both the Heian and the Kamakura were periods of feudalism similar in many ways to the Middle Ages of Europe.

The early Heian period saw the beginning of the two earliest forms of Japanese Buddhism which have lasted to the present, *Tendai* and *Shingon*. The founder of Tendai was Saicho (767–822), known to his followers also as Dengyo Daishi; and the founder of Shingon was Kukai, whose followers have called him Kobo Daishi (*Daishi* means "great teacher"). These two men set sail on the same embassy to China in 804 both seeking further study and illumination as well as sanction for their developing forms of Buddhism. Saicho returned home the following year and Kukai a year later. Each left a lasting mark upon Japanese Buddhism.

As a youth Saicho had separated himself from the Nara sects to spend twelve years in solitary meditation on Mount Hiei. Throughout his life he was devoted to the *Lotus Sutra* as a source for both study and meditation. He seems to have had the support of Emperor Kammu in going to China to seek sources and sanction for his new Buddhist foundation on Mount Hiei. On his return from China Saicho was plunged into continuing controversies with the Nara sects and later with Kukai. He apparently did not wish to form a new sect, but he was pushed into it. Saicho had great gifts for organization, devising his own form of ordination for monks and his own rigorous form of monastic rule and discipline. He was strongly nationalistic, recommending his form of Buddhism as a way of building up and sustaining the Japanese nation. His interest in esoteric forms of Buddhism led to disputes with Kukai. The Tendai Buddhism which Saicho founded continues as a living form in Japan today. According to the 1965 census of religious bodies, there are now 20 Tendai sects which claim a total of 2,261,222 family units.[15]

Kukai, who went to China with Saicho, has left a vivid personal record of his tutelage at a monastery of esoteric (in Chinese, *Chen yen*) Buddhism. Returning home in 807 with diagrams, documents, and charms (as well as a vast amount of Chinese learning on subjects ranging from calligraphy to technology), Kukai founded the Shingon sect. He was a many-sided genius who is revered by the Japanese, an authentic culture hero. His influence on Japanese life has been deep and pervasive.

He was also a wide-ranging student of man's religions whose studies embraced the main faiths of both India and China. Out of this study came his idea of these different faiths as stages in the mind's ascent to salvation. The ten main steps, in ascending order, according to Kobo Daishi were as follows:

1. The unregenerate state of no religion at all
2. The teachings of Confucius and Lao-tzu
3. The Sankhya and Vaishesika schools of Indian philosophy
4. The Kusha sect
5. The Jojitsu sect
6. The Hosso sect
7. The Sanron sect
8. The Tendai sect
9. The Kegon sect
10. The Shingon sect[16]

Building a monastery on Mount Koya, Kukai set about the propagation of Shingon Buddhism, which found a ready acceptance among the Japanese of his time. Shingon has manifested persistent vitality in Japanese history. Recent census figures show three million adherents and some twelve thousand temples.

In the Heian period esoteric Buddhism spread throughout Japan, pervading both Shingon and Tendai with its mandalas, its charms and magic words, and its secret learning, which was deemed effective to produce salvation, longevity, and immortality. Of the innumerable deities who dwelt within these holy diagrams and holy words, the number was reduced first to thirteen, then to two. These two were Kwannon (whom we have already met in India as Avalokitesvara and in China as Kuan Yin) and Fudo. Kwannon is the embodiment of mercy, and Fudo of fearsome retribution.

The closing years of the Heian period saw great disorder and anarchy. During this time, warrior monks of Tendai and Shingon monasteries contended against each other in violent conflict that would doubtless have appalled the founder of Buddhism. Men were thus afforded a vivid and grim illustration of the basic Buddhist teaching on the impermanence and misery of all worldly existence. During this time some Japanese Buddhists began to teach the idea of history as a succession of three increasingly evil ages, with the third and worst, the Mappo period, immediately impending.

In this climate of pessimism the establishment of the Kamakura shogunate with its simple but firm objectives provided Buddhism with the basis for new life. Three important new forms of Buddhism emerged in force during the Kamakura period, (1) The Pure Land Schools of Amida Buddhism, (2) Nichiren, and (3) Zen.

In the records of the later Heian period, there are stories of Buddhist monks who composed devotional poetry and often went through the streets of Japanese cities and towns singing songs to Buddha. Theirs was a popular movement which was to have great mass appeal among Japan's people. They also marked the emergence in Japanese Buddhism of a pietism similar to Hindu bhakti or Muslim sufism. Among these devotional saints were several notable figures. There was Kuya (903–972), who danced through the city streets calling on the name of Amida, singing songs of his own composition, and inviting others to join in his prayer, *Namu Amida Buddha*. There was Ryonin (1072–1132), who propagated the *Nembutsu* ("Hail Amida Buddha") through liturgical chants and popular songs; and there was also Genshin (942–1017), who wrote a famous volume, *The Essentials of Salvation,* which expounded this popular way to salvation which was open to all, laymen as well as monks, women as well as men. Genshin advocated loving trust in Amida as the power to walk this way. For reinforcement he described the pleasures of the Pure Land and the contrasting pains of the many Buddhist hells. Genshin also used a newly lifelike and realistic style of painting and sculpture to convey his message to those not able to read.

The greatest of the medieval devotional saints of Amidism were Honen (1133–1212) and his disciple Shinran (1173–1262). They were founders respectively of the Jodo and Shin sects. It was Honen who, despite his own intentions, first made a sharp break with other forms of Buddhism. He seems to have experienced a decisive religious conversion as he meditated on Zendo's *Commentary on the Meditation Sutra*. His mind was captured by the passage, "whether walking or standing, sitting or lying, only repeat the name of Amida with all your heart. Never cease the practice of it even for a moment. This is

Figure of Great Buddha in Kamakura city
Courtesy of the Japan National Tourist Organization

the very work which unfailingly issues in salvation, for it is in accordance with the Original vow of that Buddha."[17]

Honen pledged himself to the new way that opened before him and through his long life he kept this faith. He distinguished between two ways of salvation, one the path of meditation in one's own power (*jiriki*) which he characterized as the difficult path, and the other the easy path in the power of another (*tariki*). The latter depended on the mercy of Amida Buddha. It was in effect salvation by grace in contrast to man's own works. According to Honen's way, man's part was the continual confession of faith in Amida Buddha by means of the unceasing recital of the Nembutsu. Honen introduced another element into Japanese Buddhist faith and thought, namely, a sense of human depravity. In his helplessness, man cannot save himself, Honen asserted, and is therefore dependent upon the grace of Amida.

Honen set about the propagation of the new faith with characteristic vigor, thus making enemies among older Buddhist groups. His books were burned, and he was personally vilified. His success in winning converts led finally to his exile at the age of seventy-three to a remote northern part of Japan. His letter to friends and followers was a noble and courageous document in which he declined to buy clemency by silence and declared his intention to go on preaching in his new home. To his friends and converts he declared, "Mountains and seas may divide us but we are sure of meeting again in that Pure Land."[18]

Among those sent into exile with Honen was his disciple and friend, Shinran, whose offense was that he had violated his monastic vow by taking a wife. He had done so apparently at the suggestion of Honen in order to provide living demonstration that salvation depended not upon works of renunciation but on faith in Amida which transcended any outward circumstance of life. Shinran's followers have adhered to his example of marriage. Shinran believed that for his followers to marry and live in the world led to a closer identification with the people whom he sought to help on the way to salvation.

Shinran's theology resembled Honen's in most essential features. He too believed that human nature is sinful and can be saved only by the grace of Amida. He painted sin in even more vivid colors than Honen; and in his exclusive reliance on Amida, he discouraged the worship of other Buddhas. Yet in one emphasis he differed from Honen. While Honen had emphasized the recital of the Nembutsu, Shinran focused attention on the inward attitude of faith which properly found expression in this confession. Apart from this inward faith the words themselves could become a delusive dependence on self, but with this inner attitude of faith even the words might be dispensed with. Shinran's theology was a radical statement of salvation by grace alone.

While Shinran made no attempt to organize a new sect around his own faith and creed, his followers inevitably found their way into a new organization, the Shin sect, which together with Honen's Jodo sect constitutes numerically the largest bloc of Japanese Buddhism. Today some twenty-seven Pure Land sects claim a total of 16,898,289 family units.[19]

Jodo and Shin have been characterized by their emphasis on congregational worship, with sermons as a device for instruction. They have also used music and visual arts, especially images of Amida, as helps to worship. Amidist temples are used for weddings and funerals. Their people have been active in organization of schools, hospitals, and similar social enterprises.

Amida Buddha (or Amitabha as he was known in India) is one of the great gods of Asia. For popular religion he is a savior to those who heed his call and follow his way, giving both a helping hand through the vicissitudes of mortal life and a guarantee of bliss in the Happy Land beyond death. For the learned there are Sutras and commentaries to be studied, subtle distinctions to be mastered, as well as arguments with theologians of other ways, such as Zen, which regards Amida's Happy Land as, at best, a concession to human frailty. Zen theologians have sometimes argued that in Buddhism's many-storied heaven, the Happy Land is one of the lower floors, while the top is clearly Nirvana, where all mortal distinctions are left behind. Amidist theologians will not have it so, arguing back that the personal relation to Amida is the symbol of a reality altogether as true and ultimate as Zen Nirvana.

The devotional religion of Honen and Shinran in turn elicited a vigorous and violent reaction from Nichiren (1222–1282), founder of the Nichiren, or the sociopolitical, sect. Nichiren believed that the devotional piety and other-worldliness of Jodo and Shin constituted an immoral diversion of energies needed for the present life, and especially for the common life of Japan. Nichiren was the son of a humble fisherman and was educated at Mount Hiei in the Tendai tradition, which in his time had become more concerned with esoteric Buddhism than with the original teachings of Saicho. Nichiren sought to return to the founder, and was soon forced to leave Mount Hiei. Like Saicho before him, he was convinced of the sufficiency of the *Lotus Sutra*. It was apparently in meditation on this Sutra that he underwent the decisive religious experience of his life. He changed his name to Nichi-ren (literally "sun lotus") and made the following vow:

> *Finally, let the celestial beings withdraw their protection, let all perils come upon me, even so will I dedicate my life to this cause. . . . Be it in weal, be it in woe, to desert the Lotus of Truth means to fall to the hells. I will be firm in my Great Vow. Let me face all manner of threats and temptations. Should one say to me, "Thou mightest ascend the throne of Japan if thou wouldst abandon the Scripture and expect future bliss through belief in the meditation on Amida; or thy parents shall suffer capital punishment unless thou utterest the name of the Buddha Amida," etc.—such temptation I shall meet unshaken, and shall never be allured by them, unless my principles shall be shattered by a sage's refutation of them. Any other perils shall be the dust before a storm. I will be the Pillar of Japan; I will be the Eyes of Japan; I will be the Great Vessel of Japan. Inviolable shall remain these oaths.*[20]

All the energies of his intense personality were now integrated and focused. He resolved to play the role of prophet to his reluctant contemporaries and countrymen. As we have seen, he denounced Honen and Amidism in unsparing language. He sought also to arouse Japan from its apparent lethargy at the approach of foreign invasions; and he regarded the failure of the Mongol invasion as divine deliverance.

Personalities such as Nichiren often make enemies in high places. For his denunciation of the government he was twice exiled and twice condemned to death. After the second condemnation, on his way to what he thought was to be the place of execution, he paused before the shrine of Hachiman, whom he regarded as a Bodhisattva as well as a Shinto deity, but most of all the special protector of the Japanese nation. There he challenged Hachiman to save him. The execution was set aside, apparently by prearrangement, but Nichiren interpreted it as divine deliverance.[21] Characteristically, Nichiren regarded himself as "the bodhisattva of superb action."[22]

From Nichiren and a tradition of like-minded successors has sprung the sociopolitical, or Nichiren, sect of Japanese Buddhism. Like its founder and leaders, this group has been characterized by its strong adherence to Japanese patriotism and nationalism. In recent and contemporary times it has generated several significantly nationalistic sects. In 1965, thirty-eight Nichiren sects claimed a total of 25,917,097 family units.[23]

Also from the Kamakura period comes Zen, or Meditation, Buddhism. Like other forms of Buddhism, Zen was imported into Japan from China, and in this case on three different occasions: in 1191 by Eisai, the traditional founder of the Rinzai sect; in 1244 by Dogen, who founded Soto; and in 1654 by Ingen, founder of the Obaku school of Zen. Today twenty-three Zen sects claim a total of 9,578,446 family units.[24] While by no means the most popular form of Japanese Buddhism, Zen has exerted a deep and pervasive influence on virtually every aspect of Japanese culture. From swordmanship to flower arrangement, from governmental administration to the tea ceremony, every significant aspect of Japanese culture has known the quickening influence of Zen.

In the opinion of its protagonists, Zen Buddhism, far from being eccentric or esoteric, actually stands in the main line of Buddhist tradition, synthesizing in its outlook ideas and attitudes derived from India, China, and Japan. The defining idea of Zen, namely, meditation, began in India as *dhyana,* became *ch'an* in China and *zen* in Japan; and the basic practices of meditation in Zen monasteries testify to this threefold heritage.

Yet none would deny that Zen constitutes a highly distinctive interpretation of the Buddhist tradition. For one thing it is *jiriki* in contrast to the *tariki* view of Amidism. Zen has no savior; each person depends on his own power to walk the path to salvation. The nontheistic character of Zen has been of great historical significance. Zen adherents derive it from the Buddha's own teaching and example.

As noted in the last chapter, Ch'an Buddhism in China brought Indian dhyana, or meditation, down to earth, making its object not a remote transcendental realm but the present, experienced world of nature and society. This cosmic, or this-worldly attitude of China made its way to Japan, where it was given even more vivid and forceful expression. In this respect Zen Buddhism offers clear illustration of Nakamura's assertion that Japanese people seek and find "the absolute in the phenomenal world."[25] To this view the Japanese have added their own distinctive accents and their own peculiar intensity of feeling. The result is Zen Buddhism.

The Zen pioneers were Eisai (1141–1215) and Dogen (1200–1253). Eisai made two trips to China, for study and training in Ch'an as well as other forms of Buddhism. Returning home to Japan he founded temples for the practice and propagation of Zen, both in Kyoto and in Kamakura. The established Buddhists in the former city were hostile, but in the latter he and his followers gained a ready hearing from the nobles of the new Kamakura shogunate. Eisai did not hesitate to mix Zen with other forms of Buddhism such as Tendai, Shingon and Pure Land. He also brought tea to Japan, ardently recommending tea drinking as a way to health and long life. His treatise, "Drink Tea and Prolong Life" was addressed to a Kamakura shogun whom Eisai sought to win from alcohol to tea. Possibly most important of all, Eisai introduced into his native land the philosophic writings of the great Chinese neo-Confucian master, Chu Hsi.

Where Eisai was adaptable, Dogen was uncompromising. Born of noble parents, he was orphaned at the age of seven, his mother's dying wish being that he become a Buddhist monk. Ordained by the chief abbot of the Tendai school, he continued to seek for solutions of the religious and philosophic problems that concerned him. In 1223 he went to China, wandering from monastery to monastery in search of enlightenment. On the point of returning home in disappointment, he achieved enlightenment on hearing the monk Ju-ching declare "In Zen, body and mind are cast off," or in alternative phrasing, the duality of body and mind is transcended.

Returning home to Japan in 1227, Dogen spent the rest of his life in single-minded service of his interpretation of Buddhism. He regarded Zen not as a single sect but simply as basic Buddhism. Living successively at different temples he continued to write and to practice his own simple and austere form of meditation. Illness led to his death in 1253. As Dumoulin remarks, "Dogen's life was overshadowed by the sorrowful awareness of the transitoriness of all things."

He was also the greatest philosophic mind in Japanese history. His philosophy might be characterized as an unremitting effort to push beyond all dualities of thought and experience to an all-encompassing unity—a unity, we must immediately add, that must be directly experienced in order to be understood.

Primary among the dualities of thought for Dogen was what he termed the distinction between original enlightenment and acquired enlightenment. The latter is the experience of satori or enlightenment which is sought by Zen Buddhists, while the former is the innate Buddha-nature, latent in all men and all things. These two are really one, declared Dogen characteristically. Thus the achievement of enlightenment consists of the present realization of the original Buddha-nature.

Among the further dualities that Dogen sought to embrace and overcome were (2) that between body and mind, which as Ju Ching had declared must be cast off, or transcended; (3) that between the samsara world and the nirvana world, which are the same world seen from different perspectives; and (4) that between practice and enlightenment, both of which in reality are constituted by the one all-important activity of *zazen* or "meditation." In this last respect Dogen was especially opposed to sudden enlightenment or enlightenment as something apart from meditation.

The Zen tradition has produced many great leaders. Particularly notable was Muso Soseki (1275–1351), known also as Muso Kokushi ("Muso the National Master") for his role as advisor to shoguns and other government officials. He was also one of the originators of the Japanese art of landscape gardening.

The period of the Ashikapa shogunate (1333–1568), which followed the Kamakura period, was a time of extensive and intensive cultural creativity for Zen. Zen monks were leading scholars, writers, artists, and political advisors. From this age comes the development of the tea ceremony. Landscape painting was developed by such masters as Sesshu (1420–1500). Drama flowered in the No plays.

To Hakuin (1685–1768) is due credit for the modern revitalization and re-organization of Zen. His *Song of Mediation* is an admirably lucid and characteristic summary of the Zen outlook.[26]

> All beings are primarily Buddhas.
> Like water and ice,
> There is no ice apart from water;
> There are no Buddhas apart from beings.
>
> Not knowing how close the Truth is to them,
> Beings seek for it afar—what a pity!
> It is like those who being in water
> Cry out for water, feeling thirst.
> It is like the rich man's son,
> Who has lost his way among the poor.
>
> The reason why beings transmigrate
>   through the six worlds,
> Is because they are lost in the darkness of
> ignorance.

Wandering from darkness to darkness,
How can they ever be free from birth-and-death?

As Zazen taught in the Mahayana,
No amount of praise can exhaust its merits.
The Six Paramitas, beginning with
    the Giving,
Observing the Precepts and other good
    deeds, variously enumerated,
As Nembutsu, Repentance, and so on—
All are finally reducible to Zazen.

The merit of even a single sitting in Zazen
Erases the countless sins accumulated
    in the past.
Where then are there the evil paths to
    misguide us?
The Pure Land cannot be far away.

Those who, even once, in all humility,
Listen to this Truth,
Praise it and faithfully follow it,
Will be endowed with innumerable merits.

But if you turn your eyes within yourselves
And testify to the truth of Self-nature—
The Self-nature that is no-nature,
You will have gone beyond the ken of
    sophistry.

The gate of the oneness of cause and effect
    is opened;
The path of non-duality and non-trinity
    runs straight ahead.

Your form being the form of no-form,
Your going-and-returning takes place
    nowhere but where you are;
Your thought being the thought of
    no-thought,
Your singing-and-dancing is none other than
    the voice of Dharma.

How boundless and free is the sky of
    Samakhi!
How refreshingly bright, the moon of the
    Fourfold Wisdom!

At this moment what is there that you lack!
Nirvana presents itself before you,
Where you stand is the Land of Purity.
Your person, the body of Buddha.

Throughout its history Zen has placed primary emphasis on the direct experience of satori or enlightenment, which may be understood as the distinctive Zen rendering of the mystical union that we have already met in other interpretations in other faiths and cultures. Zen appeals to the example of the Buddha's experience under the bo tree in India. The whole Zen practice and philosophy point the way to having this experience. From this source the life of Zen flows. Along with teaching (or philosophy) and practice (or meditation), enlightenment is one of Zen's "three pillars."

What are the salient features of satori to those who experience it? The list which follows here has been freely adapted from the writings of D. T. Suzuki, pioneer interpreter of Zen to the West. (1) Suzuki speaks of its irrationality (but more precisely stated, the term would be transrationality), or its being beyond the rational, factual features of the world of common experience. (2) He lists authoritativeness as a feature, meaning that the experience asserts a sovereign claim over those who have known it, though not over others. Satori is addressed "to whom it may concern." (3) It is an affirmative experience. At least, those who have it testify to its affirmative or even superaffirmative quality. (4) In similar vein, Suzuki speaks of the exaltation it brings. (5) In contrast to the personal nature of Western religious experience, he characterizes Zen as impersonal in quality. Other expositors of Zen have preferred the term *transpersonal*, meaning not less-than-personal, but more-than-personal. (6) Satori is immediate or intuitive in quality, or in Whitehead's phrase, it occurs in the "mode of presentational immediacy." (7) It brings what Suzuki terms a "sense of the beyond." Yet to this we must immediately add that the reference is to the world of present experience in its inclusive totality, and not any supramundane realm or region. (8) To these features must also be added a sense of dependence. While man must walk the path to enlightenment in his own strength, satori is not so much something men do as it is something which happens to them, and it does so in ways independent of human will or volition. Such, at least, is the experience that Zen Buddhists report.

It is an experience which has renewed, reinforced, and redirected the lives of countless Japanese. They have been drawn from the secular world to Zen meditation rooms, and from these monastic halls they have moved back into the common world with new light and power.

During these centuries of Buddhist dominance, Shinto continued its quiet but pervasive influence. We have seen that as early as the Nara period the fusing of Buddhism and Shinto was under way, and during the Heian period both Shingon and Tendai Buddhism lent themselves extensively to this mixture of faiths. In many instances Shinto and Buddhist rituals took place in the same shrines or temples. There was also a merging of deities. As we have seen, Hachiman, the Shinto war god, became "the great Bodhisattva." During the

Zen garden of Ryoanji Temple, Kyoto

Courtesy of the Japan National Tourist Organization

Kamakura period these influences continued and grew in strength. Nichiren Buddhism lent force to Japanese nationalism. The failure of the Mongol invasions in 1274 and 1281 was widely interpreted as divine deliverance by Hachiman and Amaterasu.

One medieval writer and exponent of Shinto is worth mentioning. His name was Kitabatake (1293–1354) and he wrote a document called *The Records of the Legitimate Succession of the Divine Sovereigns,* in which he did not hesitate to deify his native land. Kitabatake wrote: "Japan is the divine country. The heavenly ancestor it was who first laid its foundations, and the Sun Goddess left her descendants to reign over it forever and ever. This is true only of our country, and nothing similar may be found in foreign lands. That is why it is called the divine country." [27] This growing ethnocentrism, while in no way different from that of many other lands and peoples, was destined in time to come to bring about developments which would doubtless have surprised and shocked its author, who also wrote elaborate explanations and expositions of the three imperial symbols at Ise, the sword, mirror, and jewels.

Painting of Eleven-Headed Bodhisvatta. From the Ashikaga period

Courtesy of the Metropolitan Museum of Art, Fletcher Fund, 1961

TOKUGAWA DEVELOPMENTS

The Tokugawa period of Japanese history (1603–1868) consists of two and a half centuries lying between the unification of Japan and the opening of the nation to the West and to modernity. It was an age of national integration, but also of isolation from the outside world. The Tokugawa period was ushered in by three tough-minded military men, Nobunagu, Hideyoshi, and Ieyasu, who broke the divisive power of feudalism and forcibly united the Japanese nation in a manner strikingly similar to the early modern European kings such as Henry VIII of England. The succeeding Tokugawa shoguns with their ideas of fixed order sought, like King Canute, to repress all change. Yet beneath this static surface, important changes of many kinds continued to take place, preparing the way for modern Japan.

Religiously it was a period when medieval Buddhist other-worldliness, with its goal of emancipation from all worldly bonds, gave way increasingly to more secular value systems. While Buddhism was not forcibly repressed, it was pushed away from the center of society. The Tokugawa rulers turned for religious and moral guidance not to Buddhism but to neo-Confucianism. As had so often been true in the past, this was a philosophy and code imported from China; but also as usual, the Japanese put their own stamp on what they imported.

Tokugawa neo-Confucianism began with a Buddhist monk, Seika (1561–1616), who forsook his Buddhist orders to become a lay philosopher. His disciple and successor, Hayashi Razan (1583–1657), was an advisor and counselor of Ieyasu, the first Tokugawa shogun. He was also one of the architects of the Tokugawa social system. It was his achievement to establish Chu Hsi's neo-Confucian philosophy as the orthodox system of Tokugawa Japan. In 1691 Hayashi's grandson became the first hereditary president of the Confucian University at Edo (or Tokyo). The Japanese followers of Chu Hsi professed to accept his philosophy as a whole. Some of them even practiced Chu Hsi's "investigation of things," with scientific concern for nature and for medical lore. However, the primary emphasis was upon the great Chinese master's ethical philosophy, which performed for them two very important functions, namely legitimatizing the existing political and social order and providing the individual with moral orientation within Tokugawa society.

While Chu Hsi's version of neo-Confucianism assumed the role of the official philosophy, the philosophic system of Wang Yang-ming (in Japanese, *Oyomei*) also attracted many individual students and followers. The Japanese found particularly attractive Wang's emphasis on intuition and his teaching of the unity of thought and action.

Still a third group constituted themselves as the school of Ancient Learning, rejecting both forms of neo-Confucianism and going back to Confucius himself. Chu Hsi's vast metaphysical system left them cold, but they were attracted to Confucius' ethic. Especially notable in the school of Ancient Learning was Yamaga Soko (1622–1685) in whose thought and life Confucian ethics joined forces with Japanese feudalism to produce *Bushido* or the "Way of the Fighting Knight." (The word is from *bukyo*, meaning "the warrior's creed," and *shido*, "the way of the *samurai*, or feudal retainer." [28]) Yamaga was a man of fiercely independent mind, in continual trouble with officials for his unorthodox opinions. His rejection of Chu Hsi in favor of Confucius led to his exile in a remote region of Japan for the last twenty years of his life. There he wrote not only his autobiography, but *The True Facts Concerning the Central Kingdom*, seeking to show Japan and not China to be the true center of all culture, and Japan's imperial line of rulers to be in effect divine. He expounded the lofty mission of the samurai as a dedicated servant of his lord, with the divine Emperor at the top of a graded pyramid of lordship. Yamaga was motivated by burning loyalty to Japan and her emperors.

Bushido, as it emerged in the thought and life of Yamaga and others, provided a code and way of life for the samurai of Tokugawa Japan. The Way of the Fighting Knight, originating in a fusion of Confucian ethics and Japanese feudalism, was in many ways similar to the medieval European code of chivalry, although it differed in its complete absence of romantic love. Unlike his European counterpart, the Japanese knight was not motivated by romantic dreams of his lady.

As popularized, practiced, and celebrated, Bushido may be summarized in five main tenets: (1) Loyalty: the knight is bound in personal loyalty to his lord and is thus related to the feudal pyramid of loyalty at the apex of which stands that supreme lord, the Japanese Emperor. (2) Courage: as a soldier the samurai must be brave, rejoicing to sacrifice his life for his lord. (3) Honor: again as a soldier the knight cherishes his self-esteem. He regards it as a sacred duty to revenge affronts to his honor. He also prefers death to dishonor. From this last tenet of Bushido derives the duty of ritual suicide. (The popular term *harakiri*, or "belly slitting," has in the West displaced the formal traditional designation of *seppuku*.) (4) Politeness: this generally respected virtue of Japan comes to mean for the knight not only courtesy but also a reticence which scorns any public show of feeling. (5) Benevolence: the knight is devoted to righteousness and justice and must ever stand against evildoers and evil-doing. As will be seen in the next section of this chapter, Bushido was destined for further development and application in modern Japan.

Better than by a summary of its tenets, the spirit of Bushido is shown in the popular tale of the forty-seven *ronin*. Based upon an actual happening which took place in 1702, the story soon became a popular tale celebrating the virtues of the brave and loyal knight.[29] A certain lord, goaded beyond endurance, drew his sword and wounded a shogunal officer within the Edo castle. Since to draw one's sword within the castle grounds was tantamount to treason, this lord was required to commit suicide, and his land was confiscated. His samurai thus became *ronin*, men without a master. However, forty-seven of them vowed vengeance. Knowing that they would be under suspicion, they scattered, some of them abandoning their families and even pretending to sink into lives of debauchery. Their ruse worked; a less strict watch was kept at the enemy castle. Finally one snowy night when half the castle guard had been sent away, they came together and stormed the castle, capturing the enemy of their dead lord. The leader of the ronin respectfully addressed the captive noble, stating their

identity and their mission of revenge, and asking him to perform ritual suicide.
The enemy lord sat trembling in cowardice, unable to comply. So the leader of
the ronin leaped upon him and cut off his head with the same sword with which
the lord of the ronin had killed himself. Then the ronin went as a group to the
grave of their dead lord and offered to him the washed head of the enemy.
After this the ronin waited quietly until required by the government to commit
suicide. All Japan sang their praises, and ever since they have been the peerless
exemplars of Bushido.

Still another important religious development of the Tokugawa period was
the school of National Learning, or as it is known to Western students, the
Shinto revival. This was in essence a strongly anti-Confucian and anti-Chinese
appeal to indigenous and traditional Japanese sources of thought and allegiance.
Scholars of the school of National Learning pored through Japan's ancient and
classical documents, seeking an authentically Japanese path of faith and life.
The movement may be said to have begun with Kado Azumamero (1669–
sponsor a school of National Learning. Kado's own studies began the process
of Shinto revival which his distinguished successors carried forward.

During the eighteenth and nineteenth centuries three men stood out as the
leaders and makers of the Shinto revival, Kamo Mabuchi (1697–1769), Motoori
Norinaga (1730–1801) and Hirata Atsutane (1776–1848). Kamo sought in
Japan's ancient poetry for the true national style and spirit. He also attacked
both Confucianism and Chinese influence, though ironically his attack was
expressed largely in Taoist terms. The Taoist way of nature became in his
writings the way of the divine age or the age of the gods in ancient Japan. Kamo
also attacked the Chinese language as a cumbersome vehicle of expression, inferior in every way to Japanese.

Motoori Norinaga spent more than thirty years of his life on a *Commentary
on the Kojiki,* which he sought to exalt as a national scripture. By massive yet
perceptive literary scholarship, Motoori sought to make clear to his contemporaries the simple feeling of wonder or awe in prehistoric Shinto and its innumerable kami. Indeed, Shinto faith consists of this feeling! "Man living in such a
strange and wondrous universe, wonders not about its mysteries but only about
the wonders of the Divine Age saying there is no reason for them. If this is not
senseless, what is?" Motoori argued that the Japanese myths of beginning constituted the source of the True Way which had been handed down in Japan
through the divinely descended line of emperors, but only partially and imperfectly present elsewhere in the world. He found a central place in his

Painting on scroll of Zen priest. From the Tokugawa
period

*Courtesy of the Cleveland Museum of Art,
Norman O. Stone and Ellen A. Stone Fund*

theology for the sun goddess, Amaterasu. He also studied and wrote critical interpretations of the *Tale of Genji* as a sensitive depiction of *mono no aware* or the "sadness of things." [30]

The most strongly nationalistic scholar of the Shinto revival was Hirata Atsutane, who asserted the supremacy of Shinto over all faiths, and the Japanese over all other peoples:

Shrine gate at Nikko. From the Tokugawa period
Courtesy of the Japan National Tourist Organization

People all over the world refer to Japan as the Land of the Gods, and call us the descendants of the gods. Indeed it is exactly as they say: our country as a special mark of favor from the heavenly gods was begotten by them, and there is thus so immense a difference between Japan and all other countries of the world as to defy comparison. . . . Japanese differ completely from and are superior to the peoples of China, India, Russia, Holland, Siam, Cambodia and all other countries of the world, and for us to have called our country the Land of the Gods was not mere vainglory.[31]

Hirata disagreed with Motoori in two important respects. First, he taught a creator god in ways that strongly suggest contact with Christian missionaries.

Also in disagreement with Motoori, he taught life after death. Hirata's Japanese pride was modified by an admiration for "Dutch learning," namely the modern science brought to Japan by Dutch traders. Yet he taught that the real source of this, as of medicine, was the Japanese gods who in the beginning had given these gifts to mankind.

The intense and growing sentiment of nationality on which the Shinto revival was based and to which in turn it contributed is a widely recurring human

Pottery figure of Amida Buddha. From the Tokugawa period

Courtesy of the Metropolitan Museum of Art, Rogers Fund

phenomenon; indeed there are striking parallels in American history and in the history of European peoples at approximately the same historical period. One of the differences in nationalism in Japan was its explicitly religious character. Modern and contemporary history was to witness some unique and grim expressions for the Japanese form of this recurrent phenomenon.

MODERN AND CONTEMPORARY ISSUES

The modern world came late and suddenly to Japan. In 1853 Commodore Perry appeared in Tokyo Bay with letters from President Fillmore asking for trade and the opening of ports where American ships might buy supplies. Having delivered his message, he sailed away to China. When he returned in 1854 with more ships and men, the shogun was helpless to do anything but accede to this request. This episode aroused in Japan a lively debate in which three parties emerged: anti-West, pro-West, and compromisers.

The decline of the shogunate and the death of the antiforeign Emperor Komei in 1867 brought a crisis which was resolved in December of that year with the abolition of the shogunate and the accession to the throne of the young Emperor Meiji. Under his leadership the Japanese nation undertook a comprehensive process of modernization. The only real question soon became one of the terms along which modernization should take place. Would it be under the guidance of pro-Western liberals who would replace the Japanese tradition with the secular, scientific, and liberal spirit of the modern West? Or would it be under the leadership of staunch samurai who would use Western instrumentalities for the support and maintenance of traditional Japanese values? Japanese destiny for the next century was to lie in the answers her leaders and people gave to these questions. All aspects of both Buddhism and Shinto were also to be involved.

The effective agents of the Meiji restoration were young samurai idealists for whom Shinto was a living and powerful value system. So it was that the new Emperor's statements were punctuated with appeals to the kami and to Japanese tradition. In the early 1870s these same advisors sought to make Shinto an established national faith. In the early years of the Meiji restoration it was given official status through a governmental department. There was much hostility to Buddhism as a foreign ideology, and there was even sporadic anti-Buddhist violence. The attempt at establishment and unification proved abortive; by 1875 the government had shifted its position to the modern idea of the freedom and equality of all religions, which found later official formulation in the 1889 Constitution.

However, this Western liberal façade was somewhat deceptive, for in effect what the Shintoists in the government did was to make a threefold division into (1) shrine Shinto, (2) sect Shinto, and (3) domestic Shinto, and to assert that while (2) and (3) were religious in character, (1) consisted of nonreligious patriotic allegiance and rituals. In effect, Shintoists were provided with a convenient screen of nonreligion behind which they could operate freely to influence governmental policy and popular attitudes.

This "solution" to the Meiji religious problem is significant in several ways. It is an admirable illustration of the problematic character of the word *religion* (or its Japanese translation, *shukyo*). Also it illustrates the fact that ultimate concern remains ultimate, whatever the conventional label. The loyalty to Japan and her Emperor, so jealously cherished and propagated by the traditionalists, was pushed past all limits, and became ultimate in character. The modern role of the Japanese Emperor affords perhaps the most effective illustration in modern history of the divine ruler, which has been noted as a recurring feature of nature-culture religions.

Shrine Shinto, once taken under government sponsorship, soon became state Shinto. Approximately 110,000 shrines and their 16,000 priests received governmental support—and along with it they came under governmental control. They ranged from the large and nationally important shrines like Ise, Izumo, and the Meiji shrine in the palace grounds in Tokyo to the many village shrines throughout Japan. The traditional ethnic Japanese values, many of them non-political, which had found natural expression in shrine Shinto were now twisted into the forms and necessities of nationalist and militarist propaganda. While the natural ethnocentrism of the Japanese tradition provided a basis in popular credibility, it must also be added that the exploitation of this tradition by the militarists was something new in Japanese history.

This use of the Shinto value system extended beyond the shrines to embrace all aspects of the culture. The Imperial Rescript on Education in 1890 was an intimation of things to come:

> *Our Imperial Ancestors have founded Our Empire on a basis broad and ever-lasting and have deeply and firmly implanted virtue; Our subjects ever united in loyalty and filial piety have from generation to generation illustrated the beauty thereof. This is the glory of the fundamental character of Our Empire and herein also lies the source of Our Education. Ye, Our Subjects, be filial to your parents, affectionate to your brothers and sisters; as husbands and wives be harmonious; as friends be true; bear yourselves in modesty and moderation; extend your benevolence to all; pursue learning and cultivate arts, and thereby develop intellectual faculties and perfect moral powers; further-more, advance public good and promote common interests; always respect the Constitution and observe the laws; should emergency arise, offer yourselves courageously to the State; and thus guard and maintain the prosperity of Our Imperial Throne coeval with heaven and earth. So shall ye not only be Our good and faithful subjects, but render illustrious the best traditions of your forefathers.*
>
> *The Way here set forth is indeed the teaching bequeathed by Our Imperial Ancestors to be observed alike by the Descendants and the subjects, infallible for all ages and true in all places. It is Our wish to lay it to heart in all rever-ence in common with you, Our Subjects, that we may all attain to the same virtue.*[32]

This document itself also took on a well-nigh holy quality. Shrines repeated its words, all schools had copies, and at the annual ceremonial readings of it, hearers bowed reverently.

In the popular culture, this religiously inspired and sanctioned nationalism grew with the years and decades. Successful wars against China in 1895 and 1905 imparted to it an increasing plausibility. Books like Sakurai's *Human Bullets* [33] were in effect religious tracts which served to disseminate and stimulate the popular nationalism. The Constitution of 1889 began with the fateful assertions, "The Empire of Japan shall be reigned over and governed by a line of Emperors unbroken for ages eternal. . . . The Emperor is sacred and inviolable." [34] What was even more ominous, in this Constitution the military leaders were made directly responsible to the Emperor and not to parliament.

To be sure, secular liberal voices were by no means absent in Japan during this period, but they fought a losing battle against the rising tide of nationalism. Political leaders like Baron Shidehara counseled secular and free politics at home and peace with the world.[35] Ironically the international situation in the first half of the twentieth century strengthened the position of the militarists, notably through Japan's frustrations as the result of World War I and the coming of world depression in the 1930s. At home the rise of an overtly revolutionary Japanese nationalism in such groups as the Amur Society, devoted to assassination of political opponents and to the mission of holy Japan in the Far East and the world, pushed events inexorably toward World War II.[36]

In the years before and during World War II, it was inevitable that state Shinto identify itself with the national cause. The military defeat of 1945 which hit all aspects of Japanese life with seismic force, brought fundamental changes in Shinto. In December, 1945, the American occupation authorities handed down a directive requiring "abolition of governmental support, perpetuation, control, and dissemination of State Shinto."[37] On January 1, 1946, the Emperor issued a famous rescript officially renouncing divinity. It read in part:

We stand by the people and we wish always to share with them in their moments of joys and sorrows. The ties between us and our people have always stood upon mutual trust and affection. They do not depend upon mere legends and myths. They are not predicated on the false assumption that the Emperor is divine and that the Japanese people are superior to other races and fated to rule the world. . . .[38]

The years since this historic statement have demonstrated the truth of these assertions. The "de-divinized" Emperor continues as a religious as well as a political leader, and though shorn of militaristic nationalism, as a powerful symbol of Japanese values.

During the first years of the postwar period, the newly disestablished shrine Shinto suffered a sharp decline, but in recent years the annual number of visitors to Ise and other such places approaches the prewar totals. In conscious emulation of American models, the denationalized shrines have organized into an Association of Shinto Shrines whose membership now exceeds 80,000 local shrines or parishes. Shrines are supported and attended by individuals. Religious freedom is guaranteed by the Constitution of 1947. The Kokugakuin University exists to provide education for Shinto priests and scholarly study of the faith. The new start is promising, but what the future holds for shrine Shinto only the future can tell.

Sect Shinto, officially denominated as religious in the Meiji "solution" has continued to the present to manifest considerable vitality. During the Meiji period some thirteen new sects began. Some are now only a memory, and others had little real existence even from the first. Three of the thirteen are mountain sects, two devoted to worship at Mount Fuji and a third located at Mount Mitake in central Japan. Of those which still survive, the *Tenri, Kurozumi, Taisha,* and *Konko* sects will serve as a sample of their range and variety. All of them are a blend of elements from Japan's diverse religious tradition, brought together in new ways by the mind and experience of a religious founder or leader.

Tenri kyo (literally the "Heavenly Reason" sect) was founded by an illiterate farmer's wife named Miki Nakayama (1798–1887) who appears to have been a religious genius. The movement she founded survived government persecution in the World War II period, and today reports 2,350,000 adherents and an impressive and continuing rate of growth. In 1837 on the occasion of the miraculous healing of her husband (her son, according to other accounts), she began to receive divine revelations. She devoted herself to religious work, preaching the gospel she had received and gathering a large following about her.

Her faith was based upon the Divine Parents (literally *Tsuki-hi,* or "Moon-Sun") who seek the well-being of their earthly children. Mrs. Nakayama placed great emphasis on faith and faith healing. Her followers have emulated her example in teaching and practicing faith healing, though it must immediately be added that this same practice has been a feature of many if not most of the new Japanese religious movements.

Tenri kyo's worship includes sermonic instruction and liturgical acts such as singing and dancing and uses such common Shinto objects as mirrors and god shelves, or altars, for offerings. It also features a notable liturgy of hand gestures. The headquarters of Tenri kyo's worldwide missionary activities is the city of Tenri near Nara, which is also the location of Tenri kyo's growing university.

Kurozumi kyo was founded by a man known by many names, the last being Munetada (1780–1850). A deeply devout man who believed himself the recipient of several revelations of deity, his life was crucially and suddenly changed when during what he thought to be a mortal illness he was performing his daily worship of Amaterasu. He experienced a feeling of unity with all being, which he interpreted as the grace of Amaterasu. The experience apparently healed his body as well as his spirit. Becoming a devotee of Amaterasu, he went around Japan preaching, performing faith healing, and gathering a following. After his death he was officially designated by the Japanese government as kami, or divine. During the Meiji period the Kurozumi sect grew greatly, but it now has a mere 750,000 members, and its best days have apparently passed.

The *Taisha kyo* (or Great Shrine sect) was founded in 1874 when Senge Sompuku, a priest of the shrine at Kidzuki, resigned his state office and continued Shinto ritual at his baronial mansion. In many ways it has been a sectarian adaptation of shrine Shinto. Today little remains save the headquarters of the sect in the Senge mansion.

Konko kyo was founded by Kawati Bunjiro (1814–1883), a poor farmer in a tax-ridden region of Japan, who in 1859 received a revelation from God, the Divine Parent, calling him to seek the salvation of all men. By the time of the founder's death at the age of sixty-nine, the movement had grown to several hundred thousand. A recent census figure lists some 500,000 members. Adherents maintain their faith in the Divine Parent and practice faith healing. They are also active in education and social science.

The years since the end of World War II have added a newer and vastly longer list of names to Japan's new religions. Some lists of these new phenomena run to hundreds or even thousands of items. All are complicated by the insoluble problems of what is to be counted as a religion and what as a new religion. Many of these movements are in effect novel formulations of traditional religious patterns. Many more are too transitory to be termed organizations, religious or otherwise. All of them have emerged out of what one observer has termed the "religious ferment" of contemporary Japan.[39] This ferment is the product of tradition and novelty, or the old and the new, in contemporary Japan. The people of this deeply traditional culture have been thrust forcibly and violently into an age of change bewildering in its extent and significance. One response to this situation—and a characteristically Japanese response it is —has been the emergence of new religions which claim to provide effective guidance in this new and puzzling situation.

Notable among these new religions both for its amazing size and rate of growth and for its militant or even belligerent teaching is *Soka Gakkai*, or as it now calls itself, *Nichiren Shoshu*. Beginning in 1930 as a lay movement of Nichiren Buddhism, it was founded by Makiguchi (1871–1943), who was a Tokyo elementary school principal. Conversions were few for the first years. Makiguchi and his followers refused to worship Amaterasu as was currently required of all Japanese, and they went to prison for their faith. Makiguchi died in prison during World War II and thus became a martyr. His movement came to new life in the postwar years under the leadership of Toda Josei. Soka Gakkai currently claims some 10 million to 15 million adherents, and a rapid and continuing growth. Its manifestations range from the *gohonzon*, or mandala, of Nichiren to faith healing. Soka Gakkai's militancy has been directed to politics, and it has elected a dozen or so members to the Diet on a platform of strong nationalism. Soka Gakkai has a fine new headquarters located characteristically on the slopes of Mount Fuji.

More traditional exponents of Nichiren have not hesitated to disparage Soka Gakkai as a thoroughly false form of Buddhism. Several other less extreme off-shoots of Nichiren are among the new religions. Among these are *Reiyukai*, or the "Association of the Friends of the Spirit," which claims some three million adherents, and *Rissho Kosei Kai*, whose practices give prominence to group counseling.

Another cluster of new religions consists of those which have splintered away from *Omoto* or *Omoto kyo*, "the Teaching of Great Origin." The original Omoto group was founded in Meiji times, and has lasted through severe persecution for its pacifist views. Among the half-dozen splinter forms of Omoto, perhaps the most novel is *PL Kyodan*. PL stands for "Perfect Liberty" and its adherents state with pride that the title reflects the resolution of contemporary Japan to have a modernized faith. Among the striking features are a large and excellent golf course adjacent to its national headquarters near Osaka, which has given rise to the appellation the "Golf Religion" and a creed of twenty-one affirmations beginning with "Life is Art" and ending with "Live in Perfect Liberty." PL Kyodan claims a total of 600,000 adherents.

Among the other new religions is *Tensho Kotai Jingo kyo*, or *Odoru Shukyo* as it is popularly known, the latter term meaning the "Dancing Religion." This appellation stems from the practice by the founder, Kitamura Sayo, of dancing and singing ecstatically as she preaches. This remarkable personality was clearly the focal center of the religious movement she founded in 1945 and led until her death in 1969. She claims to heal disease as well as to impart new life to her followers. Her missionary travels have brought her to Hawaii and to continental United States. The Dancing Religion claims over 100,000 members and a continuing and rapid rate of growth. While its teaching bears striking parallels to Christian doctrine, the founder understood herself to be the embodiment of a Shinto deity. She was succeeded in leadership of this religion by her grand-daughter.

Without pursuing further the endless list of new Japanese religions, it is possible to see in these phenomena several features of considerable interest and significance. These groups in all their extremes of variety testify to the unique Japanese combination of tradition and flexibility. They also provide the student of religions with a rare opportunity to study the conditions under which new religions come into being and grow.

Contrasted with the novelty and variety of the new religions, domestic Shinto has continued its quiet existence, centering on the god shelf, or *kamidana*, of countless homes throughout Japan. This is in effect an altar on which are placed such objects as a mirror, a sprig of *sakaki,* and the name of an ancestor or of a patron deity. Sometimes a curtain is draped in front of it. Daily offerings of fruits, rice, and flowers are placed on the altar. Devotions are performed before the altar by individuals or by the family as a group. Having washed the hands and rinsed the mouth, the worshiper places himself on a mat before the altar and bows and claps his hands. Actual practices vary widely according to circumstances. Some homes have in addition to the kamidana a *butsudana,* or Buddhist altar, on which are placed the names of departed ancestors and at which a Buddhist priest may occasionally say "mass."

CONCLUDING COMMENT

Looking back over our sketch of Japanese religions, what issues or themes do we see emerge as dominant in this complex picture? What emphases does Japan communicate to the student of the world's religions? To these questions a fourfold answer seems forthcoming. First of all, Shinto in the past and present of Japan provides us with what is certainly one of history's clearest illustrations of a nature-culture religion. The student notes the fateful political consequences of this fact in recent Japanese history, and then turns to see what will be the future forms of Japan's ethnic faith. Secondly, nowhere in the world is Buddhism more open than in Japan to critical scholarship and to dialog with thoughtful adherents of other faiths. While the various forms of Japanese Buddhism face real problems in maintaining themselves in the twentieth century, the general picture is one of relative health. Hence the opportunities for study and observation, as well as authentic interreligious dialog, are unique.

In the third place, no feature of Japan's tradition is more important than her sharp eye for beauty; and her achievements in the arts have been impressive to all sensitive beholders. Traditional Japanese art in painting, sculpture, architecture, literature, and music has been religious in content and spirit. Conversely the religions of Japan have sought and found expression in the arts. Nowhere on earth is there a more convincing illustration of the interfusion of religion and art than in Japan. Consequently students of both art and religion have been concerned with this relation in the past; but again they look to the present and future to see what will be the future forms, if any, of this vital historical relation.

Finally, speaking in general terms, no civilized tradition offers readier verification than contemporary Japan for the hypothesis of this volume that the human content of religion is a cluster of significant values which provide adherents with life orientation. From this, several implications follow. One is that contemporary Japan's crisis in values (and most sensitive observers agree that this is an important fact of Japan's present situation) is a genuinely religious problem. A working solution to some of Japan's urgent religious problems will provide some sort of solution to the crisis in values.

It would take us over the border which separates responsible study from oracular prophecy to say at this point what the future holds for Japan and her faiths, yet to watch that future unfold into the present is clearly within the task of study. The world holds no more significant or interesting field for students of mankind's religions than twentieth-century Japan.

NOTES

1. H. Nakamura, *The Ways of Thinking of Eastern Peoples*, compiled by Japanese National Commission for UNESCO, Tokyo, 1960, p. 527.
2. *Ibid.*, p. 438.
3. *Ibid.*, p. 527.
4. Sokyo Ono, *Shinto: the Kami Way*, Chas. E. Tuttle, Rutland, Vt., 1963.
5. Quoted from William T. de Bary (ed.), *Sources of the Japanese Tradition*, Columbia University Press, New York, 1958, pp. 23–24.
6. See *inter alia* Will Herberg, *Protestant, Catholic, Jew*, Anchor Books, Doubleday & Company, Inc., Garden City, N.Y., 1960; W. Lloyd Warner, *American Life: Dream and Reality*, The University of Chicago Press, Chicago, 1953.
7. Floyd Ross, *Shinto: The Way of Japan*, Beacon Press, Boston, 1965.
8. Daniel C. Holtom, *The National Faith of Japan: A Study in Modern Shinto*, E. P. Dutton & Co., Inc., New York, 1938, p. 106.
9. Ross, *op. cit.*, p. 23.
10. *Ibid.*, p. 28.
11. *Ibid.*, p. 75.
12. *Ibid.*, pp. 79f.
13. de Bary, *op. cit., p.* 50.
14. *Ibid.*, p. 268.
15. J. Kitagawa, *Religion in Japanese History*, Columbia University Press, New York, 1966, p. 296.
16. Kenneth W. Morgan (ed.), *The Path of the Buddha*, The Ronald Press Company, New York, 1956, p. 329.
17. Clarence H. Hamilton (ed.), *Buddhism: A Religion of Infinite Compassion*, The Liberal Arts Press, Inc., New York, 1952, p. 140.
18. de Bary, *op. cit.*, p. 207.
19. Kitagawa, *op. cit.*, p. 296.
20. Hamilton, *op. cit.*, p. 145.
21. de Bary, *op. cit.*, pp. 221, 226.
22. *Ibid.*, p. 220.
23. Kitagawa, *op. cit.*, p. 296.
24. *Ibid.*
25. Nakamura, *op. cit.*, p. 527.
26. Quoted from the *Blaisdell Institute Journal*, June, 1968, vol. 3, no. 2.
27. de Bary, *op. cit.*, p. 274.
28. *Ibid.*, pp. 351–352.
29. Edwin O. Reischauer and John K. Fairbank, *A History of East Asian Civilization*, Houghton Mifflin Company, Boston, 1960, pp. 620–621.
30. de Bary, *op. cit.*, p. 509.
31. *Ibid.*, p. 544.
32. *Ibid.*, pp. 646–647.
33. T. Sakurai, *Human Bullets*, Teibi Publ. Co., Tokyo, 1912.
34. Ross, *op. cit.*, pp. 138–139.
35. de Bary, *op. cit.*, pp. 753f.
36. *Ibid.*, pp. 761f.
37. Ross, *op. cit.*, p. 152.
38. *Ibid.*, p. 155.
39. Raymond Hammer, *Japan's Religious Ferment*, Oxford University Press, Fair Lawn, N.J., 1962.

SUGGESTIONS FOR FURTHER STUDY

Anesaki, M.: *History of Japanese Religion*, Paul, Trench, Trubner, 1931.

Aston, W. G.: *Shinto: The Way of the Gods*, Longmans, 1905.

Benedict, R.: *The Chrysanthemum and the Sword*, Houghton Mifflin, 1946.

Bunce, W.: *Religions in Japan*, Tuttle, 1955.

de Bary, W. T. (ed.): *Sources of the Japanese Tradition*, Columbia, 1958.

Hamilton, C. (ed.): *Buddhism: A Religion of Infinite Compassion*, Liberal Arts, 1952.

Hammer, R.: *Japan's Religious Ferment*, Oxford, 1961.

Holtom, D.: *Modern Japan and Shinto*

Nationalism, University of Chicago Press, 1943.

The Kojiki, trans. B. Chamberlain, Thomson, 1932.

Morgan, K. (ed.): *The Path of the Buddha,* Ronald, 1956.

Ono, S.: *Shinto: the Kami Way,* Tuttle, 1963.

Ross, F., *Shinto: The Way of Japan,* Beacon Press, 1965.

The Sacred Scriptures of Japan, trans. P. Wheeler, Abelard-Schuman, 1952.

Sansom, G.: *Japan: A Short Cultural History,* Century, 1931.

Soothill, W.: *The Lotus of the Wonderful Law,* Oxford, 1930.

Thomsen, H.: *The New Religions of Japan,* Tuttle, 1963.

Warner, L.: *The Enduring Art of Japan,* Cambridge, 1952.

Watts, A.: *The Way of Zen,* Penguin, 1947.

10

ZOROASTRIANISM

The Parsees of India, numbering slightly over 100,000, and the few thousand remaining Zoroastrians of Iran are the sole remaining representatives of Zoroastrianism, which is the smallest of the world's living religions. Parseeism does not accept converts, and maintains itself as the faith of an hereditary community located largely in and around Bombay. Small though it is, Zoroastrianism makes a strong claim on the student's attention and interest. For one thing, it is the legatee of a great tradition. Its founder, Zoroaster, or more accurately, Zarathustra, was apparently one of the great figures of the Axis age of the seventh and sixth centuries B.C. From that time until the coming of Islam in the seventh century of the present era Zoroastrianism was the religion of the vast Iranian or Persian empire. From this Middle Eastern base it reached out in many directions to influence other faiths and other peoples. Both Judaism and Christianity show Zoroastrian influences in the figure of Satan and in the hosts of angels surrounding both God and Satan. Zoroastrian gods, symbols, and cults made their way into the Greco-Roman world, Mithras being only the best known of many figures of Persian origin. The cult of Manichaeism, which was one of the rivals of early Christianity and one of the influences on the mind of St. Augustine, was a Zoroastrian sect of heretical tendencies.

Like Judaism, Christianity, and Islam, Zoroastrianism is a religion of a Book or Bible—a fact of paramount importance historically and theologically. Even a cursory reading of the Zoroastrian Bible, called the Avesta, makes it clear that the reader is in a different religious world from South Asia or East Asia. This book speaks of the one God whose sovereign will is that all men should serve him—and serve no other gods. In other words, here is the first example in our study of monotheism, or in the classification of Chapter 1 a religion of the third type. Other examples of the type in Judaism, Christianity, and Islam will follow in subsequent chapters.

In addition to the predominant metaphorical image of sovereignty or kingship, the reader notes in the Avesta the frequently recurring image of hearing. God speaks, and man hears and acts. The predominance of the metaphor of hearing over that of seeing may be said to define a religion of revelation. Revelation implies that man does not have within his own mind and self the meaning of life, and that therefore God must disclose it to him. Hence God speaks, disclosing himself and his will to man; and man's part is to hear and do the will of God. From this it is only a step to writing down in a sacred book the content of what man hears; and this book becomes the guide for all of life.

In this monotheistic understanding of religious experience, man is related to God in terms of obedience or disobedience to the divine will, and these terms may be taken respectively as the basic definitions of faith and sin. In all of this there is an active or volitional element which contrasts sharply with the contemplative or aesthetic quality of the religions of South Asia and East Asia. Most of the latter regard volition as something to be transcended in both god and man. In monotheism, the end of man is the active doing of the will of God rather than the achievement of any passive state of contemplation. This leads to a strong moral and social emphasis in the monotheistic faiths.

Zoroaster presents himself to us as a prophet, a man who out of deep conviction is called to speak for God to man. Again, the metaphor of vocation, or calling, is important to prophetic religion, and we shall encounter it in Judaism, Christianity, and Islam as well as Zoroastrianism. Here it is sufficient to point to the contrast between the prophet and other archetypal religious models such as the Hindu sadhu or sannyasin, the Buddhist monk, and the Confucian sage.

Zoroaster's faith emerged in the midst of an ancient Iranian religion which, insofar as scholarly reconstruction is possible, appears to be remarkably similar to Vedic Indian religion. If this be true, the diverging religious developments in India and Iran constitute one of the most remarkable contrasts in mankind's religious history. The mountains which separate India and Iran have been the great divide separating religions of the second and third types.

Zoroastrianism confronts the student with many tantalizing and sometimes frustrating questions. For example, it presents the clearest example in man's religious history of moral and cosmic dualism. Other faiths show tendencies in this direction, but no other has pushed this dualism to the extreme conclusion of Zoroastrianism. Thus the question arises, In what terms is the student to understand this dualism and its relation to Zoroastrian monotheism? What, in other words, are the relations between the good Ahura Mazda and the evil Angra Mainyu?

A different kind of issue is raised by the historical sources of Zoroastrianism, which are fragmentary and often speak with discordant voices. As a consequence, scholarly attempts at reconstruction are, to say the least, limited. A summary list of the main parts of the Avesta and other Zoroastrian sources is essential for the exposition which will follow. The oldest parts of the Avesta are the *Gathas*, or hymns of Zoroaster. These hymns or poems are usually attributed to the prophet himself, and together they constitute the core of the *Yasna*, or main liturgy. In addition to the Yasna, the Avesta contains four other main subdivisions: a shorter liturgy called the *Visp-rat* or *Vispered*; the *Yashts*, which are hymns or invocations; the *Khurda Avesta*, or "little Avesta," which is a series of hymns addressed to many deities; and finally the *Videvdat* (often rendered *Vendidad*), or "Law Against Demons," which is concerned largely with problems of ritual purity.[1]

In addition to the Avesta there are other texts and archaeological remains, including a notable series of inscriptions from the great Achaemenid kings such as Darius and Xerxes, which throw light on Zoroastrianism during their times. From a much later date, roughly the third through the ninth centuries, comes a series of texts in the Pahlavi language, consisting mostly of translations and commentaries on earlier documents. These primary sources are supplemented by comments of Greek historians, notably Herodotus.

There is a popular Zoroastrian tradition that the original Avesta was written in golden ink on oxhides, and that this as well as other treasures of the faith were destroyed by Alexander the Great in the sack of Persepolis in 330 B.C. However, there is no present evidence to substantiate this tradition.

IRANIAN RELIGION BEFORE ZOROASTER

Whatever is to be known of Iranian religion before Zoroaster must be reconstructed from references to it in the Gathas, and it is unfortunately true that this evidence does not yield a whole coherent conclusion. For example, the Gathas contain Zoroaster's attack on animal sacrifice and the *haoma* ritual, yet the Yasna gives a central place to these rituals.[2] Yet in many other respects a reasonably clear and coherent picture is forthcoming.

It is the picture of a religion of nature and culture strikingly similar to that of Vedic India. Even the names of the peoples are similar, for apparently the word *Iran,* like *Aryan,* means "noble," and has a similar etymology. The Vedic and Iranian languages are closely akin to each other. In both societies there was a great number of deities representing a variety of natural and social forces and objects. Two kinds of deities are referred to in both traditions, *daevas* (Indian *devas*) and *ahuras* (Indian *asuras*). It is interesting to observe in this connection that in the course of Zoroaster's prophetic criticism of his tradition he came to regard the daevas as veritable principles of evil, while among the ahuras he selected one, *Ahura Mazda,* as his one supreme and true God. As noted in Chapters 3 and 6, India took the different path of seeing a single principle manifested in and through all her innumerable deities.

Among the pre-Zoroastrian daevas was *Intar,* who like his Indian relative *Indra* was a dragon slayer and rain god. Prominent among the daevas was *Mithra* (Vedic *Mitra*), god of war and of the sun's light, who elicited from his followers the qualities of loyalty and faithfulness. Under many names and guises Mithra was destined for a long and varied life. There was *Asta,* or *Arta,* principle of order, analogous to the Vedic *Rita.* There was *Vayu,* the wind, known by the same name to the Indians. There was also *Yima,* the first man to die and henceforth king of the underworld, known to the Indians as *Yama.* Corresponding to the Indian *Pitaras,* or "Fathers," were the Iranian *Fravashi,* ancestors or ancestral principles.

Similar to the Indian *soma* was the Iranian *haoma;* both were potent drinks capable of inducing feelings of religious exaltation. Hence both were used as sacrificial libations, and both were sometimes deified. For these ancient Iranians as for their Indian cousins, sacrifice was a central feature of religion. For them too the fire of the sacrifice was of sacred significance. Unlike the Vedic Indians, they had no deity of the fire, but in the course of time the sacrificial fire itself was destined to become the supreme sacred symbol.

Reading between the lines of the Yasna the modern student may infer that the Iran of the seventh and sixth centuries B.C. was a society of cattlemen, cattle breeders, and farmers. Again the similarity to Vedic India is apparent. These Iranian cattlemen seem to have lived under continual threat from marauding nomads whom they did not hesitate to identify as the embodiment of evil. Like other societies of the time, this one was highly conservative. The traditional bonds which it placed on individuals might well seem restrictive to an outstanding person. Furthermore, beneath the surface of this traditional society, important changes were stirring. They needed the catalytic force of a great personality to bring them to overt reality.

THE PROPHET'S LIFE

Into this ancient traditional faith and society, Zoroaster was born. There is the

widest scholarly disagreement concerning the dates of his life. One estimate
places him at 1500 B.C., another at 3000 B.C., and still another at 6000 B.C.[3]
R. C. Zaehner's estimate, 628–551 B.C., accords better with existing evidence
than any alternative.[4] The crucial clue is the Zoroastrian tradition which dates
the founder "258 years before Alexander," that is, before Alexander's sack of
Persepolis in 330 B.C. This would be 588 B.C., presumably the date of Zoroaster's conversion of King Vishtaspa, which was the turning point of the
prophet's career. If this is correct, Zoroaster was a contemporary not only of
Buddha, Confucius, and Lao-tzu, but of the prophets of Israel and other men
of the Axis age around the world. It may be pointed out that if this chronology
is correct, Zoroaster's achievement of monotheistic faith followed that of the
Hebrew Moses by some six hundred years.

Zoroastrian tradition has painted a highly stylized portrait of its founder. He
received the sacred thread, symbolic of religious coming of age, at fifteen. He
was said to be a youth dutiful to his parents and of a compassionate nature.
Yet at the age of twenty he left his parents and the wife they had chosen for
him to wander forth into the world alone in search of answers to his religious
questionings. One source, admittedly late, asserts that he kept a seven-year
silence, living in a cave during this entire time.

At the age of thirty he received the first of a series of revelations which made
him the prophet of Ahura Mazda. Standing beside the Daiti River, he was
approached by the angel Vohu Manah (Good Thought), who appeared as a
colossal figure nine times human size, commanding Zoroaster to lay aside his
body and come up into the presence of the heavenly court. There God himself
instructed the prophet in the content of the new faith which he was to disseminate. This crucial religious experience is intimated in at least three of the
Gathas. In 31:8 Zoroaster sets forth his experience:

> *Through the mind, O Wise One, have I known thee as the first*
>   *and the last,*
> *As the father of the Good Mind,*
> *When I perceived thee with mine eyes as the true creator of*
>   *Righteousness,*
> *As the Lord in the deeds of existence;* [5]

Again he writes in 45:8f.

> *—For I have now beheld this with mine eye,*
> *Knowing the Wise Lord by the Righteousness of his Good Spirit,*[6]

In more detail he declares in 43:7:

> *As the holy one I recognized thee, O Wise Lord,*

When he came to me as Good Mind and asked me:
"Who art thou, whose art thou? Shall I appoint by a sign
The days when inquiry shall be made about thy living possessions
   and thyself?"

Symbol of Ahura Mazda. From a doorway in the
Council Hall, Persepolis, Iran

Courtesy of the Oriental Institute,
University of Chicago

I made answer to him: "I am Zarathustra, first,
A true enemy to the wicked with all my might,
But a powerful support for the righteous,
So that I may attain the future blessings of the absolute
   Dominion
By praising and singing thee O Wise One." [7]

Over the next ten years Zoroaster participated in a series of seven such "conferences," as he called them, with Ahura Mazda or with members of Ahura
Mazda's heavenly court such as Vohu Manah and other important angels. Tra-

dition says that with the seventh such conference the revelation was complete. During this time he also began to teach and preach the new faith he had been receiving. Results were at first painfully meager and slow; after ten years he won his first convert, who was also his cousin. In his discouragement he was visited by the evil spirit, Angra Mainyu, who bade him give up his new work and return to the old gods of his people. Like Buddha and Christ, Zoroaster was tempted, but like them he won out.

At the age of forty he began a two-year effort to win to the faith King Vishtaspa. The story here seems heavily overlaid with tradition, yet apparently there is a kernel of historic fact. Vishtaspa, a native prince, dwelt somewhere in eastern Iran surrounded by evil priests and courtiers. Zoroaster's attempts were frustrated by their magic and their influence over the King. As a consequence of these malign forces the prophet landed in prison. However, after two years of failure, virtue triumphed; tradition says that Zoroaster's miraculous cure of the King's favorite black horse, reinforced by the support of the King's consort, won the day. King Vishtaspa was converted to Zoroaster's faith, bringing with him his entire household and royal court.

Tradition says that the next twenty years were spent in the vigorous and fruitful propagation of the new faith throughout Iran. Two holy wars against the villainous Turanians were fought and won. According to one account (written a thousand years after the supposed event) Zoroaster perished during the second war. The prophet, then seventy-seven years old, was surprised by an invading soldier and met a martyr's death as he officiated before the fire altar. All that can safely be said historically is that during the course of Zoroaster's life, the new faith struck roots into the soil of Iran and began to live and grow. The rest is tradition and folklore.

Despite its meagerness, the evidence is sufficient to show that the life and teachings of Zoroaster represent a historic breakthrough from the first, or nature-culture, type of religion to the third, or monotheistic, type, comparable to the breakthrough in India from the first to the second, or monistic, type. It also accords with existing evidence to say that this ancient Iranian breakthrough to monotheism occurred independently of that which took place in ancient Israel. There were incidental contacts between Iran and Israel, but their traditions developed independently of each other.

THE PROPHET'S MESSAGE

DIVINE REVELATION

The heart of Zoroaster's message was faith in the one God, Ahura Mazda, who had revealed his will to the prophet and through the prophet to mankind.

Zoroaster took his stand firmly on the revelation which had been given him, confident that God himself had disclosed to him the faith which he held. This conviction and vocation defined his role as a prophet, or spokesman for God. Furthermore, if this faith was of divine origin, alternative, diverging faiths had to be accounted false and evil. Zoroaster did not shrink from denouncing them as such. Here again the student notes in Zoroastrianism a distinctive feature of monotheism, the clear, sharp line drawn between true and false religion. It is a line almost completely absent from faiths of the first two types.

THE ONE GOD

The one God' whom he proclaimed was named Ahura Mazda (variously translated as "Wise Lord" and "Lord of Light"). Despite the difference in name, Ahura Mazda bears striking similarity to the Vedic Indian deity Varuna. The Gathas leave us no doubt that Zoroaster regarded Ahura Mazda as the one sovereign Lord of all creation. Ahura Mazda's will defines the norm for man's life, and indeed for all creation. Lordship also meant Creatorship; the Gathas tell the story of divine creation in which Ahura Mazda called the world into being in the beginning. Like his Biblical contemporary, Deutero-Isaiah, Zoroaster asked rhetorically:

> Who set the Earth in its place below, and
>   the sky of the clouds that it shall not fall?
> Who the waters and planets?
> Who yoked the two steeds to wind and clouds?
> Who O Wise One is the creator of the Good Mind?
>
> . . . .
>
> What artificer made light and darkness?
> What artificer sleep and waking?
> Who made morning, noon, and night?
> To remind the wise man of his task?
>
> . . . .
>
> Thus I strive to recognize in thee, O Wise One
> As Holy Spirit, the creator of all things.[8]

But Ahura Mazda is not only Creator; it is he who guides both each man's life and the whole process of creation to their consummation. Last Things as well as First Things, Judgment Day as well as Creation constituted an important aspect of Zoroaster's monotheism.

ANGELS

Zoroaster's monotheism was qualified by a variety of forms which are variously interpreted as angels or messengers, heavenly attendants or servants, divine attributes, or at times simply personifications. The reader has already made the acquaintance of Vohu Manah (Good Thought), the angelic messenger who conducted Zoroaster to the heavenly court. There were many others as well. There was Spenta Mainyu (Holy Spirit) who sometimes appears as the Presence of God, but sometimes as a separate and distinguishable being. There were the Amesha Spentas (the Immortal Holy Ones), such as Asha (Right), Kshathra (Power or Dominion), Haurvatat (Prosperity), Armaiti (Piety), and Ameretat (Immortality), who seem sometimes to be understood as modes or aspects of God's being, sometimes as forces or beings, sometimes as personifications. Scholars argue inconclusively over their exact status in the mind of Zoroaster, yet it is just possible that the prophet himself never cleared up this ambiguity. In any case, the student of religions will not be mistaken in seeing here the antecedents of Judeo-Christian and Muslim angelology.

DUALISM OF GOOD AND EVIL

Zoroaster's universe was populated with evil powers as well as good powers. In the Gathas is to be found a persistent and undeniable tendency to see man's experience of the world as a conflict between two opposing principles. The basis for this dualism is variously interpreted by different writers. Zaehner, for example, finds a historical and sociological explanation in the struggle between Zoroaster's people and the hostile, marauding nomads.[9] Others profess to see here a metaphysical tendency in Zoroaster's thought.

Whatever the basis, this duality finds repeated expression in the Gathas. For example, Zoroaster says:

> I will speak of the two spirits
> Of whom the holier said unto
>   the destroyer at the beginning of existence:
> "Neither our thoughts nor our doctrines nor our minds' forces,
> Neither our choices nor our words nor our deeds,
> Neither our consciences nor our souls agree." [10]

Even more plainly Zoroaster declares:

> Now at the beginning the twin spirits have declared their nature,
> The better and the evil,
> In thought and word and deed, and between the two
> The wise ones chose well, not so the foolish.
>
> And when these two spirits came together,
> In the beginning they established life and non-life,

And that at the last the worst existence should be for the wicked,
But for the righteous ones the Best Mind.[11]

At times this duality is expressed as the opposition between *Asha* and *Druj*, Truth and Falsehood. In later times Druj became *Shaitan*, or Satan, the father of lies. The Gathas are vague on the point of Ahura Mazda's precise relation to evil and to the evil spirit, Angra Mainyu, as he came to be called. Did Ahura Mazda create the evil spirit? Or had evil existed from the beginning as an original part of creation? Do good and evil exist like light and darkness as a natural pair of opposites? All these suggestions appear, but none clearly, and none is developed in its full implications. However, on one point the Gathas are unequivocally clear; they teach consistently that Ahura Mazda and his truth and goodness will win out in the end.

HISTORIC STRUGGLE BETWEEN GOOD AND EVIL

Deriving from the lordship of Ahura Mazda together with the dualism just noted, is Zoroaster's distinctive view of all history as an agelong war between good and evil. There are good men and evil men, just as there are good and evil spirits. The daevas, or evil spirits, have joined themselves with Angra Mainyu to resist Ahura Mazda and his hosts of goodness. In this war men are urged to join the forces of Ahura Mazda and Vohu Manah against the evil forces of Angra Mainyu. This means to speak the truth, to aid other good people—and violently to resist evil and evil people. It means practical good deeds like tilling the soil, raising grain, irrigating barren ground, being kind to cows and other domestic animals. The arch-villains of this drama of good and evil are the Turanian nomads who worship the daevas, slaughter cattle, and destroy the produce of the field. The end of this war is Judgment Day, when the sovereignty of Ahura Mazda will be fully vindicated. Zoroaster seems to have believed that the struggle of good and evil was an actual and often a desperate fight, yet paradoxically at no point did he doubt the final victory of Ahura Mazda.

THE GOOD LIFE

The war between good and evil which runs through the whole world also goes through the heart of each person. Hence individual decision or commitment is a supremely important issue. Zoroaster held a fundamental and indefeasible belief in man's freedom of choice. He admonished his contemporaries:

> *Hear with your ears that which is the sovereign good*
> *With a clear mind look upon the two sides*
> *Between which each man must choose for himself.*[12]

He also emphasized the active life of man. Man is called by God not to contemplation, but to active service. Similarly, there is a strongly this-worldly, practical, indeed material emphasis in his moral values, shown in his illustrations of good conduct, which range from telling the truth to cultivating the soil; yet consistent with his practical nature, Zoroaster seems not to have been concerned with the essential or theoretical nature of the good. Truth, righteousness—surely all men know what they are! This assertion may not be satisfactory to a modern philosopher, but it seemed sufficient for this prophet.

His practical and moral nature led him also to pare away much of the traditional ritual of his people. God's first requirement of man is a good life in society with his fellowman rather than the correct performance of a ritual. He had harsh words to say about animal sacrifice and other ceremonies of his people. His views of these matters paralleled those of his contemporaries, the great prophets of Israel. Zoroaster did apparently retain one outward symbol, namely, the fire as a symbol of truth. This was destined to become the central feature of Zoroastrian worship.

DEATH AND THE AFTERLIFE

For Zoroaster, God's drama of human life moves inevitably toward consummation. The drama of each man's life will achieve its climax at the Chinvad Bridge, or Bridge of the Separator, so called because the righteous successfully pass over it to "second existence" or resurrection, while the evil people topple off to the place of misery.[13] Zoroaster also intimated an analogous consummation for the larger drama of mankind's history, speaking of Ahura Mazda's victory, dominion, and kingdom. However, these hints are not spelled out in any detail in any extant text which may reliably be attributed to Zoroaster. It remained for his later followers to describe Judgment Day in play-by-play detail.

LATER ZOROASTRIANISM

As the reader turns from the Gathas of Zoroaster to the so-called later Avesta, namely, the Yashts, the Khurda Avesta and the Pahlavi texts, he is immediately aware of being in a different environment. Important changes have taken place in Zoroaster's faith.

These religious changes took place against the background of vast historical changes. A generation after Zoroaster, the great Cyrus made his dramatic ascent to power. In 550 B.C. he toppled Astyages, the last Median king, bringing Median and Persian kingdoms together in the Medo-Persian empire. Cyrus began the Achaemenid dynasty which was destined to hold power until the coming of Alexander two centuries later. Cyrus was a Zoroastrian though not a zealous or intolerant adherent. As an empire builder, he was willing to compromise among religions in order to keep peace among the many groups of his far-flung realm.

Cyrus was followed to the throne by his son Darius I and then by his grandson Xerxes. Darius's inscriptions show him to have been a devout Zoroastrian ruling by the will of Ahura Mazda and seeking the kind of justice and righteousness proclaimed by Zoroaster. The content of Darius's Zoroastrian faith was in most respects similar to that of the prophet himself. In the case of Xerxes, there were several notable developments. One inscription tells of his suppression of the daeva cult, an act still within the framework of the original Zoroastrian faith. But others tell of widespread animal sacrifice. Xerxes is also said to have lashed the waters of the Hellespont during his attempted invasion of Greece, calling them bitter waters. This was an act some authorities characterize as conflicting with Zoroastrian reverence for water. Additional deities, including notably the goddess Anahita, make their appearance or rather reappearance, in texts of Xerxes' time.

Notable among these changes from Xerxes onward was the rise to prominence of the Magi, who were apparently a priestly group of some sort. Authoritative writers have differed sharply on the identity and significance of the Magi. Were they a tribe of Median origin, as Herodotus claims, or were they a priestly class or caste? The evidence is not decisive. Were they faithful transmitters of Zoroaster's message or perverters of it? Both views have been put forward. The Gospel of Matthew in the New Testament tells the story of their coming with gifts for the infant Christ. Herodotus recounts other less laudatory details concerning the Magi, that they made incestuous marriages, killed many living creatures (apparently animals aligned on the side of the evil Angra Mainyu against Ahura Mazda), and that they left their dead to be the prey of vultures and dogs. The original meaning of the word *magu* was "gift," implying divine grace dispensed by these priests. However, the association of the Magi with Chaldean astrologers served to give their name its historic connection with sorcery and magic.

Whatever the precise identity and significance of the Magi, they appear to have been the official priests of Zoroastrianism during the Achaemenid period. As such they were responsible for three new elements in Zoroastrianism: (1) the exposure of the dead to be devoured by vultures and dogs, (2) the practice of incestuous (or less pejoratively, endogamous) marriages, and (3) the extension of Zoroaster's dualism to include the world of animals and of material things.

Under Darius and Xerxes the historic Persian attacks on Greece were undertaken. It has often been speculated that if the Battles of Marathon and Salamis had ended in Persian rather than Greek victory the religion of Europe might have been Zoroastrian. Nevertheless, Zoroastrianism continued to be a living force in the Near East for several centuries. As noted above, Alexander the Great sacked the Persian capital Persepolis in 330 B.C., bringing the Achaemenid dynasty to an end. Following Alexander's death, his empire was divided among his generals, Persia falling to Seleucus. The Seleucid family, however, proved unequal to the task of holding power throughout their vast regions. In the late second century B.C. the Parthian dynasty rose to power in Persia, driving out the Seleucids; they held the throne until the rise of the Sassanids in the third century.

In A.D. 224 Ardashir I drove out the last of the Parthian kings and established a dynasty which lasted until the coming of Islam in the middle of the seventh century. The Sassanids were Zoroastrians and made this the established faith of their empire. A twentieth-century Zoroastrian writer speaks of the Sassanid kingdom as a theocracy, with all the weaknesses inherent in the union of political and ecclesiastical power.[14] Non-Zoroastrian religions, notably Judaism, were severely repressed by the Sassanids. During these centuries, Zoroastrianism froze into an orthodoxy whose main tenets will be summarized below.

During the Sassanid centuries there were also several dissident and heretical movements of considerable importance. Most influential for Western history was Manichaeism, whose founder, the third-century Mani, shows Zoroastrian influence. M. N. Dhalla speaks of Mani as a Zoroastrian heretic, pointing out his basic ethical and cosmic dualism.[15] Yet where Zoroaster regarded the earth and other material things as good, Mani regarded them as the root of all evil. Where Zoroaster sought the regulation of bodily desires, Mani sought their suppression. In opposition to Zoroaster's teaching, Mani practiced and taught celibacy, fasting, and other forms of asceticism.

Another dissenting movement of Sassanid times was Zurvanism. *Zurvan* has been translated as "time" or "boundless time," and the movement called Zurvanism apparently originated in a bold philosophic effort to overcome the dualism of good and evil, of Ahura Mazda and Angra Mainyu, by asserting that they both sprang from Zurvan, or the impersonal principle of Boundless Time.[16] From this principle, all things derive. Zurvanist speculations may well have been influenced by Aristotle's metaphysics, which exerted a continuing and pervasive influence on the Middle Eastern world. Another possible source for

Zurvan was the *Maitri Upanishad* of India, which asserts that Time is the Father of all.

Zurvan's combination of myth and metaphysics assumed various forms, one of which approximated philosophic materialism in its denial of spiritual and religious realities, and another of which emphasized a doctrine of fatalism. Some Zurvanist writers elaborated a mythology similar to the Gnosticism of the Greco-Roman world. While Zurvanism attracted a wide following, including even

Zurvan giving birth to Ahura Mazda and Angra Mainyu. Depicted on a chased silver breastplate
Courtesy of the Cincinnati Art Museum

some Sassanid rulers, in the end it was ruled heretical by Zoroastrian orthodoxy. Its myths and its metaphysical speculations blurred the distinction between good and evil which orthodox thinkers held to be the foundation of true faith.

During this same period Zoroastrian orthodoxy was assuming its final and definitive forms. In several notable respects it differed from the earlier teachings of the Gathas. Five such differences will be briefly summarized.

DEIFICATION OF ZOROASTER

Most important was the religious exaltation of Zoroaster himself. In the Gathas, Zoroaster appears as a man, listening to Ahura Mazda, talking back sometimes, but always declaring Ahura Mazda's will to mankind. In the later writings he is depicted as a supernatural being, a veritable god become man. His coming has been foretold 3,000 years previously. The demons are forewarned and quake

at their impending overthrow.[17] Not only Zoroaster's birth but also that of his
mother is supernatural. Once born, the infant is attacked by the demons—and
is supernaturally protected by the manifold forces of goodness. The prophet
himself performs miracle upon miracle. The great miracle of the cure of Vishtaspa's horse is elaborated in great detail. Every aspect of the prophet's life is
fitted into a framework of popular supernaturalism—a process, one adds, of
which the history of religions affords numerous illustrations.

ANGELS AND DEITIES

While Zoroaster's monotheism did admit of angels and a few other celestial
attendants, there were clear and definite limits. In later Zoroastrianism these
limits are overpassed by a vast host of gods and godlings. Many of the old
Iranian nature gods against whom Zoroaster fought return in force, though
often under different names or with different functions. For example, Vohu
Manah assumes the new function of guardian of cattle. Such powers as Asha
(Right) and Kshathra (Power) are now deities of fire and metals respectively.
The Amesha Spentas are female archangels or goddesses. The number of angels
has greatly increased.

New deities appear on the scene in force. For example, Anahita makes her
appearance in Achaemenid times, and is soon recognizable as the mother goddess and fertility goddess, known by many names in different times and places.
Haoma, a disputed element in the Gathas, returns as a god to whom animal
sacrifices are made. Mithra, never absent in Zoroastrian history, rises to new
prominence in Achaemenid inscriptions as a god of light and a recorder of
truth and faith in mankind. Still later Mithra made his migration westward
to become Mithras of the Greco-Roman world, around whom a whole new—
and different—religious movement rose and ran its course. In later Zoroastrianism there was a truly vast increase in the celestial population of the universe!

EXTENSION OF DUALISM

There is also a hardening of Zoroaster's dualism of good and evil, together
with an analogous increase in demonic population. As already noted, Zoroaster's dualism was rooted in man's experience of good and evil. In later Zoroastrian writings it becomes clearly a fixed feature of the universe. As one writer
puts it, Angra Mainyu is now a proper noun—the Evil Spirit. So too are his
numerous helpers and colleagues. As Ahura Mazda has hosts of angels and
supporters, so too does Angra Mainyu. There is Aka Manah (Bad Thought),
Andar (Successor of Intar, and relative of the Vedic Indra), Sauru, Fauru,

and the "numberless myriads" of evil spirits, daevas, and others. Druj, the Lie, has now become a female demon!

As Ahura Mazda was active for goodness at creation, so Angra Mainyu was active in pursuit of evil ends. To oppose Ahura Mazda he made the summer heat and the winter cold, human vices and diseases, demons and their evils, and witchcraft, not to speak of such evil creatures as snakes, locusts, and ants. There was an increasing tendency in later Zoroastrianism to extend the cosmic

Drawing of the goddess Anahita
Courtesy of the New York Public Library, Picture Collection

dualism throughout the realm of nature, placing all of nature's creatures on the side of either good or evil.

FINAL JUDGMENT

Later Zoroastrianism spelled out in great detail the story of Judgment Day as applied both to individual human beings and to the world at large. Individual judgment takes place at the Chinvad Bridge. Four days after death, standing before the divine judges, the soul sees its good and evil deeds weighed in the scales. Then it passes over the dread bridge. If the soul be wicked, the sharp edge of the bridge stands edgwise and gives no passage, and the soul plunges headlong to hell. If the soul be good, it is met by an amiable apparition (who turns out to be the soul's good deeds) who embraces him, leading him to bliss on the further side. Both the miseries of hell and the bliss of heaven are described in vivid detail.

As to the final judgment of the world, later Zoroastrianism told an equally vivid and detailed story. The last three millennia are to be presided over by three posthumous sons of Zoroaster, Oshetar, Oshetarmah, and most important of the three, Saoshyans (or in another transliteration, Saoshyant), who will be destined to preside over the final "renovation" of the world. All the dead will then be resurrected, heaven and hell both being emptied of their residents for the impending great Assize. In a kind of trial by ordeal, every living soul will have to walk through the river of fire. To the righteous it will seem like warm milk, but to the evil it will bring unspeakable pain as it burns the evil out of them.

In a final battle following this, Ahura Mazda and his angels will conquer Ahriman and his hosts of evil, and consume them in the final fire. Then at the last, all the survivors of these tumultuous events will live together in complete felicity. In Zoroastrian metaphor the whole universe will be made new. Even hell will be redeemed as Ahura Mazda "brings the land of hell back for the enlargement of the world; the renovation arises in the universe by his will, and the world is immortal forever and everlasting." [18]

Alone or almost so among the religions of the world, Zoroastrianism teaches a doctrine of universal salvation. In the end Ahura Mazda's power will be asserted in the salvation of all the inhabitants of the created world. It is impossible to say what relation, if any, this Zoroastrian version of last things had to the contemporaneous apocalyptic visions of Jews and Christians a few hundred miles to the west of Iran. In the absence of concrete evidence, the similarity must be judged as independent responses to similar religious problems.

CEREMONIAL PURIFICATION

In the later version of Zoroastrianism, religion acquired again many of the ceremonies which Zoroaster's prophetic zeal had purged away; and these ceremonies tended to take on a magical significance. More and more they became a kind of defense in man's struggle to avoid ceremonial impurity or guilt. In this effort the Videvdat provided *Manthras* (note the similarity to Indian *mantras*) or sacred passages of scripture used as incantations or spells to ward off the demons and their evil powers. Libations of haoma were regarded as particularly powerful means of averting uncleanness or impurity. The juice of the sacred plant was pressed and mixed with milk and holy water, then part of it was poured out as a sacrifice and the rest drunk by the officiating priest.

In religious history contact with a corpse has widely been regarded as defiling, but this feeling of ceremonial impurity developed to a unique degree in later Zoroastrianism. As we have seen, the Magi were the first Zoroastrians who exposed their dead for vultures to devour, instead of burying them. Apparently they believed that a corpse would defile the earth, which was on the side of Ahura Mazda in the agelong struggle of good and evil. Nor could a corpse be cast into water or burnt on a pyre for it would pollute the water or fire. The Videvdat prescribed the Towers of Silence, or *Dakhmas,* which became standard features of Zoroastrianism.

CONTEMPORARY ZOROASTRIANS

When Muslim conquerors swept over Iran in the mid-seventh century, the result was disaster and downfall for Zoroastrianism. It fell with the Sassanid kings with whom it was allied. A few adherents remained and withstood the fury of Muslim persecution. They called themselves *Zardustrian* (Zoroastrians) and *Boh-dinan* (followers of the good religion), but to the Muslims they were *Gabars* (infidels). Some historians of religion have used this label, but to the adherents of this faith it is pejorative. They have continued to call themselves Zoroastrians. In time the Muslim masters of Persia saw that the Zoroastrians were people of a Book, and persecution gave way to tolerance. In more modern times tolerance has become official Iranian government policy.

The Iranian Zoroastrians have clung tenaciously to their faith. Their priests have continued to officiate at the fire temples, and generations of their sons and daughters have been invested with the sacred shirt and sacred cord, symbolizing their coming of age in things religious. They have also preserved their own distinctive marriage and funeral customs and their extensive rituals of purification.

In recent times there has been increased contact with their fellow Zoroastrians, the Parsees of India, and there have been new stirrings of life in their faith, the suggestion being made that since their ancestors underwent forced conversion to Islam the present generation might change its customs and accept converts from Islam and other faiths. Estimates vary concerning their numbers, but the total is probably not more than 10,000. Of this number some two thousand live by trade, while the balance follow the time-honored Zoroastrian occupation of tilling the soil.

Some Zoroastrians fled Muslim persecution in the eighth century, making their way overseas to India, where they landed at Diu in Kathiawar. They received the permission of the local ruler to land, on condition that they not intermarry with high-caste Hindu women and avoid the killing of cows. Tradition says that they erected their first fire temple at Sanjan in Gujarat. It was subsequently moved to Udvada, where it exists today as a popular pilgrimage place for Indian Zoroastrians. The newcomers soon acquired the name *Parsee* (from the name of the Iranian province of Pars, from which "Persia" is also derived) by which they have been known ever since. At least one writer has suggested that not religion but trade inspired the original migration, and it must be added that trade between Iran and India was by no means unusual at the time of their migration.

Many of the descendants of the original migrants found their way to the vicinity of Bombay, where they have lived and prospered ever since. Apparently they turned soon to trade and commerce, for a sixteenth-century Portuguese document compares their enterprise to that of Europe's Jews. In the seventeenth century a representative of the Parsees participated in Akbar's discussions among the various Indian faiths.

The coming of the British provided the Parsees with their great opportunity, for of all Indian groups they proved best able to adapt themselves to European ways. From the beginning a middle-class group with a great respect for education, they proved to be valuable intermediaries between the British and the people of India. Their activity proved to be highly profitable, and fortunes were made in shipping, shipbuilding and later in other industries. As a consequence, the small Parsee community came to have an influence far out of proportion to its actual numbers. To its achievements in business and industry, it soon added others in education, philanthropy, and public service. Its charities, applied first to its own members, were soon extended to the wider Indian community. Some of the largest industrial and commercial enterprises of India, such as the Tatas in steel and iron and the Wadias in shipbuilding, are of Parsee ownership.

The Parsee community is ruled by a council, or *panchayat*. In some cities this includes representatives of each family, while in Bombay it consists of 100 elected members, most of whom are laymen. To the panchayat are assigned the various tasks of leadership and administration, including the dispensing of funds to needy Parsees.

The basic ceremony of the Parsee faith is worship at the fire temple, in which the worshiper brings a piece of sandalwood to the priest who with appropriate prayer and ritual places it on the fire which he and his colleagues continuously attend. Parsees hasten to point out that the fire is not a deity but a sacred symbol of Ahura Mazda. The priest gives the worshiper a spoonful of ashes to rub on his forehead. Then following a priestly benediction the worshiper retires. Entrance into a fire temple is forbidden to non-Zoroastrians. As its worship is closed to outsiders, so also Parseeism does not accept converts. It is thus an hereditary community.

The high point of the Parsee religious year is the New Year's Day festival. On this day the faithful rise early, say their prayers, don their best clothes, and join other Parsees at the fire temple, which on this day is thronged with worshipers. Following prayers and worship at the temple the rest of the day is spent in merrymaking and celebration with relatives and friends.

The Parsees have divided into three groups over a difference in the procedure for dating New Year's Day. One sect holds firmly to the vernal equinox, March 21 of each year, making the necessary changes for leap year and for shifting from a lunar to a solar calendar. The other two follow different systems which result in considerable variation in the time of year on which the New Year's Day falls. Suggestions are currently heard for a compromise solution to these differences.

There is a ritual of initiation for young people in which the boys and girls are invested with the sacred thread and girdle symbolizing full membership in the community. This ceremony is customary between the ages of seven and nine, with the result that often little of its significance is apprehended by the young person involved. There is considerable discussion of this, and of the wider problem of providing for meaningful participation by young people. For in an age of increasing secularization in India as elsewhere in the world, there are many Parsee young people who lose interest in their faith.

A related problem is that of maintaining an adequate number of qualified priests for the fire temples. The priesthood is hereditary, a fact which drastically restricts the group among which future priests may be recruited. Parsee laymen have provided funds for the education of priests as well as for scholarly research into the Parsee tradition, but the problem of religious leadership continues.

Among the other rituals of the Parsees none is better known than their funerary customs. The Dakhmas, or Towers of Silence, are stone cylinders some twenty feet in height, with a stone floor and platforms around the inside on which corpses are exposed. There are three tiers of platforms, for men, women, and children respectively. Once a body is deposited the vultures speedily reduce it to a skeleton whose bones are deposited on the stone floor where in time they crumble away. In this way the sacred earth is guarded from defilement.

The funeral ceremony is a procession to the tower, which is usually located on an otherwise vacant hilltop. The body is borne by six professional bearers, whose pay is regarded as compensation for the ceremonial impurity involved. As the bearers deposit the corpse within the tower, the company waits outside. After ritual prayers, they disperse and return home. In Indian communities too small to have a Dakhma, interment in lead coffins or stone chambers is customary.

A notable feature of the Parsee community during the nineteenth and twentieth centuries has been the rise of a liberal and reforming spirit. This has led to efforts to study their own tradition with the methods and spirit of modern scholarship. The Parsees have had fewer inhibitions against this kind of scholarship than many traditional faiths. Closely allied to these scholarly activities have been calls to go "back to the Gathas," and to infuse the often empty ritual forms with the spirit of the prophet and his writings.

Another important development of recent years has been the increasing contact between Iranian and Indian adherents of Zoroastrianism. A world conference of the faith was held in Teheran in 1960, and another in Bombay in 1964, and others are planned for the future. Zoroastrians not only worship together, but seek to plan together for the future.

The Parsee community of today faces the future with a long agenda of difficult if not insoluble problems. The attrition in membership due to the secularizing trend of the environing culture is acutely important to an hereditary religious community. Some Parsees raise questions about this aspect of their faith. Others advise more imaginative programs to hold the allegiance of their young people.

Probably Parseeism's greatest strength is the quality and interest of its lay leadership. This has led to a strong bond of community among Parsees, reinforced as it is by minority status in Indian society. For all its problems, Parseeism is by no means a dead or dying religion. Rather it remains a vital and vigorous community. Most Parsee leaders concede that it will not exert in the future the vast influence it wielded during the centuries of British presence in India. Yet their strong sense of tradition, of pride in their faith and community gives them hope for the future.

CONCLUDING COMMENT

Clearly the most noteworthy feature of Zoroastrianism is its nature as a type-three or historical religion. As the student turns from the primary sources of other religions of the first and second types to Zoroastrian documents, a basic difference immediately forces itself upon his attention. Here we meet the one God who is Lord and Creator of the world, and who reveals himself to his servant, man, calling him to active service. Here too we meet such ideas as creation, resurrection, and judgment day.

The breakthrough in ancient Iran from the preceding cosmic faith to the historical monotheism of Zoroaster is significant also as a transformation similar to, but independent of, that which occurred in ancient Israel, and which will be discussed in the next chapter. Unfortunately the ancient Iranian breakthrough is largely hidden from us by the obscurity of its source documents. However this obscurity does not prevent us from distinguishing Zoroaster from what preceded him—and also from much that followed him, such as cosmic dualism, Mithraism, Zurvan and the like.

If we ask what is the nature of ultimate concern or valuation in Zoroastrianism, the answer is that it is allegiance to the one God and the service of him, which in turn produces in man the qualities of faith, hope, and if not love, then at least active social righteousness. These are the primary values that constitute the Zoroastrian way or path. And again, they must be viewed as the basic human response to the one lord and creator of all things.

These values also constitute human fulfillment. If we ask Zoroaster and his followers, why live? How do we realize our humanity? the answer is to serve God and so achieve the values listed in the last paragraph. In all of this we see, as has been said, the clearly distinguishable features of a religion of the third or historical type.

NOTES

1. Robert Charles Zaehner, *The Dawn and Twilight of Zoroastrianism*, G. P. Putnam's Sons, New York, 1961, pp. 25f. See also John C. Archer and Carl E. Purinton, *Faiths Men Live By*, The Ronald Press Company, New York, 1958, p. 326.

2. Zaehner, *op. cit.*, pp. 37–38.

3. 6000 B.C. is the estimate of J. M. Ranina in *The Essential Principles of Zoroastrianism*, P. D. Clinoy, Bombay, 1961, p. 3.

4. Zaehner, *op. cit.*, pp. 33f.

5. J. Duchesne-Guillemin, *The Hymns of Zarathustra*, John Murray (Publishers), Ltd., London, 1952, p. 111.

6. *Ibid.*, p. 95.

7. *Ibid.*, p. 135.

8. *Ibid.*, pp. 65–66.

9. Zaehner, *op. cit.*, pp. 32, 42–43.

10. Duchesne-Guillemin, *op. cit.*, p. 93.

11. *Ibid.*, p. 105.

12. *Ibid.*, p. 103.

13. *Ibid.*, p. 79.

14. M. N. Dhalla, *History of Zoroastrianism*, Oxford University Press, Fair Lawn, N.J., 1938, pp. 318–319.

15. *Ibid.*, pp. 339f.

16. See Zaehner, *op. cit.*, chaps. 9–11; Dhalla, *op. cit.*, chap. 36.

17. R. O. Ballou, *The Bible of the World*, Viking Press, Inc., New York, 1947, p. 606.

18. *Ibid.*, p. 634.

SUGGESTIONS FOR FURTHER STUDY

Dhalla, M.: *Zoroastrian Civilization*, Oxford, 1922.

———: *History of Zoroastrianism*, Oxford, 1938.

Duchesne-Guillemin, J.: *The Hymns of Zarathustra*, Beacon Press, 1963.

———: *Symbols and Values in Zoroastrianism*, Harper & Row, 1966.

Jackson, A. V. W.: *Zoroaster: The Prophet of Ancient Iran*, Columbia, 1898.

Modi, J. J.: *Religious Ceremonies and Customs of the Parsis*, Luzac, 1954.

Moulton, J.: *Early Zoroastrianism*, Constable, 1913.

———: *The Treasure of the Magi*, Oxford, 1917.

Pavry, J.: *The Zoroastrian Doctrine of the Future Life,* Columbia, 1926.

Zaehner, R.: *Zurvan: A Zoroastrian Dilemma,* Oxford, 1955.

———: *The Teachings of the Magi,* 1956.

———: *The Dawn and Twilight of Zoroastrianism,* Putnam, 1961.

The Zend Avesta, trans. J. Darmesteter, Sacred Books of the East Series, Oxford, 1883.

11

BIBLICAL SOURCES
OF MONOTHEISM

This chapter will describe the beginnings of monotheistic faith in ancient Israel against the background of nature-culture religion of the ancient Near East.[1] The chapters which follow will consider its historical development in Judaism, Christianity, and Islam.

The history of religions has witnessed many revolutionary changes, some of which have been discussed in previous chapters of this book. Chapters 4 to 6 described the emergence in ancient India of the second, or monistic, type of religion against the background of a nature-culture tradition. The last chapter described the emergence of monotheistic faith with Zoroaster in ancient Iran. The term *breakthrough* has been applied appropriately to this type of historical change in which something new and different comes upon the scene. Use of the term *emergence* asserts a similar claim, that something new has come into being. Assertions of this kind say nothing about the superiority or validity of the new form. All that is asserted is that a historically new form of religion has broken into being. Whether the new form is good or evil, true or false is a matter for subsequent judgment.

The term *monotheism* is subject to widely variant usage. Some writers apply it loosely to all forms of faith in which one deity or one object of faith is strongly emphasized. The term *monarchical monotheism* is often used to describe religions where among many deities or half-deities there is one supreme god who is king over the whole pantheon. Other writers apply the word *monotheism* to faith which centers in a single, unique principle, as Hindu Vedantism. In this book the term is applied only to the four religions of the one God, namely, Zoroastrianism, Judaism, Christianity, and Islam. As was noted in Chapter 1's discussion of the third type of religion, several other distinctive features cluster around the allegiance to a single God. The late H. Richard Niebuhr used the term *radical monotheism* for this type of religion.[2]

The breakthrough from nature-culture religion to monotheism, from religion of the first type to that of the third type, which occurred in ancient Israel is of the greatest importance, since from this Near Eastern source have stemmed the world's three great living monotheistic faiths, Judaism, Christianity, and Islam. In this connection, the student will note the Near East, along with India and the Far East, as a main source region for man's civilized religions.

ANCIENT ISRAEL SEEN AGAINST HER ENVIRONMENT

The Hebrews were relative latecomers to the ancient Near East. Mesopotamia had known settled, civilized life for approximately two millennia when Abraham left Ur of the Chaldees (ca. 1950 B.C.). If Moses and the Exodus (ca. 1290 B.C.) be taken as the beginning of Hebrew history, they still must be seen against a long background of almost three millennia of Egyptian and Mesopotamian history. The land of Palestine, or Canaan, which became the Hebrew homeland, had known civilized life for thousands of years before the Hebrews arrived.

In modern times, all three of these areas, Egypt, Syria, and Mesopotamia, have been the scene of extensive and intensive archaeological study, as a result of which students of religion are now able as never before to see ancient Israel against her environment. The student can, for example, lay the Biblical creation story alongside the Babylonian creation story (the *Enuma Elish*), noting similarities and influences of the older Babylonian story on the Biblical story, but also noting even more fundamental differences of viewpoint and outlook in these two stories.[3] Similar comparisons can be made between the flood stories contained in the Babylonian Gilgamesh epic and the Biblical story in the Book of Genesis.[4]

The Biblical story of Israel's escape from Egyptian bondage in the Book of Exodus is told as the conflict of two kings, Israel's Lord against Pharaoh, the god-king of Egypt, ending in triumph of the Lord and the drowning of the Pharaoh and his army. The context of this dramatic conflict is the Pharaoh's well-ordered world with its priests and temples, its deities and subjects. There is significant Egyptian influence of many sorts on Israel; but even more important is their fundamental difference of outlook; it is the difference, in Eliade's phrase, between "cosmos and history." [5] The Egyptians held a cosmic outlook, or what our study terms a type-one, nature-culture religion; the Hebrews achieved a historical, monotheistic faith.

The Hebrew epic of the Lord and his people must also be seen against the Canaanite or Syrian background of the Ugaritic epic of Baal and Anath, recently unearthed at Ras Shamra.[6] While the Lord of Israel bears some similarity to the divine heroes of this epic, the differences are vastly more important. Israel's Lord has no divine friends or enemies but exists alone in solitary glory. Baal, Anath, and their kindred are deities of nature and culture, while Israel's God is envisaged as Lord of history—at first Israel's history, then mankind's history.

DISTINGUISHING THEMES IN
BIBLICAL RELIGION

Viewing the Bible against an environment in which nature and society are primary constituents of the timeless cosmos, the reader sees afresh the uniqueness of the Hebrew story of the one God who called the People of Israel to his service and whose call and service defined Israel's historical existence and historic destiny. Around this fundamental theme of Biblical religion may be grouped several observable characteristics which set ancient Israel apart from her environment. Four such differences will be listed. It is perhaps necessary to say again for purposes of emphasis that in pointing to these factual differences, no valuation, either affirmative or negative, is either asserted or implied. As historians of religion, all that we can fairly assert is that these are irreducibly different forms.

GOD AS CREATOR

One difference is that between the principle of discontinuity and the principle of continuity which characterized Egypt and other ancient Near Eastern peoples. Writing of Egypt, John Wilson has said, ". . . there was thus a continuing substance across the phenomena of the universe, whether organic, inorganic or abstract . . . the elements of the universe were consubstantial." [7] In short, gods, men, and objects of nature were conceived as members together of a single ordered and homogeneous cosmos. While Wilson is here describing Egyptian religion and society, his characterization holds good for the whole ancient Near East, and indeed for all religions of the first, or nature-culture, type.

In contrast to this viewpoint, which emphasizes the continuity of all reality, stands the clear, sharp line drawn by monotheism between Creator and creation, between the one God and the world which is his domain.[8] Seen from this viewpoint, the world is conceived not as cosmos but as creation. This is a distinction which permeates every aspect of monotheistic faith and outlook. Among its consequences is the notion of idolatry, or false religion which takes some aspect of the created world and accords it the reverence or worship which true faith reserves for the Creator alone. All three of the monotheistic faiths emphasize this idea, while none of the faiths of the first or second type so much as mention it at all. It is both pertinent and necessary to add that the monotheistic concept of idolatry implies intolerance toward all other, presumably false, religions. It is, of course, an observable fact that all religions have on some occasions fostered fanaticism and holy war. But it is also a fact frequently observed by historians of religion that monotheistic faiths have been more prone to these evils than other faiths. Here, in monotheism's exclusive claim, is to be seen one root of these problems and evils.

REVELATION

Another distinctive feature of monotheism is revelation, in which the divine will is communicated to man. To be sure, such phenomena as divination and oracular communication recur throughout the world's faiths; from this it might be argued that there is no difference between Moses receiving the Torah on Mount Sinai and Hammurabi receiving his code of laws from the sun god, Shamash, or the priestesses at Delphi receiving Apollo's oracular words. However, when these different cases are studied in fuller context, one sees in the case of Moses a faith in which the whole meaning of life, the secret of salvation, is presumed not to be in man's possession, but rather must be communicated to him by the one God. In monotheistic faiths the central importance is placed in the divine word. This is a metaphor for divine self-communication to man. God speaks to man, whose part is to hear and do the divine will. From this interpretation of religious experience as hearing and doing the divine will, it is only a step to a holy book. God discloses his will and word to man, who then writes down a record of this divine-human communication. It is not by accident that the three great monotheistic faiths are religions of a Book in a sense unique in the world's religions. Other faiths have sacred writings of many kinds, but seldom or never do these writings occupy so central a place in the whole faith as in Judaism, Christianity, and Islam.

MAN AS AGENT

From these distinctive features of Biblical monotheism derive important aspects of its view of man, such as his active, or volitional, nature and his moral and social character. If man is called to the service of God, that active service constitutes his true nature and destiny. Man is interpreted basically as a doer rather than as a contemplator or visionary; he *hears* and *does* the divine will. All of this stands in contrast to the aesthetic, contemplative attitude which predominates in religions of the first and second types.

Closely related to this distinction is the social-ethical quality of the monotheistic faiths. To be sure, some sort of ethical prescriptions and proscriptions seem to be part of all religions, though their content and importance vary greatly from faith to faith. In some religions, morality is conceived as a kind of preliminary discipline for the religious life which then rises beyond morality. Hinduism's goal of union with Brahman and Buddhism's Nirvana are both avowedly transsocial and transmoral. In contrast, monotheism asserts that God's fundamental and permanent requirement of man is a good life in society with his fellowman.

HISTORY AS DRAMA

Still another crucial difference has to do with time and history. For the cosmic religions, the recurring cycles of nature afford the crucial models for the experience of time. As noted in previous chapters, in religions of the second type men have customarily asserted an eternal reality above the common world of nature and society, in terms of which the latter is devaluated. This view has been termed an acosmic orientation. Monotheism has neither a cosmic nor an acosmic orientation, but something different from both, namely, a historical outlook.[9] Attention has already been called to the strong sense of historic destiny in the Biblical story of the one God. The next section of this chapter will sketch the plot of ancient Israel's divine-human drama of history. The reader will see that Israel's sense of time is not cyclic as those of her ancient Near Eastern neighbors, but linear and dramatic. This characteristic colors every aspect of Biblical religion. God is conceived as Lord of history, and man as an actor in that drama; and his good life consists in finding and playing his role in that drama. From this viewpoint the life of an individual human being may be construed as a piece of historic destiny; conversely, history is to be understood as the destiny of human selves.

ANCIENT ISRAEL'S DIVINE-HUMAN DRAMA

The first books of the Old Testament tell the story of ancient Israel's history, interpreted as the Lord's dealings with the people he has called to his service.

Israel's history is also set in the wide framework of world history. The resulting narrative has sometimes been called "the Hebrew epic," for there are genuinely epic dimensions in this ancient narrative.[10] One well-known student of comparative literature has compared and contrasted the epic style of Genesis with that of Homer's *Illiad* and *Odyssey*.[11] Yet the spirit and viewpoint of this narrative of ancient Israel and her God are so clearly dramatic that to call it a drama seems more appropriate than to call it an epic.

For many centuries both Jewish and Christian traditions maintained that Moses wrote the five books of the Torah, or Pentateuch. However, modern Biblical study, while recognizing a Mosaic tradition, has demonstrated clearly that many pens, many voices, and many minds living and working over long periods of time had a share in the authorship and editing of the first five books of the Bible. Beginning with songs and tales of the patriarchs sung by ancient rhapsodists, the books of the Torah gradually incorporated other parts of the present narrative, law codes, religious confessions, and the like.[12] Scholarly opinions and theories differ on details, but most contemporary scholars agree on four main strands of narrative: (1) Yahwist, ca. 950 B.C., (2) Elohist, ca. 750 B.C., (3) Deuteronomist, ca. 650 B.C., and (4) Priestly, 550 B.C.[13] Woven together by successive generations of editors, they came in time to constitute the present Pentateuch. While there are many variations in style, outlook, and historical circumstances, they all reflect the unity of a common tradition, constituting together in the view of their authors the dramatic narrative of God's dealings with his people Israel.

The first book of Moses is a book of beginnings, or literally of "genesis." It begins (chapters 1–11) with what has been called a "cosmic preface," in which the history of Israel is fitted into the larger picture of God's dealings with mankind and indeed with all creation. The divine-human drama begins with the divine Creation of man and the world. The two Creation stories (Genesis 1:1–2:3 and 2:4–3:24) are attributed by most scholars respectively to the P (Priestly) and J (Yahwist or Jahwist) authors. They differ from each other both in religious viewpoint and in factual detail, yet taken together in their overall unity, they also differ profoundly from other stories of beginnings. The Bible's first words are "In the beginning God. . . ." The Genesis "preface" moves onward from Creation and Fall to the flood story, which though clearly influenced by the Babylonian flood story differs from it as monotheism differs from polytheism. From the J writer, social pessimist that he was, have come also the stories of the Fall of man, of Cain and Abel, and the Tower of Babel.[14]

Genesis 12–50 tells the story of the patriarchs Abraham, Isaac, Jacob, and Jacob's twelve sons. While this narrative has the unity of a common heritage, it also shows an irreducible plurality, consisting as it does of many plots, characters, and viewpoints. At least some of these stories seem to be tales from the pre-

Hebrew past of Canaan, reworked to fit into the present Old Testament narrative.[15]

Early Hebrew narrators attributed the origin of their own nation as well as that of neighboring peoples to a figure named Abraham who in early days had emigrated from the Mesopotamian city of Ur northwestward to Harran in Syria and from thence south to Palestine. While Abraham appears before us as a shadowy figure, modern archaeology bears out the tradition of a westward migration into Palestine, assigning a date of ca. 1950 B.C. for Abraham.[16]

Adam and Eve. Painting
by Albrecht Dürer

Courtesy of the Metropolitan Museum of Art, Fletcher Fund, 1919

Hebrew narrators told tales of Abraham, of his life as a nomad in Palestine, of his descent to Egypt, of his generosity to his nephew, Lot, and many more episodes as well. Lot is depicted unflatteringly as the father, by incestuous union with his two daughters, of the neighboring Ammonites and Moabites. Abraham's son by Hagar, Ishmael, is identified as the ancestor of the Arabs. The Hebrew line of succession went through Isaac, the somewhat undistinguished son of Abraham and Sarah, to Isaac's more notable heir, Jacob, or Israel. Hebrew nationalism told how Jacob supplanted his twin brother, Esau, who was the progenitor of the Edomites. According to tradition Jacob's twelve sons were the ancestors of the twelve tribes of Israel. So indeed Genesis is a book of beginnings—Hebrew beginnings and those of other, neighboring peoples.

The perceptive reader will see in these stories the style which some students of religion have termed "Biblical realism." [17] There is little or no glorification of a hero, as in Greek epics, but the plain-spoken narrative of plain men, in all their strength and weakness, all their good and evil, in short, in all their poignant humanity. Under the guidance of one of Jacob's sons, Joseph, the Hebrews found their way to Egypt. The Joseph stories are notable for their unity, for their literary excellence, and for their distinctive view of a providence which guided Joseph's life to fulfillment and success.

The patriarchal stories show forms of life and social organization similar to those of nomadic groups throughout the world. For these people, life was a never-ending search for grasslands for the flocks of cattle, sheep, and goats, upon which life depended. Battles were fought over pasturage and ever-scarce water. The primary social group was the larger family under the authority of the father, who was at once priest, judge, and king. His authority in ancient Israel was somewhat limited by a council of elders. Polygamy was generally practiced, and the status of women, while not as inferior as in some societies, was clearly subordinate to that of men. The tribe was a closely knit, interdependent group in which each worked for all. While life was cheap outside the tribe, within the tribal brotherhood there was a deep respect for personality.[18]

The religious customs of these nomads included a reverent respect for natural objects such as springs, stones, wells, trees, and hills, within which *els,* or deities, were thought to dwell. Yet such polydaemonism was not the whole story of religion even at this early date. Some chiefs like Abraham conceived themselves to be in personal relation to deity, like sons before a father. In the worship of the patriarchs there was also a strong element of choice and a consequent sense of personal destiny. Here was the seed from which later religious developments were to grow.

As the reader moves from Genesis to Exodus he crosses the line which separates prehistory from history. Moses must be judged the founder of Judaism and one of the great religious figures of mankind. Out of the events of his life, principally the Exodus from Egypt and the giving of the Torah on Mount Sinai, emerge the nation Israel and the religious tradition which gave guidance and direction to the nation.[19]

While the full truth concerning Moses is obscured beneath many layers of tradition, it is still possible to discern a few salient historical facts. Perhaps the oldest account of the rescue from Egyptian bondage is contained in the following passage, often called the Pentateuch in miniature:

A wandering Aramean was my father; and he went down into Egypt and sojourned there, few in number; and there he became a nation, great, mighty, and populous. And the Egyptians treated us harshly, and afflicted us, and laid upon us hard bondage. Then we cried to the Lord the God of our fathers, and the Lord heard our voice, and saw our affliction, our toil, and our oppression; and the Lord brought us out of Egypt with a mighty hand and an outstretched arm, with great terror, with signs and wonders; and he brought us into this place and gave us this land, a land flowing with milk and honey.[20]

The Exodus version of the story as well as the account in Deuteronomy expand this tightly compressed account of Israelite history. The Book of Exodus begins with Israel in bondage in Egypt to a Pharaoh who "knew not Joseph."

The infant Moses discovered by Pharaoh's daughter
in the bullrushes. Watercolor by anonymous artist

*Courtesy of the Photographic Archive of the Jewish
Theological Seminary of America, New York.
Frank J. Darmstaedter*

The historical evidence for the date of these events does not speak with a single voice, though the end of the fourteenth century is preferred today by most scholars, with the date of ca. 1290 B.C. for the Exodus.[21]

The deliverer, Moses, was born to Hebrew parents during this time of harsh oppression. Hidden by his parents, he was discovered and adopted by Pharaoh's daughter, and given all the advantages of an Egyptian education. As a young man Moses broke forcibly with his Egyptian environment by murdering an Egyptian slave master. Fleeing to the Sinai Peninsula, he found refuge with the nomadic tribe of Midianites. He lived as a shepherd and married Zipporah, daughter of the chief Jethro (or Reuel, as he is called by one Exodus writer).

Then one day an event of crucial importance took place. On the slopes of Mount Sinai the Lord Yahweh appeared to Moses through a burning bush, commanding him to go down to Egypt to lead his people from slavery to freedom, and promising to lead them to a good future in the land of Canaan. While many of the details of the experience are obscured under several strata of tradition, clearly the narrative points to a direct encounter with God which changed the course of Moses' life and also of Hebrew history. God revealed himself to Moses by setting him this task of great moral and historic significance, promising a great destiny to Moses and his people.

There is a clear difference between J and E (Elohist) strands of this Exodus narrative concerning the beginning of Israel's worship of the Lord. E holds that the worship actually began at the time of Moses. In a crucial passage the Lord says to Moses:

> I am the Lord. I appeared to Abraham, to Isaac, and to Jacob, as God Almighty, but by my name the Lord I did not make myself known to them.[22]

It is significant in this connection to note that the divine name *YHWH* in Hebrew is translated into English as "Lord," while the Hebrew *Elohim* is rendered as "God." The Elohist writer calls deity "Elohim" or "God" throughout the Genesis period, and believes the worship of Yahweh began with Moses. Against this Elohist view, the J writer argues that Israel had "called on the name of Jahweh since the days of Enosh the son of Seth."[23] Whichever is correct, it was through the events of the Exodus and on Sinai that the Lord, or Yahweh, decisively manifested himself to his people. This was the climax of the divine-human drama as the Old Testament authors construed it.

Accompanied by his brother Aaron, Moses returned to Egypt to plead for the release of their enslaved countrymen. From this point onward, the story becomes a contest between two deities, the Lord against Pharaoh, the god-king of Egypt. Each of these deities performed mighty works or miracles, but the plagues which Moses and Aaron called down from the Lord upon Egypt moved onward to fatal climax in the death of the Egyptian firstborn. Only then Pharaoh desperately commanded Moses and his people to leave Egypt. But as they left, he changed his mind and pursued the fleeing Israelites, only to be overwhelmed by the Lord at the Red Sea.

The later conjoining of the celebration of this deliverance with a spring agricultural festival (such at least is the view of many scholars) provided ancient

Israel as well as later Judaism with its best-known and most distinctive holy day, Passover. Thus Passover was given a historical meaning in the celebration of deliverance from Egypt.

Rescued and guided by their God and led by Moses, the Hebrews made their way in a space of three lunar months to the foot of Mount Sinai. The traditional location of this mountain is the south-central part of the Sinai Penin-

Israelites worshipping the Golden Calf (Baal) in the wilderness. Silk tapestry

Courtesy of the Photographic Archive of the Jewish Theological Seminary of America, New York. Frank J. Darmstaedter

sula, and despite some scholarly controversy, this is still the most probable site. (The location and Israel's journey are noted on the map inside the front cover.) The Exodus and Deuteronomy narratives tell the story of the covenant between Israel and her Lord. While again the details of the event are obscured beneath many layers of tradition, the crucially important features are clear enough. Through these events, the Hebrew faith and nation were called into being. Ever afterward Israel looked back to Sinai as the covenant in which the Lord chose Israel, placing her under command and promise, and in which reciprocally, Israel freely chose the Lord. Thus commitment and vocation were placed at the heart of Israel's religious experience. Further, the terms of Israel's service of her God consisted of a code for social conduct; in other words, God's primary requirement of man was the ethical requirement of a good life in society with one's fellowmen.

This ethical character of Mosaic religion is epitomized in the Ten Commandments, which are surely among the most famous codes in mankind's religious history. Attention may be called to two different versions of the Ten Commandments (Exodus 20 and 34) with their great differences, and also to the fact that the first occurs in the larger context of what is usually called the Book of the Covenant (Exodus 20–23). The latter is a detailed code of social legislation and doubtless is ancient Israel's earliest written law code. In its present form it reflects an agricultural way of life and hence must be placed historically during Israel's early habitation in Palestine. Nevertheless the tendency of recent scholarship has been to push its origins back to a period close to Moses.[24]

Among its specific provisions, the Book of the Covenant recognized slavery; the lot of the Hebrew slave was easier than that of the foreigner, and male slaves fared better than females.[25] Women, while subordinate to men, were by no means without rights. The *lex talionis,* or law of equal vengeance, restrained violence against persons in this age before public law officers.[26] Property rights in animals and land were carefully defined. Throughout this code there was a strong sense of social responsibility. It is particularly noteworthy that some of the laws were stated in categorical rather than hypothetical fashion, "Thou shalt . . ." rather than "If . . . then . . . ," thus expressing the clear note of absoluteness in Israel's service of her God. At least one recent writer has contrasted this absolutism and personalism of the Mosaic code with the secularized, qualified, and somewhat impersonal tone of the Mesopotamian Code of Hammurabi.[27]

Some of the provisions of the Book of the Covenant dealt with cultic or religious duties. The Lord was to be sought and found in the Ark of the Covenant, a box traditionally supposed to contain the tablets of the Torah, which was placed in the tent of meeting.[28] Feast days and probably animal sacrifice were prescribed. Most fundamental was Israel's exclusive service and worship of the Lord; the first commandment was "no other gods before me." As has often been pointed out, this commandment presupposes the existence of other deities, and the Books of Exodus and Deuteronomy make this assumption explicitly clear. However, the important point was that Israel was categorically commanded to *serve* no other deity. Consistent with this relation the Lord was conceived as an absolute sovereign who of his own free will kept covenant with Israel. Hence also in this manner his sovereignty was qualified by his love; Israel was God's son whom he loved and chose for a great destiny. Moreover this God who was

Moses holding the Ten Commandments. 18th century German wood sculpture

*Courtesy of the Photographic
Archive of the Jewish Theo-
logical Seminary of America,
New York. Frank J.
Darmstaedter*

Lord was also the Creator; the famous words "I am who I am" should in the opinion of some scholars be translated "I am he who causes to be," or "He causes to be what comes into existence." [29]

After the giving of the Torah, Israel appears to have wandered nomadically for a generation in the wilderness south of Palestine. There was an initial and unsuccessful attempt to invade Palestine, this and other events of the period being recounted in the Biblical Book of Numbers. During this time, Israel lived as a nomadic tribe in the region of Kadesh Barnea. The Biblical estimate of forty years for this period fits with modern scholarship, for there is evidence that by ca. 1250 B.C. Israel had begun to move into Canaan.[30]

Two contrasting Biblical accounts of the conquest of Canaan are contained, respectively, in the Books of Joshua and Judges. The former describes a brief military invasion under the leadership of Joshua, who was Moses' immediate successor. It was a campaign which ended in complete Hebrew victory and the subjugation of previous inhabitants and division of territory among the traditional twelve tribes. The other account, in the Book of Judges, describes a long, slow, and fitful process of infiltration, crowned with success only two centuries later under the monarchical leadership of Saul and David.

There is doubtless some basis in fact for the account of Joshua's campaigns and the Shechem assembly at which the covenant was renewed and the land divided among the twelve tribes.[31] However, there is good reason to believe that these campaigns were local and Joshua's success temporary. Stories of total victory were the figments of later editors' imaginations.

The Book of Judges, which sketches the history of Israel's first two centuries in Palestine, was written, or at least edited, by a later writer with a different and highly distinctive viewpoint. He recognized Israel's long, hard, and fitful struggle for Canaan, but in this struggle he related good fortune to fidelity to the Lord and misfortune to infidelity. Behind this interpretation historians can discern the two-century period when Israel was locked in mortal combat with other peoples for domination of the land. At one time the Moabites achieved the mastery, and Israel rebelled against them. At another time the Hebrews, under Deborah and Barak, threw off the yoke of the Canaanites under Sisera. This battle is described in the "Ode of Deborah" which is not only a great poem, but also, as one of the most ancient documents in the Bible, an important historical source.[32] At another time Gideon arose as a leader, driving off bands of marauding Midianites.

It was an age of only minimal unity among the Hebrews, who as a result fell victim to other, better-organized peoples. It was also a time of religious conflict and transition. The Hebrews came into Palestine as a close-knit nomadic community, firm in their faith in the Lord. However they found other religious customs in the new country. Notably they encountered worship of local civic and agricultural deities called *baals* (the word *baal* in Hebrew means "lord," "husband," and "owner"). There were innumerable local baals who functioned as fertility deities of the land and were frequently wed to fertility goddesses called *asherah*. There was also a high god, or baal, celebrated in Ugaritic epic, who manifested himself in storms. It is probable that this latter was the baal whom Elijah opposed at Mount Carmel in mid-ninth century B.C.[33]

The problem confronting the Hebrews was the relation of their God, the Lord, to these new deities. Should they abandon the Lord for these new deities? Did the Lord rule the new country as he ruled the desert? Should they try to blend worship of the Lord and of the baals? It took many centuries to hammer out definitive answers to these and similar questions.

The last and most formidable opponents of the Hebrews for mastery of the land were the Philistines, who were refugees from the disaster which had overtaken Crete, and who made their way across Asia Minor and down the coast of Syria to the borders of Egypt. Repelled there, they settled on the seacoast of Palestine early in the thirteenth century B.C. Ironically they gave their name to the country, *Palestine* being a corrupted form of *Philistine*. Organized into city-states and well armed, the Philistines subjugated the Hebrews and made themselves virtual masters of the land.[34]

In this dire extremity, the Hebrew people demanded a king who could provide effective military and political leadership. To this proposal there appears to have been continuing opposition from the group in Israel which rejected a king as a competitor with the Lord for Israel's allegiance. This group asserted that only the Lord was really the King of Israel. One of the two source narratives of Saul's tragic reign appears to have been written by such an author, who did not hesitate to write his antimonarchical prejudices into history.[35]

The Bible gives two accounts of Saul's accession to the throne, according to one of which he was anointed by the seer and priest of Shiloh, Samuel; according to the other, he was selected by lot in a popular assembly of Israel's people.[36] Once in power, he showed initiative in raising an army and driving off the Ammonites from the city of Jabesh in Gilead. Turning his attention to the Philistines, Saul again had initial success, due largely to the daring and imagination of his son, Jonathan, who surprised and defeated the Philistine garrison at Michmash.

Yet Saul could not, or at least did not, follow up his first successes. He alienated Samuel, who turned his support to another aspirant for the throne, namely, David. Saul was plagued by a recurring mood of melancholy (called by the Biblical historian an "evil spirit from the Lord") which robbed him of his resolution and rendered him pathologically jealous of David. After much

David anointed
by Samuel.
7th century
Byzantine dish

*Courtesy of the
Metropolitan
Museum of Art,
Gift of J.
Pierpont Morgan,
1917*

David before
Saul. 7th cen-
tury Byzantine
dish

*Courtesy of the
Metropolitan
Museum of Art,
Gift of J.
Pierpont Morgan,
1917*

delay, the Philistines struck at the battle of Mount Gilboa. The Hebrews were routed, both Saul and Jonathan taking their own lives to avoid capture.[37] Saul's reign lasted from 1020 to 1000 B.C.

Saul's death left an open field for David, who during Saul's lifetime had carefully refrained from seeking the throne. He seems to have regarded King Saul as a sacred person, God's anointed King of Israel. When Saul died, David became king of his native Judea for seven years, while Saul's son, Ishbaal, maintained nominal power over the rest of Israel. When assassination removed Ishbaal, David grasped the opportunity to become king of a united nation. His reign (ca. 1000–961 B.C.) was the golden age of ancient Israel.

David moved quickly and decisively against Israel's enemies, the Philistines first, then the Ammonites, Moabites, and Edomites. In each case he won a decisive victory. The boundaries of the Israelite nation were extended farther than ever before or ever after. At home, stable government and a prosperous economy, aided by tribute from subjugated peoples, provided unparalleled good times.

David's reign was also marked by a flowering of art and culture. The King was a poet and musician, as well as an enthusiastic supporter of Yahweh. Hebrew language assumed its classical form; and the first redaction of Israel's national epic, that of the J writer, or Yahwist, came into being. Little wonder that David's reign became known to later generations as Israel's golden age.

David's personal and family life was not as successful as his public career. An illicit affair with Bathsheba led to his plotting the killing of her husband Uriah.[38] This sordid story is told with full realism by the Biblican historian, who also informs us of the denunciation of David by David's friend, the prophet Nathan. Here the prophet assumed the role of critic of royal injustice; it was a momentous precedent.

David's family was seldom harmonious. One son, Amnon, raped his half sister Tamar, and for this act was killed by Tamar's brother, Absalom, who was in turn ostracized from the court. Absalom subsequently rose in rebellion against his father. After coming perilously close to success, the rebellion was put down by David's military men, and much to David's sorrow, Absalom was killed.[39]

David's old age was marred by court intrigue and struggle for succession to the throne. The chief contenders were Adonijah and Solomon. The latter, with the help of his mother, Bathsheba, succeeded in gaining the support of David. Upon his accession to the throne, he proceeded to a bloody purge of his rival and his rival's followers.[40]

Solomon, lacking both his father's military ability and his democratic sensibilities, set up his court like an Oriental despot.[41] In addition to his famous temple, Solomon's extensive public building enterprises included a palace for himself, another for his favorite wife, the princess of Egypt, a hall of judgment, and many more. He built a navy with a Red Sea base, and carried on overseas commerce which featured such luxury commodities as ivory, apes, and peacocks. His extensive household included 300 wives and 600 concubines as well as a vast retinue of courtiers, all supported by public taxation. Apparently Solomon's

King David praying in the temple of King Solomon (*sic.*).
18th century woodcut

Courtesy of the Photographic Archive of the Jewish Theological Seminary of America, New York. Frank J. Darmstaedter

reputation as a wise judge was not based upon a social conscience. It is not surprising that there were repeated rumblings of rebellion during his reign.

Solomon's reign lasted from 961 to 922 B.C. When he died, his subjects met in popular assembly at Shechem to petition for redress of grievances. Meeting complete rebuff from Solomon's son, Rehoboam, the ten northern tribes did not hesitate to secede from the dynasty of David and set up their own government at Shechem (922 B.C.). Their first king and leader was Jeroboam I, a former official of and then a rebel against Solomon. This division of the kingdom disastrously split the nation. The southern tribes of Judah and Benjamin remained true to the Davidic dynasty and held the capital city of Jerusalem, while the rebellious ten tribes held most of the nation's territory, wealth, and population. Neither was a genuinely viable unit without the other.

The half century which followed the division was marked by intermittent border warfare, and also extreme instability in the northern kingdom. King followed king in rapid and violent succession until the rise of Omri. A military man who seized the throne in 876 B.C., he built Samaria as capital city and established a secure and prosperous kingdom. Omri's foreign relations with Syria to the north were cemented by the marriage of his son Ahab to the Tyrian princess, Jezebel.[42]

Ahab succeeded to his father's throne in 869 B.C. and reigned for nineteen years. Most notable event of his reign was the protracted struggle of the Yahwist party under Elijah against Jezebel and her attempt to introduce into Israel the worship of the Tyrian baal, Melkart. Jezebel was not only a forceful person, but an enthusiastic devotee of Melkart. Elijah saw the issue of Melkart versus Yahweh in uncompromising terms: Israel could serve Melkart or the Lord but not both. The worship of the Lord was connected in Elijah's mind with both national independence and social justice. When the poor man Naboth was framed and killed by Jezebel in order that she might seize his land, Elijah rose to superb heights as champion of social justice. Elijah's opposition to Jezebel and Melkart came to a climax at the trial on Mount Carmel, where he stood alone in defiance of Jezebel's 400 prophets of Baal.[43]

These and other stories of Elijah were written down not long after his death, probably by a follower. They show a figure second only to Moses among the great men of Israel. Later generations made him the symbol of prophecy as Moses was the symbol of the Torah. Elijah's prophetic career was the foundation for the work of the great prophets of the eighth and seventh centuries.

After Elijah, the northern kingdom, Israel, continued for another century and then, falling victim to Assyrian invasion in 721 B.C., disappeared from the pages of history. Her people were carried into captivity never to return, thus becoming the ten lost tribes. The tiny southern kingdom of Judah continued a tortured existence until 586 B.C., when Nebuchadnezzar captured Jerusalem and carried her people into captivity, decisively ending the national existence of the ancient Israelite people.

Apparently the divine-human drama of ancient Israel's life had come to a tragic conclusion. Yet the miracle was that this was not the end. The story of Israel did not terminate with the end of her national existence. In the historical period to which this discussion has now come, the eighth to the sixth centuries

B.C., the focus of interest shifts from national politics to another subject of para-mount importance, the rise of prophetic religion.

PROPHETIC RELIGION

What is a prophet? Many would answer immediately and without hesitation that a prophet is a divinely certified forecaster of the future. This understanding of prophecy has support in many religious traditions, from Greece and Rome to India and China. Oracles and oracular speakers are familiar figures in the world's religions. It has some basis in the ancient Hebrew tradition of the Bible, as illustrated by the stories of Balaam, and of Saul's search for his father's lost donkeys.[44]

The Greek word *prophetes* has the double meaning of "foretelling" and "forthtelling," but the Hebrew word for "prophet," *nabu* (plural *nebiim*) means unequivocally to "speak for." The latter etymology accords with the historic fact that the prophets of Israel were men who believed themselves called to speak for the Lord to Israel, and in the case of some later prophets, to mankind. The evidence for this interpretation of prophecy will be given as exposition unfolds. To be sure, the prophets of Israel did at times predict; and sometimes their predictions came true, sometimes not. However, the heart of their enter-prise lay not in predicting the future, but in declaring God's will to his recal-citrant human children.

Since the Biblical prophets were men possessed by an immediately and power-fully perceived vocation to speak for God, they have been likened to the mystic who also has an immediate, or direct, awareness of the divine. However, the Hebrew prophet contrasts sharply with the mystic in the prophet's fundamental emphasis on volition and action and hence upon specific moral and social aspects of religion. Where the mystic finds communion or union with God in some transcendent realm, the prophet encounters God in everyday moral and social relations. Holding the standard of God's will as his criterion, the prophet is led to a radical criticism of every aspect of human life and culture. For Israel's prophets, the ethical criticism of religion—as of all human culture—became a definite aspect of religion.

The prophetic principle, as it may be called, may thus be defined as the achievement of a point above all human life and culture from which all of life is held under radical criticism. The one God of monotheism has many meanings and implications, which will be developed as our study proceeds. However, the prophetic understanding involving a viewpoint from which prophetic criticism is undertaken, may be treated as basic. Many of the further meanings and impli-cations of the one God will be noted in future chapters as implications drawn from this premise.

The origins of prophecy in the Bible go far back in history. Later ages looked back to Moses as the archetypal prophet, and as has been argued, the idea of ethical religion is traceable to him. Later, during Israel's first centuries in Palestine, bands of Yahweh enthusiasts wandered the countryside prophesying ecstatically, singing, dancing, working themselves into ecstatic states. Saul is said to have identified himself with one such band.[45] It is possible that Deborah was such a prophetess.[46]

Biblical prophecy began to take on a new dimension of ethical and social criticism in such figures as Nathan in David's time and Ahijah in Solomon's.[47] It is important historically to note that this idea of a religiously inspired criticism of political power in ancient Israel is unique in the ancient Near East, if not in the religions of the whole world. Its importance for Western politics as well as religion can scarcely be overestimated.

Prophecy assumed a new importance in the great Elijah of the ninth century. As we have already noted, he was the champion of both social justice and national independence. Moreover, he pushed the Yahwist criticism of baal worship a long step further, in his assumption that Yahweh was Lord not only of history but of such natural phenomena as the weather.[48] His mordant ridicule of Baal Melkart and Melkart's priests was a step toward the conclusion of the essential unreality of the baals, and toward the corresponding conclusion that Yahweh was the absolute Lord of all reality.

A century after Elijah, the writing prophets (so called because their words and lives now form books of the Judeo-Christian Bible) burst upon the scene, and they managed to hold the center for at least two centuries. These men, beginning with Amos and continuing until Ezekiel and Deutero-Isaiah, would have rejected the title of innovator; rather they professed to recall their people to the traditional Mosaic heritage.[49] Yet the manner in which they performed this prophetic task did in fact transform Hebrew religion. It may be said that the prophets historicized, ethicized, spiritualized, and universalized Israel's religious heritage. Their historicizing emphasis took the double form of recalling Israel to the Mosaic past, and what Martin Buber has called a "turning to the future."[50] For the prophets asserted that the Lord who had ruled and guided Israel during the Exodus and on Sinai still ruled, and would yet vindicate his rule of the world. The importance for the development of Biblical religion of this looking to the future toward a time of consummation can hardly be overstated.

While the prophets inherited the Mosaic tradition of the Ten Commandments and ethical religion, they applied this standard to the life of society in new and radical ways. They were especially critical of the institutional religion of their time. Closely allied with the appeal to an ethical or moral standard for the judgment of all human life was an inward appeal to the motives or intentions which are the source of men's actions. Only if the heart be pure, argued the prophets, will action be righteous.

Finally, the prophets universalized Israel's religion. As God is one, so mankind is one human family. Thus the Lord was no longer understood as a Hebrew tribal deity, guiding and protecting his people, but as Lord of all

Wandering Elijah. Painting by Ben Zion
Courtesy of the Photographic Archive of the Jewish
Theological Seminary of America, New York.
Frank J. Darmstaedter

peoples and nations. One God, therefore one mankind: such is the logic of prophetic thought. From this point onward in Judeo-Christian history, the student sees a radical tension in thought and faith between universalism and what must be termed particularism or nationalism.

The historical background of the prophetic movement was the late Indian summer of the Hebrew nation. Jeroboam II (796–746 B.C.) occupied the throne of Israel and Uzziah (783–742 B.C.) the throne of Judah when Amos, the first of these prophets, raised his voice. On the surface, prosperity prevailed at home and peace abroad. Yet it was the momentary calm before the whirlwind of doom. As the prophets were quick to point out, the domestic prosperity was based upon the grinding poverty of the poor. Internationally, the Assyrians appeared like a dark and foreboding cloud on the northern horizon. Before the eighth century was over, the northern kingdom, Israel, had disappeared from history, and little Judah was left to another century and a half of existence as a meager pawn on the chessboard of empires and conquests. In the midst of this situation arose the great prophets of the eighth century, Amos, Hosea, Isaiah, and Micah.

AMOS (CA. 750 B.C.)

The first of the writing prophets was a farmer and shepherd from the remote Judean village of Tekoa. Making his way to the northern shrine city of Bethel, presumably at the time of a festival, he spoke out publicly against injustice and social evils of Jeroboam II's reign. Challenged by the court chaplain, Amaziah, and told to go back home, Amos replied in burning words, denying that he was a professional prophet or clergyman and putting into words his own strong sense of vocation to speak for the Lord: "Then Amos answered Amaziah, 'I am no prophet, nor a prophet's son; but I am a herdsman, and a dresser of sycamore trees, and the Lord took me from following the flock, and the Lord said to me, "Go, prophesy to my people." ' " [51] To this vocation Amos brought both a sharp eye for social realities and the fundamental conviction of ethical religion, namely, that God has written his law of justice and brotherhood into the foundations of society. He also brought a literary style which fitted his message.

In several of his prophetic oracles, Amos seemed to regard God's law of brotherhood as written into the structure of human life in such a way that to break this law is to violate the norms of human life.[52] As a wall not squarely built falls of its own weight, so an unjust society must collapse. The notes of judgment and doom are strong throughout Amos's book. Yet divine judgment is never a capricious action of some celestial judge, but rather a judgment rising from the social structure of life itself. Evil is a violation of the norms of man's life. As a destroying nemesis, God tracks down evildoers to the ends of the earth or the depths of the sea.[53]

Amos detailed his charges against his unrighteous countrymen. They have sold "the needy for a pair of shoes" and trampled "the poor into the dust," they have made "the ephah small and the shekel great," have used false weights and other sorts of sharp practice.[54]

For the leisure classes Amos had these words:

> *Woe to those who lie upon beds of ivory,*
> *and stretch themselves upon their couches,*
> *and eat lambs from the flock,*
> *and calves from the midst of the stall;*
> *who sing idle songs to the sound of the harp,*
> *and like David invent for themselves instruments of music;*
> *who drink wine in bowls,*
> *and anoint themselves with the finest oils,*
> *but are not grieved over the ruin of Joseph!*
> *Therefore they shall now be the first of those to go into exile,*
> *and the revelry of those who stretch themselves shall pass away.*[55]

Yet perhaps worst of all social evils was a ritual religion irrelevant to ethical conduct and characterized by temple prostitution and other similar evils. Amos depicts God as saying:

> *I hate, I despise your feasts,*
> *and I take no delight in your solemn assemblies.*
> *Even though you offer me your burnt offerings and cereal offerings,*
> *I will not accept them,*
> *and the peace offerings of your fatted beasts*
> *I will not look upon.*
> *Take away from me the noise of your songs;*
> *to the melody of your harps I will not listen.*
> *But let justice roll down like waters,*
> *and righteousness like an ever-flowing stream.*[56]

This unsparing denunciation of institutional religions was destined to be repeated by each of Israel's preexilic prophets.

Amos's contemporaries added to their ritual a kind of religious nationalism which found expression in the "Day of the Lord." This was interpreted as a future time when God would give the Hebrews victory over all their foes. To this Amos replied ominously:

> *Woe to you who desire the day of the Lord!*
> *Why would you have the day of the Lord?*
> *It is darkness, and not light;*
> *as if a man fled from a lion, and a bear met him;*
> *or went into the house and leaned with his hand against the wall,*
> *and a serpent bit him.*
> *Is not the day of the Lord darkness, and not light,*
> *and gloom with no brightness in it?* [57]

In dark and foreboding images, Amos foresaw the doom of a nation that had failed in essential justice and brotherhood. Presumably he viewed the Assyrians as the executors of God's judgment upon Israel.

Amos saw with equal clarity not only the divine justice but the universality of God which reduced to zero any favored status for Israel. The first chapter of Amos's book is a series of judgments of doom upon all surrounding peoples— in which presumably Amos's nationalistic countrymen could join by simply ignoring Amos's statement of the ethical character of the judgment. But then— to the bewilderment and surprise of his fellow Israelites—Amos followed with God's judgment of doom upon Israel and upon Judah for the reason that they too had failed miserably in essential morality. God's judgment plays no favorites. "Are you not to me as the Ethiopians?" Amos's Lord asks the people of Israel.[58] Indeed their previous knowledge leaves them even more blameworthy: "You only have I known of all the families of the earth; therefore I will punish you for all your iniquities." [59]

HOSEA (CA. 740 B.C.)

A few years after Amos, another prophetic voice, that of Hosea, was raised. Like Amos in his emphasis on the ethical nature of religion, Hosea nonetheless differed profoundly in other respects. He was a native of the northern kingdom, and his words suggest a priestly background. The first three chapters of his book tell of his tragic marriage and family life. These same three chapters may also be said to constitute Hosea's call to the prophetic office. The Biblical text of these chapters is obscure; reconstruction is necessary to make sense of the narrative. An attempted reconstruction of Hosea 1–3 follows in the next paragraphs.

Apparently Hosea had married a wife, Gomer, in mutual good faith. Their three children were given symbolic names with prophetic meanings. The eldest, a son, was named Jezreel, recalling Jehu's bloody rebellion a century earlier on a battlefield of that name. The other two were named, respectively, Lo-ammi, "not my people," and Lo-ruhammah, "she who is unpitied," meaning that the Lord would have no pity in his judgment of Israel. So far, Hosea had not diverged from Amos's grim conclusion concerning God's judgment on Israel.

Only then did Hosea discover that Gomer was unfaithful. The Biblical passage intimates that she became a temple prostitute. Hebrew law decreed divorce as the just fate for such a person. Sadly Hosea undertook to put the decree into effect when suddenly at a word from the Lord he felt constrained to love his erring wife through all her wanderings and infidelities and by this love to win her back to himself. By analogy Hosea saw that the Lord loved Israel despite her unfaithfulness and sought to win her back to himself. So it was that Hosea looked beyond justice to forgiving love. So too it was that through the tragic events of his marriage Hosea felt himself called to prophesy to Israel.

Like Amos before him, Hosea believed that Israel would suffer for her manifold sins; but beyond judgment he saw redemption and forgiveness. At least once in Hosea's book the marital metaphor changes and the Lord becomes the forgiving father and Israel the wayward son.[60] No other prophet declared the healing and forgiving love of God in more lyrically beautiful language than Hosea.

Hosea's viewpoint was deeply inward. Where Amos criticized evil deeds, Hosea probed the motives of the heart which found expression in such deeds, concluding that the evil affections of the heart are the source of unrighteous actions. Hosea never tired of pointing out the inconstancy of man's fickle heart, turning from God to trivial things, as the source of evil action. One consequence of all this is idolatry—false worship or false love. Also in Hosea's mind the monarchy was related to idolatry, for a king so easily confused himself with God.

In Hosea's view, the Lord is always near. If Israel persists in infidelity, God declares, "I am your destruction, O Israel, who can help you?" [61] Yet God is also always ready to take back his erring human children.

> So you, by the help of your God, return,
> hold fast to love and justice,
> and wait continually for your God.[62]

Hosea's words were a dirge for the northern kingdom. In 732 B.C. the Assyrians took Damascus and overran Israel, placing a puppet king on the throne. In 724 B.C. he rebelled, the Assyrians besieged the city, and after a long and cruel siege, took it in 721 B.C. Following their practice, the Assyrians carried the survivors captive to distant parts of their empire, bringing in foreigners to populate the northern kingdom. So the ten tribes passed from the scene of history.

ISAIAH OF JERUSALEM (CA. 742-690 B.C.)

Contemporary with Hosea there arose the mighty figure of Isaiah of Jerusalem. His words may be found in the first thirty-nine chapters of the book of the Bible which bears his name. Yet since the Book of Isaiah contains the writing of at least one and probably many other writers, constituting a kind of miscellaneous file of prophetic writings, it is necessary for the reader to distinguish the utterances of Isaiah of Jerusalem from others. Happily his style and content are sufficiently distinctive to make this possible. One of the first and most notable examples is Isaiah's description (Isaiah 6) of the experience which made him a prophet. In the temple at Jerusalem one day "in the year that King Uzziah died" (742 B.C.) he "saw the Lord." [63] The vision produced in the prophet a sense of profound awe before God which gave way first to a sense of sin, then forgiveness, and then to a sense of mission. In response to the divine question, "Whom shall I send and who will go for us?" Isaiah replied, "Here am I, send me." [64] Thus launched upon his prophetic career, Isaiah was statesman, preacher, reformer, and spokesman for God to Israel in the tumultuous decades that followed.

He spoke of God's justice and love as Amos and Hosea before him, but he introduced new notes as well. One such new emphasis was the idea of faith conceived as trust in God. Man's true source of strength was not arrogant self-trust as the nationalists asserted, nor was it trust in arms or in alliances with this or that nation. Rather it was trust in the Lord who despite all appearances to the contrary was still sovereign of history.

In a famous scene (recounted in chapter 7) Isaiah met Ahaz as the King went out of Jerusalem to secure the city's water supply and fortifications in anticipation of impending siege and war. The prophet bade the King not to fear, warning him, "If you will not believe, surely you shall not be established." [65] In the face of the King's mingled incredulity and evasiveness, Isaiah declared a sign. A child would be born, named Emmanuel (meaning "God with us"), and in the length of time necessary for the child to grow to knowledge of good and evil, the King's enemies would be brought to naught.[66] Yet what Isaiah really sought to impress upon the King was that above all kings and warriors, above all nations and empires, the Lord God rules history.

This conviction led to some of Isaiah's profoundest—and strangest—words. Like Amos before him, Isaiah believed that God would judge his own people Israel. And he plainly said that the Lord would use the hated Assyrians as his "battle axe." [67] Yet when the Assyrians actually invaded Judah, and Isaiah could see their arrogant and wanton cruelty at first hand, he cried out in change of mind: "Shall the axe vaunt itself over him who hews with it?" [68] Surely the Lord would cast off so arrogant an instrument of his purpose. Proud self-sufficiency constituted the heart of human evil, whether in Israel or her enemies. Such was Isaiah's conclusion as he looked upon the history of his troubled times.

In a famous poetic vision of the Day of the Lord, Isaiah declared that all high and arrogant human things would be brought low, and the Lord only would be exalted. God declares an absolute judgment against all forms of human arrogance.[69]

Yet this was not the prophet's last word. As he scanned the future, he saw doom and judgment in the immediate time ahead. Yet he could look beyond this darkness to a better time to come. Isaiah declared that a faithful remnant

would persist through the testing time to come, to a better future. His son bore
the symbolic name Shearjashub, meaning "a remnant shall return." [70] He spoke
of Israel as a tree cut down, from whose stump new growth would presently
come. God spoke to men in history not only in judgment but in redemption as
well.

Moreover the divine purpose in history would one day come to fulfillment.
Isaiah gave few details, but he alluded to the ideal king who would reign in
peace and justice. [71] This golden age of the future would be a time when swords
would be beaten into ploughshares and men would learn war no more. [72] In
such vivid images Isaiah probed the ways of God in human history.

MICAH (CA. 725-700 B.C.)

Beside the great Isaiah, Micah seems small and his words meager. Yet he had
a message from the Lord for the reluctant ears of his contemporaries. A country-
man, he denounced the injustices and evils of the cities. From a small town,
Bethlehem, he cried, the ideal king would come. [73] Meanwhile, Samaria and
Jerusalem would be left as rubble-heaps on the landscape. [74]

Yet these angry words softened to Micah's classic formula of prophetic religion. Its unmistakable allusion to human sacrifice places it during the reign
of King Manasseh, who practiced those barbarous rites. Whether it is from
Micah or from a disciple is thus questionable, but in either case it epitomizes the
spirit of prophetic religion:

> *With what shall I come before the Lord,*
> *and bow myself before God on high?*
> *Shall I come before him with burnt offerings,*
> *with calves a year old?*
> *Will the Lord be pleased with thousands of rams,*
> *with ten thousands of rivers of oil?*
> *Shall I give my first-born for my transgression,*
> *the fruit of my body for the sin of my soul?*
> *He has showed you, O man, what is good;*
> *and what does the Lord require of you*
> *but to do justice, and to love kindness,*
> *and to walk humbly with your God?* [75]

DEUTERONOMY (621 B.C.)

The Mican allusion to human sacrifice may well have been a reference to King
Manasseh, 687–642 B.C., for it is known that he participated in human sacrifices,
making his son "pass through fire." Manasseh was an Assyrian vassal who

brought Assyrian deities and rituals into the Jerusalem temple, pushing the altar of the Lord to one side. Also he persecuted the Yahwist party, forcing them underground.

During this time of hiding, the prophetic, or Yahwist, party formulated their own program of reform and held it in readiness for the opportune moment. That moment came when after the brief reign of Manasseh's son, Amon (642 B.C.), his grandson, Josiah, came to the throne (642–609 B.C.). In 621 he ordered long-needed repairs to the temple, during which the high priest reported the finding of a long-lost book of Mosaic law, or Torah. This event, reported in II Kings 22:8–20, is regarded by most modern scholars as the recovery or discovery of the proposals of the prophetic party as they are embodied in the Biblical Book of Deuteronomy.

The word *Deuteronomy* means in Greek "second law," that is, the second redaction of the Mosaic law. The Book of Deuteronomy is cast in the form of three sermonic addresses by Moses to the Israelites as they were about to enter Canaan. While clearly the book is in the Mosaic tradition, it is undoubtedly the work of seventh-century prophetic reformers. Its ideas fit well with what we know of seventh-century Israel. It was proposed, for example, that the remnants of foreign cults were to be rooted out and destroyed, local shrines which had been hotbeds of baal worship were to be closed, and all worship centered in Jerusalem. To the Deuteronomic reformers the worship of one God clearly implied a single sanctuary. In their insistent emphasis upon social ethics, the Deuteronomic reformers showed the influence of the great eighth-century prophets.

The Deuteronomic law code (chapters 12–26) evinced a sense of social responsibility which combined in new ways personal rights and property rights. Every seventh, or sabbatical, year debts were to be canceled, and Hebrew slaves, though not foreign slaves, were to be manumitted. A judicial system including right of appeal to a supreme court was provided. A king with limited powers was recognized. Rules of war, including a generous system of draft deferments and a military chaplaincy were sketched out. War was holy for the Deuteronomic reformers, and all prisoners and booty were *cherem*, or devoted to God.[76] There is no knowledge of the extent to which this Deuteronomic reform code was ever put into actual practice.

The religious spirit of the Deuteronomists is epitomized in the *Shema*:

> *Hear, O Israel: the Lord our God is one Lord. And you shall love the Lord your God with all your heart, and with all your soul, and with all your might.*[77]

There is in Deuteronomy a new emphasis upon the study of God's Torah, as found within the pages of this book. Indeed, precisely here may be said to be the actual beginning of the idea of a sacred scripture; here Judaism was first set upon the way of being a religion of Torah and Book. The study and practice of Torah are confidently declared to be the first duty of man.[78]

Over and over again the Deuteronomic author exhorts his fellow countrymen to avoid even the suggestion of the worship of false gods. For only so can a good life be achieved and maintained. Indeed these Deuteronomic reformers spelled out with utter consistency of detail the good fortune and prosperity which resulted from the service of the Lord, and the misfortune which they believed would follow the service of false gods. The great eighth-century prophets had argued that justice would bring a good life for Israel, and injustice would spell Israel's undoing. The Deuteronomists went far beyond this to the conclusion that a just God would, as it were, pay off the wages of righteousness and sin regularly and exactly! Some centuries later this view was to elicit the protest of the Book of Job. Later followers of the Deuteronomic dogma who edited some of Israel's historic texts did not hesitate to interpolate this over-simplified view of good and evil into such texts as the Book of Judges.

JEREMIAH (CA. 650-580 B.C.)

This great individualist among the prophets was born of a priestly family in the village of Anathoth just north of Jerusalem. The record of his call to the prophetic office makes clear his profound sense of vocation. The Lord is represented as saying to Jeremiah: "Before I formed you in the womb I knew you, and before you were born I consecrated you; I appointed you a prophet to the nations." [79] But it also makes clear Jeremiah's shy and deeply introverted nature and his reluctance to undertake so formidable a career. Yet it was to be his destiny to speak for the Lord to Israel—and to the world—during the tragic years when the Hebrew nation moved to a suicidal end with the destruction of Jerusalem and the exile of her people. During these years, Jeremiah was so consistently pessimistic that the word *jeremiad* has come to mean a doleful prediction of doom.

Jeremiah began to prophesy at the time of the Deuteronomic reform, and it is probable that he collaborated for a time with the Deuteronomists. Yet he broke with these reformers over the issue of a religious and moral code as against an inward faith of the heart. Jeremiah stood consistently for the view that faith is of the heart.

Like Isaiah in the previous century, Jeremiah pondered the ways of God in history. Like Isaiah he believed that men and nations were only instruments of the divine purpose which rules history. But Jeremiah drew a conclusion radically different from Isaiah's. Where Isaiah had declared Jerusalem impregnable, defying the invading Assyrians, Jeremiah consistently believed and taught that Jerusalem must fall to the Chaldean king, Nebuchadnezzar.[80] For Jeremiah, to trust in Jerusalem as if it were God would constitute a false and idolatrous faith. Reasoning thus, Jeremiah came to see God working in the hearts of men beyond any national boundaries. After the first fall of Jerusalem in 597 B.C., Jeremiah, still in Jerusalem, wrote a letter to Jewish exiles in Babylonia telling them to settle down in their new homes and worship God there.[81] For worship, far from being tied to a particular place, was for Jeremiah an inward relation of the heart to God. At home in Jerusalem, Jeremiah continued to oppose the popular religious nationalism of the time and to counsel complete compliance with the Chaldean conquerors—attitudes that led to charges of treason and to attempts on his life.

As events moved to their fateful conclusion, Jeremiah was led to formulate his own distinctive view of the good time coming. During the time when the Chaldeans besieged Jerusalem for a second and final capture, Jeremiah's cousin, Hanamel, offered to sell him land, it being the tradition to offer land first to a relative in order to keep the family inheritance intact. Now a man would not ordinarily buy land in a doomed nation. But strangely Jeremiah reversed his previous pessimism and bought the land, saying, "For thus says the Lord of Hosts, the God of Israel: Houses and fields and vineyards shall again be bought in this land." [82]

From this act he moved onward to depict the great good age to come, describing it as a time of a new covenant between God and Israel:

> Behold, the days are coming, says the Lord, when I will make a new covenant with the house of Israel and the house of Judah, not like the covenant which I made with their fathers when I took them by the hand to bring them out of the land of Egypt, my covenant which they broke, though I was their husband, says the Lord. But this is the covenant which I will make with the house of Israel after those days, says the Lord: I will put my law within them, and I will write it upon their hearts; and I will be their God, and they shall be my people. And no longer shall each man teach his neighbor and each his brother saying, "Know the Lord," for they shall all know me, from the least of them to the greatest, says the Lord; for I will forgive their iniquities, and will remember their sin no more.[83]

This passage was destined to have a momentous influence on the minds of both Jews and Christians.

Jeremiah's view of religion was also characterized by a new dimension of individualism. Beyond all communal and corporate aspects, religion was the communion of the individual soul with God. In his prayers Jeremiah poured out his own inner feelings to God.[84] From this stemmed a new sense of moral responsibility of the individual person which also characterized Jeremiah's interpretation of ethics.[85]

When Nebuchadnezzar captured Jerusalem in 586 B.C., he left Jeremiah among the small band of survivors in the ruined city. As previously, Jeremiah sought to reconcile his fellows to their tragic plight. But they would have none of him or his ideas. They assassinated the Babylonian governor and fled to Egypt, kidnapping Jeremiah and taking him along. Our last view of the great prophet is from Egypt as he tells his captors that even there they would not be safe from the avenging hand of the King of Babylon.[86]

EZEKIEL (CA. 625-570 B.C.)

Among the captives led into Babylonian exile in 597 B.C. was a young priest named Ezekiel, who was to become the religious leader of the little community of exiles which settled on the River Chebar in Babylonia. His own book calls him a "watchman in the house of Israel." [87] His call to the prophetic office is dated precisely, the fifth day of the fourth month of the fifth year of Jehoiachin's exile (593 B.C.),[88] and is characterized by fervor and detail, undoubtedly reflecting not only Chaldean art forms, but Ezekiel's own highly vivid and highly visual imagination. It also reflects his intense conviction of the transcendent glory of God before whom all human things are dust, ashes, and filth.

Ezekiel's prophecies can be divided sharply into those which preceded and those which followed the second and final fall of Jerusalem in 586 B.C. The former constituted Ezekiel's own distinctive interpretation of prophetic religion in its denunciation of injustice and of false worship which apparently continued among the people left in Jerusalem. God would bring such people and things to a well-deserved doom, declared Ezekiel in prophetic anger.[89]

However, the fall of Jerusalem transformed Ezekiel into the prophet of the future restoration of Israel.[90] The exile would soon end, he declared, and then the exiles would return home. Judah—and Israel—would be restored, the city of Jerusalem would be rebuilt, there would be a new temple presided over by a new and purified priesthood. In loving detail and in many vivid images, Ezekiel depicted the good time soon to come. He has been called "a priest in a prophet's mantle." Surely his affirmation of ritual religion marked a complete change in prophetic thought. It also marked the direction which postexilic Judaism was destined in fact to take. Torah, Sabbath observance, priestly ritual, rabbinate, synagogue—all of these features of developing Judaism were present at least in germ in Ezekiel's fertile mind. Small wonder that he is often called the father of Judaism.[91]

Ezekiel's vision of the future was notable for still another reason. Its vivid and often bizarre images foreshadowed a new kind of prophetic utterance, which in the course of time developed into *apocalypse,* that is, a vision of the hidden future; a form of faith and writing of great importance alike to later Judaism and early Christianity.

DEUTERO-ISAIAH (CA. 550 B.C.)

To the great anonymous prophet of the Babylonian exile, scholars have given the name Deutero-Isaiah, since his writings are to be found in the Book of Isaiah (chapters 40–66). They are easily distinguishable from the writings of Isaiah of Jerusalem by differences of style, content, and historical context. Nothing is known of this anonymous prophet and poet beyond his writings. Yet these are sufficient to characterize him as one of the great rhapsodic poets of the world's literature, as well as a mind through which prophetic faith had its culminating expression. He was a monotheist who scoffed at other "gods," and saw all history, with its rise and fall of peoples and empires, as an expression of the power of the one God.[92] Even Cyrus, the rising Persian monarch who was soon to conquer Babylon, was a servant of this universal Lord.

The prospect of Babylon's fall inspired Deutero-Isaiah with hope for his people Israel. For surely Cyrus would permit them to return to Jerusalem.

> *Comfort, comfort my people,*
> *says your God.*
> *Speak tenderly to Jerusalem,*
> *and cry to her*
> *that her warfare is ended,*
> *that her iniquity is pardoned,*
> *that she has received from the Lord's hand*
> *double for all her sins.*[93]

No Biblical writer had a more universal outlook, yet none was a more intensely loyal Jew. Between these allegiances there was a profound tension. If the Lord was sovereign of all the earth, was he in any special sense the God of Israel? And if he was the God of Israel, why had he permitted Israel to suffer so much at the hands of the nations? These questions burned their way into his mind; and his answer presents one of the profoundest conceptions of Biblical religion, namely, the figure of the Suffering Servant, or the Servant of the Lord.

In Deutero-Isaiah's writings is to be found a series of poems (42:1–4, 49:1–6, 50:4–5, 52:13–53:12) which deal with a figure called the Servant of the Lord. Whom did the prophet mean by his Servant? Christians have traditionally read these poems as a prediction of the Christ; and Jews have seen in them a depiction of Israel's role in history. To the prophet who wrote them these poems seem to have depicted either the nation Israel or a creative minority within Israel. The important issue of the poems is the Servant's vocation, which is, by means of willing endurance of suffering at the hands of the nations, to carry the knowledge of God to all the earth. This was at once an answer to the relation of Israel to universal humanity and to the question of Israel's suffering. In the last of the Servant poems, the nations speak of the Servant:

> But he was wounded for our transgressions,
>   he was bruised for our iniquities;
> upon him was the chastisement that made us whole,
>   and with his stripes we are healed.
> All we like sheep have gone astray;
>   we have turned every one to his own way;
> and the Lord has laid on him
>   the iniquity of us all.[94]

By the Servant's willing endurance of suffering the nations are won to the knowledge of God and goodness.

POSTEXILIC JUDAISM

The great watershed of Old Testament history was the Babylonian exile which extended from 586 B.C. to the capture of Babylon by Cyrus in 539 B.C. In 538 B.C. a small party of the Jewish people in Babylonia set out with the permission and blessing of Cyrus to repopulate and rebuild Jerusalem and Judah. It was an expedition fully consistent with Cyrus's generous policies with subject peoples.

The religious forms which emerged in the postexilic period exhibited both similarities to and differences from the preexilic tradition of Moses and the prophets. The same conception of God as Lord and Creator—the God of Abraham, of Moses, and of the prophets—continued to be Israel's Lord. But there were significant differences. Recovering from the critical attacks of the prophets of the eighth and seventh centuries, ritual religion reasserted itself once more. The temple with its priests and sacrifices stood at the center of society. Such features of Judaism as Torah, Sabbath, the rabbinate, and synagogue, which had been foreshadowed in the writings of Ezekiel, began to assume their historic shape during the postexilic period.

During the approximately four centuries from the end of the exile to the end of the Biblical period, the little land of Judah was a subject province successively of Persian and Greek empires, and then, after a century of independence under the Maccabees (164–63 B.C.), of the Roman empire. During this period, Israel's religious life became the central fact of her existence. Four main patterns of religion assumed definite form during this time, (1) priestly and legal Judaism, (2) devotional Judaism, (3) wisdom literature and piety, and (4) apocalypse. We shall consider them in turn.

PRIESTLY AND LEGAL JUDAISM

The first few decades of the community of Jews who returned to Jerusalem are obscure, but apparently their life was wretchedly hard, bearing little resemblance to the bright dreams of Ezekiel and Deutero-Isaiah. However in 520 B.C., two prophets, Haggai and Zechariah, arose to tell their countrymen that they had fared ill because they had not rebuilt the temple. Under the leadership of these two men, the project of a new temple to replace the one destroyed in 586 B.C. went forward with zeal, and in 516 B.C. the new temple was dedicated. It was a modest building, but it was school, law court, and general community center as well as house of worship; for it must be added that the energies which in a free people might be expressed in politics here went into one or another aspect of religion.

The priests of the temple were not only leaders in ritual but they were scholars and lawyers as well. Under their leadership the Torah was completed, and the priestly stamp was placed upon the whole document. One of their best and most distinctive products was the Creation story of Genesis 1, with its view of Creation in six days, and of the Lord's resting on the Sabbath. Sabbath observance was so important that these scholar-priests did not hesitate to write it into the structure of the universe!

These priestly editors also possessed a highly distinctive view of four epochs of history, each related to a significant aspect of priestly religion. The first age, that of Creation, centered on the Sabbath, the second in Noah and the prohibition of the eating of blood, the third in Abraham and the institution of circumcision, and the fourth climactically in Moses, the Exodus and the Passover, and the giving of the Torah on Sinai. Despite this somewhat artificial scheme, these writers did possess a view of universal history and of the God who speaks to men through the ages of history.

Sacrifice was all-important to these priestly minds, and preoccupation with the kinds and forms of sacrificial ritual in all its intricate detail was spelled out in the Biblical Book of Leviticus. The high point of the religious year was Yom Kippur, the Day of Atonement, when the high priest entered the Holy of Holies to intercede for the people.[95] Here as elsewhere the priests sought to make the people ritually holy and acceptable to the Lord.

Another project of the priestly leaders of Judaism was first the canonization and then the interpretation of the Torah. We have seen the origin of the five books of the Torah, and the beginning of the idea of sacred scripture in Deuteronomy. Under the great scribe Ezra, about the year 400 B.C., the Torah was officially designated as the sacred norm of Israel's life. In a ceremony described in Nehemiah 8–10, Ezra led in the public ceremony of reading the Torah, with the people responding by accepting it as the God-given standard for all their life.

To the Torah were added in the course of the following centuries the Prophets and the Writings, these three categories comprising the whole Bible of Judaism. Of the three parts, the Torah has always held first place. Once it was accepted as God's decisive and final word to Israel, two further developments began to take place: it began to be celebrated devotionally, and it began to be interpreted by scribes and rabbis. The interpretation led in the course of several centuries to that vast body of interpretation of Torah called the Talmud. The devotional attitudes and practices toward the Torah itself will be discussed in the next section.

DEVOTIONAL JUDAISM

While the dominant pattern of postexilic Judaism was the priestly-legal tradition just described, this was by no means the whole of Judaism. Closely related and ancillary to the dominant pattern was the devotional religion which found its main expression in the Book of Psalms. The Book of Psalms is sometimes called the hymnbook of the postexilic temple, and in fact many (though by no means all) of its psalms were written for musical rendition in the temple in Jerusalem.

Parts of the Book of Psalms, or Book of Praises, to use the Hebrew title, antedate the temple, and others show no connection with it. All, however, are religious poems bearing some relation to Israel's faith and to her Lord. There is a great variety in this vast collection. Some of the psalms are great poems; others are doggerel. The religious and ethical level likewise varies; Psalm 109 is a cry for vengeance, while Psalm 51 is a prayer for forgiveness.

Pervading the whole collection is a spirit which may appropriately be termed devotional Judaism. It is a union of prayer and poetry, in which the prayer of men's hearts finds expression in the powerful images of poetry. So one psalmist cried out,

> As a hart longs
> for flowing streams,
> So longs my soul
> for thee, O God.[96]

So also the Torah itself became the object of devotional expression as in the lines,

> *The Torah of the Lord is perfect,*
>   *reviving the soul;*
> *The testimony of the Lord is sure,*
>   *making wise the simple;*
> *The precepts of the Lord are right,*
>   *rejoicing the heart.*[97]

Amid changing scenes and shifting fortunes, in triumph and despair, Israel's heart clung to her God, and her poetry celebrated this supreme fact.

WISDOM LITERATURE AND PIETY

Bearing little relation to the priests and scribes were the sages who created the type of writing often termed wisdom literature. This was a literary type produced by many ancient Near Eastern peoples. Of the many specimens of this type in Israel, three found their way into the Old Testament, namely, Proverbs, Job, and Ecclesiastes. The sages who wrote wisdom literature spoke as old men who had seen much of the world and who out of their cosmopolitan viewpoint and mature experience offered counsel to younger men. The wisdom they offered was neither the heroic faith of prophets nor the legal prescriptions of scribes. At worst it was a pedestrian morality, and at best a cosmopolitan insight into the ways of the world. Seldom did these sages speak as Jews, usually simply as wise men. They concerned themselves with such issues as success and failure, wealth and wisdom, life and death.

A persistent theme of their writings was the relation of virtue to good fortune. The orthodox and complacent authors of the Biblical Book of Proverbs were sure that if a man were virtuous, good fortune would automatically follow. Conversely, they held misfortune to be the invariable result of some sin or misdeed. In this they continued the tradition of the Deuteronomists, celebrating a God who regularly paid off the wages of sin and righteousness, and of men who were sublimely content with these wages.

Other more perceptive men challenged this complacent optimism. Among them was the unknown author of Job, who asked: If God be good why should good men have such a bad time of it, and bad men have such a good time of it? His answer took form in the drama of the righteous man, Job, who is made the object of a wager between God and Satan.[98] Beset by every sort of evil, as a crowning affliction Job is visited by three friends who expound the orthodox line of thought that it is for some secret sin that Job suffers; or it is as a discipline from God that evil comes to him.

The Book of Job consists of a prologue setting the scene just described and three cycles of argument between Job on the one hand and his "friends" on the other. Job stubbornly maintains his innocence, resisting the friends' arguments. In search of an answer to his question, he is led even to defy God.[99] Yet he gets no answer. At the end, God appears to him giving him no answer, but rather the assurance and strength of fellowship with which he may surmount his troubles.[100]

While the author of Job clung by a thin thread to the traditional faith in God, other writers of wisdom literature were not so traditional. Among these skeptical spirits was the author of Ecclesiastes, who looked at the hard facts of evil and death and concluded that the Almighty had no concern with man. Blind chance rules man's life, and death brings extinction, so he concluded.

"Vanity of vanities! All is vanity." [101]

APOCALYPSE

Another and different pattern of postexilic Jewish faith was apocalypse. The term *apocalypse,* from the Greek word meaning "to unveil," means the uncovering or revelation of a hidden future. We have noted the origin of this form of thought and faith in Ezekiel and Deutero-Isaiah. Only one fully developed example of apocalypse found its way into the Jewish Bible, namely, the Book of Daniel; but there are apocalyptic passages which have been interpolated into other Biblical books (e.g., Isaiah 24–26), and there are many such documents which did not get into the Bible. For many centuries this apocalyptic literature was regarded as a vast enigma, but modern Biblical study has found the key and unlocked its meaning. This key is that an apocalypse is an interpretation in bizarre symbols of the time in which it was written. It was a tract for its own times.

Apocalypse grew out of prophetic thought on the problems of history. But whereas the prophet was content to see God at work in the normal processes of history, the apocalyptic seer saw all history building up to a supreme climax in the near future. This climax was presaged by an ascending series of evils, and a veritable climax of evil would be reached in the near future. Then, according to the apocalyptic seer, God would intervene, bringing to an end the present evil age and ushering in the great good age of the future. This apocalypse was a desperate way of saying amid bad times that God still ruled history. It was a cry of mingled faith and despair of men who saw no earthly way out of their troubles.

Applying these principles of interpretation to the Book of Daniel, we must note that it was written during the Maccabean revolt against a Greek tyrant named Antiochus IV in the year 164 B.C. Before this time Alexander the Great had displaced Persian hegemony of the Near Eastern world. With Alexander's death in 322 B.C., his empire had been divided among his generals, Seleucus receiving Syria and bequeathing it to his descendants. The Greeks were always more or less ardent missionaries for their language and culture. Hence there was a continuing pressure on the Jews to substitute Homer for Moses and the Greek gymnasium and theater for temple and synagogue. Yet until Antiochus IV, the Greeks were too wise to force their ways down the recalcitrant throats of the Jews.

Antiochus IV followed a different policy. In 168 B.C. he forbade the practice of the Torah and the daily sacrifices in the temple, going so far as to set up an altar to Zeus in the Jerusalem temple and to sacrifice on it a pig. This deliberate outraging of Jewish feelings brought revolt under the leadership of Mattathias Maccabee and his five sons, one of whom, Judah, proved to be a military genius.

In cryptic symbols, the Book of Daniel bade the Hebrew patriots to stand fast against Greek tyranny. Thus, for example, the lion's den of Daniel (chapter 6) and the fiery furnace (chapter 3) represent the situation of the Jewish people during the Maccabean War. Other symbols such as the colossus with the feet of clay refer to the succession of empires—Chaldean, Medo-Persian and Greek—between the time of the traditional Daniel and the Maccabean uprising.[102] The heart of Daniel's apocalyptic teaching is that the climax of history is at hand, and that soon the great good age of the future will dawn, in which the Hebrew people will live in peace, brotherhood, and world dominion.

The Book of Daniel is also notable for the first clear statement of the doctrine of the resurrection of the dead. Through most of the Old Testament period, the Hebrew people had no clear idea of man's destiny beyond the grave except the idea of *Sheol,* which was a place of shadows much like the Greek Hades, to which good and evil men alike went. Basically, religion was for the Biblical Hebrews a way of understanding and living man's life in the present world.

However, the Maccabean revolt raised the agonizing question of whether those soldiers who fell in battle against the tyrant might not have a share in the great age of fulfillment which lay ahead. The answer given in the twelfth chapter of Daniel is that the dead will rise, the righteous to a good life and the evil (i.e., the defectors and collaborators) to their appropriate reward.

In the centuries immediately following this initial statement, the idea of resurrection underwent considerable development. Basically, resurrection was a way of asserting the sovereignty of God over end as well as beginning, over last things as well as first things. Survival of death was expressed through the idea of the resurrection rather than immortality of the soul for the reason that

Hebrew thought had always construed man as an integral unity of body and spirit.

The Maccabean rebels were sufficiently successful by the middle of the year 164 B.C. to liberate most of Jerusalem and rededicate the temple, though intermittent fighting continued for several years. The Jewish festival of Hanukkah still celebrates the rededication of the temple. An independent Jewish nation under the rule of the Maccabean family was set up in Palestine. Amid varying fortunes, it lasted until 63 B.C., when Palestine became a Roman province. The Maccabean age was marked at first by a great flowering of culture, prosperity, and religion. But increasingly it was marred by civil war, so that when the Roman general Pompey appeared in the Near East, both the Pharisee and the Sadducee parties in the struggle appealed to him to bring peace to their troubled land. It was a request he gladly heeded, making Palestine a Roman province.

By now, Israel had come to the end of the Biblical period. The canon of the Jewish Bible was fixed by a rabbinical council in A.D. 90 (or as Jewish custom prefers, 90 C.E., meaning common era). The foundations of Biblical monotheism had been laid. Yet this was by no means the end of Israel's path. It was more like a new beginning. However, the unfinished story can better be told in new contexts. The next chapter will trace Judaism's way, and the following one will discuss the beginnings of Christianity. For both Jews and Christians, the persons and events of this chapter are an integral part of the divine-human drama of the one God's relation to Israel and to the world.

CONCLUDING COMMENT

As we have seen, the Old Testament centuries that comprise the content of this chapter laid the foundation for three of the world's religions, namely Judaism, Christianity, and Islam. They also constitute a primary source of the moral and religious values of western civilization, for as we shall see in later chapters, the West has its origins in ancient Greece and Israel. Still again this chapter has described a notable breakthrough or transformation from the cosmic religions of the ancient Near East to the historical monotheism of Israel and the Bible.

If we ask for the nature of ultimate concern or valuation in the Old Testament context, we must first observe that our question has come full circle. For Paul Tillich, from whom we have taken the term and idea of ultimate concern, has said that this concept is to be understood as a secularized form of the Great Commandment or Shema, quoted on page 357 of this chapter. Ultimacy in this sense of the word is expressed by the word *all* in the command to love God with *all* one's being.

Taking the expression in its original Biblical formulation, we ask the nature of religious experience or ultimate valuation, and we reply that it consists of the active service of God by the service of fellowmen or humanity. Such is the Biblical answer to this recurring question. Faith in the Biblical sense has the meaning of total allegiance of man's life to God as his source and goal, and its fruit is the love and service of mankind.

In the terms of Chapter 2's distinction, the Old Testament describes a religion of transcendence. In spatial metaphor God is above or beyond man; often he is characterized as the Most High. Nevertheless there is a humanistic content and significance for this religion in that for the men of the Bible, this divine source provides full realization or perfection to man's life. The values that flow from this source and constitute man's goal are faith (in the sense of trust leading to action), hope (in the historical fulfillment of human life) and love (in the sense of ethical concern for persons).

We have said that the Old Testament describes a breakthrough from religion of the first type to the third or monotheistic type. In the early centuries of ancient Israel's history, narrated in the Biblical books of Judges and Joshua, the question was whether to serve the Lord or the baals of Canaan. This issue was finally resolved in the writings of the prophets who provide the classical statement of historical or monotheistic faith.

NOTES

1. George E. Wright, *The Old Testament Against Its Environment*, Alec Allenson, Inc., Chicago, 1950.

2. H. Richard Niebuhr, *Radical Monotheism and Western Culture*, Harper & Row, Publishers, Incorporated, New York, 1943.

3. See *inter alia* I. Mendelsohn (ed.), *Religions of the Ancient Near East*, The Liberal Arts Press, Inc., New York, 1955, pp. 17f.

4. *Ibid.*, pp. 47f.

5. Mircea Eliade, *Cosmos and History*, Harper Torchbooks, Harper & Row, Publishers, Incorporated, New York, 1959.

6. I. Mendelsohn, *op. cit.*, pp. 223f.

7. Frankfort, and others, *Before Philosophy*, Penguin Books, Inc., Baltimore, 1949, pp. 72f.

8. Wright, *op. cit.*, pp. 20f.

9. Reinhold Niebuhr, *The Nature and Destiny of Man*, vol. II, Charles Scribner's Sons, New York, 1943, chaps. 1, 2.

10. M. E. Lyman, *The Christian Epic*, Charles Scribner's Sons, New York, 1936.

11. E. Auerbach, *Mimesis*, Anchor Books, Doubleday & Company, Inc., Garden City, N.Y., 1957, chaps. 1, 2.

12. J. Bewer, *The Literature of the Old Testament*, Columbia University Press, New York, 1922, chaps. 1–3.

13. B. Anderson, *Understanding the Old Testament*, Prentice-Hall, Inc., Englewood Cliffs, N.J., 1957, chaps. 6, 10, 14.

14. *Ibid.*, p. 164.

15. *Ibid.*, pp. 173f.

16. W. F. Albright, *From the Stone Age to Christianity*, The Johns Hopkins Press, Baltimore, 1946, pp. 179–180.

17. Auerbach, *op. cit.*, chap. 1.

18. W. Oesterley and T. H. Robinson, *A History of Israel*, The Clarendon Press, Oxford, 1932. See especially chaps. 6, 7, 10.

19. Anderson, *op. cit.*, pp. 7f.

20. Deuteronomy 26:5–10.

21. Albright, *op. cit.*, p. 194.

22. Exodus 6:2–3.

23. Genesis 4:26.

24. See *inter alia* the view of Y. Kaufman in L. Schwarz, *Great Ages and Ideas of the Jewish People*, Modern Library, Inc., New York, 1956, chap. 1.

25. Exodus 21:1–11.

26. Exodus 21:23–25.

27. W. Eichrodt, *Man in the Old Testament*, Henry Regnery Company, Chicago, 1951.

28. Exodus 34.

29. Exodus 3:14.

30. Albright, *op. cit.*, p. 194.

31. M. Buber, *The Prophetic Faith*, The Macmillan Company, New York, 1949, p. 13.

32. Judges 5:1–31.

33. I Kings 18:30–40.

34. I Samuel 1–10.

35. See *inter alia* I Samuel 12–13, as well as a more ancient statement of this viewpoint in Jotham's parable in Judges 9:7–15.

36. I Samuel 9.

37. I Samuel 31.

38. II Samuel 11.

39. II Samuel 13–19.

40. I Kings 1–2.

41. I Kings 1–11.

42. I Kings 16.

43. I Kings 18.

44. For Balaam, see Numbers 22–23.

45. I Samuel 10.

46. Judges 5.

47. II Samuel 11, I Kings 12.

48. I Kings 17.

49. R. B. Y. Scott, *The Relevance of the Prophets,* The Macmillan Company, New York, 1944.

50. Buber, *op. cit.*, pp. 96f.

51. Amos 7:14–15.

52. Amos 7:7.

53. Amos 9:1–4.

54. Amos 2:6–7, 8:5.

55. Amos 6:4–7.

56. Amos 5:21–24.

57. Amos 5:18–20.

58. Amos 9:7.

59. Amos 3:2.

60. Hosea 11:1–4.

61. Hosea 13:9.

62. Hosea 12:6.

63. Isaiah 6:1.

64. Isaiah 6:8–9.

65. Isaiah 7:9.

66. Isaiah 7:10–17.

67. Isaiah 10:5–10.

68. Isaiah 10:15.

69. Isaiah 2:6–22.

70. Isaiah 7:3.

71. Isaiah 9.

72. Isaiah 2:2–4.

73. Micah 5:2.

74. Micah 3:12.

75. Micah 6:6–8.

76. Deuteronomy 20.

77. Deuteronomy 6:4–5.

78. Deuteronomy 6:20–25.

79. Jeremiah 1:5.

80. See *inter alia* Jeremiah 19–21.

81. Jeremiah 29.

82. Jeremiah 32:15.

83. Jeremiah 31:31–34.

84. Jeremiah's prayers are to be found in several passages between chaps. 10 and 20.

85. Jeremiah 31:29–30.

86. Jeremiah 44.

87. Ezekiel 3:17.

88. Ezekiel 1:1–2.

89. Ezekiel 6–23.

90. Ezekiel 33:21.

91. Ezekiel 34–48.

92. Isaiah 44:9–20.

93. Isaiah 40:1–2.

94. Isaiah 53:1–6.

95. Leviticus 16.

96. Psalms 42:1–2.

97. Psalms 19:7–8. I have substituted the word *Torah* for "Law" in the RSV translation.

98. Job 1–2.

99. Job 31.

100. Job 38–42.

101. Ecclesiastes 1:2.

102. Daniel 2, 7, 8.

SUGGESTIONS FOR FURTHER STUDY

Albright, W. F.: *From the Stone Age to Christianity,* Anchor Books, 1957.

————: *Archeology of Palestine,* Penguin, 1960.

Anderson, B.: *Understanding the Old Testament,* Prentice-Hall, 1957.

Bewer, J.: *The Literature of the Old Testament,* rev. ed., Columbia, 1933.

Bright, J.: *History of Israel*, Westminster Press, 1959.

Buber, M.: *The Prophetic Faith*, Macmillan, 1949.

Burrows, M.: *Outline of Biblical Theology*, Westminster Press, 1946.

———: *The Dead Sea Scrolls*, Viking, 1955.

———: *More Light on the Dead Sea Scrolls*, Viking, 1958.

Gaster, T. (ed.): *The Dead Sea Scriptures*, Anchor Books, 1956.

James, F.: *Personalities of the Old Testament*, Scribner, 1939.

Kaufman, Y.: *The Religion of Israel*, University of Chicago Press, 1961.

Noth, M.: *The History of Israel*, Harper & Row, 1958.

Oesterley, W., and T. Robinson: *A History of Israel*, Oxford, 1932.

———: *Hebrew Religion*, Macmillan, 1937.

Pfeiffer, R.: *Introduction to the Old Testament*, Harper, 1941.

Pritchard, J. B.: *Ancient Near Eastern Texts*, Princeton, 1955.

———: *The Ancient Near East*, Princeton, 1958.

Robinson, H. W.: *Inspiration and Revelation in the Old Testament*, Oxford, 1946.

12

JUDAISM

From sources in the Bible have sprung the three great monotheistic faiths of the world, Judaism, Christianity, and Islam. Of the three, Judaism was the first to assume its distinctive forms and shapes. Among students of the world's religions who move rapidly from Christianity to the faiths of South Asia and East Asia, Judaism claims attention as a frequently forgotten faith. For students of religion whose experience and study has been within the Christian tradition, it claims interest as an alternative and sharply contrasting form of Biblical monotheism. Judaism will also in its own distinctive way bring forcibly to the reader's attention the recurring question, Is this a religion? It is a system of holy forms of attitude, practice, and belief, yet these forms differ sharply from those which many readers will associate with the term *religion*. In the twentieth century, it is among the world's smaller faiths, numbering some 10 million to 15 million adherents, but it is vigorously alive and making and influencing history in many regions of the world.

The last chapter noted the beginning of several basic features of Judaism. Moses is traditionally regarded as the founder of Judaism as well as the author of the Torah. Judaism as well as Christianity is a historical faith in the precise sense of a faith founded upon an event in history. In the case of Christianity

373

the event is the life of Christ, whereas Judaism is founded on the story of Israel's rescue from Egyptian bondage, of the ancient Israelite kingdom, and the development of Biblical prophecy. Some historians assert a complete continuity from these ancient Israelite beginnings to the fully developed historical forms of Judaism.[1] An alternative terminology, which will be followed here, speaks of the story of ancient Israel from Moses to the Babylonian exile as classical Hebraism, and of Judaism as emerging after the Babylonian exile.[2]

It may well be that such basic institutions of Judaism as the synagogue and rabbinate originated during Israel's exile in Babylonia. At least, they were very much in existence in the centuries following the exile. To the immediate post-exilic age also belongs the canonizing of the Torah under the auspices of the scribe Ezra (ca. 450 B.C.).[3] In the last chapter the Maccabean period of Jewish history was sketched in relation to the Biblical Book of Daniel. The festival of Hanukkah still celebrates the rededication of the Jerusalem temple in 164 B.C. after the victory of the Maccabees over Antiochus IV. This victory was followed by a century of independent national existence, often regarded as the golden age of ancient Jewish faith and culture. This century of independence (164–63 B.C.) was ended with the coming of the Roman general Pompey. From this time until the end of Israel's habitation in A.D. 135 (or C.E., meaning Common Era, as Jewish writers prefer to say), Palestine was Roman territory.

During the closing Biblical centuries, Judaism took form as the faith of the Jewish community. It is indeed this community and tradition of people from that day to this which accounts for Judaism's continued existence. The various features of this faith may be understood as aspects of the ongoing life of this people. The Torah may accurately be interpreted as the "constitution" of this community, in the American political sense of the word. This chapter will seek to sketch the history of Judaism, in the words of a recent book title, as the story of "great ages and ideas of the Jewish people." [4]

JUDAISM IN THE ANCIENT WORLD

Historically one of the most important developments of ancient Judaism was the Dispersion, the agelong process whereby Israel's people came to be scattered over the world. The process of dispersion began in 586 B.C. with the fall of Jerusalem and the Babylonian exile. With the Persian victory over Babylonia in 539 B.C. some Jews returned home to Judea. Others, however, remained in Babylonia, forming a Jewish community within Babylonian society. The process of dispersion was greatly increased two centuries later by Alexander's conquests. Soon there was a large and important Jewish community in Alexandria; and there were similar communities in Antioch, Rome, and almost all the larger cities of the Greco-Roman world.

In the first century, Philo wrote that in Alexandria two of the five areas of the city were almost exclusively Jewish. These Jews of the Dispersion, living as they did among Gentile people and ways, were much affected by their environment. Compared with their Palestinian brothers, they tended to be less strict in interpreting and observing the Torah. Yet the wonder is that they maintained any loyalty at all to Judaism. Actually they maintained their synagogues, paid the tax to support the temple in Jerusalem, respected the decisions of the council, or *Sanhedrin,* and also aspired at least once during a lifetime to make a pilgrimage to Jerusalem. Their refusal to be assimilated completely in Hellenistic culture often gained the hostility of non-Jews, and sporadically aroused the fires of anti-Semitism.

The ancient Dispersion left two enduring achievements, namely the Septuagint and the philosophy of Philo. Alexandrian Jewish scholars translated the Hebrew Bible into Greek as the Septuagint (often alluded to as "LXX"), since according to pious legend, seventy scholars working independently, produced identical translations. They are said to have been appointed by Ptolemy II, who wished a copy of the Bible for his Alexandrian library. The translation may be dated in the third century B.C. It is important for its introduction of Jewish learning and literature to the Greek world, and conversely for bringing the Bible to many Jews in the only language they knew. Intended to meet the educational and liturgical needs of the Dispersion, the Septuagint elicited the disapproval of conservative Palestinian rabbis for its Hellenistic influences and its free renderings of the Hebrew text. The Septuagint is equally important for the early history of Christianity. Not only was it the Old Testament known and used in the Christian community of New Testament times, but as Ralph Marcus points out, without the familiarity with Biblical ideas and history diffused in the Greco-Roman world by the Septuagint, Christianity would probably have been unintelligible.[5]

The other great achievement of the ancient Dispersion was the life and writings of Philo Judaeus (20 B.C.–A.D. 50).[6] Little is reliably known of Philo's life beyond the fact that he was a philosopher-statesman and one of the most honored and learned members of the Jewish community of Alexandria. Apparently he was a leader among his people, for he led an embassy to Rome in A.D. 39 to plead the religious rights of the Jews before the Emperor Caligula; and among his writings is *Against Flaccus,* which protests the anti-Semitic violence of Flaccus, Roman procurator of Egypt.

A product of Hellenistic Greek education and culture, Philo was especially a lover of Plato. However, he was also a loyal Jew who believed that God had spoken decisively to his people in the Torah and the Prophets. To such a mind there seemed great similarity between Plato and Moses. Philo believed and argued that the same God spoke through Greek philosophy and Jewish religion.

By means of the method of allegorizing, widely popular in the ancient world, Philo was able to eliminate some of the crudities and anthropomorphisms of the Bible and to exhibit an underlying compatibility between his Greek and Hebrew sources.

For Philo, God was one and spiritual in character—assertions which set the pattern for almost two millennia of theological speculation in Judaism, Christianity, and Islam. It also defined a major tradition of thought in Western philosophy. For Philo, this view of deity combined Biblical monotheism and Plato's monism. Thus the student is presented with one more illustration of attempts to combine aspects of two types of religious outlook, for monism is a feature of what our typology terms a faith of the second type, while monotheism is a feature of the third type. Philo also pushed onward in logical consistency to assert that God is absolute spirit utterly transcending all human limitation and definition. Man may say *that* God is—indeed *supremely* is—but to say *what* he is would impute an altogether undivine limitation to deity. This view of deity as the nameless and transcendent One, so appealing to mystics in all ages and faiths, may be traced from Philo to many other individuals and groups throughout subsequent Jewish and Christian history.

One problem which resulted from this conception for Philo as a Jew was the relation of God to matter. He "solved" it by interpolating between God and matter a series of intermediaries or powers somewhat similar in nature to Platonic ideas. All of these principles or powers derive from the *Logos,* or Divine Reason, which for Philo was the chief instrument of God's creative activity as well as the rational structure of the universe. This idea of the Logos spread beyond Philo, becoming one of the most pervasive features of Hellenistic philosophy and religion. It was appropriated by Christianity in the preface of the Gospel of John, and found expression in the whole theological tradition stemming from John, which asserted that the Logos, or Divine Word, was incarnated in Christ.

Ethically, Philo believed, the highest good of life consisted in emancipating man's good spirit from the trammels of evil flesh. Yet he also derived much from the spirit of active righteousness and justice to be found in the pages of the Torah and prophets of Israel. Here as elsewhere Philo sought to blend Greek and Hebraic elements. It was for this reason, too, that the conservative rabbis of Palestine had so little use for Philo. Hence his immediate influence was stronger upon Christianity than upon Judaism.

It must be added that Philo's allegorical method of exegesis opened for Jew and Christian alike a way for seeing many levels of mysterious meaning beyond the plain sense of the text of the Bible. Few men of the ancient Greco-Roman world had more pervasive influence on the subsequent religious development of the West than Philo of Alexandria.

The ancient Hellenistic dispersion, though traditionally neglected by historians of religion, has been the subject of extensive recent scholarly work.[7] The results are important for knowledge of both Judaism and the whole Western tradition. At this time in its history, Judaism was active in seeking Gentile converts. In the midst of the popular polytheism and the lax morality of the Greco-Roman world, Judaism's ethical monotheism was attractive to many Gentiles. Many of these people who shrank back from full conversion to Judaism became what Jews of the time called "God-fearers." That is, they adhered to belief in the one God and to the moral aspects of the Torah. It was among these God-fearers that Christianity got its first rootage in the Gentile world.

The Hellenistic world was, as St. Paul expressed it, one of "gods many and lords many." [8] Thus Judaism was one of the many competitors for human allegiance. Most of these faiths which found their way to the urban centers of the Hellenistic world had originated with some one of the innumerable peoples bordering this world, where they had functioned as ethnic faiths, or what Chapter 1 termed religions of the first type. In their new urban environment their clergy and first members were recruited from migrants from the home region. Many of these faiths engaged in actual missionary activities with the result that groups of adherents and sympathizers spread out from the center in concentric circles.[9] These social forms, while illustrated by Hellenistic Judaism, were by no means limited to it. They were to prove significant for the meaning of institutional religions in the West.

Hellenistic Judaism retained a remarkable loyalty to Palestine as the spiritual home of Jewish people. Jews of the Dispersion paid their annual half-shekel contribution to the Jerusalem temple. They sought to make a pilgrimage to Jerusalem, if possible for the Passover celebration. Many arranged to be buried in Palestine. In these loyalties and customs historic Zionism was prefigured.[10]

Meanwhile other developments were taking place in Palestinian Judaism. From 63 B.C. until the fall of Jerusalem in A.D. 70 (or until the final destruction under Hadrian in A.D. 135), Palestine was under Roman rule, and this political fact was of the greatest importance to Jewish faith and culture. Rome's method of ruling Palestine varied during this period. First the Romans sought to rule through an ethnarch, Antipater the Idumean, or Edomite (63–44 B.C.), and then through his son, Herod the Great (44–4 B.C.). When Herod died, his kingdom was divided among his three sons: Archelaus, who received Judea; Herod Antipas, who received Samaria and Galilee; and Philip, whose lands lay to the north and east of Galilee. Archelaus soon proved so inept that he was displaced by a series of career military governors or procurators, the most famous of whom was Pontius Pilate.

Whatever the system of rule, Rome's demands on the Jews as on other subject peoples were simple and blunt, namely, peace and taxes. In Palestine, there were continual rumblings of revolt, triggered largely by the fervent and often political messianism of first-century Judaism. Many Jews conceived the Messiah as a divinely sent military leader who would deliver the Lord's people from their Roman yoke. On at least three occasions there were large-scale revolts, in A.D. 6 in Galilee, again in A.D. 66, and still a third time in A.D. 132. All three times the Romans put down rebellion with bloody cruelty, finally bringing to an end Jewish life in Palestine and leading to the Great Dispersion, which extended from A.D. 70 (or in some reckonings A.D. 135) until the founding of Israel in 1948.

Amid its varieties of belief and practice, Judaism showed some underlying unities. Most basic was the Bible, to which Jews looked as a record of God's covenant with Israel. To be a Jew meant to be a child of the Mosaic covenant. Until its destruction in C.E. 70 there was also the Jerusalem temple, with its priests and its impressive ritual, which served as a kind of beacon to Jews of the Dispersion as well as those of Palestine. There was also the Sanhedrin or supreme council of seventy-one members under the chairmanship of the High Priest.

The destruction of the temple by the Romans produced fundamental changes in Judaism. Now the central institution was no longer the temple, but the synagogue, and the leaders of Judaism were not priests, but rabbis; a rabbi is a teacher, and the worship of the synagogue consists not in priestly ritual and sacrifice, but in the reading and interpretation of the Torah. From the rabbinical interpretation of the Torah has come the sermon in both Judaism and Christianity. In Judaism this kind of interpretation of the Torah was called *midrash,* meaning "inquiry," that is, into the meaning of Torah. The shift in the center of Judaism was not abrupt, for in many ways the center had probably already changed from temple to synagogue by A.D. 70; but it was destined to be of historic importance. From being a highly priestly or sacerdotal religion, Judaism became a faith centered in a community of laymen led by teachers.

Among the many parties and groups of Palestinian Judaism, the most important were the Pharisees and Sadducees.[11] The latter were the religious liberals of their day, advocating a tolerant and accommodating attitude toward both Roman and Greek culture. Thus they enjoyed the favor of Israel's foreign masters. Socially they were the wealthy, urban, priestly families. Odd as it seems at first glance, their attitude toward scripture was one of literalism; however, for this there was an important reason. By drawing a sharp line of literal interpretation, they could exclude from Biblical authority much of human experience not mentioned by scripture; and in such fields they were free to believe and act as they pleased. In opposition to the Pharisees, they rejected many religious innovations such as belief in angels, apocalypse, and resurrection of the dead. Prosperous in this life, they had little interest in a future life determined by a divine judgment.

Closely related politically to the Sadducees was the smaller party of the Herodians, who wished to return the rule of Judea from Roman procurators to the family of Herod. Since the Herod family had never been very popular among Jews, the Herodians were neither a large nor an influential group.

The Pharisees claimed to be the spiritual descendants of the Maccabean rebels. The name *Pharisee* probably meant "separatist," that is, one whose piety led him to separation from an evil world. The Pharisees were men of staunch faith who sought to apply the Torah to all aspects and occasions of life. Taking their stand upon the living spirit of the Torah rather than its strict letter, they accepted such innovations as angels, resurrections, and apocalypse. Morally, the Pharisees were rigorous and at times inflexible, legalistic, and exclusive. They have been compared to the Puritans of Protestant Christianity. They were deeply religious men with whom lay the future of Judaism. The popular Christian estimate of the Pharisees as hypocrites and moral monsters is wide of the mark.[12]

Probably the largest party in first-century Judaism were the Zealots, who may be characterized in modern terms as colonial nationalists. Joining together under the motto "No king but the Lord, no tax but the temple, and no friend but a Zealot," they refused compromise and collaboration with Rome, and rose intermittently in violent revolt. It was the Zealots who spearheaded the revolts of A.D. 6, of 66, and of 132. Their conception of the Messiah was a heaven-sent general and king who would throw out the hated Romans and set up the messianic kingdom in Judea and Jerusalem.[13]

Unlike the Zealots, the Essenes rejected active, military means for bringing in the Kingdom of God. Rather, they sought to escape from the present evil world and wait passively for God to bring in his kingdom. Hence they gathered in monastic communities, living under a strict religious discipline including rigid vegetarianism, celibacy, and strict Sabbath observance. They wore white garments and practiced frequent ablution rites, as well as community of property and pacifism, waiting quietly until God should bring in his kingdom.[14]

While the Essenes have long been known to students of the Bible, the recent discoveries of ancient scrolls at Qumran on the shore of the Dead Sea have greatly increased interest in this sect. The first scrolls came to light in a cave on the northwest shore of the Dead Sea in 1947. There followed the discovery of many other scrolls and extensive digging in this area.[15] Neither the archaeology nor the evaluation is as yet complete, but the discoveries point uniformly to an Essene-like community at Qumran on the shore of the Dead Sea from the second century B.C. to A.D. 68, when apparently Vespasian's Roman armies wiped them out. The scrolls constituted the library of this community.[16] Some contain hymns of worship, similar to Biblical psalms; another records this community's rigorous discipline; still others tell of a mysterious "righteous teacher" who has been persecuted by an evil priest, but who will return in future triumph. The scrolls shed valuable light on Judaism and also, by implication, on Christianity, pointing to greater variety in Judaism than had previously been supposed, and to significant parallels in Judaism to Christian beliefs and practices.

In their different ways, the Pharisees, the Zealots, the Essenes, and doubtless other groups as well, professed belief in the coming Messiah and the Kingdom of God. All of these groups held a dramatic view of history according to which a great climax of good and evil was impending. As the present evil age became progressively worse, at the crucial moment God would send his Messiah to bring in the great age of fulfillment, which was the messianic or divine kingdom.[17] Men differed widely in their views of the Messiah's coming and the nature of his kingdom. From the Zealots who expected a military king on horseback to the Pharisees who said that God would send the Messiah in his own supernatural way, messianic beliefs extended along a wide spectrum. Similarly too, men argued the nature of the coming kingdom. Few, however, doubted its nearness or its urgency.

The climate of fervent messianic expectation which characterized first-century Judaism is highly important for the understanding of both Judaism and Christianity. In the latter case, it was to form the environment in which Jesus of Nazareth and his first followers lived and thought. Its influence on Jesus' thought about the Kingdom of God, and his own messianic vocation will be considered in Chapter 13.

For Judaism, this fervent messianic expectation contributed largely to the disastrous risings against Rome. It was natural that after the disastrous defeats of A.D. 70 and 135, there should be a reaction against messianism in all its forms. It came largely in the form of an emphasis by the rabbis on the study and practice of the Torah. This aspect of Judaism, which had been important from the time of Ezra, now assumed central significance. The rabbis turned away from messianism, which had brought their people to the brink of destruction, and concentrated attention upon the practice and study of the Torah. As a consequence, the practice of the Torah became a central feature of Jewish faith, and the role of the Torah comparable in significance to the role of Christ in Christian faith. Judaism and Christianity may thus be contrasted in these terms. These two faiths have in common the one God of Biblical monotheism; Christians approach this God through faith in Christ and Jews by "doing the Torah." Out of the tradition of study and interpretation of the Torah in Judaism emerged the Talmud.

The word *Talmud* means "learning," and it refers to the interpretation of the Torah. Once the Torah had been canonized, the next question concerned its meaning, particularly as men sought to apply its teachings to all the innumerable occasions of daily life. For example, the Torah prescribed rest and no work for the Sabbath. Very well, what precisely constitutes work? When does the Sabbath begin and end? These and innumerable similar questions

A man with Torah. Painting by Marc Chagall
Courtesy of the Photographic Archive of the Jewish
Theological Seminary of America, New York.
Frank J. Darmstaedter

demanded answers in order that the Torah might be lived out. So it was that the scribes and rabbis began the agelong process of interpretation. It was a process of thinking not unlike the system of case law which characterizes Anglo-Saxon jurisprudence. For several centuries it was an entirely oral tradition. Then gradually it was reduced to writing, and the fifty-five tracts of the Talmud were the result.

In this centuries-long process, several stages may be noted. First were the oral teachings of the rabbis, the *Tannaim,* often in pairs of opposites, as for example, the teachings of Hillel and Shammai of the first century B.C. There were many other such pairs, making 148 Tannaim in all. In A.D. 69, while

Roman armies laid siege to Jerusalem, Rabbi Johannan ben Zakkai escaped to the Judean coastal town of Jabneh and founded a *Beth Din* (House of Studies). He was soon joined by Rabbi Gamaliel, who became leader of this academy, which became the intellectual center of Judaism for the next sixty years. At Jabneh, the canon of the Jewish Bible was fixed, the codification of the oral tradition of the *Mishnah* was begun. Hillel's decisions were given preference over Shammai's, and the process of interpretation continued. The famous Rabbi Akiba lived at Jabneh, prior to the war against Hadrian (c.e. 132–135), in which he was martyred.

The academy at Jabneh was a casualty of this war. Extremely repressive measures were put into force by Rome. The mere reading of the Torah became a capital offense. The survivors of this last war against Rome gathered their scrolls together and fled to the extreme north Galilean town of Usha, where, despite persecution, they worked on. As repression lessened, the Galilean schools flourished, led first by Rabbi Meir, then by Rabbi Judah, often called "Judah the Prince." Under his leadership the codification of the Mishnah was brought to completion. The word *Mishnah* means "study" and refers to that portion of the Talmud which was brought to completion at this time, ca. A.D. 200. Composed of the deposit of opinions of the Tannaim, it was arranged under six main categories: (1) "Seeds" containing mainly agricultural laws, (2) "Feasts" containing rules for observance of holidays, (3) "Women" containing rules of marriage, divorce, and inheritance, (4) "Damages" which had to do with civil and criminal law, (5) "Sacred Things" which had to do with sacrifices and rituals of the temple, and (6) "Purity" dealing with ritual cleanness and uncleanliness. Completed at the end of the second century, the Mishnah spanned nearly six centuries of Jewish life and thought. During the next two centuries, to the Mishnah was added the *Gemara* or supplementary learning. Together they formed the complete Talmud. Parallel forms of study had been going on in both Palestine and Babylonia, producing respectively the Palestinian and the Babylonian Talmud. The former was complete by the early fifth century, and the latter by A.D. 500. The latter is the more important and better known; indeed for most purposes it *is* the Talmud. By the Middle Ages even the Palestinian Jews accepted the Babylonian Talmud as their normative code.

The Talmud was the crowning achievement of the ancient Jewish community. It was the product of what has been termed "Talmudic society," the distinctive form of community which grew up in later antiquity under rabbinical leadership and found expression in rabbinical piety and scholarship.[18] The Talmud itself is a record of rabbinical discussion and argument. Its text might be termed minutes of this meeting which took place over eight centuries. Its decisions became the normative code of Talmudic society.

Talmudic society grew up in Palestine (outside Jerusalem, which was forbidden to Jews) and in other regions of the eastern Mediterranean world. It owed its existence to Roman toleration.[19] The leaders and heroes of this community within the wider Greco-Roman society were rabbis. Its main institutions were synagogue and academy. The latter was a house of rabbinical studies, and the former was not only a house of worship but school, law court, and social center. The synagogue schools carried forward the Jewish tradition of education of children.

The Torah has been the constitution of the Jewish community—as it has traditionally been treated, the divinely given constitution. In these terms, the Talmud may be likened to the American tradition of constitutional law. The simile is particularly useful in the light of the Anglo-Saxon tradition of case law, for the Talmudic method was also a case method.

In this connection a further contrast with Christianity presents itself. During the period when the Talmud was taking shape, the church fathers of Christianity were producing creeds and theology as interpretations and explanations of their faith in Christ. As previously noted, Judaism and Christianity share faith in the one God of Biblical monotheism, but approach this God by the contrasting paths of Torah and Christ. To this may now be added the further contrast of Christian creed, dogma, and theology and Jewish Talmud. Each seeks in its different way to explain, interpret, and defend the primary approach to God which stands at the center of both of these Biblical, or monotheistic, faiths.

In addition to the legal or normative aspect of the Talmud, which is called *halakah* (from the Hebrew verb *halak,* meaning "to walk"), which has been discussed, a word must be added concerning *aggada* or *haggadah,* the narrative aspects of the Talmud. These two aspects lie alongside each other with no attempt at logical systematization.

The Talmud is a puzzling document, especially to modern minds, for here law and legend, wisdom and superstitions, old wives' tales and exalted visions lie side by side. The mixture of styles and themes is doubtless the result of the oral tradition of living conversation which lies behind the written text. The Talmud may be regarded as the precipitation into writing of many centuries of talk. Its traditional authority in Judaism has been second only to the Torah which it has sought to interpret. Cursed, misunderstood, and burnt by hostile men, it has been to the Jewish people a light and guide to their path. Aside from its central religious and moral significance, it has stirred Jewish imagination, stimulating literature and other arts through many centuries.

JUDAISM IN THE MEDIEVAL PERIOD

Despite occasional harassment due to Jewish refusal to participate in the rites to Caesar, and despite the cruel repression of the Palestinian rebellions, the

Romans generally treated the Jews well. Many Romans maintained a scornful attitude toward sects and superstitions from remote parts of their empire, but their general attitude was one of cosmopolitan toleration. However, the decline of Roman power and the rise of Christianity in the late ancient and early medieval periods proved to be another and a sadder story for the Jews.

Page from a Haggadah showing a Seder
Courtesy of the Photographic Archive of the Jewish Theological Seminary of America, New York. Frank J. Darmstaedter

Worshiping a Jewish Messiah and sharing large sections of its Bible, Christianity came into the world as a movement within Judaism. The earliest Christians regarded their faith as a fulfillment of Judaism and sought to convert Jews to the new beliefs. However, the Jews resisted conversion, and relations between Christians and Jews gradually hardened into hostility. Christians charged that the Jews had rejected Christ and indeed had killed him. In the course of time, the two religions grew further and further apart. Christianity made itself at home in the Greco-Roman world. From the late first century onward, it became a religion of Gentiles. At the time when Judaism was creating the Talmud, Christianity was fashioning a very different kind of structure, namely, dogma and theology. The rabbis of Judaism scornfully rejected these Christian accommodations to Greek modes of thought and culture.

After the year 312, when Constantine made Christianity the official religion of his empire, the lot of Jews progressively worsened. Increasingly, anti-Semitism became a dark blot upon a civilization which called itself Christian. As Christian Europe became more and more intolerable, the Jews looked east-ward, in the direction of Babylonia. During the fourth and fifth centuries, the Jewish community of Babylonia became the center of Judaism. As the previous section noted, it was the Babylonian community which produced the definitive Talmud. The Parthian rulers, who were tolerant, were succeeded in the third century by the Sassanids, whose Zoroastrian faith led them to persecute other faiths, denying Jews the right to burial (lest they pollute the earth) as well as the traditional Sabbath lights. But despite persecution, the Babylonian Jew-ish community grew and prospered, providing the foundation for what was to become the Judeo-Islamic age.[20]

Islam burst upon the world in the seventh century with the inspired visions of an Arab camel driver named Muhammad, who became for his followers the Prophet. Muhammad's attitudes toward Jews and Judaism underwent change from initial toleration to pillage and harassment. However, the attitudes of his followers changed in the opposite direction within the first century of Muslim development. In the eighth and ninth centuries, at a time when Christian Europe harried and persecuted its Jews, the Muslim civilization of Baghdad offered to Judaism a large measure of freedom. In the Muslim world, Jews along with Christians were forbidden to bear arms or own Muslim slaves and were compelled to pay a poll tax, but beyond this they generally fared well. There were occasional times of intolerance and persecution, as when the fierce Almohades overran Spain in the twelfth century. However, the general rule of Muslim-Arab civilization from Babylonia to Spain was a freedom and toleration which permitted the Jewish people to build the new forms of faith and culture of the Judeo-Islamic age. As a consequence, the center of Jewish life remained within the Muslim world throughout the medieval period, and Christian Europe remained for the Jews peripheral.

The "great fusion" of elements which produced the new culture began with the widespread use by Jews of the Arabic language.[21] Maimonides and others reproached themselves for writing in Arabic rather than Hebrew, calling Arabic the "servant" and Hebrew the "mistress," but the practice continued and in-creased.[22] Hebrew was reserved for religious use and for poetry.

While Babylonia with its large Jewish community and its two distinguished academies at Sura and Pumbedita remained the dominating center of Jewish life during most of the medieval period, there were other notable centers as far west as Cordova, Spain, where also there was a great flowering of faith and culture. What was even more important, there was widespread circulation of men, documents, and ideas throughout this far-flung world. Maimonides, for example, was born in Spain, spent a greater part of his life in Egypt as court physician to Saladin, and died in Palestine. The institutional forms of the previous age, namely rabbinate, synagogue, and academy continued. Babylonia

Early medieval Jewish gravestone from Syria
Courtesy of The Metropolitan Museum of Art, Purchase, Funds from various donors, 1902

added the office of exilarch, or leader of the Jewish community in exile or dispersion.

A notable feature of the earlier centuries of the Islamic age was a heightened interest in the Bible, stimulated no doubt by the fact that Islam was also a religion of a Book, the Qur'an. It produced a great tradition of Biblical study and interpretation. This Biblical interest also produced the notable eighth-century movement called Karaism. Karaism is traditionally said to have begun ca. 750, when Anan ben David was refused the post of exilarch despite the fact that he was of a leading family and was next in line for this post. The ground for his rejection was his reputation for unorthodox views. He retaliated by organizing a faction which seceded from the main body of the Jewish community. The label *Karaite* (meaning "Reader") which was later applied to this movement referred to Anan ben David's conviction that each person had a basic responsibility to guide his life by his own reading of the Bible. The deeper protest of this movement was against the growing authority of the Talmud and the ponderous rabbis who interpreted it. Back to the Bible, said the Karaites, and each man for himself. The Karaites took their Bibles literally and seriously. They abolished the Sabbath lights (whose origin was Talmudic rather than Biblical), they ate no meat but venison, and they opposed physicians and medicine (for the Bible said "it is the Lord which healeth thee"). The Karaite movement increased and spread widely, its effect being felt from Persia to Egypt, to Russia, and Poland, and as late as 1500.[23] But probably the most important result of the Karaite protest was the response of scholastic philosophy. Karaism had asked challenging questions. What answer would orthodoxy give?

The answer was that distinctive form of philosophic defense and justification of a traditional faith called scholasticism. Both Islam and Christianity also produced notable versions of scholasticism, which will be sketched in Chapters 14 and 15 respectively. In all three cases, scholasticism made use of the philosophical heritage of Greece, which continued alive and strong throughout the Arab world.

Through most of its history Judaism has not been notably philosophical or theological in outlook. Jewish scholars have tended to be historians and linguists rather than theologians and philosophers. For the common man Judaism has been more something to *do* than something to *believe*. However, philosophical questions now began to be asked. How can God be omnipotent? How did the Devil come into existence? Can faith be rationally proved or disproved? To answer these questions, Jewish scholars used philosophic categories, Greek in origin and spirit, and preserved by the Muslim-Arab civilization of the times. While the views of individual scholars differed, the common aim of Jewish scholastic philosophers was the rational exposition and defense of faith. For them as for the scholastic philosophers of Islam and Christianity, the fundamental question was the relation of faith (or revelation) to reason.

The traditional founder of Jewish scholasticism was Saadia ben Joseph (882–942). Born in Egypt and given a Greek and Muslim education as well as a Jewish education, he gained a wide reputation as head of the Sura Academy in Babylonia. He was a vigorous opponent of the Karaites and defender of tradition. He translated the Bible into Arabic and was notable for his Biblical exposition. Above all he was a rational spirit who sought to reconcile Biblical revelation to reason. He argued the rationality of belief in the being and oneness of God, of the commandments of the Torah, and of the messianic age. Like many another rational theologian, Saadia held firmly to a belief in personal freedom.

What Saadia put in motion, others carried forward in Babylonia, and throughout the Arab world, notably in Spain. In and around the academy at Cordova, founded in the tenth century, there was a great flowering of philosophy, Biblical scholarship and other forms of study and writing. The Jewish community of Spain produced such notable figures as Ibn Gabirol (1021–1058), Judah Halevi (1085–1140), and Ibn Ezra (1092–1167). Gabirol was a poet and mystic whose volume *The Fountain of Life* expounded a Neoplatonic philosophy and whose devotion to God found expression in poetry. Halevi too was a man of letters devoted to the inner life, as well as a philosopher. His book *Kuzari* consists of dialogs between the Khazar King in search of a true religion and a Jewish teacher who expounds Judaism to him. He also wrote an ethical treatise entitled *The Duties of the Heart*.

The most important as well as the most famous figure of Spanish Jewry and indeed of all medieval Judaism was Moses ben Maimon, or Maimonides (1135–1204). Born in Cordova, he was educated in the arts and sciences as well as in Jewish studies. Driven from Cordova by the threat of persecution by the Almohades, he and his family wandered to Palestine, North Africa, and Egypt. In Egypt Maimonides rose to the position of personal physician of the Muslim ruler, Saladin. However, his deepest interest lay not in the medical sciences and arts, but in philosophy and theology. He was a learned man in an age when to be learned meant to embrace all knowledge in a single comprehensive system. He commented at length on the Torah and Talmud. Turning from Bible and tradition to philosophy, Maimonides produced the famous *Guide for the Perplexed*.[24] Maimonides was at once an honest and rational man and a devout Jew. He believed that faith and reason were aspects of a single harmonious reality.

The *Guide for the Perplexed* is precisely what its title claims. Yet Maimonides says it is not for the common reader, but for the student trained in logic and physics. The being of God is proven by inference from motion and causation, in the tradition of Aristotle's *Metaphysics*. God is the First Cause existing in pure actuality above, beyond, and before all the potentialities of the world. Philosophically, man can speak only negatively of God, stating what God is *not*. Affirmative assertions would endanger the divine unity.

Maimonides's cosmology viewed the universe as a series of concentric circles, the outermost of which and the nearest to God is Active Intellect. It is by means of this power that man comes to knowledge. Man's soul is characterized by reason, and its rational capacities and achievements are evidence for its eternal nature.

Maimonides provided rational explanations for most of the phenomena of Jewish faith, such as miracles, and the traditional food laws, which he viewed as conducive to health. The anthropomorphisms of the Biblical God, he treated as metaphors to assist the human mind. Maimonides's rationalism drew critical responses from other men who were more concerned with the possession of faith than with its rational justification. These critical attacks beginning in Maimonides's lifetime have continued within Judaism ever since.

The main features of Maimonides's faith are often summed up in a concise statement contained in his commentary on the Mishnah, often referred to as "Maimonides's Thirteen Principles" and as near to a creed as any statement Judaism has ever produced. These thirteen affirmations are: (1) the existence of God the Creator, (2) the unity of God, (3) his spiritual nature, (4) that he is first and last, (5) prayer to God, (6) prophecy, (7) Moses as the chief prophet, (8) the Torah, (9) that the Torah will never be superseded, (10) that God knows all men's thoughts, (11) that God rewards and punishes, (12) that the Messiah will come, (13) that the dead will be resurrected.[25]

Not all of the medieval Jewish community agreed with Maimonides's view that religion could be expressed and explained adequately in the categories of rational philosophy. Many found mysticism, with its appeal to immediate experience of God, a more attractive path. The record of their seeking and finding is to be found in the *Kabbala*. The word *Kabbala* means "tradition," and in this case it refers to an esoteric tradition of mysticism of which the Kabbalists believed themselves the inheritors and which they claimed went back to the Bible. Modern scholars regard the Kabbala as medieval in origin. The mystical seers of the Kabbala wrote commentaries on the Torah and other parts of the Bible, many of them claiming to come from the first or second centuries.

The common postulate was that the Bible and other ancient documents have an inner meaning, as well as their plain sense, which was accessible to esoteric inquiries. For example, the ten Hebrew numbers (*sephiroth*) are also letters of the alphabet, and applied to the proper names of the Bible they yield a luxuriant number mysticism in which from the one God proceeds a vast plurality of emanations. When the Messiah comes, he will be identifiable by his mysterious symbol, number, and name.

The most famous book of the Kabbala was the *Zohar*,[26] which means "radiance" or "splendor." Many theories of origin have been proposed, but it is now generally believed to have been written in Spain about 1285 by Moses de Leon.[27] The book purports to be an early Aramaic translation of Biblical passages and specifically claims that the Bible is not to be taken literally, an assumption which led in the course of time to wholesale allegorizing. Like other mystical documents, the *Zohar* finds mysterious meanings in Biblical names, often in the letters of the names.

The ideas of the Kabbala were drawn for the most part from ancient Gnostic or Neoplatonic sources. These sources held God to be the Absolute or Boundless (in Hebrew *en-soph*) of whom no definite or determinate predicates may be affirmed. Between God and the world is placed a series of emanations, at the world end of which is man. Man in the Kabbalist view is the microcosm who reproduces in himself the macrocosm, or world. Man is simultaneously animal, moral, and spiritual in nature, and as spiritual can rise to oneness with God. The Kabbalists saw in all natural and human things a wide range of symbols pointing to the higher, spiritual world.

The Kabbala flowed into the continuing stream of Jewish mysticism, making its contribution to this ongoing reality. As Gershom Scholem has demonstrated in *Major Trends in Jewish Mysticism*,[28] no century in Jewish history has lacked mystical souls who have sought and found immediate oneness with Israel's God. Their path to this goal has been plotted by uniquely Jewish symbols. These symbols include God, the Torah, and the main characters and events of the Bible, all woven together into what the modern reader discovers as a fantastic new fabric of mystical speculation. Undoubtedly some of the colorful threads of this fabric were added by ancient Jewish Gnostics of the Hellenistic world. Whatever its diverse origins, Kabbalism constitutes a major tradition of mystical religion and speculation, and is today studied as such.

At times this Jewish mystical tradition expresses what our Chapter 1 termed mysticism of communion, that is to say, immediate communion with Israel's God. However, at other times the viewpoint slips over to mysticism of absorption in God, or of ontological union. This latter attitude raises fundamental questions for Judaism as for Christianity. For monotheism draws a clear, sharp line between God and man, while this form of mysticism asserts their full identity. It is difficult for the student of religion to construe this relation as anything other than a head-on collision. For their part, the medieval Jewish mystics, whether exponents of ontological union or of communion, were expressing varying degrees of impatience with the ponderous scholarship of the rabbis and seeking in their various ways more immediate access to God.

The *Zohar* continued to be read and studied, particularly after the expulsion of the Jews from Spain. It has stimulated prayer and spirituality, but it has also encouraged magical superstitions (as mystical documents so often do) as well as a succession of messianic candidates. Kabbalism was particularly popular in the sixteenth and seventeenth centuries, outstanding practitioners being Isaac Luria (1534–1572) and his disciple, Hayim Vitale, who found cosmic explanations for Israel's historic exile as well as similar explanations and hope for a future return and redemption.

The most recent flowering of Jewish mysticism occurred chronologically within modern times, though in spirit it was altogether within the continuing tradition of the Kabbala. Its home was East European, or Ashkenazic, Jewry. It is usually called Hasidism (the word *hesed,* plural *hasidim,* means "pious" or "pious one"), but is not to be confused with the ancient Hasidic movement of the Maccabees. Poland and Russia were the source regions of modern Hasidism. The founder was an itinerant teacher, preacher, and faith healer, known variously as Israel ben Eliezer, Israel of Moldavia, and to his followers by the title, *Baal Shem Tob* (Master of the Good Name). Born ca. 1700 in Bukovina, he showed no inclination toward Talmudic study, being content to wander the hills, finding God in nature. After an unsuccessful first marriage, he lived happily with a second wife. But he was destined for other things. The spirit of God was with him; he began to teach, gathering followers about him, instructing them and sending them out to teach others. This informal process continued until his death in 1760.

His religious movement had the double aspect of a revolt against the ironclad authority and the massive scholarship of the Talmud and its learned rabbis and also a spontaneous revival of mystical religion. Against the ponderous learning of the rabbis, the Baal Shem Tob pitted the immediate and joyful experience of his glad heart. Never has mysticism been so affirmative in its tone. Since God is in all things, goodness also is in all things and all men. There was no ascetic world-denial in this teaching. The pervading attitude was a spontaneous and generous love for all of God's world. Informally and aphoristically the Baal Shem Tob taught that God dwells in all things in nature and in all men. Prayer was conceived and practiced not so much as petition as a cleaving continually to God in communion and fellowship. Yet by the power of prayer, miracles and exorcisms might be wrought—so at least taught the Baal Shem Tob and his followers.

The new movement evoked the violent opposition of orthodoxy. Elijah of Vilna, leader of East European Jewry, excommunicated the Hasidim and forbade all contact with them. This move led directly to the separate organizing of the Hasidic movement, whose leaders set up their own synagogues and ordained their own rabbis, called the *Zaddikim* (righteous ones). In later times, the Zaddikim tended to magic and other abuses of the master's teaching. While there is no record that the Baal Shem Tob indulged in messianic visions or prophecy, some later Hasidic seers added this accent to their message.

Hasidism grew to be a movement of several hundred thousand, and has continued to maintain a following in Poland, Russia, Israel, and as a result of immigration, the United States. Its mysticism irrigated the parched soil of Talmudic scholarship and brought spontaneous emotion back into Judaism. Its simple pietism came alive in untutored hearts for whom rabbinic study was remote and strange. Both chronologically and in outlook it showed striking similarity to Protestant pietism and to such Protestant mysticism as that of the

Society of Friends. Its permanent contribution to Jewish faith and thought, and more widely to the faith and thought of the world has been communicated through the Hasidically-based religious philosophy of Martin Buber.[29]

It is interesting to compare Hasidic mysticism with that of the Kabbala from which it sprang. Both forms found expression within the Jewish community and in symbols drawn from Jewish tradition. Yet while the Kabbala involved an alternation between the mysticism of communion with God and that of complete absorption in God, Hasidism was clearly on the side of communion. Its immediacy was that of men impatient with the ponderous learning of the rabbis, who found communion with God an immediate or direct possibility. They did not seek ontological absorption in the religious Object. Whatever the reasons for this difference, its results have been of the greatest importance. Hasidic mysticism stands as one of the clearest examples in human history of the mysticism of communion with God.

Meanwhile as mystics dreamed, philosophers speculated, and scholars pored over their scrolls, the living heart of Judaism continued to be the Jewish people and their common life, centering as ever in home and synagogue. As the Christian civilization of Europe assumed its distinctive forms, the Jews increasingly became objects of hostility and persecution. Because they resisted conversion and assimilation, they remained a small, visible, and defenseless minority, ideally constituted to serve as scapegoats for the ills of society. All of this was theologically rationalized. Were not the Jews "Christ killers"? Pope Gregory VII forbade Christians to employ Jews in any capacity. In 1215, the Fourth Lateran Council ordered the Jew badge to be worn at all times by Jews as a symbol of shame. Jews were forbidden to hold real property, a circumstance which (along with a prohibition to Christians against interest-taking) forced Jews into money-lending or banking. Some were able to make a virtue out of necessity, prospering greatly in this occupation.

The Jews were frequently subject to capricious violence, especially during the Christian Easter Week. The Crusades, for example, developed into massacres of the infidels at home—namely, the Jews. When the Black Death swept Europe in the fourteenth century, the Jews were suspected of causing it and were massacred in untold numbers. Rumors were circulated of Jewish rites in which the blood of Christian children was drunk, and of Jewish malice in poisoning wells. The Talmud was the object of the grossest misunderstanding; in Paris, it was publicly tried and burned for heresy!

Perhaps the most vivid symbol of hostility and discrimination against the Jews was the ghetto, a prescribed section of a city, usually crowded and unhealthy, where Jews were segregated. In some cities such as Rome, the ghetto went back to early medieval times; by the sixteenth century, it was a standard feature of Europe's growing cities. Jews were prohibited from living elsewhere, and were locked within the ghetto walls at nightfall. Gathering behind these walls, they developed their own community of faith and life as they were literally walled off from the common culture of Europe, to the double misfortune of both Judaism and medieval Europe. Finally, as the nations of Europe felt the first stirrings of nationalism, one after another expelled the Jews. France expelled them in 1254, England in 1290, Germany in 1298, and Spain in 1492. The harried Jews took refuge in Poland and Russia and in the Muslim world.

During these centuries of Israel's wandering among the nations, her seers and scholars continued to ponder ancient traditions and historic destiny. The mysticism of the Kabbala was for many Jews a source of light. Messianic movements continued sporadically to attract the allegiances of some Jews. The expulsion from Spain, leading as it did to the mingling of Spanish, or Sephardic, Jews with those of the Ashkenazim, or East European Jewry, was a source of new ideas and movements. In the following century the Palestinian Kabbalist, Isaac Luria, mentioned earlier, announced himself the forerunner of the Messiah. The writings of his follower, Hayim Vitale, spread Luria's teachings throughout Europe. One notable embodiment of these diverse influences was Shabbathai Zevi (1626–1676), who proclaimed himself Messiah and attracted a large following. After a varied life, he plunged his followers into disenchantment by embracing Islam. This is the most recent wave of Messianism in Jewish history to achieve a large popular following.

During the medieval period in Europe, Jewish faith and life maintained its vitality behind the ghetto walls. It was not easy to be a Jew in the Middle Ages, yet forced within the narrow confines of the ghetto, the currents of faith and culture ran deep. The modern peril of extinction by assimilation did not then exist. Moneylending and pawnbroking were traditional Jewish occupations, though they seldom were full-time activities. Many Jews plied related trades such as working with precious metals or jewels. Others were weavers, dyers, silk manufacturers, or metal workers. It is said that the Jewish quarter in Sicily and Sardinia was discernible from a distance by the sound of continual hammering.[30] The majority of Europe's Jews lived in poverty and followed the humblest forms of work throughout the Middle Ages.

While there was continuing danger of hostility and attack, it would be an overstatement to present the medieval picture as one of unrelieved persecution. In some regions Jews enjoyed special legal status and protection, and as S. Baron has written, the lot of the Jews was far less cruel than that of the serfs who constituted the majority of Europe's population.[31]

Within the Jewish community the traditional forms of religious observance, though antedating the Middle Ages in origin, came to completion during this time. No holidays in the religious year have been added since the Middle Ages. There was a high level of education, for as has been well said, Judaism viewed "study as a mode of worship." [32] There was no professional rabbinate, this office being filled by those who could meet its intellectual and religious standards and who practiced it as an avocation. Much of religious observance was based in the home. Medieval Judaism held a strong family tradition. Standards of sex morality were high, and there was general respect for women. This family tradition often persists to the present day.

JUDAISM IN THE MODERN WORLD

Emancipation from the ghetto and to full human freedom and equality came late and in reluctant steps to Europe's Jews. The Reformation brought little or no change for the better. With few exceptions, Protestants proved to be as intolerant as Roman Catholics. Martin Luther in his early years wrote favorably concerning the Jews, but when they resisted conversion, he lashed out in bitter and violent prejudice. The modicum of tolerance which Jews enjoyed in seventeenth-century Holland and England were exceptions to the continuing system of separation and discrimination.

The seeds of change were present in the Enlightenment, with its ideas of universal liberty, equality, and fraternity. But it took time for these generous ideals to bear fruit in specific social structures and actions. The application of the ideals of the Enlightenment to the Jews was by no means easy or self-evident, as Voltaire's anti-Jewish attitudes illustrate. Others, however, such as Lessing, were more consistent in their doctrines of religious freedom and toleration. Lessing's play *Nathan the Wise* was a parable of religious toleration. The relation of this play to Lessing's friend and colleague, Moses Mendelssohn, has long been a subject of controversy; but Lessing's friendship and influence on the life of Mendelssohn are beyond doubt.

Moses Mendelssohn was an outstanding example of Jews who during this age were beginning to break out of the ghetto and into the full life of European civilization. Born in 1729, the son of a scribe, a frail, hunchbacked child, but an eager and outstanding student, Mendelssohn went to Berlin in 1743. Meeting Lessing, and coming into contact with the new ideas of the age, Mendelssohn participated eagerly. He struggled to acquire an education. His rise to fame was climaxed by the removal of the customary Jewish disabilities. His writing included a dialog on immortality written in Platonic style, entitled the *Phädon,* a translation of the Torah into German, and a volume entitled *Jerusalem,* in which he pleaded the cause of Jewish emancipation. More than anyone else, Mendelssohn led Judaism away from the closed community of medieval Europe toward the open, free, and religiously pluralistic society of modernity.

Despite Mendelssohn and others like him, the old laws and old customs gave way with painful slowness. The French Revolution was a crucial chapter in this story. In 1789, the Declaration of the Rights of Man made all men, including Jews, equal before the law. Successive laws in 1790 and 1791 applied its principles specifically to Jews. Despite opposition in the years which followed, these principles spread to other European lands. Napoleon consolidated many of the gains of the Revolution. No special friend of the Jews and not above anti-Semitic attitudes, Napoleon nevertheless found it advantageous to mobilize the Jews of France behind his regime. A gathering called an Assembly of Jewish Notables in 1806 pledged loyalty to Napoleon. It was followed by Napoleon's revival of the ancient Sanhedrin. However, the historically important fact was that wherever Napoleon's armies marched, ghetto walls fell.

The fall of Napoleon and the Congress of Vienna brought a decade of reaction to Europe during which reactionary statesmen strove to set the clock of history back to pre-Revolutionary times. This decade of reaction brought with it eruptions of anti-Jewish activities in many lands, notably Germany. Then and throughout the nineteenth century the Jews sought to defend and to expand their new, hard-won gains. They joined revolutionary organizations and fought at the barricades in 1848 for democratic rights; and they read—and wrote—liberal philosophies. Nineteenth-century democracy gradually brought to Jews full admission to the life of European society. It also left a socially liberal stamp on the outlook of the Jewish community, which persists to the present.

The degree of emancipation varied widely in different Western nations. These variations were directly proportional to the degree of democracy claimed or achieved by particular nations. But emancipation also varied inversely with nationalism, which in many lands was accompanied by conscious anti-Semitism. Thus emancipation was probably most complete in Great Britain and America. It was notably less complete in Germany, in both theory and practice. In Russia and the Balkan countries, which were largely untouched by democracy, Jewish emancipation was virtually nonexistent. Russia continued a system of consistent discrimination and separation, marked by repeated pogroms during the nineteenth century. As late as 1903, the notorious forgery called *The Protocols of the Elders of Zion* was produced by an anti-Semitic monk, with encouragement by the Czar Nicholas II. In other lands, the free participation of Jews in the life of society seemed to stimulate anti-Semitism. In France the Dreyfus affair ran its sordid course from 1894 to 1906.

The impact of modernity was felt within Judaism in new views of worship and observance. During the centuries when Judaism was in effect a closed society, it was easy to maintain traditional ways of faith and life. Now, with Jews freely associating with non-Jews, this task became much more difficult. Indeed it became increasingly inevitable that the modern world should have its impact upon traditional Jewish forms of observance and worship. It is possible to place the new, emerging forms of Jewish observance and worship along a continuum representing the spectrum of responses to modernity. As these forms have taken shape in America they range from Orthodoxy on one end of the spectrum through Conservative Judaism in the center to Reform on the other end. If the institutional forms are not identical in Europe and other parts of the world, many of the same realities have none the less emerged.

Reform Judaism began in nineteenth-century Germany in groups like the Frankfurt Society of the Friends of Reform, which in 1843 issued a controversial declaration of principles: "*First,* we recognize the possibility of unlimited development in the Mosaic religion. *Second,* the collection of controversies and prescriptions commonly designated by the name Talmud possesses for us no authority. . . . *Third,* a Messiah who is to lead back the Israelites to the land of Palestine is neither expected nor desired by us; we know no fatherland but that to which we belong by birth or citizenship." [33] This statement evoked violent hostility from more traditionally minded Jews. Abraham Geiger (1810–1874) who emerged as the leader of Reform Judaism in Germany had to wage a long fight to assume his position as rabbi of Breslau, and when finally he became chief rabbi, conservatives withdrew and formed their own congregation.

In the United States similar divisions arose, with the significant difference that the institutional forms of American Judaism arose directly from successive waves of immigration during the nineteenth century. There had been a few Jews in America from early colonial days, but immigration greatly increased their numbers in the forties and fifties of the nineteenth century. Among the first immigrants were German Jews imbued with the spirit of Reform, and anxious to spread its message in America. Most notable among these newcomers was Rabbi Isaac Meyer Wise (1819–1900) often called the architect of American Reform Judaism. Rabbi of congregations in Albany and Cincinnati, Wise was also responsible for the founding of the Union of American Hebrew Congregations (1873), the Hebrew Union College (1875) for the education of American rabbis, and the Central Conference of American Rabbis (1899).

American Reform Jews sought to formulate their credo in statements made at a conference of rabbis at Pittsburgh in 1885 and somewhat less radically at Columbus, Ohio, in 1937. The latter statement, called The Guiding Principles of Reform Judaism, asserts Judaism to be "the historical religious experience of the Jewish people." The heart of Judaism is asserted to be "the doctrine of the One living God who rules the world through law and love," while man is asserted to be "created in the divine image. His spirit is immortal." Religion and ethics are said to constitute an indissoluble unity, and Jews are bidden to seek peace, the abolition of poverty, and similar social and ethical goals. The Torah is asserted to be the source of Jewish faith and life, though it is added that each age must adapt its teachings to new occasions and new needs. The

Talmud is not mentioned. The synagogue, religious observance, and religious education are urged upon the faithful in a spirit which seeks to be at the same time liberal and loyal to tradition.[34]

In the latter half of the nineteenth century, several important American Jewish leaders drew back from what they regarded as the excesses of Reform. They founded Conservative Judaism. Among them was Sabato Morais, a leading Philadelphia rabbi before he became founder and first president of Jewish Theological Seminary in New York in 1886. However, the achievement of placing Conservative Judaism on a firm footing must be ascribed above all to Morais's successor as president of Jewish Theological Seminary, Solomon Schechter. A distinguished scholar and a deeply devout Jew, Schechter became president of Jewish Theological Seminary in 1901, there consolidating what Morais and others had begun. Congregations of Conservative Judaism are joined in the United Synagogue of America, and its rabbis are members of the Rabbinical Assembly. While Conservative Jews do not adhere to tradition with the full rigor of Orthodoxy, they maintain more loyalty to tradition than does Reform.

A significant recent development of Conservative Judaism has been the rise of Mordecai Kaplan's movement called Reconstructionism. Kaplan has combined a liberal and naturalistic philosophy of religion or theology with a traditional view of Jewish culture and ways of worship and observance.[35] In 1918 Kaplan founded a synagogue center in New York, bringing together into one organization worship, education, recreation, and many other aspects of social life. In 1935 *The Reconstructionist* magazine was started to give expression to these views; and in 1945 the Reconstructionist Foundation issued a revised prayer book. While the new prayer book was less radical than the Reform prayer book, it led to Kaplan's excommunication by the Union of Orthodox Rabbis.

Orthodoxy is today numerically the strongest of the three main divisions of American Judaism, yet historically it was the last of the three to assume definite shape in America. In the closing decades of the nineteenth century, the source regions of immigration to America shifted from northern and western to eastern and southern Europe. This change brought to American shores waves of Jewish immigrants from Poland and Russia. The Judaism which they brought with them assumed definite form in America as Orthodoxy. In 1896, the first American *Yeshiva*, or Academy, known as the Isaac Elchanan Yeshiva, was founded in New York for the education of orthodox rabbis. Two years later, the Union of Orthodox Jewish Congregations was founded. In 1928, the Elchanan Yeshiva became Yeshiva College, and in 1945, Yeshiva University. It has continued to be the intellectual center of Jewish Orthodoxy in America.

Judaism has grown rapidly along with other American religious groups. According to recent figures, there are between 5 million and 6 million American Jews. Many of this number do not fall clearly into any one of the three main divisions. Indeed, for many American Jews, Jewish allegiance is more a cultural than a religious force, standing for a historic way of life rather than an institutionalized religious structure. Among avowedly religious Jews, there continues to be a wide range of faith and practice. Probably the most significant development of twentieth-century American Judaism is its changed status in American society. Through most of American history Judaism along with Catholicism was a permitted minority in a dominantly Protestant society. The waves of nineteenth-century immigration brought vast numbers of Jews and Catholics to America, changing the religious balance of society. These shifts coincided with secularizing tendencies which loosened Protestantism's grip on the society. As a result of these and other developments, America is now a land of three faiths: Protestantism, Catholicism, and Judaism.[36] This has meant a great enhancement of status for Judaism, as one of the three "religions of democracy." [37] While the smallest, it is by no means the least influential.

While Judaism was putting down roots and growing impressively in America, things were not going so well in Europe. Nineteenth-century Europe brought not only emancipation but also an ominous growth of anti-Semitism. Such ideas, endemic in the European mind from medieval times, grew to alarming proportions in the nineteenth century and became epidemic with the rise of Hitlerism in the twentieth. Hitler and his followers were avowedly anti-Semitic from the beginning, so it was no surprise that when Hitler's regime came to power in 1933, it passed immediately a series of harsh laws against Jews. Jews were deprived of German citizenship and subjected to progressively intolerable measures, culminating in the extermination camps of World War II in which it is estimated that approximately 6,500,000, or over half, of Europe's Jews perished.

Among the significant Jewish responses to anti-Semitism and more generally to the storms of twentieth-century history has been a vigorous and resurgent emphasis upon the historic tradition and community of Judaism, a response which has been illustrated by many of Judaism's leaders and thinkers. One of the first expressions of this attitude was the life and thought of Franz Rosenzweig (1886–1928). As a youth he studied Hegel and at one point was close to conversion to Christianity. However, as a German soldier in World War I, he returned in mind and heart to the faith of his Jewish tradition. The record of his return is contained in his book *The Star of Redemption,* which was written on postcards sent home to his family from the war front. In the years after the war, Rosenzweig devoted himself to the cause of Jewish education. In 1922 he was stricken with paralysis, but he continued his studies and other work until his death six years later. With Martin Buber he worked at a new German translation of the Jewish Bible. His letters and other writings have communicated to innumerable people his vivid and intensely Jewish personality. In many important respects, the historic epoch of Judaism which began with Moses Mendelssohn ended with Franz Rosenzweig.[38]

Another Jewish response to anti-Semitism has been the twentieth-century resurgence of Zionism. Throughout the centuries of the Great Dispersion, many Jews have cherished the dream of returning to their homeland, Palestine. In every century some individuals have done so. In the nineteenth century, liberal nationalism reinforced this Biblical ideal. Moses Hess wrote a book entitled *Rome and Jerusalem* in which he proclaimed Zionism as a cultural ideal for Jews. Others suggested Palestine as a solution for some of the agonizing problems of Europe's Jews. Zionism of a frankly political sort had its origin in the life and work of Theodor Herzl. Born in Budapest in 1860, by turns a lawyer and journalist, and in early life without apparent feeling for his people, Herzl was wakened to Zionism by the spread of anti-Semitism. In 1896, he wrote a book entitled *The Jewish State,* and the following year organized a Zionist Congress in Basel, Switzerland.

Herzl spent the rest of his life in apparently fruitless negotiations with European governments. Where rulers remained indifferent, many rabbis, reformed and orthodox, actively opposed his program. Herzl was succeeded in Zionist leadership by Chaim Weizmann, a British chemist, through whose efforts in 1917 the Balfour Declaration was secured. It committed the British government to "look with favour upon the establishment in Palestine of a national home for the Jewish people." [39] During the 1920s, the work of Zionism went forward despite obstacles. Jewish immigration to Palestine steadily increased; funds were raised; and the Jewish Agency, organized in 1929, gave the movement a central organization.

The rise of Hitlerism and the coming of World War II increased the tempo of immigration to Palestine, and with it the opposition of Arab states. In 1939, under pressure from the Arab states and facing the imminent prospect of world war, Britain abandoned the Balfour Declaration. Nevertheless, Jewish immigration to Palestine continued even during World War II, reaching a veritable flood tide in the years following the war. Tension between Jews and Arabs increased correspondingly. Arabs refused to cooperate with the United Nations Special Committee on Palestine.

This committee recommended partition, and this recommendation was accepted by the United Nations General Assembly late in 1947. In 1948, as Great Britain prepared to withdraw from Palestine, war broke out between Jews and Arabs. On May 14, 1948, as the British departed, the State of Israel was proclaimed. It was immediately attacked by Arab states. By January, 1949, when armistice agreements were finally reached, the outlines of a nation, recognized diplomatically by all major world powers and proven in war, had clearly emerged. Chaim Weizmann was the first President and David Ben Gurion the first Prime Minister.

During the first two decades of life, Israel faced the total opposition of the Arab states, which have firmly held the conviction from the beginnings of contemporary Zionism that the coming of the Jews represented a lawless invasion of Arab territory and confiscation of Arab property. When the fighting broke out in 1948, many Arab residents of Palestine fled their homes. These refugees, variously estimated from 300,000 to 900,000 have continued as a festering sore in Arab-Israeli relations. As a climax to continuing and growing hostility, Israeli armies attacked Egypt later in 1956, driving to Suez before being stopped by United Nations action. The armed truce between Israel and her Arab neighbors, supervised by United Nations observers, but continually broken by border episodes continues as an unsolved, and apparently insoluble problem. None of these problems was solved, and some were even aggravated, by the Arab-Israeli war of June, 1967, even though Israel's victory on the battlefield was quick, complete, and crushing.

The nation of Israel has shown an enormously wide range of religious and social beliefs. The religious spectrum extends from Orthodoxy, which is the established faith and which views the nation as a fulfillment of Biblical prophecy, to secular Jews who view the nation in a completely nonreligious light. Israel combines religious establishment with freedom in a manner similar to England's. Free entrance of Jews from all parts of the world has greatly increased the problems of Israel—not least of all the financial problems. Israel has been deeply dependent upon the economic support of the American Jewish community. Yet for Jews of all shades of religious opinion and from all parts of the world, the emergence of Israel is an event of the greatest importance. It has enhanced the vigor and morale of Judaism.

JEWISH RELIGIOUS OBSERVANCE

Judaism is a concrete way of life involving practice in a manner which is distinctive in the history of mankind's faiths. "Doing the Torah" is a recognized phrase for Jewish practice or observance. This practice has both moral and ritual aspects. What follows here is a summary of the main forms of ritual, which in varying degrees constitute the core of Jewish observance.[40]

SABBATH

Observance of the seventh day as a holy day dates from the earliest Biblical period of which there is any reliable knowledge. The Hebrews apparently took it over, along with the seven-day week, from the Babylonians. But here as else-where, the Hebrews transformed what they borrowed, for the Babylonian Sab-bath was a demon's day while that of Israel was a day of holy rest ordained by the one God. Sabbath observance has varied in its requirements, but has tradi-tionally involved rest, and no work, from the time the first stars appear on Friday until the same hour on Saturday.[41] In observing Jewish homes it begins with the lighting of the Sabbath candles by the mother, accompanied by a traditional prayer. Often the house has been cleaned on the previous day in preparation for the Sabbath. On Friday evening there is the Sabbath eve service at the synagogue, and at home a meal with the father blessing the wine and pouring the *kiddush* cup for the family and reading the scripture portion for the day. On the Sabbath day, Orthodox families go together to the synagogue, though in strictly Orthodox synagogues, the women and girls must sit apart in the gallery of women.

DIETARY LAWS

Rooted in the Torah and elaborated in the Talmud, the dietary laws are ob-served with varying degrees of strictness. In addition to the prohibition against eating pork and other animals which do not "part the hoof and chew the cud," [42] Talmudic law requires the slaughter of meat by specially certified Jewish offi-cials. Another law forbids the mixing of meat and milk dishes (based upon the Biblical commandment against seething a kid in its mother's milk [43]), a pro-hibition which in some households necessitates two complete sets of dishes, pots, and pans, and in others as many as four sets, two more being needed for the high holy days. The historical origin of the food laws is seldom probed by the faithful Jew, for whom it is enough to know that they are a part of God's Torah and, for him, a way of identifying himself with the Jewish people.

CIRCUMCISION

Circumcision has been called the single "sacrament" of Judaism, symbolizing God's covenant with Israel and the individual's membership in that covenant community. The traditional ceremony takes place when the boy is eight days old, and it may take place either at home or at a hospital. Friends are often invited to this festive occasion. A godfather holds the child while a synagogue official performs the operation. Then the father offers a traditional prayer, and announces the child's name. There is an analogous ceremony for girls in which the father offers prayer, asking divine blessing, and announces the child's name.

BAR MITZVAH

Bar Mitzvah literally means "son of the commandment" and it designates the coming-of-age ceremony for Jewish boys. According to Orthodox tradition, it occurs on the Sabbath following a boy's thirteenth birthday, and is a time of celebration and of receiving gifts. Among the gifts are a *talith,* or prayer shawl, and a *tephillin,* or small box containing the words of the Shema (Deuteronomy 6:4–6). In accordance with Deuteronomic teaching, those words are bound on

טבלא א: הארון כלי קדש וכו׳

Sixth-century floor mosaic from the Beth Alpha Synagogue, Palestine

Courtesy of the Photographic Archive of the Jewish Theological Seminary of America, New York. Frank J. Darmstaedter

the forehead and over the left arm. The highlight of the synagogue ceremony is a reading from the Torah by the Bar Mitzvah boy, often followed by an address by him. Reform synagogues also often have an analogous ritual for girls.

SYNAGOGUE

The synagogue itself epitomizes Judaism and the Jewish people, for it is a place of worship but also a school, law court, and town hall. Traditionally, a synagogue may be constituted by ten men; and ten men are traditionally necessary for any service of worship. The synagogue is organized under a layman who is president, and no synagogue has any authority over another.

The central symbolic object in the synagogue is the Ark of the Covenant, behind whose curtains are the scrolls of the Torah. Above the Ark is the eternal light. On the curtain of the Ark is inscribed the six-pointed Star of David, and beside it are often pictured two lions. Daily prayers at the synagogue vary widely according to local custom.

HOLY DAYS AND FESTIVALS

The Jewish religious year begins with *Rosh Hashanah,* or New Year, which comes late in September and is a time both for celebration and pious reflection. The first ten days of the new year are Ten Days of Penitence, the tenth being *Yom Kippur,* or Day of Atonement. It is a time of private and public prayer for forgiveness.

Later in the autumn is *Succoth,* or the Feast of the Booths, when many Jews live in cornstalk huts to commemorate Israel's time in the wilderness. It is also a time of thanksgiving, celebrating the fruitfulness of nature, during which homes and synagogues are decorated with fruits and fall flowers.

Coinciding with the winter solstice, and coming close to Christmas, is *Hanukkah,* or Feast of Lights, which celebrates the cleansing of the temple at Jerusalem at the time of the Maccabean revolt. Hanukkah is largely a family festival. For eight days a *menorah,* or candelabrum, is placed in the window, and one additional candle is lighted each night. Often the youngest child is given the privilege of lighting the Hanukkah candles. Gifts and greeting cards are exchanged among friends, and there is extensive merrymaking. In contemporary America Hanukkah has come to be widely celebrated as the Jewish equivalent of Christmas.

There is similar gaiety at *Purim,* which comes in late winter and celebrates the deliverance of Israel by Esther from its ancient persecutor, Haman. The Biblical Book of Esther is read in the synagogue at this season. The climax of the religious year in *Pesach,* or Passover, which comes in the spring, often at approximately the same time as Easter. It celebrates Israel's deliverance from Egypt, though it has also incorporated vernal rituals celebrating such events as the birth of lambs and the sprouting of grain. There are special prayers and services at the synagogue, but the central celebration is the *Seder,* or family meal, for which extensive preparations are made. The house is cleaned, Passover dishes and silver are prepared, new clothes are bought, and absent relatives return home. The central feature of the Seder is the recital by the father of the story of Israel's deliverance from Egyptian bondage. When this story is

Hannukah painting

Courtesy of the Photographic Archive of the Jewish Theological Seminary of America, New York. Frank J. Darmstaedter

Purim embroidery

Courtesy of the Photographic Archive of the Jewish Theological Seminary of America, New York. Frank J. Darmstaedter

completed a festive meal is served, and there is much singing and general merrymaking.

Fifty days after the Passover is *Shebuoth,* or Pentecost. Originally it was the festival of the barley harvest in Palestine, but in the course of time it came also to celebrate the giving of the Torah on Mount Sinai. The Jewish religious year provides concrete expression for Judaism's historic emphasis on doing, or action. These ritual observances, taken as a whole, also serve as a vehicle for the expression and communication of the value system which constitutes the content of Judaism.

CONCLUDING COMMENT

There is a central and unifying theme in all the varied phenomena of Jewish faith and life, often so perplexing to students of man's religions. This central theme is well described in the title of the notable recent volume *Great Ages and Ideas of the Jewish People,* to which this chapter has referred. This title constitutes an accurate description of the material of the present chapter. In other words, the unifying and central theme in Jewish history is precisely the common life of the Jewish people or community. Judaism constitutes the religious center of this community whose whole life conversely provides embodiment and application for Jewish faith.

To take an analogy from British and American political history, the Torah is the constitution (in both the British and American senses of this word) of this community. Hence man's basic religious obligation is to do the Torah. Man's approach to God is precisely in doing the Torah; conversely God is One who has spoken and still speaks to Israel, and to the world through the Torah.

For these reasons reliable interpretation of the Torah is crucially important. Resuming the constitutional metaphor, the Talmud may be compared to the whole body of constitutional law that relates the Torah to all the varied and changing circumstances of life, individual and social. It is interesting to observe that the Talmud, like British and American common law, follows a case method.

From the allegiance to the one God spring all the values of Jewish faith and life. They constitute the distinctively Jewish interpretation of the values of monotheistic faith.

These values are the fruit of Judaism's Biblical monotheistic faith. We have seen that this faith implies a distinctive view of man and his chief good. Much of what the West has called personality is of Biblical origin. This is personality of the sense of human dignity, inherent in a being made by God in his own image. This sentiment has always been strong in the Jewish tradition, and has had a recurring relation to strivings for human justice and brotherhood. Another notable cluster of Jewish values is a concern for learning and a respect for wisdom. As a consequence, Jews have made contributions to science and other forms of learning out of all proportion to their numbers. There has been a similar interest in the arts, ranging over music, painting, sculpture, and literature.

Yet the humanistic ideal involves important tensions for Judaism, as there must be in any monotheistic tradition where not man but God is at the center of human life. These tensions have led some Jews to break with their own religious tradition. This has been particularly true of those who have rebelled against what they have often called legalism in interpretation of the Torah. In other Jewish lives this same religious heritage centering in God has led to iconoclasm. For the tradition of "no other gods . . ." has led to critical attacks on what have been deemed false or unworthy forms of faith.

The carrier of these diverse values has continued to be the Jewish community in which faith and culture continue in distinctively Jewish configurations. Judaism continues to be a historic culture centering in a faith, or conversely a distinctive faith giving birth to the forms and values of a culture. These relations between faith and culture are sufficiently different from those of mankind's other traditions to be puzzling to non-Jews. To Jews they constitute the way of life ordained by God for his people.

NOTES

1. See *inter alia* Salo W. Baron, *A Social and Religious History of the Jews*, Columbia University Press, New York, 1952. For the same viewpoint, see also Leo W. Schwarz (ed.), *Great Ages and Ideas of the Jewish People*, Random House, New York, 1956.

2. This viewpoint is followed *inter alia* by William F. Albright, *From the Stone Age to Christianity*, Anchor Books, Doubleday & Company, Inc., Garden City, N.Y., 1957.

3. *Ibid.*, p. 266.

4. Schwarz, *op. cit.*

5. Ralph Marcus, "The Hellenistic Age," in Schwarz, *op. cit.*, p. 138.

6. For Philo's life see Erwin R. Goodenough, *An Introduction to Philo Judaeus*, Basil Blackwell & Mott, Ltd., Oxford, 1962; Harry A. Wolfson, *Philo: Foundations of Religious Philosophy in Judaism, Christianity, and Islam*, Harvard University Press, Cambridge, Mass., 1947.

7. See *inter alia* the chapter on this subject by Ralph Marcus in Schwarz, *op. cit.*

8. I Corinthians 8:5.

9. Schwarz, *op. cit.*, pp. 135f.

10. Louis Finkelstein, *The Pharisees*, The Jewish Publication Society of America, Philadelphia, 1938. See also Schwarz, *op. cit.*, pp. 108–111.

11. Finkelstein, *op. cit.*, pp. 9–11.

12. See Josephus, *The Jewish War and the Jewish Antiquities*, Harvard University Press, Cambridge, Mass., 1956. See also Louis Finkelstein (ed.), *The Jews: Their History, Culture and Religion*, Harper & Row, Publishers, Incorporated, New York, 1961.

13. Millar Burrows, *The Dead Sea Scrolls*, Viking Press, Inc., New York, 1955, pp. 227–245; also, Millar Burrows, *More Light on the Dead Sea Scrolls*, Viking Press, Inc., New York, 1958, pp. 136–142.

14. Schwarz, *op. cit.*, pp. 111f., 138.

15. *Ibid.*, p. 112.

16. Gerson D. Cohen, "The Talmudic Age," in Schwarz, *op. cit.*, pp. 143–145.

17. *Ibid.*, p. 155.

18. Abraham S. Halkin, "The Judeo-Islamic Age," in Schwarz, *op. cit.*, pp. 215ff.

19. *Ibid.*, p. 215.

20. *Ibid.*, pp. 218–221.

21. *Ibid.*, p. 227.

22. *Ibid.*, pp. 215f.

23. See A. Sachar, *A History of the Jews,* Alfred A. Knopf, Inc., New York, 1940, p. 164.

24. Moses ben Maimon, *The Guide of the Perplexed,* The University of Chicago Press, Chicago, 1963.

25. Joseph H. Hertz, *The Authorized Daily Prayerbook,* Bloch Publishing Co., New York, 1948, pp. 248f.

26. *Zohar, the Book of Splendor,* ed. Gershom E. Scholem, Schocken Books, New York, 1963.

27. *Ibid.* See also Gershom E. Scholem, *Major Trends in Jewish Mysticism,* Schocken Books, New York, 1954.

28. *Ibid.*

29. Martin Buber, *Tales from the Hasidim,* Schocken Books, New York, 1948.

30. Cecil Roth, "The European Age," in Schwarz, *op. cit.,* p. 297.

31. Salo W. Baron, "The Modern Age," in Schwarz, *op. cit.,* p. 317.

32. Schwarz, *op. cit.,* p. 283.

33. George F. Moore, *History of Religions,* vol. II, Charles Scribner's Sons, New York, 1948, p. 103.

34. Isaac E. Marcuson, *Central Conference of American Rabbis,* vol. XLVII, Jewish Publication Society, Philadelphia, 1938, pp. 97f.

35. Mordecai M. Kaplan, *Judaism as a Civilization,* The Macmillan Company, New York, 1935.

36. Will Herberg, *Protestant, Catholic, Jew,* Anchor Books, Doubleday & Company, Inc., Garden City, N.Y., 1960.

37. Louis Finkelstein and others, *Religions of Democracy,* The Devin-Adair Company, Inc., New York, 1941, p. iii.

38. See *inter alia* Glatzer (ed.), *Rosenzweig: His Life and Thought,* Schocken Books, New York, 1962.

39. Sachar, *op. cit.,* p. 367.

40. See *inter alia* S. Agnon, *Days of Awe,* Schocken Books, New York, 1948; T. Gaster, *Festivals of the Jewish Year,* Apollo Editions, Inc., New York, 1961.

41. See *inter alia* A. Heschel, *The Sabbath,* Farrar, Straus & Giroux, New York, 1951.

42. Deuteronomy 14:6; Leviticus 11:3.

43. Exodus 23:19.

SUGGESTIONS FOR FURTHER STUDY

Agnon, S.: *Days of Awe,* Schocken Books, 1948.

Baeck, L.: *The Essence of Judaism,* Schocken Books, 1961.

Baron, S.: *A Social and Religious History of the Jews,* Columbia, 1960.

Browne, L. (ed.): *The Wisdom of Israel,* Modern Library, 1956.

Buber, M.: *Tales from the Hasidim,* Schocken Books, 1948.

——: *I and Thou,* Scribner, 1958.

Cohen, A.: *Everyman's Talmud,* Dent, 1949.

Cohen, A. A.: *The Natural and Supernatural Jew,* Pantheon, 1962. ·

Finkelstein, L. (ed.): *The Jews: Their History, Culture and Religion,* Harper & Row, 1961.

Gaster, T.: *Festivals of the Jewish Year,* Apollo Editions, 1961.

Herberg, W.: *Judaism and Modern Man,* Meridian Books, 1959.

——: *Protestant, Catholic, Jew,* Anchor Books, 1960.

Kaplan, M.: *Judaism as a Civilization,* Macmillan, 1935.

——: *The Meaning of God in Modern Jewish Religion,* Reconstructions, 1962.

Moore, G.: *Judaism,* Harvard, 1930.

Sachar, A.: *A History of the Jews,* Knopf, 1940.

Scholem, G.: *Major Trends in Jewish Mysticism,* Schocken Books, 1954.

—— (ed.): *Zohar, the Book of Splendor,* Schocken Books, 1963.

Steinberg, M.: *Basic Judaism,* Harcourt, Brace & World, 1947.

Schwarz, L. (ed.): *Great Ages and Ideas of the Jewish People,* Modern Library, 1956.

13

JESUS AND
CHRISTIAN ORIGINS

THE NEW TESTAMENT SEEN
AGAINST ITS ENVIRONMENT

The New Testament, which contains the story of Christian beginnings, must be viewed immediately against the background of ancient Palestinian Judaism, and more broadly against the Greco-Roman world of the first two centuries of the Christian era.[1] Christianity and Judaism are illustrations of the third, or monotheistic, type of religion. Together, they contrast with the many Greco-Roman religions of the first and second type. Christianity began as a movement within first-century Judaism; its founder lived and died a devout, though heretical and schismatic, Jew. What is more important, Christianity has always firmly maintained its Hebraic heritage against those who would deny or distort that heritage in theory or in practice. Yet by the beginning of the second century, Christianity was a Gentile religious movement of the Greco-Roman world, expressing itself in Greek language and thought forms, and living in a society whose political institutions and leadership were Roman. Within four centuries, in the lively competition of faiths in that world, Christianity won out, becoming the official religion of Constantine's empire.[2]

The Jewish heritage of Christianity began with the full acceptance of the Jewish Bible as holy scripture, which included the authority of the Biblical images and ideas of God and man, of good and evil, or human origin and destiny. It meant that Christianity was a species of Biblical monotheism—the second of the three monotheistic faiths to assume its distinctive historical shapes and forms.

The last chapter noted some of the features of first-century Judaism, its Sadducee and Pharisee parties, its lively debates among the rabbis destined in time to develop into the Talmud, and above all, the fervent messianism of the age. All of these features left their mark on the nascent Christian movement. The New Testament might contain anti-Pharisaic assertions, yet the fact remains that on many crucial issues, Jesus of Nazareth agreed with the Pharisees and disagreed with the Sadducees. He appears to have had more serious disagreements with the prevailing interpretation of the Torah, maintaining a greater inwardness and individualism, and a clearer view of universal humanity than was popular in first-century Judaism. As to messianism, it is a too little recognized fact that Jesus of Nazareth set himself squarely against the popular and nationalistic Zealot party with its political-military messianism. In these and other respects as well, it is all important that the student of religion see Jesus and his earliest followers against the background of first-century Judaism.

However, the Christian movement must also be viewed within the context of its Greek and Roman environment. Unlike Judaism, Christianity adopted the forms of thought, of expression, and of practice of ancient Hellenism. Greek views of man, of reason, and of the world came to play a vital part in Christian faith and thought, and were thereby transmitted down the stream of Western culture.

Rome's initial contribution to early Christianity was a world of peace and order in which to operate—even though Roman political order was destined to turn violently upon the new religion several times in its first three centuries. Rome built the roads and maintained the order which allowed Paul and other Christian missionaries to go about their far-flung travels. Even more basically, Rome contributed an image of a universal community of peace and order which greatly fortified the Biblical image of a universal kingdom.

LIFE OF JESUS

Except for a few verbal shreds in classical and Jewish writings, the sole source of knowledge of the life and teachings of Jesus is the New Testament, and more particularly the Four Gospels. While there has always been some study of the Gospels, the fully free and critical study of these documents is a modern achievement; it is a fact that during the past century or so the Four Gospels have been as exhaustively studied as any writings in the world. The results of this study will be assumed in the following account of the life of Jesus. The first three Gospels, Matthew, Mark, and Luke, taken together show a common outline for the life and teachings of Jesus, in contrast to the Gospel of John, which differs radically in order and outlook.[3] Of the first three (called "Synoptic Gospels" since they "view together" the life and teachings of Jesus) the questions have been asked: Who wrote them, when, where, and under what circumstances? These questions may be taken as a definition of the synoptic problem.[4]

The answer seems to be that immediately after the life of Jesus there was a period of oral tradition or transmission. Probably the first written source was a hypothetical document to which modern scholars have given the name Q (the German word *Quelle* means "source"). According to scholarly hypothesis, Q consisted mainly of selections of Jesus' teachings, probably topically arranged and used for instructional purposes within the Christian community. Some such document was probably in existence by ten or twenty years after Jesus' death, that is, by A.D. 40 or 50.

It is well known that many more than four accounts of Jesus' life gained currency in the early Christian movement. Of these, the three Synoptics eventually won out, gaining places in the New Testament. Of the three Synoptics, Mark is clearly the oldest and is usually dated ca. 70. Matthew and Luke were written ca. 95. Both Matthew and Luke combined Mark with Q, though in independent and different ways. The three Synoptics differ from each other in style, viewpoint, and many details, though they agree in essentials such as their overall view of Jesus' life and teachings.

The Fourth Gospel, written around the turn of the second century and traditionally attributed to the disciple John, differs radically in its portrait of Jesus and in the order of events in Jesus' life. Taking up the widely prevalent Greek idea of the Logos, John interprets Jesus as the incarnate Logos, or Word of God.

The following sketch of Jesus' life and teaching will follow the Synoptic order and viewpoint as constituting our earliest and probably most reliable portrait of Jesus. True, it is not a photograph but a painted portrait, which in many details reflects the painter's interpretations and prejudices more than it does the objective features of the man who sat for the portrait. Yet there is solid critical basis for accepting as historically reliable the main features of the Synoptic portrait. The Synoptic portrait of Jesus' life will be sketched by means of six main topics: (1) nativity stories, (2) baptism and temptation, (3) Galilean teaching, (4) confession of Messiahship, (5) journey to Jerusalem, (6) last days and death.

NATIVITY STORIES

Mark, the earliest Gospel, contains no nativity story, opening its narrative with the beginning of Jesus' public career. Likewise, the apostle Paul makes no reference to a supernatural birth of Christ, alluding to Jesus simply as born of woman and of the Davidic line.[5] The Matthew and Luke stories are the sole

The Annunciation with Donors and St. Joseph. Triptych by fifteenth-century French painter, Robert Campion

Courtesy of The Metropolitan Museum of Art, The Cloisters Collection, Purchase

New Testament references to the virgin birth of Christ. It is also noteworthy that in place of a birth story, the Fourth Gospel offers a philosophic preface interpreting Christ as the incarnate Word, or Logos. Furthermore, a careful reading will show that the Matthew and Luke accounts differ sharply from each other in specific details. At most points these differing accounts do not clash, but are simply independent of each other.

For many readers the value of these stories lies not in historical accuracy but in the estimate and interpretation of Jesus which they express. Here was one at whose birth wise men came from far lands with gifts and homage, shepherds knelt, angels sang, and Herod trembled on his uneasy throne. Furthermore, for this unique son there must be a unique mother upon whom

The Journey of the Magi. Painting by fifteenth-century Italian artist, Sassatta

Courtesy of The Metropolitan Museum of Art, bequest of Maitland F. Griggs, 1943

devotion might focus. Hence, in the course of time, Mary became the chief of Christian saints.

By sifting the available historical evidence, the student may conclude that Jesus was the son of Joseph and Mary and that his home was Nazareth in Galilee. The name *Jesus* is a Hellenized form of the Hebrew name *Joshua* or

Head of the Virgin.
Drawing by Leonardo
da Vinci

*Courtesy of The
Metropolitan Mu-
seum of Art, Dick
Fund, 1951*

The Virgin and Child.
Fifteenth-century German

*Courtesy of The Metropoli-
tan Museum of Art, gift of
Felix M. Warberg and his
family, 1941*

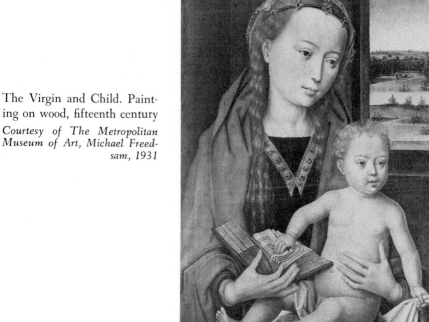

The Virgin and Child. Painting on wood, fifteenth century

Courtesy of The Metropolitan Museum of Art, Michael Freedsam, 1931

The adoration of the Magi. Painting by Hieronymus Bosch

Courtesy of The Metropolitan Museum of Art, Kennedy Fund, 1912

Yeshua, meaning "the Lord saves." Since the New Testament writers seem unanimous in the view that he was born under Herod the Great, his birth date cannot be placed later than 4 B.C. (Several centuries later when dates came to be reckoned from the birth of Jesus, an error was made in calculating the base year, A.D. 1, hence paradoxically Jesus was born a few years B.C.!)

Of Jesus' childhood in Nazareth very little is known. The Gospels refer to six other children, four brothers and two sisters. Joseph is spoken of as a carpenter, and it was the Jewish tradition for the eldest son to learn his father's trade. Since allusions to Joseph cease during Jesus' childhood, it has been inferred by some scholars that he died during this time. While the Gospels contain no specific references, one may fairly assume that Jesus had the education customary for a first-century Galilean Jewish boy. This inference is strengthened by Jesus' own teachings, including his reference to the Old Testament.

BAPTISM AND TEMPTATION

Luke dates the beginning of John the Baptist's public career in the fifteenth year of Tiberius Caesar (A.D. 29–30) thus providing a peg on which to hang the chronology of Jesus' life.[6] John was an apocalyptic preacher of the impending Kingdom of God, or messianic age. To many of his hearers he must have seemed a prophet born out of season (since the period of officially recognized prophecy had closed several centuries previously). He was a striking figure, dressed in haircloth and leather belt, and eating locusts and wild honey. His way of life as well as his words asserted his rejection of civilized society as contrary to God's will. He termed the leaders of synagogue and community a brood of vipers, and he warned his hearers to flee from the wrath to come. He taught his followers a radical social morality: a man with two coats should give to him who had none; soldiers should abstain from extortion and from wanton violence; tax collectors should take only their due.[7] John denounced Herod Antipas for living with his brother's wife—a criticism which cost him first imprisonment, then death. Ritually John taught and practiced baptism as an anticipatory cleansing which prepared men for the coming Kingdom. The similarity of John's message to the teaching of the Essenes of Qumran and the Dead Sea Scrolls has frequently been pointed out.[8]

The relation of Jesus to John the Baptist raises many questions. Beyond the fact that John baptized Jesus, the Gospels differ on some details and are silent on others. Did John recognize Jesus as the Messiah to come? Did Jesus actually become a disciple of John? Why did Jesus seek baptism by John? These and similar questions have been asked again and again for centuries, and no final answers are forthcoming.

The Temptation of Christ. Fifteenth-century engraving

Courtesy of the National Gallery of Art, Washington, D.C.

The Gospel writers agree in relating the baptism to Jesus' sense of vocation. Mark says that Jesus saw the heavens open and the spirit of God descend like a dove upon him, and he heard the voice of God saying to him, "Thou art my beloved Son; with thee I am well pleased." [9] The dove was a familiar Jewish symbol for the divine presence, and these words are from the Old Testament. The scene is clearly intended as one in which the Spirit of God came upon Jesus, giving him his vocation, or mission, leading him to his unique destiny. The parallel passages in Matthew and Luke are more objective than Mark, stating not that Jesus saw the dove descend, but that the dove descended.

The Synoptic Gospels follow the baptism with stories of temptations. Mark simply asserts that Jesus was tempted by Satan, but Luke and Matthew describe three temptations: (1) to turn stones to bread, (2) to throw himself from the temple pinnacle and emerge unharmed, and (3) to worship Satan in order to achieve world empire. It is interesting to note that each of the temptations is couched in Old Testament language, and that Jesus' replies are in effect counterquotations of scripture. Underneath these stories lie the real issues with which Jesus was apparently struggling. Should he gather a following by performing sensational miracles? Would his appeal be primarily economic—to bid men to live by bread alone? Should his movement be based on the political and military messianism so common in first-century Galilee? Each of these questions drew a negative reply as Jesus pondered his mission.

TEACHING IN GALILEE

According to Mark's Gospel, Jesus first appeared publicly in Galilee, declaring "The time is fulfilled, and the kingdom of God is at hand." [10] The Synoptic Gospels disagree on the place of Jesus' first public teaching, Matthew and Mark placing it in Capernaum on the north shore of the Sea of Galilee, and Luke in Jesus' home town of Nazareth.[11] In all three Gospels these towns as well as such others as Chorazim and Bethsaida are frequently mentioned. Apparently Jesus made his way from town to town, preaching in synagogues, in open fields, and on at least one occasion on the shore of the Sea of Galilee. The theme of his preaching was the imminent coming of the Kingdom of God and the conditions for citizenship in the Kingdom. In addition to preaching, he is reported to have healed the sick, to have performed exorcisms, and many other "mighty works." At first he traveled about alone, but soon he gathered to himself twelve intimate followers, or disciples. At one point, having instructed the twelve, he sent them out by twos to spread his message throughout Galilee. From the beginning of his public career, there were rumblings of hostility from the leaders of Judaism.

Many questions arise concerning this period of public teaching in Galilee.

How long did it last? Guesses have ranged from six months to two years. Even more important, why when this mission was proceeding successfully, did Jesus abruptly break it off and wander alone with his disciples to Tyre and Sidon and to the region of Caesarea Philippi? [12] One possible answer is that Herod Antipas, who had recently killed John the Baptist, now threatened Jesus' life. Another is that Jesus could see increasingly how Galilee, hotbed of the Zealot

Christ Preaching. Etching by Rembrandt
Courtesy of The Metropolitan Museum of Art, bequest of Mrs. H. O. Havemeyer, 1929

party with its violent and radical political messianism misunderstood him and his teachings. Whatever the reason, this period of wandering to the north effectively ended Jesus' public career in Galilee. And what is more important, in the region of Caesarea Philippi a momentous dialog took place between Jesus and his disciples.

CONFESSION OF MESSIAHSHIP

All three of the Synoptic Gospels record the scene in which as they walked along the road near Caesarea Philippi, Jesus asked the disciples, "Who do men say that I the Son of Man am?" [13] The reply was that some thought he was Elijah, there being a popular legend that Elijah would return just before the Messiah. Others thought he was John the Baptist—come back to life after his murder. "But who do you say that I am?" persisted Jesus. To this Peter, speaking for himself and the others, responded, "You are the Christ the Son of the living God."

This conversation must be understood against the background of first-century Judaism's ardent messianic expectation. Messianic claims were frequent and various; they were often treated as blasphemous by the Jewish leaders and as subversive agitation by the Romans. Under these circumstances, it was natural for Jesus to enjoin upon his disciples the strictest secrecy.[14]

According to the Synoptics this was the first time Jesus spoke specifically and directly of the Messiahship. Previous to this time, crowds had shouted messianic titles at him, but he had not responded either affirmatively or negatively. Now he spoke, though only privately, within the band of disciples, elliptically, eliciting Peter's confession rather than making a definite assertion. Later, at the end of his life, standing before the Sanhedrin, Jesus was to make his only public statement on this subject in reply to the high priest's question.[15]

The title *Christ* (or *Christos*) is the Greek translation of the Hebrew *Messiah*, which means "anointed one." The idea of the Messiah, which developed in later Judaism, was that God would send a divinely appointed king who would bring in the Kingdom of God. As previously noted, there were many first-century views of the Messiah, among the most popular of which was the military-political interpretation held by the Zealots.

The subject of Jesus' Messiahship has been much discussed in recent New Testament study, and it is generally accepted that Jesus, as the New Testament pictures him, could have little or nothing to do with most popular first-century views of Messiahship. Some scholars draw the conclusion that Jesus never made messianic claims, though such claims were ascribed to Jesus by the early Christian church.[16] Other scholars claim that Jesus did in fact make such claims, but that the force of these claims in the historical context of the first century was to assert a novel, indeed radical, reinterpretation of the nature of the Messiahship.[17]

The question of Jesus' messianic claim is of crucial significance to Christianity, for Christianity is by definition the religion of those who believe Jesus to be the Christ. Later, other terms came to be used as synonyms for this original title, such as Lord, Savior, Word, and Son of God; but they were attempts to find adequate Gentile, Greek synonyms for the original Hebrew title of Messiah. Christianity began with the apostolic confession of Jesus as the Christ, or Messiah.

The transfiguration was a sequel to the confession at Caesarea Philippi.[18] According to all three Synoptic Gospels, Jesus took Peter, James, and John to a high mountain, where in a vision they saw Moses, Elijah, and Jesus together. Moses symbolized the Torah, Elijah the prophets, and Jesus was here understood as the Messiah, who brought both Torah and Prophets to fulfillment.

PASSION AND DEATH

Following the confession and transfiguration, Jesus returned briefly and secretly to Galilee, then "set his face steadfastly" to go to Jerusalem.[19] Here Luke differs materially from Mark and Matthew in reporting the length and route of the journey; Luke's story also differs structurally from the other two Synoptic Gospels in the inclusion at this point of a large block of narrative and teaching not included in Matthew and Mark.[20] Yet all three Gospels agree that Jesus was apparently making his way to the capital city with full knowledge of the dangers involved. He seemed to be timing his arrival to coincide with the Passover festival, when Jerusalem would be thronged with pilgrims from all parts of the Mediterranean world.

Why did Jesus resolve to make this last perilous journey? Traditional Christianity has often invested Jesus with supernatural foreknowledge, and has viewed the journey to Jerusalem as conscious preparation for his sacrificial death. This appears clearly to be the viewpoint of the Fourth Gospel, though not of the Synoptics. It is belied by Jesus' response to the events of the last days as they unfolded in the Synoptic accounts. Some scholars, including Albert Schweitzer, have argued that Jesus expected a miraculous deliverance by God at Jerusalem which would vindicate him and his kingdom.[21] Perhaps the most adequate view of the matter is that Jesus was a man utterly dedicated to God who went to Jerusalem in simple trust and obedience to the will of God as he understood it.

He entered the city on the back of a donkey, on a day which has since been celebrated in Christianity as Palm Sunday. The popular demonstration of his followers had messianic implications, and his choice of a donkey may be understood as his further attempt to transform the messianic concept from a warlike, military idea to one of peace. Once in the city, Jesus went to the temple and threw out the money changers and vendors of sacrificial animals—an act clearly presupposing messianic authority, and also one which crystallized the opposition into a conspiracy to take his life.[22]

During his week in Jerusalem, Jesus lodged with friends in Bethany, over the Mount of Olives to the east. He came in to the city each day to teach on the porches of the temple, arguing his teachings with fellow rabbis, answering questions and setting forth his views like other rabbinical teachers. At least one modern writer on the life of Jesus has concluded that Jesus taught thus for a matter of several weeks in Jerusalem, then withdrew to nearby wilderness and returned to the capital city in time for the Passover Week.[23] This view can be supported from the Fourth Gospel, but there is little or no basis for it in the Synoptics.

On Thursday of the last week, Jesus' disciples arranged for a room in which he might eat the traditional Passover meal with them, within the city of Jerusalem, as Jewish custom required. According to the account in all the Gospels, he reinterpreted this meal to symbolize his own body and blood through which he believed God was making a new covenant with mankind. How much of this scene is historic fact and how much is later Christian interpretation is impossible to say with any precision or certainty.

After the meal, the disciples and their Master made their way back to Bethany; and he paused for prayer in the Garden of Gethsemane on the slopes of the Mount of Olives. There a mob, sent by leaders of the Sanhedrin and led by the traitor Judas, took him prisoner. He was taken to the home of the high priest, Caiaphas, where an illegal session of the Sanhedrin was convened to try him. The charge was blasphemy, that is, making messianic claims and threatening the destruction of the temple. When perjured witnesses failed to agree, Caiaphas asked him directly if he claimed to be the Messiah. Jesus' cryptic but apparently affirmative reply was his only public statement of a messianic claim, and it was sufficient in the view of Caiaphas and his colleagues to convict Jesus of blasphemy, an offense which in Jewish law carried the death penalty.[24]

To carry out the death penalty required Roman permission. Hence the next morning, Jesus was taken before the Roman procurator, Pontius Pilate, where the charge was not blasphemy—which would not greatly impress Pilate—but rather sedition—a matter to which Rome and her agents were extremely sensitive. Pilate's role in the trial and condemnation of Jesus is by no means clear, but at least he gave the necessary official order for the carrying out of the death penalty by the cruel method of crucifixion. So, it was thought, ended the life of one who was said to claim to be "King of the Jews." [25]

TEACHINGS OF JESUS

Jesus' primary teaching was the Kingdom of God, or as Matthew put it, the Kingdom of Heaven. In first-century Judaism, this term referred to the historic age of fulfillment which was believed to be immediately at hand, the messianic age to which all Israel looked forward. Jesus' Kingdom of God must be regarded as his particular and distinctive interpretation of this widely shared idea.

The idea of a reign of God over all the world had been a part of Biblical religion from earliest Old Testament days. If God were the ruler of all, then the world was properly his realm. But, as Israel's prophets pointed out, God's rule was not now apparent; rather, other kings seemed to be effectively in charge of the world's destiny. Hence the prophets appealed to a future age when God's whole will would be done over all the world. Such was the origin of the Kingdom of God.[26]

Christ Bearing the Cross. Sixteenth-century French enamel

Courtesy of The Metropolitan Museum of Art, Fletcher Fund, 1945

Jesus appears to have differed from his Jewish contemporaries as to many basic features of the Kingdom, notably, the individual requirements for citizenship in the Kingdom, its universality, and the basically ethical nature of citizenship in the Kingdom. He was in complete opposition to the popular political nationalistic view of the Kingdom. In Jesus' view each individual by humble repentence made his way into the Kingdom, whose membership included men of every race and nation. The requirements of citizenship as Jesus set them forth in the Sermon on the Mount were fundamentally moral in nature.

While Jesus' Kingdom of God was essentially a universal human brotherhood, there is no basis in his teachings for identifying the Kingdom with any particular kind of society or social organization. When Jesus spoke of the Kingdom of God he was not envisaging democracy, socialism, or any other ism. Rather he was dealing with a radically different sort of problem, namely, the state of man's world in which God's whole will would be done.

There is no basis in the historical record for any separation of religion from ethics in Jesus' teaching; rather, they are two aspects of a single reality, religion being the inner allegiance of the human heart, and morality or ethics, the conduct which sprang from this source.

The primary religious reality, according to Jesus, was God, conceived as Lord and Creator of all that exists, and as supreme object of human devotion. Jesus never argued the existence of God; but taking this for granted, his primary problem was man's relation to God. It was Jesus' view that the whole reason for man's existence—his purpose on earth—is to do the will of God.

The content of the divine will for man's life can be summed up in the single word *love*. Jesus used this word to mean a spontaneous, wholehearted, and complete affirmation of the selfhood of others. Contrary to much current opinion, this teaching is not unique to Jesus or to the New Testament. Several of the Old Testament books had taught God's love for man and man's for God, notably Deuteronomy, Hosea, Isaiah, and Jeremiah.[27] It must also be kept in mind that for Jesus, the concept of love had an austerity which it lacks in much modern sentimental usage. To him, love included justice and judgment as well as mercy. In the first century *father* meant an authority figure far more than in the twentieth. With these qualifications, it is accurate to summarize Jesus' God as sovereign love. It is a sovereignty which is now hidden, but which will be manifested fully in the coming of the Kingdom.

As noted above, religion and morality were for Jesus two aspects of a single integral reality. The basic moral commandments had an absolute or unqualified character based upon a divine "Thou shalt . . . ," and the commandments were all summed up in the single supreme commandment: "Thou shalt love thy neighbor as thyself."[28] Jesus had much to say about the unconditional quality of love, and the tensions which it set up with the everyday loyalties of human existence such as family, state, economic order, and the like. Far from being ascetic, he regarded these normal goods as parts of God's creation, yet he argued that all creation must be placed under the supreme goal of the Kingdom of God and its perfect goodness, which above all, he admonished his followers to seek.[29]

The content of Jesus' faith and ethic is expressed in his own summary of the

Torah and the Prophets: You shall love the Lord your God with all your heart, and with all your soul and mind and strength, and your neighbor as yourself.[30] This famous statement is a double quotation by Jesus of (1) Deuteronomy 6:4–5 and (2) Leviticus 19:18. Asked by a heckler to quote the greatest commandment in the Torah, he did precisely that with greatest accuracy. The basic moral virtue is love conceived as respect for, and affirmation of, personality as made in the divine image.

Head of Christ. Painting by Rembrandt

Courtesy of The Metropolitan Museum of Art, Mr. and Mrs. Isaac D. Fletcher Collection, bequest of Isaac D. Fletcher, 1917

Yet neighbor-love, so conceived, was for Jesus something more inward than any precise legal code. It was an attitude of the heart; and from the heart, Jesus reminded his hearers, proceed the attitudes that govern actions.[31] Moreover, it was an attitude whose universality extended beyond all barriers of race and class to the limits of humanity. It was precisely this universality which was the subject of such teachings as the parable of the Good Samaritan.[32]

In contrast to the good as love, evil for Jesus was an ever-present self-centeredness which sets man against God and his neighbor. Sometimes it is manifested as trust in one's possessions as with the Rich Fool,[33] sometimes as the pride of the Pharisees who "trusted in themselves and despised the others." [34]

Jesus' demands, both religious and moral, while not ascetic, were rigorous, indeed so rigorous that few men have claimed to fulfill them completely. Yet in the context of his teachings and life, one could see that what Jesus sought to do was to depict man's ultimate perfection. The practical problem of ethics which followed from this was how this perfection was to be related to all the changing scenes and situations of human life. It was a problem destined to concern the Christian church age after age.

Another significant issue was the relation of Jesus' faith and ethic to Judaism and to the whole Hebraic heritage of the Old Testament. For one thing, Jesus' teachings were more inward and more internationalist or universal than most first-century interpretations of the Torah. He stood against code morality and against the prevalent nationalism of his time. Yet in both respects, Jesus stood squarely on the classical tradition of Torah and the Prophets. Indeed Jesus seems to have regarded his teaching as the fulfillment of the Torah and Prophets.[35]

THE NEW TESTAMENT CHRISTIAN COMMUNITY

THE RESURRECTION OF CHRIST

Christ's resurrection was the crucial fact for the beginning of the New Testament Christian community. At the crucifixion, Jesus' followers forsook him and fled. One may imagine that they also left Jerusalem for their native Galilee, there in disillusionment to resume the occupations they had left to follow the man of Nazareth. Yet the strange fact is that only a few weeks later these same people were back in Jerusalem with an utterly changed attitude. They were the servants of a living faith which within a century was to make its impact felt from one end of the Roman empire to the other, and which in the next four centuries would turn that empire upside down.

What accounts for the revolutionary change? The answer which traditional Christianity has given to this question is the resurrection of Christ—an event which convinced the followers of Jesus that he was not dead but alive—more living and more powerful than in the days of his flesh. Hence, the resurrection might be defined as that event which certified to the Christian community the living spirit of Christ as an ever-present reality.

Precisely what occurred at the resurrection is another question to which the New Testament Christians gave more than one answer, and none without its serious problems. One answer was the story in all four Gospels of the empty tomb, the surprised visitors on the first day of the week, the appearances of the risen Christ, and finally his ascension on a cloud to heaven. Yet from the beginning there were difficulties in this interpretation of an objective physical resurrection, and an ascension of the same sort. Where, for example, did the body go, when Christ ascended to heaven?

It is also a fact that other interpretations were held. In the early 50s, two decades before the earliest Synoptic Gospel, the apostle Paul wrote to the Corinthian church:

> For I delivered to you as of first importance what I also received, that Christ died for our sins in accordance with the scriptures, that he was buried, that he was raised on the third day in accordance with the scriptures, and that he appeared to Cephas, then to the twelve. Then he appeared to more than five hundred brethren at one time, most of whom are still alive, though some have fallen asleep.
>
> Then he appeared to James, then to all the apostles. Last of all, as to one untimely born, he appeared also to me.[36]

One notes that the primary emphasis is placed here upon the risen Christ, and that no mention is made of an empty tomb. Most important of all, he also notes that Paul includes among the resurrection appearances his own experience on the Damascus road, an experience that took place long after the presumed ascension, and that Paul explicitly denies the physical nature of the resurrection: "flesh and blood cannot inherit the Kingdom of God." [37] Paul was a Jew for whom the concept of personality required some sort of embodiment. In the later verses of the chapter quoted above, he speculates about different kinds of bodies, here and hereafter, concluding that in the resurrection all men will have bodies, though of a different sort from our present bodies. Later, in II Corinthians, Paul makes a different suggestion concerning life in the resurrection; apparently his searching mind continued to look for an adequate view of this difficult and mysterious matter.[38]

THE EARLY JERUSALEM COMMUNITY

Pentecost marked the beginning of the Christian movement and community, which consisted initially of the small group of Jesus' followers who carried on religious propaganda in Jerusalem. An event of greatest importance to this group occurred on the Jewish Feast of Pentecost in the same year that Jesus died, that is, ca. A.D. 31–33. As the Book of Acts tells the story, the Christians were gathered in their upstairs meeting room when the Holy Spirit descended upon them with the supernatural accompaniments of wind, fire, and ecstatic utterance, or "speaking with tongues." [39]

Impelled to speak, Peter made a public address at the end of which, according to the Book of Acts, 3,000 converts were made to the new faith.[40] Pentecost was for Judaism the festival which commemorated the giving of the Torah on Mount Sinai and according to rabbinic tradition it had been given in the seventy languages of mankind. The Christian story was thus a kind of deliberate parallel, describing the giving of the new and universal faith in what were described as different foreign languages.

"Speaking with tongues" was a frequent phenomenon in the New Testament Christian church, as may be noted from the letters of Paul.[41] The author of the Book of Acts (writing at the end of the first century) appears to be seeking to explain the beginning of this practice; and he does so by tracing it to Pentecost and regarding it as a process of speaking in foreign tongues. Actually, a more realistic view is that it consisted of ecstatic babbling, under the stress of strong emotion. As Paul viewed this matter, speaking with tongues belonged with prophecy, visions, healings, and other preternormal phenomena, as a result of the enlargement of human power which accompanied religious revival. Yet Paul was also sensible enough to suggest that the value of all such experiences lay in their ethical and spiritual quality.

In the view of the Book of Acts, the Christian movement began in Jerusalem. The members of this earliest Christian community were good Jews in all respects except one. They went to the temple, observed the Torah, studied the Bible; but they believed that the Messiah, expected by all good Jews, had actually come in Jesus. To their contemporaries they must have appeared as one more harebrained sect. What made them appear even more eccentric was their firm conviction that Jesus had been raised from the dead, that he was spiritually present in the community of believers, and that he would soon return to earth in power to rule over God's Kingdom.[42]

This little group celebrated its faith in worship which in many ways resembled the synagogue service. There was reading of the Jewish Bible and exposition of the text accompanied by prayer to God. But all was interpreted as pointing to Christ. And there was a love feast, patterned after the Last Supper, celebrating Jesus' memory, his spiritual presence, and his expected return. This reenactment of the Last Supper grew at length into the Roman Catholic Mass and the Protestant service of Holy Communion.

Leadership of the community was by the disciples of Christ, now called apostles. (An apostle was technically defined in the early Christian community as one who had seen the resurrected Christ.) Members practiced a community of property, according to which they sold their possessions and placed the money in a common treasury from which were provided the needs of all. They also shared their meals at common tables. These practices led to abuses, as the story of Ananias and Sapphira illustrates.[43]

From the beginning the Christians were ardent missionaries. After Peter's speech at Pentecost, they carried on ceaseless activity designed to secure conversions, which activity they interpreted as their obedience to the will of Christ. However, it soon brought them into conflict with government. The authorities of Jerusalem wavered between the toleration recommended by Gamaliel and occasionally severe repression.[44] This raised an issue destined later to draw Christianity into fundamental conflict with Rome. Ordered by Jewish authorities to desist from religious propaganda, Peter and John replied, "We must obey God rather than man." [45] This conclusion was regarded by the Christians as a necessary implication of the first commandment.

Another kind of conflict was also quick to emerge in the Jerusalem church. Apparently some members began to take liberties in their observance of the Torah. Differences of opinion were reported over the daily distribution of food between members of the Christian community who were Palestinian Jews and others who were Hellenistic Jews.[46] The former were Jews who had always lived in Palestine, and the latter, those who had lived abroad in the Gentile world and then returned to Palestine. The Palestinian Jews were consistently more rigorous in their observance of the Torah.

To meet this issue, Acts reports, the office of deacon was devised. Yet it is significant that all those selected had Greek names; apparently they represented the Hellenistic group within the Christian community. It is also significant that their leader, Stephen, was soon actively engaged not only in deacon's duties, but also in teaching and preaching. He was soon in trouble with civil authorities, the charges against him being that he was disloyal to temple and Torah. As a result of these charges Stephen was lynched by an angry Jewish mob, thus becoming the first Christian martyr.[47]

This episode has significance as the beginning of the separation between Christianity and Judaism. What began with Stephen had its completion only much later when Christianity had dispensed completely with observance of the Torah and had become a Gentile religion. Other events pointing in this direction followed Stephen's death; for example, Peter in obedience to a vision deliberately breached kosher food laws and also baptized a Gentile.[48] In reaction to such events, a conservative, or Jewish-Christian, party emerged in the Jerusalem church, composed of those who asserted that in order to become a Christian a man had first to become a Jew, taking upon himself the full burden of the Torah. Thus arose the issue which was to engage Christianity crucially for a generation and on which the apostle Paul was to say the decisive word two decades later.

PAUL AS MISSIONARY

The apostle Paul's name is associated with the rise of Gentile Christianity. Gentile Christianity did not originate with Paul, since the churches of Antioch,

Alexandria, and Rome were all founded by other apostles before Paul's rise to leadership. The Book of Acts introduces Paul as the young man who held the coats of those who stoned Stephen. He had only recently come to Jerusalem from his home city of Tarsus for rabbinical study with Gamaliel. His parents were Pharisaic Jews, and his father was a Roman citizen. Paul had learned the tentmaker's trade and had received a traditional Jewish education; from the fact that Tarsus was a center of Stoic philosophy and Greek mystery religions, we may infer for him some familiarity with these phenomena. His own writings confirm this supposition. It must be supposed that on arrival in Jerusalem his attitude toward the Torah was that of any intensely loyal Pharisaic Jew. Hence it was natural for him to persecute Stephen and other Christians as renegade Jews.

Yet for Paul as for so many men, intense allegiance seems to have concealed inner conflicts. As Acts tells the story, it was on a mission to harass Christians in Damascus that Paul's conversion took place.[49] Paul's own writings agree with the Acts account in interpreting the experience as the appearance to Paul of the resurrected Christ, who said, "Paul, Paul, why do you persecute me?" Paul's response was, "Who are you, Lord?" The reply was, "I am Jesus whom you are persecuting." As Paul said many years later, he was "not disobedient to the heavenly vision."[50] At the time he was led blind into the city of Damascus, where his conversion became known.

According to Paul's own writings, he spent the next three years in Arabia, presumably in seclusion, reintegrating his shattered life and gaining perspective on what had happened to him.[51] Then he journeyed to Jerusalem for consultation with Peter and other leaders of the Jerusalem church. Following this, he settled down for fourteen years of labor in Tarsus and Antioch, presumably first as leader of the Tarsus church and then as Barnabas's assistant at Antioch. The New Testament gives no direct knowledge of these years, yet one must conclude that Paul's distinctive views on the relation of Christianity to Judaism were taking shape in these cities where Jews and Gentiles met and mingled in the Christian church.

Acts and Paul's own letters do provide more detailed knowledge of Paul's later years and missionary journeys. The thirteenth and fourteenth chapters of Acts tell of the first missionary trip undertaken by Paul and Barnabas, at the command of the Antioch church, which took them first to Cyprus then to cities of south-central Asia Minor. John Mark accompanied Paul and Barnabas to Cyprus, but then returned home. Paul and Barnabas, however, continued their journey to the mainland of Asia Minor, where they visited successively the cities of Perga, Antioch in Pisidia, Iconium, Lystra, and Derbe.[52] In each city the apostles preached and taught at the synagogue, winning converts who formed the nucleus of a Christian church.

Before venturing further afield, Paul made a journey to Jerusalem in 49 or 50 for the purpose of settling the growing dispute between him and the Jewish Christians of Jerusalem. At this meeting, often called the Council of Jerusalem, the question to be decided was whether in order to become a Christian a man had first to become a Jew, taking upon himself the full burden of the Torah. The Jerusalem church answered this question with an unyielding affirmative, but Paul had increasingly believed and taught that if a man had personal faith in Christ, he could jettison the Torah. According to Acts and to Paul's own account in the letter to the Galatians, the result of the Council was an uneasy compromise permitting Paul to work among Gentiles and the Jerusalem party among Jews.[53] The compromise soon broke down in misunderstanding, and Paul spent the rest of his life propagating his version of Christian faith among Jew and Gentile alike.

Soon after the Council, Paul returned to Antioch, then set out across Syria and Asia Minor for Europe. In Troas occurred the celebrated vision of the man from Macedonia saying, "Come over, help us." [54] From Troas, Paul crossed to Philippi in Greece and made his way successively to Berea, Thessalonika, Athens, and Corinth. Paul did not succeed in founding a Christian church in Athens; however, in Corinth he stayed for over two years, founding a thriving if turbulent Christian community. From Corinth he made his way to Ephesus, where he worked for three years, probably from 54 to 57. During these years his break with Judaism became definite and final. It was from Ephesus that he wrote the letter to the Galatians, presumably to the south Galatian cities visited on his first missionary journey. From his years at Ephesus too, may be dated his stormy correspondence with the Corinthian church. At this time or shortly thereafter, he wrote the letter to the Romans.

Paul made one more journey to Jerusalem, apparently to bring relief funds to the famine-stricken Jerusalem church. Roman soldiers saved him from lynching at the hands of an angry mob of Jewish extremists who accused him of violating essential parts of the Torah and teaching others to do so. He was held in protective custody, at first in Jerusalem, then in Caesarea, which was the Roman port for Palestine. Despairing of receiving a fair hearing for his case after two years or more, he appealed to Caesar. The Book of Acts does not tell the outcome of his trial, but a widely held tradition asserts that Paul perished as a martyr (ca. 60–64), possibly in Nero's persecution of Christians.

PAULINE THEOLOGY

Of equal significance with Paul's work as a missionary and leader of the Christian movement were his bold new patterns of thought. More than any other figure, Paul was the father of Christian theology. Not theoretical or systematic,

Paul's thinking was the plain and personal response of his mind to the events in which he played an important part. In simplest terms, Paul was a Jew who found the Messiah in Jesus. The phrases "Jesus is Christ," and "Jesus is Lord" run like a refrain through Paul's writings. To be sure, his thought showed significant influence from Greek mystery religions and Greek philosophy, but the core of it remained thoroughly Hebraic. His God was the God of his Jewish fathers, namely, the sovereign Lord who created and ruled the universe, who had spoken to man through Moses and the prophets but who had now, according to Paul, spoken a new and decisive word in Jesus Christ.

For Paul, Christianity was thus a new covenant, a new revelation of God to man. As the old covenant centered in the giving of the Torah to Moses at Mount Sinai, so the new covenant centered in Jesus Christ. Paul devoted much thought and many words to the interpretation of Christ. Frequently he used the term *Lord* (the Greek term *Kyrios,* meaning "Lord," had the basic meaning of a higher being possessing authority), saying, "Jesus is Lord." But going beyond this, Paul came at length to think of Christ as a preexistent divine figure who had condescended to take on human form, who in his death struggled victoriously with cosmic forces of evil and who now reigned with God in heavenly places.[55] By a kind of personal faith and trust amounting, according to some statements, to an identification with Christ, his human followers might win a similar victory over sin and death in their own lives.

This Pauline gospel of a dying and rising savior bore unmistakable similarity to many of the Greek and Roman mystery cults which had similar stories and saviors. Paul's description of the Eucharist as a Christian mystery lent further support to this view. But there were notable differences as well. Paul's story of the dying and rising God was not fiction but history, to which many Christians could testify as witnesses. Further, neither Paul nor any other Christian leader separated the theme of mystical union with Christ from ethical life. If a man was "in Christ," he was expected to show the fruits of faith in ethical life.[56]

According to Paul, man apprehends or lays hold upon Christ by means of faith. By faith he did not mean propositional belief or creedal assent, but rather a turning of the heart in trust and allegiance to God in Christ. In Paul's mind, faith and works stood in polar opposition. By means of works men sought to earn God's favor, to scale heaven in their own human power. Paul argued that the Torah, or Jewish Law, called on men to do exactly this.[57] Realizing the impossibility of this, a man in his helplessness turns humbly to God to receive the grace he cannot possibly earn or deserve. This crucial human act of saying a humble, receptive "yes" to God is what Paul meant by faith.

Paul taught that from grace apprehended by faith sprang freedom.[58] Freedom for Paul meant initially and primarily freedom from the Torah and its demands.

In former times, the Torah had been man's custodian or schoolmaster to Christ, but now that Christ had come, the Torah is null and void. More positively, freedom was for Paul the spirit-given power to live as "sons of God," as God calls men. Morality, Paul taught, was not a condition of faith, but its fruit. As the fruit of the tree is to its roots, so is ethics to faith. This metaphor, used repeatedly by Jesus, was also Paul's view of this matter. Moral qualities, he said many times, were fruits of the spirit.[59] For Paul and for Christ, the content of ethics is neighbor-love. Paul frequently characterized this love simply and eloquently by pointing to the figure of Christ as its great paradigm.

THE FOURTH GOSPEL

Paul's importance in the New Testament Christian movement was second only to that of Christ; yet his view of the new faith was by no means the only one in the New Testament community. Of particular importance for its contrast to Paul was the view of the anonymous Fourth Gospel. It is traditionally attributed to the disciple John, but modern Biblical study has shown this to be highly improbable. Writing around the year 100, probably in the city of Ephesus, its author appears thoroughly familiar with the language and thought of current Greek philosophy and religion. He avails himself of many of the terms and ideas of current Greek thought.[60]

Jesus was interpreted as the incarnate Word, or Logos, of God. The term *logos*, meaning "word," "thought," "rational discussion," had been common in philosophic reflection from the sixth-century B.C. figure of Heraclitus. It had been given new and distinctive meaning in the first century by such thinkers as Philo Judaeus of Alexandria, who interpreted the Logos as a cosmic intermediary between God and man, active in all creation. In effect, for Philo the Logos designated that aspect of deity which is active in all creative activity. The word *logos* was to attain widespread use in the next century in Gnostic philosophies. *Gnosticism* is a modern scholar's word for a religious and philosophical movement widely popular in the Greco-Roman world which envisaged the world as divided into matter and spirit and which sought by secret *gnosis*, or knowledge, to save men from matter to the spiritual world. It was this widely prevalent idea which the Fourth Gospel appropriated and used for the interpretation of Jesus. It asserted in effect that the basic meaning and structure of the universe was incarnated in Jesus' life.

Two motives may be observed in this novel interpretation of Christ. Clearly the author was adapting his language to that of the Hellenistic people to whom he was speaking. However, in this language he was attempting to speak his own message. His language, in short, was Gnostic (or protognostic), but the content of what he sought to say, namely, that the divine Logos had become human flesh, was utterly antignostic. It was fundamentally Hebraic.

The author's portrait of Jesus as incarnate Logos took liberties with widely accepted facts, and diverged widely from the Synoptic portrait of Christ's life. Jesus was interpreted as a preexistent, divine figure, descended from heaven, who moved mysteriously through human life, speaking in oracles and ever-conscious of his impending sacrificial death. The Fourth Gospel was destined to have widespread influence on the interpretation of Christian faith. Its view of Christ as the incarnate Word became the foundation of Christian orthodoxy in creed and theology. This book has also been a veritable fountainhead of Christian mysticism.

VARIATIONS ON A COMMON THEME

Paul and John were not the only theologians of the New Testament community. Other diverging interpretations of Christ and God were not slow to appear. For example, the Synoptic Gospels have been treated as primary historical sources for the life of Jesus; yet in their time they also represented a distinctive theological view. The second coming of Christ having failed to occur, Christians began to concentrate attention on his first coming; and it was in this connection that they wrote these Gospels. Theologically the Synoptics were distinctive for their emphasis on the human life of Jesus.

Other men, however, clung tenaciously to the idea of a second coming, or *parousia*, of Christ. In times of persecution, their views took on added relevance. So it was that during the first empire-wide persecution of Christians, under Domitian in 95–96, the Book of Revelation made its appearance. Its bizarre and vivid images, which followed the stylized patterns of apocalyptic writing and speaking, have proved a veritable gold mine of images for Christian poets and visionaries of subsequent times. In terms of its religious teaching Revelation, like Daniel in the Old Testament, was a tract for bad times, assuring that in bad times as in good, God still reigns, asserting his dominion through Christ. Revelation pictures Christ as a military commander descending from heaven on a white horse and with flaming sword to defeat anti-Christ and bring in God's Kingdom.[61]

There were still other varieties of faith and thought in the New Testament, such as the Letter of James, with its eminently practical, moral emphases and its polemic against a faith that does not result in works, and the Letter to Hebrews, with its interpretation of Christ in terms of the Old Testament sacrificial ritual and its exhortation to remain faithful under stress and persecution.[62] There were two letters of Peter, each with its own distinctive variations on the common New Testament themes of God in Christ.

CHRISTIANITY IN THE ANCIENT WORLD, A. D. 100—500

CHURCH AND EMPIRE

By A.D. 100, Christianity had found its way throughout the Greco-Roman world and had undergone persecution by Nero and Domitian. For many Romans, the Christian movement was only one more of the "oriental superstitions" which had recently flooded the empire with bizarre rites and irrational beliefs. The Romans would have been glad to let the matter rest at that point, for they were tolerant people. However, there were persistent and ugly rumors about the Christians. One was that they worshiped a king other than Caesar. Often, too, the Christians refused to perform the rites to Caesar—rites which most Romans regarded as no more religious than the modern flag salute. Many Christians refused military service and public office. Christians often incurred the charge of atheism for their scornful attitude toward the old gods. There were also ugly rumors of cannibalism at Christian worship.[63]

The Christians were willing, as they put it, to call the empire good, but not to call it God, or divine, that is, to find the whole meaning of human existence in the empire. To do so would in effect deify Roman values or the Roman way of life, which for the Christians would be a violation of the first commandment.

The conflict of Christ and Caesar extended over three centuries and ended with Christianity as the official religion of Constantine's empire. While the conflict involved systematic and empire-wide campaigns at times, at other times it was a matter of sporadic local outbreaks of public prejudice against the new and strange faith. In A.D. 64, Nero burnt Christians in Rome, but there is no evidence that his persecution extended beyond the capital city. In 95, Domitian attempted a more systematic empire-wide action. Trajan (98–117) is known for his letter to Pliny the Younger advising what both men must have regarded as a mild and lenient course against the Christian nuisance. Christians were not to be hunted out, and if they were willing to sacrifice, they were to be acquitted. Only if they persisted in their refusal to perform the prescribed rites were they to be punished.[64]

Two emperors who followed Trajan, namely, Hadrian (117–138) and Antoninus Pius (138–161) followed a similar policy. Marcus Aurelius (161–180) initiated a sharper period of persecution. There was also a continuing tradition of local mob violence against Christians. However, it was not until Decius's edict in 250 that a systematic empire-wide persecution aiming at complete destruction of Christianity was undertaken. Decius's object was to reassert the worship of the old gods who had made the empire great, and in effect to reassert the unity of Rome against this new, subversive force. There were many martyrdoms, and also many who renounced Christian faith under pressure. It was for Christianity a fearful time of trial, lasting, with intermissions, from 250 to 259. Christian assemblies were forbidden, churches and cemeteries confiscated, and church officials banished or executed. Yet the Christian movement emerged from the struggle stronger than ever.

The struggle of the empire against Christianity was resumed in earnest by the soldier-emperor Diocletian (284–311). Viewing with growing alarm the close-knit organization of the church, Diocletian acted in 303 and 304 with a series of edicts which destroyed churches, confiscated sacred books, and forced all suspected Christians to sacrifice to the Emperor. Again, as with Decius, there were many martyrs and many who "lapsed." The severity of the persecution varied widely among the local officials who carried out the edicts. But again, persecution actually strengthened what it sought to destroy.

Diocletian's retirement in 311 was followed immediately by an edict by Constantine and Licinius granting the church actual toleration. Meanwhile, among the four contestants for the imperial throne, Constantine took decisive action. Before the battle of the Malvian Bridge, north of Rome, in 312, he believed that he saw in a dream the name of Christ with the words "By this sign you will conquer." Hastily painting the monogram XP on his helmet, he won his battle. Believing that the Christian God had given him the victory, from this time onward he was in all practical respects a Christian, though he delayed his own baptism until his deathbed. The edict of Milan in 313 gave Christianity full equality with other religions. In edicts which followed, the Christian church was given an increasingly preferred position until in 319 heathen or non-Christian sacrifices were forbidden.

The new position of Christianity was a milestone in its history. Christians might now serve their God openly, without fear of persecution. But now, and for the next thousand years, there was the equal and opposite peril of being an established faith. Now that it was legal and fashionable to be a Christian, all the perils of compromise and nominal allegiance presented themselves. As the issue is sometimes stated, the question is whether at the time of Constantine, church conquered empire, or the opposite.

EARLY CHRISTIAN THEOLOGIES

The section of this chapter on the New Testament has noted the beginnings of the unceasing activity of stating, interpreting, and defending Christian faith. In the historical period now under consideration, roughly from A.D. 100 to 500, two main problems emerged: (1) What is the relation of Christian faith to its alternatives? (2) What is the nature of Christian faith? The answers to these two questions were inextricably bound up with each other.

One type of answer was given by the *Apologists*. As Christian faith came increasingly under Roman criticism, it was natural that explanations and defenses should be undertaken. They appeared in a form of writing called *apologia* (not an apology) for Christianity. Since the writers were for the most part converted pagan philosophers, notably Stoics and Platonists, they tended to construe Christianity as true philosophy. Having searched elsewhere in vain for an adequate philosophy, they found Christianity adequate or true.

Among this group of Christian philosophers were such men as Quadratus and later Aristides, both of Athens, Melito, Bishop of Sardis, the unknown author of the Epistle to Diognetus, and most notable of all, Justin Martyr. Justin, who was martyred ca. 165, was born in the Palestinian city of Schechem and spent his adult life wandering among the philosophic isms of his age. He was by turns an adherent and teacher of Stoicism, Aristotelianism, Pythagoreanism, and Platonism. In his apology he describes the way in which, while he was a Platonist, his attention was directed to the Hebrew prophets and their message.[65]

Justin was a morally-minded man for whom the righteous nature of the Biblical God was attractive. He regarded as grossly immoral the doctrine that God was neutral between good and evil. The new life to which men are called by Christ is a life of love for God and man, said Justin. Judaism had much of this ethical spirit, but was encumbered by its vast legalism. Christianity is superior in having the figure and teachings of Jesus Christ, who moreover had come in fulfillment of Old Testament prophecy.

Justin made effective and extensive use of the Logos in his interpretation of Christ. In effect, the Logos is that aspect of the divine nature by which men are guided to think rationally and live rationally and righteously. By this power, Justin argued, both the philosophers of Greece and the prophets of Israel lived and taught; any rational being, even though he profess atheism, lives by this power.[66] While universal in scope, the Logos is incarnate uniquely in Christ. So it is that Christ's coming enables man to banish ignorance and sin, and to achieve a new heart and mind. Human freedom and responsibility and reason were thus primary aspects of Justin's theology. It was Christianity which gave those qualities their highest expression.

One of the most influential and distinctive interpretations of the Christian faith emerged from the catechetical school of Alexandria. Among the most famous educational institutions of the early church, this school grew up in close connection with Alexandria's famous museum and university. It participated fully in the Platonic thought which was the dominant philosophy of Alexandria. Founded by a converted Stoic named Pantaenus, and carried on successively by Clement (150–220) and Origen (185–251), this school became famous throughout the ancient world and made a lasting impact on Christian theology. Clement taught two sources of truth, scripture and reason, with one divine Logos inspiring and guiding both. In Christ the Logos is uniquely active, making him the supreme teacher of men's minds as well as the high priest of their souls.

Clement gave the highest place to the Christian intellectual, or as he said, the Christian Gnostic. To be sure, the simple Christian might save his soul by faith, but better and higher than this was the state of the Christian intellectual who went on from faith to wisdom and for whom salvation consisted in correct knowledge of God. Clement and his successors employed an allegorical interpretation of Scripture as a means of finding faith's higher, hidden meanings within the pages of the Bible.

Origen was Clement's student, but a man of enormously greater boldness and capacity of mind than his teacher. While Origen was an avid student of the Bible, he was also a philosopher and theologian who used the Platonic heritage for the interpretation of Christian faith.[67] One of Origen's many achievements was an original and distinctive interpretation of the Christ as Logos. The problem of the interpretation of Christ had been a thorny one from the beginning of Christianity. If God is one, how is Christ related to him? If Christ be regarded as the Logos, does this involve two gods? These and other questions arose in the minds of philosophically-minded Christians. Origen met these issues by teaching that the Logos was begotten of God eternally and not created. Both Logos and God were divine, and indeed were embraced within a single divine unity. Hence worship might properly be given to the Logos as an aspect of God. However, Origen's usage of words was by no means consistent, and he left a legacy of theological questions which the church was to struggle over for several centuries.

Origen's cosmology divided the world Platonically into spiritual and material realms, and he frequently seemed to imply that spirit was good and matter evil. Man on earth was good insofar as he was spiritual; but he was also imprisoned in matter. In addition to man, Origen taught that the universe was populated by many rational spirits who had immediate and unceasing communion with God. Salvation for Origen was the restoration of man to a realm of pure spirit; and he taught that this restoration would extend to all men. Hell, or to speak more precisely purgatory, was a consequence of man's wrong choices, and in the end it will be emptied, and all men saved. At the end God will indeed be all in all.[68]

A different and opposite kind of theology was illustrated by Tertullian of Carthage (150–222). By profession a lawyer, he brought many of the ideas of Roman law into his interpretation of Christian faith. The first church father to write in Latin rather than Greek, he commanded a terse, epigrammatic style, and has often been called the father of Latin theology. Intense and rigorous in spirit, his theology expressed his personality. He viewed Christ as God's great paradox, surpassing and confounding the highest philosophical wisdom of man. Such attitudes led Tertullian to a low estimate of human reason and philosophy. "What is there in common between Athens and Jerusalem? What between the Academy and the Church?" he asked scornfully.[69] It is a fact, however, that Tertullian's own writings borrowed more than he knew from Stoic philosophy.

Tertullian possessed an intense sense of sin and so was led to reflect upon the nature of sin and grace. Grace is conferred, Tertullian declared, through the sacraments of the church. Out of his lawyer's experience he suggested that just as three persons (*personae*) might share title to property (*substantio*), so in the Godhead there were three persons and one substance. Later trinitarian theology was destined to follow his lead. Tertullian's austere puritanical nature led him away from orthodox Christianity to the Montanist heresy, yet Latin theology bore the indelible marks of his thought. He has been the archetypal model of many men since his time who have sought to understand faith and reason, religion and philosophy, as polar opposites.

HERESY AND ORTHODOXY

As Christianity made its way in the Greco-Roman world, it was inevitable that many varieties of theological interpretation should develop, some of them clearly incompatible with each other, and some viewed, rightly or wrongly, as distortions of the faith. Out of such tendencies grew the idea of heresy and its opposite, orthodoxy. It is significant to note that these ideas were clearly related to the theoretical or theological orientation of early Christianity. Judaism, developing its distinctive forms in this same period and region, had little or no sense of orthodox belief or creed, largely because it placed primary emphasis on doing or practice rather than on belief.

The modern student of religion is likely to deplore the very ideas of heresy and orthodoxy as constituting an enterprise in totalitarian thought control. He will be right about important aspects of the early Christian attitude, but he will also miss an especially important issue. The enterprise of formulating and maintaining correct belief was important in a hostile world, if the new religion was to survive at all. If it was to maintain itself as a distinctive faith, Christianity must possess what modern man might term a party line.

The earliest Christian confessions, dating from New Testament times and used as baptismal formulas, were simple statements such as "Jesus is Lord." By the middle of the second century the simple formula had grown to a series of fixed questions and answers, having many of the phrases of the Apostles' Creed, though the final formulation of the Apostles' Creed cannot be traced to a date earlier than the eighth century.[70]

Many of the issues expressed or implied in the Apostles' Creed are those of the second-century struggle of Christianity with Gnosticism and, more particularly, with the teachings of Marcion in the Roman church. As we have previously observed, *gnosticism* is a modern scholar's word for a cluster of philosophic and religious tendencies of the later Greco-Roman world. Something like Gnosticism has already been noted as the Hellenistic context of the Fourth Gospel. In general, the Gnostics maintained a dualist cosmology in which the world was bifurcated into a realm of spirit, or mind, which was esteemed both good and real, and a realm of matter, or flesh, believed to be evil or unreal or both. The realm of spirit was believed to be populated by large numbers of beings, over all of whom ruled a remote, unknowable, transcendent deity. For Gnostics, man was regarded as a good spirit imprisoned in an evil body, and his salvation was thought to consist of rescuing the spirit from its prison. This might be done by imparting esoteric knowledge (gnosis) which each Gnostic teacher and school claimed to possess. Gnosticism also often involved an ascetic morality; since flesh is evil, it must be mortified or suppressed.

While many Gnostics had no connection with either Christianity or Judaism, some of them sought to infiltrate these monotheistic religions with their teachings. For Christian Gnostics an important belief was that Christ was the divine Logos, the chief intermediary between God and man. However, in the Gnostic viewpoint it was unthinkable that the Logos should take on evil and delusory human flesh. Therefore the Gnostics characteristically denied the incarnation.[71] The human life of Christ was apparent but not real, asserted the Christian Gnostics. Christ hovered over mortal life, never really participating in birth, suffering, and death. Some Gnostics such as Marcion of Rome also denied that the God of creation is the true Lord and God of all. Rather this Jewish God who dubiously created the material world is a minor denizen of the spiritual realm.

The Christian church set itself against these Gnostic views in such affirmations of the Apostles' Creed as "God the Father Almighty, creator of heaven and earth." [72] By implication this was an affirmation of the goodness of all God's creation, material as well as spiritual. Similar affirmations concerning Jesus' birth, suffering, and death were directed against the Gnostic denial of the incarnation. So too, the assertion in the Apostles' Creed of the resurrection of the dead affirmed the salvation of the whole man and not simply the discarnate spirit. It is thus significant to see that against this ancient heresy, the church affirmed the humanity of Christ and the goodness and reality of material things.

A radically different kind of heresy arose in the second century—and one adds that it is a kind which has recurred many times since in Christian history. The second-century version was called Montanism, after its leader, Montanus, who prior to his conversion to Christianity had been a priest of Cybele, the great Mother Goddess of the ancient Near Eastern world. Montanus declared himself to be the vehicle through whom the Holy Spirit spoke. His was ecstatic utterance of a sort familiar in the New Testament "speaking in tongues." He also proclaimed that the present evil age was soon to end and that the New Jerusalem would soon be set up in his native town of Pepuza in Phrygia. His followers disposed of their worldly possessions and responsibilities, and journeyed to Pepuza to await the return of Christ in glory. Montanism taught an austere morality. Food and clothing were kept simple, and Christians were required to abstain from worldly amusements. In a time when the church had begun its agelong compromise with the world, this moral rigor had a genuine appeal to sensitive spirits. In an age when formalism had displaced personal correction, Montanist ideas of the Spirit appealed. Even the great Tertullian was led away into this heresy.[73]

The church acted to condemn Montanism, though a small Montanist following lasted on for many centuries. Meanwhile another kind of issue came increasingly to the center of the stage. Previous sections of this chapter have observed the Johannine idea of Christ as the incarnate Word of God as it continued and developed, especially among such Alexandrine fathers as Origen. Controversies of many sorts arose concerning the relation of Christ to God and to man. A particularly sharp conflict arose in early fourth-century Alexandria over the views of Arius, who seeking to preserve the monotheism of Christianity, taught that Christ, while firstborn of all creation and God's agent in the creation, was none the less a created being. As he worked out his ideas, Arius was forced to the conclusion that Christ was neither truly divine nor truly human, but a third substance inserted between God and man.

These conclusions seemed particularly unsatisfactory to Arius's bishop, Alexander, and to the bishop's secretary, Athanasius. The controversy gathered momentum and spread, until Constantine was led to convene a general council of the church in order to restore peace among the quarreling Christian churchmen. The council met at Nicaea in May, 325; it has often been regarded as the most important council in Christian history. There were three main parties, including a small group of supporters of Alexander and Athanasius and a large middle group with no strong convictions either way and more interested in harmony than in theology.[74]

After rejecting a formulation of Arius, the council proceeded to an amended form of a compromise creed offered by Bishop Eusebius of Caesarea. Among the insertions were phrases like "begotten not made," and "of one essence with the Father" (*homoousion*) which were clearly anti-Arian in both intention and significance. The council was led in the end to affirm belief

> . . . in one Lord Jesus Christ, the only-begotten Son of God, Begotten of the Father before all the ages, Light of Light, true God of true God, begotten not made, of one substance with the Father, through whom all things were made; who for us men and for our salvation came down from heaven and was incarnate of the Holy Spirit and the Virgin Mary, and became man. . . .[75]

Explicitly condemned by the Council of Nicaea were those (Arians) who said of Christ, "There was a time when he was not," or "He came into existence from what was not," or "The son of God is of a different substance from the Father." Thus Christ was definitively declared to be both God and man, both divine and human—a view which has prevailed in traditional Christianity ever since.

Once this result was generally accepted, a further question arose, namely, how this could be so. How are the divine and human elements related to each other in Christ? Again there were many answers, much conflict. For example, Apollinarius (d. 392) taught that the divine Logos took the place of a human mind in Christ. Seeking to avoid a double personality, Apollinarius did less than justice to Christ's human nature. Theodore of Mopsuesta argued that the union of two natures in Christ was one of moral attitude rather than metaphysical substance. Following this view, Theodore's student and disciple, Nestorius, denied that Mary was the mother of God (*theotokos*), since from her was born only the human nature of Christ.

After apparently interminable arguments and anathemas, the church at the Council of Chalcedon (451) declared for two natures of Christ, divine and human, perfectly blended (the document does not say how!) in one person:

> . . . one and the same Christ, Son, Lord, Only-begotten, recognized in two natures without confusion, without change, without division, without separation; the distinction of natures being in no way annulled by the union, but rather the characteristics of each nature being preserved and coming together to form one person and subsistence, not as parted or separated into two persons, but one and the same Son and Only-begotten God the Word, Lord Jesus Christ. . . .[76]

So it was that the Christian church formulated its faith. It is a long distance from the New Testament formula "Jesus is Lord" to Nicaea and Chalcedon, yet the reader can see that men walked this road in order to guard the central conviction concerning Christ from misinterpretations which they believed endangered or undercut it. It is possible to understand the concerns of the creedmakers, even though many modern men do not share their formulations or sympathize with their attitudes and anathemas.

DEVELOPMENT OF EPISCOPAL AUTHORITY

The church of New Testament times was highly informal both in organization and worship. The apostles were leaders in worship and administration; in both aspects of the church's life this leadership was charismatically exercised. However, with the passage of time, all this changed. Resident bishops claiming authority by apostolic succession supplanted charismatic leaders, and worship moved in the direction of formality. As has been recently said: "About 50, he was of the church who had received baptism and the Holy Spirit and called Jesus, Lord; about 180 he who acknowledged the rule of faith, the New Testament canon and the authority of bishops." [77]

At first, usage varied widely in different regions as to selection of bishops and the nature of their office. However, as time passed, there was greater uniformity in the office and also greater concentration of power. A clear line was drawn between clergy and laity; the ministry came to be not only a full-time occupation, but a vocation set apart by special ordination and committed to a different and higher standard of moral life. The hierarchical organization of the church developed step by step.

One step of greatest importance was the theology and practice of Cyprian, Bishop of Carthage during the Decian persecution. During the initial phases of this persecution, some Christians lapsed from the faith, performing the rites to Caesar and renouncing Christianity in order to avoid torture and death. When the terror had passed, many of these people sought reentry into the church. A crucial question was who had the authority to receive them back. In some cases presbyters had done so. Cyprian attacked this practice and maintained that only a bishop possessed this authority. As he dealt with this practical issue, his whole view of the church as centering in the authority of bishops took its distinctive shape. In his view, the episcopal authority is unitary in nature, but is exercised independently by each bishop, all bishops being united by the Holy Spirit. This principle implied the equality of all bishops as well as a harmonious order among them. It also clearly implied subjection to the bishop's authority as the mark of a true Christian. "He can no longer have God for his father who has not the Church for his mother," argued Cyprian, adding significantly "if anyone could escape who was outside the Ark of Noah, then he may also escape who shall be outside the Church." [78] So began the doctrine that salvation is impossible outside the church. Cyprian went so far as to argue that since heretics have no genuine part in the church, heretical martyrs would gain no salvation.

Cyprian qualified his view of the equal authority of all bishops by speaking of Rome as "the chief church whence episcopal unity takes its source." [79] Others had said similar things, and still others pushed the primacy of Rome still further until at length the Bishop of Rome emerged in theory and practice as the primate of all Christendom. The authority and prestige of the Roman church had always been great, for Rome was the capital of the world; also, according to tradition the Roman church had been founded by Peter, to whom Christ had given the keys of heaven and hell. The authority of the Roman church was enhanced by its successful stand against the heresy of Marcionism. At the end of the second century, Victor, Bishop of Rome, excommunicated protesting churches of Asia Minor in a dispute over the proper date of Easter.[80] Thus Rome's power continued to grow.

It grew even more rapidly as the empire declined, leaving a vacuum of leadership which was filled by powerful bishops of Rome, such as the fifth-century Popes Innocent I (402–417) and Leo I (440–461). Innocent specifically claimed authority over all Christendom. Leo not only repeated and reinforced these claims by his elaboration of the primacy of Peter among the apostles and the Petrine succession of the popes; he also acted for the people of Rome in dealing with Huns and Vandals who invaded the city. It was Pope Gelasius (492–496) who wrote to the Eastern Emperor, "there are . . . two by whom principally this world is ruled: the sacred authority of the pontiffs and the royal power." [81]

WORSHIP AND SACRAMENTS

Christian worship and devotional practices, as well as church organization, underwent similar development in the direction of formalism. A central feature was an increasing formalism in the celebration of the Eucharist. From the charismatic, spirit-filled celebration of New Testament times, both practice and theory assumed ever-increasing formalism. The Eucharist was to be celebrated only by properly ordained priests, and participation was preceded by a period of catechetical instruction and was limited to members of the church. Increasingly, men believed and asserted that the bread and wine were the body and blood of Christ, which would impart eternal life. The Eucharist was increasingly regarded as a reenactment of Christ's sacrifice on the cross. It became the central and crucial act of Christian worship.

Worship also consisted of Bible reading, prayers, hymns, and a discourse, or sermon. It was customarily held on Sunday, but also on other days as well. The great event of the year was Easter, celebrating Christ's resurrection. The forty days of Lent leading up to Easter, and even more the days of the week immediately preceding, commemorated Christ's suffering and death. Easter, by contrast, was a time of rejoicing. Prayers for the dead and the veneration of martyrs were an increasingly important theme of Christian worship.

Second only to the Eucharist in importance was the sacrament of baptism. Pre-Christian in origin, it was taken over by the church and adapted to Christian uses. Originally immersion was the general practice, but gradually it was supplanted by sprinkling or pouring. It was administered to converts and to young Christians as they came of age, though as time passed, infant baptism became more and more the common practice. Baptism was believed to cleanse the soul from original sin and to symbolize the soul's entrance into the church as the Body of Christ.

The problem of the forgiveness of sins was a persistent issue. Confession was made, at first publicly to the congregation, then later privately to a priest. With the increasing authority of the clergy came the power of the priest to grant absolution. This development was accompanied by prescribed lists of sins and prescribed practices of penance.

MONASTICISM

With the spread and popularization of Christianity came many new problems involving moral and religious compromise with the world. The problem of compromise was a primary motivation for the monastic movement. Rigorous and ascetic practices had been aspects of Christianity from the beginning. As time passed, sensitive Christians sought with varying degrees of consistency to renounce the world altogether. St. Anthony (b. 250), often regarded as the originator of Christian monasticism, lived for many years as an ascetic in his own Egyptian village before taking up a hermit's life in the desert. Pachomius (b. 292) introduced a significant change by gathering groups of hermits together into communities; ten of these communities existed at the time of his death.

The normative rule of monasticism in the West was created by Benedict of Nursia (b. 480).[82] It was notable for its combination of rigor and common sense. Benedict's monks were among the first men in the West to affirm the dignity of labor. They were important also for their intellectual pursuits. Their threefold discipline of work, study, and prayer placed Benedictine monasticism among the primary formative impulses of Western civilization.

EARLY CHRISTIANITY IN PERSPECTIVE

By the end of the fifth century the decline of Rome was a fact too plain for denial. By this time too, the foundations of the Christian church had been firmly laid, and the historic edifice erected on these foundations, if not complete, had put up its main structures. Out of the ruins of Greco-Roman antiquity was to come a new civilization called the West, in which Christianity was destined to play a central role. This story will be related in Chapters 15 and 16 following.

Early Christianity as sketched in this chapter contained elements which are of general human interest. The figure of Christ stands along with Buddha, Confucius, Muhammad, and others as one of mankind's great religious founders; and conversely Christianity demands to be understood as a personally founded religion. To the Christian, Christ stands as the embodiment of God and the living answer to the question of man's humanity and humanization. The forms of church, creed, and theology which ancient Christianity elaborated represent one more system of holy forms constituting a religion. These forms were destined for many developments and changes in subsequent times and places. At least three distinguishable religious communities sprang in the course of time from this single source, namely, Roman Catholicism, Protestantism, and Eastern Orthodoxy.

EASTERN ORTHODOX CHRISTIANITY

Almost from the beginning of Christianity there was an observable cleavage between East and West. It was as though an invisible line had been drawn through a map of the Christian world, extending from Europe in the north through the Adriatic Sea, across the Mediterranean Sea to Africa in the south. To the west of this line lay Spain, Gaul, and Italy, centering on the Western capital, Rome; east of it lay the Balkan Peninsula, Asia Minor, and the Near East, with the Eastern capital, Constantinople. The Christianity of the West tended to be active, pragmatic, and legal, while that of the East tended to be contemplative, mystical, and passive. As centuries passed, East and West drifted further apart. Their differences widened and deepened until two forms of Christianity emerged as historic facts.

From the first, Eastern bishops resisted the claims to primacy of the Bishop of Rome. In the East the Pope's pronouncements were often ignored and sometimes openly flouted. At length, the papal claims, so central to Western, or Roman Catholic, Christianity, came in the East to be regarded as schismatic. These trends were reinforced by events of secular history. As the Western empire sank into decline, the papacy was thrust into the vacuum of power, wielding both political and religious leadership for the people of Rome and Italy. In the East there was no such decline, the imperial structure being revived and maintained by such able rulers as Justinian (527–565). The Byzantine Emperors of Constantinople held the church in close embrace, thus in effect creating the intimate and dependent relation of church to state which was to become characteristic of Eastern Orthodoxy.

One of the first results of this relation was a new compound of faith and culture often called Byzantine civilization. This new synthesis had significant features ranging from the law code of Justinian to the new style of architecture brilliantly illustrated by Justinian's new church, *Hagia Sophia* (Holy Wisdom). It was also poignantly expressed in the mosaic art which adorned the walls of Hagia Sophia and other churches. Byzantine civilization provided the cultural context for the development of Eastern Orthodox Christianity. No comparable style or culture emerged in the West.

Another notable difference between East and West lay in their responses to the ecumenical councils of the church. Beginning with the Council of Nicaea in 325 and extending through seven such meetings to the Second Council of Nicaea in 767, they were regarded in the East as primary and authoritative sources of doctrine or teaching. While the West respected the councils, it dared to disagree with or even to ignore some of them.

The coming of the Muslims in the seventh and eighth centuries posed serious problems, military, political, and religious, for all Christendom. However, these problems were more urgent in the East than in the West. Constantinople itself was placed under Muslim siege many times before its final fall to the Muslims in 1453. As Muslims captured extensive regions inhabited by Eastern Orthodox Christians, these people became minority groups within Muslim culture, a fact that greatly affected the nature of their Christian faith.

The alienation between East and West was widened and deepened during the seventh and eighth centuries by controversies over the *filioque* clause in the creed and the use of icons in Christian churches. The former problem was created by the insertion, in the West, of *filioque*, ". . . and the Son . . .," in the creed, asserting thereby that the Holy Spirit proceeds from the Father "and the Son." Eastern Christians, while not necessarily opposed to this interpretation, nevertheless regarded the insertion as improper. The iconoclastic controversy was aroused by a decree of the Eastern Emperor, Leo III, in 726, banning the use of icons, both pictures and images, in Christian churches. Leo's motive was apparently to purify the church of pagan elements which had crept in, but his decree stirred up violent opposition in both regions of the empire. In the East he and his successors were able to force compliance, though at times military power was required. In the West, resistance to the iconoclastic decree was more general and more successful. The Pope excommunicated iconoclasts. The issue continued in one form or another for a century or more. The second Council of Nicaea expounded what came to be the accepted position on icons, namely, that they might be used and honored as visible representations of the invisible power and reality of God. Yet from this time onward the Eastern church restricted her use to pictures, while both paintings and sculptures continued to be used in the Western church. Icons of the saints became a notable form of art in Eastern Christianity.

The final break between East and West came in 1054 over the issue of the rights of Roman Catholic Christians in Constantinople. The Patriarch of Constantinople closed Roman Catholic churches in that city. Papal messengers responded with a bull of excommunication from the Pope deposited on the high altar of Hagia Sophia. The Patriarch responded in kind with a decree anathematizing the Pope, and the breach was final.

Meanwhile, geographically the Eastern and Western churches continued to move farther apart. While Western Christianity moved northward and westward into France, Germany, and Great Britain, Eastern Christianity pushed into Russia. So it was that in 1453, when Constantinople, the second Rome, fell before the Muslims, the capital of Eastern Christianity was moved to Moscow, which called itself the third Rome.

The divergent ways of faith which emerged in East and West present a bewildering pattern of similarities and differences. Four main contrasts may be briefly observed. As noted above, the Eastern church was bound to government in relations both close and dependent. As will be seen in Chapters 15 and 16 on Roman Catholicism and Protestantism, the relation of church to state in the West was neither as close nor as dependent as in the East. In Western Christendom, many men over many centuries fought with swords and with ideas to maintain the independence of the church. One result has been a tradition in the West of religious criticism of society which is almost wholly absent in the East.

Related to these issues have been different views in East and West concerning the nature of the church. In the East there is no Pope or supreme ruler over all the church; rather each of the fourteen or more national churches is self-ruled, or *autocephalous*. A kind of big brotherhood, or informal primacy, has at times been exercised by the Patriarchs of Constantinople or of Moscow. However, no power except that of influence over the whole Eastern Church resides in these offices.

Eastern Orthodoxy agrees with Roman Catholicism and Protestantism in calling the church the Body of Christ. Of these three the first two, but not the third, hold the church to possess a divinely given infallibility. However, Eastern Orthodoxy differs from Rome in having no organ of infallibility. Since infallibility exists in the church in general it has little effective meaning. Eastern Orthodox Churches claim to be holy, apostolic, and catholic Christianity; they also believe that both Roman Catholicism and Protestantism have deviated from these divinely given norms.

Eastern Orthodox teaching regarding the church differs notably from the

West in emphasis. It regards the church as a divine mystery which is the central fact of human history and whose eventual, or eschatological, aim is the full divinization of man. At the center of the church is the mysterious God-man, Jesus Christ. The church communicates his divine life to its members through the sacraments. Like Roman Catholicism, Eastern Orthodoxy celebrates seven sacraments. However, their list differs, for they include anointing, or chrismation, and place the Roman sacrament of confirmation under baptism. For both Eastern Orthodoxy and Roman Catholicism the central sacrament is the Eucharist. Yet there are notable differences of interpretation. For Eastern Orthodoxy, the Eucharist is the celebration of the incarnation of God in Christ. It is thus by implication an anticipation of the eventual divinization of man.

Another notable difference between East and West is the absence in the former of any continuing tradition of theological discussion and thinking. By contrast, the West continued for many centuries to argue and discuss theological problems. Eastern Orthodox theology was summed up in the system of John of Damascus, who lived in the first half of the eighth century. His book, *The Fountain of Knowledge,* gave definitive expression to the Christianized Neoplatonism which had long been popular in the East. After John of Damascus there was intellectual stagnation. The creative energies of Eastern Christianity turned from thought to liturgy.

East and West present contrasting patterns of monasticism and asceticism. Both inherited from ancient Christianity the tradition of moral athleticism and rejection of the world sketched earlier in this chapter. Yet in the West, men like Benedict of Nursia gave to monasticism an active and social direction, with the result that monks were among the formative influences on nascent Western civilization. Monasticism in the East was by contrast more individualist, more contemplative, and more otherworldly. Even in centers of monasticism like Mount Athos in Greece, monks pursued their upward paths alone. In Eastern as in Western Christianity monks remained important figures, but they were not so much active agents as pilgrims of eternity reminding men of their eternal destiny.

Modern times have brought new problems and fiery trials to Eastern Christianity. In the twentieth century the coming of Marxian communism has frequently resulted in severe repression and persecution of the church. In Russia, new currents of religious thought and feeling during the nineteenth century did little to alter the massively conservative posture of the Russian church and its close relation to the decadent czarist government. These attitudes only served to verify for the communists their view of religion as the opiate of the people. Hence it was not surprising that the first decades of Marxian rule in Russia should be years of harsh repression of the church. The record was similar in lands adjacent to Russia. However since World War II, many of these restrictions have been removed, and Russian Christians are permitted to practice their faith. In 1961 the Russian Orthodox Church joined the World Council of Churches, reporting that it had 30,000 priests, 73 bishops, and 40 million adherents.

At present there are some fourteen independent, autocephalous Eastern Orthodox Churches, extending from Moscow to Czechoslovakia, and from Lithuania to Jerusalem. To these are joined several smaller kindred groups from places as distant as Finland, Japan, the United States, Canada, and Australia. It is estimated that the total number of Eastern Christians is approximately 180 million. Increasingly these groups are leaving their former isolation for new contacts with other Christians and other religious groups.

CONCLUDING COMMENT

Seeking to summarize this long chapter that has depicted the origin and rise to power and prominence of the Christian religion, we ask: What distinctive forms of ultimate concern or value are to be found in early Christianity? Our answer must first repeat what has been said in Chapter 2, namely that ultimate concern is a secularized formulation of the Great Commandment to love supremely or give total allegiance to the one God. From this source spring the primary values of faith, hope, and love that fulfill or perfect human life.

As we saw in the previous chapter, Judaism and Christianity share this basic monotheistic faith, but the symbolic forms in which this faith finds expression differ. Where the Jew approaches God by doing the Torah, the Christian has faith in Christ; where the Jew interprets Torah by means of the Talmud, the Christian interpretation of Christ has taken the form of creed and theology.

This latter difference leads directly to still another difference, namely that while Judaism drew away from the Greek culture of the ancient Mediterranean world, early Christianity moved into the midst of that world, stating its case in terms of Greco-Roman thought and culture. In this way Christianity effected a synthesis of Greek and Hebraic elements of fundamental importance to all subsequent Western civilization. The ideas and events of this chapter thus constitute a formative phase in the history of the West.

Embodied in this Christian synthesis of Greek and Hebraic elements is a humanistic ideal concerning man; he is made in the divine image and capable of fulfilling and perfecting his life by values drawn from both Greek and Hebraic sources. But in tension with what may thus be termed Christian humanism, there were other tendencies present in early Christianity, illustrated by extremists like Tertullian. These men tended to push the new religion toward the kind of transcendence that does not fulfill, but negates, man's humanity. Both the humanistic, and the anti-humanistic trends have continued in tension through medieval and modern ages.

If we ask now which type of religion has been described in this chapter, the answer is that early Christianity is clearly and centrally an example of historical monotheism. However the Christian synthesis also contained trends or tendencies toward both cosmic and acosmic types. In the Hellenistic world which was the environment of early Christianity both Gnosticism and Neoplatonism were acosmic; this tendency persisted within Christianity. Popular religion in the ancient Mediterranean world, as in other times and places, was notably cosmic in outlook, and this tendency too continued within Christianity.

NOTES

1. Floyd V. Filson, *The New Testament against Its Environment,* SCM Press, London, 1956.

2. Samuel Angus, *The Religious Quests of the Graeco-Roman World,* Charles Scribner's Sons, New York, 1929.

3. See *inter alia* Ernest F. Scott, *The Literature of the New Testament,* Columbia University Press, New York, 1932, p. 21; Eric Titus, *Essentials to New Testament Study,* The Ronald Press Company, New York, 1958, p. 28.

4. Scott, *op. cit.,* pp. 21–32.

5. Romans 1:3; Galatians 4:4.

6. Luke 3:1.

7. Luke 3:10–18.

8. See *inter alia* Theodor H. Gaster, *The Dead Sea Scriptures,* Doubleday & Company, Inc., Garden City, N.Y., 1956, p. 12.

9. Mark 1:11.

10. Mark 1:15.

11. Luke 4:16.

12. Mark 8:27f.

13. Matthew 16:13f.; Mark 8:27f.; Luke 9:18f.

14. Matthew 16:20.

15. Matthew 26:64.

16. See *inter alia* John Knox, *The Man Christ Jesus,* Willett, Clark & Co., Chicago, 1942, pp. 28f.; and John Knox, *Christ, the Lord,* Willett, Clark & Co., Chicago, 1945, p. 36n.

17. John Wick Bowman, *The Intention of Jesus,* The Westminster Press, Philadelphia, 1943, pp. 159ff.

18. Matthew 17:1f.; Mark 9:2; Luke 9:28f.

19. Luke 9:51.

20. Luke 9:37–18:31.

21. See Albert Schweitzer, *The Quest of the Historical Jesus,* A. & C. Black, Ltd., London, 1936, pp. 7–11.

22. Matthew 21:12f.

23. Vincent Taylor, *The Life and Ministry of Our Lord Jesus,* The Macmillan Company, New York, 1955, pp. 179–182.

24. Mark 14:64.

25. Mark 15:26.

26. Martin Buber, *The Prophetic Faith,* The Macmillan Company, New York, 1949, pp. 96ff.

27. See *inter alia* Deuteronomy 6; Jeremiah 31; Hosea 11.

28. Leviticus 19:18.

29. Matthew 6:33.

30. Mark 12:28–31.

31. Matthew 5:17f.

32. Luke 10:30–37.

33. Luke 12:42–48.

34. Luke 18:9.

35. Matthew 5:17.

36. I Corinthians 15:3–8.

37. I Corinthians 15:50.

38. II Corinthians 5:1–6.

39. Acts 2:4f.

40. Acts 2:41.

41. I Corinthians 13:1, 14:2.

42. Acts 1:4.

43. Acts 5:1–11.

44. Acts 5:34.

45. Acts 4:19.

46. Acts 6:1–3.

47. Acts 7.

48. Acts 10.

49. Acts 9:1–10.

50. Acts 26:19.

51. Galatians 1:17.

52. Acts 13:13f.

53. Acts 15; Galatians 2.

54. Acts 16:9.

55. Philippians 2:6–11.

56. Galatians 5 and 6.

57. Romans 2 and 3.

58. Galatians 5:1f.

59. Galatians 5:22.

60. John 1:1f.

61. Revelations 19:11f.

62. Hebrews 5:1f.

63. Pliny's letter to Trajan regarding Christians in Bithynia, in Henry B. Bettenson, *Documents of the Christian Church*, Oxford University Press, Fair Lawn, N.J., 1947, pp. 5–7.

64. *Ibid.*, p. 7.

65. Justin's "Apology" in *ibid.*, pp. 8f.

66. *Ibid.*, p. 8.

67. Charles Bigg, *The Christian Platonists of Alexandria*, Oxford University Press, London, 1913, p. 276.

68. Williston Walker, *A History of the Christian Church*, Charles Scribner's Sons, New York, 1954, p. 76.

69. Bettenson, *op. cit.*, pp. 9f.

70. Walker, *op. cit.*, p. 59.

71. Bettenson, *op. cit.*, p. 51.

72. John H. Leith, ed., *Creeds of the Churches*, Doubleday & Company, Inc., Garden City, N.Y., 1963, p. 24.

73. Walker, *op. cit.*, p. 56.

74. *Ibid.*, p. 108.

75. Bettenson, *op. cit.*, p. 37.

76. *Ibid.*, pp. 72–73.

77. Walker, *op. cit.*, p. 57.

78. *Ibid.*, p. 67.

79. *Ibid.*, p. 67.

80. *Ibid.*, p. 62.

81. *Ibid.*, p. 124.

82. *Ibid.*, p. 127.

SUGGESTIONS FOR FURTHER STUDY

Ayer, J.: *A Source Book for Ancient Church History*, Scribner, 1913.

Bettenson, H.: *Documents of the Christian Church*, Oxford, 1947.

Bornkamm, G.: *Jesus of Nazareth*, Harper & Row, 1960.

Bowman, J.: *The Intention of Jesus*, Westminster Press, 1943.

Bultmann, R.: *Theology of the New Testament*, Scribner, 1955.

———: *Primitive Christianity*, Meridian Books, 1958.

Chadwick, H. (ed.): *Alexandrian Christianity*, Westminster Press, 1954.

Cochrane, C.: *Christianity and Classical Culture*, Oxford, 1940.

Enslin, M.: *Christian Beginnings*, Harper, 1938.

Ferm, R.: *Readings in the History of Christian Thought*, Holt, 1964.

Kee, H., and F. Young: *Understanding the New Testament*, Prentice-Hall, 1958.

Klausner, J.: *From Jesus to Paul*, Macmillan, 1943.

Knox, J.: *Jesus: Lord and Christ*, Harper & Row, 1958.

Latourette, K.: *A History of Christianity*, Harper & Row, 1945.

McGiffert, A.: *A History of Christian Thought*, Scribner, 1933.

Nock, A.: *Conversion*, Oxford, 1933.

———: *Early Gentile Christianity*, Harper & Row, 1964.

Richardson, C.: *The Church through the Centuries*, Scribner, 1938.

——— (ed.): *Early Christian Fathers*, Westminster Press, 1953.

Scott, E. F.: *Literature of the New Testament*, Columbia, 1932.

Streeter, B.: *The Four Gospels*, Macmillan, 1930.

Walker, W.: *A History of the Christian Church* (rev. ed.), Scribner, 1954.

Zernov, N.: *Eastern Christendom*, Weidenfeld and Nicolson, 1961.

14

ISLAM

The present chapter on Islam may appear to interrupt our continuous account of the Judeo-Christian tradition in the Western world. The immediate reply is that history first made this interruption. That is to say, in the seventh and eighth centuries Islam burst upon Christian Europe—and many other lands as well. The rise of Islam to a position of imperial rule which was maintained for a longer time and over more extensive territory than Rome constitutes a large fact of human history. If Western history textbooks accord meager and grudging acknowledgment of this large historic fact, this is only one more bit of evidence for provincialism on the part of Western historians and Western peoples.[1]

The classification of Islam among the world's faiths and hence the placing of the present chapter in this book constitutes a thorny problem. Clearly Islam is a monotheistic or type-three religion, and is of Near Eastern origin. But it is also a fact that today Islam's four hundred odd million adherents are scattered over the world in utter disregard for typological considerations. There is a Muslim zone extending along the equator from Morocco in North Africa through the Arab states to Iran, Pakistan, and India and thence to Indonesia and the Philippines, which comprises the vast majority of the world's Muslims. Outside this zone are the approximately fifty million Muslims of China, another thirty million in Negro regions of Africa, and approximately 800,000 in the Western world. Whatever else it may be, Islam is a world religion and demands attention as such.[2]

It makes many other forceful and valid claims to attention. Toynbee has characterized the Muslim Near East as a foil for the West.[3] In recent times many Muslim nations, from the Arab countries to Pakistan and Indonesia, have risen to challenge Western ways of politics and society. In Negro regions of Africa, Islam's genuine commitment to racial equality has gained a ready hearing for this faith at precisely the time when Negro Africans have come to view Christianity as a pious front for white racism.

Looking over the course of Muslim history the student may observe here in concentrated form many of the issues inherent in type-three, or monotheistic, faith. For example, allegiance to the one God leads to the rejection of other gods as false idols. Islam's expression of this principle is the idea of *shirk,* which is the unforgivable sin. *Shirk* means "association," that is, the association of anything creaturely with the absolutely unique and holy God, or what in previous chapters we have termed idolatry. While all of the monotheistic faiths are conscious of this idea, Islam may be said to develop its implications in most consistent—and extreme—form.

There is also an expression of this extreme monotheism in the rejection of *Muhammadanism* and insistence on *Islam* as the name of this faith.[4] *Islam* means "submission," that is, to the one God, and a Muslim is accordingly one who submits. Muslims regard their founder as prophet and ideal man, denying any imputation of divinity or deification as inconsistent with monotheism; hence they reject *Muhammadanism* as a name for what is properly Islam, the faith, founded by the Prophet, and consisting of those who joyfully submit themselves to God's will.

Again, the monotheistic faiths are religions of a Book, yet only in Islam is this taken to the extreme implied in the idea of an original Qur'an, perfect and in heaven, of which the earthly Arabic Book is only a divinely certified copy. While "Biblical literalism" is by no means limited to Islam—or for that matter, to monotheistic religions—it does find particularly vivid illustration in Islam.

Still again, monotheistic faiths in their zeal and activism have not infrequently produced fanaticism, and in particular that concentrated form of fanaticism called "holy war," in Arabic, *jihad.* Holy wars have by no means been limited to monotheism; indeed there seems to be a recurrent human tendency to put God on our side, rather than putting us—and all men—under God. Yet fanaticism and holy war do seem to find particularly ready sanction from monotheistic faiths, as the Judeo-Christian Bible, the Zoroastrian Avesta, and the Qur'an all show. None of these phenomena is limited to Islam, yet all of them find significant illustration in Muslim history.

ARABIAN SOURCE REGION

Like all religions, Islam has been significantly influenced by its social and historical context. Indeed, like other monotheistic faiths—and unlike such faiths as Buddhism—Islam has affirmed and not denied or annulled the particular geographical and historical facts that lie at its base.

A glance at the map of the Arabian peninsula shows several inhabited and civilized regions surrounding the desert quarter. At the end of the sixth century these regions were roughly as follows. To the east lay Iraq, and beyond it the powerful Persian empire under the Sassanid dynasty. The Persians controlled the trade routes to central Asia and China. To the west lay Syria and Asia Minor, which were parts of the Byzantine empire. Across the Red Sea from Mecca was Abyssinia, which was generally friendly to Byzantium. At the southwest corner of Arabia lay Yemen, often under Persian influence.

The Arabs of the region of Mecca were thus caught between the two great powers of Byzantium and Persia. Mecca also lay on the economic crossroads, along the caravan routes between east and west. As a consequence, her people prospered in commerce and finance. Mecca was a flourishing, enterprising center of trade. It was also a religious center for extensive regions of Arabia, possessing as it did the large cube-shaped temple called the Ka'ba with the famous Black Stone set in the southeast corner. Pilgrims came from afar on *hajj*, or pilgrimage, to circumambulate the temple, to kiss the Black Stone, and worship the many icons within the temple. So important to Mecca was this custom that tribal wars and raids were suspended for four months of pilgrimage each year.

Pilgrims could also visit the well *Zemzem,* which popular tradition said had originated with Ishmael, son of Abraham and Hagar. Arabs believed themselves the sons of Ishmael, who, when he and his mother were driven out by Sarah, had come to Mecca. One story had it that as his mother frantically searched for water, little Ishmael lay on the ground and kicked. Where his heel struck, there the water of Zemzem sprang up. This well, which had been filled with rubble for centuries, was relocated and dug out by Muhammad's grandfather. Pilgrims also could run with shaking shoulders between two nearby hills as Hagar had done; and they could throw stones down a gorge at evil spirits and their chief, Satan.

The wider pattern of Arab religion was a mosaic of diverse beliefs and practices. Many in the Arabian region were at least nominally Christian, and there were also Jewish communities from Asia Minor to Yemen and to Iraq. For many Arab peoples there was a distant Supreme Being named Allah. The term *Allah* means not "a god" but "the God." For popular piety there were other deities closer at hand, and more influential in human behavior. At Mecca there were three goddesses, sometimes called daughters of Allah: Al Lat, a mother goddess, Al Manat, a female deity of fate, and Al Uzzah, of the morning star. There were also innumerable fairies, jinn, and ghouls who inhabited innumerable objects of nature and society. Fairies were generally favorable to men, jinn were capricious, and ghouls consistently malignant. All this constituted an animism (and animatism) in which the world was alive with all kinds of spirits and powers.

THE PROPHET'S LIFE

Into the Arabian scene Muhammad was born, according to Muslim historians on April 20, 571.[5] The name means "highly praised." His father had died before Muhammad's birth, and his mother died six years later. He was taken into the family of his grandfather, Abd al-Muttalib, and on his death three years later into the family of his uncle, Abu Talib, who became his lifelong friend and supporter.

Muslim tradition tells many stories of the Prophet's piety, sensitivity, and integrity. Apparently well founded is the report of the name *al-Amin,* meaning "the true and reliable one," which his friends gave him.[6] As a youth he was a shepherd and camel driver, making trips to Yemen and to Syria. Also as a young man he participated in tribal councils and affairs.

On the recommendation of his uncle, Abu Talib, he went to work for a rich widow named Khadijah, managing caravans for her. So well did he perform his duties and so great was their mutual attraction that when he was twenty-five he married Khadijah, who was fifteen years his elder. The marriage was eminently successful. During Khadijah's lifetime the Prophet took no other wives, and even after her death he spoke so well of her that his other wives became jealous. She bore him five children, two sons and three daughters, of whom only one daughter, Fatima, survived infancy. The Prophet was a devoted husband and father.

During the years of his marriage to Khadijah, his religious interests were maturing. Beneath the surface were developing those forces which burst forth in his call to be the Prophet. Apparently his faith in the one God deepened, and with it his repulsion at idolatry and his sense of an impending Judgment Day. It was a period of increasing spiritual stress. What influence, if any, came from Christian or Jewish sources is beyond reliable knowledge. For several years he retired for a month to Mount Hira for solitary meditation—the practice which lies behind Muslim celebration of Ramadan. During this time he was sustained and stimulated by Khadijah.

Then in February, 610, on what Muslims call the Night of Power and Glory, the angel Gabriel, chief messenger of Allah, appeared, confronting him with an awe-inspiring summons. As recorded in the Qur'an, the Voice said:

> Read; In the name of thy Lord who createth,
> Createth man from a clot.
> Read: And thy Lord is the Most Bounteous
> Who teacheth by the pen,
> Teacheth man that which he knew not.[7]

So was given the first fragment of the Qur'an. The angel disappeared, leaving Muhammad in deep distress. Then outside the cave he heard the same Voice assuring him, "O Muhammad, Thou art Allah's messenger. . . ." [8] The experience had a shattering impact. Muhammad hastened home to tell Khadijah of his experience—and of his fear that he had been duped by demons or that he had gone mad. She reassured him. Then, according to tradition, they both went to her elderly cousin, Warakah, who was familiar with Jewish and Christian scriptures. When they told him of Muhammad's encounter with Gabriel he affirmed his belief, saying "Doubtless it is the beginning of prophecy, and there shall come upon him the Great Law like as it came upon Moses." [9]

As so often in the history of religions, it is doubtless impossible here decisively to separate fact from traditional interpretation. Yet one may safely assume a time of anguished questioning, then of reintegration and redirection as Muhammad took to himself the full force and significance of his experience and came to recognize himself as what the Voice had called him, namely, the Prophet (nabi) and Apostle (rasul) of Allah.

Other messages from God followed, though slowly at first. In obedience to the divine Voice which had put him under orders, the Prophet began to preach, proclaiming the message he had received. During the first years, results were meager. A few converts were made—but only a few. First was his wife Khadijah, then his cousin, Abu Talib's son Ali, then a servant and adopted son Zaid, then his friend Abu Bekr.

As for the people of Mecca, at first they laughed—as men have so often laughed at those who come with a message from God. Surely this dreamer with his dire warnings of impending judgment was a madman! They smiled and turned away.

But scornful laughter turned to hostility as they saw in the Prophet's public words a threat to the popular religion and the profitable pilgrimage trade. His uncompromising monotheism with its austere moral demands were deeply disturbing to men of the world. Hostility took the form of persecution. Hoodlums broke up his public meetings. His followers became the victims of discrimina-

tion and attack. On at least two occasions during this Meccan period the
Prophet sent small groups of followers abroad to Abyssinia to escape persecution. At home the Prophet's tribe, the Hashimites, were confined to a single
section of the city. Only the courageous stand of Abu Talib prevented more
aggressive action against the Prophet and his followers.

Meanwhile revelations continued to come. They have found their way into
the Qur'an, and are identified by modern scholars of Islam as revealed at Mecca.
Many of them have a strong sense of social justice, and all are pervaded with
a foreboding sense of doom and judgment. Here is a sample of *Suras,* or sections
of the Qur'an, received by the Prophet in Mecca.

> *When the sun is overthrown,*
> *And when the stars fall,*
> *And when the hills are moved,*
> *And when the camels big with young are abandoned,*
> *And when the wild beasts are herded together,*
> *And when the seas rise,*
> *And when souls are reunited,*
> *And when the girl child that was buried alive is asked*
> *For what sin she was slain . . .*
> *(Then) every soul will know what it hath made ready.*[10]

> *Every soul is a pledge for its own deeds;*
> *Save those who will stand on the right hand.*
> *In gardens they will ask one another*
> *Concerning the guilty:*
> *What hath brought you to this burning?*
> *They will answer: We were not of those who prayed*
> *Nor did we feed the wretched.*[11]

> *Nay, I swear by this city—*
> *And thou art an indweller of this city—*
> *And the begetter and that which he begat,*
> *We verily have created man in an atmosphere:*
> *Thinketh he that none hath power over him?*
> *And he saith: I have destroyed vast wealth:*
> *Thinketh he that none beholdeth him?*
> *Did We not assign unto him two eyes*
> *And a tongue and two lips,*
> *And guide him to the parting of the mountain ways?*
> *But he hath not attempted the Ascent—*
> *Ah, what will convey unto thee what the Ascent is!—*
> *It is to free a slave,*
> *And to feed in the day of hunger*
> *An orphan near of kin,*

Or some poor wretch in misery,
And to be of those who believe and exhort one another to
*   perseverance and exhort one another to pity.*
Their place will be on the right hand.
But those who disbelieve Our revelations, their place will
*   be on the left hand.*
Fire will be an awning over them.[12]

In obedience to the Divine Voice the Prophet continued to preach and teach. The year 619 (or 3 B.H., meaning three years before the *Hegira*) was a low point in his life. Abu Talib died, and shortly thereafter Khadijah. Small wonder that Muhammad afterward called it "the year of suffering." During this year he took another wife, Sawdah, widow of a follower who had just returned from the Abyssinian migration.

During this same year, he was also visited by a delegation of six men from Yathrib, a city some three hundred miles to the northwest. Their city needed new leadership; perhaps Muhammad would come to take charge. A delegation of twelve returned the following year and took an oath to abstain from all polytheism and vices and to observe the strict discipline required of the Prophet's followers. A Meccan follower returned to Yathrib with them, and the following year, the first year before the Hegira, a larger delegation, seventy-five men, came from Yathrib to swear allegiance and confess their faith—and to urge the Prophet to come to their city.

Muslim tradition tells of a change in the Prophet's tactics. Until now he had relied upon teaching and preaching to put his message into effect. Now he began to plan in terms of political and even military action. Tradition also tells of a last desperate attempt of his enemies to prevent his leaving Mecca. However, he was warned of a plot to assassinate him, and hid out with a few friends in a cave on Mount Thaur. When his enemies had passed, he together with Abu Bekr and a few other followers mounted camels and made the Hegira (withdrawal) to Yathrib, customarily a journey of eleven days, in only eight days. Thus occurred the crucial event of Muslim history. *Anno Hegira* 1, or A.H. 1 (A.D. 622) marked the beginning of the Muslim era, from which dates are still reckoned. The way of Islam was launched upon the world.

The problems in Yathrib were vast and uncharted, but the Prophet moved decisively and with a unique kind of authority which combined religious and ethical leadership with political and social leadership. He and his followers created in Yathrib (now renamed Medina, "the city") a new state and a new social order which is still regarded as the archetypal model for Muslims every-where. Records of the Muslim community of Medina in Qur'an and tradition have been studied by Muslims throughout their history as the model for all men to emulate.

While the Prophet was accorded an authority well-nigh absolute, Muslim writers point out that he acted only upon careful consultation and in full cooperation with others.[13] He proceeded first to reorganize, literally to re-form, the religious practices of the city. He erected a house of worship, the first mosque, and worked out a cultus and institution which would be pleasing to Allah. Weekly services on Friday, prayer five times daily, the call to prayer from the mosque roof, prostration during prayer, alms for the poor—these and other arrangements followed in order. At first the direction in which one faced while praying (*qibla*) was toward Jerusalem, for the Prophet had both understanding and respect for Jewish or Biblical tradition, thinking of his movement as a fulfillment of it. He was first puzzled then incensed when the Jewish community of Medina scorned him. He broke with them openly, ordering the direction of prayer to be toward Mecca.

The Prophet's great gifts of leadership were soon turned outward to foreign relations, in which he made many wise treaties of alliance with neighboring peoples, and also organized an army for Medina. Muslim writers point out the essentially defensive character of these moves, adding quotations from the Qur'an deprecating war and violence.[14]

However this may be, Medina was soon involved in military operations. Again the Prophet proved himself a brilliant leader. In the celebrated Battle of the Ditch, he used trench warfare in the successful defense of his city. Soon however the enemies of Medina, including Meccans, were intercepting and plundering Medina's caravans. Military operations back and forth seemed to be halted by Muhammad's proposal of a ten-year truce between the cities, in exchange for which the followers of the Prophet were to have the right of pilgrimage to Mecca. However, when an ally of Mecca attacked a friend of Medina the agreement broke down. The Prophet denounced the truce, marched in force on Mecca, and captured it in the year 630.

One of his first acts was to go to worship in the Ka'ba. After circumambulating the temple and honoring the Black Stone, he ordered the destruction of the many idols within and the obliteration from its walls of paintings of Abraham and others. But the Prophet proved to be a magnanimous victor. His previous enemies were pardoned, and the Meccan pilgrimage was opened to all who would accept Islam. Pagan tribes within the city were given a grace period of four months to accept the new faith. If they refused they would thereafter be subject to attack as threats to Islam. This new principle of jihad was qualified in the case of Jews and Christians. Since they were also "people of a Book," they had the option of retaining their faith if they submitted to Muslim government and paid a special tax. Muhammad continued to believe that Jews and Christians were not idolaters, but members of the tradition which was being completed in his own revelations.

Muhammad was now well on the way to his goal of the unification of all Arab peoples. In the last ten years of his life he personally led no less than twenty-seven military campaigns, and planned thirty-eight others. In A.H. 9 (A.D. 631) he personally led a campaign against Byzantine forces at Tabouk which seemed about to attack his Muslim forces. Other such attacks were being planned when the Prophet succumbed to mortal illness.

An Episode From the Life of the Prophet. Sixteenth-century Turkish painting

Courtesy of the Museum of Fine Arts, Boston

In A.H. 10 (A.D. 632) he made his last pilgrimage to Mecca. On Mount Arafat he gave a farewell discourse to his followers, warning them as ever of the impending Last Judgment, and admonishing them to hold to the beliefs and duties incumbent upon all Muslims, concluding with the words: "O ye men! hearken unto my words and take ye them to heart! Know ye that every Moslem is a brother to every other Moslem, and that ye are now one brotherhood." [15]

It was Abu Bekr who bore to the gathering of stunned followers the news of the Prophet's death. Bluntly he declared: "O people! Lo! as for him who used to worship Muhammad, Muhammad is dead. But as for who used to worship Allah, Allah is alive and dieth not."[16]

MUHAMMAD'S TEACHING: THE MUSLIM CREED

The teachings of the Prophet—or as he and his followers would hasten to correct us, the teachings revealed by Allah to the Prophet—comprise the 114 Suras of the Qur'an. If to this be added the authenticated hadiths, or "traditions," the student has all the primary sources of the Muslim faith. It is a characteristically simple and forthright faith. The faithful Muslim responds to God by saying, in effect, "I hear and do." Muslim doctrine is what is heard, and Muslim duty is what is to be done.

The absolutely fundamental beliefs are remarkably few and simple, comprising in one traditional formulation, belief in the unity of God, in the prophetic mission of Muhammad, and in the impending Judgment Day for all men.[17]

Any exposition of Muslim doctrine must begin—and end—with the one God, Allah, majestic, holy, transcendent, absolutely unique. He alone is absolute sovereign of the universe, and to him alone must be given man's absolute allegiance and service. As previously noted, the word Islam means "submission," that is, submission to Allah. Not only does he rule all that exists, but he created the universe in the beginning, calling it into being out of nothingness, and he will bring it to the awful consummation of Judgment Day. Truly Allah is Lord of beginning and end.

As noted above, for Islam the unforgivable sin is shirk, or association of anything creaturely with the unique and transcendent glory of Allah. Islam is monotheism that is as pure—and as extreme—as any monotheism in history.

Of this one God, man can speak only by negation and metaphor. From man's creaturely viewpoint, he can say what God is not, thereby illustrating what many faiths have termed the via negativa. Thus it may be asserted that Allah does not partake of any creaturely limitation. By metaphor or analogy, human tongues may say a few things about Allah. Muslim piety has elaborated "The Ninety-Nine Beautiful Names."[18] Of these, clearly the most frequent is "The Merciful," or "The Compassionate." Each Sura of the Qur'an begins with the words "In the Name of Allah, the Beneficent, the Merciful."[19] To secular readers of the Qur'an, Allah often seems stern and harsh rather than compassionate. Nowhere does this stern demeanor appear more clearly than in the pictures of Judgment Day and its consequences, heaven and hell. Yet even here, followers of the Prophet assure us that Allah's compassion is manifested in warning men of the wrath to come.

The Qur'an's descriptions of Judgment and of heaven and hell are vivid and
concrete, as the following samples show:

When the heavens shall be rent asunder,
And when the stars shall be dispersed,
And when the seas shall be commingled,
And when the graves shall be upturned,
A soul will know what it has sent forward and kept back.
O man, what has led thee away from thy generous Lord?
Who created thee and formed thee and shaped thee rightly,
Building thee up in such form as He willed?
Nay, indeed, but ye count the judgment as something false,
Yet over you, indeed, are guardians,
Noble ones, those who write.
They know what ye do.
Verily, the righteous [shall be] in delight,
While the wicked assuredly [will be] in Jahim [a name for Hell],
Where they will roast on the Judgment Day,
And they may not be absent therefrom.
What will teach thee what the Day of Judgment is?
Again, what will teach thee what the Day of Judgment is?
It is a Day when no soul will avail aught for another soul,
    but the matter on that Day will be with Allah.[20]

When that which must inevitably come has come,
[And] as to its coming there is no falsity,
[A coming which will cause] abasing [for some and for others] exalting.
When the earth will be shaken a shaking,
And the mountains will be pounded a pounding,
So that they become as scattered dust,
Then ye will be three groups.
The Companions of the Right Hand, what are the Companions
    of the Right Hand?
And the Companions of the Left Hand, what are the Companions
    of the Left Hand?
And those who have precedence, those who have precedence,
They are those who are brought near
In gardens of delight,
Quite a number from the former generations,
And a few from the latter,
On couches inlaid [with jewels]
On which they will recline facing one another,
While around them circle immortal celestial youths (wildan)
With goblets and ewers and a cup from a flowing spring,
From which they will suffer no headache nor will they become intoxicated.
Also with such fruits as they may choose,
And such flesh of fowl as they may desire.
And large-eyed celestial damsels (huris)
Like unto hidden pearls,
A reward for what they have been doing.[21]

The mercy of Allah is also shown in his sending messengers or prophets to mankind. The Qur'an mentions some twenty-eight prophets of whom eighteen are Jewish, three Christian, and four Arabian. One, incidentally, is Alexander the Great. Five prophetic predecessors of Muhammad are accorded special homage: Adam, Noah, Abraham, Moses, and Jesus. Concerning Jesus, the Qur'an affirms his virgin birth, but teaches that his crucifixion and resurrection were apparent rather than real. It repeats some of his moral teachings but says nothing concerning his lordship or divinity, which for Muslims would constitute shirk, or violation of monotheism. According to Muslim views, to Jesus was given a portion of the truth more completely to be revealed to Muhammad; therefore Christians are in Muslim eyes heretics who cling to partial truth when the full truth is available.

Muhammad is in this succession "the Seal of the prophets," the final decisive prophet after whom no more will come. He is God's decisive messenger to

Sixteenth-century Persian Qur'an cover
Courtesy of The Metropolitan Museum of Art, gift of Henry G. Marquand, 1891

whom the oracles of the Qur'an were vouchsafed. Muslim piety has also cast him in the role of ideal man, who went through all the stages of life and all its varied roles, leaving a model for all mankind to emulate. It would violate Muslim monotheism to claim more than this.

In addition to prophets, the Qur'an teaches the existence of other incidental but by no means unimportant messengers from God, namely, angels. It was the angel Gabriel who addressed Muhammad on the Night of Power and Glory. But Gabriel is only one of the heavenly court of angels. While angels are superhuman, they are creatures whose function, like that of other creatures, is to serve and praise the one God. They also serve such functions as recording human actions, witnessing for or against men at Judgment Day and guarding the gates of hell.

In addition to angels, according to the Qur'an, there are also jinn, similar to men but of different substance. Some jinn are believers, and some are infidels. The latter are called *shaitin* and their leader, "the Shaitin," is God's adversary and the tempter of humankind. Muslim teaching is that until the Last Day he has authority over all the souls which he can seduce.

Page from Qur'an
Courtesy of The Metropolitan Museum of Art, Rodgers Fund, 1942

Allah makes known his will to mankind in the Qur'an. The word *Qur'an* means "recital" or "reading," that is, of Allah's words, given to the Prophet, which in its written form becomes *Kitab,* or "scripture." Muslims point to the fact that as he was receiving these messages from God the Prophet was in a state of divine inspiration which included such accompaniments as physical exalta- tion, changes of weight and state, and not least of all his own testimony that the words were not his but God's. Many of the Prophet's own words have been preserved in *hadiths,* to be discussed later. Islam has taught that the words of the true Qur'an are "uncreated" or divine words. Of this the earthly Arabic book is only a supernaturally certified, earthly copy.

All this is true despite the miscellaneous character of the Qur'an, where lofty speculations or somber reflections on the Last Judgment lie side by side with directions on how to enter a house or other equally homely details. To the secular reader these features reflect details of the Prophet's biography and especially his particular religious experience. This particularity of detail has never deflected Muslims from their traditional view of the Qur'an as Allah's Word to mankind, and the Prophet as the divinely appointed though entirely human vehicle of this communication.

The power and style of the Qur'an are marks of classical Arabic literature at its best. These features are often adduced by Muslim scholars as evidence of its unique inspiration: only God could create anything so uniquely good. Only recently have some Muslims sanctioned the translation of the Qur'an into other languages, and even so it is held to be the "meaning" which is thus rendered, rather than the text which is translated.[22]

As for the process by which the Qur'an was committed to writing, the Prophet's hearers memorized many passages as they heard them, thus becoming "Qur'an bearers." [23] Many of them wrote down what they heard on pieces of parchment, wood, leather, or whatever was available. Tradition has counted up twenty-nine such recorders in Medina and a smaller number in Mecca. During the first years a process of oral transmission took place, but as death took more and more of the Qur'an bearers, the need for a written record became apparent. Under the second Caliph, Umar, the Qur'an was put into writing. Only passages certified by two witnesses were accepted.

Modern critical scholarship has not proceeded far in the study of the Qur'an. Different Suras have been identified as early or late, and as given in Mecca or Medina, and some developments in the Prophet's thought have been noted. The Meccan Suras tend to be shorter, more rhythmic, and poetic, and to deal

Qur'an stand
Courtesy of The Metropolitan Museum of Art,
Rodgers Fund, 1910

with fundamental aspects of Muslim faith. The Medinian Suras are generally longer and tend to deal with specific issues and problems of the first Muslim community. Some Suras cannot be placed with any degree of precision.

Turning from doctrine to duty, the student encounters the so-called Five Pillars of Islam: (1) confession, (2) prayer, (3) fasting, (4) almsgiving, and (5) pilgrimage. They will be described in order.

The first Pillar, confession, is the lifelong obligation laid upon all Muslims to confess their faith, or bear their witness to the faith. This customarily consists of a recital of the *shahada: "la ilaha illa'llah muhammadun rasulu'llah"*— "There is no god but God (Allah), and Muhammad is his Prophet (or Apostle)." These words are omnipresent in the Muslim world, and it is often asserted that simply to repeat them is to convert to Islam. However, orthodox theologians insist that to be effective six conditions must be met: they must be (1) repeated aloud, (2) perfectly understood, (3) believed in the heart, (4) professed till death, (5) recited correctly, and (6) recited without hesitation.[24]

The second Pillar is prayer, which is the daily enactment in word and deed of the Muslim's living relation to Allah. In communities where there is a mosque, which is primarily a house of prayer, the call comes from the *muezzin* atop the minaret, yet solitary Muslims must fulfill this duty without such visual and auditory reminders.

Daily prayer occurs five times: at dawn, noon, mid-afternoon, evening, and night. Liturgical prayer (*salat*) is preceded by ritual purification; and the customary use of prayer rugs is an effort to secure purity of place. In a state of purity the Muslim faces the Ka'ba, the sacred shrine of Mecca, and performs the prescribed prayers, prostrations, and recitation of Quranic passages. Besides the five prescribed daily prayers, many devout Muslims observe additional daily periods of prayer, some individual and some at the mosque.

Friday is the day of public prayer at the mosque, though it must be added that unlike the Jewish Sabbath or Christian Sunday, Friday has never been a "day of rest" in Muslim lands. The service is customarily held at noon or at sunset in the mosque's paved courtyard, under the leadership of the *imam*. The faithful assemble at the call from the minaret, remove their shoes, perform ablutions, and sit quietly while a reader (*qari*) recites passages of the Qur'an. When the imam appears, he may preach a sermon. However, he is basically not a priest or clergyman but rather a leader of prayer, and his chief function is to lead the congregation in this form of worship. As he repeats the ritual words with bowing and prostration, the congregation follows his actions. Mosques are marked with a niche indicating the direction (*qibla*) of the sacred shrine of Mecca. Attached to the mosque may also be teachers, or *ulama*, who are learned in the Qur'an and Muslim tradition. They are men of great importance in Islam; and the great Muslim universities are related to the faith by this means.

In addition to daily and Friday prayers, Islam prescribes prayers for all occasions of life such as births, weddings, and funerals. Like many other faiths, its ideal is to hallow all of life.

Muslims at prayer in the Mosque of the 'Amr. Painting by nineteenth-century French artist, Jean León Gérôme

Courtesy of The Metropolitan Museum of Art, bequest of Catharine Lorillard Woolfe, 1887

The third Pillar is fasting during the sacred month of Ramadan, in commemoration of the Prophet's practice. This obligation is considered binding upon all Muslims, and consists of abstaining from food, drink, and sex from a time in the morning when a white thread may be distinguished from a black one until that time in the evening when they can no longer be distinguished. The essentially nonascetic character of Islam is emphasized by the relaxation of these prohibitions and the general rejoicing and festivity which take place at night. In the lunar calendar of Islam, the holy month may come at different times of the solar year, and its occurrence during the hot months of summer renders the discipline stringent indeed.

The fourth Pillar is almsgiving (*zakat*), which is an obligation like the Biblical tithe on the individual person to contribute a fixed portion of income to such good causes as the relief of the poor or the freeing of slaves. The amount is normally one-fortieth of one's annual income. In early times the zakat was a tax levied on the faithful, but now it is a purely personal and private obligation.

Linked to almsgiving in some formulations of Muslim faith is the wider principle of social responsibility and social welfare which it illustrates. The traditional operation of zakat has led to the broader idea of law (*shari'a*) as the constitutive principle of the Muslim community. To these moral and social principles we shall return presently.

The fifth Pillar of the faith is pilgrimage (*hajj*). At least once during his lifetime the Muslim should make a pilgrimage to the sacred mosque at Mecca, during the twelfth month of the lunar year, called *shu'l-Hijja*.

Groups of the faithful gather at Jedda or elsewhere beyond the sacred environs of Mecca. Their heads are shaved, they put on the seamless white robes of pilgrims, and take vows of ritual purity. In the sacred city the pilgrim first circumambulates the Ka'ba seven times, touching or kissing the Black Stone each time around. Next comes the Lesser Pilgrimage, which is a visit to the two hills outside the city, Safa and Marwa, where tradition says that Hagar desperately sought water for Ishmael before the well Zemzem appeared. In emulation of Hagar, pilgrims run seven times with shaking shoulders between these hills.

Next comes the Great Pilgrimage. Following ceremonies in the Great Mosque, pilgrims proceed to Mina, a gorge, and Arafat, a mountain, some five and thirteen miles, respectively, from the city. In an open area at Arafat, the pilgrims listen to sermons, after which they spend the night in the open on the way back to Mina. Here each pilgrim casts seven stones down a gorge, celebrating Abraham's victory over, and stoning of, Satan. Then there follows the sacrifice of a goat, sheep, or camel, and after that the return to the city. Three days of festival celebration follow, but before leaving for home the pilgrim reenters the state of ritual purity for a final visit to the Great Mosque.

The significance of pilgrimage in maintaining the vitality and unity of Islam is incalculable. On his return home the pilgrim is called by the coveted title *Hajji*. He will be much in demand as a speaker to describe his experience. The numbers of pilgrims continue unabated from all parts of the Muslim world. In one recent year Saudi Arabia had 250,000 pilgrims and the Malays some 300,000.

Closely related to the Five Pillars is a variety of other obligations which are either often or always regarded as binding on the Muslim conscience. For example, a distinguished student of Islam remarks that for at least one extreme Muslim sect, the Kharijites, the holy war is regarded as a sixth Pillar.[25] The holy war is repeatedly enjoined by the Qur'an as for example in the following passage:

> *Fight in the way of Allah against those who fight against*
> *you, but begin not hostilities Lo! Allah loveth not aggressors.*
> *And stay them wherever ye find them, and drive them out*
> *of the places whence they drove you out, for persecu-*
> *tion is worse than slaughter. . . .*
> *But if they desist, when lo! Allah is Forgiving, Merciful.*
> *And fight then until persecution is no more and religion*
> *is for Allah. . . .*[26]

In contrast to Kharijite literalism, some modern Muslims interpret the jihad in sublimated or metaphorical fashion as striving for the Muslim cause or "fighting the good fight" in a metaphorical rather than literal sense.

Muslims generally have observed the Quranic prohibitions against alcohol, pork, and gambling. Islam has in this connection been called the most successful total abstinence society in history. As is well known, polygamous marriage is permitted by the Qur'an, which puts the matter thus:

> *Give unto orphans their wealth. Exchange not the good*
> *for the bad (in your management thereof) nor absorb*
> *their wealth into your own wealth. Lo! that would*
> *be a great sin.*
> *And if ye fear that ye will not deal fairly by the*
> *orphans, marry of the women, who seem good to you,*
> *two or three or four; and if ye fear that ye cannot*
> *do justice (to so many) then one (only) or (the*
> *captives) that your right hands possess. Thus it is*
> *more likely that ye will not do injustice.*[27]

If the Prophet's teachings concerning the ethics of sex and family be interpreted in historical context, they will be understood as a prophetic defense of the cause of women and children. "Two, three or four" wives meant in this historical context "not more than four." The Prophet was a defender of the rights of such defenseless persons as women, children, and orphans.

As the reader makes his way through the pages of the Qur'an, he detects considerable similarity between the ethics of the Prophet of Islam, and the ethics of the Biblical prophets of ancient Israel. In both races, allegiance to the one God carries the primary obligation of living a just or righteous life in society with one's fellowmen; injustice is a sin against God.

In Islam, these moral values are given a definite structure and a wide application to politics, economics, and other basic aspects of society through the shari'a, or law, to be described in the next section. In Islam as in other faiths, moral ideals undergo qualification and compromise as they are applied to the wider areas of society. In the modern world a process of attrition of traditional morality has gone on in Islam as in other faiths. Nevertheless Islam offers eloquent illustration of the fact that monotheistic religion has fundamental and inescapable moral and social implications.

THE FORMATIVE CENTURIES

The Prophet's sudden death posed the problem of a successor (*caliph*). There were three groups from which a Caliph might be chosen: (1) companions of the Prophet, (2) the Prophet's family, (3) the Prophet's tribe, the Quraysh, or its subdivision, the Ummayads. The companions acted first, placing in the Caliphate Muhammad's longtime friend and associate, Abu Bekr. He moved with decisiveness to bring remaining Arab tribes into line. He also ordered the gathering of the miscellaneous Suras of the Qur'an. During his short reign (632–634) he continued the Prophet's organization of an army and preparation for an assault on the outside world. Abu Bekr lived in patriarchal simplicity, receiving no stipend, and transacting all state business in the courtyard of the Prophet's mosque at Medina.

Abu Bekr died in 634 and was succeeded by another companion, Umar, who ruled (634–644) until his assassination by the poisoned dagger of a Christian slave. Like his predecessor he was simple and frugal, and also a devout and austerely righteous man. Under his direction the expansion of Islam began in earnest. He sent the great Khalid ibn-al-Walid, called "the sword of Allah," against Damascus, the capital of Syria, in 634.[28] After a forced camel-march from Iraq, Khalid and his fighting men appeared before the gates of Damascus. After a six-months siege it fell (635). Other Syrian cities and towns then fell. The decisive battle for Syria was fought on August 20, 636, a fiercely hot summer's day on which the soldiers of the Prophet routed the Byzantine army sent against them. Jerusalem fell in 639 and the seaport town, Caesarea, was betrayed by a Jewish defector in 640.

Egypt was conquered next (639–640), and Muslim armies continued their push across North Africa. By 710 they were knocking at the gates of Spain, and in 732, having conquered Spain, they were finally checked at Tours in central France. On the north-central front, Arab armies marched as far as the gates of Constantinople, which they placed under year-long siege (716–717).[29] Meanwhile still other Arab armies pushed eastward, conquering Iraq, then toppling the decadent Sassanid rulers of Iran (640–649) and bringing Islam to the borders of India.

Meanwhile Umar was succeeded by Uthman, who ruled from 644 to 656. Uthman was a companion but also an Ummayad; and he appointed so many Ummayads that serious opposition arose, in the midst of which he too fell victim to assassination.

He was succeeded by the Prophet's son-in-law and cousin, Ali, who was the first legitimist Caliph—a fact portentously significant in Muslim history as will be seen in the section of this chapter on the Shi'ites, who are Muslim sects claiming that the first three Caliphs were usurpers. Ali fell victim in 660 to a poisoned dagger wielded by an extremist follower who disapproved of Ali's leniency to a defeated foe. His assassin was a Kharijite, one of a group whose violence and fanaticism the student will have frequent occasion to observe in Muslim history.

The vastness and the speed of the Muslim conquests are difficult even to comprehend, let alone explain. In a century's time the Muslims ruled an empire two or three times the size of Rome's empire. No single cause suffices to explain so large a fact of history. In part this vast conquest is to be attributed to Muslim faith. The warriors of the Prophet believed themselves to be the servants of Allah, and they further believed that if they died in battle they would go straight to Paradise. If they survived they could keep four-fifths of their booty—often wealth beyond the wildest dreams of avarice for these Arabian nomads. The military genius of the Arab generals, their mastery of new techniques such as camel cavalry, plus the frequent ineptitude of their opposition constituted an important contributing cause. Whatever the combination of causes, the result was a century of conquest unparalleled in history before or since.

It is important to bear in mind that Islam is a universal religion which has interacted with many cultures. Among these is what is often termed Arab civilization [30]—though historians from other parts of the Muslim world hasten to challenge any suggestion that *Arab* and *Muslim* are equivalent terms. Actually, even the so-called Arab civilization was a synthesis of many elements fused into a unity by Muslim faith and presided over by Arab rulers. Here is occasion to observe once more what our study has shown many times in human history, the interaction of faith and culture to form a significant compound.

Arab civilization had its first stable center in the Ummayad Caliphate founded by Muawiyah and located in Damascus. It lasted for almost a century, from 660 to 750,[31] then was overthrown by the Abbasids (from the Prophet's uncle, named al-Abbas) who moved the Caliphate to Baghdad, where it remained until Mongol invaders destroyed the city in 1258. There, in the "glory that was Baghdad," flowered an affluent and civilized culture.[32] Situated at the crossroads of the world, between East and West, Baghdad could draw upon the cultural legacies of both. Under such leaders as Harun al-Rashid and al-Mamun (813–833), Baghdad became the center of the civilized world.

Two other Caliphates also became notable centers of Muslim faith and Arab civilization: (1) the Fatimid in Cairo, Egypt (909–1171), and (2) the Ummayad (founded, incidentally, by a survivor of the Abbasid liquidation of the Ummayads) in Cordova, Spain (929–1031). As aspects of these civilizations, there grew and developed many of the essential structures of Islam, such as the hadiths, or traditions, and the shari'a, or law. To some of these features of Islam as an organized religion, attention must now be given.

While Islam has resolutely refused to deify the Prophet, his teachings, by precept and practice, have always carried the highest authority. Many of the precepts are contained in the Qur'an and hence are regarded not as Muhammad's but as the revealed will of Allah. However, the Qur'an does not cover every human situation. Further, many of the Prophet's contemporaries recalled words or deeds from him or from close companions which could serve as models for belief or behavior. Many such hadiths (the word means "narrative") were undoubtedly accurate recollections, but as time passed and their numbers grew, many hadiths appeared which were either plainly spurious or suspiciously slanted for or against this or that partisan viewpoint. As a Muslim writer has said, "it is remarkable to note the facility with which even men of undoubted piety did not hesitate to attribute to the Prophet sayings made up by themselves to promote sectarian interests." [33] One imaginative Muslim confessed to outright fabrication of some four thousand hadiths!

The need for critical sifting led to the rise of a science for testing the veracity of hadiths. The method of testing was to establish a chain of reliable attestors by which a hadith could be traced back to the Prophet or a companion; and on this basis hadiths were judged "sound," "good," or "weak." It was vital to Islam to have reliable hadiths as a basis of Muslim law as well as of personal devotion and morality. Out of this process of critical inquiry emerged several collections of hadiths, of which the best known and most authoritative were those of al-Bukari (d. 870) and al-Muslim (d. 875). The former was an Iranian Muslim who traveled throughout the Near East gathering a vast number of hadiths (some said 600,000!), sifting them to some 7,300 reliable ones, which in eliminating repetition were reduced to 2,700. Al-Bukari's collection of hadiths has commanded an authority in Islam second only to the Qur'an.

Muslim law, or *shari'a*, arose out of the essential nature of Islam. If Allah has revealed his will for mankind, then the eternal destiny of every man consists in hearing and doing the divine will. Such is the austere logic of Muslim monotheism. However, it is equally important that all aspects of man's life, corporate as well as individual, be brought into relation to the divine will. It is at precisely this point that Muslim law emerges as a way of relating the divine words of the Qur'an to all the varied circumstances of human society. This is, incidentally, a problem which has emerged analogously in other monotheistic religions. Talmudic law in Judaism, canon law in Roman Catholic Christianity, and scriptural law or norms in Calvinistic Christianity arose to solve similar problems.

Four systems of jurisprudence (*fiqh*) have arisen in Islam, differing in methods, in the degree of liberality or rigor in interpretation of Qur'an for changing circumstances, and in their respective understanding and combination of four aspects of interpretation. These are (1) dependence on Qur'an, (2) dependence in hadiths, (3) reasoning by analogy, and (4) consensus of the Muslim community. The most liberal school, the *Hanifite,* was founded by Abu Hanifah (d. 767), an Iranian who lived and taught in Iraq and whose teachings were recorded by followers. His interpretations began with the Qur'an, taking little notice of hadiths, and relying heavily on analogy and current consensus. For example, if no Quranic teachings were available for a situation, or if an apparent conflict arose, this type of interpretation dealt with it by analogical reasoning from different parts of the Qur'an or by consulting current consensus (*ijma*). The Hanifite interpretation still prevails in Iraq, Iran, India, Pakistan, and Central Asia.

The second school, the *Malikite,* was founded in Medina by Malik ibr-Anas (d. 795) and based its interpretation upon Qur'an and hadiths taken together. Where problems arose, Malik consulted Muslim opinion. In particularly difficult problems, he resorted to analogy or even appealed to the principle of public advantage. This school of interpretation is followed in North Africa, in parts of Egypt, and in eastern Arabia.

The *Shafiite* school of interpretation was founded by al-Shafi of Egypt (d. 820), who preferred hadiths to Qur'an when differences arose, for the reason that the hadiths reflect Muslim opinion during developing periods. Yet Shafiite interpretation rejects consensus in all forms as unwarranted speculation. The Shafiite principles of interpretation have been followed in Lower Egypt, east Africa, south Arabia, Palestine, south India, and Indonesia.

The most strictly conservative school of legal interpretation, the *Hanbalite,* was founded by Ibn Hanbal (d. 855) a student of al-Shafi who reacted strongly against the liberality—and laxity, as he saw it—of the Baghdad of his times. Hence he rejected all but a strictly literal interpretation of Qur'an and hadiths. For his uncompromising attitudes he was scourged and imprisoned. His followers, notably in Saudi Arabia, have continued his austere attitudes and principles.

During the formative centuries of Islam, controversies and conflicts, sometimes bitter and violent, made their first appearances. Many of them have continued to wrack the Muslim community through the centuries. First was a dispute between the Kharijites (separatists or secessionists), and the Murjites (advocates of delayed judgment, that is, delay until Judgment Day in deciding

who is and is not a faithful Muslim). Ali's assassin has been noted as a Kharijite who believed that Ali had no right to arbitrate his differences with Muawiyah. The Kharijites were literalists in their adherence to Islam and the Qur'an.[34]
They believed that people who disagreed with them concerning the consequences of mortal sin should no longer be accepted as Muslims and should be
killed on sight. Some went even further and said that the families of such
renegades must also be liquidated. The Kharijites also believed that the Caliph
should be elected by the whole Muslim community without respect to race,
family, or social status. But Caliphs must be good Muslims and not trimmers
or children of expediency. These fierce fanatics of Islam have frequently
found the full force of Islam deployed against them. They have lived on
the fringes of the Muslim world and have periodically erupted into violent
action.

The Murjites asserted more moderately that only Allah really knows who is
a good Muslim and who is an infidel. Thus man should delay judgment and
action against suspected infidels. Better leave these matters to Allah at the Last
Judgment, meanwhile treating all professing "submitters" as true Muslim
brothers.

Growing out of the quarrel between Kharijites and Murjites was the Mutazilite movement, which sought a middle ground of responsible freedom between
conformity and fanaticism. But in their development the Mutazilites went on
to other more philosophical and theological issues. Authorities differ in their
judgment concerning this movement. Apparently our knowledge of these ancient Muslim liberal theologians is less than adequate.[35] However, some of their
main issues are reasonably clear.

Related to their insistence on man's freedom and responsibility was their
advocacy of reason and rational method for the study of things religious. The
latter was in all probability influenced by Greek thought which had permeated
the Near Eastern world.

The major tenet of the Mutazilite school was an insistence upon the absolute
unity and justice of God. A combination of both rational and religious factors
led them to this conclusion. From it they drew conclusions which were highly
controversial. True, they insisted that no final or absolute position be taken
interpreting the justice of Allah. However, in the Mutazilite insistence that
Allah is just, opponents saw a compulsion over Allah. They argued that if
justice were required of Allah, he would in that case not be absolutely free as
all good Muslims know him to be.

Mutazilites argued against literal anthropomorphic descriptions of Allah, as,
for example, having human features or sitting on a throne. They asserted that
no attributes external to Allah, as they stated the matter, may be allowed to
conflict with his absolute unity. Hence the concrete imagery of the Qur'an con-

cerning Allah (and concerning heaven and hell, too) must be taken figuratively rather than literally.

From the absolute unity of God they argued against the popular notion of the Qur'an as uncreated and eternal. Truly this would deify the Qur'an and thus conflict with the absolute unity of the one God. Rather, insisted the Mutazilites, the Qur'an is this side of the line which separates creation from Creator. Mutazilite theologians in the court of Caliph al-Mamun influenced him in 827 to proclaim the created character of the Qur'an as established doctrine, purging from public life anyone who held contrary views.

Among those who stood out against this official view was Ibn Hanbal of the Hanbalite school of shari'a. Chained, scourged, and thrown into prison, he continued to espouse the eternal and uncreated Qur'an. However, the man who turned the tide against the Mutazilites was one of their number, al-Ashari (d. 935). After many years of study and practice of the rational method of the Mutazilites he found himself at the age of forty in violent disagreement. It was his achievement to use their rational methods for the construction of a thoroughly conservative, traditional philosophy which was destined to become the foundation of the *Sunna,* or Tradition. For al-Ashari, Allah became not only one but all, in that he is the true cause of all that happens in both nature and society. Inasmuch as he created man in the first place, it is he who acts in and through them.

Al-Ashari asserted in his own way the absolute uniqueness of Allah. He is not like anything in the universe. Since he causes all events, it is he who causes men to think of him as the Qur'an bids them do. Following the full implications of this line of reasoning, Ashari concluded that Allah literally has hands and feet and sits on a throne. A similar literalism was applied to heaven and hell. As for the Qur'an, Ashari asserted that as an idea in the divine mind, it was indeed eternal and uncreated. Of this true Qur'an, eternal and heavenly, the book of Arabic words is a divinely guaranteed copy. Staunch literalist that he was, Ashari did not even shrink from asserting Allah as the cause of evil. As the cause of all that is, it is he who causes the unfaithfulness of the infidel and the evil deeds of the sinner. Further, having caused these deeds, Allah then proceeds in his own good pleasure to damn the evildoer to hell. All this must simply and plainly be accepted without question as a part of the Muslim's submission to the inscrutable decrees of Allah. From al-Ashari's time onward, the Sunna was a massively conservative tradition.

SHI'A

Among the differences which emerged during Islam's formative centuries none was more important than that which separated the Shi'ites from other Muslims.

The Shi'ites are followers of Ali (*shi'a* means "followers") who believe that he was the first true Caliph, his three predecessors being regarded as illegal usurpers. The Shi'a regard Muhammad as Prophet, and Ali as Imam, or divinely appointed leader and model for the faithful. The divinely ordained Imamate of Ali is justified by a Shi'ite hadith which represents the Prophet as saying just before his death: "I shall soon be called back to heaven; I leave you two important bequests, the *Koran* and my family." [36] Needless to say, non-Shi'ite Muslims reject the authenticity of this hadith.

Secular historians point to the origin of the Shi'a not in theology or faith, but in history and society. When Muawiyah (arch-villain for the Shi'ites) moved the Caliphate from Kufa in Iraq to Damascus in Syria, he aroused the opposition of the Arabs of Iraq. The Shi'ite name served as a rallying point for many different causes and traditions whose common element was opposition to the *Sunni,* or majority party. To this was added in the course of time the distinctive feature of the Shi'a, namely, belief in a divinely-sent Imam or leader of the Muslim community. Indeed the Imam came to be regarded as the authoritative source of Muslim doctrine. There has been, however, a considerable disagreement about the identity of some of the succession of twelve Imams. The Shi'a have been riven by sectarian divisions, often of an extreme and violent kind. Usually the resulting sects have gathered about particular Imams.

All Shi'ite sects accept Ali as the first Imam and his two sons, al-Hasan (d. 669) and al-Husain (d. 680) as the second and third respectively. Actually al-Hasan was led by Muawiyah to resign his Imamship for a pension—a fact not often recognized by Shi'ites. His younger brother, al-Husain, was not so easily diverted; both he and his young son died in battle against Muawiyah's successor, Yaze'd. The martyr's death of al-Husain is an event annually commemorated in the Shi'ite world by ten days of lamentation and a passion play depicting the suffering and death of the third Imam.

Al-Husain's son, Ali Zain al-Abidin (d. 713), was the fourth Imam. One of his two sons was Muhammad al-Bakir (d. 731), through whom according to most Shi'ites the succession continued. However, the sect of Zaidites reject him, accepting his brother Zaid as the true fifth Imam. Known as "Fivers," the Zaidites continue in small numbers in Yemen and in the past have existed from Morocco to Tabaristan. The succession of Muhammad al-Bakir proceeded through his son Ja'far al-Sadik (d. 765), who in turn had two sons, the older Ismail (d. 760) and the younger Musa al-Kasir (d. 797). Ismail would legitimately have followed his father, as seventh in the line, but he was set aside for drunkenness, a clear and serious violation of Muslim law. His followers have consistently denied the allegation, and when Ismail died five years before his father, they said he was not dead, but hidden, and would come again as the *Mahdi,* or Expected One, who would set the world right.

Several important Muslim groups have been Ismailis, or "Seveners." A ninth-century Persian named Abdullah ibn-Mamum (d. ca. 874), who claimed to be the earthly representative of the hidden Imam, built up a secret society devoted to the violent destruction of the Abbasid Caliphate. He failed in this ambitious project, but his descendants founded the Fatimid Caliphate of Egypt.

A related group of Ismailis, or Seveners, were the Karmatians. Their founder, Hamdan Karmat, had been a disciple of Abdullah. In the ninth century he built up in south Arabia an independent kingdom which extended from Iraq to Yemen. The Karmatians successfully defended themselves against the armies of the Baghdad Caliphate. They cut the pilgrimage routes to Mecca and exacted a fee for safe passage. On one daring sortie, they invaded Mecca during the pilgrimage season and carried off the Black Stone, holding it for twenty years and returning it only on the request of their fellow Karmatians, the Fatimids of Egypt.

Another, similar group of Ismailites were the Assassins of Alamut of Persia, founded and led by Hasan Sabah (d. 1124). The Assassins (the name is taken from *hashish,* name of the narcotic which they imbibed in order to induce states of religious exaltation) made the practice of killing a fine art. As practitioners of this dread and bloody art, the Assassins were feared throughout the Near East. Working his way into his victim's confidence, the Assassin struck him down with a poisoned dagger on some public occasion. He was undeterred by the fact that he too was immediately killed, for he believed that he would go directly to Paradise. The Persian stronghold which was the home of the Assassins was visited and described by Marco Polo on his way to China. Today some twenty thousand Assassins survive as a peaceful sect, living in the mountains of Lebanon. Another 250,000 live in India. Half of this number are followers of the Agha Khan, lineal descendant of the last Assassin leader of Alamut, and annually paid his weight in gold by his devoted subjects.

In contrast to the Ismailis, or Seveners, the majority of Shi'ites accept the whole succession of twelve Imams, thus acquiring the designation of "Twelvers." The twelfth Imam, Muhammad al-Muntazar (d. 878) is reputed by Shi'ites not to have died but to have withdrawn into a cave in Samarra up the river from Baghdad. Believers assert that he is not dead, but hiding, and that he will return as the Mahdi to set the world right and prepare for the Last Judgment. In Iran, where some seven million Twelvers live, the shahs have since the sixteenth century asserted themselves to be earthly representatives of the hidden Imam.

In addition to these main sects, the Shi'a have produced other smaller and less important groups. Loyalty to their Imams has often been deep and stubborn, even to the point of sanctioning dissimulation (*taqiyah*) which in times of persecution has permitted outward conformity and inner dissent. They have agreed with the Mutazilites in denying the eternity of the Qur'an and asserting freedom of human will. They have also shared in the tradition of Muslim mysticism called Sufism.

MYSTICS AND PHILOSOPHERS

Despite its massive conservatism, it would be grossly inaccurate to suppose that Muslim faith means mainly or solely assent to the traditional credo or that all change and development stopped with al-Ashari. Quite the contrary, the Muslim tradition has continued to generate many sorts of new responses to, and interpretations of, its dominant theme of submission to Allah. Two of these responses, that of the mystic and that of the philosopher-theologian, plus some combinations of the two, must now be considered.

In some of its forms, Muslim mysticism has been a way of cultivating immediate communion with Allah, who is not only transcendent, distant, and alone, but according to the mystics' favorite Quranic passage also "nearer than one's jugular vein." But in other, bolder forms, Muslim mysticism can be regarded as nothing less than a frontal challenge to Muslim monotheism. Some mystics in their journey to God move past direct communion with God to forms of absorption which pass roughly over the line fixed between Creator and creation, or between the one Lord and his dominion. So it is that some mystics have involved themselves in the unforgivable sin of shirk.

Islam has also produced a great tradition of philosopher-theologians who have in bold freedom sought rational grounds for belief. Al-Ashari might command the faithful to "believe without question," but some bold spirits have refused to accept so anti-intellectual a view of Allah's requirement of his children.

In the case of both mystics and philosophers, the Greek tradition of thought from Plato and Aristotle to Plotinus was a strong contributory cause, though often it is difficult to discern its precise role. In turn, Muslim mystics and philosophers have had important influence on other traditions, notably Judaism and Christianity.

Mysticism began early in Muslim history. Within the first century, ascetics who practiced celibacy and fasting resigned themselves to the care of Allah and concentrated their minds on the "Ninety-nine Beautiful Names of Allah."[37] The term *Sufi*, literally "wool wearer," probably refers to the coarse wool garment which was worn as an ascetic exercise. That these Muslim ascetics and mystics were influenced by Christians of the same bent is very probable, though the lines of influence are hard to trace in detail. Gibb is undoubtedly correct in interpreting Sufism as a popular religious movement aimed at countering the intellectualism of lawyers and theologians.[38] Such indeed has been mysticism's historic function in Islam as well as other religious traditions. However there is a further element of protest in Sufism. Against the austere and transcendent monotheism of the Tradition, the mystic placed the immediacy of God's presence in his heart— in the words of the Qur'an "nearer to us than our jugular vein."

In addition to innumerable anonymous pilgrims on the path to Truth, as Muslim mystics like to characterize themselves, this way has produced some great names who have left records of their pilgrimages and explorations. Among the earliest was a woman saint, Rabi'a al-Adaurya (d. 801) in whom the mystical theme of the love of God found expression in such lines as the following:

> I love Thee with two loves, love of my happiness,
> And perfect love, to love Thee as is Thy due.
> My selfish love is that I do naught
> But think on Thee, excluding all beside;
> But that purest love, which is Thy due,
> Is that the veils which hide Thee fall, and I gaze on Thee,
> No praise to me either this or that,
> Nay, Thine the praise for both that love and this.[39]

A development of the greatest significance was taken by Abu Yasid al Bistami (d. 815), who taught *fana* or the annihilation of individual human consciousness during the mystical experience. Proclaiming the identity of soul and God, he cried out "How great is my majesty!" Some students of mysticism have suggested that he was influenced by Indian mysticism.

Another mystic named Harith al-Muhasibi of Basrah (d. 857) described the stages on his path to Truth. They began traditionally enough with repentance, renunciation, poverty and the like, and continued through trust or faith to God. However, what was most notable was the culmination of the mystical journey in a state called illumination and consisting of an ineffable experience of light and love in which human individuality seemed lost or absorbed in its divine object.

The orthodox culmination of the Sufi tradition was the thought of al-Ghazzali, who in life and thought fused Sufism and tradition. Al-Ghazzali was born in Iran, but lived and taught in Baghdad. His life story and life work how both similarity and contrast with his great predecessor al-Ashari. Al-Ashari had been a Mutazilite and made his way by logical method to traditionalism; al-Ghazzali was an Asharite theologian whose creative contribution was to "reestablish theology on the basis of personal mystical experience."[40]

Born in Persia in 1058, he was educated in both law (of the Shafiite tradition) and in Asharite theology.[41] His reputation for learning and brilliance led to his appointment at the newly founded University of Baghdad. A period of spiritual struggle and crisis led him first through skepticism and then onward to Sufi mysticism. Apparently he found the intellectualism of the theologians sterile and dead. But he also found in mystical experience a way of breathing life into its dry bones.

Becoming a simple Sufi, al-Ghazzali left the university, journeying to Syria for meditation and prayer among Sufi communities. After two years he celebrated his return to faith by making the pilgrimage to Mecca. Then he returned home. For a time he taught again at the university. He began again to write, completing his monumental volume, *The Revivification of the Religious Sciences*. He died at the age of fifty-three in 1111.

Al-Ghazzali's achievement consisted in his reaffirmation of Muslim orthodoxy by infusing it with the vitality of Sufi mysticism. Taken alone, the intellectual approach to God was flat and stale. One of al-Ghazzali's books was *The Incoherence of the Philosophers*, a work in which the author pointed out many alleged inner contradictions of the rational systems and speculations of philosophy. From this impasse al-Ghazzali—and his philosophy—were rescued by the mystic daily communion with God. The core of faith, al-Ghazzali believed, was to turn one's heart in contrition to God, and by Sufi disciplines to maintain this continuing communion with the divine source of all truth and goodness. From this religious experience also sprang al-Ghazzali's great philosophical synthesis, which Muslim thinkers ever since have taken as their definitive formulation.

Other Muslim mystics were not so sympathetic to tradition. Particularly notable was al-Hallaj (d. 922), who pressed beyond communion and illumination to complete absorption in God, and was scourged and killed for his public declaration, "I am the Truth," which was understood by his Muslim hearers as equating himself with Allah who alone is Truth. In the writings of al-Hallaj, the reader finds a record of direct communion with Allah rising at length to union in which no duality is experienced or claimed. Al-Hallaj frequently used the metaphor of love for this relation, crying out, "I am He whom I love and He whom I love is I."[42]

Similar reports of the climactic experience of mysticism are given in the writings of Ibn Arabi (d. 1240). He writes:

> *Just as he who dies the death of the body, loses all his attributes, both those worthy of praise and those worthy of condemnation alike, so in the spiritual death all attributes, both those worthy of praise and those to be condemned, come to an end, and in all the man's states what is Divine comes to take the place of what was mortal. Thus, instead of his own essence, there is the essence of God and in place of his own qualities, there are the attributes of God. He who knows himself sees his whole existence to be the Divine existence, but does not realise that any change has taken place in his own nature or qualities. For when you know yourself, your "I-ness" vanishes and you know that you and God are one and the same.*[43]

Ibn Arabi also boldly drew out conclusions that must have seemed to his Muslim friends a complete denial of the faith:

> *There was a time when I blamed my companion if his*
> *religion did not resemble mine.*
>   *Now, however, my heart accepts every form: it is*
> *pasture ground for gazelles, a cloister for monks,*
>   *A temple for idols and a Ka'bah for the pilgrim,*
> *thy tables of the Torah and the sacred books of the Koran.*
>   *Love alone is my religion, and wherever their beasts*
> *of burden go there is my religion and my faith.*[44]

Many of these notes found similar expression in the songs of the Persian mystical poet Jalal al-Din Rumi (d. 1273) who was also the founder of the *Maulawi* (also called *Mevlevi*) order of dervishes. Using the love of friends as his metaphor he sang of mystical union in these words:

> *When the rose is dead and the garden ravaged, where shall*
>   *we find the perfume of the rose? In rose-water.*
> *Inasmuch as God comes not into sight, the prophets are*
>   *His vicars.*
> *Do not mistake me! 'Tis wrong to think that the vicar and*
>   *He Whom the vicar represents are two.*
> *To the form-worshipper they are two; when you have escaped*
>   *from consciousness of form, they are One.*
> *Whilst you regard the form, you are seeing double: look,*
>   *not at the eyes, but at the light which flows from them.*
> *You cannot distinguish the lights of ten lamps burning*
>   *together, so long as your face is set towards this light alone.*
> *In things spiritual there is no partition, no number, no*
>   *individuals.*
> *How sweet is the oneness of the Friend with His friends!*
>   *Catch the spirit and clasp it to your bosom.*
> *Mortify rebellious form till it wastes away: unearth the*
>   *treasure of Unity!*
> *Simple were we and all one essence: we were knotless and*
>   *pure as water.*
> *When that goodly Light took shape, it became many, like*
>   *shadows cast by a battlement.*
> *Demolish the dark battlement, and all difference will*
>   *vanish from amidst this multitude.*[45]

Words such as these could be taken as little less than a frontal challenge to Muslim monotheism, and there have been many austere orthodox followers of the Prophet who have taken them as precisely that. Yet it is also a fact of Muslim history that others, to use a favorite metaphor of mystics, have drunk at this fountain, refreshed their thirsting souls, and then continued their way along Islam's straight path.

Mystics have often been individualists, defying communal restrictions. Yet inevitably, too, they gather into communities and formulate rules and ways for their common life. So it has been with the Sufis. They have gathered into communities, sometimes in cities but sometimes too in solitary deserts. Usually the communities or orders bear the impression of some striking, attractive person who gathered other men around him. Usually they have begged for food, hence they are called dervishes (from the Persian *darwash*, "one who comes to the door"). Often they have used music and dancing to induce mystic exaltation. Local orders and communities of Sufis too numerous and too various in their practices for description here have sprung up in all parts of the Muslim world. Three orders of dervishes must serve here as illustrations of the range and variety of these orders: (1) The *Kadirites* were founded by Abd al-Kadar (d. 1166) in Baghdad. Loosely organized, devoted to philanthropy and piety, and generally shunning extremism, the Kadirites have spread over the Muslim world from Algeria to Java. (2) The *Rifa'ites* were founded by Ahmad al-Rifa'i (d. 1182) and have gained for themselves the designation of Howling Dervishes. In addition to howling, they have been given to such extremes as fire-walking and playing with serpents, as well as many forms of self-mortification. (3) The *Maulawites,* or Whirling Dervishes, were founded by the Persian poet Jalal al-Din Rumi (d. 1273), who passed on to his followers the use of music and dancing to induce mystical ecstasy.

The history of Sufism has not been free of bizarre aberrations, magic, and superstition. Sufi reverence for saints has also drawn violent reactions from traditionalist reformers. Yet at its best, Sufism has produced many good works and renewed piety.

As in other religious traditions, so also in Islam questions addressed to tradition or to mysticism served to generate philosophy. We have alluded to al-Ghazzali's great theological synthesis. He was a theologian in the precise sense of thinking and studying within Muslim tradition and authority. Other Muslim thinkers, both before and after al-Ghazzali, were less deferential to tradition. They studied and reasoned in ways independent of religious authority and tradition. In a word they were philosophers.

Islamic philosophy began in the attempt of Arab scholars to reclaim the classical Greek philosophic heritage. It is, indeed, to these Muslim scholar-philosophers from al-Kindi to Averroes that the West owes the preservation of Greek philosophy and its transmission through Jewish and Christian scholastics to the modern world.

The founder of Muslim philosophy was al-Kindi (800–870), tutor to the son of the caliph of Baghdad, who was also the owner of a large library of Greek science and philosophy and friend of Mutazilite theologians, and himself a Neoplatonist. One significant feature of the philosophy of al-Kindi and his successors was the assertion of the literal creation of the world by God at a moment in time. This idea seemed to these philosophers a necessary implication of Muslim monotheism.

In al-Farabi (875–950), Islamic philosophy achieved maturity. His system was a blend of Aristotle, Plato, and Plotinus. At the center was First Being or Absolute One which was taken as equivalent to God. He also taught that philosophy and not theology was the highest knowledge, and that man's highest goal is to develop and realize his rational powers.

Abu ali ibn Sina (980–1037), known to the West as Avicenna, was a Persian physician, advisor to rulers, a student of Greek philosophy, but most of all, the greatest and most original classical Islamic philosopher. He made and argued the distinction, all-important for subsequent religious philosophy, between Necessary Being and contingent being. He also argued that in God essence and existence are conjoined while in contingent beings they are separated. Avicenna sought to translate monotheistic faith into the language of scholastic philosophy.

The last great Muslim philosopher was Ibn Rushd (1126–1198), or as he is known in the West, Averroes. He was chief judge in Seville and Cordova, Spain and wrote on Malikite jurisprudence. He responded to al-Ghazzali's *Inconsistency of the Philosophers* with a polemical tract entitled *The Inconsistency of the Inconsistency*, which sought to show the capacity of human reason to attain knowledge of the world including the things of faith. Averroes was convinced that philosophy and religion were both true and may therefore be harmonized with each other. After Averroes no philosopher of comparable stature emerged in Islam. Historians have no fully adequate explanation for this lack, but the fact is clear.

MUSLIM EXPANSION IN ASIA AND AFRICA

Islam advanced across Iran to the gates of India during its first century of existence. There is some evidence that Muslim travelers and traders brought their faith to India during this period. However, as noted in Chapter 6, the decisive arrival of Islam in India was in 999, with the armies of Mahmud of Ghaznin. Mahmud was the Muslim Turkish ruler of a small kingdom in Afghanistan, and during the first two decades of the eleventh century his armies carried out a series of devastating raids into northwest India, resulting in a Ghaznavid government in Lahore in 1021. Mahmud's armies smashed and plundered Hindu temples and slaughtered both Hindus and Buddhists in ways that etched themselves permanently on the Indian imagination.[46]

The Ghaznavids were unable to hold their prize, losing out during the eleventh century to another small Turkish Muslim kingdom of Ghoz. In the twelfth century the Ghorid Turks established themselves in northwest India. Rule passed from the first Ghorid king to his servants, or slaves, who as the so-called Slave dynasty established the Delhi sultanate. Under successive waves of Muslim invaders the Delhi sultanate held power in northern India until the coming of the Moghuls in the sixteenth century.

It is not surprising that Islam, carried thus to India by invading armies, remained to a great degree the faith of these alien invaders and rulers. Only very slowly did it put down roots into the Indian soil. The relations between Islam and Hinduism were not satisfactory to either faith. Nor indeed has satisfactory relation been achieved at any subsequent time. Islam and Hinduism remain at an impasse in twentieth-century India. For Islam, only conversion could be a satisfactory conclusion, and Hindu India has remained unconverted. For Hinduism, assimilation of the new faith would have been satisfactory, but Islam has remained unassimilated. What has occurred has been aptly characterized as "apartheid" between these two faiths, modified only by peripheral meeting and mingling at the level of popular religion.[47]

As it has developed historically, Islam in India has not differed in fundamentals from Islam elsewhere in the world in belief or practice. One notable characteristic has been the development of an especially strong tradition of Sufism. To this it must be added that despite the mutual alienation of Islam and Hinduism, the common man of India has sometimes been unable to distinguish the Muslim Sufi from the Hindu devotee of bhakti.

In 1526 Babur won the first battle of Panipat and established the Moghul dynasty. The Moghuls were Muslims of varying degrees of devotion and orthodoxy. The greatest of the Moghul rulers, Akbar (1555–1605), was notable not only as an enlightened emperor but as an avid student of India's and mankind's religions. As a boy in Kabul, Afghanistan, he had been instructed in the teachings of Persian Muslim mystics. He married a Hindu Rajput princess and recoiled from the religious policies of repression and persecution followed by his predecessors. His interest in the many faiths of his far-flung empire led to a notable series of discussions among exponents of the Muslim Sunna and Shi'a, Jainism, Sikhism, Hinduism, Parseeism, and Christianity. The result of these discussions was the proclamation by Akbar in 1582 of his own syncretistic "Divine Faith." While it did not outlive its founder, it stands as a monument to his breadth of mind, his tolerance, and to his insatiable curiosity. The reader may recall that Sikhism grew out of the same historical situation which elicited Akbar's concern. It may also be added that Sikhism succeeded where Akbar's Divine Faith failed, probably largely because it was the faith of a real community and tradition of people.

Akbar's son Jahangir (1605–1627) shared none of his father's breadth of mind. He returned to an official policy of intolerance and repression of non-Muslim faiths, which was passed on in turn to his son Shah Jahan (1627–1658) (the builder of the Taj Mahal) and his grandson Aurangzeb (1658–1707).

As the Moghul empire sank into decline, the European nations arrived in force in India. The first arrivals had been the Portuguese who seized Goa in

Muslim pilgrim to Mecca meets a Brahman on the
road. Sixteenth-century Indian miniature

*Courtesy of The Metropolitan Museum of Art, Alexan-
der Smith Cochran, 1913*

1510. They were followed within a century by the British and French who battled for the domination of India, the British achieving victory by the middle of the eighteenth century. As noted in Chapter 6, with the West came modernity with all its manifold challenges to India's traditional culture. The story of its challenge to Indian Islam will be sketched in the next section of this chapter.

Meanwhile one important premodern Indian Muslim, Shah Walli-ullah of Delhi (1703–1762), must at least be mentioned. He lived among the crumbling ruins of the Moghul empire and sought the reform of Indian Islam.[48] Combining in his own life a steadfast loyalty to the Sunna with ardent Sufi practice, he advocated a reconstruction of Muslim faith. His writings were aimed against the inner distortion and deterioration of Islam and against its loss of influence in Indian society. Muslim reformers and builders of the next two centuries built on the foundations he laid.

The onward march of Islam in Asia paused, but did not stop in India. In southeast Asia it pushed into Indonesia and onward to the Philippines; and in East Asia it drove onward to China. Today the Muslim population of China is variously estimated at from 50 million to 70 million, while another 75 million are to be found in Indonesia, and between 1 million and 2 million in Mindanao of the Philippines.

Islam is said to have reached China by 651 in the person of Said Ibn Abi Waqqas, a companion of the Prophet who made the long journey by sea.[49] It arrived in force over the land trade routes of central Asia during the first two centuries of Muslim history. Muslim fortunes in China have ebbed and flowed with the passing centuries and dynasties. A high point was reached during the Yüan, or Mongol, dynasty, when it was said that eight of twelve Chinese regional governors were followers of the Prophet. The Ming dynasty was a time of acclimating or sinification of Islam. The Manchu, or Ch'ing, dynasty was by contrast anti-Muslim. There is little reliable knowledge as to how Islam in China fares under China's present Marxist rulers.

During the centuries when Islam was making its impact upon China, it was also pushing into Indonesia. Marco Polo's thirteenth-century travel reports tell of a Muslim community in Sumatra.[50] A Chinese traveler two centuries later describes Java as Muslim. In the absence of reliable historical records one can only conjecture that between the thirteenth and sixteenth centuries, Islam expanded its beachhead and conquered the islands of Indonesia. This chronology is further indicated by the account of Islam's expansion from Indonesia to the Philippines in the thirteenth century, where it found lodgment among people of Mindanao whose new faith gained for them the name of Moros.

Islam's advance into Africa, if less sudden and dramatic than the sweep into Asia, is nonetheless of comparable magnitude and significance. We have noted the initial thrust of Muslim armies across North Africa from Egypt to Morocco during the first Muslim century. From this base the expansion into Africa continued in three main directions. In east Africa Islam followed Arab mariners, traders, and colonists as far south as Zanzibar. In central Africa Islamic penetration followed the Nile to Sudan then made its way westward to the modern nations of Chad and Niger. The Islamization of West Africa began with the conquest of Ghana by Almohavid armies in 1076. The ruler of Mali in early fourteenth century made Islam the established religion. Other nations followed. African Islam was not hindered but helped during the eighteenth and nineteenth century period of European imperialism. For Islam's record in race relations has been better than that of Christianity, and it has not been identified, as has Christianity, with western imperialism. Contemporary estimates of the number of Muslims in Africa range from 35 to 90 million!

ISLAM CONFRONTS THE MODERN WORLD

The coming of modernity has posed multiple problems for Islam. Islam's massively conservative tradition has often reacted instinctively in antimodern ways. Often modernity has been carried by Christian peoples, making it doubly unpalatable to the sons of the Prophet. From the Arab world to Indonesia, Islam has made common cause with colonial nationalism against what is often termed "Western imperialism." For these reasons and others, Islam has not found it easy to adjust to the modern world.

Many of these attitudes found early expression in the militantly antimodern Wahhabi movement of Arabia. The founder, Ibn Abd al-Wahhab (1703–1783), has been called a Muslim Puritan. Austere, rigorous, and simple in his faith, he protested alike against inner corruption of the faith, such as he observed in popular forms of Sufism, and against compromise with the world. The slogans of the Wahhabi movement were "Back to the Qur'an," and "Back to the pure Sunna." Yet this return was both narrow and militantly intolerant. In the historic tradition of the Kharijites, the Wahhabis restored the principle of jihad, or holy war. Aligning themselves with the kings of Saudi Arabia, they broke out of central Arabia and were finally contained only by the combined military forces of Turkey and Egypt after two decades of fighting.

The Wahhabi movement has left a continuing legacy in Saudi Arabia. In 1924, when the deposed Caliph ceded Mecca and Medina to Saudi Arabia, the Wahhabis in their iconoclastic zeal turned the birthplace of the Prophet into a resting place for camels and demolished the grave-markers of the Prophet and

Sixteenth-century Muslim prayer rug from Persia

Courtesy of The Metropolitan Museum of Art, Mr. and Mrs. Isaac D. Fletcher Collection, bequest of Isaac D. Fletcher, 1917

his companions. This extremism finds expression in Saudi Arabia's continuing adherence to the Hanbalite school of interpretation of shari'a. Wahhabi extremism is generally repudiated elsewhere in the Muslim and Arab worlds, though it has stimulated other efforts at reform in many parts of the Muslim world, and it has doubtless stimulated Arab nationalism.

Coming to more recent times, the Arab world has been characterized as the locus of "Islamic crisis." [51] By this is meant the widely held view of Arab peoples that their whole way of life is being attacked, chiefly by the West. In this complex attitude there are strands of feeling as old as the crusades of medieval Europe, but there are also events of history as new as the founding of the state of Israel. Arab peoples and their leaders have responded defensively; and a part of their defense is a close identification of Islam with the Arab cause. This is an identification which non-Arab Muslims often find questionable. Yet it is a combination which often adds a religious dimension to Arab nationalism. It also has generated a vigorous and varied apologetic defense of Islam in books, pamphlets, and journals, and also such universities as Al Azhar.

Among popular organizations, the *Ikwan al Muslimum*, or Muslim Brotherhood, has played a role of political activism in the United Arab Republic, though it is necessary to add that its policies have sometimes lacked realism and have promoted violence. Less extreme, and less influential, are such other organizations as the Association of Muslim Youth.

In Turkey and Turkish areas the problems are utterly different from the Arab world. In 1924 the so-called Young Turks under Kemal Ataturk overthrew the Ottoman empire, abolished the Caliphate, and established a new government on a secular and constitutional basis. Church and state were separated, the shari'a was supplanted by secular law, and many new laws on matters ranging from education to marriage, divorce, and the status of women achieved drastic modernization.

Turkish Muslims insist, however, that these changes have in no sense constituted a desertion of Islam, but rather a Muslim reformation.[52] They point out that Islam, separated from state support and state encumbrances, continues to live a vigorous life in Turkey. In towns and cities, mosques continue to thrive, and scholars expound the faith in ways compatible with modern life. Concerning the validity of these claims only the future can decide.

Islam in India has in modern times generated its own unique issues and problems. Much that has happened in the nineteenth and twentieth centuries has been based, as we have seen, on the life and thought of Shah Walli-ullah. Likewise of great importance, not only to Indian Islam but to the whole Muslim world, is Jamal ad-Din al-Afghani (1839–1897). In his life and teachings he was both Sunni and Sufi, and characteristically he founded the pan-Islamic movement designed to draw together all Muslim peoples in mutual defense against

European domination, and to meet the challenge of the modern world. Afghani's influence extended throughout the Muslim world.

Nineteenth-century India produced a notable Muslim modernist in Sir Sayyid Ahmad Khan (1817–1898), whose lifelong purpose was to demonstrate the compatibility of Islam with the new world that was dawning upon India. He remained faithful to the British during the 1857 mutiny and thereby gained British favor. In 1875 he founded the Muslim University of Aligarh. In journals, pamphlets, and books he proclaimed the compatibility of Islam and its Qur'an with modern science, education, and life.

In this same tradition stood Sir Muhammad Iqbal (1873–1938) poet and philosopher, and often called the "father of Pakistan." Born to pious Muslim parents in the Punjab, and educated in Europe as well as India, Iqbal combined ideas and attitudes drawn from Sufism with the philosophies of Nietzsche and Bergson. In addition to his volume *The Reconstruction of Religious Thought in Islam*,[53] which is a classic of Muslim liberalism, he soon became well known for his poetry, which gave eloquent expression to Sufi devotion.

Through the writings of both Sayyid Ahmad Khan and Muhammad Iqbal is to be seen a growing fear of India's Hindu majority. This note of anxious concern grew as the Indian Congress grew in influence and became more extreme in attitudes. Indian nationalism in many of its forms became increasingly Hindu. The reaction was an equally increasing Muslim nationalism.

Out of these attitudes the All-India Muslim League was founded in 1906. At a 1930 meeting of this organization, Iqbal declared for a separate Muslim state in northwest India. The name *Pakistan* was coined by a Muslim student at Cambridge University, Chandri Rahmat Ali, with *P* standing for Punjab, *a* for Afghania, *k* for Kashmir, *s* for Sind, and *tan* for Baluchistan. The synthetic word also has the meaning "Land of the Pure."[54] Rahmat Ali's first manifesto was issued in 1933, and by the late years of the same decade was being seriously discussed by Indian politicians. In 1947 Pakistan came into existence as a Muslim state whose sovereign power was asserted to derive straight from Allah. It must immediately be added that like certain other states (such as England) with established religions, Pakistan also has freedom of religion.

Widespread rioting and massacres accompanied the partition of India and founding of Pakistan; and the legacy of hostility continues to the present day. Within Pakistan there are some sixty-six million Muslims. They are divided between a conservative and a liberal party on issues having to do with the relation of Islam to the body politic. As has usually been true of religious establishments, Pakistan has raised fundamental issues concerning compromises between the ideal and the existing situation. Whether Islam has been strengthened or weakened by this emergence of an Indian Muslim state is still an open question.

One result of partition for Islam in India is that the Muslim minority is pro-
portionately much smaller than in the old India, and anti-Muslim feeling on the
part of Hindus has greatly increased. Indian Muslims also confront the issue
of participating politically in a non-Muslim and professedly secular state. Cul-
turally they seek to preserve their own ways, ranging from their Urdu language
to their Muslim faith. As one sympathetic writer describes their situation, they
are in India what the Muslim community is in the total world, namely, an
"important minority." [55]

CONCLUDING COMMENT

In conclusion and summary let us underscore some of the main issues and themes
of our study of Islam. Beyond its intrinsic importance as the religion of some 500
million people, Islam is significant as a particularly clear statement of the monotheistic or historical type of religion, including the problems peculiar to this type.
(1) In Islam's effort to be unqualified and uncompromising monotheism, it
has unwittingly brought to light some of the problems of monotheism, or in our
typology, faith of the third kind. Some of these problems are the divine Sovereignty, leading in extreme forms to fatalism or to tyranny; the Book, leading to
literalism and legalism; and the exclusive claim for one Faith against all others,
often leading to fanaticism and holy war. (2) Islam has frequently placed powerful religious sanctions behind extremely conservative social traditions. To be sure,
it is by no means unique in this attitude. And the example of modern Turkey
makes clear that there is no stark inevitability in this Muslim attitude. (3) Islam
involves a relation of faith to culture for which there are no precise parallels in
other religions. The traditional Muslim ideal is a wholly Muslim society; however, unlike other instances of this total claim, Islam has no priestly or hierarchical
administrators of religious domination of society. To a very great extent it is a
laymen's faith. (4) Islam has taken social justice and equality seriously. One consequence of this attitude is its record on racial justice, with its consequent popularity in twentieth-century Africa. It is also a clearly universal religion in which
the reasoning from one God to one humanity is accepted clearly and unequivocally. (5) Islam has its own distinctive and great tradition of learning, scholarship,
and philosophy. (6) It also has its own indigenous tradition of mysticism, which
in its milder forms has often revitalized Islam, but in its more extreme forms has
caused a severe tension if not an open conflict with submission to Allah. (7) If it
be asked whether there can be a Muslim humanism, the answer will be that there
is a Muslim answer to the question, What must I do to be human? The Muslim
answer is to obey Allah. But if by humanism is meant any allegiance to Man as
against God, it is by definition excluded from Islam.

NOTES

1. One recent volume is a notable exception, namely, W. McNeill, *The Rise of the West,* The University of Chicago Press, Chicago, 1963.

2. Kenneth Morgan (ed.), *Islam—The Straight Path,* The Ronald Press Company, New York, 1958, p. 84.

3. Arnold Toynbee, *Civilization on Trial,* Oxford University Press, Fair Lawn, N.J., 1948, pp. 184f.

4. See *inter alia* H. A. R. Gibb, *Mohammedanism,* Mentor Books, New American Library of World Literature, Inc., New York, 1955.

5. Morgan, *op. cit.,* p. 6.

6. *Ibid.,* p. 7.

7. Qur'an XCVI, 1–5, in *The Meaning of the Glorious Koran,* trans. Mohammed Marmaduke Pickthall, Mentor Books, New American Library of World Literature, Inc., New York, 1953, p. 445.

8. *Ibid.,* p. x.

9. Sir William Muir, *Life of Mahomet,* Smith Elder Company, London, 1878, p. 132.

10. Qur'an LXXXI, 1–14, in Pickthall, *op. cit.,* p. 431.

11. Qur'an LXXIV, 38–44, *ibid.,* p. 421.

12. Qur'an XC, *ibid.,* pp. 440f.

13. Morgan, *op. cit.,* p. 13.

14. *Ibid.,* p. 14.

15. Philip K. Hitti, *The Arabs,* Gateway Editions, Henry Regnery Company, Chicago, 1956, p. 40.

16. Pickthall, *op. cit.,* p. xxvii.

17. J. Hutchison and J. Martin, *Ways of Faith,* rev. ed., The Ronald Press Company, New York, 1960, p. 295.

18. Arthur Jeffrey (ed.), *Islam: Muhammad and His Religion,* The Liberal Arts Press, Inc., New York, 1958, p. 93.

19. See *inter alia* Qur'an I, in Pickthall *op. cit.,* p. 31.

20. Jeffrey, *op. cit.,* pp. 138f.

21. *Ibid.,* p. 140.

22. Pickthall, *op. cit.,* title.

23. Morgan, *op. cit.,* p. 22.

24. Jeffrey, *op. cit.,* p. 155.

25. Hitti, *op. cit.,* p. 54.

26. Qur'an II, 190–3 in Pickthall, *op. cit.,* p. 50.

27. Qur'an, IV, 2, 3, *ibid.,* p. 79.

28. Hitti, *op. cit.,* p. 65.

29. *Ibid.,* p. 81.

30. *Ibid.,* p. 72.

31. Historians disagree on this date. H. A. R. Gibb says A.D. 762. See his *Mohammedanism,* p. 15.

32. Hitti, *op. cit.,* pp. 105f.

33. Morgan, *op. cit.,* p. 59.

34. *Ibid.,* p. 53.

35. See *inter alia* Gibb, *op. cit.,* pp. 88f.; Shafk Ghorbal in Morgan, *op. cit.,* pp. 57f.

36. Quoted in S. Archer and C. Purinton, *Faiths Men Live By,* The Ronald Press Company, New York, 1958, p. 483.

37. Jeffrey, *op. cit.,* p. 93.

38. Gibb, *op. cit.,* p. 100.

39. Quoted in Gibb, *op. cit.,* p. 103 (attributed to R. Nicholson, *Literary History of the Arabs,* p. 234).

40. Gibb, *op. cit.,* pp. 108–109.

41. P. K. Hitti, *History of the Arabs,* The Macmillan Company, New York, 1937, p. 45.

42. Arnold and Guillaume, *The Legacy of Islam,* Oxford, The Clarendon Press, 1931, p. 218, as quoted in J. B. Noss, *Man's Religions,* 2nd ed., The Macmillan Company, New York, 1956, p. 723.

43. W. T. Stace, *The Teachings of the Mystics,* Mentor Books, New American Library of World Literature, Inc., New York, 1960, p. 212.

44. I. Goldziher, *Mohammed and Islam,* Yale University Press, 1917, p. 183, as quoted in J. B. Noss, *op. cit.,* p. 724.

45. Stace, *op. cit.,* pp. 213–214.

46. *Encyclopedia Britannica,* vol. 12, p. 161.

47. W. T. de Bary (ed.), *Sources of Indian Tradition,* Columbia University Press, 1958, p. 370.

48. W. C. Smith, *Islam in Modern History,* Mentor Books, New American Library of World Literature, Inc., New York, 1959, p. 51. See also de Bary, *op. cit.,* p. 455.

49. Morgan, *op. cit.,* p. 344.

50. *Ibid.,* pp. 375f.

51. Smith, *op. cit.,* pp. 97f.

52. Morgan, *op. cit.*, p. 285.
53. de Bary, *op. cit.*, pp. 747f.

54. *Ibid.*, p. 827.
55. Smith, *op. cit.*, p. 292.

SUGGESTIONS FOR FURTHER STUDY

Adams, C.: *Islam and Modern Egypt*, Oxford, 1933.

Andrae, T.: *Mohammed*, G. Allen, 1936.

Arberry, A.: *The Doctrine of the Sufis*, Cambridge, 1935.

———: *Sufism*, G. Allen, 1950.

Arnold, T., and A. Guillaume: *The Legacy of Islam*, 2nd ed., Oxford, 1948.

Cragg, K.: *The Call of the Minaret*, Oxford, 1956.

———: *Sandals at the Mosque*, Oxford, 1959.

de Bary, W.: *Sources of Indian Tradition*, Columbia, 1958.

Gibb, H.: *Modern Trends in Islam*, University of Chicago Press, 1947.

———: *Mohammedanism*, Mentor Books, 1955.

Guillaume, A.: *Islam*, Penguin, 1954.

———: *Life of Muhammed*, Oxford, 1955.

Hitti, P.: *History of the Arabs*, 5th ed., Macmillan, 1951.

Iqbal, M.: *Reconstruction of Religious Thought in Islam*, Oxford, 1934.

Jeffrey, A. (ed.): *Islam: Muhammad and His Religion*, Liberal Arts Press, 1958.

The Meaning of the Glorious Koran, trans. M. Pickthall, Mentor Books, 1953.

Morgan, K. (ed.): *Islam—The Straight Path*, Ronald, 1958.

Padwick, C.: *Muslim Devotions*, Society for Promoting Christian Knowledge, 1961.

Schimmel, A.: *Under Gabriel's Wing*, Brill, 1961.

Smith, W. C.: *Islam in Modern History*, Mentor Books, 1959.

Von Grunebaum, G.: *Islam*, Menasha, 1955.

———: *Modern Islam*, University of California Press, 1962.

Watt, W. M.: *Muhammad: Prophet and Statesman*, Oxford, 1961.

15

THE MEDIEVAL
CATHOLIC SYNTHESIS

At the end of Chapter 13 we left Christianity newly emerged from the cata-
combs and the established faith of the empire of Constantine and his successors.
During the same period it was also splitting into Eastern Orthodoxy and
Western, or Roman, Catholicism. Now we return to Catholic Christianity as
the formative faith of the new civilization which historians were to call Europe
or the West.

It is clearly impossible to date the birth of a civilization or culture as one
dates the birth of an individual human being. Yet it accords with the prevailing
usage of historians to assert that sometime between the years 500 and 1000 a
new civilization took shape in the ruins of the ancient Greco-Roman world.
While no civilization on earth has undergone changes and transformations
more vast than those of the fifteen hundred years of Western history, there has
nonetheless been a continuing historical tradition from the West's beginnings
to the present.[1]

The next three chapters will deal with some of the varied relations between
Christianity and the West. In the present chapter our concern will be with
what Christopher Dawson has termed "religion and the rise of Western cul-

ture." [2] Christian faith played a crucial role in the formation of the new culture. What we call the medieval synthesis had an all-important religious center, namely the Catholic emphasis on creating, sustaining, and guiding a culture. In contrast, as the next chapter will point out, is the Protestant emphasis on the criticism of culture. Taken together these two emphases define one of the sharpest contrasts between Catholicism and Protestantism.

It is important to note that the defining forms of Roman Catholic Christianity both antedate and have long outlived their medieval context. They came into being in the ancient Greco-Roman world many centuries before the Middle Ages. Today the Middle Ages are long dead, but the Roman Catholic sacramental system culminating in the Mass, and the Catholic pyramid of authority rising to the Pope at the apex are still living religious forms in every corner of the earth.

Of the approximately fifteen hundred years of Western history, the first thousand are embraced by the terms *medieval* or *Middle Ages*. It is palpalby impossible to discover any single unifying feature in so long and various a period. However, more modestly one may suggest significant contrasts between medieval and modern attitudes, particularly as they relate to religion and religious tradition. One such contrast is that between transcendence and immanence. By this is meant that medieval men sought for the source of life's meaning above or beyond the actual process of human experience rather than within it, as is the predominant tendency of modern men. From this it follows that medieval men lived naturally within a system of authority, in contrast to the modern attitudes of criticism and rebellion against authority and tradition. Again, the medieval mind showed an affinity for mysticism, defined as an immediate apprehension of spiritual realities, in contrast to the empirical habit of modern thinkers.[3] As discussion proceeds through this chapter and the two following, the reader will wish not only to test these contrasts, but to make his own list of similarities and differences between medieval and modern traits.

AUGUSTINE'S LIFE AND THOUGHT

Nowhere is the historic transition from Greco-Roman antiquity to the nascent civilization of the West more clearly visible than in the life and thought of St. Augustine (354–430). On the one hand, he looked back in retrospect and summary to ancient Christianity and to its Greco-Roman context; on the other hand his main ideas and attitudes looked forward to the age to come, that is, to the Middle Ages, and in some notable respects beyond them to the whole Western tradition down to the present day. Augustine was one of the founders of the West. Through his life and thought ran many of the lines of tradition connecting the Greco-Roman past with the ages yet to come.

Augustine's life is recorded in his *Confessions,* which has the form of a dialog between Augustine and God. It was the first autobiography in the Western tradition, if not in all history. It was also the first of a long series of similar autobiographical works. In the presence of his God, Augustine discovered his human self, in all its intense and discordant passions and in all its inner depths.

Augustine was born in Tagaste, Numidia, in North Africa, the son of a devout Christian mother and a pagan father. After education in his home city and at Carthage, he began a career as a wandering rhetorist, teaching successively in Carthage, Rome, and Milan. At the same time he rejected as childish his mother's Christianity and began a period of spiritual wandering among the faiths and philosophies of the time. His first excursion was into the dualistic system called Manichaeism. Disenchanted by the inability of its leading exponent, Faustus, to answer his questions, Augustine shifted to the skepticism of the New Academy.[4] From skepticism Augustine moved on to Neoplatonism, a philosophy of which he later remarked, "There I read, In the beginning was the Word, but not the Word was made flesh." [5] His time of wandering was also a time of deep personal unrest in which he was torn between asceticism and worldliness. His own agonized prayer was "Lord, give me chastity but not yet."[6]

Augustine's complex life found a new center and new meaning with his conversion to Catholic Christianity in 354. He was baptized and received into the Catholic Church by Bishop Ambrose of Milan. Already an admirer of the monastic ideal, he withdrew to seclusion for meditation and dialog with sympathetic friends. Then, accompanied by his mother, Monica, he began the journey back to his native North Africa, where he planned to start a monastery. Monica died at the Italian seaport of Ostia after a dramatic mother-son conversation culminating in mystical illumination.[7]

Augustine spent the remainder of his life in the service of the Christian church, first as monk, then priest, then for thirty-five years as Bishop of Hippo. He preached, he shepherded his flock, he wrote voluminously, producing the first great Christian philosophical synthesis. He died in 430 as the Vandals besieged the city of Hippo.

Augustine's vast body of writings reveal a many-sided genius who addressed himself to all the main problems of Christian faith, and whose interpretations were to determine the course of Western thought for a millennium. His earliest Christian writings were concerned with the problems of faith's relation to reason, and of the truth of faith, which were destined to become the defining problems for medieval Scholasticism and for the whole tradition of Christian thought. Augustine's position was that faith had primacy but was fully subject to rational criticism. "I believe in order to know," said Augustine, meaning that the activity of knowing has its own foundations of faith. Indeed the very activity of doubting presupposes faith, having its own premises or assumptions, argued Augustine, anticipating Descartes by a thousand years. In the new context of faith, human reason had its own distinctive role, that of understanding faith.

Augustine was churchman as well as philosopher, and in the course of defending the church against those who would split it apart, he gave expression to views which are still normative for Roman Catholicism. The Donatists were a North African sect who maintained that the validity of the Christian sacraments was dependent upon the moral character of the officiating clergyman. This moral rigor stemmed from the previous century's persecution under Decius in which some clergymen as well as laymen had defected. Augustine saw in these views not only schism which would shatter the unity of the church, but a perilous subjectivism. On the Donatist basis, how would the Christian ever be sure that the sacraments he received were valid? In opposition, he argued that the sacraments of the Catholic Church were independent of the character of the priest who administers them. In bold objectivity the Catholic Church was asserted to be the Ark of Salvation whose sacraments alone can effectively guarantee eternal life. Augustine also did not hesitate to invoke the help of civil government in repressing the Donatists—a fateful precedent.

While Catholic Christianity accepted Augustine's view of the church and rejected (or seriously revised) his view of man and. sin, precisely the opposite was true of Reformation Protestantism, which rejected his view of the church and accepted wholeheartedly the great Bishop of Hippo's grim view of human nature. Augustine's ideas of man were worked out in conflict with Pelagius, a high-minded monk who was repelled by widespread laxity, particularly among the monks of his day, and who sought to achieve higher moral standards by teaching man's freedom and responsibility. In sharpest opposition, Augustine replied with his teaching of man's total depravity and consequent total dependence on God's grace. This view was autobiographical; Augustine believed out of his own tortured experience that God had given him the unmerited gift of faith. He asserted more generally that ever since the fall of Adam, man is so far sunk in evil that except for God's grace, perdition is his just and inevitable end. God extends his grace to those whom he predestines to receive it and his stern justice to the rest of humanity. Thus arose the austere doctrine of double predestination, of some men to Heaven and other men to Hell.

In many ways Augustine's most important single work was *The City of God,* which he began in 410 as a response to charges that Christianity was responsible for the barbarian sack of Rome. The book, completed in 426, showed Augustine's view of history as the dramatic interaction of the City of God and the city of this world, each of which is constituted by its own distinctive form of love, the city of this world by self-love, and the City of God by the love of God and the neighbor. This was the first Western philosophy of history. The

Middle Ages were destined to interpret the relations of church and empire in terms of Augustine's two cities. Even more fundamental throughout the whole course of Western history has been Augustine's view of mankind as actors in a kind of divine-human drama, of which God is both author and producer-director. The curtain went up on this drama at Creation, the climax is achieved in the coming of Christ, and the final curtain will fall at Judgment Day. The plot may be understood as God's relation to his erring human children. Each man's destiny consists in finding his proper role in the divine-human drama and playing it out with fidelity.

The sense of historic destiny expressed in Augustine's *City of God* was clearly derived from the Bible and its distinctively historical view of human existence. Through Augustine's book this view was channeled into Western culture, where in subsequent centuries some of its many implications would be spelled out. For example, the many and often bizarre views of millennialism in medieval and modern history derive largely from the Bible and Augustine's *City of God*. Even such modern ideas relating to human destiny as progress and Marxism stand in the Augustinian tradition.

THE MONASTIC ORDERS

The beginnings of Christian asceticism and monasticism as well as their distinctive formulation in Eastern Orthodoxy were noted in Chapter 13. In broadest perspective the Christian styles of asceticism and monasticism must be understood as distinctive variations on themes which recur throughout the world's religions. In many faiths men have been led to deny and mortify the flesh, devote themselves to celibacy and fasting, and with varying degrees of consistency reject or flee the common life of the secular world.

In the medieval West, monasticism was to become a basic institution of society. Many men in successive generations took monastic vows rejecting the world. Yet ironically, these monks helped powerfully, often in ways beyond their knowing, to build the new culture of Europe. During the Middle Ages they helped to maintain and guide its life.

In a notable essay, Lynn White has sought to interpret medieval Christianity as a succession of three great waves of reformation. He writes:

> The history of the Western Church since apostolic times has centered about three great crises: the Monastic Reformation, the Medieval Reformation and the Protestant Reformation. The early Middle Ages were dominated by the results of the first, the eleventh to thirteenth centuries by the accomplishment of the second, the later Middle Ages by preliminary symptoms of the third. Each of these three reformations marked a vigorous reaction of the Christian yearning for spiritual perfection to its changing environment and resulted in

mutual adaption between Christianity and the dominant social and intellectual forms. While none of these movements can be properly understood without reference to its general historical context, nevertheless, no purely secular economic or sociological interpretation of them is adequate. In each case the initiative towards change came from within the Church itself, arising out of deep spiritual discontent and concern lest the purity of religious life be sullied by worldly influences. Consequently, each of these reformations was essentially ascetic although, since each was dominated by a quite different view of religious perfection, each produced its characteristic type of ascetic in the monk, the friar, and the Puritan respectively.[8]

The first reformation was organized and led by Benedict of Nursia (ca. 470–ca. 547). As a student in Rome he was repelled by the evils of the time and fled as a hermit to a cave in nearby mountains. As the fame of his holiness spread, he reluctantly became head of a monastery. About 529 he founded the mother monastery of the Benedictine order on Monte Cassino and formulated its famous rule, which was destined to be the model for all subsequent Western monasticism.

Benedict's rule showed his insight into human nature and his genius for organization as well as his dedication to monasticism. It contained wise provisions for all the multifarious aspects of the monastic community, from its daily worship to the daily rations of food and drink and the interpersonal relations of the monks. The great achievement of the Benedictine rule was to make the ascetic aspiration for spiritual perfection a socially constructive and useful instrument for the service of the church and incidentally of Western civilization.[9]

Benedict's threefold rule of daily work, study, and prayer was characteristic. Monks did much of the hard work necessary to lay the foundations of a new civilization. What was even more far-reaching was that in this new context, manual labor was no longer slavish or servile (as it had been in the Greco-Roman world), but rather acquired new dignity as a way of serving God. Study too was a form of obedience to God. In the studies and libraries of monasteries the classical heritage of Greece and Rome was preserved through the Dark Ages, to quicken and guide subsequent ages of the European tradition. The worship and devotion of the monks was a spring from which the life of Christendom was periodically renewed.

The Benedictine rule spread northward, first to England and Germany, then to France. Its monks were the missionaries and pioneers who brought these lands into the Christian fold and laid the foundations for the new civilization.

Yet with passing generations, ardor cooled and had to be periodically revived. Monasticism, which was a protest against worldliness, found the world reasserting itself within the cloister. The sociopolitical organization of the new civilization was feudal, and increasingly the church was caught in the web of feudalism. In the next section of this chapter a few of the chains of this bond-age will be described. Here we note that it was a new wave of monastic protest and reform which freed the church from these feudal bonds.

The reform movement began in 910, when Duke William of Aquitaine founded a small abbey at Cluny, populating it with monks from the pure Bene-

Medieval monks at work on manuscripts
Courtesy of the Pierpont Morgan Library

dictine tradition and placing the new house under direct papal authority. The time was ripe for change; the new order spread rapidly, becoming the Cluniac movement, and had at one point almost a thousand houses scattered over France, Germany, Switzerland, and Italy. The Cluniac movement brought to the medieval church a new vitality and also a new freedom from feudal domi-nation. It was a Cluniac monk who as Pope Gregory VII brought the Emperor to his knees at Canossa. From Cluniac cloisters the leaven of a new faith was spread abroad into the life of Christendom.

In its turn, however, the world reasserted itself in Cluniac cowl and cloister.

But again the worldliness elicited protest and reform. This time the source was a new monastery founded at Citeaux, near Dijon, in 1098. Its discipline was strict, its way of life austere. But its devotion was strong, and like Cluny before it, the Cistercian movement brought a new spirit into monasticism, and thence into church and world.

In great measure the success of the Cistercian movement was due to the influence of a single man, Bernard, Cistercian abbot at Clairvaux. Born of knightly ancestry in 1090, he entered the monastery at Citeaux in 1112. Bernard was indefatigable as preacher and church leader. Impeccably orthodox, he was the sworn enemy of heretics and schismatics. A man of undeniable integrity, his piety was guided and moved by mystical vision, which will be described later in this chapter.

The second great wave of monastic reform which broke over Europe, called by White the "medieval reformation," showed significant differences of form.[10] It found expression not in cloistered monks who forsook the world, but in friars who in obedience to their orders went out into the burgeoning cities and universities of thirteenth-century Europe to teach and to serve the people. The two most important new orders were the Dominicans and the Franciscans.

The Dominican order was founded by Dominic, a devout Spaniard (1170–1221) who on a trip through southern France was appalled at the contempt shown to Catholic Christianity by a widespread movement of heresy and schism whose members were called the Albigensian Cathari. Dominic sought to do something to win these people back to the church. The outcome was the Order of Preachers, popularly known as the Dominicans, founded in 1215 and given the official sanction of the church the following year. The Dominicans emulated the Franciscans in adopting the rule of mendicancy; its members should beg even for daily bread. The new order was organized into provinces with elected officials, thus combining authority with representative government.[11]

The new movement spread rapidly to all European nations, and particularly to university centers. Some of the greatest figures in medieval faith and thought were Dominicans, among them being Albert the Great and Thomas Aquinas, who were Scholastic philosophers, Tauler and Eckhart, who were mystics, and Savonarola, the preacher. Ironically, it was the intellectual quality and integrity of the Dominicans which led to their selection as inquisitors, servants of the Holy Office of the Inquisition.

Equally influential in the thirteenth century were the Franciscans. Their founder, Giovanni Bernadone, or Francis, as he came to be called, was born in 1182, the son of a cloth merchant of Assisi in Italy. To the dismay of his sober father, the young Francis lived a gay life. The circumstances of his conversion are obscure, though illness and military service are said to have played a part in turning his mind from the pleasure and business of the world to the love of Christ.

Hearing what he believed to be a command of God to restore the fallen house of God, Francis sold cloth from his father's shop to rebuild the church of St. Damian near Assisi. His outraged parent took Francis to the bishop to be dis-

St. Francis in Ecstacy. Painting by Bellini
Courtesy of the Frick Collection

inherited. Francis responded by saying that henceforth he had no father but the Father in heaven. His conversion took place in 1206 or 1207.

The following year, on hearing Christ's command of poverty (through a reading of Matthew 10:7–14), Francis took a vow of mendicancy, and more broadly, of imitation of Christ's love and service to men. He drew a group of friends about him in allegiance to this vow. Two by two, members of the group went about the countryside, singing, aiding peasants in their work, caring for sick and needy people, and praising God. The movement spread, and more extensive journeys were undertaken. Drawn by the example of Francis' life, more and more men came into his group. His own travels widened, and in 1219 he journeyed to Egypt, where he preached before the Sultan.

Unlike Dominic, Francis was not an effective organizer, and it remained for others to give structure to the movement he founded. A revised rule for the society was approved by the Pope in 1223.[12] Meanwhile Francis withdrew increasingly from the world, spending his time in prayer and singing. He died in 1226, and was proclaimed a saint two years later.

The structure of his order was similar to that of the Dominicans. Similarly too, the Franciscans came soon to have widespread and profound influence. But the nature of the influence differed. Whereas the Dominicans were teachers and philosophers, the Franciscans devoted themselves to works of service and mercy in Europe's cities. The influence of the Franciscans was greatly increased by their third order, or tertiaries, that is, lay supporters who took some of but not all the vows and who provided support and carried on teaching activity.

From its founder the Franciscan movement received a legacy of significant feeling and imagination. Francis had made the first Christmas crèche, and he celebrated his devotion to Christ in song, picture, and story. He was far ahead of his time in romantic feeling for nature. The stories of his preaching to the birds are entirely consistent with what is known of his life and thought. These and similar impulses lived on in his movement, and through his movement found their way into the mainstream of Western life.

The monastic orders effected successive transformations and revitalizations in medieval Europe, but their significance was not limited to this. Once in existence, they were available for new tasks and new functions which the church might set for them. In days to come these tasks were to be ever-changing and worldwide.

AUGUSTINE'S TWO CITIES: MEDIEVAL CHURCH AND STATE

While Augustine never gave precise details on the relation of the two cities, the Middle Ages did not hesitate to interpret the City of God and the city of this world respectively as church and empire. In the medieval interpretation each was a society complete in itself, with respective systems of authority rising to the Pope and the Emperor.

The beginnings and development of the papacy were sketched in Chapter 13. During the Middle Ages the papacy achieved its greatest power and prestige. In the very early medieval period, as the Roman empire crumbled and barbarian invaders overran Europe and the Byzantine Emperor became more and more remote and unrelated to the West, there were periods when temporal authority lapsed into anarchy. At these times the Bishop of Rome was virtually the only center of stability for wide areas of Italy. The result was a steady rise in the Pope's power.

In the eighth century there appeared a document called the *Donation of Constantine* purporting to be a deed of gift in which Constantine, in gratitude to Pope Silvester for curing him of leprosy, gave him not only the primacy of the Catholic Church but also the city of Rome and somewhat ill-defined environing regions.[13] The truth and authority of this document went unquestioned until the fifteenth century, when the Renaissance scholar, Lorenzo Valla, demonstrated its falsity. Meanwhile, by the ninth century the Papal States had become a well-established political fact.

Papal power increased in numerous other ways. Gifts of land, the basic form of wealth in feudal society, were numerous. Christian missionaries sent by Rome won new lands to Christianity from Ireland and Scotland to Germany, thus widely extending papal authority.

Christmas Day of the year 800 saw the symbolic origin of the Holy Roman Empire. Charlemagne had conquered wide regions of France, Germany, and Italy. He was in Italy to protect the Pope and subdue dissident nobles, and as he knelt in prayer in St. Peter's on Christmas Day, the grateful Pope Leo III placed upon his head the Roman imperial crown. To many men in Rome and throughout the West, it was the restoration of the imperial power which had been Rome's. To Charlemagne it seemed a fulfillment of Augustine's City of God.

Yet it must be added that for the two centuries following this event, the church was drawn even further into the network of feudal society. Lacking the power to act for itself, it became increasingly one element among others in European feudalism. Church offices were bought and sold, a practice called simony, and bishops were appointed by temporal rulers. The Pope himself was uniformly subordinated to the Emperor.

It was under the Cluniac reform party that the church forcibly broke these shackles and asserted its independence, and indeed its domination. The Cluniac monk Hildebrand became Pope as Gregory VII in 1073, with an avowed program of reform and reassertion of the church's power and, as he saw it, her integrity.

The right of investiture, that is, appointment of bishops, was the crucial issue. The Emperor, Henry IV, appointed a bishop of Milan without Gregory's knowledge or assent. The Pope responded by excommunicating Henry and absolving his subjects from their allegiance. In 1077 Henry, surrounded by rising political troubles, made the dramatic move of coming to the north Italian castle of Canossa, where the Pope was lodged, and standing barefoot in the snow as a penitent on three successive days until Gregory released him from excommunication.

This dramatic event of 1077 stands as a symbol of papal power over the Emperor. However, the outcome of the dispute was a compromise in which the supremacy of the Pope in spiritual matters and of the Emperor in temporal matters was recognized. In effect a bishop must be approved by both Pope and Emperor.

The Hildebrandian ideal of the Pope's universal supremacy was destined to come close to full realization in Innocent III (1193–1216), whose words and deeds made him the most powerful man in Europe. He forced King Philip of France to put away a wife considered unlawful by the church. In a quarrel with John of England over the appointment of the Archbishop of Canterbury, he placed John under excommunication, took his kingdom from him, and gave it back to him as a feudal grant on Innocent's terms. Other measures failing, he proclaimed a military crusade against the Cathari of southern France, which the French King gladly carried out. Within the church, Innocent was also supreme. All disagreements among the higher clergy were subject to his final decision. He called the Fourth Lateran Council in 1215 and required it to do his bidding. Truly his reign was the high-water mark of the medieval papacy. Innocent himself put the issue in these words:

> The Creator of the universe set up two great luminaries in the firmament of heaven; the greater light to rule the day, the lesser light to rule the night. In the same way for the firmament of the universal Church, which is spoken of as heaven, he appointed two great dignities; the greater to bear rule over souls (these being, as it were, days), the lesser to bear rule over bodies (these being, as it were, nights). These dignities are the pontifical authority and the royal power. Furthermore, the moon derives her light from the sun, and is in truth inferior to the sun in both size and quality, in position as well as effect. In the same way the royal power derives its dignity from the pontifical authority; and the more closely it cleaves to the sphere of that authority the less is the light with which it is adorned; the further it is removed, the more it increases in splendor.[14]

A century later Boniface VIII (1294–1303) stated the spiritual authority of the Pope in equally clear terms:

> We are obliged by the faith to believe and hold—and we do firmly believe and sincerely confess—that there is one Holy Catholic and Apostolic Church, and that outside this Church there is neither salvation nor remission of sins. . . . In which Church there is one Lord, one faith, one baptism. . . .

> *For this authority, although given to a man and exercised by a man, is not human, but rather divine, given at God's mouth to Peter and established on a rock for him and his successors in Him whom he confessed, the Lord saying to Peter himself, "Whatsoever thou shalt bind," etc. Whoever therefore resists this power thus ordained of God, resists the ordinance of God. . . . Furthermore we declare, state, define and pronounce that it is altogether necessary to salvation for every human creature to be subject to the Roman pontiff.[15]*

Yet it is a fact that even as Boniface spoke these bold words, new forces such as nationalism were swirling about the church. Some of these issues will be sketched in a later section of this chapter. Meanwhile it must be noted that the absolute spiritual authority of the Roman pontiff thus achieved in the Middle Ages became a permanent part of Roman Catholic Christianity. However, what this supreme authority might mean, how it was to be interpreted and reinterpreted, were destined to be continuing questions in ages to come. Indeed no question is more pertinent to twentieth-century Roman Catholicism than what is and is not involved in the Pope's supreme spiritual authority.

Two further aspects of the medieval church's temporal power must at least be mentioned. These are the Inquisition and the Crusades. As to the Holy Office of the Inquisition, it grew up in the thirteenth century during and after the suppression of the Cathari, as a device for ferreting out heretical and schismatic ideas. As already noted, its officials were mainly Dominicans—an order formed with a very different aim. The Inquisition constituted in effect a secret court in which the defendant had no right to confront his accusers or examine evidence against him and where he was subject to torture. While the physical punishment of those convicted was committed to temporal government, responsibility lay clearly with the church. The confiscation of the convict's property as spoils to be shared by lay authorities doubtless further fed the fires of persecution. The Inquisition was a highly successful instrument for stamping out or at least repressing dissent. At least, it was successful for the duration of the Middle Ages.[16]

The Crusades were a series of military expeditions against the Muslim Near East numbering at least six, with many other expeditions too small for enumeration, the whole series occurring between 1095 and 1291. In 1095 Pope Urban II proclaimed the First Crusade at the Synod of Clermont in France, and in 1291 the last of Latin holdings in Palestine was retaken by the Muslims. Between these two dates, the six major Crusades set out from Christian Europe to rescue the Holy Land from the infidel hands of Islam, ostensibly so that Christian pilgrims might have free access to the Holy Land. Actually many kinds of motives contributed to the Crusades, ranging from religious idealism to the love of adventure, and to the desire for economic gain, loot, and pillage. Many sorts of men, from warrior saints to dashing kings or common criminals participated. Many sorts of results followed from these expeditions, most of them unexpected. One consequence was the legacy of ill-will between Christianity and Islam, as we noted in the last chapter, which persists to the present day. However, another result was increasing contacts between Europe and the Near East ranging from trade to exchange of learning. Also, the Crusades make indelibly clear to the student of mankind's religions that Christianity no less than Islam sometimes practices holy war.

LIFE AND WORSHIP IN THE CITY OF GOD

From earliest days, Catholic Christianity has taken with utmost seriousness the nature and significance of the church. St. Paul, writing in the New Testament, called it the Body of Christ,[17] and Cyprian, third-century Bishop of Carthage, termed the church the Ark of Salvation, outside of which there was no salvation. To these metaphors were added the Augustinian view of the church as the City of God.

Citizenship in the heavenly city has been, and still is, construed as extended to the faithful of all places and times, past, present, and future. From Augustine's time onward, it was customary to speak of the church on earth as the Church Militant, the church in purgatory (a doctrine mentioned by early church fathers and elaborated in medieval times) was called the Church Suffering, and the church in heaven was called the Church Triumphant.

The structure of authority within the City of God might be likened to a pyramid the base of which is the ordinary citizens, the Chrisitan laity. At successively higher levels stand clergy and bishops, and at the apex the Holy Father at Rome. As noted in the preceding section, membership in the Roman Catholic Church has from medieval times involved submission to the supreme spiritual authority of the Pope.

Life on earth is construed by Roman Catholic Christianity as a preparation for blessedness hereafter. Hence the faithful Catholic perseveres to the end in the hope of the beatific vision in heaven. The Roman Catholic Church's chief function is that of an authoritative, unerring guide through earthly life to heavenly blessedness. For salvation, membership in the Catholic Church is a necessary condition, though as will be seen, more modern interpretations have substantially qualified this requirement by reinterpretation of both words, *membership* and *church*. However, medieval Catholics did not shrink from more literal interpretations. For example, Dante placed Socrates, Plato, Aristotle, and Vergil as righteous pagans in the first circle of hell. Other less righteous pagans together with heretics and schismatics were located in lower and less comfortable regions.

Within the official community of the faithful, authoritative guidance begins with clear definitions of sin and salvation. Sin for Roman Catholics as for Protestant Christians is defined as any violation of God's will or law, and salvation is God's free gift through Christ to man, to be appropriated by human faith. The basic difference between these views lies in the Roman Catholic view that the church acting through her priests has the sole authority to absolve men from sin, and more affirmatively to communicate to them the sacraments which are essential to sustain the human soul in grace and prepare it effectively for bliss hereafter. Many features of this view of sin and salvation are premedieval, going back to the earliest Christian church or to the Bible. Yet the full elaboration of this architectonic system as well as its full practice was the achievement of medieval Christianity.

Only a few salient features of the Roman Catholic road map to heaven and hell can be mentioned here. For example, the church has distinguished between venial and mortal sin from an early historical period onward. Venial sins, less serious violations of God's will, came to be viewed as not depriving the soul of sanctifying grace and therefore susceptible of remission by prayer and good works. Mortal sin, which was defined as a serious breach committed with full awareness, came to be construed as depriving the soul of its supernatural life of grace. Therefore the church has taught that men who die in mortal sin go not to purgatory or heaven, but to hell. Attention must be called to the conditional nature of this assertion. *If* a man dies in mortal sin, *then* he goes to hell. However it is the view of many knowledgeable Catholic theologians that no human knowledge, not even the Pope's, is sufficient for the knower to assert with complete certainty that any man has in fact died in mortal sin. Only God knows for sure concerning this matter.

THE SEVEN SACRAMENTS

The indispensable guideposts along life's way and the vehicles through which grace is communicated to man, according to the Roman Catholic Church, are the seven sacraments. All were premedieval in origin, yet the full delineation and interpretation of the sacramental system was one of the great achievements of medieval Catholicism. The seven sacraments are: (1) baptism, (2) confirmation, (3) penance, (4) marriage, (5) holy orders, (6) last anointing, and climactically (7) the Mass, or Eucharist. A sacrament is by definition a sign or symbol which when properly performed mediates the grace of God to man.

BAPTISM

Baptism is both logically and chronologically the first of the sacraments. It is the symbolic act of pouring water upon the person, while stating that it is done in obedience to divine command and in the name of Father, Son, and Holy Spirit. Its effect is spiritual regeneration and inclusion in the community of the faithful, so that in time the person may proceed in order to the other sacraments. The service of baptism is customarily also a christening in which the child receives his Christian name.

Roman Catholic Christianity recognizes the validity of non-Catholic baptism of several sorts. Under extreme circumstances, such as impending death, some person other than a clergyman may perform the ceremony. Under certain circumstances the church accepts the Baptism of Desire, that is, the intention of the person or his parents to have the sacrament, or even the Baptism of Blood, in which unbaptized persons who give their lives for Christ and the church are received into the Heavenly City.

CONFIRMATION

Confirmation is the sacrament by which the church confers spiritual adulthood. It is usually preceded by a period of instruction in the nature of Roman Catholic faith. The symbolic action consists of the laying on of hands and anointing with holy oil by the bishop as he says the words of confirmation. While not necessary for salvation, it is considered an important step in an individual's growth in grace.

PENANCE

Penance is the sacrament in which God through a priest absolves a person from sin. Four elements are deemed essential, namely confession, contrition, absolution, and satisfaction. That is to say, the person must confess his sins fully and in good faith to a priest who is his confessor. The priest on hearing the confession has authority from God to grant absolution, remitting the eternal punishment which is the just penalty of mortal sin, and remitting also, in part or whole, the "temporal punishment" of sin, which is to say, penal time in purgatory.

This last aspect of penance involves the widely misunderstood Roman Catholic doctrine of indulgence. It is, of course, not permission to commit sin or payment in advance for future sin. Rather it is a substitution of specified acts such as prayers or other devotions for the temporal consequences of sin. The church's right to extend indulgences depends in turn upon the idea of the treasury of merit which is a special fund of goodness accumulated by saints (who have had more than enough for their salvation) and now at the disposal of the whole church to be dispensed under papal authority.

MARRIAGE

Marriage is a sacrament performed by two baptized persons who commit themselves to each other in permanent monogamous matrimony. The officiating priest is regarded as a witness; the contracting parties actually perform this sacrament. In extreme circumstances the sacrament can be performed with no priest present. Not only is marriage a permanent union of two souls like the union of Christ and the church, but it is the means by which new souls are brought into the world, and hopefully, prepared for the heavenly city. Therefore the Roman Catholic Church has always taken a very serious view of marriage. No divorce is permitted (though under carefully defined circumstances annulment is possible), and the duties of the married estate are carefully and fully set forth by Christian morality.

ORDINATION

Holy orders, or ordination, is the sacrament by which priests are consecrated to the ministry of the church. The laying of the bishop's hands on the head of the candidate, with appropriate prayer and solemn ritual, places the priest in the apostolic succession, which goes back through Peter to Christ. The sacrament is irrevocable—"once a priest always a priest." The priest is empowered to perform the sacraments and stands under the authority of his bishop and ultimately of the Pope.

LAST ANOINTING

Last anointing is the sacrament by which the soul is prepared for death and the life hereafter. It consists of anointing the body with holy oil, accompanied by prayer. Usually too, if possible, it is accompanied by a last confession and a last communion, or *viaticum*. Under special conditions such as warfare, a person other than a priest of the Roman Catholic Church may offer to the dying some of the comforts of this sacrament, hearing the prayers of the dying and assuring him of the faith of the church.

MASS

The Eucharist, or Mass, is the central and climactic sacrament of the church. The word *mass* is English for "missa," and is apparently derived from the words of dismissal at the end of the Mass, *Ite, missa est*. The official name of the sacrament, Eucharist, is derived from the Greek word for giving thanks, which points to a central act of the Mass, man's thanksgiving to God for salvation in Christ. Actually, the Mass incorporates a great many aspects of worship, such as confession, contrition, adoration, and praise, but clearly the climax is the reenactment of Christ's sacrifice for the sins of the world.

Normally the Mass is said by a priest, each of whose garments symbolize some aspect of his priestly function or preparation. Colors of some of the priest's vestments change according to the season of the Christian year, or for special occasions such as a nuptial or requiem mass. There must also be an altar containing the relics of some saint.

The Mass, or Eucharist, has a definite dramatic structure, rising to climax in the Fraction of the Host and moving on to conclusion in the communion of priest and laity and the postcommunion prayers. This dramatic action begins with Mass of the Catechumens, which continues the ancient custom of including in the first part of the service the catechumens, or those who are receiving instruction in Christian faith. These portions of the Mass include the Kyrie ("Lord, have mercy on us . . ."), the Gloria, the Collects, or prayers appointed for the day on which Mass is being said, the Epistle, and the Gospel, which may be followed by a sermon. In ancient times, catechumens were dismissed at this point, only baptized and confirmed Christians being free to remain through the Mass of the Faithful which followed. Today anyone who maintains an attitude of reverence is welcome to stay throughout the entire ceremony, though only baptized Catholics who have made preparation by confession are permitted to receive Holy Communion.

The Mass of the Faithful begins with the saying of the Nicene Creed, followed by the offertory. Then the priest ritually purifies himself in the *lavabo* and offers prayers called the Secret. Next come the Preface and the Sanctus ("Holy, holy, holy . . ."). The Sanctus, Kyrie, Gloria, Credo, and Agnus Dei taken together constitute the Ordinary of the Mass, which does not change from day to day. The Proper consists of those features which change with changing seasons and occasions. The Canon of the Mass, which is always and everywhere the same, begins with the prayer of consecration and Pater Noster which follow the Sanctus. The Canon moves on through the mysterious divine-human drama of the Mass; it includes the Fraction of the Host, the Agnus Dei ("Lamb of God who taketh away the sins of the world . . .") and the dramatic climax of the Mass, in which the priest elevates the host, saying, "This is my body. . . ." At this moment the wafer and wine are believed to be miraculously changed to the body and blood of Christ, which are offered as a holy sacrifice to God for the sins of the world. So Christ's sacrifice is reenacted whenever and wherever the Mass is said.[18]

The theological theory by which this mystery is explained is called transubstantiation; and it was officially proclaimed as doctrine of the Roman Catholic Church at the Fourth Lateran Council in 1215. It was formally explicated by Thomas Aquinas as a change, not in the external properties and accidents of the bread and wine, but in their inner substance (their "breadness" and "wine-ness").[19]

The climax of the Mass is followed by the communion of the priest and then of the people. After this come the postcommunion prayers, and the Last Gospel, which consists of parts of the first chapter of John's Gospel. The church encourages participants in the Mass to follow the action by means of Missals or Mass Books. By decree of the Second Vatican Council, large sections of the Mass may now be said in the vernacular language, though the Canon is still uniformly said in Latin. Whatever the changes or alterations, the celebration of the Eucharist continues to be the high point of Roman Catholic worship. This ceremony, which had its origin in the ancient world and came to its full development and significance in the Middle Ages, still continues to provide a living center for the faith of the world's 500,000,000 Roman Catholics.

CHRISTIAN SCHOLASTICISM

The term *scholasticism* is often used negatively to mean a type of thought which is preoccupied with insignificant details or which subordinates reason to ecclesiastical authority. While at times scholasticism has deserved this negative valuation, it is in historic fact a much larger and more significant phenomenon than these modern prejudices indicate. As we have seen in previous chapters, scholasticism may be defined as the use of philosophy for the exposition and defense of religious faith. In this sense we have met it twice already in this study of the world's religions, in Judaism and Islam. Both of these occurrences had significant historical influence on medieval Christian scholasticism.

Augustine is frequently called the father of Christian scholasticism. While he had historical influence, scholasticism actually came into being many centuries later. From the age of Charlemagne, schools played an ever-increasing part in Christianity. From them emerged the medieval universities. Out of the discussions of the medieval schoolmen emerged scholastic philosophy, or theology. It looked back upon a heritage of Greek philosophy and Biblical religion and sought to synthesize them into a single whole—and in the process produced something new.

Here we cannot do more than hint at the great magnitude and range of medieval Christian scholasticism, pointing to a few major thinkers and their handling of important recurring problems. One such issue was the relation of faith to reason. Closely related was that of faith's object, or God; and scholasticism found a close relation between the nature of God and that of man. Taken together these constitute a cluster of issues never far from the center of scholastic thought.

Among earlier Scholastics none was more influential or characteristic than Anselm of Canterbury (1033–1109). An Italian by birth who was for many years abbot of the monastery of LaBec in Normandy and who ended his life as Archbishop of Canterbury, he illustrates the international character of the movement. Anselm's approach to philosophy is epitomized in his dictum *fides quaerens intellectum,* "faith seek understanding." By this he asserted his thought on the basis of faith, but sought philosophically to understand its nature and implications. Philosophy in this interpretation is faith's effort at self-understanding. Paraphrasing Augustine, Anselm declared *Credo ut intelligam,* "I believe in order to understand." In this manner, he sought a middle way between the extremes of uncritical belief and faithless reason.

His approach may be illustrated by his famous ontological argument for the existence of God. Anselm had already written a treatise expounding the cosmological argument, that is, arguing from the world to God. But dissatisfied, he sought a better, surer way, and in the ontological argument he believed that he had achieved it.[20]

This argument began from the idea of God as perfect being, a being greater than which is inconceivable to man. Now the object of this perfect or greatest idea either exists or does not exist. But if we take the second option, we violate the assumption that this idea is greatest or perfect. For if to the idea we add existence, we get a result greater than the idea without existence. Therefore we must assume the greatest idea to include the existence of its object. Therefore God exists. So reasoned Anselm!

His position was immediately attacked by a monk named Gaunilon. In an effort at reduction to absurdity, Gaunilon applied this same line of thought to the idea and existence of a perfect island. However, Anselm responded by limiting his argument to the single idea of absolute perfection, that is, to the radically unique God of monotheism. Only to this idea does the argument apply. Since its formulation the ontological argument has been argued and reargued, accepted and rejected, down to the present moment.

Anselm applied his thought to the theological problem of atonement in a book entitled *Cur Deus Homo* ("Why God Man?").[21] His answer was that God properly demanded satisfaction for human sin, meaning a satisfying of offended honor such as might characterize a feudal noble. Now a being who was simply man could not offer satisfaction, nor could satisfaction be achieved by the sacrifice of a being who was simply deity. Hence only one who was both God and man could achieve the desired result. Anselm's answer was less important than the question he raised—how to understand the sacrificial death of Christ.

Anselm was also deeply concerned with another issue of scholastic philosophy, namely, the nature of universals, of general ideas or concepts. One party in this dispute, the realists, asserted with Plato that ideas have a reality apart from their basis in sense experience, but the opposing party, the nominalists, asserted that only the objects of sense were real, ideas being simply shorthand expressions for recurring sense experiences. The issue was important to medieval thinkers for the reason that many significant religious objects such as God and the church partook of the same sort of supersensible reality as Platonic ideas. Anselm ranged himself squarely on the side of realism.

An intermediate position on this continuing issue was taken by the best-known scholastic figure of the next century, Abelard (1079–1142). A searching spirit, but by no means an irreligious man, Abelard attracted a large following as teacher and lecturer. Like many another academic, he had a penchant for criticism. His work *Sic et non* quoted contrary passages from the Church Fathers on many great doctrines, with no attempt to harmonize them. His view of the atonement differed from Anselm's idea of satisfaction; Abelard argued that Christ's death represents the highest expression of God's love for man, and its efficacy in salvation derives from this fact.

Abelard's bold views brought him into conflict with the strictly orthodox St. Bernard of Clairvaux, who after years of trying, secured Abelard's condemnation as a heretic. This, combined with his personal life, which included the famous love affair with Heloise, made Abelard's life a turbulent one.

Scholasticism achieved its greatest heights in the thought of St. Thomas Aquinas (1225–1274). His career must be seen against the background of new issues of the thirteenth century as well as against the earlier developments of Scholasticism, which have just been sketched. By this time new Aristotelian ideas were seeping into Christendom from Muslim Spain, largely through the writings of Ibn Rushd, known also by his Latin name, Averroes, whose thought we noted in the previous chapter. Previous medieval thinkers had possessed only part of Aristotle's thought; but Averroes, who was himself a bold speculative mind as well as a scholar on the writings of Aristotle, expounded such Aristotelian ideas as the eternity of the world and the mortality of the human soul. These and other similar ideas were eagerly seized upon by skeptical thinkers in Christian Europe as grist for their mill, with the result that the reading of Aristotle was proscribed at many European universities. For example, the Bishop of Paris thrice banned the reading of Aristotle by students of the university during the first two decades of the thirteenth century.[22]

Into this conflict as a mediator came Thomas. He was born of noble parents in the south Italian town of Aquino and educated at the Benedictine abbey at Monte Cassino. Then, to the consternation of his parents, he joined the new Dominican order and went off to the equally new University of Paris to study with the Dominican master, Albert the Great. He followed Albert to Cologne, then back to Paris, where he achieved the license to teach. During his brief life, Thomas taught in Paris, Naples, and Rome. He died in 1274 en route to the Council of Lyons, where he was to have been advisor to the Pope. Of his vast body of writings, the *Summa contra Gentiles* and *Summa Theologica*, the latter unfinished at his death, are characteristic. Many centuries later, in 1879, his work was proclaimed by Pope Leo XIII as the norm for Catholic theological teaching.

The key idea of Thomas's vast and architectonic system of theology is the relation of faith to reason. Much of religion—though not all—is susceptible of rational proof. Using Aristotelian reason on the facts of the natural world, it is possible to demonstrate the existence and unity of God. To be sure, reason comes presently to the limit of its capacity, and then man must continue his spiritual journey by faith, which though it goes beyond reason is never contrary to it.

Aquinas's use of reason and argument is illustrated by his five arguments for the existence of God, which occur in slightly variant forms in both *Summas*. They may be briefly summarized as follows:

1. Motion entails or presupposes an Unmoved Mover. For Aquinas, motion did not mean simple physical displacement, the mathematical formula s/t of modern physical equations, but rather the whole fact of change whereby, beginning with potentiality, the process of development toward a *telos*, or goal, occurs. Like Aristotle, Aquinas conceived the world as a process moving toward fulfillment, the source of this process being the Unmoved Mover.[23]

2. Thomas also followed Aristotle in an analogous inference from the fact of causation to a First Cause. By *cause* Aquinas (and probably Aristotle before him) meant the whole productive agency in terms of which a process is brought into being and takes place. In both of these arguments, from motion and from cause, Aquinas also followed Aristotle in denying the possibility of infinite regression; it was inherently irrational and therefore impossible.

3. Aquinas argued from the fact of contingency to necessary being. Obviously, contingent beings exist; but equally clearly, it is not rationally possible to conceive of a universe in which literally everything is contingent. Rather, contingency presupposes necessity, and Necessary Being constitutes one aspect of deity.

4. A similar argument in the field of qualities, values, or proprieties moves from the degrees of perfection to Perfect Being. The argument presupposes that adjectives, such as *hot* and *cold*, *red* and *blue*, *good* and *bad*, designate real entities in the world, and on this basis proceeds to argue for the existence of their comparative and superlative degrees. Common human experience of goods and betters clearly and certainly points to an Absolute Best, which again is part of what men mean when they say God. So, at least, Aquinas taught.

5. In contrast to the preceding formulations of the cosmological argument,

that is, the argument from the world to its cause in God, the fifth argument is
teleological; that is, it argues from the supposed fact of design to a Divine Designer who, once more, is an aspect of what men mean by God. Design exists,
ergo the Divine Designer exists.

Thomas believed it possible to prove with complete logical certainty the
existence of the one God. He also traced the way by which the human mind

St. Thomas Aquinas
Aided by St. Peter and St.
Paul. Fifteenth-century
Italian painting
*Courtesy of The Metropoli-
tan Museum of Art, Fletcher
Fund, 1923*

ascended the path leading from the world to God. It is by way of negation of
that which is finite, mortal, and conditioned to the *in*finite, *im*mortal, and *un*-
conditioned. This way of negation consists of stripping away the limitations of
finitude, literally of placing a negative prefix before all the adjectives designating
human limitations. To the way of negation he added the way of analogy; and
Thomas's carefully worked out view of analogical speaking is an essential part
of his philosophy.[24] It is a way of taking certain carefully defined aspects of
man's life such as reason and love, and referring them metaphorically to the

infinite being of God. Thomas's views of analogy have become a major subject of study and writing among his modern followers.

Yet however carefully or adequately carried out, reasoning comes at length to the end of its road. At that point man continues his journey by faith, which for Thomas seemed to consist of belief accepted on the reasonable, well-founded authority of mother church. Concerning God, such truths of revelation which go beyond natural reason may be illustrated by the creation of the world by God, God's incarnation in Christ, and his threefold manifestation in the Trinity. These and the many other truths of revelation are to be taken on faith and lived out as aspects of the Christian's life and his preparation for blessedness hereafter.

There are few things in heaven, earth, or hell that Thomas's all-encompassing system did not treat. Indeed the idea of a *summa,* that is, an encyclopedic summary of all knowledge of all reality, in heaven above, in the earth beneath, and in the waters under the earth was inherent in his scholastic viewpoint. Thomas's all-encompassing philosophical-theological synthesis was by no means the only attempt of this kind in medieval Christianity. Other scholastic philosophers wrote Summas. But in many ways Thomas most nearly succeeded in this ambitious undertaking. After him the medieval synthesis began to crack, then to fall apart, as illustrated in the philosophies of such men as Duns Scotus and William of Ockham.

Many students have observed significant parallels between Scholasticism and another characteristic achievement of the Middle Ages, the Gothic style in architecture as embodied in the great medieval cathedrals. The Gothic style, which grew out of the Romanesque, was distinguished by its pointed arch and soaring height. Never before or since has stone been used in structures whose vertical lines so seemed to defy the laws of gravity. The Gothic style of cathedral and cloister has seemed to many students of the Middle Ages to express the religious aspiration of the times. The great Gothic cathedrals were also an expression of the communal life of this highly unified society and were a work of common labor and common devotion of the people. Small wonder that these great churches should exhibit the same inclusive architectonic unity and the same devotional spirit which found expression in scholasticism.

Even as men had labored together to create these vast churches, so also men of all stations knelt together within them in common worship of the one God to whom they were devoted. The humble, unlettered serf might not understand the subtleties of scholastic philosophy, but his spirit was moved by the soaring arches of the cathedral, by its amazing organization of parts into a coherent whole, or by the breathtaking beauty of its stained glass windows and sculpture.

All Christian men were drawn together by the faith celebrated in solemn mystery at the high altar of the cathedral. Like the center which draws all the

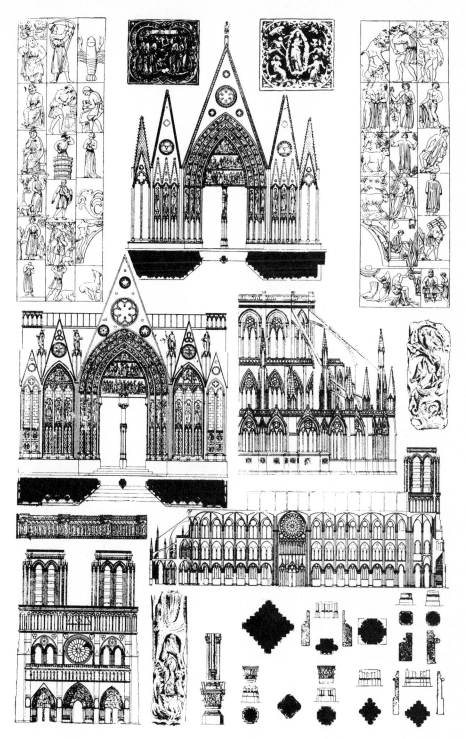

Details of the Cathedral de Notre Dame, Paris
Courtesy of New York Public Library, Picture Collection

radii to itself, this altar was the center of medieval society. The faith celebrated here was proclaimed in sermon and other forms of teaching. It was notably expounded in the glass and sculpture and the symbolic shapes of the cathedral, which was often termed a sermon in stone.

True, the common man might differ in his apprehension of the faith from his more learned brothers, yet there were impressive continuities even here. So it was that the cathedral was the focal center of thought and life in medieval Europe, the living center of the medieval synthesis. Today, when this is no longer true, these great churches still stand in the midst of Europe's cities as mute memorials to this once great and significant social fact.

MEDIEVAL CHRISTIAN MYSTICS

Mysticism and mystical attitudes have been observed in several of the religious traditions so far studied; it is not surprising to note their emergence in medieval Christianity. Indeed, all three of Chapter 1's categories of mysticism find illustration in medieval Catholic Christianity. These, the reader will recall, are mysticism (1) as an emphasis on the immediacy of religious experience, (2) as immediate communion with the religious object, and (3) as ontological union or absorption in this object.

Mysticism in the first sense has often been asserted to be a primary feature of the Middle Ages, whether the reality involved be the real presence of Christ in the Eucharist, or the presence of the Virgin Mary in devotions offered to her, or of some other saint in some particular holy place. Holy or spiritual things were of immediate and vivid reality to the people of this age. For this reason religion held the central place in their society.

The second and third meanings of mysticism found embodiment in particular men and traditions of the Middle Ages. Some men sought and found immediate communion with God, but others pressed on to complete absorption.

The tradition of medieval mysticism may be traced to Plotinus and other similar figures in the ancient world, and notably to an anonymous fifth-century Christian mystical document ascribed to Dionysius the Areopagite. The Pseudo-Dionysian treatises spoke of three kinds of knowledge of God, linear, spiral, and circular. The first might be termed inductive, the second dialectic or philosophical, but in the third, or circular, way the thinker retired within himself and in his inner life ascended the path to God.[25] Plotinus's goal had been absorption, but his Christian followers remained ambiguous on this important point. Whether the "circular path" ended in union or communion was seldom clear.

Among the many mystics destined to follow this circular path was the ninth-century Johannes Scotus Erigena, who envisaged God, in a classical mystical metaphor, as a fountain from which all reality bursts forth. Even better known was the twelfth-century Bernard of Clairvaux, for whom mysticism as immediate communion of the soul and God became a way of bringing new vitality into the increasingly sterile dogmatism of his time.[26] In his sermons on the Song of Songs Bernard spoke of Christ as Bridegroom of the Soul, and in a variety of vivid ways used the love relation to characterize religious experience, thus permitting mystics to understand their raptures as ideal or heavenly love. Bernard taught that this love had three stages, purgation, illumination, and union, though he was not clear whether union meant communion or absorption.

Other mystics hastened to walk the path which Bernard opened up. Bonaventura (1221–1274), bishop and Minister General of the Franciscan Order, was the author of a life of St. Francis and of a mystical tract called *The Journey of the Mind to God*.[27] In this journey he found six stages, beginning with the discovery of traces of God in the common world and moving inward and upward through religious gifts of grace to reflection upon the names of God and the Trinity, and thence to a consummation in which all the affections of the human heart pass "on to God."

Bolder, and more clearly an exponent of the third view of mysticism, was the Dominican Meister Eckhart (1260–1327).[28] Eckhart was celebrated both as a popular preacher and a writer in the then new German language. In his view, the goal of the religious life was the absorptive union of man and God in what he termed the rebirth of Christ within the soul. From this viewpoint, human individuality was something ultimately to be laid aside. Only the rebirth of God in the soul is finally real. Eckhart also taught two aspects of deity, one the traditional Father of Christianity but the second termed "Deity" (*Gottheit* in German) which was virtually the God above God.

These views seemed to Meister Eckhart to be in accord with orthodox Catholic teaching, but others did not think so. He was accused of heresy and died during the proceedings. The subsequent censure by the church did not lessen Eckhart's influence upon a large and continuing group of followers from his own time to the present.

Other mystics with many different emphases, and in many different regions, arose during the later medieval period. There was the fourteenth-century Catherine of Sienna (1347–1380), and her contemporaries in Germany, Johann Tauler (1300–1361) and Henry Suso (1295–1366), who continued in Eckhart's path. There were the Brethren of the Common Life, whose members practiced a monastic and celibate discipline aiming at a mystical religious life. A notable product by a member of this group was a volume by Thomas a Kempis entitled *The Imitation of Christ*, which may be characterized as a combination of the first two of our three types of mysticism.

While these mystical currents of thought and feeling revitalized Christian life, they also had the effect of loosening allegiance to the church. For if men

could come immediately into God's presence why take the longer, more labo-
rious route through the church with its seven sacraments and its many obligations? While it was not clearly intended so, mysticism contributed to the
dissolution of the medieval synthesis.

For the student of mankind's religions, the medieval Christian flowering of
mysticism shows lines of relation with mysticism of other times, places, and
faiths. A few lines of actual historical relation have been traced to mysticism in
Eastern Orthodox Christianity and to Jewish mysticism, and even to Islam.
Mystics, it seems, are often careless of the ties that bind them to particular religious groups or organizations.

When comparison is made between Christian mysticism and the great mystical traditions of south and east Asia, both similarities and differences emerge.
First, it appears that mystics tend to use the symbols of their own religious
tradition. Hence the Christian mystics speak of God and Christ, the Jewish
mystic of the Torah, the Hindu mystic speaks of Brahman and perchance of
Shiva or Krishna, the Chinese mystic of Tao, and the Buddhist of the Buddha-
nature. However, in these variant formulations, recurrent themes emerge. Of
these recurrent themes, none is more important than that of communion versus
absorption. The significant fact is that the Christian mystic (together with his
monotheistic brothers of Judaism and Islam) tends to speak of mystical communion with the one God. When as in the case of Meister Eckhart, the mystic
goes beyond communion to ontological union, theological problems of greatest
gravity are raised. Yet what is forbidden or at best problematic in monotheism is
the avowed and approved goal of the Eastern mystics. Their goal is complete absorption in the religious object. From this transcendent viewpoint a negative
valuation is expressed toward the present world with its experience of individuality, personality, and action. One corollary of this difference in goal is the
contemplative character of Eastern mysticism as against the active social character of Western mysticism.

THE BREAKUP OF THE MEDIEVAL SYNTHESIS

The thirteenth century was the great period of the medieval synthesis of faith
and culture. During this time Thomas Aquinas thought out and wrote his
comprehensive philosophical-theological synthesis. It was the age when papal
power and prerogative reached its highest point. Men worshipped God in the
newly finished cathedral of Chartres and in other brilliant representatives of
the new Gothic style. Dominicans and Franciscans argued with each other and
taught the Catholic faith to men of the growing universities and cities of Europe.

Yet as so often happens with great achievements of human civilization, cracks
soon began to appear in this imposing structure. In the fourteenth century

these cracks widened and deepened. Within two centuries it became apparent that the medieval synthesis was a thing of the past.[29]

Among the many contributing factors, one of the most important was growing European nationalism, especially in France and England. King Philip IV, "the Fair" (1285–1314), of France was drawn into bitter quarrel with Pope Boniface VIII (1294–1304) over the issue of the King's right to tax church property. It was during this quarrel that Boniface issued his *Unam Sanctam* (quoted earlier

Chartres
*Courtesy of the French Embassy Press and Information
Division, New York*

in this chapter) which, though it was the high-water mark of papal claims to supremacy over civil power, must be regarded as a monument to an age which was passing away, even at the moment when it was promulgated. For Philip summoned the French Estates-General and called the Pope a common criminal, and then dispatched an army which held the Pope a prisoner. This episode came to be unforgettably etched on men's memories.

Soon afterward Philip persuaded the subservient Pope Clement V (1305–

1314) to leave Rome for Avignon in southern France. The seat of the papacy was destined to remain there from 1309 to 1377, during the so-called Babylonian captivity, a time when the popes were French and under the domination of the French King. It was a disaster from which the medieval papacy never recovered.

Nationalism stirred in other lands as well. In England Wyclif (1328–1384) protested against papal taxes and prerogatives and attacked the corruption of the church. Arguing that the Bible was the law of the church, he and his followers translated the Bible into English. To give the Gospel to the people, Wyclif began sending his "poor priests" out to the cities and villages of England.

Wyclif's influence spread to Bohemia, in the writings and activities of John Huss (1373–1415). The church condemned Huss and burnt him at the stake at the Council of Constance, but this martyr death only caused the fires of Bohemian nationalism to burn more brightly. Once more in human history persecution actually spread what it sought to stamp out.

The inner deterioration and corruption of the church, apparent to every perceptive man, were further illustrated by the so-called Renaissance Popes,

men who rose to the papal office by intrigue and bribery and who in its exercise were more concerned with the new Renaissance art and with Italian politics than with Christian faith or love of Christ. Of the several examples of this phenomenon during the fourteenth and fifteenth centuries perhaps the most notable, or notorious, was the Borgia pope, Alexander VI (1492–1503) who gained the papal office by bribery and used it to advance the fortunes of his illegitimate children, Lucrezia Borgia (by advantageous marriages) and the murderous Cesare Borgia (by assisting him to carve out a political principality within the States of the Church).

As early as Marsilius of Padua (d. 1342?), the author of *Defensor Pacis,* thoughtful men were seeking to call a church council to check the inner corruption as well as the irresponsible power of the papacy. Similar voices were raised during the next century or two, but other voices rose to defend papal prerogatives. The contest between them was a drawn battle, with the result that no action was taken. When finally councils were called, the situation had disintegrated too far for reform to be possible. The councils did little or nothing to check the disintegration.

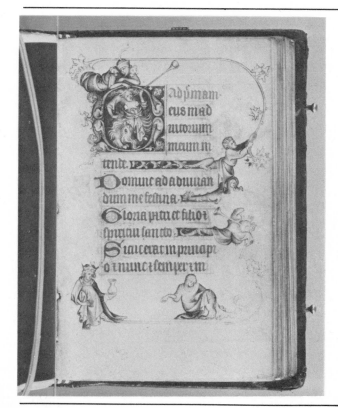

The House of Jeanne d'Evreux (14th century), a book of private services with prayers for each hour of the day. Such books were used by the nobility, who commissioned fine artists to prepare them
Courtesy of the Metropolitan Museum of Art

Probably more important than any single person or event in the breakup of the medieval synthesis was the subtle but persistent and pervasive shift of human interest from the next world to this world which took place during the Renaissance. It is impossible to assign exact dates for the beginning of the Renaissance or to give precise definition to its nature or significance. However, the reader sees in men and documents of the fourteenth century a new interest in the world of nature and society, and in Greek and Latin antiquity. Petrarch (1304–1374) was interested in Latin literature, especially Cicero, but was also a poet of great gifts himself. Petrarch's friend and admirer Boccaccio (1313–1375), best known for the earthy tales of his *Decameron,* was also a student of Greek who promoted humanistic studies in Florence and Naples.

The Renaissance came to full flower in the arts of painting, sculpture, and architecture in the Italian cities. In Florence under the Medicis, such scholars as Marsilio Ficino sought to combine Christianity with Platonism, even to the point of celebrating Plato's birthday as well as Christ's. In Rome, John Pico della Mirandola, avid and omnivorous student of literature, language, and history, proposed to debate all comers in defense of the dignity of man.[30] From Italy the Renaissance spread northward and westward to embrace all of Europe.

In most of its manifestations the Renaissance was by no means anti-Christian. There was no conscious break with the Christian tradition. Yet it represented a shift of interest from that of the high Middle Ages. Not God but man was the new center of interest. Not blessedness hereafter but fulfillment during this life was its message. As there will be occasion to note in Chapter 17, this was a trend destined to increase and develop throughout the Modern age. Here we note its function in disrupting (perhaps *undermining* or *eroding* would be a more descriptive verb) the medieval synthesis.

CONCLUDING COMMENT

As we have seen in the course of this chapter, the Middle Ages of Europe (approximately 500–1500 A.D.) produced a synthesis of Chistian faith and human culture unique in history. It was also a unity of faith and culture to which men in less integrated, more disordered modern times have looked back in nostalgia. Christian faith informed and guided culture, and so found expression not only in personal piety but in philosophy, literature, sculpture, architecture, and other arts. Christian humanism, to which we alluded at the end of the previous chapter, came to full flower in the Middle Ages, uniting Greek and Hebraic values.

The particular forms of ultimate concern or valuation produced in this situation were those of historical monotheism, as discussed in previous chapters, modified and qualified by the cultural situation. In the service of the one God, men achieved faith, hope and love. However their service of God took place not just in individual life, but in and through the great works of human culture. These works ranged from the writing of Thomas Aquinas' *Summa Theologica* or Dante's *Divine Comedy* to the construction of the Chartres Cathedral.

Yet despite its supreme achievements medieval European civilization had its dark side too. It was officially intolerant of dissent; hence the Holy Office of the Inquisition employed torture to disclose or to silent dissent. Heretics were harried, Europe's Jews were spasmodically persecuted, and a holy war or Crusade against Muslim Arabs of the Near East continued for approximately two centuries.

In the end the medieval synthesis was shattered by the dynamic forces that it nurtured. Burgeoning nationalism, especially in France and England, burst the bonds of medieval unity. The middle-class energies of Europe's cities had a similar effect. The energies of autonomous humanism pressed against the medieval limits, and then in the Renaissance (as we shall see in the next two chapters) burst this tight unity. If the twelfth and thirteenth centuries marked the medieval synthesis, the fourteenth and fifteenth marked its disruption, and presaged the coming of the Modern age.

Yet the Middle Ages did not perish utterly. Roman Catholic Christianity, which received definitive expression during this age, still continues as a vital force in the lives of men across the world. The philosophy of Thomas Aquinas and other scholastics is still a living option for many twentieth-century minds.

Finally, if we ask now which of the three main types of religion are to be observed in the medieval Catholic synthesis, the answer is that while historical monotheism obviously predominates, there are interesting and significant traces of both of the other types as well. Some of the great mystics of Catholic Christianity are virtually indistinguishable from acosmic mystics. The close relation in medieval times between church and culture pushed in the direction of cosmic religion, a direction that was powerfully supported by popular religion in this as in other times and places.

NOTES

1. Arnold J. Toynbee, *Civilization on Trial*, Oxford University Press, Fair Lawn, N.J., 1948, p. 15.

2. Christopher Dawson, *Religion and the Rise of Western Culture*, Image Books, Doubleday & Company, Inc., Garden City, N.Y., 1958.

3. Paul Tillich, *A History of Christian Thought*, unpublished manuscript, n.d.

4. Augustine, *Confessions*, V, 3.

5. *Ibid.*, VII, 9.

6. *Ibid.*, VIII, 7.

7. *Ibid.*, IX, 10.

8. Lynn White in George Thomas (ed.), *The Vitality of the Christian Tradition*,

Harper & Row, Publishers, Incorporated, New York, 1945, pp. 88–89.

9. Henry Bettenson (ed.), *Documents of the Christian Church*, Oxford University Press, Fair Lawn, N.J., 1947, p. 164.

10. White in Thomas, *op. cit.*, pp. 88–89.

11. Williston Walker, *A History of the Christian Church*, rev. ed., Charles Scribner's & Sons, New York, 1959, pp. 232–238.

12. Bettenson, *op. cit.*, p. 181.

13. *Ibid.*, p. 137.

14. *Ibid.*, pp. 157–158.

15. *Ibid.*, pp. 161–163.

16. *Ibid.*, pp. 188–189.

17. I Corinthians 12:27.

18. See any authorized Missal or catechetical manual. As to the latter, J. Killgallon and G. Weber, *Life in Christ*, 720 N. Rush Street, Chicago 11, Ill., is striking for the quality of its writing.

19. Bettenson, *op. cit.*, pp. 199f.

20. *Ibid.*, p. 195.

21. *Ibid.*, p. 196.

22. E. Gilson, *Reason and Revelation in the Middle Ages*, Charles Scribner's Sons, New York, 1938.

23. For this and others of Thomas's arguments for the existence of God, see A. Pegis (ed.), *Introduction to Thomas Aquinas*, Modern Library, Inc., New York, 1948, pp. 20–27. See also Jacques Maritain, *Approaches to God*, Harper & Row, Publishers, Incorporated, New York, 1954.

24. Pegis, *op. cit.*, p. 701.

25. Dionysius the Areopagite, *The Divine Names and Spiritual Theology*, trans. C. E. Rolt, The Macmillan Company, N.Y., 1951.

26. Ray Petry (ed.), *Late Medieval Mysticism*, Library of Christian Classics XIII, The Westminster Press, Philadelphia, 1957.

27. Bonaventure, *Journey of the Mind to God*, The Liberal Arts Press, Inc., New York, 1953.

28. W. Blakney, *Meister Eckhart*, Harper & Brothers, New York, 1941.

29. Walker, *op. cit.*, chaps. 10–16.

30. John Pico della Mirandola, *Oration on the Dignity of Man*, Henry Regnery Company, Chicago, 1956.

SUGGESTIONS FOR FURTHER STUDY

Adam, K.: *The Spirit of Catholicism*, Image Books, 1954.

Augustine: Confessions and Enchiridion, trans. A. Outler, Westminster Press, 1955.

Battenhouse, R. (ed.): *A Companion to the Study of St. Augustine*, Oxford, 1955.

Bettenson, H. (ed.): *Documents of the Christian Church*, Oxford, 1947.

Dawson, C.: *Religion and the Rise of Western Culture*, Image Books, 1958.

Ferm, R. (ed.): *Readings in the History of Christian Thought*, Holt, 1964.

Fairweather, A. (ed.): *Nature and Grace: Selections from Thomas Aquinas*, Westminster Press, 1955.

Fairweather, E. (ed.): *A Scholastic Miscellany*, Westminster Press, 1956.

Gilson, E.: *The Spirit of Medieval Philosophy*, Scribner, 1936.

———: *Reason and Revelation in the Middle Ages*, Scribner, 1938.

———: *God and Philosophy*, Yale, 1959.

Latourette, K.: *A History of Christianity*, Harper & Row, 1945.

Maritain, J.: *True Humanism*, Scribner, 1936.

———: *Degrees of Knowledge*, Scribner, 1939.

———: *Approaches to God*, Harper & Row, 1956.

Martindale, C. C.: *The Faith of the Roman Church*, Sheed, 1950.

Panofsky, E.: *Gothic Architecture and Scholastics*, Meridian Books, 1957.

Pegis, A. (ed.): *Introduction to St. Thomas Aquinas*, Modern Library, 1948.

——— (ed.): *Basic Writings of St. Thomas Aquinas*, Random House, 1950.

Petry, R. (ed.): *Late Medieval Mysticism*, Westminster Press, 1957.

Walker, W.: *A History of the Christian Church*, rev. ed., Scribner, 1959.

16

THE REFORMATION
AND PROTESTANTISM

Like many other large historical events, the Protestant Reformation is hard
even to locate with precision, let alone to understand. This is particularly true
of the Reformation since there are so many disagreements among historians.
Secular historians have generally been content to consider the Reformation
along with the Renaissance as an aspect of the vast and often violent process of
change by which the medieval world of church and empire was transformed
into the modern world of nation-states and territorial churches. Roman Catholic
historians have often interpreted the Reformation as a story of error and delusion, while many Protestants have viewed it as the recovery of original Christian
truth and virtue. There is doubtless a germ of truth in all of these approaches,
but none is fully adequate.

The late H. Richard Niebuhr once made the seminal remark that the Reformation might best be approached as a religious revolution within a social
revolution.[1] The latter is, of course, the transformation in Europe's history from
medieval to modern world; undoubtedly the Reformation was deeply and inextricably involved in this revolution. This social revolution had many causes,
ranging from the burgeoning nationalism of European peoples and the rising

importance of the middle classes, to technological advances such as the printing press, and to geographical discovery and expansion such as the opening up of America to European exploration and colonization. Yet the social revolution even in its widest sense is not the whole story of the Reformation.

The inner revolution may be characterized as the eruption of what Paul Tillich has called the "Protestant principle"[2] (or what Chapter 10 of this book termed the "prophetic principle") in the religious life of sixteenth- and seventeenth-century Europe. Tillich has defined the Protestant principle as the conviction that all human things must be held under God's judgment or criticism, and accordingly that if they are to find affirmative relation to God, God must take the initiative. H. Richard Niebuhr has called this outlook "radical monotheism"[3] and has asserted that as its consequence, human life is placed in a state of "permanent revolution."[4] Man's life under God is forever being shattered and remade. Such is the prophetic or Protestant principle of never-ceasing criticism of all human things, when they are held under the one God.

The Reformation had its own particular applications of this principle, often involving extensive adaptation, and compromise with local forms of thought and life. In the history of the Reformation, aspects of the inner religious revolution were inextricably mingled with aspects of the outer, or social, revolution. The result was the period of Western history called the Age of the Reformation.

This age began when on October 31, 1517, an obscure monk named Martin Luther posted a list of ninety-five theses on the church door (which served as the university bulletin board) at the new German University of Wittenburg, thus inviting public debate. It ended on the continent of Europe more than a century later with the Peace of Westphalia in 1643, and in England with the Glorious Revolution of 1688. By this time, men who were weary of religious war and fanaticism resolved to tolerate differences—and to turn to other interests. Christianity entered this age structurally as one church. What emerged were five main traditions of Christianity as follows: (1) Lutheranism, (2) Calvinism, (3) Anglicanism, (4) Sectarianism, and (5) Roman Catholicism.[5]

LUTHER AND LUTHERANISM

As noted above, Luther's Ninety-Five Theses were the spark that set the Reformation off with explosive violence—incidentally, somewhat to the surprise of Luther.[6] As in all explosions the causal factors were many and complex; in this case they ranged from low clerical morality and the general need for reform to nascent German nationalism and the rise of humanism. Certainly one causal factor was the personality and mind of Martin Luther.

Luther was born in 1483 in Eisleben, of peasant stock. He had the advantage of a good education, preparing for law at the University of Erfurt. A narrow escape from death in 1505 diverted him from this career and led him to pledge himself to the monastic life. He entered the Augustinian order the same year, and two years later was ordained a priest. He continued his theological studies, concentrating attention on the Book of Psalms and the Pauline Epistles. In 1510–1511 Luther made a momentous trip to Rome for his order, seeing at first hand the need for reform of the church.

However, the deepest problem of these years of his life was inward and psychological in nature. Luther felt himself increasingly and desperately cut off from God and hence plunged into despair, from which his rigorous practice of ascetic discipline was powerless to rescue him. Many modern readers see psychopathological states in his recurrent periods of despair. Luther's superior in the Augustinian order, Staupitz, was sympathetic, but to no avail. What did avail was what Luther found in the Bible, namely, the momentous idea that God's free gift of grace, which sinful man could not in the least earn or deserve, could give him back the lost meaning of his life. Thus he came to believe that man was justified not by works but by God's grace, which was appropriated through man's faith. Faith for Luther, as for Paul and Augustine before him, was a process of turning away from proud self-centeredness to God; it was man's humble but joyful "Yes" to God, in answer to God's original "Yes" to man. This revolutionary conception took shape in Luther's mind as he pored over the pages of the Bible, and it rendered useless all the elaborate aspects of the Roman Catholic system.

Many of these issues came to a climax when the Dominican monk, Johann Tetzel, appeared in Germany peddling indulgences with lurid salesmanship in order to raise money for the new St. Peter's Basilica in Rome. It was Tetzel's appearance just across the river from Wittenburg that elicited Luther's Ninety-Five Theses, many of which dealt specifically with the issues of indulgences and God's forgiveness of human sin.

As noted in the last chapter, an indulgence was not an ecclesiastical permission to sin, but rather a remission of part or all of the temporal penalty of sin, which is to say, man's sentence in purgatory. In no case did it claim to remit sin's eternal penalty, that is, condemnation to hell. To grant indulgences was, moreover, a right of the Pope, based upon the medieval idea of the treasury of merit. The Pope presumably might issue checks on this special account of merit, accumulated by the saints. What the age of the Reformation added to these ideas was the abuse of high-pressure salesmanship. But when Luther protested, he soon found himself increasingly driven to protest against the whole system, in the name of his own personally discovered view of grace as the favor of God to be appropriated by man's faithful and obedient heart.

While the Ninety-Five Theses challenged abuses, but not the Pope's right to issue indulgences, they did characterize repentance as an inward and continuing attitude of the believer toward God rather than any external act. However, in debate with official spokesmen of the church, notably in 1517 at Leipzig with Johann Eck, Luther maintained the Scripture as an authority over the church. In 1520 he was excommunicated, and he remained under this ban for the rest of his life. He responded by a public burning of the papal bull of excommunication in the town square of Wittenberg. In this same year he wrote three of his most important tracts, *On Good Works, On Christian Liberty,* and *On the Babylonian Captivity of the Church.*[7] The following year, 1521, he was summoned to appear before the highest authorities of the Holy Roman Empire at Worms. Shown his writings and given a chance safely to recant, Luther courageously refused, declaring, "Here I stand. I can do no other. So help me God." [8]

As he returned home from the imperial Diet at Worms, Luther was abducted by friendly hands at the command of his ruler, Frederick the Elector of Saxony, and was hidden for several months in the Wartburg castle. He used his time to translate the New Testament into German. It was the core of the epoch-making Luther Bible—a monument of German language and literature as well as of Christian faith and theology.

By 1523 Luther was back in Wittenburg, taking an active role in reforming the church. He wrote new liturgies for the church and sought to give constructive direction to the processes of change he had released. This led him to resist the radical efforts of colleagues like Carlstadt who sought to push the change to extreme conclusions. Luther called these men *Schwärmerei,* "enthusiasts," and denounced them unsparingly. In return, they regarded him as a halfway reformer.

In 1525 Luther married a former nun, Katherine von Bora. The marriage was arranged in haste, thus evoking Erasmus' jibe that the Reformation which at first seemed a tragedy was really a comedy ending in the wedding of a priest and a nun. Actually Luther's marriage was a completely honorable one and evoked some of the most attractive and winsome aspects of his life and thought, records of which are preserved in his *Tischreden,* or "Table Talk," recorded by theological students who lived with the Luthers.

As the German Reformation developed momentum and direction, it took on increasing political significance. This led Luther to seek to separate the Gospel from the world of politics, the world of faith and grace from the bloody and ugly world of German politics. He was also increasingly unhappy with the never-ceasing quarrels of the reformers. Yet his great contribution had been made in his proclamation of the message of God's grace and man's faith. Luther died in 1546 on a visit to Eisleben, the town where he had been born sixty-three years before.

Luther's theology bore a close relation to the volcanic personality and life that gave birth to it. He was scornful of the elaborate systematic formulations of

Scholastic philosophies of the church, based as they were on "that blind pagan Aristotle." [9] His own theology was based not on a system, but on his own intense, extreme, and undeniable experience. It began where Luther had begun, with the experience of sin, which Luther regarded as the arrogance of the human heart which cuts man off from God and raises idols in proud self-worship. Luther's view of sin was more extreme and less measured than Roman Catholic doctrine.

Luther disagreed with Catholic thought on the relation of faith to reason and thus on the use which Christian faith should make of philosophy. Luther's own training inclined him to the nominalism of William of Ockham, against the speculative reason of Thomas Aquinas; but at a deeper level Luther opposed all confidence in scholastic philosophy as a rival of faith. Such a use of human reason is depraved and sinful, or in Luther's phrase, a "devil's harlot." [10]

Not reason or philosophy, but faith alone was for Luther the instrumentality by means of which man approaches God, or more properly, the way in which man responds to God's grace. By faith Luther did not mean primarily a mystical experience (though he was much influenced by late medieval forms of mysticism), but rather the trustful allegiance and obedience of man's heart. It was Luther's fundamental conviction that God had acted in Christ to reconcile man to himself. Therefore he spoke of Christ as "God's Word," meaning the divine self-utterance or self-expression to man. So it is that when man responds with faith in Christ, he is reconciled to God.

The record of this redemptive activity of God is contained in the Bible, which for this reason assumed in Luther's thought a place of priority over Pope and church. It was for Luther the final authority. The Christian man has only to read its pages with an honest and seeking mind to find amid its words the Word of God. Luther made a clear and sharp distinction between the words of the Bible and the Word which God speaks through them. Thus he declared the words of the Bible to be the cradle of Christ. Luther was clearly not a literalist, as were some others of the reformers and some of his Lutheran followers. Moreover, he did not find the Word of God equally in all parts of the Bible, but regarded Hebrews, James, and Revelation as inferior. James was a "right strawy" epistle which he would have liked to exclude from the canon of Scripture. [11]

The life of faith which follows from God's grace not only makes philosophical speculation trivial and otiose, it is a great leveler. For this truth from God is not the monopoly of priest or theologian, but is every man's possession. Rather, every man is possessed by this truth, and in this service finds freedom, as Luther declared in On Christian Liberty. The corollary of justification by faith was the priesthood of all believers, in which not only was every man his own priest, but every man was a priest to his neighbor.

Martin Luther

Courtesy of New York Public Library, Picture Collection

From grace and faith sprang love. Christian love, or charity, was for Luther not a condition of earning God's favor, but rather the by-product in human life of God's grace or love to man. Luther believed that in gratitude to God for his divine love to man, love welled up spontaneously in man's heart. Few men have described the virtue of love more eloquently than Luther; yet few men have been as vividly aware of the tensions of love and hate in man's heart and of the desperate difficulty in any detailed attempt to apply love to the affairs of the world.

Mention has already been made of the growing duality in Luther's thought of law and gospel, or of the fallen world where group relations are determined by self-will and power, or at best by order backed with force, and the hidden world of God's grace and love which is foreshadowed here on earth in the relations of love in family and church. As Luther himself expressed the matter, he put law on earth and gospel in heaven. As the Reformation developed, Luther assumed an increasingly conservative social and political viewpoint. Drawing back in horror at the prospect of anarchy during the Peasants' Revolt of 1524–1525, Luther wrote *Against the Murderous and Thieving Peasant Bands*. He denounced unsparingly what he regarded as the radical aberrations of other reformers. The result of these tendencies was acceptance of the duality of church and state, in which the church asks of the state only the liberty to preach the gospel and administer the sacraments. On the other hand, having turned over the problems of social order to the prince or politician, the church refrains from criticism of the existing order, limiting its function to praying for the state and its ruler. Thus denied any social gospel at its beginning, the Lutheran tradition has been one of social acceptance often termed "quietism." Only when the basic rights of the church are threatened may the church speak out on political or social issues. Nevertheless Lutherans have sometimes spoken and acted in courageous defiance of state power, as was the case in recent history in Nazi Germany and Scandinavia. These events have led to extensive rethinking of the traditional Lutheran social position.

The Reformation in Germany was soon thrust into the troubled waters of interstate politics. By the late 1520s there was a league of Catholic princes and an opposing league of Protestant princes. It was the *protestatio* of the latter group at the Diet of Speier in 1529 which fixed the name *Protestant* upon the proreformation party. Dubious political maneuvering alternated with even more dubious military battles until the Peace of Augsburg in 1555 resolved the struggle on the basis of the formula, *cujus regio ejus religio,* "whose the rule, his the religion." Germany was divided between Catholicism and Lutheranism on the basis of the faith of the rulers of her several states. If the common man was dissatisfied with the local religion, he might choose to move to another region, though the choice was only between Catholicism and Lutheranism. It did not extend to Calvinism or sectarianism. But at least this solution brought peace to a people tired of religious strife.

From Germany, the Lutheran form of faith spread to the countries of Scandinavia, where it became the established church. From Scandinavia and Germany it emigrated to America, where it has continued to exert strong influence among Americans of German and Scandinavian descent.

Lutheran worship as well as theology has continued to bear the stamp of Luther's mind. In marked contrast to some other types of Protestantism, Lutheran worship has maintained a strong liturgical foundation. As to the sacraments, Luther recognized only two of the seven sacraments of Roman Catholicism as Biblically based, baptism and the Eucharist. In the whole issue of worship it may be said that Luther sought to simplify and purify Roman practice, but that as an intensely devout man he sought forms which would nourish and sustain the Christian spirit. He was particularly fond of music and wrote many hymns both as an expression of his own faith and for use in congregational worship. Choral singing has historically played a significant part in Lutheran worship.

CALVIN AND CALVINISM

As with every other aspect of their life, the cantons of Switzerland proceeded independently with the issues of reforming the church, some maintaining their Roman Catholic faith and others turning to one of the varieties of Protestantism. Leadership among the latter was assumed by canton Zürich under the soldier-humanist Huldreich Zwingli. In 1519 Zwingli became priest and pastor of the Zürich Cathedral, a post which he occupied until his death in battle with Roman Catholic cantons in 1531. Zwingli led the people of Zürich in abolishing many Roman Catholic practices and beliefs, and in establishing a Biblically based Christian faith, whose ultimate authority lay with the Christian community. Progress of the Reformation in German-speaking Switzerland was halted with the defeat of the Zürich army by Catholic opponents in 1531 in the Battle of Kappel, in which Zwingli was killed.

In French-speaking Switzerland, notably in Geneva, events took a different direction. During the late 1520s and early 1530s, Geneva was torn by dissension between Catholic and Protestant parties, due in part to the preaching and activities of the fiery Protestant, William Farel. Matters came to a head in 1535–1536 with anti-Catholic and iconoclastic rioting and with the city council torn between Catholic and Protestant parties. By the middle of 1536, Geneva had decided for Protestantism, though probably more for political than religious reasons.

In July, 1536, Farel was visited by a young French friend who was en route to visit fellow Protestants in Italy. His name was John Calvin, and Farel persuaded him to stay in Geneva and help with the work of reforming the city. Except for three years, 1538–1541, the rest of Calvin's life was to be identified with Geneva and the Genevan Reformation.

Calvin, born in 1509 of middle-class parents in Noyon, Picardy, had been educated first for a clerical then for a legal career. His youthful interests at the Universities of Paris and Orleans were those of a serious and brilliant young humanist. His first book, published in 1532, was *Commentary on Seneca's Treatise on Clemency*. During the year following, Calvin underwent an experience of "sudden conversion."[12] Nothing is known of this momentous event beyond Calvin's conviction that God spoke to him through the Bible and that God's will must be obeyed. The impact of this experience was to be seen in the whole subsequent life and thought of Calvin. From this time onward his own austere Christian faith had an altogether central place in his life. During the same year, Calvin's friend Nicholas Cop, newly chosen rector of the University of Paris, delivered an inaugural address so Protestant in tone that both Cop and Calvin were forced to flee. There is no basis for the assertion that Calvin wrote the address, though doubtless he sympathized with its sentiments.

Calvin went into hiding in France, then fled to Basel, Switzerland, where in 1536 he wrote the first edition of his famous *Institutes of the Christian Religion*, destined to grow through many successive editions until the final and definitive edition of 1559. Composed at first as a defense of French Protestantism against groundless charges of the French King, Francis I, the *Institutes* grew into the classical statement of Reformed Protestantism.

Calvin's first position in Geneva was as lecturer on the Bible. A year later he was appointed one of the city's pastors, the only official post he ever held, but one from which he launched a program destined to revolutionize the city's life and to be felt throughout the Western world. Calvin and Farel moved slowly at first, in 1537 securing passage by the Little Council of Geneva of a measure to excommunicate unworthy people and to impose a catechism and creed on the city. However, the following year the party opposed to Calvin won in the elections, and Calvin and Farel were banished. Calvin spent the next three years with his friend Butzer in Strassburg.

Returning to Geneva after victory in the 1541 elections, Calvin consolidated his position, soon becoming the most powerful man in the city. He moved to establish an ideal Christian commonwealth where all of life, individual and social, would be conducted according to his own severe interpretation of Christianity. It regulated individual conduct down to matters of speech, clothes, and manners.

Calvin's way with opposition is illustrated by the famous, or infamous, case of Servetus. Servetus, an erratic genius, had written against the Trinity in ways similar to modern Unitarians. Condemned to the stake in Roman Catholic Lyons, France, Servetus escaped, and for reasons hard to understand made his way to Geneva, where his presence was a deliberate political challenge to Calvin and was so interpreted by the opposition party. Calvin accepted the challenge. Servetus was tried, convicted of heresy, and burnt at the stake in 1553. It was an intolerant act in the midst of an intolerant age, though it was also at the time a great political victory for Calvin.

John Calvin

Courtesy of the New York Public Library, Picture Collection

Calvin's work at Geneva included many achievements which must be judged affirmatively by any civilized standard. While certainly no democrat in any modern sense, he did sanction the choice of pastors and elders by popular vote of the congregation, thus providing a thin opening wedge for democracy; it is a historic fact that democracy did develop notably in Calvinist lands. Calvin also removed the medieval Catholic ban against interest-taking by Christians, thus making possible a great growth of Protestantism among the rising business classes of Geneva and all of Europe. He also founded the Genevan Academy, which later became the University of Geneva.

Protestants from all parts of Europe, many of them refugees, gathered under

Calvin in Geneva, there imbibed his distinctive and vigorous version of Protestantism and then carried it back home with them. In this way Calvinistic Christianity got its start in France, the Netherlands, Germany, England, and Scotland, and from these bases, in America. In all of these lands the disciples of Calvin were strong men, convinced of their election to be fellow workers with God, and sure that in the Bible God has given an unerring guide for human faith and life.

In Calvin's native France, Reformed fortunes fluctuated with politics. By the middle of the sixteenth century the Huguenot party, under the able leadership of Admiral Coligny, was said to number almost half a million people. Untold numbers of them fell victim to the massacre of St. Bartholomew's Day in 1572. Through the action of the tolerant King Henry IV, they won legal existence in the Edict of Nantes in 1598. Almost a century later Louis XIV felt powerful enough to revoke the Edict; as a consequence the Huguenots became a martyr church until the French Revolution. What was even more important, through this intolerant act of Louis XIV Protestant influence in French life was almost wiped out.

In the Netherlands Calvinism provided courage to resist Spanish tyranny through more than a decade of savage war. Dutch Protestantism was Calvinist in both belief and church organization. Many influences, including a rising and successful business class, combined to produce in Holland a larger measure of religious toleration than elsewhere in Europe at the time.

Calvinism was taken to Scotland by John Knox, who had served a year and a half as a French galley slave for youthful Protestant activities. Upon release he found his way to Geneva, where he was pastor to other British refugees and also was one of the translators of the Geneva Bible. Returning to Scotland he became the chief foe of Mary, Queen of Scots, and main architect of the Calvinistic Church of Scotland.

Calvinism found its way to England during the reign of Henry VIII (1509–1547), and flourished during the brief following reign of Edward VI (1547–1553). Violently repressed by Edward's successor, Mary, it emerged again under Elizabeth and her Stuart successors as Puritanism. The Puritan revolution of the seventeenth century will be discussed in a later section of this chapter. From England, Scotland, and Holland, Calvinistic Christianity made the voyage to America, where it entered deeply into the fabric of church and society.

Calvin's thought, as contained in the *Institutes* and his many other writings, constitutes a different and more thoroughgoing type of Protestantism than Luther's. Calvinist worship and church organization were more thoroughly stripped of Roman Catholic features. The pulpit with the open Bible became the center of worship, and the service centered around prayer, scripture, preaching, and congregational singing. Like Luther, Calvin recognized two sacraments, baptism and the Lord's Supper; but Calvin went further than Luther in his rejection of such Catholic doctrines as transubstantiation. For him the sacraments were signs of God's promise to man. The Calvinist churches are ruled by elders elected by the people.

The center of Calvin's interpretation of Christian faith is the absolutely sovereign will of God. God rules the world and everything in it. It is he who called the world into being at Creation, and he sustains it through every moment of its existence. His will is inscrutable, and from man's viewpoint, God seems to follow his own mysterious good pleasure. Yet in fact the divine will is holy, righteous, and just. All things are ordained to serve God's glory.

Calvin taught that enough of the divine will is visible by human reason from the order of creation to render man responsible, yet it is also a fact that human understanding is very greatly dimmed by the depravity of sin. Hence God has taken the trouble to communicate his will to man with complete clarity in the Bible, which in Calvinistic Christianity constitutes a final and infallible authority. Indeed Calvin seemed at times to regard the specific words of the Bible as the revealed will of God, differing in this respect from Luther. In the Calvinist tradition a literalist view of Biblical inspiration was destined to be a continuing problem. In the struggles of Catholics and Protestants, it was perhaps inevitable that the absolute authority of the Pope should be countered by the Bible as a "paper pope."

Like Luther, Calvin believed in the total depravity of man—that is, no part of human nature is exempt from the ravages of sin. This idea of Calvin has been subject to many misunderstandings, especially in modern times. It is traceable to Augustine, to Paul in the New Testament, and even to such figures as Jeremiah in the Old Testament. Even in Calvin's extreme formulation it did not deny or obscure the fact that the natural man is capable of high achievements in many realms of life. However, since no part of man's life is exempt from the self-centeredness and evil of sin, man is incapable of the crucial religious act of turning to God through his own power. If man is to be saved, God and not man must take the initiative.

Like Luther, Calvin fervently believed that in the Bible, centering in Christ, God has done this. Indeed salvation is wholly of God, and man must believe that even his own turning to God is of divine grace rather than of human works. Yet according to Calvin if man is not saved by his works, he is saved to them. Calvin taught that salvation is fulfilled in righteousness of life. Hence a Calvinist was expected to be fruitful in works of righteousness, to show forth his election to salvation by the quality of his life. Righteous character was for Calvin and his followers an evidence that man has been justified, or saved.

Calvin's characteristic emphasis on the divine initiative in salvation led him to the austere doctrine of double predestination, to salvation and to damnation. He taught that God in his inscrutable will has predestined some men to damnation—a fate which divine justice would decree for all men—and others to salvation—as an expression of his unmerited love. Calvin was always careful to point out that predestination is not a doctrine of speculative philosophy but rather an inference from the glory and sovereignty of God.

Reformed Christianity produced a morality of great vigor and of equal rigor. The Puritan has been termed a "moral athlete."[13] Zealously he strove to make all of human life conform to the righteousness of his God. Max Weber has termed Calvinism "this-worldly asceticism."[14] The Calvinist sometimes fell victim to self-righteousness, and sometimes to a hard and loveless legalism in ethics. Nonetheless the popular American picture of Calvinists as humorless fanatics is a crude caricature which does little justice to the humane learning and the catholicity of Calvinism.

As previously suggested, Calvinist Protestantism made an alliance with the rising middle classes.[15] It emphasized the virtues of thrift, hard work, and industry as signs of election, and the vices of laziness and improvidence as signs of perdition. As many writers have pointed out, there has been a close relation between Calvinism and the rise of Western capitalism.[16]

Politically Calvinism proved to be the seed plot of modern constitutional government. As previously noted, Calvinism was democratic in its church government. Moreover, Calvinists had the best of reasons for opposing the arbitrary power of rulers. To all forms of political absolutism they said, "God alone is lord of the conscience." [17] The Calvinist view of human sinfulness led many Calvinists to a deep suspicion of all forms of power and hence to the political idea of checks and balances. Calvinist conscience and social responsibility proved to be a good soil in which grew many of the virtues essential to modern democracy.

THE ENGLISH REFORMATION

The English Reformation produced no single great figure such as Luther or Calvin and was even more deeply involved in political and national factors than the German or Swiss Reformation. It was the response of the English people as a whole. English churchmen often point to its source in an ancient tradition of English Catholic Christianity, allegedly independent of Rome.

The occasion of England's break with Rome was Henry VIII's desire to be legally rid of his wife, Catherine of Aragon, in order that he might marry Anne Boleyn and hopefully have a male heir to his throne. Yet beneath these personal events lay many deeper causes. English dissent to Rome was of long standing, going back at least to Wyclif (d. 1384). English nationalism flexed its muscles in the sixteenth century. The humanism of Erasmus, Colet, and More had a ready hearing in English universities and created a climate of opinion highly critical of the church. The writings of Luther were widely read. Incidentally, Henry VIII wrote a refutation of Luther which gained for him from the grateful Pope the appellation Defender of the Faith.

Henry, who has been called a tyrant under legal forms, was not a man to be denied. Refused a legal separation by the Pope, he resolved to break with Rome. A dutiful Parliament acceded to the King's demands with the Act of Supremacy in 1534. The strongly Calvinist Archbishop of Canterbury, Thomas Cranmer, performed the marriage ceremony of Henry and Anne Boleyn. Henry followed up these acts by confiscation of the extensive lands of the monasteries, which he divided among his subservient nobles. However, at this point Henry sought to clamp the lid on the process of reformation. In theology and church government he was no Protestant, and he harried and persecuted those who were.

Henry died in 1547 and was followed by his son, Edward VI, who was a child, and whose Protestant advisors made the most of their opportunity. A *Book of Common Prayer* adapted from many traditional sources was adopted in 1549, and an even more strongly Protestant edition was issued in 1552. More than any other factor the *Book of Common Prayer* has given unity and direction to Anglican Christianity. It combined a Protestant emphasis on the Bible with traditional Catholic forms of liturgy. Typical of the *Book of Common Prayer* was its designation of the Eucharist as "the Lord's Supper, or Holy Communion commonly called the Mass." The real presence of Christ in the Eucharist was proclaimed, but the Roman Catholic doctrine of transubstantiation was expressly denied. Forty-two Articles of Religion, revising Henry VIII's articles, were passed by Parliament in 1552; they affirmed three orders of clergy—bishops, priests, and deacons—and the Anglican clergy standing in valid apostolic succession.

Edward died in 1553 and was succeeded by his devout Roman Catholic sister Mary, who was intent upon undoing the Protestant mischief, as she saw it. Protestants who under Edward had persecuted Catholics were now burnt at the stake and harried from the land. The persecution was severe but brief, for Mary died in 1558.

England's next queen was Elizabeth, daughter of Henry and Anne Boleyn, and similar to her father in ability, insight, and personal popularity. Her long reign (1558–1604) was one of England's greatest ages. Religiously she sought a middle course between the extremes of Roman Catholicism and Calvinist Protestantism. The Act of Supremacy of 1559 declared the Church of England to stand politically under the Crown, the *Book of Common Prayer* to be the

KING HENRY THE EIGHTH.

OB. 1547.

King Henry VIII

Courtesy of New York Public Library, Picture Collection

standard for public worship, and the episcopate and a revised Thirty-nine Articles of Religion to be the norms of the Church of England. The foundations of Anglican Christianity were laid in these decisions.

While the English Reformation produced no Luther or Calvin, nonetheless the middle way of Anglicanism did find remarkable expression in a single book, Richard Hooker's *Laws of Ecclesiastical Polity*, published in 1594–1597. The author was a graduate of Corpus Christi College, Oxford, and between 1585 and 1591 he was Master of the Temple, a position which enabled him to preach to the university community. His disappointed rival for the same post, a Puritan named William Travers, spoke from the same pulpit Sunday evenings, thus provoking the quip, "The forenoon sermon spoke Canterbury, the afternoon Geneva." [18] In 1591 Hooker left the University for a country parish in order to devote himself to writing his *Laws*.

In this volume he deliberately sought a middle way between Rome and Geneva. In reaction to Calvinist emphasis on the Bible alone, Hooker based his case on the threefold foundation of the church in scripture, tradition, and reason. While deeply critical of many aspects of Roman Catholicism, he nonetheless refused to reject any idea simply because it was Roman Catholic.

His emphasis on reason found expression in the idea of natural order, or natural law, which had its origin in the mind of God. God has written the idea of natural order into the structure of his creation, or in other words, creation has a rational structure, expressible as natural law. Hooker asserted that the positive enactments of governments or churches were based upon divine and natural laws. The later conception of natural laws or self-evident truths in the thought of men like Locke and Jefferson owed much to Hooker's formulation.

In worship, Hooker's combination of law and tradition led him to vigorous defense of the *Book of Common Prayer* against what he saw as the Puritan desire to thwart all beauty and pleasing forms. Beauty and dignity of worship were worth maintaining, argued Hooker. From his time, Anglicans have placed a higher priority on worship than have most other non-Roman forms of Christianity. For Anglican Christianity the celebration of Holy Communion according to the *Book of Common Prayer* is the central act of worship and of the church's life.

The Anglican tradition which found expression in Hooker was destined to be tested, tried, and developed in subsequent history, but Anglican history has not strayed far from the formulations of Hooker. From England this form of Christianity spread to America, where it produced the Protestant Episcopal Church, to Scotland, where it became the Scottish Episcopal Church, and to mission stations in all parts of the world. Anglican Christians find a common center in Canterbury, and their bishops meet in periodic conferences at Lambeth Palace. Yet each national church, indeed each diocese and parish, enjoys a large measure of autonomy. Anglicans frequently regard their church as the bridge between Protestantism and Catholicism. Anglican high churchmen regard themselves as true Catholics, with Roman Catholics and Protestants alike diverging from the true norm. Low and broad churchmen, by contrast, emphasize the Protestant aspect of their tradition.

Queen Elizabeth's pragmatic solution of the religious problem was not destined to go unchallenged. Many of her subjects, dissatisfied with her middle-of-the-road position, sought to push the Reformation further. Their announced intention to purify Christian worship and teaching gained them the name *Puritans*. Standing on a Calvinist theology and opposing the episcopal form of church government, the Puritans carried on increasing activity throughout Elizabeth's reign. In the next century they played a dominant role in English history.

Elizabeth was followed to the throne by the Stuarts, James I (1603–1625) and Charles I (1625–1643). James struggled throughout his reign with growing religious dissent, and under Charles it broke into open rebellion which cost the king his throne and his head. Under the soldier-statesman, Oliver Cromwell, the Puritans made England a commonwealth (1642–1660). Cromwell's own religious views were somewhat to the left of the Puritan majority in Parliament, but politically he favored a national church which would exclude only papists and irreconcilable Anglicans, with a large measure of toleration for dissenting sects such as Baptists and Congregationalists.

The Westminster Assembly, named for its place of meeting, was a notable Puritan gathering of 121 clergymen and 30 laymen called by Parliament in 1643 for advice on religious matters. Excepting a few Episcopalians on one extreme and a few Separatists on the other, the majority were Calvinist in theology and presbyterian in church organization, that is, favoring the rule of the church by elected elders (the Greek word *presbyteros* means "elder") in a representative though centralized democracy. The Westminster Assembly produced the Westminster Confession of Faith, a notable statement of Calvinist Christianity, as well as a longer and shorter catechism and a Directory of Worship. All of these documents were much influenced by men and ideas from north of the Scottish border. In the Cromwellian period, English Presbyterianism assumed definitive form as the established faith of England. But when the Commonwealth fell in 1660, giving way to the Stuart restoration under Charles II, English Presbyterianism became the faith of a small minority—a position from which it has never recovered. However, during its period of ascendancy it sent many colonists overseas to America, where it grew with the growing nation. In addition to influencing the Presbyterian churches of America, English Calvinism exercised a strong influence on the theology (though not the church organization) of New England Congregationalism.

The Commonwealth had given way in 1660 to the restoration of Charles II; but the militant Roman Catholicism of Charles's successor, James II, led to the Bloodless Revolution of 1688, which brought the Protestant monarchs, William and Mary, to the throne. Even more importantly it produced the Act of Toleration and Bill of Rights of 1689. England continued to have an established church, but religious toleration and freedom were the law of the land. At first the range of freedom and toleration was narrow, excluding Roman Catholics, Jews, and atheists. Toleration was extended only to dissenting or free churches. Nonetheless a beginning was made for the distinctively modern idea of religious freedom, which once experienced and practiced was to spread, and as men came to understand its meaning, to widen and deepen its meaning.

SECTARIAN PROTESTANTISM

In addition to the three forms just described, the Reformation produced a fourth, namely, the small sects. Throughout the centuries of Christian history there have been small groups of men who have arisen to protest the compromises and evils of existing church and society. Indeed, this difference of outlook between church and sect has served as a focus for much fruitful study of Christian history and ethics.[19] According to this view, a church tends to be the religious organization of a whole society—to be, as it were, the society at worship. The church tends therefore to be closely related to the world, thus necessitating compromises and adjustments, but providing religious orientation and guidance for all men. In sharpest contrast, sects scorn compromise and adjustment as signifying an alliance with the devil. They have generally insisted that their members join voluntarily; and their customary ceremony of adult baptism has symbolized this feature. Once he has joined the sect, the member is rigorously disciplined. In their repudiation of the world of human society, most sects have been pacifist, rejecting as unchristian the evil of war. Some have also rejected private property as evil, others have taken the view of philosophical anarchism, rejecting the institution of government, and still others have even renounced the family as inconsistent with Christian morality.

No century of Christian history has been without its sectarian protests. The Christian movement of the first three centuries has been interpreted as a persecuted sect. Only with Constantine did Christianity take the form of a church. Thereafter, throughout the Middle Ages there were groups such as the Waldenses in twelfth-century Italy, the Albigenses of thirteenth-century France, and the Lollards of fourteenth-century England that illustrated the sectarian pattern. The early Franciscan movement showed some signs of becoming a sect, but the church was wise enough to reach out and draw it back into the fold. It is with this background of agelong sectarian activity in mind that attention is now turned to the sectarian groups which arose during the age of the Reformation.

Characteristically this form of Protestantism produced no single great leader or form of organization, but rather sprang up locally and in great variety in many parts of Europe. Many sectarians held the conviction that Luther and Calvin were only halfway reformers and therefore to be regarded along with Rome as evil. Most of them rejected infant baptism as a meaningless ritual and insisted upon adult or believer's baptism as an expression of an individual's decision to enter the community of believers. From this insistence was derived the label *Anabaptists,* or rebaptizers.

Groups of Anabaptists sprang up over large areas of Germany, Switzerland, and the Low Countries. Typical was the community which existed for some years in Waldshut, Switzerland, under the leadership of Balthazar Hubmaier. Later the saintly Hubmaier was hounded out of Switzerland to Moravia and thence to Vienna, where he was put to death. In Zürich, Anabaptist leaders were put to death by drowning, in hideous parody of their faith. Generally both Roman Catholic and Protestant leaders cruelly persecuted the Anabaptists. Yet, as often happens, persecution only spread abroad what it sought to destroy.

In addition to believer's baptism, these groups stood for rule of the church by a self-governing congregation, free of control by state and ecclesiastical hierarchy alike. They studied the Bible and sought rigorously to live by its teachings. For the most part, they were quiet, God-fearing people.

For some Anabaptists the Bible led them to politically radical conclusions. Such was the case in the Münster rebellion of 1534–1535. Under the leadership of Melchior Hofman, Jan Matthys, a baker of Haarlem, and Jan Beukelssen, a tailor of Leyden, these sectarians seized control of Münster and set up a new order based largely upon the Biblical Book of Revelation. Polygamy and community of property were established, and opponents were forcibly repressed. This radical experiment was put down with great cruelty by combined Catholic and Lutheran military forces. The Münster rebellion served to discredit widely such radical sectarian leadership and to divert European Anabaptist groups to peaceful, indeed passive, ways. The leader in this new path was a former priest, Menno Simons, who spent his life as the itinerant leader and guide to communities of sectarians in Germany and the Netherlands. His followers were called Mennonites. Many of them emigrated to America and other regions of the world in search of religious freedom.

Sectarian ideas and activities emerged in England as well as on the European continent during the sixteenth and seventeenth centuries. Some Puritans tended to become more radical as they continued to develop their criticisms of the established church. One such was Robert Browne, who in 1581 founded a church in Norwich, England, dedicated to the radical idea of separation of church from state. His preaching soon landed him in jail. Subsequently he sought refuge in the Netherlands, where his writings argued the case for the autonomy and self-government of the local congregation. Browne is claimed as the father of Congregationalism.

The term *Separatist* was applied in England to those who advocated complete separation from the established church and from governmental control of religion. One such group, under the leadership of John Smyth, fled England for Amsterdam in 1607. There Smyth adopted the practice of adult baptism, and in 1612 he and his flock returned to London to become the first Baptist Church in England. Throughout the seventeenth century, Baptists suffered severe repression in England, as illustrated by John Bunyan's long life in jail. In America Roger Williams founded Rhode Island on Baptist principles, including religious freedom, in 1636. Baptists have generally been characterized by adult baptism, autonomy of the local congregation, and a generally Calvinist theology. Beyond these common features, they have shown enormous variety.

Another Separatist group which fled persecution in Scrooby in 1609 found a temporary home in Leyden, Holland, under John Robinson, William Brewster, and William Bradford. But their eyes turned toward the New World, and in 1620 they sent their bolder and more adventurous members across the Atlantic on the *Mayflower* to a place to be called Plymouth, Massachusetts.

As the seventeenth century unfolded, many varieties of sectarian groups flourished in England and on the continent of Europe. So far, attention has been called principally to what have often been termed millennial or apocalyptic sects, that is, sects which stake their being on the imminent coming of Judgment Day and the New Age. Needless to say, the New Age has been conceived in widely different ways. Attention has also been called to the fact that following the Münster debacle, the Mennonites emerged as a pietist sect, that is, one which emphasized individual emotive experience of religion on the part of all members without reference to any claims of an impending millennium. Other noteworthy pietist sects were also to emerge.

In addition to apocalytic and pietist types were the mystical sects, illustrated by the Quakers, or Society of Friends, founded and led by George Fox (1624–1681). Fox experienced a mystical conversion in 1648, convincing him that true religion consists not in creed or church but in illumination by the Holy Spirit. He spent his life in obedience to this vision, organizing and propagating a religious society without formal clergy or sacramental worship. True worship consists, said Fox and his followers, in sitting in silence until the Divine Spirit moves someone to speak. Fox also bequeathed to his followers a strong sense of equality within the whole society and a passion for brotherhood among men. From the beginning, Quakers rejected all titles and differences in social rank; they also rejected and opposed both war and slavery. Among the early leaders of the Society of Friends was William Penn (1644–1718) under whom the Pennsylvania colony was founded as a haven for harried Quakers. Since Quakers also believed in religious freedom for all men, Pennsylvania soon became a refuge for many religious groups from England and Continental Europe. Among American Quaker leaders, John Woolman (1720–1772) was notable for his *Journal* as well as for his opposition to Negro slavery. Quaker zeal for the cause of peace and justice among men has been rekindled more recently by Rufus Jones (1863–1948), philosopher of mysticism and founder of the American Friends Service Committee. In America and Europe, and indeed throughout the world, the Quakers have exerted a moral influence out of all proportion to their numbers.

On the continent of Europe during the seventeenth century another notable pietist movement sprang up, in part at least as a response to the sterile intellectualism of orthodox Lutheran and Calvinist theology. In both Lutheran and Calvinist traditions, the vital convictions of earlier days gave way to rigidly correct intellectual beliefs. To all this, Pietism was an emotional reaction. For Pietism, true religion was not assent to a creed but personal, individual, and usually emotional experience of religion. In Germany Philip Spener (1635–1705) and later Hermann Francke (1663–1727) organized small groups of devoted people for Bible study, prayer, and devotions. For the Pietist movement, ideas such as sin, salvation, and faith in Christ took on intense and vivid personal reality.

Similar to the Pietists were the Moravian Brethren founded by Count Zinzendorf (1700–1760), who was influenced by Pietist education. Permitting a group of Moravian Hussites to establish a community on his Saxon estate, he was led to join with them. Under his leadership the Moravian Brethren were founded in 1727. Several communities of Moravians settled among the English colonists of North America. Throughout their history they have been notable in sending missionaries to all parts of the world. Through John Wesley they also exerted a vast influence on the Methodists of England and America.

The Methodist revival of eighteenth-century England was begun and led by John Wesley (1703–1791) and his brother, Charles Wesley (1707–1788). The sons of an Anglican clergyman, they attended Oxford, where they were members of a student religious society whose aims were worship and visitation of local jails. This group was known derisively as the Holy Club until someone dubbed them "Methodists" as a scornful characterization of their methodical customs of worship.

Despite his pious habits, John Wesley's religion was destined to be worked out through a decade of agonized seeking. On shipboard bound for the American colony of Georgia, Wesley was deeply impressed by the personal conviction as well as the calm courage of a group of Moravian Brethren, who were also bound for the New World. In Georgia controversy over a woman reduced his usefulness as a priest and missionary, and he sailed for home. In 1738 his religious seeking was answered by a conversion experience at a meeting of an "Anglican Society" in Aldersgate Street, London. Wesley recorded in his journal

John Wesley
Courtesy of the New York Public Library, Picture Collection

the details of the experience in which he felt his heart "strangely warmed." This experience transformed his life and left its stamp indelibly upon him and the movement he led.

Beginning to preach to the unchurched multitudes of England's growing cities, Wesley soon found himself organizing his converts into religious societies. The Wesleyan movement attracted scant interest in the Church of England, and Wesley, always a devout Anglican, found himself forced, step by step, to found a new sect. A decisive step in this process was his act of ordaining clergymen to carry on the work of Methodism in America, Anglican ordination being the exclusive prerogative of bishops. Yet once the first step had been taken,

Wesley proceeded to ordain other clergymen for the Methodists of Scotland, Newfoundland, and finally England. The Wesleyan movement combined a pietist concern in personal religious experience and conversion, with an interest in the people of England's industrial cities and America's frontiers. For both of these groups, Methodism offered new hope and salvation.

Still another and different kind of sect is illustrated by the Unitarians. From the first days of the Reformation, there had been intellectual radicals who questioned traditional dogmas as irrational. The doctrine of the Trinity drew their heaviest fire. One such person was Michael Servetus, executed by Calvin's Geneva. Faustus Socinus (1539–1604), member of a noble Italian family, was another. Moving from land to land seeking asylum from official intolerance, he found his way successively to Switzerland, Transylvania, and Poland. As a result of his labors, the Polish Brethren Church was founded with a unitarian creed. In the centuries which followed, individuals and small groups rose in many parts of Europe to espouse liberal and unitarian ideas. The eighteenth-century Enlightenment gave great impetus to unitarian ideas and societies. In 1773 Theophilus Lindsey withdrew from the Anglican Church and organized a Unitarian Church in London. Closely associated with him was Joseph Priestley, a dissenting clergyman, also an eminent chemist and the discoverer of oxygen. Priestley spent his last ten years in America. Thomas Jefferson is often listed as a Unitarian. In the nineteenth century such Americans as William E. Channing, Ralph Waldo Emerson, and Theodore Parker gave the Unitarain movement an influence far greater than the size of its membership indicated.

THE ROMAN CATHOLIC REFORMATION
AND COUNTER—REFORMATION

It is a fact often overlooked that the process of reformation went on within the Roman Catholic Church as well as among those groups which seceded from that church. It is also a fact that as the Protestant forces picked up momentum and seemed in a position to win most of Europe, Roman Catholic forces mounted what in military metaphor may be termed a successful counteroffensive, winning back for their church Italy, France, and extensive areas of Germany. Nineteenth-century historians gave the title "Counter-Reformation" to these events.[20] From these events the Roman Catholic Church emerged in a massively defensive posture which has defined her characteristic attitude until almost the present. In other words, the Roman Catholic Church of modern times is as much a product of the Reformation as any of the four main types of Protestantism just considered.

Some aspects of the process of revival and reform within the Roman Catholic Church, such as the work of Cardinal Ximenes to revive the Spanish church and educate her clergy, antedate by a full generation Luther's breach with Rome. A notable aspect of revival within the Roman Church was a number of new orders and organizations, the Theatines, the Regular Clerics of St. Paul, the Oratory of Divine Love, and many more.[21] Of these new orders, the Society of Jesus, founded by Ignatius Loyola, was the most important and best known.

Loyola was one of the great figures of the age. Born Inigo Lopez de Recalde of a noble Spanish family in 1491, he had a notable career as a soldier. Wounded in battle, he spent his recuperation studying the lives of Christ, St. Francis, and St. Dominic. Ideals of chivalry were still alive in Spain, and Ignatius resolved to be a knight of the Blessed Virgin. Hanging up his soldier's armor on her altar he set forth to serve her. As a good soldier and a man of intense faith, he began the rigorous discipline of life which subsequently found expression in his *Spiritual Exercises*. In 1523 he made a pilgrimage to Jerusalem, seeking to be a missionary to Muslims, but was refused by the Franciscans who were in charge of this mission.

Realizing that education would increase his effectiveness, he went to school, advancing rapidly to the university. A born leader, he gathered followers about himself and thus incurred the suspicion of the revived Spanish Inquisition. In 1528 he entered the University of Paris—just as John Calvin was leaving it. Again he gathered a group of like-minded students about himself. In 1534 these companions took a vow to go to Jerusalem to labor for church and fellowmen, or failing that, to put themselves at the disposition of the Pope. The Society of Jesus was finally recognized by Pope Paul III in 1540, and Ignatius was made its first "general," an office he held until his death in 1556.

The Society of Jesus spread rapidly throughout Catholic regions of Europe and was instrumental in reviving Catholicism and holding these regions for the church. Members encouraged frequent confession and communion, and they used their position as confessors to nobles and kings to advance their own intense and sometimes extreme interpretations of Catholic faith and to oppose both Protestantism and defection among Catholics. The Jesuits were active and influential at every level of education. The international character of their order made them particularly effective servants of the church.

Nowhere were Jesuits more active or was their record more glorious than in foreign missions. Within a century of the order's founding there were Jesuit missionaries on every continent on earth, where they preached and taught and made converts for their faith. The Jesuits were also intrepid explorers and travelers. Francis Xavier (1506–1552) reached India by 1542, went on to Japan in 1549, and died in 1552 just as he was entering China. Matteo Ricci reached China in 1581. In North and South America, French and Spanish Jesuits traveled, explored, and observed, founded missions and schools, and ministered to many human needs.

A second main instrument of the Catholic Reformation and Counter-Reformation was the Council of Trent. Ecumenical or universal councils of the church extend in a long tradition back to the Council of Nicaea. The last chapter noted the effort of the conciliar party which sought in vain to reform the church by convening a council. Such calls continued to be heard in the sixteenth century in efforts to heal the breach between Catholic and Protestant and restore the lost unity of Christendom. It is ironical that when a council finally met, its function turned out to be not the reconciliation of Catholics and Protestants, but the definition and assertion of the Roman Catholic position against Protestantism. The Council met in the north Italian city of Trent, and had three distinct periods, 1545–1550, 1550–1552 (when German Protestant delegations were admitted), and 1562–1564.

On every disputed point the Council took a hard line against Protestant thought and practice.[22] Against the Protestant view of the supremacy of the Bible, the Council reasserted the Roman Catholic doctrine of the equal authority of scripture and tradition. It denounced the views of Luther and Calvin on justification by faith alone. In the interpretation of the Eucharist, transubstantiation was stoutly maintained. On the issues of penance, purgatory, and indulgences, the Council of Trent conceded nothing. The major conclusions of the Council were summarized in the *Tridentine Profession of Faith,* acceptance of which has since been required of all converts to Catholicism.[23]

In keeping with this new militancy of Roman Catholicism, Pope Paul III reorganized the Holy Office of the Inquisition for use in any part of Europe where governmental officials would support or permit it. It proved to be an effective device for purging a country of Protestantism. Italy was the first country to be thus cleared. Another instrument of great effectiveness was the Index of Forbidden Books. Beyond their immediate effectiveness at the time, the significance of these and similar measures of Roman Catholicism was to indicate the defensive posture which that church was taking and was destined to maintain throughout the modern centuries of European history.

The nineteenth and early twentieth centuries witnessed a series of events which brought Roman Catholic defensiveness to a climax. In 1846, Pope Pius IX came to the papal throne, supposedly a liberal. However, disenchanted by the Revolution of 1848, he turned to policies which were not so much conservative as reactionary. In 1864 he issued the famous *Syllabus of Errors,* which was a list of errors to which the Roman pontiff—and presumably all Christians—must never be reconciled.[24] Lumped together in this list of errors and evils were pantheism, naturalism, absolute rationalism, moderate rationalism, indifferentism and toleration, socialism, Biblical societies, and in summary "progress, liberalism, and civilization as lately introduced." Seldom has a great religious body taken so completely negative a view of its environing world.

The climax of Pius IX's pontificate was the Vatican Council of 1869–1870, or as it is now called, Vatican I; and the most significant action of this Council was the affirmation, by a vote of 533 to 3, of the doctrine of papal infallibility. This doctrine, frequently subject to popular misunderstanding, asserts:

> The Roman Pontiff, when he speaks ex cathedra (that is, when—fulfilling the office of Pastor and Teacher of all Christians—on his supreme Apostolical authority, he defines a doctrine concerning faith or morals to be held by the Universal Church), through the divine assistance promised him in blessed Peter, is endowed with that infallibility, with which the Divine Redeemer has willed that His Church—in defining doctrine concerning faith or morals— should be equipped: And therefore, that such definitions of the Roman Pontiff of themselves—and not by virtue of the consent of the Church—are irreformable. If anyone shall presume (which God forbid!) to contradict this our definition; let him be anathema.[25]

Ironically, during the same year, 1870, the Italian army and people under King Victor Emmanuel put a forcible end to the States of the Church. Pope Pius IX responded by declaring himself the "prisoner of the Vatican." This issue was settled a half-century later by the Vatican Concordat with Mussolini.

In the same spirit of opposition to modern trends was the encyclical *Pascendi* of Pius X in 1907. Its objective was to destroy Catholic modernism. This was a movement of Roman Catholic Biblical scholars, theologians, and philosophers seeking to reconcile Roman Catholicism with modern scientific and critical knowledge. Among Catholic modernist leaders were George Tyrrell in England, Alfred Loisy in France, and Friedrich von Huegel in Germany, all of whom were excommunicated. As late as 1950 Pope Pius XII expressed similar attitudes toward Biblical scholarship in the encyclical *Humani Genesis*. These events underscore the historic importance of the change of attitudes initiated by Pope John XXIII and the Second Vatican Council of 1963–1965. It is doubtless too early to assess the results of these contemporary happenings, but it can be safely asserted that they reverse a direction maintained for the 400-year period from the Council of Trent to the very recent past. A posture of resistance to the modern world has been replaced by one of engagement with that world. Previous to Vatican II the relation of Roman Catholicism to other forms of Christianity was one of divergence and conflict; now the ways are convergent.

PROTESTANTISM IN AMERICA

While Roman Catholicism might stand in resistance to the modern world, such a position was hardly possible for Protestantism, which lacks any organ of central authority such as the papacy. Furthermore, Protestantism has always placed

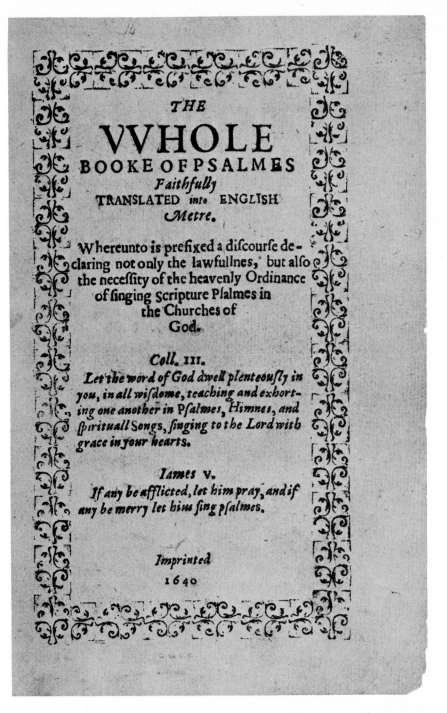

Title page of the Bay Psalm Book. It was the first book printed in the colonies

Courtesy of New York Public Library, Picture Collection

great emphasis upon freedom as an inherent part of faith. As a result of these features, Protestantism has interacted significantly with many aspects of the modern mind and world, sometimes rather indiscriminately taking to itself the latest colors and fashions of this world to produce what has been termed culture Protestantism. At the other extreme have been Protestant forms of well-nigh total rejection of the world of modern culture in what is often called "fundamentalism," and in some forms of sectarianism. However, at its best, Protestant Christianity has interacted with modern culture to produce significant forms of liberal religion.

Nowhere has the interaction of Protestant faith and modern culture been more important than in America. It is known to every American schoolchild that the English colonization of America was carried out largely by Calvinist and sectarian Protestants in search of the religious freedom which was denied them in Europe. This interaction of faith and successive forms of culture has constituted a large portion of American history. One of the first and most ironical chapters in that history deals with the New England establishment, or theocracy. The Puritans responded to their new environment by establishing a tyrannical rule over every aspect of human life. The rule of God through his ministers was extended over church, state, and even men's private lives. Illustrative of this Puritan establishment was the Mather dynasty in Massachusetts, begun with the migration of Richard Mather from England in 1635 and extending to his son, Increase Mather (1639–1723), and his grandson, Cotton Mather (1663–1728). All the Mathers were clergymen and leaders of the community. Increase Mather was President of Harvard College, a position which he was forced out of in the midst of political dispute. Both Increase and Cotton Mather were authors of several books. Both of them played somewhat dubious roles in the Salem witchcraft trials of 1692. By the later years of Cotton Mather's life, it was apparent to others, if not to him, that he was the spokesman for an age which was rapidly passing away. Secularizing trends were apparent in many aspects of society. In short, the Puritans were becoming Yankees.

Puritanism was soon to give place to other, more indigenous patterns of religion. In this historic transformation the role of leadership passed to Jonathan Edwards (1703–1758). A precocious child who entered Yale College at the age of thirteen, with a philosophic mind of great originality, Edwards became a devoutly religious man. Upon graduation from Yale he went to assist his grandfather, Solomon Stoddard, as pastor of the church in Northampton, Massachusetts. Stoddard had sought to accommodate himself sensibly to the cooling zeal of his parishioners. Edwards, by contrast, attacked their growing self-sufficiency. Out of his sermons from 1731 to 1735 emerged America's first religious revival— and what is even more important, the pattern of revivalism in American religion. Edwards's position eventually forced his resignation at Northampton, which he left for the frontier town of Stockbridge, Massachusetts.

Meanwhile similar events had been taking place in other American colonies, notably with Theodore Frelinghuysen in New Jersey and the Tennents, father and son, in Pennsylvania and New Jersey. Many of the currents of revival converged in the visit to America from 1739 to 1741 of the celebrated English preacher and revivalist, George Whitefield. Out of all these events emerged the Great Awakening. Not only did this revival result in renewed faith, it had many other fruits in the founding of schools and colleges and in varied humanitarian causes.

A Puritan Governor Interrupting Christmas Sports
Courtesy of New York Public Library, Picture Collec-

The Great Awakening was followed at the end of the century by the Great Revival, or Second Great Awakening, whose effects were felt especially on the frontier. The revival pattern of religion might be termed a result of the interaction of Protestant faith and frontier society. American pushed westward, and the frontier was the edge of this thrust into the wilderness. Frontier society was rough, simple, and mobile. To be relevant to these conditions, religion had to partake of these same qualities.

Methodist and Baptist circuit riders went from settlement to settlement, preaching, saving souls, baptizing, marrying, burying the dead—in short, bringing what religion they could to these outposts of civilization. In vast camp meetings people of the American frontier gathered from wide areas to hear sermons exhorting them to make their own acquaintance with religious realities. Traditional Protestant revivalism was charged with high emotional voltage, and behavior frequently became ecstatic. Men shouted, jumped, rolled, or even passed into unconsciousness as they "got religion." The pattern of revivalism had a clear and functional relation to American frontier society; today this pattern continues in less clearly functional ways in such figures as Billy Graham.[26]

Another milestone in American religious development was the achievement of religious freedom and toleration. As noted above, the New England Puritans were intolerant, and yet the modern idea of tolerance was born in seventeenth-century England. From England it was imported to America, where it was

A Revival Meeting
Courtesy of New York Public Library, Picture Collection

destined to find more pervasive and radical application than in Europe. Many men and many factors cooperated to apply and develop this idea in America. Ideas of Baptists such as Roger Williams and Quakers such as William Penn were supplemented by the more secular and rationalist viewpoints of Thomas Jefferson, Benjamin Franklin, and Tom Paine. Even more than as an ideal goal, toleration was demanded as a necessity of American social life. These and other factors all converged to make religious freedom the "lively experiment" of American Christianity.[27] While religious freedom has a "made in America" label, it has in recent times been exported to many other parts of the world.

Another decisive influence on American religion was the nineteenth-century immigration from Europe. Beginning in the 1830s and 1840s this immigration brought to American shores first Roman Catholic and then Jewish immigrants.[28] At first these groups existed as minority groups in a dominantly Protestant culture, sometimes tolerated and sometimes the victims of cruel intolerance. Yet these newcomers were destined to make their impact. For in the twentieth century America was to develop a threefold religious pluralism. This is a theme to which we shall return in Chapter 18.

Grave rubbings taken from early eighteenth-century gravestones in Massachusetts

Courtesy of the Abby, Aldrich, Rockefeller Folk Art Collection, Williamsburg, Va.

The nineteenth century brought also the large-scale urbanization and the industrialization of America with all their attendant social problems. These vast new movements elicited many religious responses.[29] The revivalists moved their activities from the frontier to the new cities—with notably diminished results. Another response was what has often been called the Social Gospel. Reclaiming the heritage of Christianity as a religion addressed to society as well as to individual people, many nineteenth-century American Christians sought Christian solutions for the new problems of society. Their suggestions varied widely, from settlement houses in America's teeming cities to industrial YWCAs and YMCAs, to the advocacy of social and political reforms and even to the suggestion that Christianity entailed a socialist reorganization of society. Among the leaders of the Social Gospel movement were the pastor Washington Gladden (1836–1918) and the theologian and teacher Walter Rauschenbusch (1861–1918). We shall return in the last chapter to this and similar trends as aspects of the contemporary situation in religion.

Amid the diverse forms of Protestantism, it is perhaps significant to note that Protestant emphasis upon freedom has been an important factor in creating this fragmentation. Yet it is important also to understand Protestantism as a form of Christianity. The term *Protestantism* is misleading; rather we should understand *Protestant* as an adjective modifying *Christian,* and the Protestant Christian as sharing many beliefs, attitudes, and practices with other Christians, of Roman Catholicism and Eastern Orthodoxy.

CONCLUDING COMMENT

The Reformation was one of the events (along with the Renaissance and the rise of modern natural science, to be discussed in the next chapter) that shattered the medieval Catholic Christian synthesis and set the Modern age of the West on its way. But as we have noted, within this social revolution was a religious revolution that demands to be understood in its own terms, as a reassertion of the Protestant or prophetic principle that only God is lord. From this principle follows the implication of faith as trust in God, and as the source of all life's meaning and value. In Protestantism, as in other forms of monotheism, the primary human values of faith, hope and love are derived from God.

The Reformation placed its own prophetic emphasis on the idea of ultimate concern, saying in effect that *only* God is truly ultimate, and that other claims to ultimacy or absolute allegiance must be judged false and evil. To the Reformers this charge was aimed at the church, but the principle is capable of wider and more general application. Also, as we have seen, this prophetic or Protestant principle must be viewed as an adjective modifying the noun, Christian.

From the Reformation emerged at least five differing types of Christian faith and organization: Lutheran, Calvinist, Anglican, sectarian, and Roman Catholic. What is even more important, divided Christendom faced an increasingly secular Europe and America, less interested in religion, and more interested in business and politics. In the case of Calvinist societies, Protestantism infused the new concerns with religious meaning and mission.

Protestant responses to the question, what must I do and be to be genuinely human? have varied across a wide spectrum from genuinely humanist responses to types of transcendence that can only be considered anti-humanist in significance.

As to our three main types of religion, the Reformation must be said to have sharpened or accentuated the monotheistic character of the faith and the cultures it has informed and guided. Sometimes, as for example in extreme Puritanism, this led to actual iconoclasm. Nevertheless, other tendencies, notably those of the cosmic type, have also found expression in Protestant cultures.

NOTES

1. I have been unable to locate this assertion in any of his published works. It was a remark made in a meeting of the Society for Theological Discussion in New York City, ca. 1956 or 1957.

2. Paul Tillich, *The Protestant Era,* The University of Chicago Press, Chicago, 1948, pp. 161f.

3. H. Richard Niebuhr, *Radical Monotheism and Western Culture,* University of Nebraska Press, Lincoln, Nebr., 1960.

4. H. Richard Niebuhr, *The Meaning of Revelation,* The Macmillan Company, New York, 1941, p. 118.

5. See Albert Outler's essay "The Reformation and Classical Protestantism" in George Thomas (ed.), *The Vitality of the Christian Tradition,* Harper & Row, Publishers, Incorporated, New York, 1945, for a discussion of the Reformation under the first four of these topics. To Outler's list I have added the fifth.

6. H. Bettenson (ed.), *Documents of the Christian Church,* Oxford University Press, Fair Lawn, N.J., 1947, pp. 259f.

7. *Ibid.,* pp. 272f.

8. *Ibid.,* p. 285.

9. Martin Luther, *Works of Martin Luther,* The St. Louis Edition, vol. II, Concordia Publishing House, St. Louis, 1956, p. 146.

10. *Ibid.,* vol. XX, p. 232.

11. *Luther's Works,* vol. 35, *Word and Sacrament,* vol. I, ed. by E. Theodore Bachman, Muhlenberg Press, Philadelphia, 1959, "Prefaces to the New Testament," p. 362.

12. Williston Walker, *History of the Christian Church,* rev. ed., Charles Scribner's Sons, New York, 1959, p. 349.

13. Ralph Barton Perry, *Puritanism and Democracy,* Vanguard Press, Inc., New York, 1944.

14. Max Weber, *The Protestant Ethic,* trans. Talcott Parsons, George Allen & Unwin, Ltd., London, 1930.

15. *Ibid.* See also R. H. Tawney, *Religion and the Rise of Capitalism,* Harcourt, Brace & World, Inc., New York, 1947.

16. See *inter alia* Ernst Troeltsch, *The Social Teachings of the Christian Church,* trans. Olive Wyon, The Macmillan Company, New York, 1931.

17. Calvin, J., *Institutes of the Christian Religion,* vol. 2, ed. John T. MacNeill, trans. Ford Lewis Battles, The Westminster Press, Philadelphia, 1960, p. 1520.

18. Harry Emerson Fosdick, *Great Voices of the Reformation,* Modern Library, Inc., New York, 1954, p. 335.

19. Troeltsch, *op. cit.*

20. The term "Counter-Reformation" is by Leopold von Ranke, the great nineteenth-century German historian.

21. K. S. Latourette, *A History of Christianity,* New York, Harper & Row, Publishers, Incorporated, 1953, pp. 855–6.

22. Bettenson, *op. cit.*, p. 381.

23. *Ibid.*, pp. 370–72.

24. *Ibid.*, p. 381.

25. *Ibid.*, p. 383.

26. Franklin Littell, *From State Church to Religious Pluralism*, Anchor Books, Doubleday & Company, Inc., Garden City, N.Y., 1962.

27. Sidney Mead, *The Lively Experi-ment: The Shaping of Christianity in America*, Harper & Row, Publishers, Incorporated, New York, 1963.

28. Will Herberg, *Protestant, Catholic, Jew*, Anchor Books, Doubleday & Company, Inc., Garden City, N.Y., 1955.

29. *Ibid.*, pp. 81–82. See also Mead, *op. cit.*, for a different interpretation of these trends.

SUGGESTIONS FOR FURTHER STUDY

Atkinson, J. (ed.): *Luther: Early Theological Works*, Westminster Press, 1957.

Bainton, R.: *Here I Stand*, Abingdon, 1950.

Bettenson, H. (ed.): *Documents of the Christian Church*, Oxford, 1947.

Brauer, G.: *Protestantism in America*, Westminster Press, 1954.

Brown, R.: *The Spirit of Protestantism*, Oxford, 1961.

Calvin, J.: *Institutes of the Christian Religion*, ed. J. T. MacNeill, trans. F. L. Battles, Westminster Press, 1960.

Ferm, R. (ed.): *Readings in the History of Christian Thought*, Holt, 1964.

Herberg, W.: *Protestant, Catholic, Jew*, Anchor Books, 1955.

Latourette, K.: *A History of Christianity*, Harper & Row, 1953.

Littell, F.: *From State Church to Religious Pluralism*, Anchor Books, 1962.

MacNeill, J. T.: *The Character and Spirit of Calvinism*, Oxford, 1954.

Nichols, J.: *A History of Christianity 1650–1950*, Ronald, 1956.

Niebuhr, H. R.: *Social Sources of Denominationalism*, Hamden, 1954.

————: *The Kingdom of God in America*, Harper & Row, 1959.

Pauck, W. (ed.): *Luther: Lectures in Romans*, Westminster Press, 1961.

————: *The Heritage of the Reformation*, Free Press, 1961.

Perry, R. B.: *Puritanism and Democracy*, Vanguard, 1944.

Tawney, H.: *Religion and the Rise of Capitalism*, Mentor Books, 1950.

Tillich, P.: *The Protestant Era*, University of Chicago Press, 1948.

Troeltsch, E.: *The Social Teachings of the Christian Churches*, trans. O. Wyon, Macmillan, 1931.

Walker, W.: *A History of the Christian Church*, rev. ed., Scribner, 1959.

17

MODERN CRITICISM
OF RELIGION

The Modern age is usually dated from the Renaissance and Reformation (ca. 1500) to the present, or as will be argued at the end of this chapter, to the recent past (ca. 1900). While it was initially a period of Western history, modernity in many of its important aspects has been exported so extensively to the non-Western world that it has become virtually a worldwide phenomenon.

Like all large historical entities the Modern age is difficult to define with precision. However, the aim of this chapter permits us to bypass these larger issues by limiting the exposition to the tracing of a few of the threads and patterns in the large and complex pattern of modernity which show the implications of the modern spirit for traditional religions or faiths. Initially these implications were limited to Western faiths, but more recently the Oriental faiths have been drawn within the scope of modernity and modern criticism.

The Modern age has seen criticism, pervasive and radical, of every aspect of human culture including politics, economics, art, science, philosophy, and religion. This criticism has been so pervasive and so intense that it will not be wide of the mark to call it the defining feature of modernity. The Modern age is the Age of Criticism. While our present concern is with criticism of traditional religion, this has been part and parcel of the general criticism of tradition in all its manifold aspects.

Criticism of religion did not begin with the modern West; rather it appears as a pervasive and recurring human phenomenon, rooted in the fact that even as man is a self, needing some faith or value system to guide the course of life, so also he is a critical mind seeking truth in this as in other areas of experience. Since this double fact is so, it is not surprising to observe the recurrence of criticism in many of the cultural traditions studied in this book. It was particularly significant in ancient Greece and in China, yet the reader will recall that even the heavily sacral tradition of India has had its anticlerical, materialist, Carvaka philosophy. Such attitudes and ideas, often mordantly critical of religion, recur in virtually ever civilized tradition in human history.

Despite these facts, the criticism of traditional religious faiths which has arisen in the Modern age is so enormously more extensive and intensive than any previous historical instance that it must be judged in effect to be something radically new. Thus for the first time in human history, men have been able to assert the possibility and desirability of the complete abolition of religion. Today in all parts of the world men have been divorced from their religious traditions in numbers and to a degree unparalleled in previous history.

This modern attitude toward traditional religion involves several necessary presuppositions. In a few summary words, the success of modern science and technology and the philosophical ideas of such men as Marx and Freud—along with many other factors as well—all converge in the novel assertion that mankind both can and ought to effect the complete abolition of traditional religion.

Whether in its new, modern form or its recurring historical form, the criticism of tradition raises an important but seldom recognized issue concerning the relation of criticism and the traditional values which it criticizes. A. N. Whitehead has remarked ". . . if men cannot live on bread alone, still less can they do so on disinfectants." [1] Criticism of tradition may be likened to a disinfectant whose function is to kill harmful bacteria; criticism has for its purpose the destruction of irrational and inhumane aspects of tradition, in religion and all else. These are worthy objects, but they have limits. As Whitehead's aphorism implies, disinfectant cannot serve as food, and criticism does not provide for that affirmation of value which is distinctively the content of faith. Indeed, precisely the opposite appears to be the case: criticism presupposes the existence of the values and faith which are its proper business to appraise and test. With reference to the vast numbers of twentieth-century people who have no relation to any historic faith, the crucial problem, stated in secular terms, is that of value creation and value maintenance. This is an issue to which it will be necessary to return during the course of this chapter and the next.

ELEMENTS OF MODERNITY

Since the modern spirit did not spring into existence all at once, but developed historically over a period of several centuries, it will be illuminating to glance quickly at three main historical phases in its development, namely, (1) the Renaissance, (2) the rise of natural science, and (3) the Enlightenment. Their cumulative impact will be sufficient to provide us with a working definition of the modern spirit, particularly in its relation to traditional religion.

THE RENAISSANCE

The Renaissance was primarily a movement of revival in European art, literature, and learning of the fourteenth, fifteenth, and sixteenth centuries. It began in the city-states of Italy but spread to other parts of Europe; it also spread to embrace more and more aspects of the culture. Since it was a many-sided affair emphasizing freedom and variety, exception may be taken to almost any generalization about it.

The Renaissance was basically Christian in outlook. While it involved tensions with the Christian past at many points and also many new emphases, nevertheless there was no break, either conscious or unconscious, with the tradition. While it deliberately sought to recapture ideas, attitudes, and forms from ancient Greece and Rome, many of its essential ideas were Christian in origin and nature. Such for example were the idea of the dignity of man made in the image of God, the sense of the infinite meaning of the individual human self, and the joyful affirmation of the whole panorama of the world of man and nature as God's creation.

Yet it is important to note the new elements and changed emphases of the Renaissance. There was an implied criticism of medieval ideas and attitudes even as early in the Renaissance as Petrarch (1304–1374), divided as he was between his love of poetry and of faith, between this life and eternal life, between love of Laura (to whom he wrote sonnets) and love of God.

The Renaissance criticism of medievalism involved increasingly radical attacks on the ideal of monasticism. Erasmus pilloried the vices and follies of monks, and with vastly less restraint Rabelais pursued this same theme.[2] Such criticism was also directed at medieval Scholastic theology, with its vast flights of overgeneralized speculation and its logic-chopping methods. The intellectual ideal of the Renaissance was not Thomas Aquinas writing his *Summa Theologica*, but Erasmus poring over manuscripts in order to achieve a critical text of the New Testament; or it was Lorenzo Valla exposing the forgery of the *Donation of Constantine*. It was Marsilio Ficino, of the Florentine Academy, adding the study of Plato to that of the Bible and proposing to celebrate the birthday of Plato as well as Christmas.[3]

The most fundamental change of the Renaissance was its shift of interest and attention from God to man and from heaven to earth. For some thinkers, such as John Pico della Mirandola (1463–1494) writing his *Oration on the Dignity of Man*, God's chief distinction was to have created man, who becomes virtually divine in his own right.[4] Pico and others were scornful of the traditional idea of original sin. Not man's sin and God's forgiveness, but human possibilities and achievements constituted the faith of the Renaissance. Its central tenet was man's boundless and creative freedom. Erasmus spoke for the Renaissance when he wrote *On Free Will*. The contrast between Renaissance and Reformation became clear when Martin Luther replied with an essay on *The Bondage of Will*, asserting a position even more extreme than that of the Roman Catholic Church.[5]

The Renaissance developed in detail the implications of its central tenet of belief in man. Not preparation for the hereafter, but the enjoyment of the rich goods of the present life is man's chief end. The fine arts of painting, sculpture, architecture, and literature became primary human pursuits, and their flowering was both cause and confirmation of the belief in man. Not even the papacy was secure against the new faith. Of the so-called Renaissance Popes, Julius II commissioned Michelangelo's "Moses" and the Sistine Chapel murals; Leo X, of the Medici family, shared his family's interest in art and also its involvement in Italian politics; and Alexander VI, father of Cesare and Lucrezia Borgia, was a great patron of the arts.

The significance of the Renaissance for subsequent periods of the West lay in its new and distinctive view of man which was, in the defining metaphor of the movement, man reborn, or renewed, and hence standing in the presence of an open future with its infinite possibilities beckoning him forward.[6] This aspect of the Renaissance is to be seen in its many Utopias. In addition to Sir Thomas More's *Utopia*, there were such pictures of the perfect society as Campanello's *City of the Sun* and, in earthier style, Rabelais' Abbey of Thelme with its motto, "Do what you will." There was also Giordono Bruno's similar idea of the infinite worlds which opened before the human mind. In these writings there was not yet the idea of actual historical progress, but there was clearly the basic image of man's renewal or rebirth. This vision of renewal carried its own seminal implications, including an ever-increasing criticism of the past, from whose fetters man must be freed in order to fulfill his limitless possibilities. The Modern age is the story of the development of these implications in theory and in practice.

The Renaissance also showed another fundamentally modern trait in its increasingly secularized view of man and society. *Secularization* is a word of many meanings and uses. Probably the most basic meaning is "freedom from ecclesiastical control." Thus a school or educational system is secular when it is free from church control. Closely related but not identical to this is the freedom from appeal to religious sanctions, rules, or motivations. In this meaning of the term, the modern West has seen a progressive secularization of such concerns as politics, economics, and art. One by one, these major human concerns have left the medieval household of the faith and, coming of age, have set up housekeeping on their own. Obviously this development is closely related to the modern belief in human autonomy, which is a still further meaning of the term *secularization*. In most general terms of all, secularization may be characterized as any movement of man's mind or life away from the conscious religious center of personality or culture. As such it is a generally observable and recurring trend in many cultures and persons. For example, ancient Greece of the fifth century B.C. shows a secularizing trend, as does Tokugawa Japan. In America the movement of New England culture from the seventeenth to the eighteenth century, from Cotton Mather to Benjamin Franklin, is another illustration of a secularizing tendency. Yet the general movement of the modern West, from the Renaissance onward is surely the most massive and all-inclusive secularizing movement in history. As such, it is one of the defining features of modernity. Modern man is secular in outlook, feeling no need to relate his interests to any religious center. While at times antireligious, his general attitude is more adequately described as nonreligious.

In all its essential traits the Renaissance stands as the spring from which the modern spirit has flowed—in religion as in all else. Yet it must also be asserted with equal force that it involved no open break with traditional religion. Rather, it may be asserted that in the Renaissance the paths of modernity and tradition began to diverge. In the following centuries they were destined to move further and further apart.

THE RISE OF NATURAL SCIENCE

Many leaders of the Renaissance, such as Erasmus and Rabelais, were scornful of the nascent natural science of the times, but others such as Leonardo da Vinci were scientists and engineers as well as artists and scholars. There were important lines of relation, both positive and negative, between the Renaissance and the rise of modern natural science; yet the two must be approached as distinguishable historical phenomena.

The new way of thinking which was to become modern natural science developed quietly and gradually in laboratories and studies throughout Europe. Its course was influenced by many interests and many causal conditions, ranging from technological needs to new mathematical speculation. Then suddenly in the seventeenth century—"the century of genius," as it has been called—science burst upon the world.[7]

In its first impact, particularly as related to religious tradition, the new science took the form of a revolutionary new view of the physical universe. For the common man of the Middle Ages the world had been a three-storied affair, with God and heaven above, man in the middle, and Satan and his minions in the basement. If Ptolemy's—or Dante's—cosmology involved refinements or revisions in this picture, they did not greatly alter its overall significance. For man still occupied the center of the stage, solicitously watched over by the divine management of the universe.

This man-centered view of the universe was rudely shattered by the revolutionary discoveries of early modern natural science. Copernicus's volume *Concerning the Revolution of the Celestial Spheres* (1543) placed the sun rather than the earth at the center of things. However, this view remained a mathematical speculation until Galileo developed its implications and tested them with his newly constructed telescope. The clash between the new science and the old theology came into the open when Galileo was summoned before the Holy Office of the Inquisition in 1616 and again in 1633 and was forbidden to teach that the earth revolved about the sun. Galileo's writings as well as those of Kepler and Copernicus were placed on the Index of Forbidden Books— where, incidentally, they remained until 1822, when as one writer put it, "the Sun received the formal sanction of the Papacy to become the centre of the planetary system."[8]

What Copernicus began and Galileo greatly advanced came to brilliant fulfillment—to final completion, it seemed at the time—in Isaac Newton's *Mathematical Principles of Natural Philosophy* (1687). By means of the law of universal gravitation, Newton construed the universe as a single realm of mathematical order. Here was convincing mathematical proof that the universe is one vast harmoniously ordered mechanism. Few new ideas in human history have had implications more vast and more revolutionary than this. While scientists pushed onward from this victory to new problems and new territories to conquer, other men sought during the Age of Reason, or the Newtonian age as it was called, to develop the implications of the triumphant new Newtonian or scientific reason for all aspects of human life and society. Earlier, Pascal had spoken for traditional religion concerning the new cosmology when he exclaimed, "The eternal silence of these infinite spaces frightens me."[9] Other men had very different reactions and responses.

Meanwhile, natural science moved onward, proving itself to be not simply a body of results—impressive as the Newtonian results might be at the time—but a dynamic and ongoing new method for knowing. As such it was capable of rendering any and all particular results obsolete and of constituting a kind of permanent revolution in human knowledge. The scientific method as it developed showed two aspects, one mathematical and rational, and the other empirical and experimental. Contrary to many popular views of science the rational aspect had been the first to take shape. For example, Copernicus's heliocentric view of the universe was the product of his deductive, or mathematical, search for a logically simpler view than that of Ptolemy. In a similar spirit Galileo explored nature, seeking illustrations for his conviction that the great book of nature is written, as he put it, in geometric terms.[10] Different sciences and scientists combined the rational and the experimental aspects of science in widely different ways. Yet in the whole historical movement of modern natural science, it has been the interaction of these two aspects of the method that has accounted largely for the enormous power and creativity of science.

From the beginning, science grew out of technological needs and problems, and its answers greatly influenced technological development. As science moved forward, technology continued to force vast changes in society and to remake the face of the earth—sometimes for human welfare, often for apparently opposite results, but always in ways that no man could ignore. The revolution in science and technology still goes on, at an ever-accelerating pace and with no end in sight. It continues to force changes in every aspect of human life. To many men around the world modernity means scientific technology, whether embodied in automobiles, in steel mills, Coca-Cola coolers, or in nuclear fission.

In the continuing relation of science to traditional religion and theology, the publication of Darwin's *Origin of Species* (1859) and the coming of evolutionary theory constituted an event in biological sciences of comparable magnitude to the discoveries in physics of Copernicus, Galileo, and Newton. From thinking of himself as a fallen archangel, man was rudely called by this new theory to view himself as an ape who had made good—and whether he had made good became increasingly problematic. The furor created by Darwin's theory began the year after its publication, when at the meeting in 1860 of the British Association for the Advancement of Science, Archbishop Wilberforce sought to ridicule the new view, and was thoroughly castigated and refuted by Thomas Huxley, soon to be known as "Darwin's bulldog." The controversy continued until the Bryan-Darrow encounter at the Scopes trial in Dayton, Tennessee, in 1925, and for some surviving Biblical literalists to the present moment.[11]

As theologians, philosophers, and others continued to ponder the implications of science, science itself continued to move onward. Beyond Newton and Laplace lay Einstein; beyond Darwin lay Freud and his explorations of man's inner life. Beyond every present achievement lies the future. By renouncing absolute truth and asserting all its results to be provisional and tentative, science has been able to push forward into an ever-open future.[12] This open future of science has been sometimes promise and sometimes threat, but in either case has become in the twentieth century the largest, most momentous fact in man's world.

The clash of science with religion has constituted a major and pervasive theme of modern thought, affording one more illustration of the general theme of modern criticism of tradition and modern rebellion against traditional authority. Most writers have seen the science-religion struggle as a battle of the free and progressive scientific mind against the fetters of prescientific authority. A. D. White's monumental *A History of the Warfare of Science and Theology in Christendom* envisioned the struggle in precisely these terms.[13] A. N. Whitehead, who wrote of these matters from his own novel viewpoint, remarks that "for over two centuries religion has been on the defensive and on a weak defensive," and concluded that "it will not regain its old power until it can face change in the same spirit as does science." [14] Until then religion's long retreat, step by step as science advances, is likely to continue. Such at least is the dominant modern image of the relation of science to religion and theology, and no candid observer would wish to deny that it contains much important truth.

Only as a student of this problem takes full account of this truth has he a right to go on to other aspects of the multifaceted relation between science and religion. Yet much current writing on science and religion has proceeded to some of these other aspects. Some writers have called attention to the fact that science originated in the Western tradition, which has been infused and informed by the Judeo-Christian tradition. Accordingly they point to significant aspects of the latter tradition which have served—or so it is claimed—as necessary presuppositions of modern science. For example, the Judeo-Christian God transcends the world, thus opening the way to a secularization of the world, which is a necessary precondition to scientific understanding and control of the world.[15] Man does not scientifically manipulate a world which is "full of gods"; and this phrase may be taken as descriptive not only of ancient Greece but of all nature-culture, or type-one, religions. Attention is also frequently called to the Biblical doctrine of creation, with its affirmation of the reality and goodness of the world of nature in contrast to faiths which regard nature as illusory appearance; this contrast expresses the difference between views of the world in religions of the second and third types. Still other writers call attention to the need for moral guidance of science if science is to be used for human welfare rather than ill-fare. Meanwhile, however these issues may finally be resolved, it is safe to characterize the Modern age as the Age of Science. The creation of modern natural science is surely the most important achievement of the Modern age. It remains for man to learn to live with his achievement.

THE ENLIGHTENMENT

Reference has already been made to the Age of Reason, as an attempt to apply the spirit and method of triumphant Newtonian science to all aspects of human society and life. The men of the eighteenth-century Age of Enlightenment sought rationality in politics, in philosophy, in religion, and in ethics. Not even art escaped the influence of rational form, as the poetry of Pope, the music of Handel and Haydn, or the formal patterns of an eighteenth-century garden all testify. It was a century in which European men devoted themselves to the ideal of universal and harmonious rational order in all human things; and they had few doubts that man's reason was sufficient for this ambitious undertaking.

The Enlightenment had varying impact upon different European nations. In England, which had had its social revolution during the previous century, the Enlightenment was a moderating process. In France it was revolutionary, producing Voltaire, Diderot and his Encyclopedia, and the French Revolution, with its battle cry of "Liberty, Equality, Fraternity!" and the goddess Reason replacing traditional Catholicism. In America, it produced such varied figures as Benjamin Franklin, Thomas Paine, and Thomas Jefferson. Both the Declaration of Independence and the United States Constitution may be said to express varying moods of the Enlightenment.

In its basic affirmations the Enlightenment continued and extended the faith of the Renaissance in man, his freedom, and the infinite possibilities that open before him. The new ingredient in the Enlightenment was science, both as rational method and as achievement. Science was also doubtless the primary basis of the Enlightenment's basic belief in human progress. For natural science offers concrete examples of intellectual progress. Science was and still is mankind's clearest example of progressive or cumulative knowledge. From the intellectual progress of science, it was an easy and natural step to human progress. For as scientific knowledge increased, so also human happiness and well-being would increase; such at least was the optimistic credo of the eighteenth century. Proclaimed cautiously and moderately by the English, and with lyric enthusiasm by such French writers as Condorcet, the belief in progress expressed well the Enlightenment's confidence in man and reason.

As for sources of this belief, many contemporary writers trace it to the Bible and its linear and dramatic view of history. Chapters 11 and 12 noted the Biblical sources of this idea, and Chapter 15 sketched Augustine's formulation of it in his *City of God*. This view of history gave expression to millennial and messianic beliefs that have continued to erupt throughout Jewish and Christian history. Belief in progress emerged from belief in the millennium, as Carl Becker has written, when early in the Enlightenment, belief in God became belief in Nature, and belief in original sin was transformed into its opposite, belief in human perfectability.[16] As a consequence, the City of God became the City of Man and was relocated somewhere in the human future. To state the matter theologically, progress might be characterized in Augustinian terms as grace, prevenient, immanent, and at least in some formulations, irresistible.

The Enlightenment differs from the Renaissance in two important ways relating to religion, namely, its strong humanitarian ethic and its conscious break with the Christian tradition of theology and faith. As to the former, the Enlightenment held a firm conviction of universal humanity, based no doubt on the Judeo-Christian idea of God's universal Kingdom, but expressed more often in rationalist terms than in traditional religious terms. The belief implied a critical attack on all irrational institutions and practices of society. Specific applications of this rule varied widely from person to person, but they included such causes as opposition to absolute monarchy or sometimes more radically to all monarchy, to war, to slavery, and to maltreatment of criminals and the insane. Affirming a cosmopolitan or universal ideal, the Enlightenment was hostile to all forms of provincialism or parochialism, ranging from political nationalism to religious dogmatism.

No other issue was more characteristic of the Enlightenment than its passionate opposition to bigotry and intolerance, that is, to all particular forms of religion held on grounds which were deemed irrational or "dogmatic," and which led to actions which violated freedom and humanity. In practice, these convictions led to strong advocacy of religious toleration and freedom.

In this cause the men of the Enlightenment found allies among Protestant sects such as the Quakers and the Baptists who for their own compelling reasons opposed religious establishment and intolerance. As a result of their combined efforts, the traditional patterns gave way in some Western nations to systems of freedom and toleration. England had made a start in 1688 with the Act of Toleration, though toleration was limited to non-Anglican Protestants and did not extend to Roman Catholics, Jews, or atheists. While Great Britain subsequently extended toleration and freedom to all her people, she has continued to combine this tradition with an established church.

In America the lively experiment of religious freedom has been a central theme in the national tradition. It was rooted in historical origins and has been demanded by practical necessity. As every American schoolchild knows, many of the colonists were Protestant sectarians fleeing intolerance and seeking religious freedom. Also, the American nation came into being in the eighteenth century under Founding Fathers who were men of the Enlightenment. The idea of religious freedom in America owes its origin to an alliance of such religious figures as William Penn and Roger Williams with rationalists such as Jefferson, Madison, and Franklin.

American religious freedom and toleration did not come into being all at once, but gradually, as a step-by-step process. Some American states did not relinquish religious establishments until the 1820s. Furthermore, the meaning of religious freedom was greatly widened and deepened as immigration increased the diversity of the American population during the nineteenth century. In the storms of twentieth-century history, Americans are finding still new meanings and implications in their system of religious freedom and diversity. Thus the lively experiment continues to the present moment.[17] The idea of freedom of religion, which bears the stamp "made in America," has been widely exported to all parts of the world, with the result that today, however much it may be distorted in practice, religious freedom is widely regarded as a fundamental human right.[18]

It is difficult for Americans born and nurtured in religious freedom and diversity to see how genuinely revolutionary this idea is. With very few notable exceptions, such as King Ashoka's reign in ancient India, the overwhelming practice in human history has been religious uniformity and establishment, with prohibition of dissent. The new position must be seen as one of the great achievements of the Modern age.

The Enlightenment not only criticized religious intolerance and bigotry, but also mounted a massive attack upon traditional Christian faith and theology. This criticism began during the seventeenth century with the moderate liberalism of men like Lord Herbert of Cherbury, who taught that human reason operating in the manner of Newton could establish such tenets as the existence of one God, his creation and government of the world, and the immortality of the soul. Deists likened the relation of God to the world to that of watchmaker to watch. Revelation might go further than reason and tell man more about God. For example, it might certify the Biblical miracles and prophecy, but natural reason laid the foundations upon which the edifice of faith and revelation was erected.

In the course of time the rationalists' criticism of traditional religion became more and more radical. First, all supernatural aspects of religion were attacked as superfluous and repugnant to reason; then the argument from watch to watchmaker was subjected to withering critical attack by skeptics such as David Hume.[19] In France the course of eighteenth-century thought moved onward not to the cautious and careful skepticism of Hume, but toward the dogmatic materialism of Holbach and the equally dogmatic rationalism of Diderot or Robespierre. In both cases the critical spirit of the Enlightenment made a clean and conscious break with the Christian tradition. After the eighteenth century, thoughtful Westerners might be Christians, but only consciously and by a deliberate effort of mind. Clearly this was something new in Western history.

Indeed it was something new in human history. The absence of an Enlightenment in the religious history of India and other Oriental cultures marks a fundamental contrast between East and West.

David Hume

Courtesy of the New York Public Library, Picture Collection

THE RADICAL CENTURY

In some important ways the nineteenth century reacted against the dominant Newtonian rationalism of the eighteenth. Nineteenth-century Romanticism was a way of saying that not only science but also art, history, and religion are legitimate concerns which in their distinctive ways illuminate and enrich man's life. Not only scientific reason, but also feeling, imagination, volition are legitimate aspects of human experience. Nature is the object not only of scientific study, but of poems, of landscape paintings, or indeed of contemplation.

True as this may be, and important as the Romantic reaction was, with specific reference to the issue of this chapter, namely, modern Western man's criticism of traditional religion, the nineteenth century continued and drove deeper the Enlightenment's criticism of traditional religion. So true is this that the nineteenth is clearly the radical century. It is so in the etymological sense of going to the roots of this issue.

The radical impact of nineteenth-century criticism of religion will be outlined here through a few important individuals. Back of most of these radical critics stood the imposing figure of Hegel, whose system of philosophic idealism dominated much of nineteenth-century thought. Hegel had deserted theological education for a career in philosophy, in which his great achievement was the construction of a comprehensive, all-embracing system of metaphysics. Hegel's philosophy, sometimes called absolute idealism, was his ambitious attempt to embrace all of reality in a single systematic whole, the key concept of which was Mind, or Spirit (the usual English translations of the untranslatable German word *Geist*). It is impossible here even to hint at the rich suggestiveness of Hegel's philosophy, except to say that while both nature and self were expressions of Mind, it was history which provided its most significant manifestation. Hegel treated history as the progressive unfolding of Mind. Hegel's Mind resembled the traditional God of Christianity in some significant ways but differed sharply in others. For all its suggestiveness, Hegel's philosophy was also extremely ambiguous in its key terms.

It is therefore not surprising that his students, followers, and interpreters should be divided into two warring camps, the "right," or "old," Hegelians, and the "left," or "young," Hegelians.[20] Hegel's own social outlook was massively conservative; he believed that the Prussian state of his time was the unique embodiment of the World Spirit. It is therefore ironical that the left Hegelians should include some of the most revolutionary figures of the nineteenth century. Among the young Hegelians was Ludwig Feuerbach, who greatly influenced the criticism of religion. Like Hegel he began as a Protestant theological student and then rebelled. Going from Heidelberg to Berlin, he came under the influence of Hegel. Feuerbach taught for a short time at Erlangen, but for the greater part of his life held no academic position. He sought to recast radically Hegel's philosophy in the direction of naturalism and materialism, the view of the world which asserts the sole reality of nature and denies any supernature or transcendence. His most important book, *The Essence of Christianity*, was published in 1841 and translated into English by George Eliot.[21]

While avowedly hostile to traditional Christian theology, Feuerbach regarded himself as a friend of religion, and he regarded his book as a viable reformulation of its living and human essence. In its traditional forms religion is both illusory and delusory, that is, both false and misleading. As to the real existence of God or gods, Feuerbach was explicitly atheistic. They do not exist! Only nature exists, said Feuerbach, meaning man's material and biological environment together with his own body and those of other human beings. The gods are "wish-entities" (*Wunschwesen* in German), products of the wishful bent of man's imagination. Religion, in short, is a result of wishful thinking or wish-fulfillment. This idea was by no means original with Feuerbach. In one form or another, the reader has seen it emerge in several of the traditions studied in this book. The significance of Feuerbach was to give explicit, full, and systematic expression to this view. From his time onward this explicitly atheistic approach to religion was ready at hand for others to accept, to work at, and to develop further.

One reader of Feuerbach was Karl Marx, who punned that all the young Hegelians had been baptized in Feuerbach (*Feuer-Bach* means in German "fire-spring"). Marx (1818–1885) was also a left Hegelian, who studied at Berlin in the years after Hegel's death, becoming deeply involved with other left Hegelians. Marx received his doctorate in 1841, but was destined never to occupy an academic position, spending his life rather as a radical newspaper editor, a revolutionary agitator and organizer, and an exiled, poverty-stricken scholar in the British Museum. No one in the twentieth century is ignorant of the worldwide and revolutionary impact of his thought, for it has become the official dogma of the communist movement. It is by this sequence of events that explicit and militant atheism has become the official creed of millions of twentieth-century men.

Marx's religious ideas were decisively influenced by Feuerbach. Following Feuerbach, he asserted that material nature was the sole reality, thus denying any possible existence to any transcendent or spiritual reality. Like Feuerbach he believed deity, or the supernatural, to be a figment of man's subjective and wishful imagination. However, Marx went beyond Feuerbach in his analysis of the ways in which religious experience is sociologically formed, conditioned, and used or misused. In Marx's own words, religion is the opiate of the people.[22] Inherently delusory in nature, religion, like opium, has the function of deadening pain—the social pain of the masses—thus making them less rebellious, more acquiescent to their misery. For Marx religion, along with education, art, and all of culture, is simply and plainly a tool by which the dominant classes of society maintain their domination. It is accordingly not simply delusory but also fundamentally immoral and therefore ought to be completely abolished.

That Marx and his followers have deemed this result not only desirable, but also possible and feasible, has been due in part to their confident faith in man. Marx regarded his views in this respect as in direct line of succession from the Enlightenment. He concluded that once man has broken the chains of his social slavery and stepped into the new world of freedom and communism, he will have no further need for the crutch of religion. Incidentally, many of Marx's specific judgments concerning religion are shared by people who are by no means Marxist in social outlook, or in fact to whom this social philosophy is repugnant.

Sigmund Freud (1856–1939) shared Marx's debt to Feuerbach's psychological understanding of religion, but he gave this idea a profoundly different

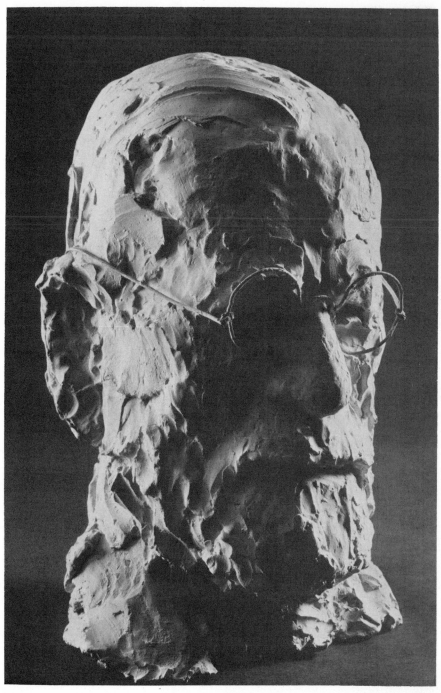

Sigmund Freud. A contemporary sculpture by Jack
Gregory, photograph by Seymour Mednick
Courtesy of the Smith, Kline, and French Laboratories

formulation. Freud was the founder of psychoanalysis, which is both a technique for curing mental illness and a general theory of the human self in its total relation to the world. The latter aspect of Freudian teaching has significant similarities to both philosophy and religion. Freud shared Feuerbach's view of reality as limited to nature, denying categorically the reality of anything supernatural or transcendent. To the psychological processes which produce and sustain religion, Freud gave his own detailed interpretation. Religion, he argued, is an infantile neurosis in which the image of an almighty and omniscient father is projected onto reality;[23] it is a delusion born of neurotic dependence. Freud shared with Marx the humanistic view that since man is alone in the world he ought to be content to stand alone. However, Freud was vastly less certain than Marx of the possibility of attaining this goal—at least for most men.

Freud also differed from Marx in his lack of antireligious feeling, and in his genuine though somewhat furtive interest in the subject. He read widely in the anthropology of religion and used mythical terms and symbols in meaningful ways in his psychoanalytic studies. If Marx's attitude was angrily antireligious, Freud's was melancholically nonreligious. One of Freud's early students, Carl Jung, broke with his master on this issue and produced a version of psychoanalytic doctrine of considerable significance to both the practice and the study of traditional religion.[24] As a consequence, the total impact of psychoanalysis has been less hostile to traditional religion than Marxism has been. Indeed in some versions it has been a device for providing fresh interpretations of traditional religions. However, for Freud and his followers, the conclusion was nonreligious. Mature men will learn to stand upon their own feet and face the tragedy of human existence in their own strength, assert Freud and his followers. This view must be counted as a late aspect of the radical century's criticism of traditional religion.

The impact of Darwin and the theory of evolution was of a different sort from that of Marx or Freud, but in the end was no less radical. Darwin was a dedicated scientist, with no conscious desire to criticize or disturb traditional ideas. Yet as noted earlier in this chapter, Darwinian evolution collided head-on with prevailing theological views of human origin and divine creation. However, Darwinian evolution had other implications as well. Marx was convinced that it lent support to Marxian ideas of human social development. Herbert Spencer argued with equal assurance that laissez-faire capitalism constituted the application of the Darwinian idea of survival of the fittest to human society; and a whole generation of social Darwinists echoed his claim. Spencer also generalized Darwin's idea of biological evolution to a universal law of progress, which operated as a beneficent cosmic escalator. Spencer did not doubt that the highest point in this universal progress was nineteenth-century Europe. He combined his dogma of progress with agnosticism toward the traditional God.

The idea of evolution was given a radically different direction by the German philosopher Friedrich Nietzsche (1844–1900), with his idea of Superman, or Overman (the German word is *Übermensch*). The son of a Lutheran pastor, Nietzsche was educated as a classical philologist. He was an angry rebel against the established values of nineteenth-century middle-class Europe, regarding them as a conspiracy against the vital powers of the creative minority

Charles Darwin
Courtesy of the New York Public Library, Picture Collection

of men. Nietzsche angrily attributed the hated way of life to Christianity and middle-class rationalism in philosophy. As a consequence his arch-villains were Jesus and Socrates. In relation to the former, Nietzsche boldly called himself an antichrist.[25] Christianity he castigated as slave morality and as a rebellion of the weak against the strong. Both Christian love and philosophic rationalism he viewed as a betrayal of man's creative vitality to the mediocrity of the human herd.

Nietzsche's own credo was expressed in the ambiguous and much misunderstood phrase "will to power." [26] What he meant was not the will to dominate other people, but the will to create, a vitality of the sort that finds embodiment in a great artist. In terms of these values, Nietzsche called present humanity a disease and lyrically foretold the emergence in the future of Overman, or Superman.[27]

Nietzsche was militantly anti-Christian. "God is dead," he shouted in *Thus Spake Zarathustra*, meaning the God of traditional Christianity.[28] However, Nietzsche was by no means antireligious. Indeed he did not hesitate to cast himself in the role of prophet of a future faith. The outlines of this faith are not altogether clear, but it appears to have been a hard Dionysiac vitalism to be espoused by a minority of men with whom the future was alleged to lie. In terms of this faith, Nietzsche called for a transvaluation of values.[29] The reader does not need to accept all that Nietzsche had to say in order to see that in his writings the criticism of traditional Western religion had reached its most radical point.

SOME MODERN CREDOS

This chapter has advanced the thesis that the Modern age and spirit have involved a process of ever more radical criticism of traditional faiths. This criticism has also involved doubt of varying kinds and degrees. Sometimes it has been the purely intellectual doubt of Descartes, employed as a means for establishing his own individual existence, "I doubt, therefore I am."[30] For other thinkers the process of criticism involved doubt of a more existential and personal quality. For them doubt became a kind of polar opposite to faith.

Some modern men have devoted themselves to criticism and doubt with little apparent need for any more affirmative attitude. However, others have felt the need to affirm in words as well as in action of the faith which guides their lives. They have felt the need to say *"Credo"* as well as *"Dubito."* What follows here is a sampling of modern credos selected from the many possibilities for their contemporary interest and pertinence.

THE THOUGHT OF SPINOZA

Baruch (or Benedict) Spinoza (1632–1677) stands as one of the supremely great figures in the history of philosophy, both for the creative power of his thought and for his single-minded personal dedication to the life of thought, or as he put it, to "eternal things." Spinoza was born in Amsterdam, where his Portuguese Jewish family had fled from the Spanish Inquisition. He studied for the rabbinate, but encountering the radical scientific views of his Dutch teacher, Van der Ende, Spinoza developed a philosophy widely rumored to be heretical, which led to his excommunication in 1656 by the synagogue. He responded by changing his name from the Hebrew *Baruch* to the Latin *Benedict*; in both languages it means "blessed." He was to know the blessedness of dedication to the faith of his own choosing. Earning his living by lens-grinding, which aggravated a tubercular condition, he died at the age of forty-five as

piously and humanely as he had lived. But Spinoza left in his writings a philosophic and religious vision of the world, breathtaking in its bold originality and
brilliant in its clarity.

Spinoza's integral vision had two components: (1) his study of the new,
modern scientific view of the world, and (2) his traditional Jewish piety. He
used traditional religious terms like *God, salvation,* and *immortality,* but he
filled them with new content drawn from scientific study. The result was a
reinterpretation of traditional Judeo-Christian faith, radical in its criticism of
anthropomorphic views of God as well as other self-centered and childish ideas,
but also of unquestioned authenticity in its deep spirit of piety and devotion.[31]

Spinoza defined God, or Nature, as infinite substance, or that which alone is
capable of self-existence. Maimonides and Aquinas before him had approached
deity as Ultimate Reality or Absolute Reality, and Spinoza followed in this
succession. His boldness lay in his reinterpretation of this old idea. He took
as Ultimate Reality the universe revealed by the new modern natural science
and proposed to treat as Supreme Reality the object-matter of science. True,
such a God is not personal, and Spinoza rejected as childish any view of deity
as being personal in nature. Nevertheless, he continued to use the traditional
religious language for his new views. Perhaps he would say that it is not more
inaccurate to use personal than impersonal language to point to the altogether
unique divine object.

Spinoza distinguished between knowledge of God, which is the province of
philosophy, and obedience to God, which is the goal of religion. To help attain
the latter, the Bible and its traditional language are well suited. Philosophy
and religion accordingly supplement each other in the service of God.

Spinoza viewed man as the slave of ignorant craving, and his description of
bondage recalls Buddha's description of man's misery. Spinoza believed that the
path from bondage to freedom lay in the passionate devotion to truth for truth's
sake, or as he expressed it, to the "intellectual love of God." [32] This allegiance
he believed capable of leading man out of his warring affections and disaffections to the sunlit life of reason in which man dwells amid eternal things.
Again in his new terms, Spinoza rejected as childish bondage all popular ideas
of life after death. The new view constituted not only immortality in the only
defensible meaning of that term, namely life with a timeless or eternal quality
in the present moment; but it also constituted freedom, which is the life of
rationally determined choices. Such was Spinoza's bold modern credo.

He was modern in many other ways than in his reinterpretation of tradition
in the face of new scientific knowledge. His Biblical studies anticipated by two
centuries the development of the higher criticism of the Bible.[33] He knew no
other way of study than by use of the free human intellect. Also, he formulated
his own credo of religious toleration as alone consistent with the reason and

freedom which were integral aspects of his own philosophy and religion. Truly Spinoza was a modern saint; and as saints sometimes are, he has been an inspiration to many men since his time.

PROTESTANT LIBERALISM

Another modern credo may be labeled Protestant liberalism. Attention has already been called to the attitude of weak defensiveness which has so largely characterized Christianity during the modern period. In Roman Catholicism, decisions of the Council of Trent, enforced by the church's system of authority, may be said to have institutionalized this largely defensive and negative attitude. The Roman Catholic Church seemed to be saying a continuing and insistent "No" to all that was modern, liberal, and forward-looking. As noted in Chapter 16, this negative attitude grew until the middle of the nineteenth century, when in the Syllabus of Errors (1864) the Pope listed the modern trends condemned by the Church and forbidden to Catholic Christians. The Vatican Council of 1869–1870 declared the Pope infallible and irreformable when he spoke to the whole church on matters of faith and morals. These attitudes were continued in the papal denunciation of Catholic modernism in 1905. In the light of these persistent attitudes, the new direction of Roman Catholicism under Pope John XXIII (1958–1963) and Pope Paul VII and the second Vatican Council are of the greatest historic importance. While it is too early to offer detailed appraisal of the new trends, it is not too early to assert that a historic trend of four centuries' duration has been reversed.

Protestant Christianity, having no central authority and being less shielded from the new developments of modern culture, has been shaped and reshaped by that culture. Protestant responses to the thought and practices of the modern world must be placed along a wide and continuous spectrum ranging from well-nigh total negation to an equally total and uncritical affirmation. During the present century, the Fundamentalist movement in American Protestantism will serve as ready illustration of Protestant negativism, with its rejection of Darwinian evolution and, in some formulations, of Copernican astronomy, and with its rigid assertion of Biblical inerrancy.[34]

For other Protestants a more affirmative alternative has long been available. By *affirmative* is meant here simply more congenial or congruent to the modern world. Whether this is a good or a bad thing—indeed what good and bad would mean in this context—is another and a different question which will have to be answered by each reader in the light of his own primary valuations. Our task here as elsewhere is to characterize significant historical developments. In this particular case, thoughtful men have disagreed over the question of whether liberal religion is to be judged good or bad. In any event, in Protestant Christianity there has grown up over the past two centuries a liberal attitude and outlook which seeks to maintain the Protestant faith's relation to the Christian tradition but to make it acceptable and relevant to the modern world.

Protestant liberalism has developed in a great variety of forms which can only be sketched in here. The intellectual foundations of Protestant liberalism were laid by the German philosopher Immanuel Kant (1740–1804) in his *Critique of Practical Reason*. The first of Kant's three great critiques ended as negatively for traditional theology as did the skeptical philosophy of David Hume. However, in the second critique Kant traced a path from moral experience (which for Kant was indubitable and inescapable) to the religious affirmations of God, freedom, and immortality. Kant's own religious faith thus was in effect cautious eighteenth-century rationalism. Yet his great importance was that he reopened the gates of possibility for forms of religious thought and experience which his contemporaries had deemed closed.

Among those who moved on, seeking to develop the new possibilities was Friedrich Schleiermacher whose *Addresses on Religion To Its Cultured Despisers* (1799) and *Christian Faith* (1834) are often termed the foundation of modern theology. Schleiermacher began not with God or the Bible, but with religious experience; and God entered the picture as the object of religious experience or, as Schleiermacher put it, of religious consciousness. Clearly this was a new approach to an old subject. It was remarkable how much of traditional Christian faith found its way back into Schleiermacher's theology through his new approach and method. What Schleiermacher began, others carried forward in their own ways. Albrecht Ritschl, for example, distinguished between judgments of fact and of value, interpreting faith as derived from value judgments.[35] The influence of Ritschl and his student and successor Wilhelm Herrmann was particularly strong on American Protestant theology. Both in Europe and America what emerged from this theological movement was the means for relating the Christian tradition to the Modern age.

Other developments within Protestantism served the same objective. The higher criticism of the Bible, that is, the free and critical study of the Bible with a view to answering questions of authorship, began in the eighteenth century and came of age in the nineteenth. Rejected and viewed with alarm at first, it was subsequently accepted and adopted within Protestantism.[36] The free study of other religions, called history of religions or comparative study of religions has undergone a similar development.[37]

Still another aspect of liberal Protestant thought and practice has been its fresh consideration of the ethic of Christianity. Christians had never been completely oblivious of the ethical implications of their faith. In modern times a succession of reforming groups and movements have sought to focus attention on specific social problems, ranging from slavery to the excesses of the Industrial

Immanuel Kant. Painting by Richard Linder
Courtesy of the Continental Can Company

Revolution. As noted in the last chapter, in post-Civil War America, there grew up a liberal Protestant movement preaching what its proponents called the Social Gospel, and determined to relate the Christian ethic to the whole of society.[38] The movement attracted some of the best minds in American Protestantism, it spread to other parts of the Protestant world, and in the course of development it has become an important aspect of the life and thought of the National and World Councils of Churches. While questioned and ignored in some quarters, it has undoubtedly given to Protestant thought and faith a fresh approach to the world.

HUMANISM

While liberal Christianity has sought to mediate between tradition and modernity, other men have believed that the conflict is irreconcilable and hence have broken with traditional faith. Within the past century many such men have called themselves Humanists, thus providing another new meaning for this already multivalued word. By use of the term, these modern Humanists have sought to assert that, unable in the age of modern science to believe in the traditional Judeo-Christian God, they propose still to believe in Man, or Humanity.

Humanism in this sense of the word has had several organizational or institutional forms. The French philosopher and sociologist, Auguste Comte (1798–1857), organized in Paris a Church of Humanity, in which the Great Being or Humanity replaced the traditional God and which taught that altruism would conquer egoism.[39] Comte created for his new faith an elaborate cultus, borrowed largely from Catholicism, with priests and sacraments and even a Positivist calendar in which the names of scientists and scholars replaced saints. However, this contrived faith never attracted a following and as a consequence did not outlive its founder.

There has been a different outcome for the Ethical Culture Society founded in 1876 in New York City by Felix Adler.[40] Adler was a student for the rabbinate who rebelled against what he thought to be Judaism's excessive legalism, and turned to philosophy. Accepting the ethical philosophy of Kant, he sought to give it concrete expression in the various areas of society from family to school, economic order, and state. At the center of society Adler envisaged a religious organization, voluntary in nature, whose leaders would be ethical teachers rather than priests and whose purpose would be to inculcate moral values in its members. Adler's New York Ethical Society grew to over a thousand members, and it spread to other cities of America and Europe. The Ethical Culture movement engages in educational, philanthropic, and social reform activities. Its worship is simple, combining readings from inspirational literature, music, meditation, and addresses on topics of ethical significance. There are no doctrinal requirements for membership.

Similar to Ethical Culture, but specific in its rejection of traditional theism as a religious belief, is the American Humanist Association.[41] Recruited mainly from left-wing Protestants and Jews, its members are held together by common ideas and purposes more than organizational ties. A bimonthly magazine, *The Humanist,* is published, conferences are held, and propaganda is carried on.

Humanism is not only an organized movement and creed but also the unexpressed outlook of countless modern people. This outlook has its basis in the method and achievements of science. This belief is sometimes consciously expressed but often exists simply as a confident acceptance of the scientific outlook and a willingness to live and act in these terms. Frequently related to this is an allegiance to Humanity either explicit or implicit in quality, and generating a wide range of social concerns and reforms. Among the attempts to give explicit formulation to Humanism are Corliss Lamont's *Humanism as a Philosophy,* John Dewey's *A Common Faith,* and Julian Huxley's *Religion Without Revelation.* In wider, more pervasive form the humanistic outlook has functioned as the climate of opinion of the modern world, thus finding acceptance in countless minds and lives that have never given it conscious articulation.

This exposition of liberalism and humanism has been limited to their expression in the Judeo-Christian tradition both because these tendencies have been developed furthest in this tradition and because this tradition probably stands closest to the experience of most readers of this book. Yet the fact is that the spirit of liberal accommodation to modernity and of humanist rebellion against tradition has increasing application to all of mankind's religions. Increasingly the issues outlined here have relevance to the Oriental faiths. The only question is what kinds of responses these faiths will be capable of making to the challenge of modernity.

THE END OF MODERN TIMES

In recent decades many writers have asserted that the Modern age is now past and that mankind has embarked upon a post-Modern period. Berdyaev wrote *The End of Our Times* in 1933.[42] Some years later and in a somewhat different context Norman Cousins wrote *Modern Man Is Obsolete.*[43] However, others have responded with what Charles Frankel has called "the case for modern man." [44] The issue is evidently controversial, and happily no wholesale judgment is necessary for the purposes of this chapter. Nevertheless, understanding of the contemporary situation in religion requires that we begin to appraise some of the issues involved in the wider situation.

One central fact is that the criticism of tradition which has been so pervasive and fundamental an aspect of the modern spirit seems to have run its course. There are very few uncriticized beliefs or traditions left for critical treatment. To be sure, there is a perennial critical function of reason which must be exercised by every generation and every individual. But criticism in its radical and avowedly modern sense seems to have done its work. In the opinion of some observers the acids of modernity have eaten away the fabric of traditional beliefs and acceptances so completely that little or nothing is left.

This appraisal of the contemporary situation has been expressed in various ways. Tillich has spoken of a "cultural void," which might be identified as the empty place in many contemporary minds and hearts where traditional faiths or values used to be.[45] It was this aspect of modernity that led to T. S. Eliot's metaphor of the wasteland. Writing from a very different perspective, David Riesman has diagnosed the present situation as a shift from tradition-directedness and inner-directedness to outer direction, or conformity to social context.[46] Having no values or faith of his own, the contemporary human being is content simply to conform to his social context. Lonely and naked men huddle together in crowds. Whatever the specific formulation, these various diagnoses all point to a seismic change in contemporary man's basic attitudes and orientation, in his faith, or value orientation.

This change in attitude may be expressed as the shift away from criticism of tradition and rebellion against authority to a profoundly new kind of issue. The new issue may perhaps be formulated as the question: Where amid the storms of our times can genuine meaning be found? Having completed that rebellion against tradition and authority defined as modernity, man now asks a different question, What is the meaning of life? What shall I live for? The reader will recall this as one formulation of what Chapter 1 termed the fundamental religious question. However, the problems of the twentieth century have given it a peculiar urgency and timeliness and significance.

The contemporary search for meaning takes many forms. One of the most significant is the Existentialist movement in contemporary philosophy, literature, and theology, for which the question, What is man? or more personally, Who am I? is the common and central feature. Many answers are given, including the specific avowal of no-answer, but it is the question which is the significant and common feature of this movement.

It is not possible for any except oracular or prophetic persons to see what forms the future will take. Yet it is significant for whatever future may come to be that our present situation is characterized by a question. This question defines a new opportunity and challenge for mankind's traditional faiths. It was asserted in Chapter 1 that the perennial function of religion has been to provide life orientation, to give men a convincing answer to the question, Why am I alive? This question is being asked today in new and urgent ways which give relevance to those faiths which are bold and wise enough to adapt their traditional answers to the new situation.

CONCLUDING COMMENT

As this chapter has shown, the modern spirit has been one of criticism, aimed at tradition, at the Middle Ages, and indeed at any and all affirmations of faith. What is the nature of ultimate concern and value in such a situation? Several responses demand to be made. In one sense, the spirit of criticism is hostile to the attitude of faith or ultimate concern. Hence just to the extent that criticism predominates, ultimacy of concern recedes into the background. So it is that in this modern world, religion has occupied less of men's attention than, say science, politics, or business.

However at another level of response, modern men have revealed in their lives structures of faith or ultimate valuation. While they have been less concerned with God than were the men of the Middle Ages, they have committed themselves passionately (shall we also add, ultimately?) to science, to reason, to humanity and progress, and sometimes to nation or race. Apparently, ultimate concern, shut out the front door, forces entrance through the back door. We shall say more on this theme in the next chapter.

As to humanity and humanism, as we have seen in this chapter, modern men have given the term *humanism* the new meaning of faith in humanity or mankind as against faith in God. Proponents of this new use claim that it is continuous with the traditional meanings that we have set forth in previous chapters. However, opponents deny this, claiming that it is through traditional faith in God that man fulfills or realizes his humanity. Students of religion observe that this argument continues to the present moment.

In the modern period what has happened to our three main types of religion? To answer we must first recall that modernity originated in the West, which has been informed and guided by historical monotheism. While the one God of this faith has receded during the Modern age, the drama of history that we have noted in past chapters as central to this third type of religion has continued significant. It has done so in the secularized forms, first of eighteenth-century progress, then of nineteenth-century evolution or evolutionary progress. As a consequence these ideas have assumed great importance both philosophically and religiously for many modern people.

NOTES

1. A. N. Whitehead, *Science and the Modern World*, The Macmillan Company, New York, 1927, p. 87.

2. Desiderius Erasmus, *In Praise of Folly*, Reeves and Turner, London, 1876. François Rabelais, *Gargantua and Pantagruel*,

trans. Jacques Le Clercq, Heritage Press, New York, 1942.

3. See John Herman Randall, Jr., *The Making of the Modern Mind*, Houghton Mifflin Company, Boston, 1940, p. 122.

4. John Pico della Mirandola, *Oration on the Dignity of Man*, Henry Regnery Company, Chicago, 1956.

5. Desiderius Erasmus and Martin Luther, *Discourse on Free Will*, ed. and trans. Ernst F. Winter, Frederick Ungar Publishing Co., New York, n.d.

6. This point is developed in detail by Reinhold Niebuhr, *The Nature and Destiny of Man*, vol. II, Charles Scribner's Sons, New York, 1943.

7. Whitehead, *op. cit.*, pp. 57f.

8. W. C. Dampier, *History of Science*, Cambridge University Press, London, 1942, p. 124.

9. Pascal, *Pensées* 25:18, as quoted in Ernst Cassirer, *An Essay on the Dignity of Man*, Yale University Press, New Haven, Conn., 1944, p. 14.

10. Quoted from Randall, *op. cit.*, p. 237.

11. See *inter alia* Andrew Dickson White, *A History of the Warfare of Science and Theology in Christendom*, George Braziller, Inc., New York, 1955.

12. On the open future of science see Karl Popper, *The Open Society and Its Enemies*, Princeton University Press, Princeton, N.J., 1963; Henri Bergson, *The Two Sources of Morality and Religion*, Henry Holt and Company, Inc., New York, 1935.

13. White, *op. cit.*

14. Whitehead, *op. cit.*, p. 270.

15. See M. Polanyi, *Science, Faith and Society*, The University of Chicago Press, Chicago, 1964, and *Personal Knowledge*, The University of Chicago Press, Chicago, 1958.

16. Carl Becker, *The Heavenly City of the Eighteenth-Century Philosophers*, Yale University Press, New Haven, Conn., 1932.

17. See *inter alia* Sidney Mead, *The Lively Experiment*, Harper & Row, Publishers, Incorporated, New York, 1963; Franklin Littell, *From State Church to Religious Pluralism*, Anchor Books, Doubleday & Company, Inc., Garden City, N.Y., 1962. Will Herberg, *Protestant, Catholic, Jew*, Doubleday & Company, Inc., Garden City, N.Y., 1960.

18. It was one of the Four Freedoms of Roosevelt and Churchill; and it is one of the rights recognized in the UNESCO Universal Charter of Human Rights.

19. David Hume, *Dialogues Concerning Natural Religion*, Social Sciences Publ., New York, 1948.

20. See Karl Löwith, *From Hegel to Nietzsche*, Holt, Rinehart and Winston, Inc., New York, 1964.

21. Ludwig Feuerbach, *The Essence of Christianity*, Harper Torchbooks, Harper & Row, Publishers, Incorporated, New York, 1957.

22. Karl Marx, *Kritik der Hegelschen Rechtsphilosophie*, Introduction. Quoted from Karl Marx, *Early Writings*, trans. and ed. by T. B. Bottomore, McGraw-Hill Paperbacks, 1964, p. 44.

23. Sigmund Freud, *The Future of an Illusion*, Anchor Books, Doubleday & Company, Inc., Garden City, N.Y., 1957.

24. For Carl Jung see *inter alia* his *Psychology and Religion*, Yale University Press, New Haven, Conn., 1938; and *Modern Man in Search of a Soul*, Kegan Paul, Trench, Trubner & Co., Ltd., London, 1933.

25. Friedrich Nietzsche, "The Genealogy of Morals" in *The Philosophy of Nietzsche*, Modern Library, Inc., New York, 1937, pp. 92–93.

26. Friedrich Nietzsche, *Will to Power*, vol. I, ed. Dr. Oscar Levi, George Allen & Unwin, Ltd., London, 1924.

27. Friedrich Nietzsche, "Thus Spake Zarathustra" in *The Philosophy of Nietzsche*, p. 27.

28. *Ibid.*, p. 27.

29. Nietzsche, *Will to Power*, vol. II, pp. 390–391.

30. Descartes, *Meditations and Selections from the Principles*, trans. John Veitch, The Open Court Publishing Company, La Salle, Ill., 1941.

31. See *inter alia* his *Treatise on God, Man and His Wellbeing*. For a more detailed exposition of Spinoza's philosophy see his *Ethics*.

32. Spinoza, *Ethics*, preceded by *On the Improvement of the Understanding*, ed. James Gutmann, Hafner Publishing Company, Inc., New York, 1949. (Prop. XXXII–III)

33. Spinoza, "Tractatus Theologico-Politicus," in *Chief Works,* trans. R. H. N. Elwes, Dover Publications, Inc., New York, 1955.

34. See *inter alia* N. Furniss, *The Fundamentalist Controversy, 1918–1931,* Yale University Press, New Haven, Conn., 1954; L. Loetscher, *The Broadening Church,* The Westminster Press, Philadelphia, 1954.

35. Albrecht Ritschl, *Christian Doctrine of Justification and Reconciliation,* T. & T. Clark, Edinburgh, 1902.

36. *Encyclopaedia of Religion and Ethics,* ed. by James Hastings, Charles Scribner's Sons, New York, 1919, vol. X, p. 665.

37. *Ibid.,* pp. 664–665.

38. C. Howard Hopkins, *The Rise of the Social Gospel in American Protestantism,* Yale University Press, New Haven, Conn., 1940.

39. Auguste Comte, *Positive Philosophy,* Franklin, 1875–1877. See also J. S. Mill, *Comte and Positivism,* The University of Michigan Press, Ann Arbor, Mich., 1961.

40. Felix Adler, *An Ethical Philosophy of Life,* Appleton-Century-Crofts, Inc., New York, 1918.

41. Johannes Auer, A.C.F., *Humanism States Its Case,* Beacon Press, Boston, 1933.

42. Nicholas Berdyaev, *The End of Our Time,* Sheed & Ward, Ltd., London, 1933.

43. Norman Cousins, *Modern Man is Obsolete,* The Viking Press, Inc., New York, 1945.

44. Charles Frankel, *The Case for Modern Man,* Harper & Row, Publishers, Incorporated, New York, 1956.

45. Paul Tillich, *The Protestant Era,* The University of Chicago Press, Chicago, 1948, pp. 55f.

46. David Riesman, *The Lonely Crowd,* Yale University Press, New Haven, Conn., 1950.

SUGGESTIONS FOR FURTHER STUDY

Becker, C.: *The Heavenly City of the Eighteenth-Century Philosophies,* Yale, 1932.

Bergson, H.: *The Two Sources of Morality and Religion,* Anchor Books, 1954.

Dampier, W.: *A History of Science,* Cambridge, 1942.

Descartes, R.: *Selections,* ed. R. Eaton, Scribner, 1927.

Feuerbach, L.: *The Essence of Christianity,* Harper & Row, 1957.

Freud, S.: *The Future of an Illusion,* Anchor Books, 1957.

Hume, D.: *Selections,* ed. C. Hendel, Scribner, 1927.

Huxley, J.: *Religion without Revelation,* Mentor Books, 1957.

Kant, I.: *Selections,* ed. T. Greene, Scribner, 1929.

Lamont, C.: *Humanism as a Philosophy,* Philosophical Library, 1950.

Mackintosh, H.: *Types of Modern Theology,* Fontana, 1963.

Marx, K.: *Basic Writings,* ed. L. Feuer, Anchor Books, 1959.

Niebuhr, R.: *The Nature and Destiny of Man,* Scribner, 1943.

Nietzsche, F.: *The Philosophy of Nietzsche,* Modern Library, 1937.

Polanyi, M.: *Personal Knowledge,* University of Chicago Press, 1958.

———: *Science, Faith and Society,* University of Chicago Press, 1964.

Popper, K.: *The Open Society and Its Enemies,* Princeton University Press, 1963.

Randall, J.: *The Making of the Modern Mind,* Houghton Mifflin, 1940.

Schleiermacher, F.: *Speeches on Religion,* Harper & Row, 1958.

———: *The Christian Faith,* Harper & Row, 1960.

Spinoza, B.: *Selections,* ed. J. Wild, Scribner, 1930.

White, A.: *A History of the Warfare of Science and Theology in Christendom,* George Braziller, 1955.

Whitehead, A.: *Science and the Modern World,* Macmillan, 1927.

18

TRADITIONAL FAITHS
AND THE HUMAN FUTURE

THE POST—MODERN PROSPECT

At the end of the last chapter it was suggested that the Modern age is past
or passing, and that mankind is now moving into a new period of history
which is post-Modern. The task of the present chapter is to sketch some of the
implications of the new situation for man's traditional faiths.

Many of the fundamental issues of modernity have ceased to be crucial and
have been pushed aside by new issues and problems. The central issue of
modernity, emancipation from tradition, has largely achieved its goal. Yet this
modern emancipation has brought with it consequences unforeseen by the great
pioneers of modernity. In degree and numbers unparalleled in previous history,
men of every land and tradition have been emancipated from their old allegiances, but in the absence of any effective substitutes have been cut adrift on
the sea of existence, their lives guided only by impulse, pleasure, and conformity. Cities around the world number such people by the million. For these
people, servile allegiance to tradition is no problem. Indeed for many there appears
to be no felt problem at all. For the more sensitive individuals a new problem

593

has emerged, namely, where amid the turbulence of our times is any human meaning to be found in existence? As noted in the last chapter, this change from the Modern to the post-Modern, or contemporary, situation is marked by the shift from the question: How shall I free myself from servile allegiance to tradition? to the question: Where and how shall I find meaning in existence? In the changed situation, some aspects of the Modern age remain as secure achievements while others have become obsolete. Our first task is to take cognizance of the new landscape. This section of the present chapter will be concerned with a few important features of the contemporary religious landscape.

FREEDOM AND RESPONSIBILITY

The enduring achievement of modernity has been its emphasis on freedom. True, many men of previous ages have known that man is free and responsible, but the Modern age has made this fact altogether central, and has at least begun the task of its detailed application to all the various aspects of individual and social life. Despite the twentieth-century popularity of totalitarianism, this is an achievement which will not be undone. Having once tasted freedom, Homo sapiens is unable completely to forget it. However, it is to be expected that the emphases and accents given to freedom will change with changing times and situations.

Most modern interpretations have emphasized, quite properly in historical terms, the negative aspects of freedom. Freedom has meant, in Erich Fromm's terms, "freedom from." [1] It has been defined as the absence of hindrances to or interferences with the individual, whether these be of political, ecclesiastical, or other origin. Men will be free, it has been urged, when they are out of prison and rid of all chains.

Yet one of the first lessons of the post-Modern age is that while such negative aspects are necessary, they are by no means sufficient, conditions of freedom. Freedom is not only "from" but "to" and "for." It has not only its negative but its positive requirements. It is possible for men to be out of prison and rid of chains, yet to fall short of freedom. Among the many positive requirements of freedom is a principle of allegiance strong enough to hold the human self together in unity and to give it purpose and direction. By a principle of allegiance we mean what in other connections we have termed an ultimate concern. The terms are synonymous. However characterized, it is what holds the self together in functioning unity. The perplexing problem is to find some such principle which will perform this function without again reducing the self to bondage. Having suggested that the traditional faiths have performed this function for their adherents, we may now extend the suggestion to say that they may continue to fulfill this function in the present and future.

For some men of the present as of every past age, freedom and its corollary, responsibility, are a burden and a task too great to be borne. Such men will always be looking for some higher power or authority upon which they can unload this burden. Contemporary religious and political history shows many movements which are, like the Grand Inquisitor, all too ready to assume this power over men. Yet this chapter and this book are written on the assumption that to the extent to which men are willing to shed their freedom and responsibility, to precisely the same extent they divest themselves of their humanity. To say this is not to advocate any one faith or to condemn others, but to set conditions for any faith which a man may hold without sacrificing that central core of freedom which constitutes his humanity. Accordingly our primary concern is with forms of faith, actual and possible, which address men in and through and not outside their fundamental freedom. Whether there are or can be such forms of faith is a central issue before thoughtful men today.

Paul Tillich has sought to deal with these issues in his threefold category of heteronomy, autonomy, and theonomy.[2] Heteronomy is the situation, as the etymology of the word suggests, in which an alien norm stands over the self, whether this norm be religious, political, or of some other sort, and reduces the self to servility or bondage. Since it stands in tyranny over the self, it frequently provokes the rebellion of autonomy. In autonomous situations, there is no authority over the human self, which provides its own norms or laws. Yet it is a fact of human history that autonomy has frequently been unstable, being little more than a point of transition from one heteronomy to another. Hence Tillich has been led on to the category of theonomy, the ideal situation, in which there is an equivalence between the commands of God and the aspirations of human selfhood. The term *God* suggests a monotheistic faith, yet Tillich's formulation can easily be generalized to cover all religions or value systems by substituting the neutral term *religious object* or *object of ultimate valuation*. That such a "theonomous" situation is difficult is undoubtedly true. Yet, it may be added, so are many other good things. But they are possible. Our task here is achieved if we recognize this as one human possibility among others in the contemporary situation.

SUBSTITUTE RELIGIONS

Another very important feature of the contemporary situation is the rise to power of what Tillich has called the "quasi-religions," namely, systems of allegiance like communism and Nazism which have some of but not all the traits of religion.[3] Here these systems will be called "substitute religions," which may be defined as systems of allegiance or valuation which function religiously, in part or in whole, in the lives of their adherents but are not recognized by their adherents as religious. They have also been called "unconscious religions" and "tacit religions." Whatever the designation, it is important to see that in the contemporary world they constitute the strongest rivals to the traditional faiths for men's allegiance.

This whole region is fraught with pitfalls and controversies, but it lies so clearly across our path as to be unavoidable. Attention must first be called to the fact that use of the term *religious substitute* or *substitute religion* is descriptive and in no way evaluative. It is meant to suggest no judgment as to the good or bad qualities of such phenomena, but only to recognize that there are such systems of value and thought, which function religiously (as this volume has defined and expounded religious functioning) but are not recognized as religions by their adherents. Surely it does not require extensive factual observation to verify the existence of such phenomena. While they are by no means limited to communism and extreme nationalism, these two systems probably constitute the most important existing religious substitutes in the contemporary world. They will be considered in turn.

Karl Marx's thought was discussed in the last chapter as a part of the radical century's criticism of traditional religion and as marking a historic development in atheism. It will now seem ironic if not contradictory to assert that Marxism constitutes a substitute religion providing a functioning system of life orientation or life valuation for countless millions of men. Indeed some observers of communism have offered the blunt evaluation that its evil is not atheism but idolatry.[4] What they mean is that behind the façade of atheism stands an absolutism which functions in much the same way that monotheistic religions assert idolatry functions. It would take us far beyond our present field of study to evaluate this charge. Yet it is an important feature of contemporary religious history that such claims are made.

The assertion of communism's religious significance is by no means novel. Almost four decades ago Middleton Murry called it the world's one living religion.[5] During the 1930s such writers as William Temple, Reinhold Niebuhr, and Paul Tillich were characterizing communism as an unconscious religion and were attempting to lay bare what they thought to be its false and misleading character.[6] More recently such diagnoses have become widely popular.

Assuming the religious significance of Marxism, it becomes important to ask what kind of religion this is. In many important ways it is a by-product of the Bible and the Judeo-Christian tradition. Many observers have agreed in calling it a Judeo-Christian heresy. In terms of our typology of religions, Marxism offers clear illustration of the third type. This designation seeks to call attention to the view of historic destiny which Chapters 11 and 13 observed in the Bible and Chapter 15 in Augustine and his *City of God*. Communism is the inheritor of this tradition. To call it heretical is to assert that it gives distorted expression to the basic ideas involved. For example, both Biblical and Marxist myth tell stories of the original perfection and fall of man. In contrast to the Biblical story, the communist story begins with primitive communism; and the fall of man occurs when the landlord and soldier combine to subjugate the worker. Evil is here characterized by Marxism as acquisitiveness, or lust for property, rather than arrogant pride, or rebellion against God.

Again, Marxism's explicit atheism does not obscure the messianism which centers in Karl Marx. From this, other traits of religion follow in succession. The Communist Party functions as a kind of church, or sect, whose sacred scriptures are the writings of Marx and Lenin, and whose leaders function sometimes as priests and sometimes as prophets. Some writers have even commented on the emergence of holy places such as the tomb of Lenin to which the faithful go on pilgrimage. These and other aspects of Marxism provide impressive verification for the thesis of this volume that religion as ultimate concern is a perennial and undeniable feature of man's life. Deny overt expression to religion, and it is not destroyed but rather forced underground, where it finds expression as covert or substitute religion. Truly man is *Homo religiosus!*

Of religious significance comparable to communism is modern nationalism in its various guises, particularly in extreme forms such as German Nazism, Italian fascism, Japanese militarism, and the radical right of the United States. In most modern nations nationalism has functioned as "man's other religion," providing a functioning value system which men need to render life meaningful.[7]

To readers familiar with recent world history, the religious quality of nationalism will be sufficiently clear in Nazism and Fascism. Here are systems of ultimate concern and valuation or of total orientation exhibiting many of the features of traditional religion, ranging from a holy leader surrounded by a context of ritual and myth to total devotion to the cause on the part of faithful followers. While Nazism and Fascism were unconsciously religious, modern Japanese militarism had direct and conscious continuity with the national religious tradition. Chapter 9 noted the distinctive Japanese formulation of the recurring themes of sacred ruler and sacred nation or land and sketched the ways in which these traditional elements were used by Japanese ultranationalists in the period culminating in World War II. The question may be asked, When does loyalty to the nation become religious in quality? The answer is, When a man's concern becomes ultimate in the sense described in Chapter 1.

Many Americans who recognize the religious significance of nationalism elsewhere in the world have given little or no thought to its place in their own situation. Asserting the traditional American doctrine of the separation of church and state, they apparently consider the matter solved. It does not exceed the bounds of factual or historical study to point out that this conclusion is premature. For whatever the official formulation, whenever loyalty to the nation is taken as total or absolute it may be assumed to have religious significance. Whenever any concern becomes ultimate, it takes on religious significance. That American nationalism functions in this way for many groups of the so-called radical right, some ostensibly secular, others avowedly religious, will be clear on observing their writings and their behavior. Whatever their conscious religious professions, the American nation is their actual object of ultimate concern. Again it will be well within the bounds of historical study to assert that Uncle Sam functions as their god.

The religious quality of American nationalism is by no means limited to extremist groups, but rather runs like a major thread through the fabric of American tradition. The New England Puritans believed that God had called them to found a new order of life in this new land. The great seal of the United States proclaims a *novum ordo saeculorum,* a new order of the ages. The tradition of America's manifest destiny has frequently assumed the significance of a religious substitute from Polk to McKinley. Lincoln proclaimed American democracy as the last great hope of mankind, and Eisenhower remarked that America is a missionary society to the world.[8]

Many of these valuations have found expression in what is often called America's civic religion. Writers as different as Lloyd Warner and Will Herberg point to the religious significance of American national holidays such as Memorial Day, July Fourth, and Thanksgiving Day.[9] They also point to the ways in which such ostensibly Christian festivals as Christmas and Easter are invested with ethnic significance. In American churches and synagogues men call upon God, but the actual value-content of their religion invests him with the significance of Uncle Sam, their faith becoming in effect a religion of American values or the American way of life. Robert Bellah has given thoughtful expression to the central American value system as a "civil religion."[10]

The kind of religion constituted by nationalism is sufficiently clear from what has already been said. It is not, like Marxism, a new form of Biblical religion, but is rather a powerful reassertion of religion of the first, or nature-culture, type. In this respect the Japanese experience is illuminating, for it presents actual historic continuities with such an ethnic tradition. But the value-content is similar in other national traditions as well. The ghosts of the divine Pharaoh of Egypt, of the Roman Caesar, of the Chinese Son of Heaven, and of countless tribal chiefs walk the earth again in contemporary nationalism. To make the same claim in value terminology, the national values are asserted to constitute the whole meaning of life; beyond the borders of the nation, nothing of any significance exists. Such is the nationalist credo. The historian of religion may note here a clear conflict with all the universal religions, that is, those which address man as a member of the human family. In a day when continued human existence depends upon global solidarity of mankind, such faiths pose a mortally serious practical problem to all who are concerned with the human future.

While communism and nationalism probably constitute the most significant religious substitutes of the contemporary world, the list by no means ends here. Like the ancient Romans, contemporary men have constructed a populous pantheon. This is even true of the academic community, despite its professions of agnosticism. On many university and college campuses are professors and students whose conventional academic agnosticism is belied by an allegiance which is virtually total and final to Science, to Democracy, to American Values, to Progress, or to Humanity. They provide effective illustration of Robin Williams' remark that every community has its functioning religion.[11]

Whatever the reader's evaluation of these substitute religions, their presence in the twentieth century in great numbers and force makes one fact abundantly clear. It is that man's need for religion shows no sign of abating. He still needs some faith to guide the course of his life, to provide him with life orientation. If overt religious forms or symbol systems are denied him, or if they do not speak with light and power, he will cleave to covert religions. The chief contenders for the allegiance of man's heart, for his ultimate commitment and concern today, are not traditional faiths (these are often regarded as polite embellishments of a civilized life) but the quasi-religious, or religious substitutes.

THE STATE OF TRADITIONAL FAITHS

While the religious substitutes flourish, what can be said concerning the contemporary condition of man's traditional faiths? What is their present state of health or disease? How have they responded to the challenge of the modern world? Which of the traditional faiths appear capable of creative responses to this challenge—and which ones do not? How effectively are they performing their function of providing men a reason for living? What are some of the values now being engendered and sustained? Can the traditional faiths continue to perform this function in the contemporary climate of opinion and feeling? Space limits the present discussion of these issues to raising a few questions and sketching a few main trends.

First, it seems clear that at least some traditional faiths are dead or dying. Chief among these is Taoism, which has been slowly expiring for several centuries. In the opinion of one authority the chief reason for its demise is the long absence of any capacity for new thought.[12] In the present lack of communication between China and the West we do not know the condition of Taoism, but it may well be that the Marxist rulers of China have already interred its moribund remains. Surely Taoism fits well the Marxist view of what religion is and does.

As to Confucianism, there is much evidence that it too is in its death agony. W. T. Chan's reports of the decrepitude in which he found Confucianism in 1948–1949 have been confirmed by later shreds of information passed through the bamboo curtain that separates China from the West.[13] Throughout the nineteenth and twentieth centuries, as China has felt the impact of modernization, the enormous conservatism of the Confucian way has seemed to many modern-minded Chinese of both democratic and communist outlooks to be a vast roadblock to progress. One can think of few more extreme contrasts on earth than that between Confucius and Marx. In Marxist China Confucius can have little future.

If some religions appear to be dying in the twentieth century, others apparently are being born. Here the scene shifts from China to Japan, which during the past century has been a matrix for many new religions and religious movements. Chapter 9 noted the thirteen Meiji sects as well as innumerable, even newer religions which have emerged since World War II. Apparently the combination of intense traditionalism and rapid, wide-ranging social change which characterizes contemporary Japan constitutes precisely the kind of soil in which new religions germinate and grow.[14] Which of these will endure and which will wither and die remains to be seen. In any case, contemporary Japan presents itself to the student of religions as a veritable laboratory experiment in the birth and growth of religions.

Still another group of religions and religious phenomena are those which continue very much alive but whose life appears to be totally identified with a particular group of people. This is true of three Indian communities of faith, the Jains, the Parsees, and the Sikhs. All three are apparently holding their own, but are doing so as the established faiths of definite communities. Hence these faiths are limited by the bounds of these communities. This is true despite the presence of other values and other ideas in the literature and traditions of Parseeism, Jainism, and Sikhism.

Another closely related group of religious phenomena consists of those in which nationalism finds expression in terms of traditional religion, in many cases being the principal ingredient or actually determining the contemporary course of religious development. Examples may be selected at random from the newly developing nations of Asia and Africa. Southeast Asian Buddhism is an illustration familiar at the present time to Americans. In Japan, the rise to prominence of Soka Gakkai or Nichiren Shoshu continues a nationalistic tendency which has had numerous illustrations in Japanese history. Islam lends a religious quality to Arab nationalism in such organizations as the Ikwan, or Arab Brotherhood. In Judaism the net effect of some forms of extremist Zionism is Israeli nationalism. In Hinduism, the list extends from Swami Dayananda and the Arya Samaj to the Jana Sangh and numerous other organizations which identify

Hindu religion with Indian nationalism. The reader will recall that Tagore and Gandhi disagreed over this issue, and also that Gandhi was assassinated by a fanatical Hindu extremist who believed that Gandhi had conceded too much to India's Muslims.

Mention may also be made at this point of a notable contemporary instance of what may perhaps be termed denationalization. The use (or misuse) of Shinto by the Japanese militarists of the nineteenth and twentieth centuries was pointed out in Chapter 9, as was the fact that during the American occupation the Emperor renounced his divinity and Shinto was disestablished. These latter developments were the crucial events in a process of denationalizing Shinto, transforming it into a relatively nonpolitical religion which provides expression for the Japanese way of life. The transition has been difficult, but statistics indicate an impressive measure of success. There is even a university, Kokugakuin, which is devoted to the scholarly study of this faith and tradition.[15] Here again contemporary Japan affords another instance of significant religious experimentation.

Turning to the larger and historically more important religions, what signs of health and sickness, of vigor or morbidity, does the observer find? Of the world faiths Hinduism is perhaps the hardest to observe. Clearly it is under attack by modern and scientific persons and trends. In India's cities caste is being eroded, though in villages it is very far from dead. Many modern-minded Indians point impatiently to the massive conservatism of Hinduism. India's need is not for religion, they argue, but for steel mills, scientific agriculture, and population control. Yet it is also a fact of contemporary history that new life has been breathed into old Hindu ideas during the great century that began with Ram Mohan Roy and ended with Gandhi. The Ramakrishna Order carries on good works and active Hindu religious propaganda both in India and around the world. The Arya Samaj and Jana Sangh continue very much alive. Apparently oblivious to modern criticism, most of India's millions continue to be Hindus in their traditional ways.

The picture is equally mixed with Buddhism. Some Buddhist ideas and groups seem moribund. To Western students the present state of Chinese Buddhism is obscure, but there are few indications of vigor. The Chinese Communists appear to have succeeded in their attempt to liquidate Tibetan Buddhism along with the rest of Tibetan culture. Opposing such trends is the Buddhist revival in central India, where adherents are reliably estimated to number three million people, though critics point to the primarily sociopolitical significance of this form of Buddhism. Southeast Asian Buddhism shows stirrings of new life from Ceylon to Cambodia and Vietnam, though it must be added that in every case there is a strong admixture of nationalism. The state of Japanese Buddhism, while controversial, appears on the whole to be one of health. After making the necessary discounts for Western faddism, Zen presents a picture of considerable vigor, both intellectual and religious. The larger and more popular Amidist groups are at least holding their own among the people. There is no lack of new movements attempting to interpret Buddhist tradition in fresh terms to contemporary Japan. There are some signs of an ecumenical spirit in Buddhism which attempts to bridge the gap between Mahayana and Theravada.

Islam's monumentally conservative posture was noted in Chapter 14. In recent times it has generated a great deal of defensive behavior among Muslims, particularly in their dealings with the West. The central contemporary question is whether this massively conservative posture can be changed sufficiently to facilitate real adaptation to the contemporary world. There are some signs of adaptive rather than defensive behavior in Islam from Pakistan to Turkey, and there is vastly greater variety in Islam than is usually supposed by Western observers. As has been true before in Muslim history, it may be that Sufism will be the agent of creative change. Yet if the opinion of as sympathetic and perceptive an observer as Wilfred Cantwell Smith is to be accepted, this crucial issue still hangs in the balance at the present moment. In Black regions of Africa Islam prospers as the vehicle of racial equality and justice.

For Judaism the emergence of the state of Israel is the crowning fact of contemporary history, and it has quickened many other movements in Jewish faith and culture. The vast tragedy of modern anti-Semitism culminating in Hitlerism has evoked many kinds of Jewish responses, ranging from fanatic nationalism to a deepening of Israel's historic faith and thought about her faith, and to a general strengthening of the bonds which hold Jewish people together in a living community and tradition. Another feature of the present situation is the emergence to maturity and leadership of American Judaism. Thus Judaism continues as a relatively small religion, but very much alive and exerting an influence in the world altogether out of proportion to its numbers. It is probably more vigorous and vital today than for many centuries past.

In Roman Catholic Christianity the overarching fact is Pope John XXIII in all his unique and powerful impact upon church and world. Chapter 16 suggested that Pope John and the second Vatican Council marked a historic change of attitude, from the defensive outlook of the Council of Trent to an outgoing and affirmative approach to the world. Here it may be added that these events have provided a center for many and diverse movements for renewal in Catholicism. These have included a notable flowering of the arts in such men as Georges Roualt, creative philosophical and theological study in Maritain, Gilson, Kueng, and Rahner, and renewed religious forms and activities ranging from liturgics to social work and missions. There is also inertia and resistance to the new trends in faith and thought, yet despite these, the Roman Catholic Church today seems clearly to face forward rather than backward, toward the world rather than away from it. Likewise the lines of relation toward other Christian groups are convergent rather than divergent.

In Protestantism, the ecumenical movement antedated its emergence in Roman Catholicism, and it has assumed somewhat different forms and emphases. Beginning as far back as the first decade of the present century, it sought at first to draw the different Protestant bodies together in common tasks at home and on mission fields. From this it moved onward to press toward unity of creed, institutions, and organizations. Many other streams of influence fed into the ecumenical movement. Among these was a notable revival of theological thought and study, embodied in such men as Karl Barth, the Niebuhr brothers, and Paul Tillich. Still another influence was the Social Gospel, as noted in Chapter 16.

In recent years there have been many moves toward rapprochement between Protestants and Roman Catholics. These have ranged from mutual consultations among theologians to meetings for mutual fellowship and exploration between adherents of the two forms of Christianity or to official and quasiofficial representation at each others' ecclessiastical gatherings. What the future holds is not clear, but Protestants and Roman Catholics today appear to be facing toward each other rather than away from each other.

In American Protestantism during the years after World War II (as well as in American Catholicism and Judaism) there was a rate of growth at times twice that of population growth, with the result that religious adherence, church attendance, and almost every other index of participation stand at all-time highs. However, more recently this increase has slackened or ceased altogether. Also it must also be recorded that despite the quantity, the quality of this faith has been widely questioned, for this return to religion has not been accompanied either by any significant increase in knowledge of the faith or in any of the significant fruits of genuine religious faith.

In Protestant Christianity in America and, one suspects, elsewhere as well, the greatest single problem today is not antireligion but nominal adherence. It is not excessive to say that the effectiveness of religion in the contemporary world will be measured by the degree to which the gap between the concerned minority and the masses of adherents is overcome. While this gap exists in every religion on earth it appears to be particularly serious and significant in contemporary America.

CHALLENGE AND RESPONSE

The contemporary situation makes clear that the human need for religion shows no signs of abating. It has been a hypothesis of this book that traditional faiths have sought to provide men with functioning answers to the question: Why am

I alive? This perennial function of religion has acquired a new and peculiar urgency and relevance in the post-Modern situation of the twentieth century. Many circumstances have converged to create this new relevance.

It was Hegel and after him Marx who spoke first of dehumanization, applying it to the impact of nineteenth-century industrialism on the lives of the workers. By this term they sought to call attention to social conditions which in their opinion prevented men from fulfilling their human lives. The idea has been applied more widely in the twentieth century than in the nineteenth. Moreover these trends in the political and economic areas of society are powerfully reinforced by factors deriving from man's mind and spirit. The last chapter depicted the way in which the acids of modern criticism have eaten away the fabric of traditional faith and values. The result of all these converging causes is the widespread contemporary sense of meaninglessness. Man stands alone and naked in a world denuded of all human meaning or value.[16]

This, or something like this, constitutes the challenge to which contemporary man must find some adequate response if human life is to continue, at least if it is to continue in a distinctively human or humane way. It would of course be presumptuous to suppose that religion, or indeed any single thing, could provide a solution to what is a major crisis in man's history. Nevertheless the traditional faiths have the opportunity to make a significant contribution.

It is important in this connection to be clear that man does not receive his humanity all at once or as a gift of nature. Rather his humanity or his personal stature may be characterized as an aspiration and a task. Thus a newborn baby is not so much a person as the potentiality of becoming such. The late Teilhard de Chardin gave the synoptic expression *hominization,* humanization, to the process by which man achieves and sustains his full human stature.[17] While Teilhard gave no special emphasis to the negative process of dehumanization, there is no reason why these two terms and ideas should not be juxtaposed, thus bringing to full articulation the elemental struggle between humanization and dehumanization.

Here then is a warfare which goes through every individual heart and through the large patterns of contemporary human affairs, economic, political, and social. Each human being makes a bid for humanization, yet no man's bid is made alone, apart from fellowmen. Rather he is a small part of the web of life, which is social and in our time increasingly global in nature.

What now is the role of the traditional faiths in this dramatic situation? This volume has repeatedly argued that the various faiths may legitimately be construed as value systems, symbolically expressed, and proposed as answers to the existential questions: Why am I alive? What must I do and be to be genuinely human?

To say the same thing by means of a different model, man may be imagined at the center of a circle around the circumference of which stand representatives of all the religions. The man in the middle asks his existential questions, and from their positions around the circumference, each of the faiths makes its answer. From among these answers man must choose, and in terms of his choice must live out his life.

Will the traditional faiths be capable of recasting their messages to fit this novel context? Indeed, an even more fundamental question may well occur to the reader, namely, *Ought* they to try to do so? For—so runs the thought— religions traditionally have had to do with gods or God. Is it then proper to reinterpret them as having to do centrally with man or human life? As we have seen, Feuerbach and his disciples, the Humanists, have sought such a transformation. Many readers may regard this as an attempt to stretch traditional words and ideas beyond their elastic limits.

To do justice to this last question would take us far beyond the limits of our present discussion, though it is well to note it as a significant topic for possible study. We can, however, observe that it accords well with common sense and traditional faith to assert that religion deals with the way men are to live their lives. It is also possible to note in passing that many of the best-known contemporary theologies assert that the proper content of faith is not man's view of God, but a kind of God's-eye view of man, and the proper understanding and conduct of human life. In such approaches the term *God* stands as a way of certifying or authenticating this view of man. Karl Barth, for example, once remarked that the Bible contains not the correct human thoughts about God, but the correct divine thoughts about man. Thus it must suffice here to note that some traditional faiths are in fact construing themselves in the manner suggested by this hypothesis.

It may also be noted that there is an increasing tendency on the part of several of the traditional faiths to speak in terms of alternative kinds of humanisms. For several decades Roman Catholic thinkers have worked with a concept of Christian humanism which might be defined as a Christian answer to man's existential question.[18] Voices of this kind are increasingly being heard among Protestants. Jewish thinkers have proposed a Jewish humanism.[19] There is increasing emphasis among significant Buddhist thinkers on the humane tradition of their faith.[20] Much the same can be said of Hinduism. It does not take too much extension of present trends to envisage a situation in which each of the faiths will present its own distinctive answer to the question: What must we men do and be to become human? In any case this constitutes the challenge of the contemporary situation. Whether mankind's traditional faiths can respond effectively remains to be seen.

THE SHAPE OF FAITHS TO COME

In the past, times of radical change have sometimes produced new religions. The coming of civilization brought with it numerous religions of the nature-culture type from China to Mesopotamia to Greece. The Axis age of the ancient world brought Confucius, Lao-tzu, Buddha, the prophets of Israel, and others. Will the present period of human history, which is surely a crisis as deep and pervasive as any other in human history, produce some radically new religion or religious orientation? Or will man's future be one of non-religion or secularism? The only factual answer that can be made is that there are no signs of such new developments visible at the present time.

If we concede mankind's continuing religious need and interest, the alternative to some new development is that the traditional faiths speak their old words in some new way to the new situation. Assuming this kind of change, is it possible to project any lines of probable future development? On some such basis let us ask, What is the shape of faiths to come?

It is important to be clear concerning what we do and do not mean by this question. For one thing, it does not commit us to crystal gazing or oracular prophecy. Even more important, we are not engaged in recommending or prescribing what faith or kind of faith men ought or ought not to have. Indeed if the reader places either of these interpretations on the paragraphs that follow he will be misunderstanding what is meant and said. Rather, we seek on the basis of our study of the past and present to project a few lines of development into the foreseeable future. Obviously such thinking is highly fallible. If the reader is inclined to disagree with the expectations to be projected here, he is invited to set out his own alternatives. Both of us will have the task of comparing our expectations with the unfolding course of events.

The only preferences or valuations assumed here are those necessary for the continuance of civilized humanity. There must be men in order for any faiths to continue, and this assumption commits us to some underlying minimal valuations. However, it does not in any sense commit us to recommending one faith or denigrating another.

We shall glance briefly at five themes which bear importantly on the shape of faiths to come: (1) ultimate valuation or concern, (2) man's paradoxical situation of freedom and dependence, (3) the holy, or sacred, (4) the symbolical expression of religious experience, and (5) morality, or the implication of ultimate values for man's action.

ULTIMATE CONCERN

At the center of any future faith will be a core of functioning values which will provide life orientation for its adherents. Whether this function can be fulfilled without any of the negative or disfunctional features of past faiths is a matter of much interest. The definition of faith as ultimate concern has had as one of its objectives to call attention to this central function of faith in contrast to such classical aberrations as defining faith primarily as propositional belief beyond or against the evidence, that is, "believing what one knows is not so." By contrast, to characterize faith as ultimate valuation makes clear that this process may be reasonable or unreasonable, wise or foolish. There is nothing inherently irrational about ultimate concern as such.

However, it is a fact of history that the traditional forms of ultimate concern emerged in ages of history when it was easy or indeed inevitable for them to be mixed with now outmoded cosmology. God and heaven, for example, were "up there" just out of sight and reach. The emergence of modern science has rendered such cosmologies implausible and untenable. It will accordingly be interesting and significant to observe the response of religious experience to the new situation. Some students of religion, including the theologian Rudolf Bultmann, with his program to demythologize Christian belief, and John Robinson, Bishop of Woolich, with his recommendation that Christian believers be "honest to God," have sought to develop the implications of the new situation. In polemical discussion of some traditional theories of the human mind, Gilbert Ryle has been led to characterize one view as the fallacy of the "ghost in the machine."[21] By analogy, at least, one view of deity might be characterized as the fallacy of the "Big Spirit out there." Such ideas at least are obsolete.

For monotheistic faiths like Christianity the status of belief in God is a crucial question. However, as the study of this volume has pointed out, the problem of God impinges differently upon faiths of the first two types. In some of them, as for example Zen Buddhism, the problem of God does not arise at all. The current popularity of Zen among Western intellectuals is undoubtedly to be understood in part because of this. Stated in most general terms to cover all the faiths studied in this book, we may say that the problem is that of the nature of the object of ultimate concern. The question is how to construe the object of ultimate concern in ways that do not contravene or stultify the experience itself and that do not contradict known facts concerning the world.

Some current Christian theologians have laid hold upon Nietzsche's dictum that "God is dead" and teach a form of Christian faith in which the traditional belief in God is deleted from the Christian confession.[22] Whether this development is an indication of the shape of things to come or merely a current fad remains to be seen. At least these students of Christian faith may be said to be attacking obsolete ideas and images of deity. Whether other ideas and images will replace them, or whether the whole idea of deity will go into oblivion, remains to be seen. The problem may be stated in most general form as that of the status in existence of the object of ultimate concern. Whether the future will lie with nontheistic forms of faith or whether new images and ideas of the object of ultimate concern will rise to lay hold upon men's allegiance is precisely the issue that only future events can decide.

MAN'S FREEDOM AND DEPENDENCE

Closely related to the God-problem is that of the paradoxically related experiences of freedom and dependence which find expression in religion. As previous sections of this chapter have argued, the central feature of modernity has been its application of freedom to man's life. If this is the case, it follows that no form of faith which avoids this issue can hope to hold the allegiance of thoughtful men in days ahead. It is easy enough to make the general assertion that any faith of the future will have to establish satisfactory relations with human freedom and responsibility. But it is something enormously more complicated and difficult to give this assertion detailed and full application in the life of religion.

It is so particularly because of the paradoxical combination of freedom and dependence in human life. If there is any single issue on which all traditional faiths have agreed, it is that man does not stand alone, but rather is dependent on powers external to himself, whatever the name or nature of these powers. Man as a finite creature chooses neither the circumstances of his birth nor (excepting suicide) his death, and between birth and death many things are thrust upon him independently of his will or against his will. Important elements of all traditional faiths have been involved in the interpretation of these aspects of the human situation. Often, to be sure, the traditional faiths have counseled a premature acquiescence to conditions which man in his freedom and intelligence can ameliorate. Yet equally, it must be urged, some forms of dependence seem unavoidable, as inherent in the human situation. As long as man is man, he will be born and die, and will suffer good fortune and ill fortune. Each of the different faiths will have its own characteristic interpretation of human dependence, involving its own way for man to adjust to his fate.

The attitude of faith also involves dependence upon the religious object, however conceived. A persistent problem for future as for past faiths is that of giving expression to this form of dependence without falling headlong into what psychology likes to call neurotic dependence. This term means kinds of dependence, often compulsive in nature, that undermine the normal free and responsible functioning of the self. Some contemporary writers seem to regard all religious dependence as neurotic. By contrast, it may be urged that there is such a thing as normal dependence, involving a real relation to real aspects of the world. Hence to distinguish normal from neurotic dependence constitutes an important problem for future faiths.

Similarly the acknowledgment of authority has often conflicted with man's freedom and responsibility. So much is this the case that some writers assert authority and freedom to be mutually contradictory. To be free means to be out from under authority; to be under authority means to be unfree. This view coincides with what Tillich calls autonomy, and as previously noted it is a view which often occurs in rebellion against heteronomy. In opposition to this view it is not difficult to see that finite, mortal existence entails some recognition of authority. It has been said that the realistic formulation is not: Authority or no authority? but rather: Under which authority will I live? The quality of the authority is also important. It is possible to distinguish among religious, political, and other sorts of authority, those kinds whose acceptance is fatal to freedom and responsibility, and those whose acceptance fulfills freedom.

This is by no means only a verbal distinction. Many historic forms of religion have been plainly authoritarian, asserting a kind of authority which destroys man's freedom and responsibility. In effect they have been religious tyrannies. Dostoyevsky gave poignant expression to such a relation in his story of the Grand Inquisitor, who took away man's freedom in exchange for mystery, miracle, and authority. It will be significant to observe whether future forms of faith will be able to achieve systems of authority under which man may stand in his full stature as a free and responsible self.

THE QUALITY OF THE SACRED

Another cluster of issues concerning faiths to come centers in the quality of holiness, or sacredness, and its relation to the secular world. Chapter 1 identified this unique affective quality as the common feature of religious phenomena. Yet in the past the holy has lived a very dubious life, associating with some of the most disreputable and dehumanizing forces in history, such as superstition, obscurantism, and injustice. The holy has served as a screen to hide the manipulations of the magician, it has served as a roadblock in the road of human intelligence, it has been a device for enforcing acquiescence in tyranny and injustice. Tyrants, shamans, and diseases have all been interpreted by countless human beings as authentically sacred. Sometimes the division of human society and human experience into two realms, the sacred and the secular, has been a way of putting up "no trespassing" signs over large areas of human experience.

Accordingly it is a fair question whether there can be expressions of the sacred which successfully avoid these historic pitfalls. Again, only future events can give the actual answer, yet it accords with past experience to assert this possibility. For if anything is observably true of the sacred, it is the infinite variety of its expressions. The quality of holiness attaching to voodoo differs from that which inheres in the Zen meditation hall. That which is to be seen in the person of Christ differs qualitatively from that of Buddha or Muhammad. Since this is so, it is at least possible that there may be forms which do not conflict with man's sense of reason, justice, and humanity. In one set of symbols or another, man must make his peace with the universe in which his lot is cast. The holy will be the emotive accompaniment of this ultimate adjustment, as it may perhaps be termed. And if this quality be combined with man's highest values, the result will be a quality of reverence which does not conflict with, but fulfills, man's humanity.

Expressions of the sacred of this sort will involve no conflict with the modern idea of the secularization of society. They would, of course, conflict with the negative dogma of secularism which categorically denies any legitimate existence to the sacred. It may be argued with much justification that a secular society is not hostile to religion, but provides a kind of neutral environment in which different faiths are free to pursue their ways and works. For faiths that are vital and vigorous, such an environment is an opportunity and a challenge. The problem is accordingly not to combat secularization as an evil, but to discover new ways of communicating sacred value in this new historic context. For there is every indication that the agelong drift toward secularization will continue into the future.

It is a view frequently argued in these pages that no form of the holy is experienced as a direct object of human interest. That is, men do not say "Let us have an experience of the holy," or "Let us be reverent." Rather, these emotions occur as by-products of situations of ultimate commitment and concern. Also they occur through the mediation of powerful symbols or symbol systems. To the symbols of faith attention must now be turned.

SYMBOLISM

Previous pages of this study have argued that ultimate concern demands and receives expression in powerful and concrete symbols. It was also pointed out in the last chapter that the Modern age has carried out a radical, devastating criticism of traditional symbols and faiths. The result is that the hold of these symbols and symbol systems upon men's minds and hearts has been greatly loosened. Tillich has spoken of this contemporary situation as one of "broken symbols," that is, symbols which are recognizable as such, and not as literal truths. The great question is whether in this radically new kind of context, religious symbol systems can maintain their power over their adherents. This question is a genuinely open one, the answer to which will lie in the actual destiny of the world's traditional faiths. For literally, a dead faith is simply one whose symbols no longer speak with light and power to the minds and hearts of men.

To these observations it is necessary at this point only to add that in the world of the mid-twentieth century a great deal of significant free play and experimentation with symbols is taking place in both religion and the arts. One result of the contemporary mingling of religions has been the syncretist or eclectic effort to combine symbols and traditions, by such groups as Theosophy, Bahaism, Christian Science, Religious Science, and the like. To date, the results of this kind of experimentation have not been impressive. From these processes has emerged no single, authentic style, but a hodge-podge of many styles jumbled together in incoherence. Such symbols and symbol systems do not successfully communicate ultimate concern or conviction to very many people.

A radically different and unrelated kind of experimentation which is taking place in many of the contemporary arts has vastly greater promise for the future of religions. One cannot read a poem by Eliot or Rilke without realizing that the author is actively seeking for fresh symbols which will adequately express what he has to say; and what the poet has to say is often strikingly similar to what traditional faiths have said through their respective symbol systems. This observation, made about poetry and other literature, is equally or even more true of the visual arts of painting, sculpture, and architecture. In all of these arts there has been a deliberate abandonment of old symbols as worn out and an exploration in search of new images or symbols. Often this search has seemed revolutionary or nihilistic, as in Picasso's painting and sculpture, in which the ordinary forms of things are twisted and distorted beyond all recognition. Yet the search that underlies these apparently strange pictures and shapes is not nihilistic but genuinely humanistic. Free imaginative play with new forms has been a characteristic of artists like Chagall and Rouault and of architects like Le Corbusier. Often these men and others like them have worked with traditional religious themes, but even when this is not true their work has an undeniable religious significance. In their various ways contemporary men seek images and symbols by means of which they may communicate the meaningful character of life.

The work of philosophical theologians such as Tillich, Buber, and Suzuki reveals an analogous search and experimentation in the world of ideas for new symbols, or for new interpretations of old symbols which will provide light and power for contemporary men. Here, in the free play of images in the contemporary mind, the possibility of negative results is always present—as it is in any experiment. Yet also as in any real experiment, the situation before the experimenter is genuinely open. Clearly the last word has not been spoken. The part of honest and sensitive men is to find expression as adequately as

The First Day. Woodcut by Ernst Barlach

Courtesy of Collection, Museum of Modern Art, New York

Crucifixion. Etching by Marcello Muccini

Courtesy of Collection, Museum of Modern Art, New York, Purchase

Jonah. Woodcut by Jacob Steinhardt

Courtesy of Collection, Museum of Modern Art, New York, Purchase

Tobias and the Angel. Wood engraving by Leonard Baskin

Courtesy of Collection, Mr. & Mrs. Rawell Schleicher, New York

Benediction. Acquatint by Georges Rouault

Courtesy of Collection, Museum of Modern Art, New York, Purchase

Christ Mocked by Soldiers. Painting by Georges Rouault

Courtesy of Collection, Museum of Modern Art, New York, Purchase

The Ark Brought to Jerusalem. Etching by Mark Chagall

Courtesy of Collection, Museum of Modern Art, New York, gift of Mr. & Mrs. Bernard J. Reis

Guernica. Mural by Pablo Picasso

On loan to the Museum of Modern Art, New York, from the artist

they can for what they believe to be meaningful and true and to stay in communication with other seekers. In some such terms as these the contemporary
experiment with life symbols goes on. The results lie in the lap of future
history.

Le Corbusier's modern Church of Notre Dame du
Haut, Ronschamp, Alsace

Courtesy of George Holton

MORAL AND ETHICAL VALUES

Turning attention to the moral and ethical aspects of ultimate concern, the
contemporary situation seems as fluid as in other aspects. At least a part of the
modern criticism of traditional faiths has been moral in its inspiration. Traditional faiths have been criticized because they have violated their own moral
values. Teaching justice and love, they have often practiced fanaticism and
hate. The details of these criticisms are well known to any thoughtful person,
whatever his own estimate of them. The commonly accepted conclusions of
these criticisms may seem as agenda for the moral features of future faiths.

It has been a feature of most traditional faiths to provide moral values to guide the footsteps of its adherents in their active and interpersonal life. The values to which man gives allegiance in the experience of faith also provide him with moral guidance. Religion and ethics are not two different enterprises but two aspects of man's experience of value.

Such considerations as these point to important moral and ethical requirements for future faiths. If the assertion repeatedly made in previous pages regarding man's nature as a free and responsible being is tenable, it sets awesome moral tasks for any future faith. For such a faith will have to find expression in social life for precisely this estimate of human personality. Furthermore the future forms of human relations, both intrapersonal and interpersonal, involve vast unprecedented problems. Questions of right and wrong and moral good and evil emerge in such novel areas as the chemical alteration of consciousness. Psychedelic drugs appear as only the first and simplest of vast new developments. Similarly the global dimensions of human relations, which must be dealt with if the human race is to have a future, will have their distinctively moral aspect. It is not our purpose to prescribe or even to hint what these moral valuations of future faiths will be, but only to say that as long as man remains man the moral aspect of his nature will also remain. Therefore any faith that claims to offer guidance to human life will have to speak pertinently to man's moral problems.

The suggestions of the preceding paragraphs concerning future faiths might perhaps have been labeled present indications of things to come. To go beyond present evidence would be an exercise in augury and necromancy. Yet to observe the future as it unfolds into the present, and to play one's part in the process, is not augury but responsible humanity, in which every man has the duty and privilege of participation.

LET THE BEST FAITH WIN

A noteworthy feature of the present situation is a new kind of meeting of the world's peoples and faiths. One need not go beyond a metropolitan airport in any part of the world and there listen to the announcements of arrival and departure of planes, in order to take in this fact. True, peoples have met and mingled peripherally since the beginning of civilization. However, the contemporary phenomenon is not peripheral, but so central and thoroughgoing as to constitute a new thing. Not only air travel but all the modern means of communication combine to put an end to isolation. Hence any faith which depends on sealing off its followers from outside influences seems doomed to extinction.

The new meeting of faiths poses important problems of interreligious relations. It is probably necessary to add once more that our intention here is not to advocate this or that policy or solution but to indicate what kinds of solutions seem possible or, at most, what kinds of interreligious relations seem consistent with those human values necessary for the continuance of the human race.

These problems of interreligious relations are so new and so large that it would be presumptuous even to speak of a solution here. We can, however, begin to be aware of some of their aspects. To date three kinds of approaches to interreligious relations have been undertaken: (1) missionary programs of particular religions, (2) attempts at the synthesis of some or all religions, and (3) proposals for the unbiased scientific study of all religions.

Missionary programs to convert all men to one particular religion have been undertaken at various times and places in human history. Of the monotheistic faiths both Christianity and Islam are overtly missionary in nature, while Judaism has been so only in a highly qualified sense since ancient times. Of the other faiths Buddhism has engaged in missionary activity of various kinds from King Ashoka to the present. With Hinduism the picture is unclear. Some Hindus declare plainly that the only door of entry is being born an Indian. However, groups like the Ramakrishna Order do engage in their own forms of teaching work in America and Europe. Some, though by no means all, missionary programs aim at what Hocking has called the radical displacement of one religion by another. They are based on a conviction of the truth of one particular religion in contrast to all others. While such programs have varied widely in spirit and in detail, they have at times been characterized by an attitude of exclusive and arrogant particularism which especially in modern times has drawn drastic criticism from men devoted to universal human values.

A second approach to interreligious relations is illustrated by syncretist proposals in many times and places. The Moghul Emperor Akbar sought this kind of fusing of religions in seventeenth-century India. Bahaism and Theosophy are more recent attempts of the same sort. The Parliament of the World's Religions which met at the Chicago World's Fair in 1892–1893 undertook explorations of a similar sort to find the common elements in the world's religions. While this way of dealing with interreligious relations successfully meets the objections to the missionary approach, it has its own characteristic weakness, namely, in its search for breadth it overlooks the conviction which finds expression in specific or concrete symbols and symbol systems. As a result it has never attracted a widespread following, and does not appear likely to do so in the future.

Another approach to interreligious problems is the scientific study of religions, illustrated by such organizations as the International Congress on the History of Religions, with its scholarly journals, its periodic conferences, and other activities. The main instrument of this approach is objective study similar to that which takes place in all the scholarly disciplines. This is highly useful as far as it goes, namely, in the acquisition of a body of reliable knowledge concerning all the religions. But clearly it is based on a student's or an observer's approach to religion, and it deliberately stops short of participation. While the knowledge thus amassed may well be of use to the participant, scholarly knowledge offers no sufficient guidance for interreligious relations.

The search for an adequate approach to interreligious relations leads on to other suggestions and other aspects of religious experience. Any approach which seeks to be adequate in the twentieth century may well begin with the freedom of religion which has been the great achievement of the Modern age. It will bid each faith not only to enjoy this freedom for itself but also to defend it for every other faith, and to think through its implications for the life of faith in a world of religious freedom, pluralism, and mutual meeting.

Among these implications of freedom is that any faith has the right to speak its message to the world—its words of conviction and witness—in any way it sees fit, consistent with peace and social order. This right stems from the nature of religious conviction. For it may be said that all deep and genuinely held convictions have a missionary quality. If a man genuinely believes something he is impelled by this conviction to tell others. Often he believes that he *must* do so. As was said in earlier chapters, there is a close relation between the experiences of vocation and mission, of being *called* and being *sent*. It is of course a long distance from these basic qualities of religious experience to all the apparatus and instrumentalities of organized missionary programs, but this is the foundation upon which such programs are erected.

Yet there is a further implication in this quality of religious experience which is often overlooked by religious people. It is that if as a result of this quality of my faith I have a right and duty to speak my word of witness, so too does the other man, the adherent of another, competing faith. If he is an object of my witness, I stand in a reciprocal relation to him. I am an object of his missionary word and work. Out of this situation may well arise a new dimension of conversation or communication among the world's faiths, consisting not just of an amiable exchange of opinions but of genuine dialog of faiths.

There are signs that such a conversation among faiths is actually beginning to take place. Its rules are those of freedom and fair play and a genuine desire for dialog. No one can predict the result of this nascent conversation. Yet if it is carried on, one result is bound to be a better mutual knowledge of each other among the participants, and also by implication a new kind of self-knowledge for each. Sometimes the conversation will end in agreement, sometimes in disagreement. Where the former is the consequence, it may have the further result of common action. For example, Toynbee has proposed that Christianity and Buddhism stand together in mutual defense against the totalitarian political systems which threaten both. Other similar common objectives will arise in the future.

But dialog may also arrive at fundamental disagreement. The value systems proposed to man by the various religions do in fact differ fundamentally at many important points. No amount of dialog will remove the differences between the Buddhist Nirvana and the Judeo-Christian heaven. At all such points, the proposal here presented implies a relation of mutual respect and friendly competition. Justice Oliver Wendell Holmes once spoke in a classic aphorism of a free market in ideas. There is no reason why there may not be a free market in faiths and in the symbolic images which constitute their vehicles of expression and communication. Any faith is, as it were, addressed: To whom it may concern. Let each faith address itself to all who are concerned to hear and heed its message. In the resulting competition for men's allegiance, let the best faith win.

Among the many complex and difficult issues involved in this proposal is the question of what is meant by the best faith. It could be taken to mean simply that faith which in fact wins out in the competition of faiths, in which case the phrase *best faith* would be a tautology. While a full answer is impossible in present limits of space, it may be briefly answered that *best* faith means "most true" or "most adequate." Adequacy in its most inclusive sense requires the capacity to live in the presence of facts, to respond to facts, to take full account of them in thought and action. It leads the faithful not to avoid facts, but to seek them out, and having found them to weave them into even wider patterns of coherence. A fact, as we have previously had occasion to observe, is simply and plainly whatever the mind finds and does not make, discovers and does not invent, in its encounter with reality. Accordingly a fact is a piece of reality, and conversely, reality is the total structure of facts.

The most adequate faith or best faith is that which takes fullest account of reality in all its many aspects. Here in the religious region of experience as elsewhere a wise man's life is a lifelong quest for adequacy. The best faith is that which proves itself most adequate in all man's varied encounters with reality. Who is to be the judge of adequacy? Obviously each man must judge for himself.

A TIME OF WAITING

The present post-Modern age has been variously characterized as a time of waiting—for God, for Godot, or for whatever surprising new value systems the future may bring. This chapter has sought to trace a few of the implications of this time of transition for the faiths of mankind.

Some of the readers of these pages are doubtless adherents of some one of the world's faiths. Others in equal probability stand apart from all such adherence. Still others will have begun and/or ended the study as seekers for a faith not yet achieved or clearly articulated. Whatever one's own view it is well for each person to realize that there are men of eminent intelligence and integrity who disagree with him. It is also well for him to realize that for all mankind and for all aspects of the human situation the present is a time of rapid and unprecedented change toward a future so radically open and novel that no man can descry the shape of things to come. In such situations it has been said that men must simply expect the unexpected.

In the things of faith or religion two or three further words may be added. We must face this future with integrity and candor as the only possible basis on which an authentic faith may be erected. Let each person be what he is seriously led to be, stand where he is seriously led to stand, on whatever convictions form the base of his being. It is well also to face the future with the openness of intellectual and spiritual freedom. Such receptivity is hazardous, for what a man takes into himself he becomes. Yet the opposite attitude of the closed mind and spirit is more than dangerous, it is fatal.

The attitude of combined openness and conviction involves inner tensions which must not be underestimated. Yet many men can testify from personal experience that such tensions can be creative rather than destructive. Recent and current psychology has made much of the viewpoint of participant-observer, that is, the participant in group activities who simultaneously seeks to observe what takes place in the human interactions involved in the group. Students of religion might well consider the viewpoint of the participant-observer as an approach to faith. They may find here valuable clues for both study and practice.

NOTES

1. Erich Fromm, *Escape From Freedom*, Farrar & Rinehart, Inc., New York, 1941, p. 134.

2. Paul Tillich, *The Protestant Era*, trans. James Luther Adams, The University of Chicago Press, Chicago, 1948, pp. xvi, 56–57.

3. Paul Tillich, *Christianity and the Encounter of the World Religions*, Columbia University Press, New York, 1963, pp. 5–6.

4. See *inter alia* John Bennett, *Christianity and Communism*, Association Press, New York, 1948, pp. 81–82.

5. J. Middleton Murry, *The Necessity of Communism*, Jonathan Cape, Ltd., London, 1932.

6. Reinhold Niebuhr, *The Nature and Destiny of Man*, vol. I, Charles Scribner's Sons, New York, 1943; Paul Tillich, *The Religious Situation*, trans. H. Richard Niebuhr, Meridian Books, Inc., New York, 1956. For Temple's writings on this subject, see *The Christian Newsletter* for the 1930s.

7. Edward Shillito, *Nationalism: Man's Other Religion*, Willett, Clark & Co., Chicago, 1933.

8. Will Herberg, *Protestant, Catholic, Jew*, Doubleday & Company, Inc., Garden City, N.Y., 1960, p. 92.

9. Will Herberg, *op. cit.*; W. Lloyd Warner, *American Life: Dream and Reality*, The University of Chicago Press, Chicago, 1953.

10. Robert Bellah, *Beyond Belief*, Harper & Row, Publishers, Incorporated, New York, 1970, p. 168f.

11. Robin M. Williams, *American Society: A Sociological Interpretation*, Al-

fred A. Knopf, Inc., 1951, p. 312.

12. W. T. Chan, *Religious Trends in Modern China,* Columbia University Press, New York, 1953, chap. 4, pp. 136–156.

13. *Ibid.*

14. Raymond Hammer, *Japan's Religious Ferment,* Oxford University Press, Fair Lawn, N.J., 1962.

15. Floyd Ross, *Shinto: The Way of Japan,* Beacon Press, Boston, 1965. Sokyo Ono, *Shinto: The Kami Way* in collaboration with Wm. P. Woodward, Bridgeway Press, Rutland, Vt., 1962.

16. Tillich, *The Protestant Era,* p. 60.

17. Pierre Teilhard de Chardin, *The Phenomenon of Man,* Harper & Row, Publishers, Incorporated, New York, 1959.

18. Jacques Maritain, *True Humanism,* Charles Scribner's Sons, New York, 1938.

19. Will Herberg, *Four Existential Theologians,* Doubleday & Company, Inc., Garden City, N.Y., 1958.

20. D. T. Suzuki, *Zen Buddhism,* selected writings ed. by William Barrett Anchor Books, Doubleday & Company, Inc., Garden City, N.Y., 1956; Kitaro Nishida, *A Study of Good,* trans. V. H Viglielmo, Printing Bureau, Japan Government, Tokyo, 1960.

21. See *inter alia* Paul van Buren, *The Secular Meaning of the Gospel,* The Macmillan Company, New York, 1963; Thomas J. Altizer, *The Gospel of Christian Atheism,* The Westminster Press, Philadelphia, 1965; Gabriel Vahanian, *The Death of God,* George Braziller, Inc., New York, 1961.

22. Gilbert Ryle, *The Concept of Mind,* Hutchinson and Co. (Publishers), Ltd., London, 1949, pp. 15f.

SUGGESTIONS FOR FURTHER STUDY

Bellah, R. (ed.): *Religion and Human Progress in Asia,* Free Press, 1964.

Berdyaev, N.: *The End of Our Time,* Sheed, 1933.

Buber, M.: *I and Thou,* Scribner, 1958.

——: *Between Man and Man,* Macmillan, 1948.

Chan, W.: *Religious Trends in Modern China,* Columbia, 1953.

Cousins, N.: *Modern Man is Obsolete,* Viking, 1945.

Cragg, K.: *Sandals at the Mosque,* Oxford, 1961.

Frankel, C.: *The Case for Modern Man,* Beacon Press, 1959.

Hammer, R.: *Japan's Religious Ferment,* Oxford, 1961.

Kaplan, A.: *New World of Philosophy,* Random House, 1961.

Kramer, H.: *World Cultures and World Religions,* Westminster Press, 1961.

Hocking, W.: *Living Religions and a World Faith,* Harper & Row, 1940.

Littell, F.: *From State Church to Religious Pluralism,* Anchor Books, 1963.

Marx, K.: *Basic Writings,* ed. L. Feuer, Anchor Books, 1959.

Mead, S.: *The Lively Experiment,* Harper & Row, 1963.

Niebuhr, R.: *Faith and History,* Scribner, 1949.

——: *The Self and the Dramas of History,* Scribner, 1955.

——: *Pious and Secular America,* Scribner, 1958.

Riesman, D.: *The Lonely Crowd,* Yale, 1952.

Smith, W. C.: *Islam in Modern History,* Mentor Books, 1959.

——: *The Meaning and End of Religion,* Macmillan, 1963.

Suzuki, D.: *Zen Buddhism,* Anchor Books, 1956.

Thomsen, H.: *Japan's New Religions,* Tuttle, 1963.

Tillich, P.: *The Protestant Era,* University of Chicago Press, 1948.

——: *The Courage To Be,* Yale, 1952.

——: *Christianity and the Encounter of the World Religions,* Columbia, 1963.

——: *Theology of Culture,* Oxford, 1963.

——: *The Future of Religions,* Harper & Row, 1966.

GLOSSARY

The following key interprets the symbols which are used in this glossary to designate the various religious traditions with which particular terms are to be identified. The emphasis has been upon relevance rather than exhaustiveness in specifying the path or paths of faith within which a term is commonly encountered. The absence of any symbol whatsoever denotes either that the term is meaningful in most if not all of the major historic religions or that its individual referent is not included among the symbols employed herein. The identifying definitions provide the necessary explanations in either case. The extensive cross references are provided as aids in placing unfamiliar terms into their respective contexts.

B: Buddhism
Ch: Christianity
Co: Confucianism, Neo-Confucianism
F: Folk religion
G: Greek religion
H: Hinduism
I: Islam
Ja: Jainism
Ju: Judaism
M: Mesopotamian religion
Sh: Shinto
Si: Sikhism
T: Taoism, Neo-Taoism
V: The religion of the Vedas
Z: Zoroastrianism

Abhidhamma Pitaka: (B) The "Metaphysical Basket" consisting of philosophical treatises, the third section of the Pali canon of scripture (*Tipitaka, q.v.*).

adharma: (H) Evil, vice, lack of merit; the opposite of *dharma* (*q.v.*). (Ja) The principle of rest as a constituent of the universe (see *ajiva*), inertia entailing a lack of value, thus, evil.

adhvaryu: (V, H) Altar-building priest.

Adi Buddha: (B) Primordial Buddha-nature; see *Dharmakaya.*

Adi Granth: (Si) The sacred book of the Sikh faith.

advaita: (H) Nondualism; the monistic school of Vedantic philosophy founded by Shankara.

Agni: (V, H) Fire god; sacred fire, of the altar as well as the sun.

agnidh: (V, H) Fire-kindling priest.

agnosticism: Denial of the possibility of knowing (or suspension of judgment concerning) whether there is a transcendent power grounding all finite reality.

ahimsa: (Ja, B, H) Nonviolence; the ethic of noninjury to any and all living beings.

Ahriman: (Z) See *Angra Mainyu.*

Ahura Mazda: (Z) "Wise Lord," "Lord of Light," the one supreme deity who is sovereign over all creation. (For origin of the name, see *asuras.*)

ajiva: (Ja) All that is not living (*jiva, q.v.*), comprising space, time, matter, *dharma* (*q.v.*), and *adharma* (*q.v.*).

alaya-vijnana: (B) In Yogacarya (*q.v.*), the absolute consciousness or cosmic all-mind which, as the repository of all possible ideas and perceptions, makes individual human consciousness possible; pure consciousness.

Allah: (I) The one, true, sovereign God; exalted by Muhammad in contradistinction to the polydaemonism of earlier Arab religion.

Amaterasu: (Sh) Sun goddess, chief among the pantheon of *kami* (*q.v.*).

Amesha Spentas: (Z) Immortal holy ones, modes of divine activity or divine personifications; forerunners of Western angelology.

Amitabha (Chinese, *Omito*; Japanese, *Amida*): (B) An aspect of universal Buddha-nature, Buddha's Body of Bliss (*Sambhogakaya, q.v.*); deity of the Sukhavati Heaven (*q.v.*), widely honored throughout the East as a savior-Buddha; one of the Dhyani Buddhas (*q.v.*).

623

anatta: (B) The ultimate unreality of a substantial self or soul; no-ego, no-soul.

anekantavada: (Ja) The manysidedness of reality; an epistemological doctrine, composed of *nayavada* and *syadvada* (*q.v.*), which affirms that the world's complexity or multiformity transcends human conceptualization of it.

Angra Mainyu: (Z) The Evil One; the chief personification of the spirit of evil in opposition to Ahura Mazda (*q.v.*), engendering an ethical dualism which took on cosmic proportions in later times; known also as *Ahriman.*

anicca: (B) Impermanence, transitoriness, the absence of substantiality in the external world.

animatism: (F) See *manism.*

animism: (F) The primitive belief that everything in nature has a soul (*anima*); the attribution of selfhood to inanimate beings; misplaced personalism. Also, the theory that religion had its origin in such a belief.

anthropomorphism: The attribution of human characteristics to deity.

antinomianism: The practice of seeking salvation in complete freedom from obedience to moral laws, or in deliberate flouting of such laws.

Anu: (M) The god of heaven and erstwhile ruler of the gods.

apocalypse: (Ju, Ch, Z) A vision or revelation of a hidden future, employing bizarre symbolism of its own times, in which present history is seen to be leading up to an impending end.

Apollo: (G) A member of the Olympian pantheon, variously worshiped as a pastoral deity, an archer god, the god of revelation associated with the Delphic oracle, and later a sun god.

Apsu: (M) The primordial god, one of the original divine pair (the other being Tiamat, *q.v.*) from whom all other deities derived.

Aranyakas: (V, H) "Forest Books," transitional writings between the Brahmanas and Upanishads (*q.v.*); a portion of the Vedic tradition.

Artemis: (G) Goddess of wild nature, protectress of animals as well as lover of children.

artha: (H) Material prosperity, success; one of the four acceptable aims of human life (*purushartha, q.v.*).

Asana: (H) Correct posture and bodily control, the third stage of Yoga discipline.

asat: (V, H) Nonbeing, unreality, chaos; untruth. (See also *sat, satya.*)

Asha: (Z) Truth, the Right, in opposition to *Druj* (*q.v.*); later personified as a deity of fire.

asherah: (M) Canaanite fertility goddess; consort of *baal* (*q.v.*).

ashramas: (H) Stages of life, particularly in *jnana marga* (*q.v.*), the four stages being, successively, that of student, householder, hermit, and ascetic holy man (*sannyasin, q.v.*).

ashva medha: (V) The horse sacrifice, a late Vedic ritual assuring salvation to its accomplisher.

Asta, Arta: (Z) See *Rita.*

asuras (Iranian, *ahuras*): (V, Z) In pre-Aryan India, the spirits of natural forces, which came to be regarded in Vedic times as evil spirits and by Zoroaster as the opposite. (See also *devas.*)

Atharva Veda: (V, H) The fourth Veda, consisting of magic incantations.

atheism: The denial that there is a transcendent power grounding all finite reality; also, frequently, an attitude functioning as a basis for opposition to particular religious institutions.

Athena: (G) Warrior maiden and, in the Homeric pantheon, goddess of wisdom.

Atman: (V, H) Selfhood; Absolute or Universal Self; the foundation of individual subjecthood and therefore the true self; the ultimate as discovered within oneself; the transcendental ego. (See also *Brahman-Atman.*)

Aum, Om: (V, H) Mystic syllable, symbolizing the fundamental reality of the universe. Its three letters came to represent the three major Vedas as well as the unity of the three major deities, Brahma, Shiva, and Vishnu. The word is considered to exert mystical power when meditated upon. (B) The threefold body of the Buddha (*Trikaya, q.v.*).

autonomy: The situation in which there is no authority over and beyond the human self which provides its own norms or laws. (See also *heteronomy, theonomy.*)

Avalokitesvara, Lord Avalokita: (B) The Mahayana Bodhisattva of great compassion, mercy, and love; known later in feminine form, as *Kuan Yin* in China and as *Kwannon* in Japan.

avatara: (H) "Descent," incarnation, particularly of Vishnu. (B) The coming to human birth of a Bodhisattva (*q.v.*).

Avesta: (Z) The sacred scriptures of the Zoroastrian faith, fragmentary and uncohesive in their transmitted state.

avidya: (B, H) Ignorance, consisting in the delusion of the separate existence of the self and a corresponding confusion about the true nature of reality. (See also *vidya.*)

baal: (M) Canaanite fertility deity, often local in scope.

Bar Mitzvah: (Ju) "Son of the commandment"; the male coming-of-age ceremony.

belief: Propositional faith; an assent of the intellect to convictions concerning the character of reality.

Bhagavad Gita: (H) "Song of the Lord"; India's most cherished religious document, an epic poem of multiple authorship incorporating a wide variety of philosophical viewpoints; a prime source of *bhakti* (*q.v.*).

Bhaisaguru: (B) One of the three principal Dhyani Buddhas (*q.v.*), the Buddha of healing.

bhakti: (H) Religious devotion; worshipful adoration of a particular deity as a means of obtaining grace.

bhakti marga: (H) The way of devotion, one of the three paths to salvation.

Bo (or *Bodhi*) *tree:* (B) "Wisdom tree," the tree under which Gautama was sitting when he attained enlightenment.

Bodhisattva: (B) In Theravada, a Buddha-to-be, such as Gautama prior to his enlightenment and Maitreya (*q.v.*). In Mahayana, a candidate for Buddhahood who, on the verge of enlightenment and having attained an almost inexhaustible store of merit, delays entrance into Nirvana in order to help suffering humanity.

Bonism: (F) The indigenous folk religion of Tibet prior to the advent of Buddhism.

bot: (B) Meditation hall in a Theravada monastic complex (*wat, q.v.*).

brahma: (V, H) Prayer; the holy power believed to inhere in the sacrificial prayers of the Brahman priests.

Brahma (masculine): (H) The four-faced creator god in popular Hinduism, a member of the *Trimurti* (*q.v.*).

Brahman (neuter): (V, H) Absolute Reality, that which is ultimately and supremely real; Being-as-such, Being stripped of all its qualifying predicates, hence Being-in-and-beyond-beings. (See also *Brahman-Atman.*)

Brahman (or *Brahmin*): (V, H) A member of the priestly class, at the head of the caste system, which rose to prominence through control of the holy power (*brahma, q.v.*) invoked in the performance of sacrifice and ritual.

Brahman-Atman: (V, H) The unity of the self with Absolute Reality, the ultimate lack of distinction between self and not-self; the oneness or absorptive union of the objective and the subjective.

Brahmanas: (V, H) "Priestlies," prose appendices to the Vedas composed by the Brahmans, containing detailed instruction in the meaning and performance of sacrificial rites.

Brahmanaspati: (V, H) "Lord of the Ritual," deification of the power of the sacred prayer-word (*brahma, q.v.*) in sacrificial ritual.

Buddha: (B) The Enlightened or Awakened One; originally descriptive of Siddhartha Gautama, founder of Buddhism, but in subsequent developments in Mahayana the term came to encompass a variety and multiplicity of Buddha-figures which are manifestations of an all-pervading Buddha-nature underlying the universe. (See, *inter alia, Trikaya, Manushi Buddhas, Dhyani Buddhas, Bodhisattva.*) (H) The ninth avatar of Vishnu.

Bushido: The Way of the Warrior, a Japanese code of chivalry incorporating Confucian ethics, Japanese feudal traditions, and Zen Buddhist self-discipline. Its classic expression is in the tale of the forty-seven ronin.

butsudana: (B) The "Buddha-shelf," an altar often found in private homes in Japan.

Caliph: (I) Successor to Muhammad as religious and political leader of the Muslims, though in later times only the latter; any of several successions of such leaders. The last Caliphate was ended in 1924 with the overthrow of the Ottoman Empire.

Carvakas: India's indigenous tradition of materialism, heterodox in its rejection of the Vedic tradition.

chaitya: (B) Chapel or temple commemorating a holy place and often housing a Buddha-relic; a characteristic form of Indian Buddhist art.

Ch'an: (B) "Meditation" (*dhyana, q.v.*) sect of Mahayana in China. (See also *Zen.*)

charisma: An extraordinary power spontaneously emanating from an individual, which thereby invests him with an influence and authority within the religious community.

Chen yen: (B) "True Word," esoteric sect of Mahayana in China, which became *Shingon* in Japan.

ch'eng: (Co) Sincerity, truthfulness.

cheng ming: (Co) "Rectification of names," semantic precision in the use of language as a basis for social order.

ch'i: (Co) Material force, vital energy pervading all existence; one of two elements generating the universe (the other being *li, q.v.*).

chih: (Co) Knowledge, wisdom, insight.

ch'ih: (Co) Conscience; sense of shame for what is evil.

ching: (Co, T) Classic; the term which designates the most honored writings of the Chinese religious tradition.

Ching-tu: (B) "Pure Land" sect of Mahayana in China, whose adherents are devoted to Amitabha (*q.v.*).

Chinvad Bridge: (Z) Bridge of the Separator, upon which the soul's fate is determined after death.

Christ: (Ju, Ch) See *Messiah.*

chthonic: (G) A type of deity or divine power that inhabits earth or subterranea.

chun tzu: (Co) "Magnanimous man," the ideal man who embodies all the virtues in their proper combination.

Ch'un Chiu: (Co, T) "Spring and Autumn Annals," one of the Five Classics of Chinese tradition.

chung: (Co) Moderation, balance, the mean; being in accord with one's true nature, conscientiousness.

Code of Manu: (H) An important *dharma shastra* (*q.v.*).

cosmogony: Theory and lore concerning the origin of the universe.

dagoba: (B) See *stupa.*

daimon, daemon: (G) A secondary divinity ranking between gods and man; a godling (*q.v.*).

dakhma: (Z) Tower of Silence where bodies of the dead are exposed to birds of prey.

darshana: (H) "Point of view"; a system of philosophical thought, sometimes one which is orthodox in its acceptance of the Vedic tradition.

Day of the Lord: (Ju, Ch) In prophetic literature, the expected decisive intervention of God in history when humanity would be severely judged; in apocalypse (*q.v.*), the last judgment at the end of this evil historical aeon.

Deism: (Ch) A type of natural religion, which is limited to what can be known rationally apart from special revelation.

Demeter: (G) Mother Earth, goddess of fertility.

demiurge: (G) A subordinate deity to whom was ascribed the creation of the material world.

demon: An evil spirit, often indwelling some element or force of nature and causing misfortune or destruction.

devas (Iranian, *daevas*): (V, Z) "Shining ones," gods; Vedic personifications of beneficent powers of nature, which came to be regarded by Zoroaster as principles of evil, demons. (See also *asuras.*)

Dhammapada: (B) "The Way of Truth," an important moral treatise within the *Sutta Pitaka* (*q.v.*) of the Pali scriptures.

Dharana: (H) Concentration of attention upon a single object of meditation, the sixth stage of Yoga discipline.

dharma (Pali, *dhamma*): (Ja, B, H) The cosmic moral order or Law of Righteousness which sustains the universe. This word, strictly untranslatable into English, is to be further identified as follows:

(Ja) The Good, understood as the principle of motion and accordingly one of the constituents of the universe (see *ajiva*). (B) Truth; the Norm; the Doctrine of the Buddha; duty; justice. (H) Personal righteousness, virtue, duty, the first of the four ends of man (*purushartha, q.v.*).

dharma shastra: (H) A manual for moral guidance teaching the way of *dharma,* a prime example being the *Code of Manu;* such treatises are *smriti* (*q.v.*).

Dharmakaya: (B) The Body of Essence, one of the three aspects of the cosmic Buddha (*Trikaya, q.v.*); the primordial Buddha-nature, known also as Adi Buddha; sometimes identified with Nirvana.

dhyana: (H, B) Meditation, contemplation. (H) (*Dhyana*) The seventh stage of Yoga discipline. (B) The method of enlightenment in the meditation sects of *Ch'an* and *Zen* (*q.v.*).

Dhyani Buddhas: (B) Buddhas of Meditation, who have achieved Buddhahood as cosmic spirits without human manifestation.

Digambaras: (Ja) The stricter "Skyclad" (unclothed) sect of monks and their lay followers.

Dionysus: (G) The god of wine and ecstatic rites, around whom a savage mystery cult developed.

docetism: (Ch) The doctrine that the humanity and suffering of Jesus Christ were only apparent and not real, adjudged heretical by the early church.

Druj: (Z) Falsehood, a spirit of evil who in later times became Satan (*q.v.*).

dukkha: (B) Misery, suffering, which is the true nature of existence.

Durga (or *Thaga*): (H) The fierce patroness of the cult of Thugs, one of the numerous manifestations of *Shakti* (q.v.).

Dyaus Pitar: (V) Father Heaven, comparable to Greek Zeus but suffering an early decline in importance.

Elohim: (Ju, Ch) One of the names by which God was known to early writers of the Old Testament; later identified with *Yahweh* (*q.v.*).

Enuma Elish: (M) "When on high," the first words of the Babylonian creation story, by which it is known.

Fa Chia: Legalists, the Chou school of political realism in China.

faith: Ultimate or primary valuation, ultimate or unifying concern, embracing the whole of human experience; that life-orientation which is determinative of all other allegiances. The expression of this concern in some historic religious community. A set of statements or propositions expounding the content and meaning of this concern (see also *belief*).

fetish: (F) An inanimate object in which supernatural power, invocable through magic (*q.v.*), is believed to or induced to dwell.

filioque: (Ch) "And from the Son," a phrase inserted in Western texts of the Constantinopolitan Creed affirming that the Holy Spirit proceeds from the Father *and* the Son.

fiqh: (I) A system of jurisprudence interpreting the *shari'a* (*q.v.*).

Fravashi: (Z) Ancestral principles, preexistent external souls of living beings; similarly known in Vedic India as *Pitaras.*

Gaina Sutra: (Ja) One of the source documents of the Jain faith.

Ganesha: (H) Elephant-headed deity in the Indian popular pantheon.

Garuda: (H) Bird god of popular Indian religion and vehicle of Vishnu.

Gathas: (Z) "Hymns of Zoroaster," the oldest part of the *Avesta* (*q.v.*).

Gemara: (Ju) "Supplementary learning" added to the *Mishnah* (*q.v.*) to form the *Talmud* (*q.v.*).

Gilgamesh: (M) Semidivine hero of a Babylonian epic structured around man's futile quest for immortality.

Gnosticism: (G, Ch) A modern term for a diversified religiophilosophical movement, widespread in the Greco-Roman world, which proclaimed a matter-spirit dualism and a salvation from the former to the latter through secret knowledge (*gnosis*).

godling: A divine spirit or minor deity of considerably restricted dimension, often local in scope.

guna: (H) In *Sankhya* (*q.v.*), a constituent, quality, or "strand" of matter (*Prakriti, q.v.*), of which there are three:

sattva (intellect, harmony), *rajas* (active power, passion), and *tamas* (inertia, darkness). These three *gunas* in distinctive combination in a human soul (*Purusha, q.v.*) define a personality.

gurdwara: (Si) "Gate of the Guru," the Sikh temple.

guru: (H) Spiritual teacher. (Si) (*Guru*) The spiritual and temporal leader of the Sikh community until the termination of the guruship in 1708.

hadith: (I) Tradition, narrative; a recollected saying of Muhammad, of varying authenticity.

haggadah, aggada: (Ju) The nonlegal or narrative traditions incorporated into the *Talmud* (*q.v.*).

hajj: (I) Pilgrimage to Mecca, the fifth Pillar of the faith.

Hajji: (I) One who has completed the *hajj* (*q.v.*).

halakah: (Ju) The legal or normative aspect of the *Talmud* (*q.v.*).

Hannukkah: (Ju) Feast of Lights, eight-day celebration at the winter solstice commemorating the rededication of the Temple during the Maccabean revolt.

Hanuman: (H) The monkey god of Indian popular religion.

haoma: (Z) See *soma.*

Hasidism: (Ju) A mystical and pietistic movement originating in eastern Europe out of the tradition of the *Kabbala* (*q.v.*).

Hegira: (I) The withdrawal of Muhammad from Mecca to Medina in 622, the pivotal occasion which marks the beginning of the Muslim era according to that system of dating.

Hera: (G) Maiden goddess who became the wife of Zeus and patroness of married women.

heteronomy: The situation in which an alien norm or law is imposed upon the self, subjecting the self to bondage. (See also *autonomy, theonomy.*)

Hinayana: (B) The "Lesser Vehicle" or "Small Ferryboat." See *Theravada.*

holy: The quality of reverence, the emotive accompaniment of ultimate concern and commitment.

homoousion: (Ch) "Of the same essence," a phrase in the Nicene Creed referring to the substantial identity between the Son and the Father in the Godhead.

Hosso: (B) See *Yogacarya.*

hotar: (V, H) God-invoking priest.

hsiao: (Co) Filial piety.

hybris: (G) Pride.

hylozoism: The doctrine that all matter has life.

i: (Co) See *yi.*

I Ching: (Co, T) "Classic of Changes," a handbook of divination, one of the Five Classics of Chinese tradition.

icon: An image or picture of an object of religious devotion.

idolatry: Devotion to idols or images of deity, regarded as objectionable in monotheistic religions but widely accepted in other types.

ijma: (I) Consensus; agreement by the knowledgeable concerning the validity of a religious opinion.

imam: (I) Leader of prayer in Muslim worship. (*Imam*) In *Shi'a,* a divinely appointed successor to Muhammad, comparable to the *Caliph* (*q.v.*) of the *Sunni* (*q.v.*).

immanence: The doctrine that deity indwells the phenomenal universe. (See also *transcendence.*)

Indra: (V, H) Storm and war god, of major importance in the Vedas but later declining to the status of a minor rain deity.

Indrani: (V, H) Wife of Indra.

Isatpragbhara: (Ja) The state of bliss attained by souls beyond the cycle of transmigration; the Jain heaven.

Ishtar: (M) The great mother goddess of the ancient Near East, known under a variety of names.

Ismailis: (I) "Seveners," Shi'ites who regard Ismail as the seventh Imam and authentic successor of Muhammad.

Izanagi: (Sh) The "Male Who Invites," the Sky Father among the Japanese *kami* (*q.v.*).

Izanami: (Sh) The "Female Who Invites,"the Earth-Mother among the *kami* (*q.v.*), wife of Iza-nagi.

Japji: (Si) The traditional morning prayer silently repeated daily by the faithful.

jen: (Co) Human-heartedness, humaneness, concern for humanity; perfect virtue, true humanity, the essential foundation of all moral qualities in the individual.

jihad: (I) "Holy war" waged against non-Muslims.

Jina: (Ja) Conqueror, one of the titles accorded *Mahavira* (*q.v.*).

jinn: (I) Supernatural spirits of either good or evil. (See also *shaitin.*)

jiriki: (B) In Jodo (*q.v.*), the difficult path to salvation through reliance on one's own human power. (See also *tariki.*)

jiva: (Ja) Life, soul; all that is living, constituting along with *ajiva* (*q.v.*) the two ultimate, eternal categories of the Jain dualistic universe.

jivan mukti: (H) One who has achieved emancipation from the burden of *karma-samsara* (*q.v.*) while still living, through the experience of *samadhi* (*q.v.*).

jnana: (H) Saving knowledge, wisdom; comprehension of the all-embracing unity of reality. (See also *vidya.*)

jnana marga: (H) The way of knowledge, one of the three paths of salvation.

Jodo: (B) A Japanese Pure Land sect founded by Honen, emphasizing human depravity and devotion to Amida through recital of the *Nembutsu* (*q.v.*).

Ka'ba: (I) "Cube"; the large cube-shaped shrine in Mecca in which the sacred Black Stone is embedded.

Kabbala: (Ju) "Tradition," writings of medieval origin giving expression to an esoteric tradition of mysticism.

kalacakra: (Ja, B, H) "Wheel of time," the cosmic symbol of the cyclic character of history.

Kali: (H) Fierce black goddess and consort of Shiva, whose devotees worship her also as the great mother; a particular exemplification of *Shakti* (*q.v.*).

kama: (H) Love, pleasure, desire, sensuous or sensual fulfillment; one of the four traditional aims of human life (*purushartha, q.v.*); (*Kama*) in Indian popular religion, the god of love.

kami: (Sh) Holy power, sometimes personalized; the name given to an innumerable host of entities or phenomena widely ranging from ostensible deities or godlings to mere manifestations of extraordinary or awe-inspiring potency.

kamidana: (Sh) The "god-shelf," an altar in the private home which is the center of worship in domestic Shinto.

kandhas: (B) See *skandhas.*

karma (Pali, *kamma*): (V, Ja, B, H, Si) The law of the deed, action and its inevitable consequence; the chain of cause and effect which holds man in bondage to delusion.

karma marga: (H) The way of works, one of the three paths to salvation.

karma-samsara: (V, Ja, B, H, Si) The fated cycle in which the consequences of human deeds continually result in subsequent incarnations.

karuna: (B) "Feeling with others," compassion, mercy.

kevala, kaivalya: (Ja) A trance-like state of emancipation and perfect knowledge, similar to the Hindu *samadhi* (*q.v.*).

Khalsa: (Si) The Community of the Pure, a strictly disciplined brotherhood whose members bear the name of Singh ("lion").

koan: (B) A riddle or puzzle on which the Zen pupil concentrates as a guide to enlightenment. Known in Ch'an as *kung'an.*

Kojiki: (Sh) Record of Ancient Tales, sacred writings dealing with ancient and prehistoric Japan.

Krishna: (H) God-hero of the *Mahabharata* and divine charioteer of Arjuna in the *Bhagavad Gita*, the eighth avatar of Vishnu and also a god in his own right.

Kshatriya: (V, H) A member of the noble or warrior class, second in rank in the caste system.

Kshitigarbha: (B) The Mahayana Bodhisattva who has vowed to deliver all humanity, especially children and the wicked, from suffering. Known as Ti Tsang in China and as Jizo in Japan.

Kuan Yin, Kwannon: (B) See *Avalokitesvara.*

kung'an: (B) See *koan.*

kwei: (T) Evil spirits in Chinese popular religion.

Lakshmi: (H) Wife of Vishnu and giver of good fortune; an exemplification of *Shakti* (*q.v.*).

lama: (B) "One who is superior," the Tibetan monk.

li: (Co) (1) Good form, propriety, ceremony, decorum, correct order, not only in man and society but extending also to the very fabric of the universe. (2) Principle, form, very similar to the Platonic idea, one of two elements which generate the universe (the other being *ch'i, q.v.*). (These are two separate and distinct characters in the Chinese language.)

Li Chi: (Co, T) "Record of Rites," the last of the Five Classics of Chinese tradition.

lien: (Co) Integrity, honesty.

lingam: (V, H) Phallic symbol, particularly prominent in the worship of Shiva.

Logos: (Ju, Ch) Divine Word or Reason, the chief instrument of God's creative activity; regarded in the Christian tradition as having been incarnated in Jesus.

Madhyamika: (B) Central School of Indian Mahayana philosophy, founded by Nagarjuna, which emphasizes the ultimate unreality of all appearances and the universality of the void (*shunya, q.v.*).

Magi: (Z) The official priesthood in later times, whose origins and precise identity are clouded in mystery.

magic: The endeavor through fixed ritual to bend or control natural phenomena to one's own purposes.

Mahabharata: (H) Epic of over 100,000 stanzas, the world's longest poem, recounting the great war of the Bharatas; one of India's chief religious classics (*smriti, q.v.*).

Mahadeva: (H) "The Great God," the title accorded Shiva (*q.v.*) by his devotees.

Mahasthama-Prapta: (B) The Mahayana Bodhisattva who represents the wisdom and mercy of the Buddha.

Mahavira: (Ja) "Great Hero," the name by which Mataputta Vardhamana, the founder of Jainism, is primarily known.

Mahayana: (B) The "Great Vehicle,"

"Great Ferryboat"; the larger, more widespread, more speculative, and less conservative of the major sects; the more inclusive vehicle of salvation. (See also *Theravada.*)

Mahdi: (I) The Expected One, the hidden Imam (*q.v.*) whose coming will set the world right.

maithuna: (B, H) Sexual intercourse, of a sacramental character in tantrism (*q.v.*).

Maitreya (Pail, *Metteya*): (B) The compassionate Buddha of the age to come.

maitri (Pali, *metta*): (B) Loving-kindness, true friendliness, compassion.

mana: (F) Holy power; mysterious, impersonal power indwelling objects, persons, or events, causing them to be regarded as sacred.

mandala: (B, H) A symbolic pictorial representation of the universe, into which the gods are sometimes diagrammatically placed.

manism: (F) The theory that religion originated in the perception of *mana* (*q.v.*) in holy objects; also called *animatism.*

Manjusri: (B) The Mahayana Bodhisattva of wisdom; the personification of supreme wisdom. Known in China as *Wen-yu.*

mantra: (V, B, H) A sacred word, verse, or formula mystically embodying a deity or divine power.

Manushi Buddhas: (B) Figures such as Gautama who have begun from a human base in their attainment of enlightenment and complete Buddhahood.

mara, Mara: (B, H) Death, sometimes personified as the god of death.

Marduk: (M) Babylonian war god who rose to prominence as creator god and chief deity.

marga: (H) Path, road, way of salvation.

Maruts: (V, H) Storm spirits, attendants of Indra (*q.v.*).

maya: (H, Si) Illusion; the delusory appearance of the phenomenal world.

Messiah: (Ju, Ch) "Anointed One," the divinely appointed ruler who was expected to usher in the Kingdom of God on earth; the title accorded Jesus by his followers. Known also, from the Greek, as *Christ.*

michi: (Sh) Path, way.

midrash: (Ju) "Inquiry" into the meaning of the Torah; rabbinical, homiletic interpretation, from which the sermon has been derived.

Ming chia: The Chou school of Names in ancient China.

Mishnah: (Ju) "Study," the earlier portion of the *Talmud* (*q.v.*), containing codified collections of laws.

Mithra: (Z, G) Iranian god of war and light, who migrated westward to the Greco-Roman world as *Mithras,* the focus of a widespread mystery cult.

Mohists: Followers of the Chou philosopher Moh tze, who taught universal love and a personal Heaven.

moira: (G) Fate, the impersonal law which controls the destiny of gods as well as men.

moksha: (V, Ja, B, H) Emancipation; salvation as liberation from the bondage of finitude, the ultimate goal of man, which is completely attainable only after death.

monism: The doctrine that all reality is ultimately of a single character, that all is One.

monotheism: (Z, Ju, Ch, I, Si) The doctrine that the transcendent power grounding all finite reality is unitary and personal in character.

mysticism: The doctrine of the achievement of religious experience involving an immediacy of apprehension of the religious object, either in communion or in ontological union and absorption.

myth: Sacred story or narrative which serves as a vehicle for the authoritative expression of central values that provide meaning and direction for human life.

Nandi: (H) Bull god in Indian popular religion and the principle vehicle of Shiva.

nayavada: (Ja) "Viewpoints"; an aspect of the doctrine of manysidedness (*anekantavada,* *q.v.*) which affirms that an object of thought may be considered from seven distinct but equally valid points of view.

Nembutsu: (B) "Hail Amida Buddha," the ritual invoking of Buddha's name.

nemesis: (G) Doom, tragic fate, an important element in ancient tragic drama.

neti neti: (V, H) "Not this, not that"; the process of arriving at the true nature of Absolute Reality by stripping away every qualifying (and therefore, limiting) predicate until one reaches Being-as-such. (See also *via negativa.*)

Nichiren: (B) Japanese sociopolitical sect, characterized by patriotic nationalism combined with Buddhist devotion.

nihilism: Nothingness; the doctrine that nothing exists or is knowable or meaningful.

Nihongi, Nihon Shoki: (Sh) Chronicle of Japan, sacred writings.

Nirmanakaya: (B) The Body of Manifestation or Appearance, the aspect of the cosmic Buddha (*Trikaya,* *q.v.*) which appears on earth.

Nirvana (Pali, *Nibbana*): (B) "Blowing out" of the flame of passion in the cessation of ignorant craving and the attainment of emancipation from finite limitation; the transpersonal state of release from all attributes of phenomenal existence; the supreme goal of human existence.

Niyama: (H) Observance of self-culture, the second stage of Yoga discipline.

Noble Eightfold Path: (B) The formula of moral and intellectual development leading to enlightenment and emancipation.

Nyaya: (H) "Inference"; the orthodox *darshana* (*q.v.*) of logic and semantics.

Om: (V, B, H) See *Aum.*

Om mani padme hum: (B, H) An extremely potent *mantra* (*q.v.*) incorporating the sacred syllable (see *Aum*), "the jewel (*mani*) is in the lotus (*padme*)," and a petition for protection (*hum*).

Omito: (B) See *Amitabha.*

omophagia: (G) A rite of some mystery cults, in which a live animal is torn asunder, its blood drunk, and its flesh eaten by frenzied worshipers.

pagoda: (B) A tower-like structure with a characteristic multiform roof, which may have originated as a *stupa* (*q.v.*) but which has become important as a center of ritual activity and festival celebrations.

palyopama: (Ja, B, H) A single twelfth-turn of the cosmic wheel of time (*kalacakra, q.v.*).

Parinirvana: (B) The full realization of Nirvana (*q.v.*), attainable only at the end of earthly existence.

parousia: (Ch) The eschatological second coming of Christ.

Parvati: (H) A consort of Shiva, kind and gracious in demeanor.

path: A cluster of life values which provides man with convincing and illuminating answers to the fundamental questions of life's meaning.

Persephone: (G) Maiden goddess, daughter of Demeter.

Pesach: (Ju) Passover, vernal festival celebrating Israel's deliverance from Egypt.

Pitaras: (V) "Fathers"; see *Fravashi.*

polytheism: The concept that the powers or gods governing the universe are multiple in number; the practice of being apparently committed to a plurality of ultimate values.

Poseidon: (G) God of the sea and of horses.

Prajapati: (V, H) "Lord of creatures," a creator god in late Vedic tradition.

Prakriti: (H, Ja) Matter; one of the two basic elements of the universe in *Sankhya* (*q.v.*), the other being spirit (*Purusha, q.v.*).

Pranayama: (H) Regulation of the breathing, the fourth stage of Yoga discipline.

Pratyahara: (H) The freeing of the senses from all objectivity, the fifth stage of Yoga discipline.

Prithivi: (V) Mother-Earth, an early goddess linked with *Dyaus Pitar* (*q.v.*).

prophecy: (Z, Ju, Ch, I) The activity of "speaking for" the one God in monotheistic religions; the "forthtelling" of the divine will by keenly sensitive interpreters of their historic situation, occasionally but not necessarily involving future predictions.

Proto-Shiva: (F) Horned god of pre-Aryan India.

puja: (H) Worship; devotion externally manifested.

Puranas: (H) "Ancient Tales," writings which are extremely important for popular piety.

purdah: (I, Si) The veiling and seclusion of women.

Purim: (Ju) Late winter feast associated with the Biblical Book of Esther.

Purusha: (V) Cosmic person, the soul of the universe. (Ja, B, H) Spirit, mind, the human soul in its essential immateriality. (See also *Prakriti, guna.*)

purushartha: (H) The four permissible goals of human life, the traditional ends of man. See *artha, dharma, kama, moksha.*

Purva Mimamsa: (H) "Interpretation of the first part [of the Vedas]"; the least philosophical and most conservative of the orthodox *darshanas* (*q.v.*), characterized by atheism and an emphasis upon the literal validity of the Vedas.

Q, Quelle: (Ch) "Source," a hypothetical document containing teachings of Jesus which scholars believe was used in the composition of two of the Gospels, Matthew and Luke.

qari: (I) Reader of the Qur'an at mosque services.

qibla: (I) The direction in which the worshiper faces in prayer (toward Mecca).

Qur'an: (I) The Holy Book containing the divine revelation to Muhammad, of which the earthly Arabic text is considered to be only a copy of the eternal perfect Book in Heaven.

rabbi: (Ju) A teacher, expert in the exposition of the Torah.

rajas: (H) One of the *gunas* (*q.v.*).

Rama: (H) The ideal man, hero of the Ramayana (*q.v.*) and the seventh avatar of Vishnu, sometimes worshiped as a deity in popular religion.

Ramayana: (H) "The Adventures of Rama," an epic poem which serves as a major source of popular devotion in Indian religion.

religion: A system of holy forms providing an all-embracing life orientation as a community of ultimate concern (*q.v.*) gathered about a single cluster of concrete symbols.

revelation: (Z, Ju, Ch, I, Si) Divine disclosure of previously unperceived truths, such as the will of God or the meaning of human life.

Rig Veda: (V, H) The earliest and most significant of the Vedas and the oldest source of Aryan religion, comprising a wealth of religious poetry of multiple authorship, dating from the second millenium B.C. though remaining in oral tradition for a number of centuries.

rishi: (V, H) Seer, sage, inspired poet; one of those who were originally responsible for the composition of the Vedas.

Rita: (V) Cosmic order or the deified personification thereof, known similarly in Iran as *Asta* or *Arta.*

ritual: The ceremonial observance of formal symbolic actions relating to some particular occasion or aspect of individual or social life.

Rosh Hashanah: (Ju) The New Year observance in the religious calendar.

Rudra: (V) A storm god who later became *Shiva* (*q.v.*).

Sabbath: (Ju) The seventh day of the week, observed as a holy day of rest.

sacred: The accompanying attribution of that which is valued as of ultimate concern.

sadhu: (H) Holy man, one who has achieved an experience of undifferentiated unity with the Absolute. (See also *sannyasin, samadhi, jivan mukti.*)

salvation: The attainment of a wholeness of being in which the vicissitudes of human existence are overcome, whether in ultimate fulfillment of one's true personhood, in a transpersonal emancipation from bondage to phenomenality, or in realization of other conceptual models.

Sama Veda: (V, H) The third of the Vedas, consisting of selections from the Rig Veda used in ritual.

samadhi: (Ja, B, H) A trancelike state in which the individual achieves an experience of absorption into Ultimate Reality while still living; in Yoga, emancipation, the eighth and final stage of self-discipline.

Samantabhadra: (B) The Mahayana Bodhisattva of compassion and mercy; known in China as *P'u-hien.*

Sambhogakaya: (B) The Body of Bliss,

one of the three aspects of the cosmic Buddha (*Trikaya, q.v.*), known also as *Amitabha* (*q.v.*).

samsara: (V, Ja, B, H, Si) Transmigration of the human soul through successive rebirths; perpetual reincarnation. (See also *karma-samsara.*)

samurai: (Sh, Co, B) The military or warrior class of Japanese feudalism. (See also *Bushido.*)

Sangha: (B) The monastic order founded by the Buddha, continuing to the present day in Theravada and in some other Buddhist groups.

Sanhedrin: (Ju) The council of elders, a rabbinical body with religious jurisdiction in post-exilic Judea.

Sankhya: (H) "Distinction"; the orthodox *darshana* (*q.v.*) which emphasizes the attainment of salvation through properly distinguishing between spirit or soul (*Purusha, q.v.*) and matter (*Prakriti, q.v.*).

sannyasin: (H) The fourth stage (*ashrama, q.v.*) of life in which the individual experiences *samadhi* (*q.v.*), thereby becoming *jivan mukti* (*q.v.*); consequently, an ascetic holy man similar to the *sadhu.*

Sarasvati: (H) Wife of Brahma and patroness of wisdom; a manifestation of *Shakti* (*q.v.*).

sat: (V, H) Being, the existent, the ordered universe.

Satan: (Z, Ju, Ch, I) Originally, the father of lies (see *Druj*), who migrated from Iran to become identified with the chief spirit and personification of evil in a cosmic framework of moral dualism. (See also *shaitin.*)

sati: (H, Si) The self-immolation of a widow on her husband's funeral pyre.

satori: (B) In Zen (*q.v.*), the immediate experience of enlightenment or awakening, transrational and transpersonal in character.

sattva: (H) One of the *gunas* (*q.v.*).

satya: (V, H) Truth, the real.

satyagraha: (H) "Truth-force" of Mohandas Gandhi, known in the West as the doctrine of nonviolent resistance.

Savitar: (V, H) A solar deity who functions as stimulator, generator, vivifier.

Seder: (Ju) Family meal which is the

major element in the Passover celebration (*Pesach, q.v.*).

shahada: (I) The fundamental confession, "There is no God but God (Allah), and Muhammad is his Prophet," the recital of which constitutes the first Pillar of faith.

shaitin: (I) The evil *jinn* (*q.v.*), whose leader is "the Shaitin," God's adversary and mankind's tempter. (See also *Satan.*)

Shakti: (H, B) "Female power"; the personification of a god's power or energy; the essential mother goddess in all of her various exemplifications.

shaman: (F) Sorceror priest who endeavors to secure desired results through the practice of magic (*q.v.*).

Shamash: (M) Babylonian sun god, from whom Hammurabi was presumed to have received his famous law code.

Shang-ti: "Lord on high," pre-Chou Chinese designation of Heaven. (See *T'ien.*)

shari'a: (I) The whole body of religious law which is conceived to have authority over all human life, individual and social.

Shebuoth: (Ju) Pentecost, the celebration of the giving of the Torah (*q.v.*) on Mt. Sinai.

shen: (T) Good spirits in Chinese popular religion.

Shi'a: (I) "Followers"; the Muslim party whose adherents (*Shi'ites*) are followers of Ali as the divinely appointed first successor (*Imam*) to Muhammad. (See also *Sunni.*)

Shih Ching: (Co, T) "Classic of Songs" or "Book of Odes," a poetic miscellany which is one of the Five Classics of Chinese tradition.

Shin: (B) A Japanese Pure Land sect founded by Shinran, similar to *Jodo* (*q.v.*) but with a stronger emphasis upon the importance of inward faith.

Shingon: (B) See *Chen yen.*

shirk: (I) "Association" of anything creaturely with the one true God; hence, idolatry, the cardinal sin.

Shiva: (V, H) "The Auspicious One," the Destroyer; a major deity in the popular pantheon and a member of the *Trimurti* (*q.v.*). (See also *Rudra, Mahadeva.*)

shruti: (V, H) "Heard," referring to writings believed to have been divinely revealed to an inspired individual (*rishi, q.v.*); hence, sacred literature in distinction from uncanonical writings (*smriti, q.v.*).

shu: (Co) Reciprocity, a moral principle comparable to the Golden Rule of Christianity.

Shu Ching: (Co, T) "Classic of Documents" or "Book of History," a collection of chronicles and the like, one of the Five Classics of Chinese tradition.

Shudra: (V, H) A member of the servant class at the bottom of the caste system, generally non-Aryan in race.

shunya: (B) Void, emptiness; that which is devoid of all distinguishing characteristics and thus has no phenomenal existence; hence, blessedness beyond existence. (See also *Madhyamika.*)

Shvetambaras: (Ja) The less conservative "Whiteclad" sect of monks and their lay followers, which comprises the majority of the Jain faithful.

sikh: (Si) Disciple, student; specifically, (*Sikh*) a follower of the way of Nanak.

Sita: (H) The supremely virtuous wife of Rama in the *Ramayana* (*q.v.*).

skandhas (Pali, *kandhas*): (B) The five personality components which enter into temporary and nonsubstantial combination to form an apparent soul or self.

smriti: (V, H) "Remembered," referring to writings which have arisen out of the teachings of ancient sages; hence, religious classics as distinguished from canonical scripture (*shruti, q.v.*) on which they are largely based.

soma (Iranian, *haoma*): (V, H, Z) A potent drink used as a sacrificial libation because of its tendency to induce visions and feelings of religious exaltation; (*Soma, Haoma*) sometimes deified, as the lord of the drink who is responsible for its intoxicating potency.

Spenta Mainyu: (Z) Holy Spirit of *Ahura Mazda* (*q.v.*), sometimes conceived of as a separate angelic being.

Sthanakvasis: (Ja) An iconoclastic sect of late origin which has rejected ritual and temple worship.

stupa: (B) An earth mound enshrining a relic of the Buddha, sometimes constructed with a *wat* (*q.v.*), which usually tapers upward gracefully to a pointed pinnacle; known similarly in Ceylon as the *dagoba.* (See also *pagoda.*)

Succoth: (Ju) Feast of the Booths, an autumn celebration commemorating Israel's sojourn in the wilderness.

Sufi: (I) "Wool wearer," the name given to the communities of mystics after the clothing which their ascetic predecessors originally wore.

Sukhavati Heaven: (B) The Pure or Happy Land, a paradise of the intermediate realm between Nirvana and the world, presided over by *Amitabha* (*q.v.*).

Sunna: (I) The body of orthodox tradition incorporating prophetic teachings outside the Qur'an; the traditionalist party which constitutes the major Muslim way.

Sunni: (I) A member of the majority party which adheres to the entirety of the *Sunna.* (See also *Shi'a.*)

Sura: (I) A section or chapter of the Qur'an, of which there are 114.

Surya: (V, H) The sun or sun god; often linked with *Ushas,* the goddess of the dawn.

Susa-no-o: (Sh) The storm kami and brother of Amaterasu (*q.v.*).

Sutra (Pali, *Sutta*): (B) A discourse attributed to the Buddha or a disciple which now holds the status of scripture.

Sutta Pitaka: (B) The "Basket of Discourses," a collection of didactic material which constitutes the second section of the Pali canon of scripture (*Tipitaka, q.v.*).

svarna: (B, H) Heaven; a concept employed, in lieu of Nirvana, both by King Ashoka and by *Purva Mimamsa* (*q.v.*).

swadeshi: (H) Loyalty to one's own land or tradition, a central concept in the thought of Gandhi and his followers.

syadvada: (Ja) "Perhaps," conditional or relative predication; an aspect of the doctrine of manysidedness (*anekantavada, q.v.*), which affirms that reality expresses itself in multiple forms so that no absolute predication concerning an object of thought is possible (wherefore "perhaps" or "somehow" must be prefixed to every statement).

symbol: A word, object, or event which mediates an experience of the holy by evoking and sustaining a conscious awareness of ultimate concern.

syncretism: The intentional merging of elements from two or more separate traditions or religious movements into a single path of faith.

taboo: (F) That which is forbidden to ordinary use because of the presence of holy power therein.

tadekam: (V) "That One [Thing]," the impersonal creative impulse in late cosmogonic speculation, which as primal reality is neither being nor nonbeing and out of which arises even the gods as well as all phenomenal reality.

T'ai Chi: (Co) The Great Ultimate, the one supreme ultimate reality which is infinitely manifested throughout the universe.

Talmud: (Ju) "Learning," the multivolume interpretation of the Torah (*q.v.*) put together by rabbinical scholarship of several centuries.

tamas: (H) One of the *gunas* (*q.v.*).

Tannaim: (Ju) Oral rabbinic teachings, often in pairs of opposites, which became codified in the *Mishnah* (*q.v.*).

tantra: (B, H) Any one of a considerable number of religious texts and ritual manuals of late origin which are the basic treatises for tantrism (*q.v.*).

Tantrayana: (B) The "Vehicle of the Tantras," a name for tantric Buddhism (see *tantrism*).

tantrism: (B, H) An esoteric religious movement which places particular emphasis upon magical rites and formulas, erotic practices, and mystical experiences as aids to the achievement of salvation.

Tao: (T, Co) Cosmic way or path; the eternal dynamic way of the universe and its preordained rational structure. To tread the Tao is to live in perfect harmony with the cosmic order.

Tao te ching: (T) "Classic of the Way and its Power," a brief cryptic poem attributed to Lao-tzu which functions as the authoritative source for Taoist tradition.

tapas: (Ja, H) Asceticism, practiced as a means of achieving emancipation of the soul from bondage to material things.

tara: (B) Savioress, consort of a deity,

comparable to the Hindu *Shakti* (*q.v.*).

tariki: (B) In *Jodo* (*q.v.*), the easy path to salvation through relying on the power of another, *i.e.*, dependence on the grace of *Amida* (*q.v.*). (See also *jiriki.*)

tat tvam asi: (V, H) "That art thou"; the ultimate identity between self and objective reality. (See *Brahman-Atman.*)

tathata: (B) "Suchness," the Yogacarya (*q.v.*) concept of the Absolute, the positive aspect of the Void (*shunya, q.v.*); pure undifferentiated being, which alone truly exists and which is the source of the phenomenal world.

Tendai: (B) Japanese sect founded by Saicho, emphasizing the teachings of the *Lotus Sutra.*

theism: The view of reality which affirms a transcendent power grounding all finite being. (See also *monotheism, monism.*)

theocracy: Government of a people by leaders who claim to rule according to divine authority.

theology: Rational inquiry into matters pertaining to deity and to the relations of deity to man; the endeavor to achieve critical understanding of the object of the ultimate concern of oneself or of others.

theonomy: The ideal situation in which the normative demands of the object of one's ultimate valuation are identical to the fundamental aspirations of human selfhood. (See also *autonomy, heteronomy.*)

theophany: The visible manifestation of God or a god to man, usually in some tangible form.

theotokos: (Ch) "Bearer of God," a title applied to Mary the mother of Jesus in the early church.

Theravada: (B) "Way of the Elders," the more conservative of the major sects, which insists on the sole authenticity of the Pali canon of the scriptures (*Tipitaka, q.v.*) and claims direct descent from the Buddha. (See also *Mahayana.*)

Tiamat: (M) Primeval goddess whose slain body becomes heaven and earth in the cosmogonic myth of the *Enuma Elish* (*q.v.*).

T'ien: (Co, T) "Heaven" as the source of human destiny and object of natural piety, conceived in terms of impersonal divinity.

T'ien Ming: (Co, T) "Mandate of Heaven," the divine sanction under which a Chinese ruler was considered to govern.

T'ien t'ai: (B) "Heavenly Terrace" sect of Mahayana in China, similar to the Japanese *Tendai* (*q.v.*).

Tipitaka (Sanskrit, *Tripitaka*): (B) "Three Baskets," the Pali canon of scripture which is recognized as authoritative by Theravada, and which is partially accepted in its Sanskrit version by most Mahayana sects.

tirthankara: (Ja) 'Fordfinder," one who discovers a way across the stream of human misery to the far shore of salvation. Tradition mentions twenty-four of them, the last having been Mahavira (*q.v.*).

Torah: (Ju) The Law; the first five books in the Hebrew canon, comprising the Pentateuch.

totem: (F) An animal or natural object from which a tribe envisages itself to be descended and around which group life is centered.

transcendence: The doctrine that deity stands over against all finite reality as its ground and source. (See also *immanence.*)

transubstantiation: (Ch) The Roman Catholic doctrine of the miraculous transformation of the inner substantial reality of the eucharistic elements into the body and blood of Christ in the priest's performance of the Mass.

Trikaya: (B) In Mahayana, the "Three Bodies" of the Buddha, comprising the primordial and ultimate Body of Essence (*Dharmakaya*), from which emanate its heavenly manifestations constituting the Body of Bliss (*Sambhogakaya*), from which in turn has emanated the Body of Appearance (*Nirmanakaya*), which alone has been present in earthly existence. (Cf. also *Trimurti, Trinity.*)

Trimurti: (H) The great triad of Brahma, Shiva, and Vishnu, sometimes regarded as the threefold manifestation of Absolute Reality (*Brahman, q.v.*) or as the Universe in its triple role as creator, destroyer, and preserver. (Cf. also *Trikaya, Trinity.*)

Trinity: (Ch) The doctrine of the three-fold character of the Godhead as Father, Son, and Holy Spirit, traditionally understood as three eternal and ungenerated manifestations of a single personal reality.

trishna: (B) Ignorant craving; the desire for self-gratification in separateness from one's cosmos, which is the root of human misery (*dukkha, q.v.*).

Tushita heaven: (B) A heaven below the level of the Buddha-realms, from which the pre-existent Buddha descended to earth and where the future Buddha now resides.

Tvashtar: (V, H) The divine blacksmith.

ulama: (I) Conservative scholars learned in the Qur'an and the Tradition (*Sunna, q.v.*).

ultimate concern: Ultimate or primary valuation, unconditional and unqualified values or loyalties; those all-embracing convictions which give unity and meaning to the life of an individual or an entire culture.

Uma: (H) Goddess of light and a consort of Shiva.

Upanishads: (V, H) Highly philosophical writings, originally appendices to the *Aranyakas* (*q.v.*), which complete the body of Vedic literature recognized as *shruti* (*q.v.*).

Ushas: (V, H) Goddess of the dawn. (See also *Surya.*)

Utnapishtim: (M) Narrator of the Babylonian flood story in the Gilgamesh epic.

Vairocana: (B) A solar deity and manifestation of the primordial nature of the cosmic Buddha (see *Dharmakaya*).

Vaishesika: (H) "Particular"; the orthodox *darshana* (*q.v.*) which teaches an irreducible plurality of particular entities in the universe and a fundamental spirit-matter dualism.

Vaishya: (V, H) A member of the working class of merchants, artisans, and farmers, third in rank in the caste system.

vajapeya: (V) A royal rejuvenation ceremony in late Vedic ritual.

Vajrapani: (B) The Mahayana Bodhisattva of power.

Vajrayana: (B) The "Thunderbolt Vehicle," the esoteric sect of tantric Buddhism (see *tantrism*).

Varuna: (V) Sky god, who became morally important as the source of all righteousness, the revealer of sin, the judge of truth, and the one who rewards and punishes.

Vayu: (V, H) Deity of the wind.

Veda: (V, H) "Knowledge"; the most ancient of India's sacred writings, regarded as divinely revealed to inspired seers (*rishi, q.v.*) and therefore *shruti* (*q.v.*). The four Vedas proper (*Rig, Yajur, Sama,* and *Atharva, q.v.*) constitute *Veda Samhita,* whereas the entire corpus includes also the interpretive appendices of the *Samhita* (the *Brahmanas, Aranyakas,* and *Upanishads, q.v.*).

Vedanta: (H) "End of the Veda"; the most influential and significant of the orthodox *darshanas* (*q.v.*), which is primarily interested in the doctrines of the Upanishads (which are the culmination of the Vedas); characterized by philosophic idealism and varying degrees of monism (see *advaita*).

via negativa: The "way of negation," wherein one endeavors to comprehend the nature of God or Absolute Reality by discerning what it is not. (See also *neti neti.*)

vidya: (B, H) Knowledge as comprehension of the ultimately real. (See also *avidya, jnana.*)

vihara: (B) Monastery, chapel.

Vijnanavada: (B) See *Yogacarya.*

Vinaya Pitaka: (B) The "Basket of Discipline" consisting of monastic rules, the first section of the Pali canon of scripture (*Tipitaka, q.v.*).

Vishnu: (V, H) The Preserver, and exemplar of divine love, who descends to earth in numerous incarnations (see *avatara*); a member of the *Trimurti* (*q.v.*) among the pantheon of deities.

Vishvakarman: (V, H) "Maker (or doer) of all," an apparent creator deity of later Vedic writings.

Vohu Manah: (Z) The angel of Good Thought, through whom Zoroaster received many of his divine revelations.

Vritra: (V) The chief of the demons,

slain by Indra in a Vedic cosmogonic myth.

wat: (B) The characteristic walled cluster of buildings constituting a monastic complex in Theravada lands.

Wei Shih: (B) See *Yogacarya.*

wu: (T) Nothingness, nonbeing, emptiness, with which the *Tao* (*q.v.*) is sometimes identified.

wu wei: (T) Nonaction, passivity, "action without action," which constitutes the core of the Taoist ethic.

Yahweh: (Ju, Ch) "Lord"; the English rendition of the Hebrew *YHWH* by which God was known among the Israelites particularly after the Exodus.

Yajur Veda: (V, H) The second Veda, which contains sacrificial formulas.

Yama: (V, H) Lord of the dead. (H) Restraint, self-control, the death of desire, the initial stage of Yoga discipline.

yang: (T, Co) The cosmic energy mode which is the active, bright, warm, dry, masculine principle, comprising with *yin* (*q.v.*) the *Tao.*

yantra: (B, H) A geometrical diagram employed in Tantric magic rites.

YHWH: (Ju, Ch) See *Yahweh.*

yi, i: (Co) Duty, obligation, righteousness, right relationship; the correct form of social relations as concrete expressions of *jen* and *shu* (*q.v.*).

yin: (T, Co) The cosmic energy mode which is the passive, dark, cold, wet, feminine principle, comprising with *yang* (*q.v.*) the *Tao.*

yoga: (H) The way of salvation through inner discipline; (*Yoga*) the specific *darshana* (*q.v.*) which teaches a rigorous

system of self-discipline aimed at developing one's powers of insight in meditation as a means of emancipation, sometimes regarded as the practical counterpart of the philosophy of *Sankhya* (*q.v.*).

Yogacarya: (B) The Way of Union, the Indian Mahayana philosophy of idealism emphasizing an essential or absolute consciousness (*alaya-vijnana, q.v.*) as being the ultimate character of reality (see *tathata*); known also as *Vijnanavada* (Consciousness Only), which became *Wei Shih* in China and *Hosso* in Japan.

Yom Kippur: (Ju) Day of Atonement, the tenth day of the Jewish New Year.

yoni: (V, H) Ring-shaped female sex symbol. (See also *lingam.*)

yu wei: (T) Activity, active doing, the undesirable opposite of *wu wei* (*q.v.*).

Zaddikim: (Ju) The "righteous ones," the rabbinical leaders of Hasidism (*q.v.*).

zakat: (I) Almsgiving, the fourth Pillar of the faith.

zazen: (B) In *Zen* (*q.v.*), the technique of sitting for long periods in disciplined meditation as a necessary preparation for *satori* (*q.v.*).

Zen: (B) "Meditation" (*dhyana, q.v.*) sect of Mahayana in Japan, nontheistic in character and this-worldly in orientation, wherein the truth is sought in the unity of immanent reality.

Zeus: (G) Father Sky; chief of all the deities in the Olympian pantheon.

ziggurat: (M) Pyramidic edifice at the center of a temple compound, symbolizing the earth mountain.

Zurvan: (Z) "Boundless Time"; in late developments, the impersonal principle of Time from which all reality derives.

INDEX

DATE DUE